THE GREGG/McGRAW-HILL MARKETING SERIES

Gillespie and Hecht
RETAIL BUSINESS MANAGEMENT, Second Edition

Troxell
FASHION MERCHANDISING, Second Edition

Burke
ADVERTISING IN THE MARKETPLACE, Second Edition

Reece and Manning
WILSON RV—AN IN-BASKET SIMULATION FOR MANAGEMENT AND SUPERVISORY DEVELOPMENT

ADVERTISING IN

John D. Burke
Former Head, Creative Department
Compton Advertising, Inc., New York, NY

THE MARKETPLACE

Second Edition

Gregg Division

McGraw-Hill Book Company

New York Atlanta Dallas St. Louis San Francisco
Auckland Bogotá Düsseldorf Johannesburg London
Madrid Mexico Montreal New Delhi Panama Paris
São Paulo Singapore Sydney Tokyo Toronto

Sponsoring Editor/Sylvia L. Weber
Editing Supervisors/Mary Levai and Christine Douglas
Design Supervisor/Karen T. Mino
Art Supervisor/George T. Resch
Production Supervisor/S. Steven Canaris

Cover Design/Jack Weaver

Library of Congress Cataloging in Publication Data

Burke, John D [Date]
    Advertising in the marketplace.

    Includes bibliographical references and index.
    1. Advertising. I. Title.
HF5823.B855 1980   659.1   79-18152

ISBN 0-07-009035-1

ADVERTISING IN THE MARKETPLACE, Second Edition

3 4 5 6 7 8 9 0 DODO 8 8 7 6 5 4 3 2

CONTENTS

PREFACE

Most advertising textbooks describe the field of advertising and seek to develop the reader's understanding of the advertising process. *Advertising in the Marketplace, Second Edition,* has a different and more exacting goal. It concentrates on the ways to complete the advertising task. Although it presents advertising theory, it emphasizes how to get the job done.

This practical approach gives students the tools that will help them solve the problems they will encounter when they enter the field of marketing. For example, if students become merchants, they must know what to advertise and why, be familiar with proper advertising budget procedures, and be able to determine advertising costs from rate cards. They must also be able to establish advertising objectives, know the sources to call on to help ''make'' ads, select media, and measure results. If students obtain entry jobs in the advertising department of a retailer, manufacturer, or supplier of service, or in an advertising agency, they should be familiar with advertising department organization, advertising plans, Standard Rate and Data Service, and creative processes. This book supplies these basic types of information in a logical and readable manner.

Advertising in the Marketplace, Second Edition, differs from all other advertising textbooks in two other important ways. First, since many students will face the advertising task on the local level, the text covers local advertising thoroughly. Second, since the essential part of advertising is its selling message, it stresses the creative rather than the technical side of advertising. By studying the text and completing the end-of-chapter activities, the student can actually produce simple but effective print and broadcast copy. The text supplies the student with checklists that can help in judging whether an ad is effective.

Objectives

Advertising in the Marketplace supplies the student with the necessary knowledge and proficiency to handle the advertising task either as a small advertiser or as a member of a large marketing organization or advertising agency. Since all advertising requires the completion of nine basic steps, the student learns what these steps are and how to perform each one. Although this text has been prepared for use in a basic course in advertising, it can be used as a practitioner's guide for the businessperson who wants to develop more creative advertising programs.

Basic Premises

Advertising is a lively, exciting industry constantly involved in new developments. The author has been eager to write and update this new edition so that students and all those interested in the subject can be aware of and can understand the relative importance of changes in this field. In addition, the passage of time permits some objectivity. Certain areas of this textbook have been expanded and strengthened to help students in the most constructive way possible.

In spite of the many innovations in advertising, the basics of the industry have not changed at all. The original plan of this textbook remains valid.

Organization

The new edition of *Advertising in the Marketplace* is organized into nineteen chapters, which are grouped in four units, and an appendix. It also contains a glossary.

Unit I, "The World of Advertising," defines advertising, explains its history, and demonstrates how it works. The local and the national advertisers are discussed, and the ways in which each organizes to complete the advertising task are fully described.

The industry has made strides in self-regulation, and the activities of the National Advertising Division of the Better Business Bureau, along with those of the National Advertising Review Board, are documented in this revision. Federal Trade Commission corrective advertising has been covered. Cooperative advertising, including its procedures and the legislation that affects it, is treated at length. Advocacy advertising and advertising by professionals are discussed in new sections.

In the advertising agency field, the commission-fee controversy is explored, as are the alternatives to using an ad agency, including house agencies, creative boutiques, and media buying services.

Unit II, "Advertising Media, Research, and Budgets," covers the technical side of advertising. Beyond describing the various media and their capabilities and limitations, this unit includes simple guidelines that are helpful in making advertising media decisions. In this edition, "wave," or "pulse," scheduling of advertising is described and evaluated. "Qube" cable, the two-way medium, is described at length, and many other media innovations are covered. The research activities of both local and national advertisers are described, along with suggestions on when and how to use research. An entire chapter is devoted to budget procedures.

Unit III, "Creating Practical Advertising," explores the creative process. It probes where ideas "come from" and tells how ideas can be stimulated. It then stresses the need to identify an advertising objective and instructs the student in ways to evaluate such an objective. Chapters 12, 13, and 14 present the essentials of writing print and broadcast advertising copy. Examples of all principal types of copy are given in the text and illustrations. "Teaser" copy, special incentive copy, and the controversial area of comparative copy are discussed. The discussion of the creative processes is then supported by technical information on ad production. Layout, illustration, and type are discussed in Chapter 15, and Chapter 16 covers the fundamentals of print production. Chapters 17 and 18 explain television and radio advertising production.

In Unit IV, "Your Future in Advertising," Chapter 19 discusses career opportunities in advertising, supplies checklists for use in measuring individual potentials for various careers, and outlines preparatory steps that aid a student's entry into this exciting field. It also discusses future trends in advertising.

The appendix, "Local Advertising," organizes the principal categories of local advertising in accordance with the nine steps of the advertising process. The style, preferred media, and advertising methods of each of these industries are described and illustrated. The format, new to this edition, permits the student to concentrate on areas of particular interest.

Teaching Aids

The chapters conclude with the following activities: (1) a list of significant advertising terms that the students are asked to define, (2) a series of questions that help students to recall information presented in the text, (3) several exercises that encourage students to apply principles they have learned and that require submission of tear sheets or descriptions of advertisements, (4) assignments that call for individual research, and (5) "Career Ladders" describing typical situations encountered by people throughout their advertising careers and requiring creative solutions.

Each unit concludes with a case history that requires the students to analyze and interpret the data presented and to make advertising decisions. These cases involve students in the kind of practical advertising problems that will be faced in their future careers; the cases make the nine basic steps of the advertising task come alive for the students.

An accompanying instructor's manual and key contains answers to all end-of-chapter activities and provides ready-to-duplicate midterm and final examinations. It also contains general teaching suggestions, a bibliography, and ditto or transparency masters of forms used in preparing advertisements.

Acknowledgments

This book could not have been written without the cooperation and assistance of scores of local merchants, the advertising media trade organizations, the advertising trade journals, many national advertisers and their agencies, and marketing educators. I am especially appreciative of their help. Peggy Fincher, Peggy Fincher Promotions and Fashion Institute of Technology, New York; Vivienne Manias, Montour Senior High School, McKees Rocks, Pennsylvania; Louis P. Ruggiero, State University of New York at Farmingdale and Farmingdale Senior High School; and Dr. Ralph D. Wray, Illinois State University, Normal, Illinois, reviewed the entire manuscript. They offered many helpful recommendations for improving the usefulness of the text as a teaching tool.

Felix Kent was most helpful in reading manuscript covering legal matters and the prickly field of advertising regulation, and many of his suggestions have been included. Spencer Bruno, of Spencer Bruno Associates, has given me valuable advice, particularly in the research sections. I am indebted to various Compton department heads, including Thomas Dunkerton, head of marketing, research and media services; Ruppert Witalis, head of art services; and Charles Capuano, head of television and radio production, for their suggestions. Others at Compton, particularly Vivian Barr, Arnold Behrman, Joel Fisher, Ivan Glick, Graham Hay, Maggie Lacey, Myrna Omang, and Chaunce Skilling, answered many questions. Halbert Paine, marketing consultant, and Dana Redman and Robert Lidell, media consultants, also have made many helpful contributions that have improved this book. Finally, I owe a debt of gratitude to my wife Betty, whose encouragement made it all possible.

John D. Burke

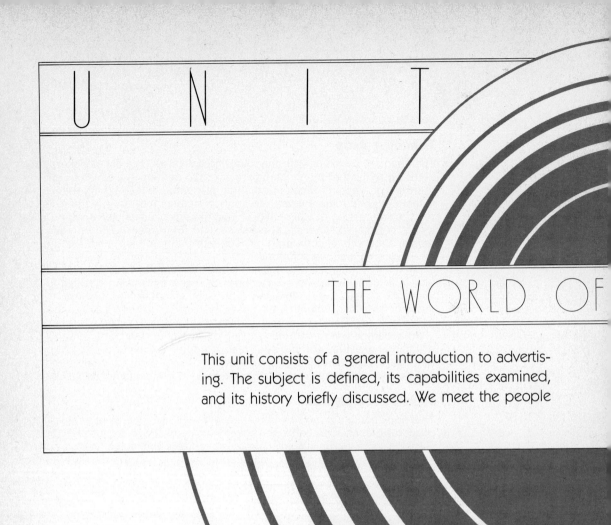

U N I T

THE WORLD OF

This unit consists of a general introduction to advertising. The subject is defined, its capabilities examined, and its history briefly discussed. We meet the people

O N E

ADVERTISING

involved in local and national advertising, learn about the jobs they perform, and discover how their work is organized to complete the advertising task.

CHAPTER ONE

ADVERTISING: WHAT IT'S ALL ABOUT

The basic needs of people are simple: food, clothing, and shelter. In many of the countries of the world today, these basic needs have been satisfied for most of the population. These are the industrialized countries, of which the United States is a good example. Mechanization and the factory have freed the inhabitants of these lands from the necessity of spending all their waking hours providing for their own individual needs. The machine does much of their toiling for them and produces goods at a rate undreamed of before the Industrial Revolution.

The masses of goods thus produced must be distributed to the people who will use them. Various systems of distribution have been created. Nations with a socialized form of government rely on a planned economy, where the power to determine what is produced and how goods and services are distributed is in the hands of government specialists. In the nations of the free world, such decisions, for the most part, rest with individual businesspeople and producers, who plan production and distribution according to their own evaluation of what can be sold to the consumer, the individual who ultimately uses an article or service. The latter nations have a *free* rather than a *planned* economy.

In nations with a free economy, the business science of marketing has come into being. *Marketing* has been defined as "the performance of business activities that direct the flow of goods from producer to consumer."[1] It is a broad area that includes the development of products, distribution of goods to the marketplace, and promotion. Included in promotion is a mixture of activities designed to persuade a customer to buy a product or service. This *promotional mix* includes display, sales promotion, publicity and public relations, personal selling, and advertising. Each area of the promotional mix employs its own practitioners and

[1] American Marketing Association, *Marketing Definitions: A Glossary of Marketing Terms,* Chicago, 1960, p. 15.

engages in its own activities. Table 1-1 shows some of the major activities involved in each area of promotion.

All the activities in the promotional mix, including advertising, are part of the marketing process because they are a form of selling. It is no coincidence that the most industrialized free-economy nations use the most promotion —and the most advertising.

Why is advertising necessary? Since advertising is a form of selling, the real question becomes: Why is selling necessary? In the days before the Industrial Revolution, when goods were made by individual craftspeople and artisans, all the needs of the *consumer,* the ultimate user of a product or service, could not always be met. It was as common for a buyer to seek a seller as it was for a seller to seek a buyer. There was not much need for selling ability, and although there was advertising, it did not play an important role. When machines and factories replaced production by hand, however, goods and services could be produced in quantity. The mass production of products and services requires constant selling pressure to keep consumption high. Goods

are produced that may well appeal to the public, but unless the public is informed about them and persuaded to try them, the goods remain unsold.

Thus the growth of advertising parallels the growth of industrialization. Advertising grew because it was needed to sell goods and services. Its twin jobs of informing and persuading help keep the factories and stores busy.

Let's think about the advertising done by the local merchant in your own area.

As a service to readers, local newspapers often list in their news columns what is playing at the neighborhood drive-in movie theater and the time schedule. Isn't this enough? The drive-in owner doesn't think so. The owner wants to persuade the consumer to come, so advertising in glowing terms is used to interest the reader. In the ads, quotes from favorable reviews may be listed along with the price of admission. And the sign at the drive-in itself is as big and as visible as possible. The drive-in owner would probably be out of business without advertising.

The supermarket owner is one of the heaviest users of advertising. The newspaper is used to

TABLE 1-1 Promotional Activities

Display	Sales Promotion	Publicity and Public Relations	Personal Selling	Advertising
Exterior:	Price reductions	Publicity releases	Retail salespeople	Newspapers
Signs	Premiums	Previews	Outside salespeople	Magazines
Banners	Trading stamps	Community events		Radio
Window	Coupons	Community partici-		Television
Interior:	Contests	pation		Direct mail
Counters	Samples	Special events		Outdoor
Shelves	Trade shows	Guides		advertising
Walls	Exhibits	Consumer advisory		Transit
Buildups	Dealer incentive	boards		advertising
Hangers	programs	Customer relations		Specialty
	Sales staff	Employee relations		advertising
	incentive			Directories
	programs			and programs

announce popular items and low prices, in the hope that the homemaker will do weekend shopping at the owner's store rather than at the competitor's. Is this advertising necessary? A food store manager says, "My ads take plenty of my time and money. But they bring the folks in, and if our service stays good and I sell quality items, the customers keep coming back. I've got to have the ads every week. They pay off for me."

Prevalence of Advertising

Advertising surrounds us during all our waking hours. Whether it's the sign on the diner that simply says "Eat," the matchbook with its sales message, the advertising letters and pamphlets that arrive in the mailbox, or the sequences of commercials on television that break up the movie into 10-minute segments, we are in constant contact with advertising messages of one sort or another.

It has been estimated that a typical family is exposed to 1,500 advertising messages a day.[2] Now this is a very conservative figure. If you traveled even a short distance to the campus today, you could have passed 100 shop signs and posters on the way. If you stopped at a drugstore, you could have seen a myriad of counter advertising cards, interior signs, and packages printed with advertising messages. Glancing through a monthly magazine, you

would be exposed to at least 100 ads. And if you read the local evening paper, the total number of advertising messages you were exposed to during the day becomes even more impressive. For example, a tally of the ads in the Friday edition of a newspaper that sells 10,000 copies a day revealed 134 ads measuring more than 4 square inches in size and 471 smaller ads.

Every advertisement is intended to persuade the consumer to take some positive form of action favorable to the advertiser. But each consumer responds to only a very small number of these advertising appeals. The mind rejects what does not interest it, and one does not see what one does not want to see.

If a person has eaten lunch and then passes a restaurant, the window sign advertising the luncheon specials holds no appeal and isn't noticed by that individual. A man is not aware of the sign for a shoeshine parlor unless his shoelace has broken or he needs a shine. Nor is a homemaker particularly conscious of the local appliance dealer's ads for refrigerators until her old one breaks down and she needs a new one. Then she reads the refrigerator ads. The "sorting" mechanism in our minds screens out material that is irrelevant to us. As with other things, we become aware of advertising, read it, and respond to it only when it relates to our needs or wants.

In another study, consumers were asked to count the number of advertisements that they saw or heard in a day—ads, in other words, of which they were aware. The average was seventy-six ads per consumer.[3] This is quite a reduction from the estimate of 1,500 messages that the average family is actually exposed to.

---

[2] The director of research at Batten, Barton, Durstine & Osborn, a leading advertising agency, labeled the figure 1,500 a "myth," according to a news story in *Advertising Age,* October 19, 1970. His research indicated men "saw, heard or viewed" 285 advertisements a day and women, 305. The author upholds the validity of 1,500 or more daily advertising exposures. The BBDO study confuses awareness with exposure, two quite different matters, as discussed above.

[3] Raymond A. Bauer and Stephen A. Greyser, *Advertising in America: The Consumer View,* Division of Research, Graduate School of Business Administration, Harvard University, Boston, 1968, pp. 175–176.

Would you pay attention to these ads and read them if you had no need for what is advertised? (Courtesy I. Protovin/Maternitique Ltd.; The Pilchuck School; Gould Inc., Rolling Meadow, IL; Philadelphia Sheraton Hotel)

But both figures are logical and reasonable; the sorting mechanism in our minds is at work, and we are ignoring the vast majority of the ad messages that surround us.

Definitions of Advertising

Back in the 1890s, advertising was thought of as "news about products and services." This definition is partially true. Advertising often gives consumers news: news about the new car models, news of the grand opening of a supermarket or bank, or news about a clearance of summer furniture at a department store. But advertising is more than just news, and a famous advertising writer, John E. Kennedy, revolutionized the advertising business in 1904 when he unveiled his own definition. "Advertising," he said, "is salesmanship in print." Nobody had looked at advertising this way before, and Kennedy's statement astounded businesspeople.[4]

But there was truth in Kennedy's definition. Advertising is a form of selling, for its job is to persuade the consumer to take some action favorable to the advertiser: to buy the product, use the service, or accept an idea about a company or an industry. John E. Kennedy's definition was good for advertising because it influenced advertising writers to concentrate on the persuasive aspect of advertising, and it

was good for Kennedy because it made him rich. But it is not good enough for advertising today. We now define advertising as follows:

Advertising is a sales message, directed at a mass audience, that seeks through persuasion to sell goods, services, or ideas on behalf of the paying sponsor.

Let's take a closer look at some of the terms in this definition:

Advertising is a Sales Message The advertising message must act as a salesperson and do its best to convince the consumer of the merits of the product or service described. (See Color Plate 1.)

Directed at a Mass Audience Advertising differs from its close relation, personal selling, in an important way: a salesperson can make only a limited number of calls in a day. But the advertising sales message can reach perhaps millions of consumers through the advertising *media* (a term used to cover all the vehicles that advertisers use to carry and communicate their messages—radio, newspapers, magazines, television, posters, and even matchbooks).

Goods, Services, or Ideas When the advertising message asks the consumer to buy a car, a tube of toothpaste, or a soft drink, goods, or products, are being advertised. When it asks the consumer to open a bank account, or patronize the dry cleaner, business services are being advertised.[5] Sometimes an ad sells neither goods nor services; its job is to sell an idea about a company, a store, or an industry. The local electric utility runs a message about

---

[4] Kennedy was apparently aware that Albert D. Lasker, the famous advertising agent who later became head of Lord & Thomas, was obsessed with the problem of defining what advertising was. One day an office clerk handed Lasker a note from Kennedy reading, "I am in the saloon downstairs and I can tell you what advertising is." Intrigued, Lasker proceeded to the saloon and emerged after several hours of conversation with the now famous definition. Kennedy, a former Canadian mountie and natural-born advertising writer, was hired by Lasker at a salary of $28,000 a year, a fantastic amount for those days. John Gunther, *Taken at the Flood,* Popular Library, New York, 1961, pp. 55–57.

[5] Certain businesses sell both goods and services. The jeweler sells watches but also repairs them. The service station sells gasoline but also services cars with oil changes and lubrication jobs. The car dealer sells cars but may also be in the rent-a-car business. In such instances, the advertising may feature both goods and services.

saving electricity. Smokey the Bear says, "Only you can prevent forest fires." IBM advertises the concept of "word processing." These are all ideas that the advertiser wants the consumer to "buy," or accept.

An ad can serve more than one purpose. E. I. du Pont de Nemours & Co., for example, advertises Lucite, a clear plastic product. The ad begins by telling all about Lucite's advantages. But it ends with an idea it wants the reader to accept about du Pont as a whole: "du Pont—better things for better living . . . through chemistry." Thus one advertisement can sell both a product and an idea. The ads on the following two pages show examples of advertisements that sell goods, services or an idea.

The Sponsor The *advertiser,* or sponsor, pays the cost of preparing an advertisement and the cost of inserting it in the chosen media. Advertising thus differs from *publicity,* a message about a product, company, industry, or service that is placed in editorial or news columns of media. Sponsors pay for the space or time when they advertise. They do not pay when the message appears as publicity.

Who Ultimately Pays for Advertising?

The advertiser pays the bill for preparing and running an ad. And this is just one of the many costs the advertiser faces in the course of making an article or setting up a service to be sold. There are manufacturing or preparation costs—raw materials to buy or process, payrolls to meet, or, for a merchant, a store to rent and stock with goods. Then what is to be sold must be distributed or marketed, and in this process advertising is used along with other promotional activities. All these efforts

cost money, money that returns only when products or services are sold at prices that cover all these costs and provide profits as well.

When buying a product or a service, the consumer pays for the costs of making it and distributing it. As advertising is part of the distribution costs involved, the consumer ultimately pays for the cost of advertising.

But advertising serves several important functions. Besides being one of the important tools that industry uses to help bring about the distribution of goods and services, it also supports the communications media. A medium-size newspaper receives 25 percent of its income from the price charged per copy and 75 percent from the advertising it carries. The same ratio applies generally to magazines. In the commercial broadcast media, radio and television, the only source of income is advertising. If there were no advertising, a newspaper might cost four times its present price, and television and radio would be available to the public only on a fee basis. So advertising pays for the contents of newspapers and magazines as well as the evening's television fare.

Cost of Advertising

The cost of advertising is high in some industries and low in others. Even within industries, there is sometimes great variation. Some businesses advertise heavily, others very little. The amount of advertising and its consequent cost are determined by the methods of distribution used by the manufacturer or retailer.

A manufacturer of cosmetics, for example, may choose to sell products through salespeople who personally call on women at home. This method is called *direct selling.* Such a manufacturer will probably use advertising of two kinds. The manufacturer will advertise to obtain salespeople and also run advertisements that support them in their work.

HOW TO REDUCE RUST

YOU MAY BE WASHING THE WRONG SIDE OF YOUR CAR.

Spring is a perfect time to do something about rust.

Rusting is a year-round problem, and corrosive conditions have become a lot worse in the last five years.

If you live where salt is used to melt ice on the roads, that is speeding up corrosion on your car. If you live in the country, it's the calcium chloride that's spread on dirt roads to hold down dust. And corrosive chemicals in the air are causing rust in every part of America.

We're doing something to help prevent rust on the new cars we're building. Meanwhile, you can do something about reducing rust on your car.

It's important to wash your car often. Use a mild soap and lukewarm or cold water. **Please don't neglect the underside of your car.** The worst rusting happens from the inside out. That's because salt, slush, and even mud tend to collect in the crevices underneath the car, in the door creases, and inside the fenders. Moisture gets trapped in those places and causes rust. So try to wash the underside of your car, too. In winter, if you can, and at the first opportunity in spring. Even if it's only a few times a year, that would help some.

If your car gets dented, scratched, or chipped, try to get it repaired as soon as possible. Even a "small" scratch is bad. Because once a car starts to rust, the damage spreads fast. The paint around a dent or scratch can look okay, but rust is spreading underneath. In the long run, it's cheaper to fix the car right away.

A lot of people think that parking a car in a heated garage during the winter will help prevent rust. But it's just the opposite. Cold slows down the rusting process, as it does most chemical reactions.

We're doing more now to protect GM cars from rust. For one thing, we're using more rust-resistant materials, including different types of zinc-coated steel, in places where rust usually occurs. Also, our new paint primers and the way we apply them are designed to provide a thorough finish, even on some parts of the car you can't see.

Our goal is to protect your car so that it lasts longer and gives you the most value. And fighting rust helps.

This advertisement is part of our continuing effort to give customers useful information about their cars and trucks and the company that builds them.

General Motors
People building transportation to serve people

Which ad sells goods? Service? An idea? (Courtesy General Motors; The Bell System; Konica Camera Co.)

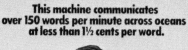

Most of this manufacturer's efforts in distributing cosmetics are thus entrusted to salespeople. Most of the sales budget is devoted to direct selling. Advertising to the consumer is less important to this manufacturer as a method of distribution.

Another cosmetic manufacturer uses more usual methods of distribution through discount houses, drugstores, and supermarkets rather than from door to door. Unless these cosmetics are heavily promoted to the consumer, they will languish unsold on shelves of the stores for a time. Then they will disappear from the stores altogether. Stores will not stock them because shelf space is valuable and the store management cannot afford to display slow-moving items.

Advertising is thus very important to such a cosmetics manufacturer and is the primary method of distribution. This maker will spend much more on advertising than the competitor who uses salespeople to distribute cosmetic products.

An example will make this clear. Avon Products is a large manufacturer and marketer of cosmetics. Its method of selling is to employ sales representatives who call on consumers in their homes. Avon cosmetics cannot be purchased in stores. Avon does advertise but on a smaller scale than other cosmetic manufacturers and for particular purposes as noted above. One primary intent of its ads is to "introduce" the Avon Lady to the consumer in an effort to make her welcome when she rings the doorbell. Another purpose is to recruit sales representatives for its direct selling operation. Refer to the Avon ad (Color Plate 2).

Note the Drug and cosmetics section of Table 1-2. Avon's advertising costs are 5.7 percent of sales. Bristol-Meyers, with its many brands, including the Clairol line of products, is a very large company in the toiletries field selling through retail stores. It must support its products on the shelves and create consumer demand through advertising. As a result, its ad costs are 9.5 percent of sales. Revlon also protects and enhances its consumer franchise with heavy advertising at an advertising cost of 9.9 percent of sales. The methods of distribution of these companies are completely different from Avon's, and their advertising consequently plays a different role.

Cost Differences among and within Industries

Note in Table 1-2 that the companies marketing oil and petroleum products spend less than 1 percent of sales on advertising, while makers of gum and candy and soap products spend much more. The basic reasons are their methods of distribution and types of products.

TABLE 1-2 Advertising Costs as Percentages of Sales for Selected Companies, 1977

Company	Advertising Costs	Sales	Advertising Costs as Percentage of Sales
Cars:			
General Motors	$312,000,000	$54,961,300,000	0.5
Ford	184,000,000	37,841,000,000	0.4
Chrysler	127,100,000	16,708,000,000	0.7
Volkswagen of America	52,700,000	11,522,827,824	0.5
Toyota	49,175,900	10,872,000,000	0.5
Food:			
General Foods	300,000,000	5,380,000,000	5.6
General Mills	160,500,000	3,243,000,000	4.9
McDonald's	122,157,600	3,241,477,000	3.8
Kraft	99,000,000	5,238,807,000	1.9
Kellogg	69,804,000	1,533,442,000	4.6
Soaps, cleansers (and allied):			
Procter & Gamble	460,000,000	8,099,687,000	5.7
Unilever	145,000,000	1,355,072,000	10.7
Colgate-Palmolive	120,000,000	3,837,204,000	3.1
S. C. Johnson & Son	48,860,500	450,000,000	10.9
Drugs and cosmetics:			
Warner-Lambert	201,000,000	2,542,728,000	7.9
Bristol-Myers	203,000,000	2,191,433,000	9.3
Johnson & Johnson	91,800,000	1,713,583,000	5.3
Revlon	80,000,000	809,810,000	9.9
Avon Products	55,000,000	959,227,000	5.7
Block Drug	31,000,000	135,919,000	22.8
Gum and candy:			
Mars	51,000,000	790,000,000	6.5
Wrigley	31,036,900	397,941,000	7.8
Oil:			
Mobil	142,722,470	34,442,935,000	0.04
Exxon	35,270,800	58,458,000,000	0.006
Shell	26,800,000	10,193,685,000	0.03
Others:			
General Electric	112,210,300	17,518,800,000	0.6
CBS	93,379,000	2,776,331,000	3.5
Eastman Kodak	85,471,800	4,763,500,000	1.8
Anheuser-Busch	75,437,000	2,231,230,000	3.4

Source: From *Advertising Age*, August 28, 1978, p. 30; reprinted by permission.

Advertising is relatively less important to the petroleum marketer than to the maker of packaged goods sold through stores. Gasoline can be considered a commodity, and differences between brands are relatively unimportant to motorists, particularly when gasoline shortages are prevalent. Advertising, therefore, gets little emphasis in petroleum company distribution planning.

The soap manufacturer and the candy manufacturer rely much more heavily on advertising to force distribution and create consumer demand in stores. Because there is such a wide variety of these products grouped together on the shelves of the store, consumers are more likely to pick up a brand that they have heard of—through advertising.

Besides differences of distribution methods in various industries, other factors influence the amount of advertising expenditures. Competition may be more severe in one industry than in another, and when competition thrives, so does advertising. Company management may adopt a policy of heavy advertising, judging this to be the best way to increase business. Or, in a particular year, a company may bring out one or more new products. New-product introduction invariably means heavy initial advertising expenses; advertising, it is hoped, will make the unknown brand accepted and familiar. Reasons like these have important bearing on advertising costs. For example, S. C. Johnson's policy of heavy advertising plus their frequent introduction of new products make this company's advertising expenses high, as can be seen in Table 1-2.

Advertising Costs per Unit

It is difficult to obtain advertising costs for the separate brands a company may market so that we can examine ad costs per brand or per unit sold. Companies usually consider this information confidential. But we do have available ad-cost figures for the automobile industry (Table 1-3).

If we divide the money spent on advertising for each make of car by the number of cars of that make sold, we see that advertising costs ran from $23.09 for an Oldsmobile all the way to $68.34 for a Chrysler. Advertising did part of the job of distributing these cars to the purchaser, and it cost these amounts per car to accomplish the task.

These figures do not seem particularly high in proportion to the total cost of buying a car these days. But why not stop advertising and pass the savings on to the buyer in lower car prices? We still would buy cars; after all, they wear out and need replacing. But we must remember that advertising stimulates demand for a product. With no advertising fanfare, the introduction of new car models would be a tame matter indeed. Car makers could rely only on publicity releases that would announce changes in styling and new advances in engine design. Without advertising to whet our appetites for the new models, we would probably wait longer to get our new cars, and it is reasonable to assume that sales would eventually suffer. With lower sales, costs of making cars would rise, and the prices of cars would be higher than those that now include the advertising cost.

Information on advertising costs of brewers is listed in Table 1-4.

Competition is severe in the brewing industry, and without promotional activities, the brewer would find it difficult to survive. Yet the costs of an advertising program, the most important part of brewery promotional activities, range from 2 cents to 14 cents per case. These are relatively insignificant amounts when the retail cost of a case of beer is considered.

It is logical to assume that if a brewer ceased advertising, sales would fall off. With smaller volume, brewing costs per unit would increase, costs which would be passed on to the consumer in higher retail prices.

Is Advertising Hypnotic?

The power of advertising is often exaggerated by its critics, who cast advertising people in the role of superpsychologists, able to manipulate the minds of consumers at will. In reality, the consumer is far from dumb and docile; actually, the consumer is sophisticated and discriminating in buying goods and services. We have seen that the vast majority of advertising is ignored and that people respond to advertising only when it interests them. This is hardly what one would expect if advertising people could manipulate consumers' minds.

But there is additional evidence that merely spending money on advertising does not automatically ensure business success. Of every ten major new products introduced into the

marketplace, according to a survey made by the National Industrial Conference Board, three do not develop satisfactory sales, and one is completely withdrawn from the market. The most important reasons for failure are "inadequate market analysis and product defects." "Inadequate market analysis" means that companies didn't do their homework properly. Products were conceived that did not have the hoped-for appeal to the consumer. And if a product contains defects or fails to meet expectations and consumer standards, the public is quick to reject it. Advertising cannot overcome these business mistakes.

The experience of the Ford Motor Company is a case in point. After elaborate analysis of the automobile market, the Edsel car was introduced with much publicity and heavy advertising backing. The car was an astonishing failure. Ford had not gauged the public's interest properly. On the other hand, Ford's Granada and Fairmont, both heavily promoted, have enjoyed sales success. They were what the public wanted. As Jules Backman says, "The pub-

Company	Number of Cars Sold	1972 Advertising Investment	Ad Cost per Car 1972
American Motors	312,271	$ 25,508,200	$43.72
Chrysler	1,517,610	64,209,000	42.31
Chrysler	201,094	13,742,300	68.34
Dodge	583,392	25,508,200	43.72
Plymouth	733,124	24,958,500	34.04
Ford	2,666,594	133,728,000	50.15
Ford	2,157,118	102,565,900	47.55
Mercury	409,171	24,909,000	60.88
Lincoln	100,305	6,253,100	62.34
General Motors	4,823,127	132,073,000	27.38
Buick	681,065	18,442,600	27.08
Cadillac	269,127	7,557,100	28.08
Chevrolet	2,345,134	69,178,400	29.50
Oldsmobile	771,280	17,812,400	23.09
Pontiac	756,521	19,082,500	25.22

TABLE 1-3 Ad Costs per Car

Source: From *Advertising Age*, December 31, 1973; reprinted by permission.

TABLE 1-4 Ad Costs of Brewers

Company	Number of Barrels Sold	1977 Advertising Investment	Ad Cost Per Barrel	Per Case
Anheuser-Busch	36,600,000	$58,687,200	$1.60	$0.11
Miller	24,200,000	43,283,400	1.78	0.12
Schlitz	22,130,000	43,928,800	1.98	0.14
Pabst	16,003,000	10,969,789	0.68	0.04
Coors	12,830,000	4,355,333	0.33	0.02
Olympia	6,831,000	8,830,050	1.29	0.09
Heileman	6,245,000	4,736,473	0.75	0.05
Stroh	6,114,000	7,310,516	1.19	0.08
Schaefer	4,700,000	4,325,193	0.92	0.06

Source: From *Advertising Age,* October 9, 1978; reprinted by permission.

lic must desire a product and be convinced of its superior quality before it will make large-scale purchases."[6]

What advertising can do is force initial trial; that is, it can persuade the consumer to try something once. But if the product or service doesn't satisfy the buyer by filling a need, the buyer will refuse to purchase the item again.

Brisk and Vote toothpastes; Duractin, a time-release aspirin; Radar, a hair-grooming product; Hidden Magic, a hair spray; Tanya, a suntan oil; and Double-Buffered cold tablets were all developed by leading manufacturers in recent years. They were introduced across the country with extensive advertising support. None of them is on sale today, for the public did not find the brands attractive enough to keep on buying them at a profitable rate. Many more products do not even reach the point of being distributed nationally. They are tried out by *market testing,* a method that attempts to test on a small scale in one or a few markets the sales results that might be achieved on a national level. Advertising is used within these

limited areas at a rate that is comparable to national rates. If the products fail to meet sales objectives, they are dropped. The point is that advertising alone cannot ensure success.

We have said that advertising can't sell an individual something that isn't needed or wanted, but an ad can persuade a consumer to try a product initially in the hope that it might be superior in meeting that consumer's needs. In the case of totally new products, an ad can create a need in the reader's mind that previously didn't exist. Does the consumer really need the product? Perhaps not. Can advertising sell people things they really "shouldn't have"? Of course it can.

Suppose the man of the house sees a new-model, 24-inch color television set advertised by the local appliance dealer in the evening paper. Perhaps he hadn't thought of buying a new color set, but now he thinks of it. He can't really afford it, but he can't resist it. He buys it and takes on one more time-payment plan. Or perhaps a woman has a weakness for new clothes. The ads for the new fashions sponsored by the local dress shop are her downfall. A boy might see an ad featuring a boat dealer's end-of-summer close-outs on outboard motors

[6] Jules Backman, *Advertising and Competition,* New York University Press, New York, 1967, p. 57.

Lately, some mysterious automobiles have been seen on the roads

IF you happened to be up in northern Minnesota last year, it's just possible that you might have noticed a covered car cruising smoothly along out-of-the-way county roads.

You would know if you saw it, because this automobile didn't look much like the usual run of cars you find around Bemidji.

Or maybe you were one of the few who chanced to see such a car roaring wide-open through the sand and mesquite under the high, hot Arizona sky.

And recently, more than one filling station owner in the Cumberlands has forgotten to say, "Fill 'er up?" in his hurry to ask, "Hey, what kind of a car you got there?"

Edsel is the kind.

Maybe you thought none had been built yet.

But if you did, you were wrong. For almost a year, the first Edsels have been chalking up miles. Miles of pavement and of no pavement. Of mud and slush. Of mountain and flatland. Of sub-tropic heat and sub-zero cold.

Not thousands of miles. Hundreds of thousands.

By the time it reaches your streets, the Edsel will be one of the best-tested, best-proved cars in automobiling history. And that time is not far off.

The **EDSEL** is on its way

New member of the Ford family of fine cars

EDSEL DIVISION · FORD MOTOR COMPANY · DEARBORN, MICHIGAN

Both these cars received heavy advertising support. In spite of this, the Edsel failed to sell and was withdrawn. The Ford Fairmont was a success. Advertising alone can't guarantee sales results. (Courtesy Ford Motor Company)

and water skis and spend more of his summer earnings than he had intended. Maybe the people concerned shouldn't have these things, but did advertising cause the problem? Who is wrong? Is it the advertiser who reached the individual with an effective selling message or the individual who can't live within a budget? If we say that the advertiser is at fault, someone must determine who should advertise and to whom and judge advertising (and the products that advertising sells) on the basis of social worth. If we say that individuals who spend more than they should are at fault, we are interfering with their freedom of choice and their right to make a mistake.

Is Advertising Truthful?

The words used in ads are often those that a salesperson would use in talking to a prospective customer face to face. These words praise the product or service being sold, and they are colorful, glowing words. They put the product's best foot forward, and they tell of the satisfaction to be enjoyed when the consumer does as the words ask. In persuading, they may often exaggerate. By its very nature, advertising cannot be balanced or objective. Its job is to present only the point of view of the sponsor, who pays for the opportunity to persuade the consumer to buy. Ads can be interesting, informative, helpful, inspiring, amusing, and entertaining. They can also be annoying, persistent, unbelievable, repetitive, boring, confusing, and offensive. But today they seldom are untruthful.

Such has not always been the case. In simpler, less sophisticated times, advertising often made claims that were completely unrestrained. Particularly in the area of drugs and medicines, promises of miracles were common. The following figure reproduces an example of such an ad from before the turn of the century. There is a nostalgic charm about this

THE FUTURA IS NOW.

Right now! Ford Futura gives you advanced styling with the look of tomorrow today. A sporty coupe with all the style and flair that's just right for the life you're livin'. You don't have to wait for the future to afford an expensive personal car. You're ready for Futura—now!

Now means you've got your own style... and we've got the car to match.

Now means luxury touches and high style, coming and going. Why not the optional touch of power windows?

Now is comfort. The luxury of 5-passenger roominess.

Now is a sporty way of life. Futura matches it with a sporty rack and pinion steering and an economical 2.3 litre overhead cam engine with 4-speed manual transmission.*

Now means personal style. Add your own touch. Order your own personal Futura to your own personal taste.

Now is a flip-up open air roof...open up your roof and let the sunshine in.

*EPA estimated MPG: [20] Highway estimate 31 MPG. For comparison to other cars. Your mileage may differ, depending on speed, weather and trip length. California MPG is lower. Actual highway mileage will probably be lower than estimate.

FORD FAIRMONT FUTURA

FORD DIVISION *Ford*

The future isn't someday, it's now. Why wait? Step into the '79 Futura—now!

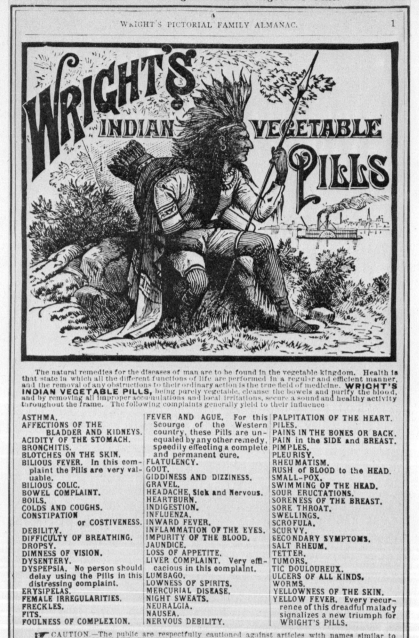

This ad is a typical example of the grandiose claims of nineteenth-century advertising. What protection do we have today against unsubstantiated statements in advertising? (The Bettmann Archive, Inc.)

copy when it is read today, but at the time, the claims that were made were taken quite seriously. Today there are several forces that work to minimize the number of untruthful advertisements that appear.

Consumer Sophistication

With the increased availability of secondary and higher education, consumers are better informed than their counterparts of the 1890s. People are better able to judge the claims of advertisers and aren't taken in by promises that have no basis in fact or by statements that have been exaggerated beyond credibility.

Business Self-Policing Activities

Business polices itself in the advertising area. In the early decades of the twentieth century, business and industry began a policy of self-discipline because it was increasingly realized that unethical and untruthful advertising reflected poorly on business as a whole. The Better Business Bureau (BBB), organized on a national and local basis, helped to curb untruthful and unethical advertising and dishonest selling methods and helped to set guidelines through its fair-trade policies.

NAD-NARB Self-Regulation A major step in industry self-regulation was taken in 1971. At that time, the Council of Better Business Bureaus joined with the American Advertising Federation, The American Association of Advertising Agencies, and the Association of National Advertisers in inaugurating a system for advertising self-regulation that has had far-reaching effects.

The National Advertising Division of the Council of Better Business Bureaus (NAD) and the National Advertising Review Board (NARB)

were established. The NAD investigates complaints concerning the truthfulness and accuracy of claims made in advertisements; in situations where a controversy is not resolved it refers the cases to NARB for decision.

By April 30, 1978, the NAD-NARB mechanism had handled 1,380 complaints from consumers, consumer groups, local Better Business Bureaus, and the advertising monitoring activities of NAD. In addition, advertisers themselves have registered complaints about competitors' advertising activities directed against them.

When a complaint is received by NAD, it is reviewed for merit. If it seems justified, the advertiser involved is asked by NAD to provide proof that the claims or statements in question are accurate. After reviewing the advertiser's explanation, NAD decides either that the advertiser's claims have been substantiated or that the claims are untruthful and inaccurate. In the latter case, NAD asks the advertiser to change or discontinue the advertising.

When the advertiser refuses to cooperate, NARB takes over and a panel is appointed to review the case. If the advertiser again refuses cooperation, NARB publicly refers the matter to an appropriate government enforcement agency for action. Advertisers have in every case cooperated with NAD-NARB decisions to change or discontinue advertising, withdrawing or modifying the advertising being questioned.

A typical case concerned a razor manufacturer's statement "So you don't have to worry about nicks and cuts" when using its disposable razor.[7] NAD was concerned that the words might convey a false sense of security to the user. After all, it was possible to get nicks and cuts when shaving with the razor. The manufacturer was unable to convince NAD of the appropriateness of the "nicks and cuts" claim

[7] *Advertising Age,* December 20, 1977, p. 18.

and agreed to discontinue it in the spirit of co-operating with self-regulation. In other instances, the claim that a tennis ball "had a roundness outside that nobody in the industry can match" was discontinued for lack of proof, and the claim made by an ice-cream maker, "Now there's a new product that tastes even better than regular ice cream," was eliminated from the advertising because of insufficient proof.

The work of NAD-NARB has been an effective self-regulatory system and has the added benefit of saving taxpayers' dollars. The method handles complaints of untruth and inaccuracy that otherwise would be the concern of overburdened government regulatory agencies and the judicial system and settles them without governmental intervention.

Trade and Industry Standards The American Association of Advertising Agencies (AAAA) is the national trade association of the advertising agency business and currently consists of 455 member advertising agencies that create advertising for manufacturers and place it in various media. AAAA has developed a code of conduct, which reads, in part, as follows:

We, the members of the American Association of Advertising Agencies, in addition to supporting and obeying the laws and legal regulations pertaining to advertising, undertake to extend and broaden the application of high ethical standards. Specifically, we will not knowingly produce advertising which contains:

1. False or misleading statements or exaggerations, visual or verbal
2. Testimonials which do not reflect the real choice of a competent witness
3. Price claims which are misleading

4. Comparisons which unfairly disparage a competitive product or service
5. Claims insufficiently supported, or which distort the true meaning or practicable application of statements made by professional or scientific authority
6. Statements, suggestions, or pictures offensive to public decency

We recognize that there are areas which are subject to honestly different interpretations and judgment. Taste is subjective and may even vary from time to time as well as from individual to individual. Frequency of seeing or hearing advertising messages will necessarily vary greatly from person to person.

However, we agree not to recommend to an advertiser and to discourage the use of advertising which is in poor or questionable taste or which is deliberately irritating through content, presentation, or excessive repetition.

Many industry organizations have accepted and endorsed this code, including the Association of National Advertisers, the Magazine Publishers Association, and the American Business Press. The AAAA code of conduct, while praiseworthy in intent, lacks the complaint mechanism of NAD-NARB. It is merely an honor system that is subject to a variety of interpretations.

Media Acceptance Standards The business magazines that specialize in covering the advertising and distribution world have done a consistently thorough job of watching over advertising activities and calling attention to unethical and untruthful advertising. And major media that serve the consumer (newspapers, general magazines, radio, and television) set their own standards on what advertising they will accept and what advertising they consider offensive enough to reject.

The *continuity-acceptance* or *commercial-*

clearance departments of the television networks pass on all advertising submitted before it is run and often ask for proof of statements made in advertising before approval to run it is given. Commercials featuring demonstrations of product superiority must be accompanied by affidavits describing the procedures used in producing the commercials. Claims of superiority must have supporting documents prepared by the advertiser's research and development staff. When the continuity-acceptance department people remain unconvinced, commercials are either rejected or revised to meet network standards.

According to Jack E. Hinton, CBS Television Network Director of Commercial Clearance, his department has six editors who review approximately 40,000 commercials a year.[8]

Three of our editors are specialists in their fields. We have an editor with an engineering degree who reviews all automotive and electronic entertainment commercials. Our food editor has a degree in nutrition and has worked as a product analyst for several large food companies. And our medical editor graduated from Fordham University's College of Pharmacy and worked as a pharmacist before joining us.

Hinton noted that formerly the department's main concern with commercials submitted for clearance was the verification and evaluation of advertisers' statements and claims. Today the department's editors are increasingly concerned with matters of taste and with stereotyped portrayals of individuals within commercials, for example, commercials that demean ethnic groups or senior citizens.

---

[8] Jack E. Hinton, "Offending People in Advertising: Do unto Others. . . ," speech at the Eastern Annual Conference, AAAA, November 19, 1975.

Government Regulation

State laws universally prohibit advertising that contains misleading or untrue assertions. The federal government relies on the *Federal Trade Commission* (FTC) to prevent business from using unfair methods of competition, and in 1938, through the Wheeler-Lea Amendment, false advertising was defined and prohibited. Superlatives and exaggeration are acceptable only when the matter being discussed is subjective in the mind of the reader of the advertisement. For example, descriptive words such as "wonderful" and "superdelicious" could be used to describe the taste of a new snack cake. Superlatives and exaggeration cannot become extreme and suggest facts that can't be proved.

Today, advertisers are careful to steer clear of advertising that violates FTC rules. The commission can bring suit against advertisers and advertising agencies and frequently does. If an order is issued, the damages for breaches of the order are severe. For example, both the advertiser and his advertising agency can be fined $5,000 a day for every day the offending advertising message appears on television.

Felix Kent, partner of Hall, Dickler, Lawler, Kent & Howley, a law firm specializing in legal problems in the field of advertising, emphasizes the care advertisers should take in avoiding untruthful advertising. He has stated to the author

---

False and deceptive advertising consists of any claim the advertiser cannot prove. You've got to have the facts, and the burden of proof is shifted to the advertiser. If you make an ambiguous or vague statement, the FTC will usually construe it against you. False disparagement of a competitor's product should be avoided at all cost. If you've said anything really harmful, not only the FTC can sue, but so may your competitor.

Corrective Advertising Even though the FTC may order an advertiser to cease making claims of an inaccurate or untruthful nature, this action may not be considered sufficient by the commission in certain instances. The commission may reach the conclusion that the advertising claims in question are of such penetrating or long-standing nature that they cannot be rectified merely by ordering the advertiser to cease making such claims in the future.

In such instances, the FTC may order corrective advertising. Statements are ordered inserted in current advertising that previous claims for a product or service were not true. A statement, or disclosure, must not be hidden in the ad by the advertiser, but must be "separated so it can be readily noticed," according to a typical FTC order. In newspaper and magazine ads the disclosure must be printed in type at least twice the size of the "principal portion of the text of the ad." This FTC order can be contested in federal court by the advertiser. However, the commission has negotiated settlements with such advertisers as Campbell Soup and Firestone without involving litigation.

In the Listerine case, Warner-Lambert, the maker of Listerine, decided to fight an FTC order in the courts. Listerine has been traditionally presented to consumers as a product for general oral hygiene and bad breath. But in addition, for 50 years, Listerine was advertised as a "cold fighter."

From medical evidence the commission concluded that Listerine did not prevent colds or sore throats or relieve cold symptoms. Research among consumers revealed that the idea that "Listerine fights colds" was widely accepted. Because of this acceptance and the length of time this idea had been advertised, Warner-Lambert was ordered to run language in $10 million worth of ads stating that "Listerine will not help prevent colds or sore throats or lessen their severity."[9]

Warner-Lambert, quoting its own favorable medical research, decided to fight the order and took the case to federal court. In doing so, it went much further, claiming that the First Amendment prevented the FTC from requiring Warner-Lambert to run corrective ads.[10] A U.S. circuit court of appeal rejected this plea and confirmed the FTC's power to order corrective advertising. Subsequently, the Supreme Court refused to review the case. The effect of this refusal was to reaffirm the circuit court's decision.

Corrective advertising acquired a new dimension in the STP Corporation case. In an agreement, the commission and STP settled charges that the manufacturer made false claims for two of its products in violation of an FTC consent order.[11] In addition to paying a $500,000 fine, STP agreed to run $200,000 worth of advertising in magazines and newspapers exclusively devoted to the fact that STP had agreed to a $700,000 settlement because of running "allegedly inaccurate past advertisements"

While this corrective advertising undoubtedly served to inform some consumers about past inaccuracies in STP advertisements, its primary purpose, as noted by FTC officials, was to warn other advertisers that violations of commission orders will be treated seriously.

TV Advertising Directed at Children The subject of television advertising to children has been a controversial one since the early

[9] *Advertising Age,* October 3, 1977, p. 6.
[10] On May 24, 1976, the Supreme Court decided that "commercial speech," that is, advertising, has First Amendment protection. See *Advertising Age,* May 31, 1976, pp. 2B, 3, and 62A.
[11] *Advertising Age,* February 13, 1978, pp. 1 and 106.

seventies. Organized consumer groups have held that children are easily manipulated by advertising techniques and lack the ability to look at advertising messages objectively. For these reasons, consumer activists have aimed to ban such advertising from television. In addition, these groups advocate forcing broadcasters to present special educational programming for children. Obviously, business interests and the television broadcasting industry have opposed these goals.

In 1974, the FTC, in an effort to decrease commercialization in this area, issued a policy statement which endorsed a limit of 9½ commercial minutes on each hour of weekend children's shows and 12 commercial minutes for weekday children's programs. Rules were issued which barred the use of personalities on children's programs as salespeople for advertised products and which prohibited mention of advertised products in program material.

By February 1978 a staff report of the FTC recommended a ban on television advertising to "very young" children.[12] The report added a new dimension to the controversy by recommending that advertising of sugared products which might cause tooth decay be banned for children up to the age of 12.

FTC hearings on the subject were initiated early in 1979, with consumerist groups such as Consumers Union and Action for Children's Television arrayed against representatives of cereal and toy manufacturers and of the television industry. FTC regulations in this area, if and when issued, will be tested in the courts. According to some legal experts, an outright ban of all television advertising directed at children will not be sustained in court because of a Supreme Court ruling that gives "truthful commercial speech" First Amendment rights. It

is probable, however, that regulation of such advertising will become increasingly stringent. This will be accomplished by FTC rules and by industry self-regulation.

FTC Guides The FTC occasionally issues guides for advertising claims and statements that national and local advertisers should follow. For example, the 1960 guide, *Deceptive Advertising of Guarantees,* states that if a guarantee is mentioned in advertising, the nature and extent of the guarantee must be fully disclosed in the advertisement and the manner of the guarantor's performance must be described. The 1964 guide, *Deceptive Pricing,* establishes consumer safeguards against advertising "former" prices of articles that are not true and valid. An example of illegal fictitious pricing in advertising would be the case of a retailer who advertises "Bargain on Ball-Point Pens! Were 12 for $3—Now 12 for $1.50." If the retailer has sold pens consistently at the former price, all is well. But if the retailer promoted at the $3 price for a few days only to establish the "cut price," the "bargain" is not advertisable or permitted. Retailers should be aware of such FTC guides and conform to them.

Guides are issued without advance notice and are an indication of attitudes on the part of the FTC rather than enforceable regulations. The FTC prefers to rely on *trade regulation rules*, which cover similar areas to guides and are enforceable by law. The issuance of such rules is a lengthy procedure involving public hearings.

Other Government Regulatory Bodies In addition to the FTC, many other government agencies regulate advertising. The Civil Aeronautics Board (CAB) has jurisdiction over airline advertising. The Securities and Exchange

[12] *Advertising Age,* January 22, 1979, p. 81.

Commission (SEC) issues regulations concerning financial advertising. The Department of Agriculture has concurrent jurisdiction with the FTC in certain areas. And the Treasury Department (Bureau of Alcohol, Tobacco and Firearms) has concurrent jurisdiction with the FTC for liquor advertising. In all, approximately eighty different federal agencies are involved in the advertising regulatory process, although many are concerned with advertising only in a minor way.

All these internal and external activities and restrictions serve to keep advertising basically truthful today. It should be stated, however, that in spite of regulations, there are advertisements that are untruthful and that do not meet industry and government standards. These occurrences, while in the minority, serve to discredit business and the advertising community.

Public Attitudes Toward Advertising

People have very strong opinions about advertising. You can undoubtedly think of several ads that you dislike or that annoy you, and if you're like the average person, you can think of others that you approve of or enjoy. The medium through which the advertisement is brought to your attention may influence the way you feel, or the product or service itself might have some bearing on your reaction.

Influence of Media on Attitudes

Where advertising is seen and heard influences the consumer's opinion of it. Advertising in magazines and newspapers is considered far less annoying than advertising on radio and television. Newspaper advertising is held to be more informative than advertising in the other major media. People working in advertising have long felt that most consumers had these opinions. Their views have been supported by the studies of Bauer and Greyser. Table 1-5 shows how consumers react to ads in the various media.

The basic reason for the difference in reactions is that radio and television ads interrupt the program, while magazine or newspaper ads can be easily escaped by just turning the page. It may comfort the local retailer to know that the newspaper, a medium the retailer uses extensively, does not deliver a high annoyance factor and that its pages contain ads thought to

TABLE 1-5 Reaction to Advertising In the Four Media

| | Nature of Reaction by Percent of Consumers | | | | |
	Annoying	Enjoyable	Informative	Offensive	Number of Ads
All media	23	36	36	5	9,325
Magazines	9	37	48	6	1,012
Newspapers	12	23	59	6	867
Radio	24	33	40	3	1,416
Television	27	38	31	4	5,929

Source: Raymond A. Bauer and Stephen A. Greyser, *Advertising in America: The Consumer View,* Division of Research, Graduate School of Business Administration, Harvard University, Boston, pp. 175–176.

be highly informative. One of radio's advertising strengths lies in its power to register a message by intruding on the listener's consciousness and compelling attention. As we shall discover in our chapter on writing radio advertisements, some types of radio advertising approaches irritate the listener more than others. Avoidance of irritating techniques can solve the annoyance problem for the individual retailer.

Influence of Type of Product on Attitudes

It's understandable that consumers consider ads for certain kinds of products more offensive and annoying than others. Ads that begin with the words "New Way to Shrink Hemorrhoids" or "Dry Up Ugly Skin Blemishes" hardly qualify for a good-taste award. But a message that sells travel ("Find Your Own Castle in Spain") will be considered enjoyable; one that sells a new refrigerator ("Combination Refrigerator-Freezer Holds 20% More") will be considered informative.

Advertising Believability

We have discussed truth in advertising; now we will look at the consumer's opinion of truth in advertising. What do consumers think about advertising claims? Do they believe what ads say and accept them?

In 1968, the AAAA commissioned a study on consumer judgment of advertising. More than 1,800 consumers were asked (among other things) the following question: Some people we've talked to say they don't like advertising and feel very unfavorable toward it. Why do you think they feel this way? The answers follow.[13]

Advertising is untruthful or exaggerated (26 percent)
Advertising is false, misleading; ads not quite truthful; trying to fool the public; they don't give a true picture; I've found it was false, or at best misleading (21 percent)
Exaggeration; products can't do all they say; they make them sound as if they were the last word[13] (5 percent)

Similar feelings on the part of the general public often are revealed when researchers undertake consumer studies of product likes and dislikes. A strong minority invariably states, "I don't believe the advertising."

One reason for this disbelief lies in the very nature of advertising. Its job, we must remember, is to do its best to persuade the reader (or listener or viewer) to take some action favorable to the sponsor. It's difficult for the consumer to admit that this persuasion has succeeded. The consumer would much prefer to believe that reasoning powers have led to the purchase of a particular product. The consumer may say that experience with a brand has proved its superiority or that the product was recommended by a friend or relative. These reasons may well be true, but they are also more comfortable reasons, and they reflect better on the individual than the admission that advertising has done its job of persuasion. It is an interesting comment on human nature to note that people who do not believe what the advertising says often go out and buy a particular brand anyway.

Practical, efficient advertising, carefully planned and executed, moves good merchandise at a profitable rate, in spite of the fact that a large percentage of the public consistently states that it is unbelievable.

[13] Bauer and Greyser, pp. 133–134.

IS THERE A DOCTOR SHORTAGE?

For awhile there certainly was. In the 1960's, all of a sudden, doctors' offices were literally swamped. Our medical care system became overloaded almost overnight.

Many factors contributed to this tremendous demand on our doctors and hospitals. The rise in population. The passage of Medicaid and Medicare. The increase in our over-65 population whose medical needs are greatest, and the rise in people with health care insurance (from 123,000,000 in 1960 to 170,000,000 in 1974).

But today we have succeeded in doubling the output of our medical schools. This has produced a 34% increase in the total number of physicians practicing in this country. A recent University of Chicago study reveals that whereas in 1963 only 49% of black Americans saw a physician, by 1976 74% saw a physician, only two percentage points below the 76% for whites. Eighty-eight percent of Americans, according to this study, are generally satisfied with the health care they receive.

Of continuing concern to your doctor is maintaining the quality of care he provides. Your doctor, through his American Medical Association, is active in insuring our high standards of medical training through a major role in the accreditation of medical schools and graduate facilities. To help him renew his capabilities and knowledge, the A.M.A. keeps him up-to-date with a dozen publications and sponsors over 35 major national and regional conferences yearly. When it comes to your health, your doctor has a partner, too.

American Medical Association, 535 North Dearborn Street, Chicago, Illinois 60610.

Your Doctor's Your Partner
Help your doctor help you

REMOVE EMBARRASSING HAIR

with **TIRETTA**

TIRETTA removes hair right from the deep roots. As this is the latest collodion gum treatment there is NO UNPLEASANT SMELL — NO PAINFUL EFFORT — NO WAITING — NO ELECTRICITY — NO COMPLICATED DEVICE — IMMEDIATE EFFECT. Tiretta is ideal for all parts of the body including legs, arms, etc., and is completely safe to use, its deep action reaches right down to the hair roots, and its effect is immediate and lasting. Follow instructions carefully when applying to face.

UNDER THE MICROSCOPE
1. *Razor Cut.*
2. *Ordinary Hair Remover.*
3. *Right down to the roots with Tiretta.*

OUR UNDERTAKING
IF WITHIN 30 DAYS, AFTER USING OUR PRODUCT, ONE SINGLE HAIR GROWS AGAIN, WE WILL TOTALLY REFUND YOUR MONEY.
Send now for this amazing discovery.

Tiretta $4.95 plus 55 cents post and packing.
Giant Tiretta $8.95 plus 55 cents post and packing.

BELGRAVE PRODUCTS LTD. Dept. A-21, 40 Grand Boulevard, Brentwood, New York, N.Y. 11717

ADVERTISEMENT

Are you constipated again?

If you are, you should do something that will be of real help. Sure, you've probably been trying lots of things Maybe even harsh chemical laxatives that can irritate your system. But they haven't given you the relief, you've been looking for.

What you need is a gentle laxative that regulates your system. And that laxative is Serutan.

Serutan works by adding the roughage your system needs to retain vital moisture. Then, Serutan's gentle bulk forms the soft stools that enable you to eliminate gently and comfortably.

There are no strong chemicals in Serutan to cause cramps or irritation. Serutan has natural ingredients for smooth, easy results.

So if you're constipated, take Serutan—you'll get the relief you've been looking for.

Good Housekeeping

Read label for directions.

Tortured 9 Years by 2 CORNS and a WART

now they are gone," writes a happy user.
Away go corns, calluses, common warts with wonder working DERMA-SOFT. This unique formula softens & dissolves those hard to remove growths so you rub off painlessly & safely, leaving skin smooth & soft. Don't suffer. Get DERMA-SOFT today at Druggists.

FREE! Househunter's Guide!

Looking for a home? You'll get lots of helpful advice in our free booklet "The Househunter's Guide." It tells you everything you need to know to become a househunting expert.

It answers some questions, and poses others you'll want to ask about the home itself, the community, taxes, schools, shopping, transportation, and recreation. Financial questions, too, about loans, down payments, mortgages, closing costs, title protection. And more.

With our booklet, and the help of real estate professionals, you're ready to shop for the largest single item you'll ever buy. Happy hunting.

Free househunter's booklet.

Please send me "The Househunter's Guide." I understand I am under no obligation.

Name

Address

City

State   Zip

Approximate month
I might buy

Chicago Title
Department HG6
111 West Washington St., Chicago, Illinois 60602

Which of these ads do you think would cause annoyance or be offensive to the consumer? Which do you think would inform, without annoying or offending? (Courtesy Chicago Title; American Medical Association; Belgrave Products Ltd.; The J. B. Williams Co., Inc.)

Vocabulary

Define the following terms and use each one in a sentence.

Advertiser
Advertising
Consumer
Continuity acceptance department
Corrective advertising
Direct selling
FTC guides
Federal Trade Commission

Marketing
Market testing
Media
NAD
NARB
Promotional mix
Publicity

Review Questions

1. What are the differences between a planned and a free economy?
2. Why doesn't a person "see" or read all the advertisements to which he or she is exposed? Discuss.
3. Give an early definition of advertising. Why is it inadequate today?
4. How does advertising differ from personal selling efforts? From publicity?
5. Why is advertising necessary in our type of economy?
6. Who ultimately pays for the cost of advertising?
7. Can advertising sell the public goods or services that are not needed or wanted? Explain why or why not.
8. What forces are there that serve to police or regulate advertising?
9. When a complaint about untruthful advertising is received by the NAD, what procedure is followed?
10. What is the job of the Federal Trade Commission?
11. What is the purpose of the Wheeler-Lea Amendment?
12. Briefly describe the Listerine case. What was important about it?
13. What types of products would be most likely to annoy and irritate the public with their ads? What types of products would be least likely to annoy with their ads?

Activities

1. List twelve different kinds of local merchants or businesses in your community (shoe repairer, auto dealer, bank, etc.). Then opposite each one note whether the businessperson or business is selling goods, ser-

vices, or both. For example, shoe repairers sell services, but you can buy laces and polish from them, so they also sell goods.

2. Look through magazines for examples of ads that sell goods, services, or ideas. Make a note of the advertiser and what is being sold in each case. Discuss the ads in class.

3. In your experience, what advertising has most annoyed or irritated you? List the products or services advertised and (if you can) the media in which the advertising appeared. Why were you irritated by these ads? How could they have been changed to overcome your reaction? Also list examples of advertising that did not annoy you and that you found acceptable or enjoyable. Where did these ads appear? Why did you like them? What makes you think they did a good job?

Project

In order to complete end-of-chapter activities and projects and to be able to answer some of the review questions, you will need a supply of actual advertisements on hand. Start now to build up a supply of ads. Save a few days' worth from your local paper and be sure that ads from either a Wednesday or Thursday morning or evening edition are included. One of these editions will carry many ads for local supermarkets that do not appear on other days. If your home is in a different community from your college, ask your family or friends to save a few copies of your hometown paper to add variety to your collection. Obtain back copies of magazines, too. Try to vary the kinds, if you can. Include women's magazines such as *McCall's, Family Circle,* and *Ladies' Home Journal;* a general magazine such as *The Reader's Digest;* news weeklies such as *Time, Newsweek,* or *U.S. News & World Report;* and men's magazines such as *Sports Illustrated, Popular Science,* and *Esquire.* The weekly magazine section of a Sunday newspaper is also a good source of advertising. If you can locate old copies of business magazines (publications that address their editorial content to specific business areas), they will be helpful.

Listen to radio commercials with an attentive ear and don't tune out when television commercials appear on the set. Write down brief descriptions of the ones that seem especially good or bad and make a note of what's being advertised. Listen or watch for commercials that sell goods or services or an idea.

Note the outdoor posters in your area and make a record of those that interest you. Briefly describe the illustration and copy the words.

In the process of observing and collecting, you will be developing your understanding of advertising and the tasks it performs. At this stage, do not clip ads from their sources. That comes after you have a good supply of ads on hand.

CHAPTER TWO

THE FASCINATING HISTORY OF ADVERTISING

Advertising is probably as old as commerce itself. Once a society became sufficiently developed to permit individuals to specialize in their trades and have goods or services to sell, tradespeople naturally wanted their businesses to be successful. This meant that they had to make the availability of these products known, and this involved using some form of advertising. Historical documents and archeological research have confirmed the existence of advertising in ancient times.

Early advertising contains all the elements used in modern advertising, with one exception. It was used merely to announce what was for sale and remind people to buy it; the attempt to convince or persuade was lacking. This important refinement seldom appeared until the development of printing in the West because, before printing, advertising was usually limited in space. With printing, the advertiser could expand and lengthen the message beyond the limitations of a simple sign.

This newfound space was used to add persuasive reasons for buying what was on sale.

Advertising in Ancient Times

Until the introduction of printing in Europe in the fifteenth century, advertising existed in three forms only: shop signs, town criers, or "barkers," and wall signs. Just as it does today, selling goods in ancient times involved personal selling ability. Merchants needed to identify their places of business with a symbol that told their trade, and so shop signs were born. And the merchant had to make a point of impressing the qualities of the wares on customers—the fact that the fish had been caught that morning or that the bread was well baked, or the wine a good vintage from a well-favored vineyard. But merchants didn't have time to tell everyone about the quality of their wares, so they hired men called *criers* to walk the streets and do it for them by calling out advertising news. Another form of advertising that is still very much with us today was used in the ancient world. On the walls of buildings near important gathering places were lettered signs advertising entertainment events, the location of taverns, and goods for sale.

Babylonian Advertisements

When Hammurabi ruled in Babylon, 2,000 years before Christ, there were artisans, bakers, shoemakers, and greengrocers, who sold the produce of the rich, irrigated farms, and a host of merchants. All were eager to exchange their goods for money, and advertising helped.

But these were not literate times. Only the top classes of Babylonian society could read the cuneiform writing. The advertising methods the merchant could use were limited and primitive. Barkers were employed to stand outside shops and spread word of their wares to those who passed by.[1] Signs using pictures were placed over shops to identify the establishment and symbolize what was sold within.

Roman Advertisements

Other ancient peoples used shop signs and employed criers to advertise the wares of the shopkeeper, but not until Roman times can we find physical evidences of advertising and actually see advertisements that were once at work.

Early in the morning of August 24, A.D. 79, a severe earthquake shook the cities of Pompeii and Herculaneum, which were resort towns as well as ports. Mount Vesuvius erupted and cast down ashes on Pompeii to a depth of 3 feet. Hot pumice fell and then more ashes. Herculaneum was obliterated by 60 feet of the same materials, and cloudbursts turned the mixture into a hard, cementlike form. It is estimated that 2,000 people died in Pompeii alone. But the cinders and ashes that covered the town preserved it magnificently, and we are thus able to see how these people lived. Excavations have revealed their homes and shops—bakeries, wine shops, and shoemakers' shops. There are many evidences of advertising.

Shop signs were made of terra cotta (an unglazed earthenware) and placed in the columns making up the shop fronts.[2] Two men carrying a huge wine jug signified a wine merchant; a cupid balancing a shoe on his head and holding the mate in his hand told the passerby that a shoemaker's shop was inside; a goat indicated a dairy; and a grain mill with a donkey turning it was the sign of a bakery. On a wall is a painted sign to catch the thirsty traveler's eye:[3]

> **TRAVELER GOING FROM HERE TO THE TWELFTH TOWER THERE SARINUS KEEPS A TAVERN. THIS IS TO REQUEST THAT YOU ENTER. FAREWELL.**

Presbrey suggests that certain walls in Pompeii may have been rented out by "advertising agents" because they were covered with painted signs that were apparently often changed. One read:[4]

> **THE TROOP OF GLADIATORS OF THE AEDIL WILL FIGHT ON THE 31ST OF MAY THERE WILL BE FIGHTS WITH WILD ANIMALS AND AN AWNING TO KEEP OFF THE SUN.**

[1] Frank Presbrey, *History and Development of Advertising,* Doubleday & Company, Inc., Garden City, N.Y., 1929, p. 3.

[2] James Playsted Wood, *The Story of Advertising,* The Ronald Press Company, New York, 1958, p. 23.
[3] Presbrey, p. 9.
[4] Ibid., p. 7.

Other evidences of advertising have been found in Rome itself. Shopkeepers and professional men would smooth an outside wall, whiten it, and paint symbols of their occupation on the surface. A cup to hold drawn blood showed that a physician lived inside. Artisans pictured the tools of their trade. And school was indicated by a boy being switched.[5] This reassured parents, who paid the tuition bills, that teachers believed in plenty of old-fashioned discipline and no new-fangled permissiveness.

Advertising in the Middle Ages

With the collapse of the Roman Empire and the advent of the Dark Ages, commerce and trade routes were drastically diminished. The people of Europe were mostly illiterate. There was thus no point in using written signs as advertisements, and since merchants' shops were often robbed and destroyed, there was not much point in putting up pictorial shop signs to direct attention to valuable goods.

[5] Ibid., p. 6.

Throughout this period, the town crier was an important conveyor of news, and references to his work are occasionally found in the writings of this period. His function was to tell the townspeople of victories and defeats, famines, and plagues. As society gradually revived and commerce and trade again became important, the town crier's methods were copied by advertising criers. They carried horns, blew them raucously to attract attention, and advertised the goods of the local businessmen.

Criers for taverns were so numerous in Paris in the thirteenth century that they formed a union and were chartered by King Philip Augustus. These men developed an interesting advertising gimmick: they carried buckets of wine from the tavern they represented and gave out liberal samples. This instance of sales promotion was based on the sound principle that one drink deserves another.

Here is King Philip's charter for the wine criers:

Whosoever is a crier in Paris may go to any tavern he likes and cry its wine, provided they sell wine from the wood and that there is no other crier employed for that tavern; and the tavern keeper cannot prohibit him.

This announcement of a gladiatorial contest, inscribed on a wall in Pompeii, is evidence that advertising has had a long history. (From *The Mad Old Ads* by Dick Sutphen, The Dick Sutphen Studio, Inc., Minneapolis, 1966, p. 9)

If a crier finds people drinking in a tavern, he may ask what they pay for the wine they drink; and he may go out and cry the wine at the prices they pay, whether the tavern keeper wishes it or not, provided always that there be no other crier employed for that tavern. . . .

Each crier to receive daily from the tavern for which he cries at least four dinarii and he is bound on his oath not to claim more.[6]

Shop signs came back into use, and soon almost every merchant had one. Wood points out that the nobility, particularly the impoverished members, often rented their houses as inns when they were away. Inns displayed the nobles' coats of arms and came to be known locally by the most obvious feature in the coat of arms. The Wild Boar, the Red Crown, and the Red Fox were typical inn and tavern names. These signs served another purpose, too. There were street numbers, but directions could be given based on signs. "Go to the street of the Gold Dagger, and hard by you will find the house of the physician," was an instruction fairly easy to follow.

Later, signs became so common that Charles II of England proclaimed, "No signs shall be hung across the streets shutting out air and the lights of the heavens."[7]

The Advent of Printing

The production of written messages on paper by mechanical means that allow for reproduction is known as *printing*. It uses type (letters or characters) that is inked, and the impression is then transferred to the paper by a press.

Printing originated in China, and the oldest known printed book is dated A.D. 868. Printing devices used were clay plates and wood

[6] Presbrey, pp. 11–12.
[7] Wood, pp. 23–24.

blocks. Movable type was developed in the eleventh century in China with type characters made of hardened clay, but this material was not particularly successful. Type was cast in metal in Korea and became widely used in China and Japan. By the middle of the twelfth century type characters were cast in bronze. It is believed that this knowledge was passed to the West through Arab traders. Yet the times were such that nothing came of it. It was not until the fifteenth century that Johann Gutenberg independently discovered the art of printing in Mainz, Germany, and printed his famous Bible in 1456.

This rediscovery, in the West, together with an increase in education was essential to the growth of advertising. New methods of advertising were now available. Printed posters, handbills, and signs came into use; pamphlets, books, and newspapers appeared; and advertising had a brand-new dimension.

Early Printed Advertising

Signs printed on paper and tacked up on boards put up to carry public notices were common in England in the late fifteenth century. The English called them *siquis,* which came from the first two words of Roman public notices. In Latin, *si quis* means "if anyone," and typical Roman notices might read, "If anyone can apprehend the slave Junius escaped April 18, a reward will be given. He is a Goth of 30 years, fair of complexion with a great scar on his left arm. . . ." "If anyone needs iron cooking pots, let him come to the shop by the baths. . . ."

The first printed advertisement of which we have a record is a siquis printed by William Caxton, an Englishman who had learned the printing trade in Germany. It was tacked up in 1480 or perhaps a few years before, and it advertised a book of clergyman's rules that Caxton had printed. Here is the "copy":

If it plese ony man spirituel or temporel to bye ony pyes of two and thre comemoracios of salisburi use enpryntid after the forme of this preset lettre whiche ben wel and truly correct, late hym come to Westmonester in to the almonestrye at the reed pale and he shall have them good chepe Supplico Stet Cedula[8]

What this message told the reader was that copies ("pyes") of divine service rules ("comemoracios") were for sale. It stated that they were printed in the same type used in the advertisement itself ("enpryntid after the forme of this preset lettre"). The Latin at the end of the message is freely translated as "Leave this notice up."

[8] Standard Rate & Data Service, *The Story of Advertising*, New York, 1944, unpaged.

Caxton had a good natural sense of advertising. He addressed his appeal to a wide market —not just the clergy, but "any man." He described what his product was. He listed important sales points. He pointed out that it was a quality product, well made and "correct." He proved to the reader that his book was legible and readable. He told where to buy it. And he said it was a bargain.

Siquis were put up wherever crowds of people got together. The advertising man of the time was using his common sense to arrive at what today's outdoor billboard salesperson calls "maximum visibility" and "consumer traffic flow." As a result, the most popular place in London for posting siquis was the center aisle of St. Paul's Cathedral, because it was the busiest gathering place in London.

From descriptions of what went on in the cathedral in those days, it seems that very little

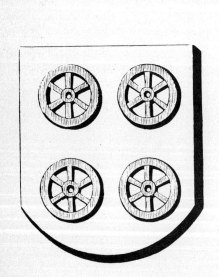
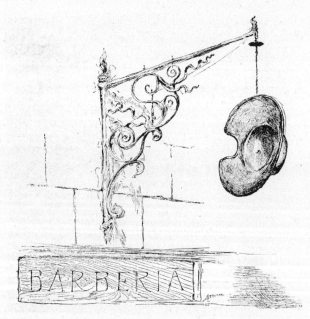

During the Middle Ages and the Renaissance, when literacy was not widespread, pictures and familiar objects were used to identify shops. Here we see the signs of a wheelwright and a barber. (The Bettmann Archive, Inc.)

time was given to religious services. Crowds gathered all day in the great church. Lawyers talked to old clients and looked for new ones. Tailors and seamstresses waited for jobs. There were tobacco shops and bookstalls. Bookmakers took bets. Ladies of quality exchanged gossip. And circulating through the crowd were pickpockets, confidence men, loan sharks, and gamblers.[9] If you were an advertiser with goods for sale, a St. Paul's location for your poster was a must—and the most important part of your advertising plan.

The Growth of Newspapers

Generally considered the first newspaper in England because it reported the news, was printed, and was issued fairly regularly, the *Weekly News* appeared in 1622. It contained no advertisements. Newspapers had a difficult time of it in the reign of Charles I because the royal party looked on any kind of news as a threat to the establishment. Cromwell's subsequent Puritan Revolution allowed more freedom of the press, however, and at the end of the seventeenth century, when newspaper censorship was lifted, hundreds of papers came on the scene.

Among the most popular newspapers was Richard Steele's *Tatler,* which was first published in April 1709. It carried foreign and local news, essays, reviews of plays, and plenty of advertisements. Joseph Addison, a regular contributor to the *Tatler,* was fascinated by advertising and wrote an article on it for the issue of September 14, 1710. He claimed to "have frequently been caught with Tears in my Eyes over a melancholy Advertisement," and he named three uses for advertising: to allow a merchant who buys space for his ad a moment of glory alongside the famous newsmakers of the day; to permit competitors to argue among

themselves the merits of their products; and to inform the world of what is necessary for life.

This last point makes the most sense today, and here are Addison's words:

The third and last use of these writings is to inform the world, where they may be furnished with almost everything that is necessary for life. If a Man has pains in his head, cholic in his bowels, or spots in his clothes, he may here meet with proper cures and remedies. If a man would recover a wife or a horse that is stolen or strayed; if he wants new sermons, electuaries, asses' milk or any thing else either for his body or his mind, this is the place to look for them. . . . The great art in writing advertising is the finding out of the proper method to catch the reader, without which a good thing may pass over unobserved.

The last sentence describes a problem that still faces advertisers today: how they can best attract attention to their message.

Addison later joined with Steele to publish the *Spectator,* the circulation of which is said to have reached 30,000 copies per issue. The *Spectator* differed from the *Tatler* in content. It contained no news; instead, it consisted of essays—comments on the life and customs of the times. Because of its large circulation, advertisers filled its pages with their messages. Here are a few from the issue of Thursday, May 29, 1712.

ADVERTISEMENTS

For the Benefit of Mrs. Saunders, the Desire of several Ladies of Quality, By Her Majesties Company of Comedians, At the Theater Royal in Drury Lane, this present Thursday, being the 29th Day of May, will be presented a play call'd THE UNHAPPY FAVORITE or THE EARL OF ESSEX. . . . With Entertainments of Comic Dancing by Mr. Thurmond, Mr. Price, Mrs. Hacknell, and others.

[9] Presbrey, p. 15.

FOR SALE BY THE CANDLE

Tomorrow the 30th Instant, at Lloyd's Coffee House in Lombard Street at 5 in the Afternoon, (one Cask in a Lot) twenty puncheons of excellent French Prize Brandy, (Bourdeaux and Coignise) full proof, rare, an entire Parcel, (not any having been sold or exposed to Sale) Just landed; now at a Warehouse fronting the Thames at Sommers-Key between London Bridge and Billingsgate.

Lost on Sunday the 25th Instant, between the Mall in St. James Park, and the Spring Garden-Gate, a large out-side Case of a Gold Watch somewhat bruised about the Spring, and in the inside a piece of red Gold-bearers Paper; whoever brings it to Charles Lillies at the corner of Beaufort Buildings on the Strand, shall receive two Guineas reward, and no Questions asked.

The Stamp Tax

Advertising was flourishing as never before. But in 1712 newspapers, pamphlets, and magazines in England suddenly received a setback that put most of them out of business. The Tory party was in power, and, to cut off criticism of its rule, the government levied a tax (called a stamp tax) of a halfpenny on every newspaper and magazine sold. In addition a tax of one shilling was levied on each advertisement carried. The *Spectator* held out for a while but went under in December 1712. Not many papers survived.

This tax lasted until 1855 and greatly curtailed the growth of the press and magazines in England. Nevertheless, advertising in newspapers continued on a limited scale. Some advertisers were willing to absorb the tax. Indeed, by 1759 Samuel Johnson had these words to say about advertising:

Advertisements are now so numerous that they are very negligently perused, and it is therefore necessary to gain attention by magnificence of promises, and by eloquence sometimes sublime and sometimes pathetic. Promise, large promise, is the soul of an advertisement.[10]

Advertising in America

The American colonies used methods of advertising similar to those in England. There were street criers, shop signs, painted signs, printed posters, handbills, pamphlets, and newspapers. But newspaper advertising was not burdened with a tax, and its volume grew along with newspaper circulations. Its value was appreciated by such notables as George Washington, Paul Revere, and Benjamin Franklin.

Washington wrote an advertisement and placed it in a Maryland newspaper in 1773, offering 20,000 acres of Ohio land for sale. He described the land in glowing terms: it had plenty of game and fish; the soil was "luxurious"; and there was much in meadowland.[11]

As for Paul Revere, it is generally known that he was a silversmith; an advertisement he placed in the Boston *Gazette* tells us that he was accomplished in making false teeth, too. Here it is, in part:

Whereas many Persons are so unfortunate as to lose their Fore-Teeth by Accident, and otherways, To their great Detriment, not only in Looks but in speaking both in Public and Private:—This is to inform all such that they may have them re-placed with false Ones, that look as well as the Natural, and answers the End of Speaking to all Intents, by *PAUL REVERE*, Goldsmith, near the Head of Dr. *Clarke's* Wharf, *Boston.*[12]

[10] Henry Darey Curwin, *A Johnson Sampler,* Harvard University Press, Cambridge, Mass., 1963, pp. 103–104.
[11] John C. Fitzpatrick (ed.), *The Writings of George Washington, from the Original Manuscript Sources,* U.S. Government Printing Office, Washington, 1931, vol. III, pp. 144–146.
[12] Presbrey, p. 157.

Benjamin Franklin understood the power of advertising as no man had before. He was a master of the art of persuasion and wrote easily and well. A modern advertiser would be lucky indeed to have Franklin's talents. When he began publishing the Pennsylvania *Gazette* in 1729, the advertising columns were very important to him and he wrote most of the ads himself. Up to this time, ads had consisted of three or four lines of text of uneven type. Franklin opened up the columns by separating the ads with white space and included headings. This made the messages easier to read. Soon he was experimenting with simple illustrations and symbols, and modern advertising was born.

Franklin was a first-rate writer of advertising and was not satisfied with the simple announcements that merchants considered advertisements. He believed in giving the reader full details on the products being sold and understood that these additions added conviction to the messages.

He had no qualms about playing on the reader's emotions and worries when he was promoting in an ad a product he had invented. Here is the text of an ad promoting the Franklin stove:

Fireplaces with small openings cause drafts or cold air to rush in at every crevice, and 'tis very uncomfortable as well as dangerous to sit against any such crevice. . . . Women, particularly from this cause (as they sit so much in the house) get cold in the head, rheums, and defluxions which fall into their jaws and gums and have destroyed early, many a fine set of teeth in these northern colonies. Great and bright fires do also very much contribute to damaging the eyes, dry and shrivel the skin, bring on early the appearance of old age.[13]

Here is the copy he wrote for a soap made by two of his brothers in Boston:

It cleanses fine linens, muslins, laces, chintzes, cambricks, etc., with ease and expedition, which often suffer more from the long and hard rubbing of the washer, through the ill qualities of the soap, than the wearing.

Franklin is important to the growth of advertising for another reason. In 1765 the stamp tax that had slowed advertising progress in England was applied to the American colonies. It was levied on newspapers, pamphlets, and, in fact, on almost any form of printing, including college diplomas. Advertising was taxed, too. Franklin was in England at the time and, realizing the paralyzing effect the tax would have on commerce, did his best to persuade influential Englishmen against it. His testimony against the tax in the English House of Commons was so convincing that the American stamp tax was repealed.

Advertising was used for recruitment during the Revolution, just as it has been used for this purpose in all of the nation's wars since. On a privateer, the sailors shared in the profits from the prize vessels they captured, and this ad for privateer enlistments stressed the profit motive.

All those jolly fellows who love their country and want to make their fortune at one stroke repair immediately to the rendevous at the head of his excellency Governor Hancock's Wharf.[14]

In colonial times, America was primarily an agricultural country, and there was little need for advertising. The total amount of advertising expenditures in the year 1777 has been esti-

[13] *Advertising Age*, April 19, 1976, p. 27.

[14] *Advertising Age*, April 19, 1976, p. 28.

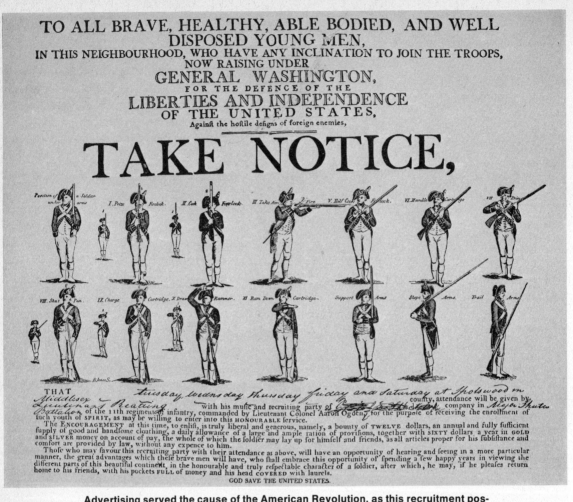

Advertising served the cause of the American Revolution, as this recruitment poster shows. (The Bettmann Archive, Inc.)

mated at only $200,000.[15] A small amount of manufacturing was done by individuals—artisans and craftspeople. The cloth they wove, the pots and pans they made, and the tools they forged were transported by wagon or barge—difficult and expensive ways to distribute goods. New methods were needed, and when they arrived, they would change the country completely.

[15] *Advertising Age*, July 5, 1976. p. 1. Other estimates in this chapter of advertising expenditures through 1945 are from the same source.

The Industrial Revolution

In the first years of the nineteenth century, the effects of the Industrial Revolution began to be felt in America. Inventions that eventually resulted in the production of goods mechanically, rather than by hand, included Cartwright's power loom for weaving textiles, the use of coke to strengthen iron, and Watts's use of steam to generate power. One application of the latter development was the invention of a steam-driven printing press that the New York *Daily Advertiser* installed in 1825. It multiplied the number of copies that could be printed. This made possible for the first time the large-circulation newspaper, with the advertising it contained reaching far wider markets than were previously available.

Mechanization and industrialization received a great boost because of increased production needs during the Civil War. New factories with "modern" machinery came into being, and there was no returning to the agricultural economy of America's youth. By 1876, the volume of annual advertising expenditures had risen to $150 million.

Now that goods were produced in quantity by mechanical means, manufacturers needed advertising more than ever before. They were able to make more articles, and wider markets were needed in which to sell them. Since the quality of these goods was unknown in distant markets, manufacturers advertised. It was possible to do this successfully because of two interlocking developments: the growth of transportation and the spread of education.

The Growth of Transportation

Shipping goods by wagon on turnpikes was costly and time-consuming, but when the steam-powered *Clermont* headed north on the Hudson River in 1807, a new era in low-cost water transportation was born. Some years later, construction of a vast network of canals was undertaken in the northeastern and central seaboard states. No longer was it necessary to bring goods up a river by barge and then laboriously transport them overland to another navigable stream. Presbrey states that the opening of the Erie Canal in 1825 cut freight rates between New York and Buffalo from $100 a ton to $15 a ton.[16]

The age of the railroads began in America in the 1830s, and when railroad building in the Midwest reached its peak in the 1850s, rail-

[16] Presbrey, p. 183

roads provided even cheaper transportation than the canals. Goods could now be distributed with relative ease and economy.

At the same time, mass circulation of newspapers allowed merchants to blanket retail markets with their advertising messages. And cheap transportation allowed magazines published in one city to be shipped and sold in all important urban areas. Here for the first time was an opportunity for the advertiser to spread news of what was for sale on a regional or national scale through newspapers and magazines.

The Spread of Education

The second development that made possible the growth of advertising was the spread of education. Schools existed in colonial America, but with an agricultural economy demanding the help of children on the family farm and with large territories sparsely settled, making distances between schools in some areas prohibitive, many Americans were simply unable to obtain an education. In 1850, it is estimated that 30 percent of the population could neither read nor write. But at this time laws were passed that required children to stay at school until the age of 11 or 12, depending on the state, and eventually literacy became almost universal. In 1880 the illiteracy rate was down to 15 percent; in 1900 it was less than 10 percent.

The consumer's ability to read and write meant that the advertiser could now easily communicate with almost every possible buyer.

The Development of the Advertising Agency

An important factor in the growth of American advertising was the advertising agency. The first agency people were no more than sellers of advertising space for newspapers. Men such as Volney B. Palmer represented a list of papers and contacted possible advertisers. When they sold the advertising space, they received a 25 percent commission on the deal. Palmer was a superb salesman, full of bluster and confidence, who told prospects tales of how merchants had doubled their business by advertising—through the papers Palmer represented, naturally. He and others like him did much to sell manufacturers on the power and effectiveness of advertising.

Another kind of advertising agent came on the scene after the Civil War. He speculated in advertising space, sometimes making a fortune and sometimes going broke. His business consisted of purchasing advertising space from publishers as cheaply as he could get it and selling it to businessmen as dearly as he could.

The Commission System F. Wayland Ayer, of the N. W. Ayer & Son advertising agency (founded in 1869), made a far-reaching change in the agency business. Instead of working for commissions received from publications, he developed the principle of making a contract with the advertiser. Ayer realized that if he received commissions from the publications he would really be a publication space salesman, with the publications' interests as his prime concern. But if he could somehow receive his commission from the advertiser, he would then be serving the best interests of the advertiser, buying space wherever it would do the most good. He thus established the present *agency commission system,* whereby the agency bills the advertiser for the cost of the space in a publication, then pays the money to the publication "less fifteen percent commission." Thus the present type of advertising agency was created.

However, the agency of this time was merely an advertising placement firm; that is, the only business the agency conducted was the pur-

chase of advertising space in publications for its manufacturing clients.

The Addition of Research In 1879, Ayer performed the first market research task. He was trying to obtain a threshing-machine manufacturer as a client and did research to find where the best markets for the product were located and which farm papers reached these markets. The research function was thus added to the advertising agency's tasks.

The Preparation of Advertising It was not until the 1890s that agencies started to prepare ads for clients. Previously the manufacturer either employed an advertising writer or hired free-lance talent to write the advertisements. Now, for the first time, writers and artists were hired by the advertising agencies. Thus all the principal departments found in agencies today were in existence.

A modern *advertising agency* is a business organization consisting of creative people and businesspeople who develop and prepare advertising and place it in advertising media on behalf of the agency's clients, who are sellers of goods and services.

It is important for the student to understand something of what advertising agencies do and how they are compensated for two reasons: (1) the agencies have had a profound effect upon advertising in America. Almost all the magazine and national television advertising and much of the newspaper and radio advertising produced today is created by the advertising agencies, and (2) a student who enters the retail business and sponsors advertising that costs over $20,000 annually may consider using the services of one of the many advertising agencies that are found in every American city.

Other developments that caused advertising to grow include the advent of mass-circulation

HOW THE ADVERTISING AGENCY COMMISSION SYSTEM WORKS

1. AGENCY RUNS CLIENT'S AD IN NEWSPAPER.

2. AD COSTS $100. NEWSPAPER BILLS AGENCY $100.

3. AGENCY BILLS CLIENT $100.   **4.** CLIENT PAYS AGENCY $100.

5. AGENCY PAYS PAPER $85.   **6.** AGENCY KEEPS $15 AS INCOME.

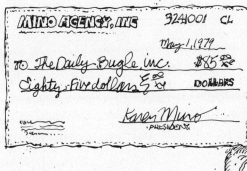

F. Wayland Ayer developed the agency commission system as a means of compensating the advertising agency for its services. (Jared D. Lee)

Ads like these were common in late nineteenth century periodicals.

MADAME DEAN'S SPINAL SUPPORTING CORSETS.

They support the Spine, relieve the muscles of the back, brace the shoulders in a natural and easy manner, imparting graceful carriage to the wearer without discomfort, expanding the chest, thereby giving full action to the lungs, and health and comfort to the body. Take the place of the ORDINARY CORSET in every respect, and are made of fine Coutil, in the best manner, in various styles and sold by agents everywhere at popular prices, Mrs. Wm. Papes, Keota, Iowa, says:—I have been an invalid for six years, have travelled extensively for health, yet never received as much benefit as I have in a few weeks wear, of your MADAME DEAN'S CORSET. I am gaining strength all the time, and could not do without it. It has proven to me a *godsend.*

FREE Our new book entitled: "Dress Reform for Ladies" with elegant wood engraving and Biography of **Worth,** the King of Fashion, Paris; also our **New Illustrated Catalogue** sent free to any address on receipt of two 2-cent stamps to pay postage and packing.

AGENTS WANTED for these celebrated Corsets. No experience required. Four orders per day give the agent **$150 monthly.** Our agents report from four to twenty sales daily. **$3.00 Outfit Free.** Send for terms and full particulars. **SCHIELE & CO., 390 Broadway, New York.**

[1885]

BOY'S SUIT
$2.75

Absolutely All Wool.

During our 25 years' experience as manufacturers and large retailers for the best trade we have never seen such a value as this suit. Made in the best manner. Fits finely and has great durability. If not perfectly satisfactory it can be returned.

Send amount by P. O. Order, Express Money Order or Draft on New York. If ordered C. O. D. send 50 cents to guarantee charges. Extra Pants, $1.10.

Boys' Shirt Waists, 60c. Boys' Overalls, 50c.
Boys' All Wool Sweaters, $1.50.

Our Men's $10.00 Suits Lead the World.

Everything in Clothing. Send for 1895 Fashion Plate.

Baldwin the Clothier, Fulton and Smith Sts., BROOKLYN, N. Y.

[1895]

magazines in the 1880s, the addition of color to magazine advertising in 1899, and the arrival of the "horseless carriage" (automobile ads in 1911 took up to 10 percent of all advertising space in magazines).[17] In 1914, advertising expenditures had grown to just over $1 billion. Advertising seemed to be everywhere, and the *Atlantic Monthly* ran an article on the subject, expressing concern about its influence on the morals and taste of society and stating that it was the most conspicuous feature of American life. There was reason for this statement. For example, in 1914, the Palisades along the Hudson River were painted with enormous advertising signs, and the Albany steamboat at night would turn on its searchlights so that passengers could read these billboards.[18] But the dynamic growth of advertising was still to come, caused by the two important developments of radio and television.

The Arrival of Radio and Television

The first commercial radio broadcasting station, KDKA in Pittsburgh, Pennsylvania, made radio history by broadcasting the 1920 election returns. Soon, owning a primitive "crystal set" radio was all the rage. *Printers' Ink* states that the first advertiser to use radio was the Queensboro Corporation, which bought time on WEAF, New York, and added a new dimension to advertising—a spoken sales message delivered not on the street by a crier but right in the prospective customer's home.

Advertisements could be even more widely disseminated with the growth of radio *networks* —groups of stations that are banded together. This enabled a program or an advertisement to be broadcast simultaneously in several markets. The first radio network of 19 stations was

[17] *Printers' Ink,* June 14, 1963, p. 2.
[18] *Advertising Age,* April 19, 1976, p. 32.

REO

4-Seat Runabout $675

You cannot match this car. You cannot find another that combines runabout simplicity and liveliness with such power and capacity; such absolute strength and reliability and such style.

This car carried four people 57 miles on 1¾ gallons of gasoline in the recent Chicago to Cedar Lake contest; and carried four people 682 miles for $3.38 per passenger in the New York Motor Club's great six-day tour, winning the gold medal for all $1,500 cars.

When the extra seat is not in use it folds down neatly out of the way. Or you can buy it as a 2-seat car for $650 and afterwards add the extra seat.

This gives you a trim, handy car with almost touring-car ability but without the complications or expense. It gives you 26 miles an hour; two speeds and reverse; ample climbing power; and positive "get there."

A combination not found in any other car

Write for the 1907 catalogue which describes it in detail. Also the REO $1,250 five-passenger Touring Car.

R. M. Owen & Co., Lansing, Mich.
Sales Agents

[1907]

BE SURE THE NAME "POPE" IS ON YOUR AUTOMOBILE

POPE *Toledo* AUTOMOBILES

The Pope-Toledo Breaks Two More Long Distance Records

Cut of 30 H. P. Front Entrance

30 H. P. Front Entrance Pope-Toledo, $3,200

L. A. Nares, with a 30 H. P. Pope-Toledo, July 19th, 1905, broke the record from San Francisco to Los Angeles, a distance of 502 miles, time 24 hours, 4 minutes, carrying full touring equipment and four passengers. The previous record was 29 hours, 51 minutes. At Columbus, Ohio, July 4th, a regular stock model, 30 H. P. Pope-Toledo, won the first 24-hour race ever held, making 848 miles in that time. Mile after mile in this race was reeled off by the Pope-Toledo in 1:05, 1:08, 1:09.

Be sure the name "Pope" is on your Automobile

Isn't it a significant thing that when two or three owners come together in Club, Country or Garage, Pope-Toledo standing is always granted by common consent? These men may own other cars, but they never think of questioning Pope-Toledo supremacy.

Send for catalogue and

20 h. p. Double Side Entrance	$2,800
30 h. p. New Front Entrance	3,200
45 h. p. Double Side Entrance	6,000

POPE MOTOR CAR CO.
Desk N. Toledo, Ohio

Members A. L. A. M.

[1905]

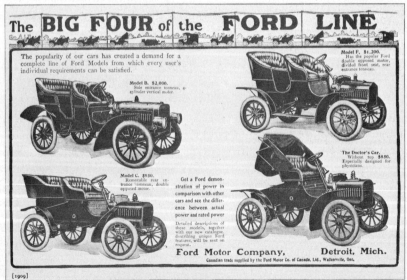

The BIG FOUR of the FORD LINE

The popularity of our cars has created a demand for a complete line of Ford Models from which every user's individual requirements can be satisfied.

Model B. $2,000. Side entrance tonneau, 4-cylinder vertical motor.

Model F. $1,200. Has the popular Ford double opposed motor, divided front seat, rear entrance tonneau.

Model C. $950. Removable rear entrance tonneau, double opposed motor.

The Doctor's Car. Without top $850. Especially designed for physicians.

Get a Ford demonstration of power in comparison with other cars and see the difference between actual power and rated power

Detailed descriptions of these models, together with our new catalogue, describing unique Ford features, will be sent on request.

Ford Motor Company, Detroit, Mich.

Canadian trade supplied by the Ford Motor Co. of Canada, Ltd., Walkerville, Ont.

[1909]

The advent of the automobile was a new source of advertising revenue for periodicals.

put together in 1926 by the National Broadcasting Company. By 1929 this network extended from coast to coast.

The thirties were the days of the big-name radio shows such as the *Carnation Hour* and the *Lucky Strike Hit Parade.* Eddie Cantor, Ed Wynn, Bob Hope, Jack Benny, and other famous entertainers were sponsored by leading advertisers; that is, a single advertiser controlled all the advertising messages included in the program, and "owned" the entire show. The costs of putting together these shows were high, and advertising budgets were not limitless, so advertising in newspapers and magazines was often cut to make room for the new kind of advertising on radio.

The thirties were the years of the great depression, and budgets for all forms of advertising were greatly curtailed as business dried up. In 1929, advertising expenditures had reached an unprecedented $2.85 billion. In 1933, at the bottom of the business collapse, ad expenditures were less than half that figure. It was not until 1945 that the 1929 figure was reached again.

Later, newspapers, magazines, and radio suffered more losses when commercial television arrived on the scene. At the close of World War II a few advertisers were already gaining experience with this new advertising form. By 1948 television hit the big time when the fiftieth television station started operation. In that year, the Procter & Gamble Company led a parade of big advertisers out of the magazine advertising pages and over to the television stations. Radio "soap operas," serial dramas of human conflict and emotion, and some other forms of radio programs were easily converted to television shows. On television, the public could see the product in use as well as hear about it.

Table 2-1 shows estimates of advertising expenditures for certain media from 1949 through 1978. Total advertising expenditures, figures that include many other kinds of advertising in addition to magazines, newspaper, radio, television and direct mail advertising, went from $5,210,000,000 in 1949 to $43,740,000,000 in 1978, an increase of 840 percent.

Some of these media did not keep pace with this growth. Advertising expenditures in magazines increased from $458,000,000 in 1949 to $2,595,000,000 in 1978, an increase of 566 percent. Radio ad expenditures were $571,-000,000 in 1949 and $2,955,000,000 in 1978, increasing 518 percent, and between the years 1949 and 1958 expenditures were "flat," hardly changing at all.

But note the incredible growth of television ad expenditures between 1949 and 1978. The growth in advertising revenues in magazines and radio was retarded as advertisers switched dollars to the medium of television. Television's fabulous growth rate is today a thing of the past, however. Escalating costs of advertising on TV have forced advertisers to seek out substitute media where advertising is less expensive.

Direct mail advertising (see Chapter 7) does not compete with the television medium for advertising dollars as aggressively as magazines and radio do because it serves a different purpose. As a result, direct mail has grown by 798 percent from 1949 to 1978, about the same rate of increase as for advertising as a whole during this period. Newspapers have had a growth of 664 percent. The bulk of newspaper advertising is advertising run by local merchants and local services and in spite of some inroads made by local television competition, newspapers are still the mainstay of local advertising budgets.

What new forms of communication will be developed in the future? We cannot imagine what they will consist of, but judging by the past, if these new forms are efficient in reaching masses of people, advertising will be part of them and will continue to grow.

TABLE 2-1 Advertising Expenditures, 1949–1978, Millions of Dollars

Totals and Amounts Spent in Selected Media

Year	Total, All Advertising	Newspapers	Magazines	Television	Radio	Direct Mail
1949	$ 5,210	$ 1,911	$ 458	$ 58	$ 571	$ 756
1950	5,700	2,070	478	171	605	803
1951	6,420	2,251	535	332	606	924
1952	7,140	2,464	575	454	624	1,024
1953	7,740	2,632	627	606	611	1,099
1954	8,150	2,685	629	809	559	1,202
1955	9,150	3,077	691	1,035	545	1,299
1956	9,910	3,223	758	1,225	567	1,419
1957	10,270	3,268	777	1,286	618	1,471
1958	10,310	3,176	734	1,387	620	1,589
1959	11,270	3,526	832	1,529	656	1,688
1960	11,960	3,681	909	1,627	693	1,830
1961	11,860	3,601	895	1,691	683	1,850
1962	12,430	3,659	942	1,897	736	1,933
1963	13,100	3,780	1,002	2,032	789	2,078
1964	14,150	4,120	1,074	2,289	846	2,184
1965	15,250	4,426	1,161	2,515	917	2,324
1966	16,630	4,865	1,254	2,823	1,010	2,461
1967	16,870	4,910	1,245	2,909	1,048	2,488
1968	18,090	5,232	1,283	3,231	1,190	2,612
1969	19,420	5,714	1,344	3,585	1,264	2,670
1970	19,550	5,704	1,292	3,596	1,380	2,766
1971	20,740	6,198	1,370	3,534	1,445	3,067
1972	23,300	7,008	1,440	4,091	1,612	3,420
1973	25,120	7,595	1,448	4,460	1,723	3,698
1974	26,740	8,001	1,504	4,854	1,837	3,986
1975	28,230	8,442	1,465	5,263	1,980	4,181
1976	33,720	9,910	1,789	6,721	2,330	4,813
1977	38,120	11,132	2,162	7,612	2,634	5,333
1978	43,740	12,690	2,595	8,850	2,955	6,030

Note: Since only the five largest media are listed in this table, the figures for these media do not add up to the figures listed in the Total column. Omitted are business publications, farm publications, outdoor, and miscellaneous media.
Source: *Advertising Age,* September 4, 1978, pp. 32–33, for figures through 1976. 1977 expenditures and preliminary 1978 expenditures are from *Advertising Age,* January 8, 1979, p. S-8.

Vocabulary

Define the following terms and use each one in a sentence.

Advertising agency
Agency commission system
Criers

Networks
Printing
Siquis

Review Questions

1. What forms of advertising were used in the ancient world and why were they used?
2. Where did the art of printing originate? Where was it independently discovered?
3. Why was Caxton's first printed poster, or siquis, a good advertisement? Give three reasons.
4. Name four forms of advertising used in the American colonies.
5. In what ways did Benjamin Franklin improve advertisements?
6. Why was there little need for advertising in colonial times?
7. Discuss why advertising was more necessary after the Industrial Revolution and list the two developments that made it possible to advertise successfully.
8. What one job did the earliest advertising agencies accomplish?
9. Explain how the advertising agency commission system works and how this serves the interest of the advertiser.
10. What new selling dimension did the use of television add to an advertisement?
11. Why was the growth of advertising expenditures in newspapers not greatly affected by the advent of television?

Activities

1. Suppose that you live in the sixteenth century in London and that you and two friends are a barber (who is also a surgeon), an innkeeper, and an importer. For each occupation, what advertising would you rely on? Draw a rough shop sign, and, using your imagination, write out a siquis for each occupation.
2. List five of the most important events, discoveries, and developments that have influenced the growth of advertising since ancient times. Explain why each was important.
3. It is late in the nineteenth century. Imagine that you are employed by the "new kind" of advertising agency developed by N. W. Ayer & Son. It is one of your responsibilities to try to obtain new clients for your agency. You have an idea that a soap company in Cincinnati, selling its products to the public, might be interested in employing an advertising agency. What would you tell this prospect about your agency, its

services, and why these services could be helpful to this manufacturer? Outline your agency's services, explaining what they offer. Be prepared to discuss your outline in class.

Project

Select two local advertisers from the following: a discount department store, a bank, a supermarket, and either a menswear or womenswear shop. By observation over period of 1 week, note the media in which their advertising appears. Check the daily newspaper and billboards and try to catch any radio or television advertising these merchants are sponsoring. If there are no radio or television messages, note this fact. Clip any examples of their newspaper advertising that you see.

Write a brief report of the advertising activities of these two advertisers as you have been able to understand them and add your opinion on (1) the quality and effectiveness of their advertising and (2) the logic of their choice of advertising media.

CHAPTER THREE

WHO ADVERTISES?

Businesspeople in every kind of commercial activity use advertising in one form or another as a selling tool, and they spend a tremendous amount of money on advertising every year. In 1978, almost $44 billion was spent on advertising in the United States. In addition, it cost almost $2.5 billion to prepare this advertising so that it could be placed in the various media.

Who uses advertising? Why do advertisers find it necessary to spend such substantial sums annually on their messages? Basically, there are two categories of advertiser, local and national, and they are motivated to advertise by many different reasons.

The Local Advertiser

Advertising sponsored by local businesses to reach possible buyers in a neighborhood, town, or city is called *local advertising*. The local merchant accounts for 40 percent of the total amount of money spent on advertising in the United States.

Much local advertising is *retail advertising*.

A retailer is a merchant who sells goods or services directly to the consumer, for example, a supermarket manager, a stationery store owner, a home appliance dealer, or a department store operator. Banks, travel agencies, real estate firms, laundries, beauty shops, and movie theaters, which are retailers of services, have advertising programs, too; their advertising is sometimes referred to as *service advertising*. And the term "local advertising" also covers the advertisements of the manufacturer whose business (and advertising) is restricted to a local market.

All merchants advertise, even when they think they don't. Consider the sign over the door with the store's name on it[1]—that's an

[1] Jim McArdle, an enterprising and enthusiastic advertiser for his local garden supply business, makes an interesting observation on the kind of names local advertisers should choose for their stores. He advocates incorporation of the owner's name in the store name, for example, "Lee Wilson Hardware" rather than a name such as "Peerless Hardware." This is because local businesspeople are usually active in town affairs, from the PTA to the local chamber of commerce. If the owner's name is used in the store name, every new person the owner meets can then associate the owner with the name of his retail store, and the owner's very presence advertises his business.

advertisement. Then there's the window display, with cards describing the merchandise shown and listing the prices. There might be a streamer across the window announcing a sale or a clearance. Inside the store the merchant may use point-of-sale advertising, that is, signs and displays that feature goods on sale. All these things are advertisements, and the merchant is an advertiser, whether consciously or not.

Primary Function of Local Retail Advertising

The primary function of local retail advertising is to bring customers into a particular business establishment.

One way the local retailer can attract a large number of customers to the store is to establish it in a location where there is a maximum flow of consumer traffic. The merchant seeks the busy part of town, where the crowds are. Traffic count, or the number of passersby during an hour or day, is an important criterion for store location. Since the merchant obviously wants to be where the action is, the most favorable location is picked that is affordable. There, because there is ample consumer traffic, the merchant multiplies chances of selling the store's goods or services.

But even if a business establishment is in a good location, not everyone who passes by it is a potential customer, and, conversely, there are some potential customers who will not come to that area unless their attention is called to something there that they want. So the merchant must reach beyond the passersby to everyone else in the locality who might be considered a potential customer, and the only way this can be done is through advertising.

The signs merchants use at their places of business serve only to identify them to passersby. To attract a larger market, retailers use the local media—newspapers, radio, television, even billboards—to tell potential customers in the area about what they have to sell. They may have handbills passed out to local consumers, or they may send letters or pamphlets by mail, which is called direct mail advertising (Chapters 4 and 7).

The local retailer who advertises differs in a fundamental respect from the manufacturers, wholesalers, or service firms who advertise on a national scale. The national advertiser wishes to convince a potential buyer of the merits of a product and hopes to persuade the buyer to ask for it wherever it can be obtained. The national advertiser has no particular interest in where the consumer buys the product or service; it can be purchased anywhere it's available. But the local merchant's advertisement says, "Buy X product or service from *me*." The retailer doesn't care so much what the consumer buys as where it's bought. The goal is to bring customers to the store for the products or services sold there.

To illustrate the different goals of national and local advertising, take the case of Zenith, a manufacturer of television sets. Zenith, a national advertiser, runs ads in national magazines and on television extolling the advantages of the new models. The company's advertising does its best to persuade the audience that Zenith is a better set than those offered by the competition. The message may wind up by urging the reader or viewer to "see the new Zenith sets at Zenith dealers everywhere." But that is the extent of recognition of local Zenith dealers. The local merchant who carries Zenith sets has a different problem. The new models will be advertised, too, but every effort is made in the advertisements to urge the local audience to buy them at the merchant's store, not someone else's. It doesn't matter which brand of set the customer buys as long as the merchant makes the sale.

Kinds of Local Advertising

We have seen that the primary function of local retail advertising is to bring customers to a local merchant's place of business. The merchant accomplishes this in two ways. One way is called *promotional advertising.* This is advertising of a specific item that is for sale. The second way is called *institutional advertising.* This is intended to convey a favorable image of the place of business itself. It is hoped that the institutional advertising will have a favorable long-range effect on the business.

Both these advertising functions are often combined in the same ad. For example, in the fall a garden supply firm can advertise rakes and lawn sweepers and in a separate part of the same ad make the point that the firm's employees "have all the answers to your gardening problems. Just ask." The firm thus combines promotional and institutional advertising.

Promotional Advertising Sometimes the term "promotional advertising" is used specifically to describe the advertising of goods by merchants in the department store, home furnishings, and wearing apparel trades, but in a broader sense it refers to any local advertisement that sells specific items or services. The specific items mentioned in a promotional ad may be products—food (supermarket); meals (restaurant); home furnishings (department store); fertilizers (farm and garden supply)—or they may be services—prices for cleaning dresses (dry cleaner); the interest rate offered on savings accounts (banker); a homeowner's insurance policy (an insurance firm).

The purpose of running promotional advertising goes deeper than merely selling the specific items featured in the ad. Suppose that a suburban hardware merchant advertises garbage pails that are "raccoon- and dog-proof—no animal alive can pry off the lid." The price listed is low, so the merchant is sure in advance that the ad will pull in customers and sell, or "move," the pails. The merchant may or may not sell enough pails to cover the cost of the ad and also make a profit. If the ad is profitable, the merchant will be happy, of course. But even if it isn't profitable, this retailer will not be particularly upset because experience shows that when an attractive price is placed on the item and its advantages are promoted properly, customers are brought to the store and store traffic is built. Once they enter, the customers are potential buyers of all the other items the store carries. Perhaps the customer thinks, "I'll get the pail, and I'll buy that gallon of paint I need, too." When on the premises, customers may do *impulse buying,* purchasing items seen on display that they had not considered buying before entering.

Promotional advertising, by bringing customers to a store, does more than sell the items featured in the ad. It's a store traffic builder, too. Promotional advertising constitutes the bulk of local retail advertising.

Institutional Advertising Institutional advertising conveys an idea or builds an image in the mind of the potential customer; in the department store field, where it is prevalent, this is known as image advertising. (See Color Plate 3.)

When promoting items or services, the retailer is concerned about "tomorrow's" sales volume in the store, that is, looking for fast selling action over a short period. When thinking "institutionally" or about the desired image, the retailer is planning for long-range sales results, built over future months and years.

When a local advertising program is consistent and long-term, with ads appearing at regular intervals, it can build a lasting relationship with the consumer, build sales volume, and encourage steady sales year-round, tending to eliminate "soft," or light, selling periods.

An example of institutional advertising is a

DON'T DESPAIR

WE REPAIR

RADIOS, STEREOS, TELEVISIONS...

All home entertainment items are carefully repaired. For all appliance repairs see . . .

the appliance department store
PARTRIDGE & ROCKWELL INC.
251 Greenwich Ave., TO 9-8877

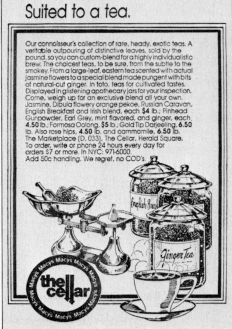

Suited to a tea.

Our connoisseur's collection of rare, heady, exotic teas. A veritable outpouring of distinctive leaves, sold by the pound, so you can custom-blend for a highly individualistic brew. The choicest teas, to be sure, from the subtle to the smokey. From a large-leaf, eastern tea scented with actual jasmine flowers to a special blend made pungent with bits of natural-cut ginger. In toto, teas for cultivated tastes. Displayed in glistening apothecary jars for your inspection. Come, weigh up for an exclusive blend all your own. Jasmine, Dibula flowery orange pekoe, Russian Caravan, English Breakfast and Irish blend, each $4 lb.; Pinhead Gunpowder, Earl Grey, mint flavored, and ginger, each 4.50 lb.; Formosa Oolong, $5 lb.; Gold Tip Darjeeling, 6.50 lb. Also rose hips, 4.50 lb. and cammomile, 6.50 lb. The Marketplace (D. 033), The Cellar, Herald Square. To order, write or phone 24 hours every day for orders $7 or more. In NYC: 971-6000. Add 50c handling. We regret, no COD's.

Are you tired of your relatives?

A NEW PICTURE FRAME CAN MAKE ALL THE DIFFERENCE. BRING IN THOSE FAMILY PORTRAITS AND YOU REFRAME THEM EXPERTLY AND INEXPENSIVELY WITH US AT YOUR SIDE TO DO IT YOURSELF AND SAVE, OR WE'LL DO IT FOR YOU.

1 DAY CUSTOM FRAMING AVAILABLE

FRAME YOUR OWN SHOP and GALLERY

56 La Salle Rd., West Hartford Center
Tel. 233-7804 Hours: Tues.-Sat. 10-5; Wed. 'til 8

These local ads are called promotional because they promote the specific goods and services of local businesses. (Courtesy Partridge & Rockwell Inc.; Frame Your Own Shop & Gallery, Inc.; Macy's)

department store in a large city running an ad telling about its buyers' attendance at the Paris and Rome showings of famous dress designers. This ad attempts to build an image of fashion leadership in the minds of its potential customers. Or a bank ad might describe the friendliness and cooperation of its employees; a real estate firm might point out that it is the largest local firm, and therefore the people looking for homes are guaranteed the widest selection in every price range to choose from. These ads are image builders. They seek to create long-range sales results.

Cooperative Advertising An important special category of local advertising is called *co-operative advertising.* Co-op advertising is generally prepared by the manufacturer or supplier of goods and services and features specific brands of items for sale, but it is run by local merchants over their own store names. The cost of a merchant's co-op advertising is shared by the local merchant and the supplier of the goods. Suppliers benefit because they can indicate specifically where their products are for sale locally. The local merchants benefit because the cost of the advertising is lower than the cost of advertising they sponsor completely by themselves. Also, if the merchant is a consistent user of co-op advertising in newspapers, the total amount of advertising that is run will increase, thus entitling the merchant to newspaper rate reductions (discussed under Newspapers in Chapter 6). Such rate reductions may also apply when the merchant runs co-op advertising on local radio and television stations.

Depending on the size of the manufacturer and the co-op program involved, a variety of materials may be supplied to the retailer. These include newspaper ads, with open space where the dealer inserts the store name and address; television and radio commercials

with time at the end for dealer identification; sample direct mail letters; publicity programs and publicity releases; window displays and counter cards and posters. Some of these materials are free, and others are supplied at cost.

Some merchants, particularly large department stores, prefer not to use the co-op advertising materials supplied by the manufacturer. A prestigious store typically develops a style of advertising that is distinctly its own. "Canned" advertising elements made up by the manufacturer's advertising department strike a jarring note when included in the store's advertisement. The store then prepares an ad featuring the manufacturer's item but interprets it, in illustrations and text, in a style in keeping with the store's advertising image. This treatment can still qualify for receipt of manufacturers' co-op funds.

Legislation Affecting Co-op Ads The amount of cooperative advertising funds available to the retailer is determined by the amount of goods ordered by the retailer from the manufacturer. In reality, this is a discount to the retailer on the prices of purchased goods, and it would be natural for the manufacturer to offer co-op funds to the firm's largest and best retail customers and to ignore the small-volume retailers. This was the case before passage of federal legislation in 1936.

The Clayton Act of 1914 had as its goal the elimination of price discrimination among purchasers of goods, and the Robinson-Patman Act of 1936 broadened and strengthened Clayton Act provisions in ways that had particular application to cooperative advertising. The Federal Trade Commission is responsible for enforcing the Robinson-Patman Act. Today, by this legislation, a manufacturer offering a concession such as co-op advertising to one retailer in a marketing area must offer it to all retailers alike on a basis proportional to sales.

Somewhere
deep under that bristling, spiny
exterior there's got to be a big-hearted
softie! We know this to be true of artichokes
and institutions and individuals.
In our era of chaos and confusing facts,
we sometimes forget that patience and
persistence usually manage to get to the
heart of matters. For our part,
more than ever before, John Wanamaker
is prepared to show you the
beauty and tenderness inside
its stone walls, and we
want to help you express your
Valentine's Day sentiment in the ways
you know best. John Wanamaker.
Ten stores that love you.

This local institutional ad for John Wanamaker concentrates on selling the store's image rather than on specific merchandise. (Courtesy John Wanamaker)

If, for example, a swimsuit maker offers in a co-op deal to pay 40 percent of a store's advertising when it is devoted to this maker's goods, it must offer the same deal locally to every retail customer. Customer A may order 5,000 swimsuits and customer B only 50. In each case, the 40 percent co-op deal will apply. It is important to note that neither of these retailers may want to take advantage of the deal. The Robinson-Patman Act's purpose is not to push co-op advertising but to ensure that all the swimsuit maker's customers are treated in the same way.

Co-op Procedures Participating retailers must sign a contract or agreement with the manufacturer to qualify for co-op advertising funds. The contract spells out in detail the basis of compensation for advertising promoting the manufacturer's goods in newspapers, on radio and TV, on billboards, in store circulars and catalogs, and the like. It contains information on treatment of the manufacturer's name or trademark in the advertising and lists minimum sizes of ads or portions of ads devoted to the products. After co-op advertising is run by the retailer, proof of performance is sent to the manufacturer. This includes invoices from the media showing cost of the advertising, tearsheets, or ads cut out of newspapers; and copies of radio or TV scripts if these media have been used. On receipt, the manufacturer sends a check to the store covering the cost of the co-op advertising.

Co-op Advantages and Limitations From the point of view of the manufacturer, the co-op program has the advantage, already mentioned, of local advertising that shows exactly where the manufacturer's goods are on sale. Co-op advertising also ties in with the manufacturer's national advertising, ideally stressing similar selling points and thus magnifying

the manufacturer's total advertising effort. It results in more advertising "impressions." Sometimes a manufacturer will benefit because the co-op advertising is run by a top store with a reputation for selling quality merchandise. This store prestige, the manufacturer thinks, is bound to rub off on the products on sale there. But not all manufacturers offer a co-op program. Their goods may be of such a quality that stores are competing to stock these items and the need for co-op incentives disappears. Manufacturers have canceled co-op programs because of difficulty in enforcing details of contracts, breaches of contract, and dishonest claims made by retailers. From the manufacturer's point of view a co-op program is difficult to administer, particularly when small accounts are involved, and this work must be weighed against results achieved.

A final disadvantage is that a manufacturer loses control to a certain extent of some of the firm's advertising funds. In a co-op program it is the retailer who determines where and how the manufacturer's co-op funds are spent. And it is often the retailer who writes the advertising and designs the illustrations for the manufacturer's products when that retailer does not choose to use the advertising materials the manufacturer supplies.

From the retailer's point of view, a co-op program has the advantages of lower cost per ad and qualification for volume media rate reductions. Through the use of co-op funds, the retailer can increase the size of the advertisements or increase the frequency of their appearance in local media. The retailer can also benefit from association, in the store's advertising, with top brand merchandise. Wedgwood china, Waterford crystal, Cuisinart, and Hart, Schaffner and Marx are prestige names that help the store's reputation when these brands are sold. A disadvantage is that the retailer may not wish to be curtailed in any way when the store's advertising is prepared, and co-op contracts often include stringent rules on how the manufacturer's products are to be treated in the store's advertising.

There is another reason why co-op advertising is not used by some retailers, particularly the smaller ones. A co-op program is work, and some retailers "just can't be bothered" and suffer from inertia. This is unfortunate but true, and as a result many retailers don't capitalize on the advantages of using available co-op dollars.

Characteristics of Local Advertising

Local advertising differs from national advertising in that it is personal, direct, and price-oriented and delivers faster results. For these reasons it has a different look from its national counterpart. It has more personality and is more people-oriented. Scores of advertisers have indicated, in conversation, that local advertising can be highly individualistic and less confining than national advertising. Local advertisers seem to find more actual enjoyment in preparing ads than national advertisers do. They can be specific and less constrained, expressing their own personalities, and talk directly to customers in ads.

Personal Local advertisers know their customers as no national advertiser ever can. They are part of the community, and their neighbors are their customers. They cater to customers' preferences. Merchants are personal salespeople who have great influence over what the customers select. Their advertising reflects this daily, personal involvement. They are free, in their ads, to convey a personalized image of their places of business.

Direct The local advertiser runs the ad and hopes it will bring customers directly to the store. Other forms of advertising do not operate as directly. The manufacturer must promote the company's products, but they are not bought from the company. They are bought from retailers, who must stock and promote these goods before they reach consumers. When retailers advertise, they talk directly to their customers and ask them to do one thing only: come to their place of business to buy what is advertised.

Price-Oriented Since prices for a product or service often vary in different parts of the country, the national advertiser cannot often include them. But local retail advertising very often includes the price of the merchandise or service. Since local merchants can often set the price of what they sell, and since they are looking for immediate action, the tendency is to list the price as an incentive to the consumer to buy. Price is important and newsworthy to the consumer. Leaf through an evening newspaper and notice how often the local advertiser lists prices and how often they are featured as a main point of the advertising message.

TRADITIONALIST MEN'S SUITS FOR FALL—$175.

BEAUTIFUL COLONIAL HOUSE—PARKLIKE SURROUNDINGS—$80,000.

CONTROL INSECTS AND CRABGRASS—20-LB BAG WAS $7.85, NOW $6.35.

REUPHOLSTER SOFA OR 2 CHAIRS—$149.

TOMATOES—59¢ A POUND. CHEDDAR CHEESE—$2.29 A POUND.

Action-Oriented The local advertiser has purchased a supply of merchandise or is equipped to render a consumer service. But no money is made until the goods or services are sold. Local advertisers look for action *now*, and their promotional advertising is geared to deliver immediate results. Profits depend on volume sales and constant turnover of merchandise. Local merchants' personal, direct, price-oriented approach to advertising helps them stay in business. Unlike national advertisers, concentrating on future sales, local merchants live in the present. Those who advertise understand advertising's power because they see its effects quickly. Selling results are immediate when the right merchandise is selected for the sales territory, when it is priced competitively, and when it is advertised aggressively. When national advertisers make mistakes in their advertising planning, it may be months before these mistakes are discovered. But when local advertisers run ineffective ads, errors are quickly discovered and seldom repeated.

The National Advertiser

Advertising sponsored by a manufacturer of goods or a supplier of services that are sold on a nationwide basis is *national advertising*. This definition covers many different kinds of national advertising, and there is much overlapping among them, as we shall see. Because of this, it is almost impossible to categorize advertising on a strict and inflexible basis. For instance (just to limber up our thinking), a national advertiser can run local advertising. Suppose the maker of Green Valley Tomato Soup, who places advertising in consumer magazines that are sold nationally, such as *Good Housekeeping* and *McCall's,* decides to add selected newspapers to the media list to support sales directly in certain cities. This food product maker is now advertising locally as well as nationally. But this manufacturer is not what is defined as a local advertiser for two reasons: (1) the ads do not tell the consumer in

what specific stores Green Valley Tomato Soup can be bought, and (2) the product is being sold at the same time everywhere throughout the country. The soup producer is merely using local advertising for selective sales support in certain cities where it's considered needed, in conjunction with the national advertising program.

Regional advertisers are classified with national advertisers. Some concerns are regional rather than national or local. Their district is not nationwide but it is larger than a city or town. Their sales area is regional because of the nature of their business or because of management policy. Many breweries such as Schmidt's, Genessee, and Iron City are regional advertisers because transportation costs limit their selling area. Treadway Inns confines its advertising to the Northeast because that is where the units of this motel chain are located. Thomas's english muffins are baked in two plants, one in California and one in New Jersey. Its advertising is concentrated on the West and East Coasts. Some oil companies have regional, not national, distribution of their petroleum products. Their advertising only covers areas where the service stations are located. Large bakeries and dairies are regional concerns because of distance limitations imposed by transportation costs and the fact that their products are perishable. These businesses use local media and national media as well, but only that portion of national media that circulates exclusively within their sales territory. Many national media—*Time* magazine, for example—have special regional editions in which such regional concerns advertise.

Direct mail advertising and catalog advertising may be national or local in scope. These particular forms of advertising are discussed in Chapter 4. A discussion of the main types of national advertisers follows.

The Brand Advertiser

The most important category of national advertising is advertising that sells a brand of merchandise. A *brand* is a distinctive name identifying the product of a manufacturer. There are tens of thousands of merchandise brands in the United States, many of which are familiar to us because they are advertised. Examples such as Plymouth, Toastmaster, Kodak, Ivory Soap, Crisco, Tide, Maxwell House, Budweiser, and Goodyear come readily to mind. Most brands and their distinctive designs are trademarked, that is, officially registered with the federal government for the exclusive use of the manufacturer, to distinguish the products from the competition.

The primary purpose of national brand advertising is to create consumer demand for the product advertised, but there are often secondary purposes, too. If a brand is nationally advertised, it is a morale booster for the manufacturer's sales force. Those in the field who call on retail stores or wholesalers are backed up by an ad program that makes the brand they are selling known and appreciated. Also, brand advertising can force distribution of a brand or product. If consumers respond to brand advertising and ask for certain brands when they shop, merchants will order the brands and carry them in stock. These purposes also apply to regional brand advertisers.

The Service Advertiser

Just as on the local advertising scene, there are national advertisers who don't sell products but who do sell their services. Insurance companies, airlines, car rental firms, moving firms, and the telephone company are examples of advertisers in this category. Their advertising job is to inform, to persuade, and to create a demand for the services that they offer.

The Corporate or Institutional Advertiser

Often a company management, coming to the conclusion that its reputation or its capabilities are not well known to the public, seeks to make the company's goals, achievements, and standards better understood. This can be accomplished through a planned publicity program and through advertising. Such advertising is called *corporate* (or institutional) *advertising* and has as its goal building a company's reputation or prestige. We have seen that local merchants also strive for this same goal in their institutional or image-building ads.

Corporate advertising, when it is developed and placed in media, is usually only a small part of the total advertising run by a manufacturer. The big job that the manufacturer's advertising must accomplish is selling the brands, or products, to the consumer. Nevertheless, corporate or institutional advertising can yield important results. It can serve to make the financial community aware of a company and enhance its prestige. It can broaden the ownership of company stock by impressing investors with a company's capacity for future growth. It can help in obtaining government contracts. It can keep the company's name before the public when its goods are not available because of strikes, war, or other reasons. It can enhance the company's reputation with the public, and this good reputation in turn can support the brand products that the company sells through its regular advertising. Sometimes the goal of corporate advertising is to describe a company's contribution to society as a whole and thus create a desirable public image.

General Electric runs a series of ads with the slogan "100 years of progress for people." Each advertisement describes one of the company's technological advances, like the development of an x-ray scanner that provides

Our fame has spread throughout the West!

After years of potting and puttering in a South San Francisco greenhouse, it was finally perfected in 1954. Since then, literally millions of trowels, rakes, hoes and hands have spread Supersoil across the west . . . and moved it to the very top. Today, in fact, it is the leading potting mix on this side of America! Why? There are many reasons:

Rich Canadian sphagnum peat. Sierra fir bark. Redwood. Granite-based river sand. A superbly balanced broad-spectrum nutrient package. And unique sterilization by pressurized steam. This is Supersoil, the finest all-around growing medium, indoors or out, for virtually any kind of greenery that ever grew beneath the western sky!

So share a little fame with your plants. Insist on the leading potting soil of the west—Supersoil! At leading nurseries, supermarkets and garden supply stores near you.

Supersoil
potting mix

"Favorite potting mix of western gardeners and their plants!"

©Copyright, Rod McLellan Co., 1979

These ads are examples of national and regional brand advertising. How do they differ from local retail ads? (Courtesy The Gillette Company; Supersoil; Sioux of America, Middlesex, NJ)

The old soft Shioux.™

In case you think we've gone a little soft, we have. We did it in the most superbly supple kidskin. Hand-lasted with an inner-sole that floats your foot on air, and an outer-sole of genuine Plantation Crepe. The entire combination is pure walking pleasure, for men whose feet prefer gentle going. In a slip-on or tie. Write for the name of your nearest dealer. Sioux of America, Dept. S2, Newington Park, Newington, New Hampshire 03801

20 Million Pairs sold 'round the World

FREE* RAZOR FROM GOOD NEWS!®

*30¢ off coupon when you buy a 2- or 3-pack Good News! Disposable Razor.

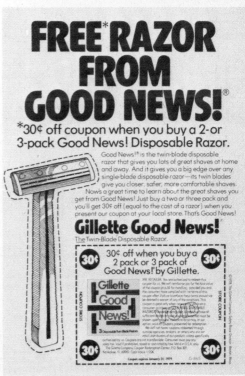

Good News!® is the twin-blade disposable razor that gives you lots of great shaves at home and away. And it gives you a big edge over any single-blade disposable razor—its twin blades give you closer, safer, more comfortable shaves. Now's a great time to learn about the great shaves you get from Good News! Just buy a two or three pack and you'll get 30¢ off (equal to the cost of a razor) when you present our coupon at your local store. That's Good News!

Gillette Good News!
The Twin-Blade Disposable Razor.

Light assurance is our business

Not only do we assure you that a Zippo lighter will give a strong windproof light . . . time after time, we also guarantee any Zippo ever made in our 47 years of business to work always or we will fix it free . . . regardless of age or condition.

Zippo®

Our Zippo guarantee is your light assurance policy.

THE FAMOUS
zippo
GUARANTEE

Zippo Manufacturing Co. Bradford, Pa. 16701 In Canada: Zippo Mfg. Co. of Canada, Ltd.

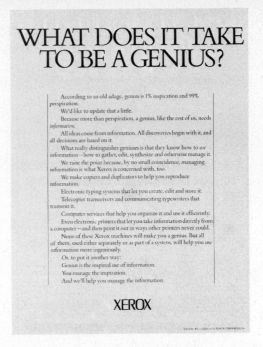

WHAT DOES IT TAKE TO BE A GENIUS?

According to an old adage, genius is 1% inspiration and 99% perspiration.

We'd like to update that a little.

Because more than perspiration, a genius, like the rest of us, needs *information.*

All ideas come from information. All discoveries begin with it, and all decisions are based on it.

What really distinguishes geniuses is that they know how to *use* information—how to gather, edit, synthesize and otherwise manage it.

We raise the point because, by no small coincidence, managing information is what Xerox is concerned with, too.

We make copiers and duplicators to help you reproduce information.

Electronic typing systems that let you create, edit and store it.

Telecopier transceivers and communicating typewriters that transmit it.

Computer services that help you organize it and use it efficiently.

Even electronic printers that let you take information directly from a computer—and then print it out in ways other printers never could.

None of these Xerox machines will make you a genius. But all of them, used either separately or as part of a system, will help you use information more ingeniously.

Or, to put it another way:

Genius is the inspired use of information.

You manage the inspiration.

And we'll help you manage the information.

XEROX

Here are two national advertisements. Which is selling goods, and which is an example of corporate advertising? What ideas are these ads trying to convey? (Courtesy Zippo Manufacturing Co., ad designed and produced by Zippo's in-house agency; and Xerox Corporation)

more detail than ordinary x rays, and helps avoid exploratory surgery. It is run in conjunction with General Electric's regular brand advertising. Philip Morris in its institutional advertising advocates the idea that corporations should be patrons of the arts and describes its own sponsorship of traveling art exhibits for the public. American Electric Power, a large utility, tells the reader in its corporate campaign of its investment in new power plants and pollution-control facilities. The General Motors ad with the caption "How to reduce rust" provides helpful information to car owners and has as its goal establishing the idea that GM is dedicated to making its cars last longer. These are all examples of corporate or institutional ads at work.

The Trade and Industrial Advertiser

National advertisers often find it necessary and important to address ad messages directly to the retail merchants and wholesalers to whom they want to sell merchandise. This kind of advertising supplements and supports the field sales force, and its name, *trade advertising,* was developed from the expression "retailers in the trade." The national advertiser is usually a trade advertiser, too. There are hundreds of special nationally circulated magazines and newspapers known as *trade papers,* with an editorial content geared to specific businesses, industries, and professions. They cover every conceivable mercantile and professional area, from accounting to yachting. The names of these publications indicate their area of specialization: *American Banker, Bakery Products and Marketing, Chain Store Age, Drug Topics, Home Furnishings Daily,* and *Women's Wear Daily.* (See Color Plate 4.)

Producers of goods and services are themselves consumers: they need raw materials, supplies of all kinds, machinery, and other equipment to do their job. Other businesses and industries supply these needs. These suppliers are national advertisers, too, but their advertising is directed to industrial customers, not the individual consumer. This is *industrial advertising.* The messages are placed in nationally circulated business or industrial magazines, such as *Fortune, Office Appliances, Industrial Machinery News, Business Week,* and *Chemical Week.*

The Farm Advertiser

There is a special category of national advertising directed toward farmers. Manufacturers of farm equipment and farm suppliers need to

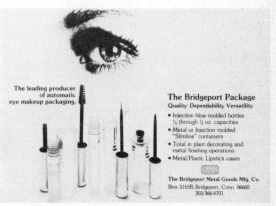

The Kodak ad is a trade ad addressed to the supermarket or discount house operator. The Bridgeport Metal Goods ad is an industrial advertisement. Its purpose is to sell specialized packaging to the cosmetics industry. (Courtesy The Bridgeport Metal Goods Manufacturing Company)

reach the farming community on a national basis in order to help sell their specialized products. These businessmen can reach the farmer and agriculturist through general, non-specialized magazines, and they can reach the farmer's wife through women's magazines such as *Good Housekeeping* or home-decorating magazines such as *House Beautiful.* But the farm press exists, and it is aimed specifically at the farm audience. The purpose of *farm advertising* is to reach a selected audience of farm-oriented consumers with selling information on farm products and services, and a specialized group of magazines and newspapers is available for this purpose. Advertisers using these media, are farm advertisers.

The Trade Association Advertiser

The dairy farmers and dairies of America have formed an association that has as one of its goals fostering the use of dairy products in general. The association turned to national advertising as a way to accomplish this objective. It places ads directed at the consumer to encourage consumption of milk, butter, and ice cream. Members of the association are assessed the costs of the ad program. This is an example of *trade association advertising,* which promotes the products of an industry in general, rather than specific brands of individual companies. The American Dairy Association promotes milk, rather than a brand of milk such as Borden's. Many industries advertise in this way. The American Iron and Steel Institute, the California Raisin Advisory Board, the Holland Cheese Export Association, the Idaho Potato Commission, and the Institute of Life Insurance promote the products or services of their industry on a nonbrand basis. (See Color Plate 5.)

Advertising with the same goal as trade association advertising has also been run by trade unions. Here the purpose is to promote in general the products made by industry union members in order to aid employment. The International Ladies' Garment Workers Union, for example, runs short campaigns at peak garment selling periods in the spring and fall. Its jingle, "Look for the Union Label" promotes the sale of clothes made in the United States rather than imports.

The Advocacy Advertiser

Advertising that presents ideas and opinions on one side of controversial social issues and marshals facts to bolster the sponsor's point of view is called *advocacy advertising.* It usually singles out an adversary and seeks to change the reader's attitudes with the goal of helping to undermine or defeat this adversary.

Advocacy advertising is popularly thought to be sponsored only by corporations and business trade associations, but other types of organizations can be advocacy advertisers as well. An environmental group such as the Sierra Club may run advocacy advertising against, or in support of, proposals that affect the environment. A labor union may place advertising that seeks to encourage restrictions on imports to protect its members' jobs. However, most advocacy advertising is run and paid for by elements of the business community.

It is important to distinguish advocacy advertising, presenting views on controversial issues, from corporate advertising, the goal of which is to enhance a company's reputation. Both types can appear in the same advertisement. A coal company, for example, places an ad which explains that its strip mining areas are restored for useful purposes after operations are completed. This is considered corporate advertising. But if the text then makes the point that strip-mining legislation is too strict and should be modified, advocacy advertising is at work.

Advocacy advertising has existed since the twenties.[2] Its volume expanded with increased public interest in the environment in the seventies and with the energy crisis of 1973–1974. The subject has become controversial. In brief, critics of advocacy advertising say that large corporations can afford to advertise in this way and that groups holding contrary beliefs generally can't. Critics hold that the costs of advocacy advertising should not be deducted as a business expense, as it is now, but should be charged against corporation profit after income taxes are paid. It is also said that such advertising should be regulated by government bodies to ensure that there is substantiation for the claims and statements that are made.

In reply, corporate management people resist any attempt that is construed as imposing censorship and restricting free speech. Limiting or prohibiting advocacy advertising or changing the taxing procedures, as critics suggest, would restrict freedom to express opinions. It is felt that when news media cover controversial social issues affecting business interests, the viewpoints of business people are inadequately presented. It therefore becomes necessary, this argument holds, to present business attitudes to the public through advertising. Then the public would be exposed to all sides of an issue and would be in a better position to make judgments on such controversial matters.

Advocacy advertising is run almost exclusively in the print media. The decision to accept or reject such advertising is the responsi-

bility of magazine and newspaper publishers, and policies vary. A different situation exists in the broadcast media. The public "owns" the airwaves, and there is a limit to the number of television and radio stations that can be accommodated. The federal government, through the Federal Communications Commission, therefore regulates the broadcast industry. The FCC's fairness doctrine requires broadcasters to make available air time to both sides when controversial public issues are presented, and this requirement has been applied to advocacy advertising. When advocacy advertising is accepted and aired, it is therefore necessary to offer time for rebuttal by the other side. Broadcasters solve the problem by not accepting advocacy advertising. A more detailed discussion of the fairness doctrine appears in Chapter 8.

The Public Service Advertiser

Various causes in the public interest receive volunteer advertising support, and such advertising is called *public service advertising*. The advertiser in many such instances is an organization called the Advertising Council, supported by the advertising communications industries and American business. The Council was established in 1942 in response to a request for help in the war effort from the government. It has continued ever since, supporting public interest causes with annual campaigns. In 1979, the Advertising Council mounted thirty major public service campaigns. The value of radio and television time and space in newspapers, magazines and on billboards, donated by the communications industry, exceeded $0.5 billion for the seventh straight year.

Campaigns promote voluntary citizen actions to help solve national problems. Each project must be noncommercial, nonpartisan, and not designed to influence legislation. The

---

[2] S. Prakash Sethi, *Advocacy Advertising and Large Corporations,* D. C. Heath and Company, Lexington, Mass., 1977, p. 14.

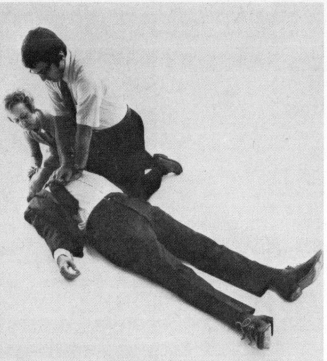

A Heart
Too Good To Die.

It's our guess you've never even heard of cardiopulmonary resuscitation—right? Well, there are some new lifeguards around these days, trained by the Heart Association in a lifesaving technique called cardiopulmonary resuscitation (CPR).

You'll see them in hospitals, industrial plants, ambulances, football stadiums . . . even large offices. Many are doctors, but others are firemen, nurses, ambulance and rescue personnel, policemen . . . and just plain people.

When someone's heart stops, his brain begins to die. Minutes count.

Prompt application of mouth-to-mouth breathing and chest compression keeps blood flowing to the brain. CPR can restore life, or sustain it until complete cardiac care can be started. Thousands of victims of sudden heart arrest have been saved by these CPR "lifeguards."

A lot is being done these days to prevent premature death, to save hearts "too good to die"— and the Heart Association is doing it. Your gift to the American Heart Association will keep us at it.

Give to the American Heart Association
WE'RE FIGHTING FOR YOUR LIFE

Could you pass this Red Cross swimming test?

SWIM:
1. Breaststroke — 100 Yds.
2. Sidestroke — 100 Yds.
3. Crawl stroke — 100 Yds.
4. Back crawl — 50 Yds.
5. On back (legs only) — 50 Yds.
6. Turns (on front, back, side).
7. Surface dive — underwater swim — 20 Ft.
8. Disrobe — float with clothes — 5 mins.
9. Long shallow dive.
10. Running front dive.
11. 10-minute swim.

Anybody who's taken a Red Cross swim course knows how tough it can be.

There's a good reason.

We believe drowning is a serious business.

Last year alone, we taught 2,589,203 Americans not to drown—in the seven different swim courses we offer all across the country. (Incidentally, most of the teaching —as with almost everything American Red Cross does—is done by dedicated volunteers.)

A good many of the youngsters not only are learning to keep *themselves* safe. Thousands upon thousands of them are learning to become lifesavers.

And the life they save—it just might be your own.

Peter Vaeth-Photography

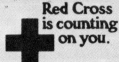

Red Cross is counting on you.

These public service messages appear in national magazines at no cost. Smokey the Bear and the American Red Cross are Ad Council campaigns; the American Heart Association message was prepared independently. (Courtesy The Advertising Council; The American Heart Association)

FIRES GROW FASTER THAN TREES.

A Public Service of This Newspaper & The Advertising Council [Ad]

purpose of the project must be such that advertising methods can help achieve its objectives.

The Advertising Council's most famous campaigns are "Only you can prevent forest fires" with its spokesman Smokey the Bear, and the antipollution campaign. This latter, with Iron Eyes Cody, the "crying Indian" has become synonymous with environmental concern to the general public. Other campaigns are the American Red Cross, aid to higher education, the American economic system, minority business enterprise, and rehabilitation of handicapped people.

The method of operation is as follows:

1. A campaign is proposed to the Council and is then accepted or rejected.

2. The Association of National Advertisers selects a coordinator from the business world.

3. An advertising agency is chosen. It contributes time and work on a volunteer basis.

4. An advertising program is developed by the agency and made available to various media.

5. Advertising space and time are contributed by magazines, newspapers, television and radio stations, business papers, outdoor advertising, and other media.

The charitable fund raiser is a substantial advertiser on a national as well as on a local scale. The March of Dimes, local Community Chest and Red Feather drives, and CARE are typical advertisers of this kind. Advertising space is sometimes donated by media, but, unlike Advertising Council projects, payment for space is generally required on the local level for charitable drives' fund-raising ads. Time involved to prepare such ads is volunteered free of charge by advertising agencies.

Advertising by Professionals

Traditionally professional people, such as doctors and dentists, lawyers, architects, and accountants, have been forbidden by their trade associations to advertise their services. *Advertising by professionals,* that is, advertising promoting the services of professional people, was considered to be unethical and undignified. But in June 1977, a U.S. Supreme Court ruling[3] struck down an Arizona Bar Association regulation that did not permit lawyers to advertise. The ruling set aside all regulations and laws that forbid advertising all other professions as well.[4]

Since the ruling, advertising by professionals has been run principally by two groups, lawyers and dentists, and the practice is not widespread. A recent poll reported that 3 percent of lawyers in the United States are advertising, while 89 percent stated they would never advertise.[5] It is highly unlikely that this will remain the case for these reasons: the number of lawyers has proliferated by almost 300 percent in the last 10 years; it is widely held that many legal firms which have advertised have increased their business; legal clinics offering an assortment of "packaged" services at relatively low cost are proliferating, and this type of operation lends itself well to promotion.

Doctors, accountants, and architects have in general not made use of their new freedom to advertise. The subject of advertising by professionals has become controversial. Besides concerns about ethics and dignity, many lawyers and dentists have other problems with advertising by professionals. They acknowledge that advertising can increase business but believe that quality of service will be sacrificed in the process. Others maintain that increased volume and standardization of service reduces costs to consumers. Committees of professional trade associations have spent months deliberating on workable advertising codes that govern how and where practitioners may advertise if they decide to do so, and many of these codes will be tested in the courts.

Indications are that television is a productive medium for generating legal business. Jacoby & Meyers, a Los Angeles legal clinic with 16 offices, spent $250,000 on TV ads in 1978 and found this expenditure profitable, according to Stephen Q. Meyers, a partner in the firm. (See the illustration on page 65.)

Advertising by professionals should not be confused with the category "professional advertising," words sometimes used to describe advertising by manufacturers and suppliers of drugs, medical and dental equipment, architectural materials, and accounting services to members of the various professions. This advertising appears in publications as *American Family Physician, Architectural Record,* and the *American Journal of Nursing.*

---

[3] *Bates and O'Steen* v. *State Bar of Arizona.* In the ruling, the Supreme Court extended the doctrine that truthful commercial speech has full First Amendment rights. The Court, by a five-to-four majority, rejected the argument that ads promoting professional services are likely to give the public an inaccurate picture. The view prevailed that present laws prevented advertising deception and that the preferred remedy for public confusion was "more disclosure, not less." Bates and O'Steen operate a legal clinic and had run a newspaper ad on February 22, 1976, that offered low-cost services for divorces, bankruptcies, wills, and other legal matters. The Arizona State Bar attempted disciplinary action, and the law firm brought suit. *Advertising Age,* July 4, 1977, pp. 1 and 51.

[4] *Business Week,* July 24, 1978, p. 122.

[5] *Advertising Age,* July 24, 1978, p. 10.

These are examples of advertising by professionals. What is your opinion as to whether professional people should advertise? (Courtesy The Legal Clinic of Jacoby & Meyers; Lawrence Irwin Frankle and Associates; Chollick Associates, Inc. for The Denture Center)

Vocabulary

Define the following terms and use each one in a sentence.

Advertising by professionals
Advocacy advertising
Brand
Cooperative advertising
Corporate advertising
Farm advertising
Industrial advertising
Institutional advertising
Local advertising

National advertising
Professional advertising
Promotional advertising
Public service advertising
Regional advertising
Retail advertising
Service advertising
Trade advertising
Trade association advertising

Review Questions

1. Name six types of advertisers and give a reason why each one advertises.
2. What is the primary function of local advertising?
3. What is the fundamental difference between national advertising and local advertising?
4. Distinguish between two kinds of local advertising, promotional advertising and institutional (or image) advertising.
5. Give examples of local promotional advertising found in your local media.
6. What can promotional advertising do for a local merchant besides sell the products advertised?
7. What effect does the Robinson-Patman Act have on manufacturers' dealer co-op programs?
8. From the point of view of the manufacturer, what advantages does a co-op program offer?
9. Name three characteristics of local advertising.
10. From your own observation, name ten nationally advertised brands or products made well known by advertising.
11. Name three reasons why a company would consider running a corporate or institutional advertising program.
12. Why does a manufacturer sponsor a trade advertising program?
13. What is the purpose of farm advertising?
14. Name three advertising programs of the Advertising Council.

15. Should advocacy advertising by business be permitted, limited, or prohibited? Give reasons for your point of view.

16. Give two reasons why it is likely that advertising by lawyers will increase.

Activities

1. Bring to class ten examples of local advertising clipped from a newspaper. Identify each and label as selling goods or services. Be prepared to discuss the basic purpose of the advertiser in each example.

2. Obtain and bring to class examples of national brand advertising and national service advertising and also one of the following: a national corporate or institutional ad, a national farm advertising ad, a trade association ad, or a public service ad. Use national magazines or a farm magazine as your source.

Project

Look over your town or city newspaper, and select a local retail advertiser who interests you. Check with your teacher; then arrange to interview the person who is in charge of advertising for this firm. Stop by in person, and ask for a few minutes of time. If the person is busy, make an appointment for a more convenient time. Your task will be to write a report of this merchant's advertising program.

Before your interview, do some preliminary sleuthing. Note the type of merchandise carried and to what kinds of people it should appeal, such as low-, middle-, or upper-income groups. For example, if you have selected a supermarket, the goods may appeal to all three income groups. If you have selected a high-fashion dress shop, the customers are from the upper-income group. Try to determine whether the merchant draws trade from the neighborhood or from a wider area.

Know the questions you're going to ask before you arrive. Ask why the merchant advertises and where and when the advertising is run. Ask the merchant's opinion of the effectiveness of the program and how the pulling power of the media is evaluated. Probe for examples of success or failure experienced in the course of the merchant's advertising program.

Your report should start with a brief description of the merchant's business and the type of customer appealed to. It should then outline the advertising program, including the answers to the questions posed above. Finally, it should be accompanied by an ad that the merchant has run.

Career Ladder

Assume that you are attending a community college and are looking for a summer job between semesters. Eventually, you would be interested in working in the advertising or marketing fields. If you had your choice for summer employment in the following three areas, which would you choose, and why?

Salesperson in a local discount house

Part-time interviewer for a local research firm which has some clients in the marketing area

Bank teller (pays better than the other two)

Be prepared to discuss your reasons in class.

CHAPTER FOUR

THESE ADVERTISING PEOPLE

A popular conception of the advertising worker is that of a cynical, high-pressure person in a glamorous field. But at the risk of destroying illusions, we must state that advertising and advertising people are not like this at all. Advertising is a business, and a very practical one. Its purpose is to help sell goods and services. Because it is always challenging, and because, to be successful, advertising requires the application of creativity, it can often be stimulating, exciting, and rewarding. It can also be routine and humdrum, and, in any case, it invariably requires hard work.

This is not to say that some people in advertising do not sometimes lead exceedingly glamorous lives. Advertising writers for ad agencies might travel all over the world with a camera crew and director to shoot television commercials for oil companies, airlines, and car makers. Photographers who specialize in advertising sometimes travel widely. Task force coordinators from industry and ad agencies go to the White House to consult with spe-

cial assistants to the President on Advertising Council public service programs. People who have the responsibility for supervising television programs for advertising departments of leading companies must spend a certain amount of time in Hollywood and New York with the actors and entertainers involved in producing television shows. These ad people are experienced professionals, at the top of their field, who have earned these sometimes quite pleasant experiences. But even they have to meet tight deadlines, and they carry heavy workloads. They shoulder considerable responsibility, and this always involves the risk of failure.

Perhaps you will be able to shape your business career in directions that entail a certain amount of glamour and excitement. But in any case, if you enter advertising you will find that the processes involved in creating, placing, and eventually evaluating even the simplest advertising can be rewarding and productive if they are approached with an attitude of determination to take fullest advantage of what practical advertising can offer in sales results.

Many different kinds of people are involved in this advertising business, some on a part-time basis and some on a full-time basis. Who are they, and what are the advertising tasks they perform?

The Do-It-Yourself Part-Time Advertiser

Local merchants with small-volume businesses are part-time advertising people who nevertheless perform functions similar to those of the very largest advertisers. They usually do all the work themselves. They may spend as little as 2 hours a month thinking about their advertising and taking the steps necessary to produce it, or they may spend 30 percent of their business hours on advertising tasks. The time spent is determined by the kind of business they are in, the size of the business, and their own judgment concerning the importance of advertising to business success.

No matter how much or how little time is spent on advertising matters, no matter how large or how small the advertising expenditures are, local merchants take these basic advertising steps:

1. Establish an objective, or goal, for the advertising

2. Select the goods and services to be advertised

3. Determine how much should be spent (establish an advertising budget)

4. Choose the advertising media

5. Prepare the advertising

6. Produce the advertising in the form required by the media

7. Place the advertising in the chosen media

These signs are examples of identification advertising used by retailers. (Courtesy The Kroger Company; Gino's, Inc.; John Wanamaker; Mobil Oil Corporation)

8. Pay bills and take care of other paperwork

9. Evaluate the results of the advertising[1]

Note that in this list of tasks, we do not give local merchants the choice of whether to advertise or not. When merchants go into business, they must use advertising in some form or another. As we have pointed out in Chapter 3, every merchant is an advertiser, even if only because of the sign on the storefront. The choice merchants have is to what extent they will advertise beyond this fundamental and necessary advertising.

Advertising That Goes Beyond Identification

How does the local merchant in a small business determine whether advertising should be used beyond what we may call identification advertising, the signs and window cards that tell passersby what is being sold in the store? Often such a decision is purely arbitrary. But there are certain fundamental business criteria that determine whether advertising beyond the identification stage can be profitable.

Is the merchant's sales volume capable of expansion? If the answer is yes, advertising is well worth considering as a method of expanding sales volume. Does the merchant sell some items that deliver generous profits, that is, what is termed a high profit margin? Again, an affirmative answer will offer a reason for advertising. The generous return received when an item with a high profit margin is sold allows higher selling expenses, one of which can be advertising.

Let's examine some businesses located in an imaginary row on a busy shopping street

[1] Research is not listed as a separate category because it can help determine decisions at several points in the nine advertising steps. See Tables 9-1 and A-1 for research applications to the advertising process.

and discover how answering the above questions can help us determine whether or not the merchants should advertise beyond the identification stage. We shall consider a drugstore, a luncheonette, a florist, and a hardware store.

The Drugstore The drugstore is on a corner and has show windows on two sides, filled with merchandise that is priced competitively. The prices are as low as or lower than those featured by the other drugstores in town. The interior selling area is about 1,200 square feet, and there is ample storage room for stock in the rear. The druggist, Mr. Gonzalez, can expand his sales volume through advertising. To do this he needs no more selling area than he already has. What he hopes is that through advertising he can increase the turnover of his competitively priced merchandise; in other words, he wants to sell his stock faster. The druggist also carries items with high profit margins. His prescription department, for example, delivers a high profit margin, and Mr. Gonzalez therefore wants to build up his prescription business.

This merchant can place two forms of advertising to increase sales, product advertising and institutional advertising. Examples of product advertising would be ads featuring suntan lotions in the summer, back-to-school items in the fall, vitamins and cold remedies in winter, and beauty aids year-round. For the prescription department, institutional advertising is run. These institutional ads stress experience of the pharmacist in carefully filling prescriptions and the fact that medicines will be delivered in emergencies.

The druggist has decided to go beyond identification advertising because some of his merchandise offers high profit margins and because his sales volume is capable of expansion with no additional investment in space.

The Luncheonette The luncheonette next door, run by Mr. Clarke, caters mainly to a breakfast and lunch trade, and at noon all the tables are taken. It's near the high school, so the owner does a good fountain business at 3 p.m. Practically no one stops in at dinner time, as the place just doesn't have a "restaurant look." The food isn't particularly good, anyway. The owner finds his profit margins low on the food he sells. In the unlikely event that he tried advertising, perhaps by featuring luncheon specials, he couldn't accommodate more customers unless he expanded his luncheonette.

Advertising can't help a business facing these conditions. Mr. Clarke can't use advertising unless he expands and also improves the quality of what he sells.

The Florist Although the store selling area is small (500 square feet), the florist, Mrs. Bruno, runs advertising in the local newspaper on a regular basis. In this field, a selling area of this size can support an expanded volume of business. The location is good because visitors at the large hospital around the corner often stop in and make purchases. The greenhouse is near enough to replenish the florist's stock if her sales are so good in the course of the day that she runs short. And there's a generous profit margin to be made on cut flowers and potted plants. This florist can afford advertising and can profit from it, so for her it is a good investment.

The Hardware Store The hardware store is large and has recently been expanded by the owner-operators, Mr. and Mrs. Meyerson. They now have floor space to carry items with a generous profit margin, such as power mowers, snow blowers, and a full line of kitchen utensils. They have added a decorator section featuring wallpaper and tiling. The Meyersons are promoting their expansion with a "grand re-opening" ad in the local newspaper and a series of commercials on the local radio station, and they now run ads regularly on items that carry a good profit margin. Their ads are increasing store traffic and building business.

Conclusions

We see from these examples that some local businesspeople are not in a position to advertise profitably beyond the store-identification stage, either because the way they do business does not offer the possibility of expanded sales volume or because the products they sell do not offer a high profit margin. Their sales volume is usually very small and remains that way. But this is not to say that all merchants who are not limited by these factors do advertise in their local media. Some who could advertise and profit by it do not do so because of inertia, lack of knowledge, or the fact that they just don't see any point in it. Advertising does entail a risk—money is spent without any guarantee of profit—and there are merchants who decide not to use this sales aid.

Do-It-Yourself Small-Business Advertising

Local merchants who run small businesses and who decide to advertise beyond the identification stage become part-time advertising people who spend a limited amount of time accomplishing the task and do all the work themselves. In small businesses it is usually the owner who assumes the responsibility of carrying out the advertising program. The task is important because it bears directly on business success and growth, and it involves decisions on expenditure of funds. The owner likes to make these decisions. This task is often interesting to a proprietor. The work involved is

These do-it-yourself local advertisements were placed in newspapers by merchants in their role as part-time advertising people. (Courtesy Lyman Orchards; Morse; Sullivan & Son Carpet; House of Light)

enjoyable, and this is another important reason why the owner handles the advertising program himself or herself.

The Time It Takes There is no hard-and-fast rule that determines the amount of time local merchants spend on their ad programs. It might take less than 1 hour for a men's apparel store owner to prepare an ad for the local newspaper if all the information and materials were at hand. If two or three ads are placed each month, all the necessary steps involved in advertising can be accomplished in about 6 hours a month. The kind of business involved and the owner's decision whether or not the advertising program will be minimal or elaborate are the time determinants.

Here is how Paul Leone, a local Ford car dealer in a city with a population of 70,000 saw the problem:

I spend about four hours a week on advertising. I write up a full-page ad for the paper almost every week, and run some commercials on the radio station. I wrote the radio spots myself some time back, and I keep repeating them. I don't spend too much time thinking about my ad budget. The treasurer gets into the act when she thinks I'm spending too much money.

This dealer also spends a certain amount of time speaking or writing to his Ford distributor about the newspaper advertisements and what to feature; he also spends an hour or so every month checking over advertising bills from the media and approving payment. He takes an informal and relaxed attitude toward his advertising, as do most local merchants, and exerts a minimum effort on it.

The ad program for Reliance Home Appliances two blocks away is somewhat similar. This is a family-run business. Joe Kruger handles service and repairs; his wife, Mary, the

billing and some of the accounting. Joe Jr. does all the buying; manages the store; takes care of inventory, pricing, and delivery and also runs the ad program. Although the retail appliance business is extremely competitive and has traditionally relied heavily on advertising, Joe Jr. can do the job "in about 2 hours a week, plus 5 or 6 hours a month on claims." The work on what he terms "claims" is concerned with his cooperative advertising (Chapter 3). This co-op advertising, supplied by the manufacturers of the brands he sells and run locally by him over his store's name, accounts for a good deal of his total advertising. Since the costs of co-op advertising are shared with the manufacturer or distributor after the ads are run, this merchant makes a claim on the manufacturer for part of the costs involved.

In contrast, Jim McArdle, a garden supplies merchant in the same town, spends a total of 30 percent of his business hours on his advertising program. His tasks in general are similar to those of the car dealer and appliance store manager. He could accomplish them in a few hours each month, but he doesn't choose to. He has evolved a more complicated, time-consuming program that calls for his direct involvement and has been profitable for his store.

His newspaper ads are seasonal in nature—placed when consumer demand for an item is greatest. Since he relies heavily on prepared co-op advertising material, these ads require a minimum of preparation time. But instead of merely placing commercials on the local radio, this merchant has developed his own 5-minute program twice weekly on which he chats with his audience on gardening topics and delivers his own commercials. This activity is time-consuming, but because of it he has become a well-known local personality. His store dominates the local field, and business is growing. In addition, this merchant relies on a spring store catalog that he mails to his customers annually. He likes to write and prepare it himself. It takes him 6 weeks each year to accomplish this task, but his catalog has a noncommercial "folksy" flavor.

The total effect of this ad program has been the building of an image and a character for the store that is unique and that has contributed to business success.

The Effort It Takes The three ad programs described above are all practical and efficient. As we have noted, the advertising job can be accomplished with minimal effort. However, local merchants are in an unusual position in the advertising field. There are opportunities here to make business grow by applying more than a minimal amount of time to an ad program. Within the limits of creative ability and the time that they can afford to spend on ad programs, merchants can build their store's reputation and image through unique and nonroutine advertising promotion methods, like the garden supplies merchant. Ideally, every local merchant should take the time to look long and hard at the ad program and try to determine whether or not it holds such opportunities. Most programs do.

Advertising Departments in Larger Retail Stores

The advertising "department" of small local stores usually consist, as we have seen, of owners themselves, who handle their program on a do-it-yourself basis and spend a small portion of their time accomplishing their advertising tasks. In larger retail businesses these tasks are delegated to a retail *advertising department,* that part of a business charged with planning, preparing, and executing its adver-

tising program. The number of people employed in this department range from two or three in a small city home furnishings or department store to the 100 advertising people who

pacesetter on 2
Jeff Sayre: American in Paris.

His clothes don't hint that he's a native Californian. Because exciting young designer, Jeff Sayre, has incorporated so much of the European, less-layered look into his menswear, he's produced a whole new approach. An approach that says Jeff Sayre is his own man. His collection, just arrived at Macy's, shows off his flair for translating continental élan into a great, simple, de-accessorized freedom. Fine news for Americans! Just a sample of his light touch with original color and fabric: The Veste de Ville (in New York: the city jacket), 100% wool flannel in seafoam or dusty blue, $165. Jacquard stripe shirt with a trace of antique striping in black/blue or red/green on ecru, $75. Pacesetter Shop, 2nd Floor at Macy's Herald Square.

Macy's welcomes the American Express Card **macy's**

What people in the advertising department of Macy's were involved in the preparation of this ad? What were their tasks? (Courtesy Macy's)

work for Macy's department store in New York City. It is important to realize that in spite of the numbers of people found in large retail ad departments, the functions performed are similar to those performed in the smallest ad departments.

The most important activity the retail advertising department performs is the preparation of the store's advertising. To accomplish this, three kinds of people are needed: copywriters, who write the words in the advertisements; artists, who produce the illustrations for the advertisements; and production people, who prepare the advertising material for reproduction in print. There are various jobs in each category, depending on the size of the department.

The Copy Section

Written words are a basic ingredient of a printed advertisement. They are the primary means of communicating information about the product or service being sold. *Copy* is a general term that applies to all written material appearing in an ad. The copywriter is a key person in the department, being responsible for preparing all that is written about the item being advertised: headings, captions, its features, and prices. When the information needed isn't forthcoming, the copywriter must dig it up, getting in touch with the manufacturer if necessary. The copywriter develops the approach to be used to the consumer and writes in a style that matches the product's image. In large departments, the copy section may be headed by a copy chief, a supervisor of copywriters' work, who evaluates the copy and who may do some copywriting too. In the very large stores, writers specialize in writing copy on certain areas. For example, there may be an appliance group of writers, a home appliance group, and a group of copywriters who concentrate on high-fashion items.

The Art Section

The art section of the department is usually headed by an art director, or art supervisor. Reporting to this person are artists who rough out the physical appearance of an advertisement. These artists produce *layouts,* or approximate resemblances of finished ads, that remain as a guide during the preparation of the final advertisement. The layout artists plan the "look" of the ad, determining where and how large the illustration will be; where the headline or lead statement of the ad is to appear; where the copy should be placed in relation to the illustration; how much space should be allotted to the copy; and where to place such elements as merchandise, price information, and the store name and address. Their job is to use the space of the ad in the most efficient and attractive way possible. Also reporting to the art director are artists who produce finished artwork, final illustrations that are used in the finished advertisement. And there may be one or more photographers, who photograph merchandise for use in ads whenever this service is called for.

The Production Section

Working under a production manager and following the layout, specialists prepare the art and copy so that the ad can be placed and run in print media: newspapers, local magazines, pamphlets, and catalogs. Typographers specify the typefaces the printer will use in setting the copy (typefaces and type selection are discussed in Chapter 15). The production manager or an assistant will determine specifications for photoengraving, the process that reproduces the illustrations and ultimately the entire ad in a form called a plate that is sometimes used by media to print the final ad. Use of the photoengraving process has decreased, and most papers today are printed in offset. In this process, production people need only submit a *mechanical* of the advertising material to the newspaper or printer of catalogs and pamphlets for reproduction. The mechanical consists of type and illustrations pasted up as the layout indicates and prepared in the department. (Printing processes are discussed in Chapter 16.) In the production section, too, is the proofreader, who reads the typeset copy against the original and checks for errors. In larger stores, there is a traffic person who, as the title implies, "traffics" or transmits the elements of each ad as it goes through the department on the basis of a prearranged schedule so that deadlines are met. The traffic function may also be assigned to the department manager's staff.

The Production Line

These three sections—copy, art, and production—constitute the production line of the retail ad department. Life for people working here is anything but slow and leisurely. Their department is dominated by deadlines. Copy and layout may be prepared in the morning, illustrations drawn in the early afternoon, type set and plates made before evening, and the ad run in the newspaper the next morning. Usually, however, the schedule is not quite this hectic.

To operate the three sections of the production line, an advertising manager, or advertising department head, is required. This person has overall responsibility for the operation of the department and spends much time in planning the advertising program and in working with the store buyers of merchandise and the merchandise managers of the various retail departments. In larger stores the ad manager is assisted by a planning staff, and also on the staff are such people as secretaries, clerks, and messengers, none of whom are directly engaged in the preparation of advertising.

The Broadcast Advertising Section

We have stressed print media in our discussion of the retail advertising department because retail stores rely on newspapers as their basic advertising medium. Reasons for this reliance will be discussed elsewhere. The term *broadcast media* refers to the media of television and radio, and retail advertising in these forms can be a valuable adjunct to an ad program. Large stores have a broadcast section, because preparing advertising copy for television and radio is a specialized form of advertising. Copywriters are assigned to this section, as well as an artist who draws *storyboards,* which are a series of sketches that detail the sequential action of a television commercial, with accompanying copy.

The Sign Section

The sign section might be a part of the advertising department, or it might be part of another department, the display department. If it is in the advertising department, it is the responsibility of the copy and art staff. In either case, the sign section produces the posters, signs, and cards that are used to identify and sell merchandise throughout the store and in the display windows. These signs and posters are a vital part of the store's advertising. They often are used to feature items currently being advertised in print or broadcast media, and they may tie in, via words and illustrations, with the day's ads.

The One-Person Department

Some stores are not large enough to warrant fully staffed advertising departments. These stores maintain only one-person departments, where the manager must play most of the roles filled by specialists in the advertising departments of larger stores. The manager is copyrighter, planner, type specifier, production expert, and traffic manager. Usually outside free-lance sources can be relied upon for art help, but some talented managers are able to handle this job, too. In any case, the manager is ultimately responsible.

Chain Store Advertising Departments

Chain stores are sales outlets for a large merchandiser or seller of goods. The store units of the chain are pretty well uniform in physical appearance, and all units sell similar merchandise. Planning, buying, and advertising are centralized at chain headquarters or, in the case of very large chains, at regional headquarters. Chain store operation can vary in size from the many hundreds of store units constituting F. W. Woolworth and the A & P to the three- or four-store local chains.

Employees in chain store advertising departments must perform tasks similar to those performed by people who work in retail store advertising departments. They are concerned with the planning, preparation, and executing of an advertising program. But in the case of chain stores, they are not performing these functions as part of a retail store. They are producing advertising for the individual chain store units. The manager of the chain store unit has no advertising department and relies on chain store headquarters or regional headquarters for advertising materials and promotion.

Advertising People in Manufacturing and Service Businesses

Manufacturers and service businesses with nationwide operations invariably have an advertising department that handles and supervises an ad program. Such advertising departments are usually involved with overseeing, rather than preparing, the company's main advertising program. They differ in this important way from the ad departments of retail stores and chain store headquarters. As we have seen, the main task of the ad department of Macy's, for example, is preparing ads. In contrast, the ad departments of Eastman Kodak, Pan American World Airways, or the Bank of America do not prepare the company advertising that appears in national or local media. Manufacturers and service businesses rely on advertising agencies to perform this service for them. The tasks the ad departments in these businesses do perform are the direction, supervision, and approval of the ad program prepared by their companies' advertising agencies.

It is not correct to say, however, that advertising departments of manufacturers and service businesses never prepare advertising materials. They often do, but in a specialized way. The department may be responsible for preparing any or all of the following advertising and advertising-related promotional devices, collectively referred to as *collateral material:* point-of-sale material; package designs; consumer, dealer, or retailer brochures, catalogs, specification sheets, pamphlets, etc; dealer cooperative (co-op) advertising; advertising brochures directed at the company sales force; material to describe the company ad program to employees; and direct mail advertising.

Sometimes these activities are assigned to the company's advertising agency, but sometimes they are undertaken by the company advertising department if it is staffed to perform them. How to handle the activities is management's decision, and variations exist among companies and industries. Many copywriters, artists, and production people find employment preparing this type of advertising material with company ad departments.

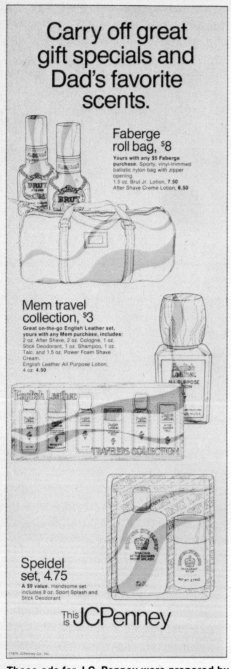
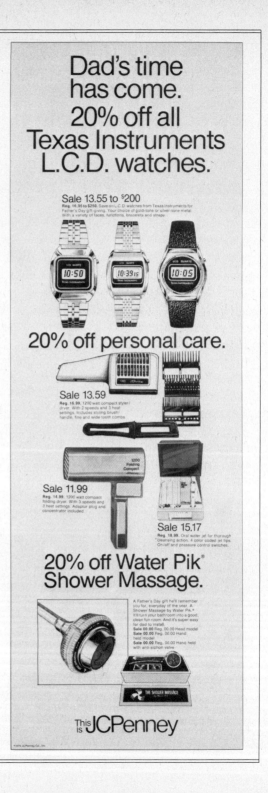
These ads for J.C. Penney were prepared by the advertising department at chain headquarters. (Courtesy J.C. Penney Co., Inc.)

Advertising managers, or advertising directors, of manufacturing and service businesses thus have two responsibilities. They and their department people, working with the advertising agency, supervise the development of their companies' ad programs. They also supervise those who prepare the collateral material.

Ad managers work with the company management and the ad agency in developing company advertising goals. Ad managers prepare annual advertising budgets, and approve copy, artwork, and finished advertisements submitted by the agency. Bills are approved in this department for payment. Finally, managers do their best to analyze the results of the ad program after it has run. In a small company, all these tasks must be done by the ad manager, perhaps with the help of an assistant.

Advertising Agencies

Advertising agencies prepare almost all national advertising and much local advertising. They are employed by companies to perform this service, and their list of clients may consist of hundreds of manufacturers and service businesses, or just two or three. Agencies can range in size from small-city two-person outfits to the giant agencies, such as J. Walter Thompson Company and Young & Rubicam, Inc., who employ thousands of people all over the world. Small or large, their functions are similar. They are engaged in creating, producing, and placing advertisements for the companies that employ them.

A manufacturer need not hire an advertising agency. Ads can be prepared within the company, and placed directly—in other words, placed in the media by the company rather than through an agency. Before 1875, this was, in fact, the usual procedure, with the manufacturer sometimes employing a free-lance, or independent, writer in the process.

Today, as we shall explore later in this chapter, there exist alternatives to hiring advertising agencies. But there are two reasons why the great majority of advertisers work with, and use, agencies. The first reason is concerned with the ways agencies are reimbursed for their services. The commission system (Chapter 2) is the prevalent method of payment. Although the agency is employed by an advertiser, under this system it receives most of its income from the media in which it places the client's advertising.

It may seem strange, but when a manufacturer places an ad in a magazine, for example, the cost is the same as when an agency places an ad for that same manufacturer. No savings are made by direct placement. In the negotiated fee system, an increasingly used alternative to the commission system, the agency receives a fee for its work from the client and rebates to the client the commissions it receives from the media when ads are placed. In both these methods of payment, the company gains advantages that would not exist if the company prepared and then placed advertising in media. When the commission system is used, the services the client receives from the agency are in a sense free, because, as we have stated, the agency receives income in the form of commissions from the media that covers the cost of this work. When the fee system is used, the client, receiving commission rebates, ultimately may pay less for the ads.

A second reason why companies utilize ad agencies is that the preparation of national advertising requires specialized talent. It would be expensive and uneconomical for individual companies to maintain on their ad department staff a sufficient number of specialists to accomplish the tasks that an advertising agency is equipped to perform in their behalf.

The Commission-Fee Controversy

"There's nothing in the commission system that is really in the best interest of the client. . . . It's archaic." This statement was made by Kenneth J. Griggy, president of Wilson & Co., the meat packaging company. "The commission system is doomed—not long for this world," stated Ira C. Herbert, president of the Foods Division of Coca-Cola.[2]

These important advertisers, and many others as well, are strongly against the commission system method of recompensing agencies. In truth, this method has been under attack from clients almost from the day it was invented. Why do advertisers find the system unsatisfactory? There are two important reasons.

First, clients hold that agencies, when paid by commissions, are overcompensated for certain kinds of work, receiving money that should rightfully go to the client. If an agency purchases two million dollars worth of commercials on a network television program, the task is accomplished without great difficulty and the agency receives $300,000 in commissions. In a "spot TV plan" the agency buys specific time slots for its commercials in a list of markets. These purchases might cost $500,000 but entail many individual negotiations that are very time-consuming. The agency in this case receives $65,000 in commissions. Advertisers have trouble rationalizing why agencies should be "overpaid for the easier jobs."

Second, there is the question of conflict of interest. Under the commission system, the more expensive the media plan the agency recommends the more commission the agency makes. If the agency recommends that $1.5 million be spent in consumer magazines when the client feels strongly that half that amount will do, the client may wonder whether the

agency is objectively serving the client's interests or whether the agency people are thinking of their own net profits. It should be noted that there is a factor that keeps agencies from recommending overblown media plans. If a client is convinced that an agency is merely looking for bigger commissions, that agency will lose the account.

In the *fee system,* the usual method of determining agency income is to estimate the amount and kind of service needed for an individual account and agree on the number of people needed to do the job. Through negotiations, a "price" is put on this work. The client does not specify what salary the agency people make who work on the account; that is the agency's business. The agency's bookkeeping on the account is regularly reviewed by the client.

Although the commission system is still widely used, fee accounts are growing in number. The fee system is very often used by local advertisers, and many large national advertising agencies work with both methods.[3]

The du Pont Experience

The fee system does not necessarily save clients money, but may be the only way an agency can be fairly recompensed. But changing to a fee system can improve the entire advertising program in special situations, as the experience of E. I. du Pont de Nemours & Company shows. According to H. Lloyd Taylor, Director of the du Pont

[2] *Advertising Age,* December 29, 1975, p. 19.

[3] Agencies also receive income for handling production of advertising materials. When a bill is submitted by suppliers such as a typesetter, a film production house, or a photographer, it is generally marked up by 17.65 percent as a service charge. If the charge for three photographs is $1,000, the client is billed $1,176.50 by the agency. This rate of fee is exactly the same as the agency would receive from the 15 percent commission system on media buys. If the cost of inserting an ad in a trade paper were the same ($1,176.50), the agency would bill the client this amount, pay the magazine $1,000 and keep the balance of $176.50 as its commission.

Advertising Department,[4] du Pont moved to a fee arrangement with its several agencies in the mid-1960s. "du Pont is overwhelmingly a marketer of *industrial* products and services. Our industrial advertising budgets outnumber those for consumer products by about fifteen to one," Taylor states.

It was discovered that under the former commission system client personnel asked for all kinds of services from the agency in order to get their "money's worth." The agencies also tended to overservice the business. Productivity studies and elimination of unnecessary tasks resulted in increased output per person and reduction of the work force at the agencies. As a result, according to Taylor, none of the du Pont agencies has lost money on the account, agency productivity is higher, and the fee system has never resulted in substantial overpayments or underpayments for du Pont.

The fee system is particularly advantageous to both client and agency on industrial accounts, where it is necessary to prepare many different ads, which then appear in small-circulation industrial and trade magazines. The commission system can be a fair way to recompense agencies on many accounts requiring advertising directed to the consumer.

Policy on Competitive Accounts

If an agency serves a swimsuit account such as Cole of California, can it accept business from Jantzen, another leading swimsuit maker? After all, the agency, through its Cole experience "knows the market" and should be able to do a good job for Jantzen. The rule that prevails, however, is that an agency cannot handle *competitive accounts,* the accounts of cli-

ents that compete directly in the marketplace with the goods and services of clients already on the agency's roster. It's clear that the client naturally wants the agency people to concentrate on Cole of California business and not spend time helping a competitor. And no client can tolerate a situation in which information on plans and future campaigns might become available to a competitor using the same shop.

An agency might solicit a large airline account or a large soft drink account when it already has a small one. The intent would be to resign the small competitive account if it obtains a big one in the same field. Not only does this raise ethical questions, but it also can result in a delicate situation. A small client may leave the agency when the above situation becomes known, and agency accounts have been lost for this reason. One way to solve the problem with fairness to all has been developed by a few of the very large agencies. Interpublic is a large corporate entity which includes McCann-Erickson, a large agency, and also three separate agencies, Campbell-Ewald, Marschalk, and Erwin Wasey. Accounts that would normally be considered competitive when under one roof can be accommodated in the separate agencies with no conflict of interest. Some clients agree to such a relationship.

Creative People in an Agency

Fundamentally, an advertising agency depends for its success on the quality of its creative output. The usual reason for the loss of a client is that the client feels that the creative work is not satisfactory. Accounts are usually acquired because the prospective client feels that a better creative "product" will be obtained from one agency instead of another. Thus great emphasis is placed by agency management on the creative end of the business. The copywriters, copy supervisors, and

[4] H. Lloyd Taylor, "One Client's Pragmatic View about His Agencies, or Fun and Games with Fees and Friends," speech made at the annual meeting of the AAAA, May 13, 1976.

art directors in the creative department are often well paid for their work, and salaries in creative departments are generally higher than salaries of people working on somewhat similar tasks in department stores and company advertising departments. The companies the agencies serve are referred to as *accounts,* and a copywriter or an art director in an agency may be assigned to one account or several.

The Copy Department A copywriter does not devote the entire day to writing. A good deal of time is spent preparing to write, gathering information about the product, reading research reports, talking to other people in the agency who can help explain the copy problem, and discussing copy with a supervisor, the art department people, or the client. Writers often spend time in the field to broaden their perspective by talking to consumers and store managers about the product. Many women are in the copywriting business. They predominate in fashion, cosmetic, and food product accounts, while men often staff accounts for liquor and cars.

The Art Department The key individual in an art department is the art director. He or she plans, or "visualizes," the ads and works closely with the copywriter in the conceptual stage of an ad, trying out the copy in rough layouts, or *thumbnails,* quickly drawn miniature experimental layouts that serve to convey a feeling or a look. The art director is responsible for the final appearance of the ad and orders the necessary artwork from outside suppliers. The art director is in constant contact with the print production department when the ad is being produced for publication and also is heavily involved in visualization of television commercial copy.

Other people in the art department are layout artists and sketchers, who render semifinished art for use in *comprehensives,* layouts closely resembling the finished ads that are often used in presenting the proposed advertisement to the client. There's usually a bullpen where the newer art people gain experience by assembling the *mechanicals,* ads in the final stages of production. After layout and copy have been approved by the client, copy set in type, and final art or photography completed, the ad is assembled in mechanical form. The type and artwork are placed in position according to the layout and prepared for reproduction in proper form for use by media. There are also storyboard artists, who specialize in turning out the storyboards for television commercials. Art directors often perform this task, too.

Larger art departments employ specialists, such as lettering people, who are skilled in printing ad headlines and captions by hand in a clear and attractive fashion closely resembling type.

It is important to realize that the finished artwork is not usually produced in agency art departments. Outside photographers and illustrators are used for this purpose. An important part of an art director's job is the selection of the right art talent to produce a particular piece of artwork, and it is rare for such a person to be found on an art department staff.

The Account Handling Department

The account handling department is responsible for contact with the client. *Account executives,* or contact people, represent the agency at the client's organization and represent the client's point of view at the agency. Their function is often a sales function, presenting or helping to present agency recommendations to the client companies. They are organizers and expediters who use the other agency departments to provide service to their accounts. Much of their work involves advertising budgets and relations with media representatives. They spend time in the field, trying to know almost as much about their clients' business as the clients do themselves. Because of the nature of their jobs, contact people become knowledgeable about all the agency departments and are consequently a good source to tap for management positions.

Creative Responsibility

Since the agency depends for success on its creative work, thorny questions of responsibility exist in the interaction between the creative department and the account handling department. The account management staff, with its intimate knowledge of the clients' problems and objectives and its control over work flow within the agency, is in a strong position to influence creative work and to determine which creative plan is presented and recommended to the client. But account people do not get their good jobs because of creative ability; they are there primarily because they are business-oriented. Who, then, judges the copy, the creative people who develop it or the account people who face the music when creative work does not do its expected job of selling products in the marketplace?

When disagreements occur, the problem can be resolved in several ways, depending on the approach of the agency management. The head of the creative department can make final decisions on copy if backed by management. Final decision may be made by a plans board or a creative review board. Or the agency head, in certain cases, may decide to take on this responsibility alone.

The problem of creative responsibility is eliminated in one unique agency job that combines both creative work and account handling. *Copy-contact people,* usually considered members of the account handling department for purely organizational purposes, are often hired or trained for specialized advertising tasks. If, for example, the agency has a client manufacturing surgical equipment, or industrial chemicals, or offset lithography presses, the trade and industrial advertising tasks involved can most efficiently be handled by people who contact the client and write the copy. Copy-contact jobs are preferred by some advertising people who enjoy writing in technical areas because they are usually left alone to do their job independently without a great deal of supervision. There is also more job security in copy-contact work. Even when an agency loses an account, the copy-contact people often go with the account to the new agency.

The Media Department

The primary task of the men and women working in the media department is the development of the most efficient media program possible for a client within the confines of the client's advertising budget. The media people deal in circulation figures of newspapers and magazines, areas covered by the circulation, and the *coverage areas* that television and radio stations blanket with their signals. They become expert on subjects such as the proper location of advertising within the pages of magazines and newspapers and the best time slots on television and radio for the client's product. They are buyers of space and time for advertising messages and, depending on their experience and ability, can often determine the success or failure of an advertising program.

The Research Department

The research department is the "information factory" of an ad agency. Its responsibility is the development of information needed to make proper advertising decisions. Research people gather the facts a copywriter needs in order to understand who buys the product or service and why it is bought. They develop intricate methods that attempt to pretest advertising before it actually appears in the marketplace. They interview consumers to discover their likes and dislikes about the brands the agency services and about competing brands. They do their best to take the guesswork out of the advertising business, and they work closely with the creative, account handling, and media departments.

The Print Production Department

Print production people are an important part of the agency operation. The production manager and staff assistants see to it that ads are produced for use in magazines and newspapers according to art department specifications. There are specialists who order engravings and typesetting, proofreaders who check the set copy against the original, and often traffic people who prepare schedules for producing ads.

The Television Production Department

The advertising agency does not physically produce its own television commercials. It relies on film studios, which have the specialized facilities and the directors, camera crew, and film editors to do this work. The agency producer selects the right studio for each job and sees the commercial through the production process. The producer starts work before this, however, by talking to copywriters and artists about storyboards and ideas and lining up specialists for musical backgrounds if they're called for. The producer is often involved in casting, or selecting the right actors and actresses for the commercials, although this task is sometimes handled by a separate casting department. When commercials are

made, they are often shot on location. The producer, as the person responsible for the final film, must be there. He or she must know a great deal about the costs involved in making films because film studio bids must be analyzed when work is under consideration and bills must be approved when submitted for completed work. The production person often produces radio commercials, too, and the procedure is similar. Art directors and sometimes copywriters often act as producers, particularly when they have been responsible for the creative work up to the time of production.

Advertising people at work: A print production supervisor checks on the progress of a job; a creative group goes over storyboards; a television producer observes the taping of a commercial; a research interviewer discusses product preference with a consumer. (Courtesy J. Walter Thompson Company; Morgan Guaranty Trust Company, from an ad produced by Henderson, Roll, Friedlich Inc., photography by Carl Fischer; Teletronics International, Inc.; Robert Capece)

Other Agency Departments

There are several other departments in large ad agencies. They include the merchandising department, which consists of experts in the retail sales area who work closely in the field with clients' salespeople; the checking department, which checks to see that advertising is actually run as ordered; the program department, which contracts for the purchase of television programs; and the accounting department. In the larger agencies there are librarians, film projectionists, and dieticians and cooks who work in the test kitchen, developing recipes for food products and preparing food for use in photographs and television commercials. The large agencies with these departments and specialists are called *full-service agencies.*

In contrast, in the smallest ad shops, there may be no departments at all. The contact staff will do the media work, often write the copy, and spend some time on research in the field. If there's a person responsible for media, he or she may serve as a research "department." When tasks beyond client contact, copywriting, and media purchasing need to be performed, outside temporary help is solicited.

Specialized Advertising Agencies

Most advertising agencies try to obtain accounts in any field of commerce that the agencies have the ability and experience to serve. Some are specialists, however. There are industrial agencies, which concentrate in preparing ads for industrial marketers, and medical agencies, dealing in the ad programs of makers of drugs and manufacturers of hospital and surgical supplies and equipment. These shops rarely prepare advertising directed to the consumer; most of their ad output appears in trade, industrial, or professional magazines. There are also a few specialist agencies in the soft goods and fashion fields. Here the rule of not handling competitive accounts is suspended, probably because the individual manufacturer's business is not large and the size of the account is relatively small. Experience in servicing such accounts outweighs the factor of handling competitive business.

Black Agencies

In the early seventies, black agencies appeared on the scene. These agencies not only helped advertisers reach an important market segment that had previously received little attention but have also provided career opportunities for black advertising workers. They offer specialized knowledge and abilities to clients who wish to sell products and services to the black segment of the market reached by black media. Assignments of part of the advertising account have been given to black agencies by such companies as RCA, Heublein, General Motors, R. J. Reynolds, Miller Beer, and AT&T.

Alternatives to Advertising Agencies

A company may choose to accomplish the advertising task without using an independent ad agency, or may use such an agency for only part of the advertising program. Such a choice is invariably motivated by a company's desire to cut costs. Many advertising people have jobs in these companies that offer alternative methods of preparing and executing advertising. However, the bulk of national advertising today, as in the past, continues to be handled by independent advertising agencies.

The House Agency An advertiser can build an organization that resembles an independent advertising agency with all its depart-

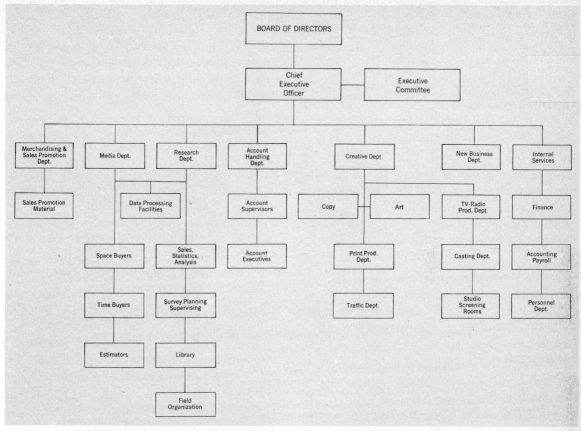

This chart shows the organization of a typical large full-service advertising agency.

ments and functions. The difference is that this organization is owned by the advertiser and consequently the advertiser receives the profits from its operation. Known as a *house agency,*[5] it usually serves only one client, the company that owns it. Sony and Singer Sewing Products are examples of companies following this route. American Home Products has for many years owned the John Murray agency, which places advertising for Anacin and other company brands. American Home, however, also uses independent advertising agencies.

While this system obviously satisfies the companies listed and others as well, there are traditional arguments against use of a house agency. It is pointed out that independent thinking on the part of the agency is discouraged when its only client owns the premises. House agencies have problems in hiring top advertising talent because such people prefer the environment of an independent advertising agency and because salaries are higher there. The advertising produced by the

[5] The term *in-house agency* is often used to describe this type of operation, but this term leads to some confusion. When advertising materials such as collateral or even advertisements themselves are prepared within a company's advertising department, the company is said to prepare the materials in-house.

house agency may be narrow and lacking in creativity; in independent ad agencies, personnel are often exposed to the stimulation of working on a varied client list.

Creative Boutiques   A few highly paid creative people have in recent years left their agencies to form small "creative-only" shops, called *boutiques,* that offer copy and art direction services, usually including television and radio production facilities. A company can therefore rely on such a shop for creative work and handle the rest of the advertising through a house agency. Boutiques come and go rapidly. Excellent campaigns have come about through their use, temperament abounds, and boutiques are not famous for businesslike procedures. If a creative-only shop attracts profitable clients, it may soon choose to add departments, service the whole account, and become a full-fledged advertising agency.

Media Buying Services   A company may separately hire a media buying service, performing basically the same functions as an agency media department. The balance of the advertising task is performed by the company's regular agency or house agency. It is the claim of these media service people that their buying procedures are faster and more efficient than agency media departments. These specialists work in the fields of radio and TV spot announcement purchases, where availabilities of time slots change with lightning speed.

Agency Service "à la Carte"   One agency reaction to the minor splinterization that has occured in the advertising business caused by boutiques and media buying services has been the development of the *à la carte concept.* Some large agencies will offer their services to prospects on a partial basis. Agency management in such a case prefers to service *all* phases of a client's advertising business but will handle creative, research, or media tasks individually for a fee. The hope is that a client using part of the agency will like the agency's work and will eventually give the agency the entire account.

Media Advertising Departments

Magazines, newspapers, television and radio stations, and other media are all heavily involved in the advertising business. They depend, in some cases almost completely, on advertisers to supply the revenue that permits them to operate, and they must sell advertisers on placing their advertisements in the vehicle they offer. Thus the media need sales forces to call on prospective advertisers and advertising agencies and present and explain the reasons why advertising in the particular publication or medium they represent is a wise expenditure of advertising dollars. These advertising people are known as *media representatives,* or reps.

Media also advertise *themselves.* Individual magazines, newspapers, television stations, radio stations, and outdoor advertising companies run ads regularly in the advertising trade press and in newspapers in Chicago and New York where the advertising agency business is concentrated. The goal of these ads is to show what the particular medium offers advertisers—in market coverage, quality of readership, or other subjects believed to be important to the advertiser. Some media advertising budgets are substantial, and advertising agencies compete for this business. The advertising of a small-town radio station or newspaper will be prepared by the station or newspaper ad department.

Newspaper Advertising Departments

Important members of newspaper advertising departments are the advertising salespeople, often called *space reps* because they actually are selling space in the newspaper to advertisers.

There are two kinds of newspaper advertising, display and classified. Display ads are those including illustrations, headlines, and subheadlines, and other elements that stand out. Large-city newspapers have staffs equipped to assist local advertisers in the preparation of copy or layout for display ads. On papers with smaller circulations, the space representative or the advertising manager often performs this preparation service. If there are copy and layout people on the staff, they perform additional tasks, such as producing promotional pamphlets describing the newspaper's advantages and charts and cards listing sales points. They thus support the space rep in the selling task.

Classified ads are simple, small-space, non-illustrated messages that contain a brief headline or lead-in to the copy and are arranged in newspaper columns according to the category of the goods or services involved. Help wanted, lost and found, real estate offerings, and used cars for sale are typical classified ad categories. Classified advertising people take the copy by phone or receive it by mail from the people who wish to run a classified ad, and they revise and condense the copy as needed.

National Media Advertising Departments

The national media sales representatives are supported by sales promotion people who help them in many advertising-related tasks. Advertising-related tasks undertaken by these sales promotion people fall into two broad categories: (1) extending the effect of the advertising carried by the medium through promotion of the ads with retailers or at point of purchase and (2) selling the advantages of the advertising medium itself to advertisers and agencies. Copy people on magazine staffs, on behalf of advertisers, prepare direct mail letters to retailers that describe the advertising effort placed behind a brand. Cards for retail counter displays featuring advertisements in a particular magazine are prepared and placed in stores. Promotions are developed for supermarkets and drugstores that tie in with product advertisements run on the pages of the publication. Research studies are made of consumer buying habits. These seek to prove the advantages of advertising in certain media.

Traditionally, the broadcast media do not offer the quantity of promotional activities to their advertisers that magazines do. Their advertising departments do much, however, to support their sales representatives with research and sales presentations to prospective and current advertisers.

Direct Mail Advertisers

Direct mail advertising consists of letters, catalogs, brochures, and pamphlets sent to potential buyers by mail. Every type of advertiser can make use of this form of advertising. Involved in it are the same kinds of people that prepare advertising in other forms. Direct mail requires copy, layout, and production; and specialists are needed to perform these tasks.

There are thousands of advertising people who spend their business careers in the direct mail field, offering their specialized knowledge to manufacturers and service companies. They

THE BUNK BED:

FOR TWO.
FOR ONE.

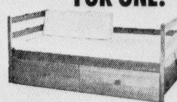

Bunk bed with two massive storage drawers. Double bunk can sleep two, or single bed can be used alone to seat or sleep. Three foot storage drawers on wheels hold plenty. Available in teak, polished pine, or red stain.

the children's room

318 East 45th St., N.Y.C. 10017 (212) 687-3868
Send one dollar for our brochure

What are the similarities and differences between the display advertising and classified advertising shown here? (Courtesy The Children's Room)

act as an outside source and plan, create, write, and design direct mail material. In many cases they handle the production and mailing tasks involved. One person can do most of these operations, farming out the artwork to free-lance photographers and artists. The work may be done on a part-time basis while the person holds down another kind of advertising job in normal working hours. Or these people may be in business for themselves, devoting all their time to the work of producing direct mail advertising.

There are large firms, too, that specialize as direct mail counselors. Often large printing firms have direct mail people on their staffs in order to offer a well-rounded service to pro-spective customers.

Catalog Advertisers

When we think of merchandise catalogs, we think of the big catalog houses such as Sears, Roebuck and Company and Montgomery Ward. In previous times, these firms relied on their catalogs exclusively to sell their goods, but today three selling methods are used: (1) catalogs are mailed to customers; (2) catalog "stores" are available where customers can leaf through catalogs and order the products they want; and (3) the firms have established their own retail outlets, similar to department stores, where goods and even services can be purchased directly.

Advertising Departments of Catalog Houses

The catalog advertising people in catalog houses perform the same functions of preparing and producing advertising as people who work in department store advertising departments. Here are found copywriters who specialize in writing copy for lines of merchandise, layout designers and artists, and production people involved in producing the copy and artwork in catalog form. Because of the wide variety of experience offered and the heavy volume of work, the catalog field, as well as the retail store advertising field, has traditionally been a training ground for advertising agency creative department people. While some copywriters and artists spend their entire business careers profitably working for catalog houses, others move to the agencies. Many top agency writers received their basic training at Sears, Alden's, Spiegel, and Montgomery Ward.

Other Specialists in Catalog Advertising

Many business firms, retail merchants, industrial manufacturers, and industrial trade groups rely on catalogs for part of their promotional effort, and specialists in preparing and producing catalogs can be found in all these types of businesses. A steel manufacturing company will produce catalogs of its products for use by the sales department on calls or as mailings to customers and prospects. A department store may mail out a series of catalogs to its charge customers for such seasonal needs as Christmas gifts, January white-sale items, Mother's and Father's Day gifts, and back-to-school items. A nursery and garden supply house may feature a catalog of bulbs for fall planting. Sometimes printing houses find profit in preparing and producing catalogs for their customers and take on this work as a sideline

to their printing business. Buyers' cooperatives, organizations that act as central purchasing agents for groups of independent retailers to make lower purchasing prices of merchandise items possible, often offer catalog services to their members. For example, a general hardware and housewares catalog is prepared, and the independent retailer imprints the store name on it. Thus the retailer has available a "personalized" catalog.

Mail-Order Advertisers

There is an overlapping of terminology and jobs when we come to consider mail-order people. In *mail-order advertising,* the ad itself produces the sales results. Mail-order advertising "asks for the order" and offers a means by which the consumer can buy the product directly. Such advertising usually contains a coupon that is filled out by the reader and mailed to the advertiser. While much mail-order advertising uses the media of direct mail and catalogs, it is not by any means restricted to such vehicles. Newspapers and magazines carry mail-order advertising, as do local radio and television stations. The important fact that separates most mail-order advertising from other forms of advertising is that the goods or services advertised are not offered through stores but only by mail. (See Color Plate 8.)

Many advertising people specialize in mail-order advertising. Some advertising agencies concentrate their entire efforts on this field. The Book-of-the-Month Club, International Correspondence Schools, the Columbia Record and Tape Club, and many other merchandisers characteristically sell by this method. These heavy users of mail-order advertising employ creative and production people devoted to the preparation of mail-order ads, direct mail, and brochures.

These mail-order advertisers rely on coupons or offers to sell their goods to consumers. In the case of Montgomery Ward, another step is involved. The reader orders a catalog and uses it to order goods. (Courtesy The Schoenheit Company; Montgomery Ward; L.L. Bean, Inc.)

Butcher Block

34" high work table
36" x 24", $142.00
48" x 24", $156.00
60" x 30", $194.00
or choose 30" dining
height table at
same prices.
Locking Shepherd
Casters,
$30.00 additional

Two-inch thick maple butcher block top, durable bench-construction frame. Sent express collect. In Illinois, add applicable taxes. Send check or money order, no C.O.D.'s please.
For complete catalog of exciting butcher block furniture, send 50¢ to:

butcher block & more

The Schoenheit Company
Dept. HG-68A, 1600 S. Clinton, Chicago 60616

Smart Shopping

"Wards Catalog shopping saves me time, energy and money!"

Join the millions of satisfied Wards Catalog shoppers! It's easy to get your own copy of Wards new 1978 Spring and Summer Big Book. Just send in the coupon below with a $2 check or money order. We'll send you the Catalog and $2 in Catalog Merchandise Certificates good on your next order.

Wards new Big Book has what you want for the warm seasons ahead—1,200 pages of fashions for the whole family, home furnishings, appliances, sporting goods and more. And, you can shop from the comfort of your home . . . just phone or mail in your order!

Mail in the coupon today. You'll find thousands of fine products, great values and have a handy comparison shopping guide right at your fingertips. That's catalog shopping convenience with Montgomery Ward!

THIS OFFER EXPIRES FEB. 27, 1978
Montgomery Ward, M & A Dept., Sec. F, Oakland, CA 94616

ORDER YOUR WARDS CATALOG TODAY!

Fill in this coupon and mail to: **Montgomery Ward M & A Dept., Oakland, California 94616**

A ☐ check or ☐ money order for $2 is enclosed.

NAME _____

ADDRESS _____

CITY _____

STATE _____ ZIP CODE _____

Please send me Wards new Spring and Summer Catalog and $2 in Catalog Merchandise Certificates valid until the end of this June.   S78FC

MONTGOMERY **WARD**

Creative people in the mail-order field rapidly become practical advertising men and women. Since the selling effectiveness of the headline, illustration, and copy in a mail-order ad can be measured quickly by the number of coupons mailed in, various advertising appeals can be evaluated on the basis of business actually obtained. This direct confrontation with sales results is unlike advertising in other fields, where results are more difficult to measure. Good ideas for a mail-order piece may turn out to be not so good when coupon returns fail to come in, and life is full of surprises and learning experiences for the young mail-order writer.

Free-Lance People

When assistance is needed temporarily for a particular advertising project, an outside specialist may be called in. *Free-lance* people are men and women not regularly on a company payroll but hired on a special-assignment basis. Almost every kind of advertising specialist has a free-lance counterpart, but the main job categories are in the copy and art areas. Copywriters in ad agencies or ad departments often undertake free-lance assignments to add to their income, working on copy for booklets, catalogs, direct mail pieces, and special writing assignments in their spare time. Art directors and layout artists with the ability to produce finished artwork—cartoons, drawings, package designs, and other illustrative material—are much in demand. They also undertake extra part-time assignments designing or laying out ads and brochures, and act as consultants to smaller companies on projects requiring art direction. Some advertising men and women prefer the independence of free-lance work and devote all their working hours to these assignments, developing a list of regular clients in the process.

There are free-lance television commercial producers, fashion and beauty stylists who help art directors and television producers, research people who do interviewing for research departments on a temporary basis, and even food "stylists" who prepare foods for use in print advertisement photographs and television commercials. The availability of these free-lance specialists is particularly important to small agencies that cannot ordinarily afford to have such people on their staff full time. Free-lance advertising artists and layout artists are found in every city, and their presence enables local merchants to obtain the contributions of experts in the performance of various advertising tasks. Free-lance work, if diligently developed, can be profitable and stimulating either on a part-time or full-time basis.

Advertising's Progress Toward Equal Opportunity in Employment

Prejudice, as exemplified in discrimination against minority groups, was evident in various fields of advertising until recent years, but some progress has been made to eliminate it. A basic attitude held by people in the creative end of the business has been helpful in overcoming prejudice. As we have seen, good copy and art ideas or high-caliber creative output are essential to advertising success, and no one group—race, creed, or sex—has a monopoly on good creative thinking. The average supervisor of creative people is unconcerned about an individual's ethnic background or race. It is the supervisor's job to obtain good advertising work from the people in the department he or she supervises, and job performance is the standard by which these people are judged.

Studies have been made by the advertising agencies to encourage minority groups' interest in the field of advertising. In 1968 the percentage of minority-group members employed in the 15 largest New York agencies was 4.9. In 1969, the figure was 10.5. Progress since that time has been slow. In 1974, the latest period available, minority employment totaled 12.9 percent of agency employees in New York City, according to the New York City Human Rights Commission.

Vocabulary

Define the following terms and use each one in a sentence.

Account
Account executive
Advertising department
À la carte concept
Broadcast media
Collateral material
Comprehensive
Copy
Copy-contact people
Coverage area

Creative boutique
Direct placement
Fee system
Free-lance
House agency
Layout
Mail-order advertising
Mechanical
Media representative
Thumbnail

Review Questions

1. What is identification advertising?
2. What are the two criteria a local merchant applies in deciding to advertise beyond identification advertising?
3. What three sections form the production line of retail advertising departments? What are the tasks each performs?
4. Who prepares the advertising for a chain store?
5. By what two methods can an advertising agency be reimbursed for the work it does?
6. Why can't agencies handle competitive accounts?
7. Name two kinds of specialized agencies.
8. Give one reason why an advertiser finds the commission system an unsatisfactory method of agency reimbursement.
9. Name three alternatives to using all the services of an advertising agency that are available to an advertiser.
10. How do advertising departments of manufacturers differ from advertising departments of retail stores?
11. Name four kinds of advertising materials that are often prepared in a manufacturer's advertising department. What types of advertising people prepare them?
12. What are the functions of an advertising agency?
13. Name five kinds of specialists employed by advertising agencies and indicate the tasks each performs.
14. What advertising jobs are available on newspapers and magazines?
15. What kinds of advertising people are needed to produce direct mail?

Activities

1. If you are interested in a career in advertising, select a job you would like to hold based on information given in this chapter. Write out the job description; state why you would like to be employed in this capacity and what talents or abilities you have that would be helpful to you in this work.
2. The three local businesspeople described below do not currently advertise. On the basis of the information supplied, which ones should be reasonably expected to be advertisers and which ones should not? Should the owner run product or service ads, institutional ads, or a combination of both? What media should be used? Give your reasons.

a. George Reeves rents an empty lot in the business section with 100-foot frontage on South Street and a depth of 150 feet. He operates a parking lot there as one of his businesses. An office building is on either side, and a movie theater is in the rear. The theater will probably close because of lack of business. Reeves nets, after expenses, approximately $8,500 a year. While he does a fair business in the daytime, activity dries up at night. His customers are office workers and shoppers.

b. Charlie Wong, an experienced restaurateur, has just opened a Chinese restaurant, the Golden Palace, in a new shopping center in the suburban area. The capacity is 100 diners, and his evening trade is fair and building. The location of a bowling alley and a movie theater in the shopping center helps considerably. He does a take-out business that also peaks at night. Luncheon business is terrible. Within a half-mile of his location is an industrial park. It includes a research lab of a large drug manufacturer employing 200 white-collar workers. A large group of management people also works at companies located in the park.

c. Sheila Doscher runs a medium-size travel agency with a street-front office well located in the downtown business section. Sales of individually tailored travel plans constitute the bulk of her business. These are relatively expensive personalized trips for upper-income customers from the suburbs and city high-rent districts. Low-cost package tour and group tour business, which would turn up a high profit margin, is not done on a large scale. Sales volume could stand improvement. There is an opportunity to rent space next door if business picks up.

Projects

1. Visit the advertising department of your local newspaper and on the basis of the information you are able to obtain draw up an organizational chart of the department. Write out a brief explanation of the jobs on the chart. This project is best handled when you and your classmates visit the newspaper as a group.

2. Go to a local department store and obtain information on the organizational structure of the advertising department. Chart the departmental setup and write out an explanation of the jobs involved.

3. If there are advertising agencies in town, contact one of them and obtain information about its departmental structure. Chart the organization, and describe the departmental responsibilities.

Career Ladder

As advertising manager of a medium-sized newspaper, you have a job opening in the classified department. Work consists of taking information from people wanting to run classified ads and shaping their thoughts into basic, nonrepetitious selling copy. Some writing ability is desirable, and the person hired should enjoy dealing with all kinds of people. You are considering two applicants, both of whom have had 2 years of higher education.

Applicant 1 has had experience as a sales clerk in a drug store for two summers and worked on the community college biweekly newspaper as a reporter and news editor. This applicant did well in advertising and merchandising courses.

Applicant 2 was elected a class officer each year (first as treasurer, second as vice-president) and made the dean's list, specializing in business administration courses.

Which applicant would you hire for the job in the classified department and why?

CHAPTER FIVE

ORGANIZATION FOR ADVERTISING

Faced with the necessity of producing an ad or a series of ads, how does the advertiser go about the task? Whether the advertiser is large or small, big-league manufacturer or local merchant, service company or department store, similar basic steps are involved (Chapter 4). The order of these activities may change,or some of the steps may be subdivided and enlarged. But the steps must be taken by everyone who advertises.

To understand fully how advertisers accomplish these steps, we shall have to consider three important areas of business advertising activity:

1. The local merchant's advertising program.

2. The advertising activities of a department store.

3. The advertising activities of a consumer-product manufacturer using an advertising agency.

Organizing for Advertising: The Local Merchant

The local merchant of a small business who is just starting in business and is a beginner in the advertising field often uses a trial-and-error approach to advertising. Although advice and assistance may be available from representatives of manufacturers and the media, the decisions of when and how to use this help rest with the advertiser. However, there are definite guidelines that can be followed in order to achieve more consistently satisfactory results.

Establishing a Goal and Choosing the Media

Step 1, establishing a goal for advertising, and step 4, choosing the advertising media, are interrelated. To be successful local merchants must know their customers well. They must know the market, that group of individuals who are buyers or potential buyers of the merchants' goods and services. The selling objective is to offer these buyers the right merchandise at a competitive price when it's needed in the marketplace. A merchant's task might be to maintain existing sales volume against competitive pressures. Even so, there should be a larger goal, that of expanding existing sales volume. This can be accomplished (1) by getting more business from present customers and (2) by attracting new customers to the store. Advertising can reach both these groups and help expand volume. This is the marketing objective, the plan that is followed to speed up a store's movement of goods and services to consumers. The advertising strategy must evolve from the merchant's marketing objective in order to achieve the store's marketing goals.

In advertising to present and potential customers, the local merchant has a wide choice of media. One or all or a combination of the following media are available: the local newspaper; the suburban weekly newspaper; shopping guides; the local television station; the local radio station; local magazines; outdoor posters and signs; ads placed on public transportation facilities and at stations; direct mail; catalogs; handbills, fliers, and the like; advertising specialties (giveaways such as calendars, ball-point pens, matchbooks, and other items).

The merchant must be guided in the selection by an evaluation of which medium or combination of media delivers the maximum number of potential customers for the expenditure the merchant can afford. Some of these media are basic media. They blanket the entire local market. In this class are newspapers, outdoor posters, radio stations, television stations, and possibly local magazines. They reach through their circulation, or through their coverage area in the case of radio and television stations, most of the store's potential customers. The balance of the media available are selective or supplementary. They do not reach everybody, and they deliver the message to only part of the potential market.

Local merchants still use the newspaper as the keystone of their advertising program. It reaches almost all their prospects—and at a price that the advertiser can afford. The reader can see illustrations of the items advertised. The advertising is placed in a familiar and accepted setting, surrounded by news stories and features. Also, advertising for this medium can be prepared relatively easily and quickly, allowing the merchant, because of daily newspaper publication, to capitalize on fashion news when it happens and feature timely merchandise regularly.

But in newspaper advertising, as in all basic media advertising, some of the advertising will be wasted; that is, some part of the audience that the media reaches will not be interested in what a particular merchant has to sell. One way of looking at local media selection is to determine which media deliver the least wasted circulation. A high-fashion dress shop featuring quality, expensive merchandise has relatively few customers in the average town or city. The owner knows that most of the people who read the local paper will not come to the shop, but the people who do come all read the local paper. The owner weighs buying an advertising schedule, or series of ads, in the paper appearing at predetermined intervals against running an ad schedule in a local magazine, which is directed at local club women and features local social events. This latter possibility offers a more selective audience. The cost of the schedule is a determinant. The owner may test advertising in each medium to try to determine which sells more goods. The newspaper might prove to be the better advertising buy even though much of its circulation is wasted.

Selecting the Product or Service to Be Advertised

Step 2, the selection of what to advertise, presents no problem to the merchant whose business is concentrated on a single product or service or on a limited number of products or services. The moving and storage company, the movie theater, the real estate firm, the hamburger chain, the dry cleaner, the car rental outfit, the landscape architect, the home oil heating company, and the bowling alley all have clear-cut advertising programs determined by the single-minded nature of their businesses.

It is a far different matter for merchants who sell a wide variety of goods or who offer multiple services. In such cases, knowing what to advertise is an important determinant of business success. Fortunately, there is a simple rule that tells us which goods and services should be backed by advertising expenditures, and it applies to every kind of retail business. This rule is: *advertise best-selling goods and services.* Advertising should be concentrated on articles that have good sales records behind them, items the public wants and comes to the store to obtain. As Edwards and Brown state:

No matter what direct sales are expected, the surest way to secure immediate volume at a profit is to select best-selling items—articles of proven desirability. The items that people are already buying in quantity in a store are the articles that the people want. These items should be "pushed for all they are worth" as long as demand for them continues.[1]

[1] Charles M. Edwards, Jr., and Russell A. Brown, *Retail Advertising and Sales Promotion,* Prentice-Hall, Inc., Englewood Cliffs, N.J., 1959, p. 66.

Edwards and Brown also point out that advertising best-selling items draws people to a store in volume, thereby creating desirable customer traffic and consumer exposure to nonadvertised articles on display. A few examples will make clear the importance of advertising items or services with known popular appeal.

A travel agent sells package tours to places all over the world. Although there is an exotic tour to India and the Republic of Indonesia, it isn't advertised because of its limited appeal; in the past year, this tour has been sold only once, to a group of wealthy dowagers who had "been everywhere" and were desperate for a change. The travel agent advertises cruise packages to the Caribbean in the winter, trips to Europe in the late spring and summer, and travel to Hawaii all year round. These trips deliver the firm's current sales volume.

A druggist concentrates the advertising on fast-moving beauty aids, volume-generating branded drugs, dentifrices, and, on occasion, such items as bathroom scales and hair dryers. The old-fashioned remedies and proprietary drug items that are gathering dust on shelves are not promoted. Few people want them or could be made to want them by advertising.

A bookstore owner buys the best sellers in volume and promotes them. Other new books that appeal to limited audiences will be stocked in small numbers but will not be advertised, no matter what their quality.

Determining the Advertising Budget

In determining advertising budgets (step 3) local merchants are guided by trade practices, the competitive environment, and their own experience based on sales results in proportion to ad expenditures. Budget guideposts and procedure are discussed in Chapter 10. At this point, we will assume that our local merchant's

The brass bed advertiser has no difficulty deciding what to advertise; the store fulfills only one consumer need. The West End Shop sells many items. A choice must be made of which items to advertise. (Courtesy The Brass Bed Factory; West End Shop)

judgment on what to spend is supported by practical considerations.

Preparing the Advertising Material

Assume that a merchant has developed advertising goals, determined what goods or services will be advertised, established an ad budget, and selected the media where the advertising will be run. What must now be done is to prepare (or *create,* as it is termed in the advertising business) the advertisement itself (step 5).

In the case of print media, headline, copy, subheads, and all other written material that appears in the ad must be prepared. Ideas for illustrations must be developed. The copy and illustrations must be organized into some form of layout, rough or otherwise, and illustrative material must be obtained that can be used in the production of the finished ad.

For the broadcast media the tasks are different. The merchant prepares scripts, or copy for radio and television. For radio, production elements such as sound effects, musical background, or a selling jingle may be required. For television these same elements may be needed, and in addition a rough or partial storyboard should be put together that indicates the visualization of the script or copy. Then the merchant must see to it that the merchandise and props indicated in the storyboard are available when the television commercial is produced.

These requirements may sound difficult, but the local merchant has many resources available that help. How many of these tasks the merchant or a delegated employee actually accomplishes is a matter of preference. The advertiser may do all of them, some of them, or none of them, in the latter case merely accepting, changing, or rejecting the advertising material prepared by others outside the merchant's business. Following is a description of the advertising resources available to the local merchant from outside sources.

Newspaper Advertising Services Local merchants can subscribe to advertising services that supply entire ads or parts of ads, such as display elements, headlines, and borders, from which an ad can be assembled. Companies in this business are also called *mat services.* This is a holdover from the time when most newspapers were printed by the letterpress method, and the word *mat* is an abbreviation of *matrix,* a paper mold of type and other elements making up an ad. When molten lead is poured into the mat, it produces a duplicate printing plate that can be used by the newspaper to reproduce an advertisement.

Today, most newspapers are offset-printed, a method that does not require mats or printing plates. Instead, offset uses a proof, or *slick* of the ad, printed on heavy coated (or glossy) paper.

There are scores of mat services covering every conceivable type of retail business. Metro Associated Services, Inc., New York, the largest service, supplies advertising for men's, women's, and children's apparel and accessories; supermarkets; home furnishings; furniture; variety store merchandise; and many other business areas. SCW, Inc., Los Angeles and New York, another large service, covers many retail business and specialty areas. Adplans, a small outfit in Portland, Oregon, specializes in local insurance advertising. Banker and Brisebois, Detroit, concentrates on furniture store advertising and carpet promotions. The House of Ideas, Atlanta, supplies the supermarket field.

The subscriber receives a monthly or quarterly brochure reproducing the ads and display elements available. This brochure is prepared with a heavy emphasis on seasonal advertising material. The material is ordered, and when received, the local merchant need take only one step before the ad can be run in the local media. A space has been left for the store name and address. The familiar lines "store name here" or "name advertiser" appear on the proof. This element is eliminated, and the merchant's store and address is typeset and inserted. Typical ads are shown on pages 106 and 107.

If the merchant prefers to assemble elements and "make" ads from the illustrations, headlines, and borders shown in the brochure, that's a simple task too. In this case, a rough layout must be made and accompanying copy written and set in type.

The independent supermarket owner can, for example, order illustrations of meat cuts, poultry, dairy and bakery products, and other top-selling categories from an advertising service. At the local newspaper there are literally volumes of such display elements on hand to choose from. Note the food store display elements shown on page 108.

The Manufacturer as a Resource It is in the interest of the manufacturer to supply the retailer with advertising help. When the retailer places an ad that features the manufacturer's merchandise, it is still another impression made on the consuming public on behalf of the maker of the item. The manufacturer therefore supplies a wide range of advertising materials to the local merchant, some free, some at cost, and some on a cooperative advertising basis. These are the kinds of advertising materials most frequently supplied:

1. Portfolios of ads in various sizes featuring the manufacturer's merchandise and including space for the dealer's name and address. The dealer orders mats or coated proofs.

2. Scripts for use on local television or radio stations in various commercial lengths. The dealer adds the store identification to the script.

3. Recorded radio commercials and filmed television commercials in various commercial lengths. On each, time is left for local dealer personalization and identification. When available, they are supplied on a request basis or a cost-shared basis.

4. Catalogs, pamphlets, and direct mail programs that can be personalized by surprinting local dealer identification.

5. Advertising specialties (giveaways) supplied to the dealer, usually in quantities determined by the volume of goods ordered from the manufacturer.

6. In-store displays, window displays, signs, and counter cards featuring the manufacturer's products. Often such material is included automatically in the shipment of goods. More elaborate display material usually is offered to the local merchant via a brochure with an order form included and is cost-shared with the merchant.

Media Resources The advertising manager and the advertising sales force of local media are motivated to help local merchants solve their advertising problems for sound business reasons. By giving this assistance, they encourage advertisers to place business with the media they represent. Individual newspaper sales reps sometimes write headlines and slogans for their advertisers and help them select illustrations from the mat services to which the newspapers subscribe. Often a newspaper has a copy and art section that will prepare advertising for local merchants. Television and radio station reps can also help in copy preparation, but there is usually a program promotion or continuity writer on the staff who supplies copy for local advertisers. At the station, libraries of recorded music are available to supply musical background or themes for commercials.

These ads are typical of material supplied by an advertising service for use by local merchants. The name of the store is added where indicated. (Courtesy Metro Associated Services, Inc.)

Local supermarket owners who prefer to build their own ads can order elements like these headlines and captions from pages of a monthly bulletin of Metro Associated Services. (Courtesy Metro Associated Services, Inc.)

Television station people make up lettered dealer identification cards to tag film spots supplied to dealers by manufacturers. When radio or television advertising is needed, the local dealer should spend some time at the local stations becoming familiar with studio facilities and determining their usefulness.

Retail Advertising Clipping Services The merchant or the newspaper can subscribe to ad clipping services that reproduce retail ads already run in newspapers throughout the United States. These clipping services are, in some instances, supplied by the mat service outfits. *Men's Clip Review,* featuring menswear and boyswear, is published twice monthly. *Discount Promotions* appears weekly. *Shoes on Parade* is a weekly publication. *Jewelry Clip Review* appears twice monthly. There are many other ad clipping services, covering a wide range of retail businesses.

The clippings are supplied to help subscribing retailers keep up with advertising current in the field and to suggest ideas for headlines, copy, and illustrations. The general term for such material is *swipes,* and retailers borrow extensively from these clip sheets.

Advertising Agencies A merchant or small manufacturer can use the services of a local advertising agency, which will prepare the advertising, produce it, and place it in the required media. For a manufacturer, we have arbitrarily chosen $20,000 as the minimum annual amount necessary for an advertising budget if a local advertising agency is to be used. This budget would generate an agency commission of only $3,000 on the account, but some small agencies are geared to make a profit on this amount of billing.

The local merchant faces a special situation when using an advertising agency. Local advertising is not "commissionable" to an ad agency. In national advertising, the agency is allowed a 15 percent commission by the newspaper or broadcast media; but this is not the case in local advertising. Retail ad rates are invariably lower than national rates, and, in order to be paid for its services, the agency must charge the advertiser the 15 percent commission it would otherwise receive from the media. Or, instead of following the 15 percent system, the advertiser and agency may work out a fee for the work involved. This makes advertising agency services relatively expensive for the small local advertiser, and since small merchants have many other resources available to aid them in preparation of advertising, some of which are free, very few use ad agencies.

Free-Lance Resources In most areas, free-lance copywriters and artists are available to retailers if they care to avail themselves of these resources. Usually local merchants running small businesses prefer to write their own copy, but when it comes to the artwork they are not likely to have the skill and training required to do a satisfactory job. If the retailer does not wish to use any of the artwork resources we have discussed, the assignments may be farmed out to an artist or sketcher. In the women's fashion field, particularly, merchants use local fashion artists to supply sketches of their merchandise. Sometimes the merchant will commission a local artist to design the base of the ad, including the store name and a slogan in hand-lettered form, and perhaps an illustrative device. This is then produced in offset proof form, or as a *cut,* or engraving. Once this base is available, it remains constant in the advertising, serving as a distinctive identifier that sets the ad apart from others on the page.

Completing the Advertising Steps

Step 6, producing the advertising in the form required by the media, step 7, placing the advertising in the chosen media, and step 8, paying the advertising bills, are mechanical functions that involve no creative decision or judgment. Step 9, evaluating the results of advertising, is based on short- and long-range sales results and estimates of store traffic developed as a consequence of advertising.

Organizing for Advertising: The Department Store

Whether a department store is small or large, its advertising department is organized to complete the nine basic advertising steps listed at the beginning of Chapter 4. The only difference is that in a small store the tasks must be handled by fewer people. The person responsible for production does the proofreading and has no assistant to traffic the jobs; the art director does finished sketches; the ad manager writes much of the copy; and so on.

Establishing an Advertising Program, or Plan

If advertising for a department store is run on a hit-or-miss basis, profit will also depend on chance. A definite advertising program that is geared to the calendar must be established. This program can cover a period of time ranging from a week to a year (although the latter interval is too ambitious). It should include the following information: specific times when ads are to run, or the *insertion dates;* in what media the ads are to appear; the store departments that will advertise; the merchandise that each department will promote; the amount of money the ads will cost; the size of the ads; and a forecast of sales of advertised items.

The preparation of this program of advertising activity takes care of several basic steps, namely, establishing goals, establishing a budget, selecting goods to be advertised, and choosing media. This advance planning is subject to change; it is not a straightjacket. In the world of retail selling, opportunities for special merchandise purchases often arise quickly; fashion trends develop faster than sometimes foreseen; and items sometimes do not sell as anticipated. The advertising plan must adjust to these developments.

This program of advertising activities, or advertising plan, is often developed on a store-wide basis, and additional department plans are based on it and expand it from the departmental viewpoint. There can be an advertising plan for home furnishings, lingerie, housewares, misses' fashions, and each of the other store departments. It is prepared by the buyer of the department (the man or woman responsible for purchasing all the items the particular department sells) and the department manager, with the aid of the advertising manager.

Processing the Departmental Advertising Request

The departmental plan alerts those involved in the preparation and production of the store's advertising to departmental advertising needs in the near future. About a week before the insertion date of a scheduled advertisement, the department buyer initiates a departmental *advertising request.* This contains a wealth of necessary information for the advertising department. It lists the department, the date of insertion, the names of the media, the size and cost of the space involved, the amount of merchandise on hand, the type of ad (image, regular promotion, or special sale), the price of the merchandise, and a description of the merchandise. And most important, it lists the selling features of the merchandise that the buyer believes will be of interest to the prospect and describes what should be featured in the illustration. The advertising request, to be helpful, should contain maximum available information about the merchandise.

Following Through with Advertising Department Procedures

When the advertising request is received by the advertising department, the ad manager checks it against the departmental advertising plan, questions items that are not clear, and takes a long, hard look at the selections of merchandise the buyer is proposing to advertise, to see whether in the ad manager's judgment these items are appropriate for promotion. This done, the advertising request is passed on to the copy and art people. Let us assume that the request is received by the advertising department 1 week before the date of insertion.

Assignment of the Project to Copy and Art The advertising manager or the copy chief and head art director, if these are staff members, may become directly involved in a particular advertisement when it is considered important. The extent of involvement is determined by the individuals and their working habits. But the key people in an advertising department cannot conceivably do all the creative work themselves, much as they might want to. Unless there are special considerations, the ad manager assigns the advertising request to a copywriter who will prepare the copy. The manager may also compile (or have an assistant compile) a schedule of all ads planned for each insertion date, based on the advertising requests received from buyers. This schedule goes to the production people, alerting them to requirements and giving them the information they need to traffic the job, or see that it is completed on time.

Preparation of Copy and Layout The copywriter has the very important responsibility of producing copy that will result in satisfactory sales of the merchandise involved. There may be sufficient information on the advertising request, or there may not. There usually is a sample of the merchandise on hand for the writer and the art director to examine. The writer may need to question the buyer more fully or talk to salespeople on the floor to obtain information about the merchandise, or it may be necessary to check with the manufacturer. It's up to the copywriter to obtain all the necessary information to do a good job on the copy.

Some copywriters prefer to talk over the assignment with the art director first. This is always a good idea. Preliminary *roughs,* or rough layouts, may be made at this point. Perhaps the conversation with the art director will spark a headline idea or a layout approach. Two minds are often better than one in producing good department store ads, particularly if the individuals work well together. After this preliminary get-together, the copy is written and turned over to the art director for a final layout. The illustration on page 76 shows a typical department store layout.

Approval of Copy and Layout In the schedule of 1 week from receipt of advertising request to insertion date, 3 days have now passed, and the copy and layout are presented to the advertising manager for approval—or to the copy chief and head art director, if the store is a large one. Copy and layout should also be scrutinized by the department buyer to check for accuracy.

Production of the Advertisement After approval of copy and layout, illustrations are made by staff artists, or photographs are taken of the featured merchandise. The production people are now in charge of the operation. The production manager or the typographer specifies the type, marking up the copy to indicate the typefaces and type sizes and indicating on the layout where cuts or plates are to be made of supplied illustrative material. The production manager writes out any other instructions that the medium (or the photoengraver) needs to produce the ad. Marked-up layout and copy are illustrated in Chapter 16. This material, plus finished art work, is then sent to the newspaper accompanied by a *wait order*. This gives approval for production of a printing plate but does not give approval to insert the ad. In the offset method, a mechanical plus illustrative elements are sent with a wait order.

Receipt of Proofs It is now 1 or 2 days before insertion date, and the newspaper returns a *proof,* or hand-printed copy, on newspaper stock of the assembled type and cuts of the advertisement. The proofreader checks the proof against original copy. Other proofs of the ad are seen by the writer, art director, ad manager, production manager, and buyer. Corrections are made on the proof as needed, and it is returned to the newspaper. Sometimes a second corrected proof for verification is required by the store. When approvals are given, an advertising order authorizing the insertion is sent to the newspaper.

The day before the insertion date, store personnel concerned with the merchandise featured in the ad are informed via presentation of a proof.The ad should be "merchandised," or promoted within the store, to the maximum extent possible in order to obtain the greatest possible sales results. Salespeople should be aware of advertised items and should be informed of the selling features. The display section, already informed of the proposed advertising, should be rechecked to ensure that selling-floor and store-window support is being given, if authorized. Enlarged copies of the ad may be posted at high-visibility locations in the store.

Performing Post-Insertion-Date Activities

After the ad has appeared in the newspaper, actual advertisements cut from the pages of the publication, called *tearsheets,* are received by the individual responsible for advertising accounting procedures. These are advertisements as run, and they are measured to see if their size was actually run as ordered. Only after checks such as these have been made can payment for advertising be authorized. The cost of the ad is covered by the departmental budget. Meanwhile, the buyer, observing the sales results of the advertised merchandise, will write up the history of the selling activity. It is essential to accumulate these sales records to establish satisfactory guides for the expenditure of future promotion dollars.

Organizing for Advertising: Manufacturer and Agency

To understand how a typical consumer-product manufacturer and the advertising agency it employs are organized to accomplish the advertising task, a theoretical *advertising campaign,* a series of advertising messages devoted to the same idea, concept, or theme, will be traced from inception to results in the marketplace. For this purpose, we shall invent a company.

Background Information

The Green Valley Soup Company is a medium-size firm by national standards but important in the Midwest, where it distributes and markets regionally and where some of its products are dominant in sales. It produces a full line of soups, a line of frozen prepared high-quality items, and a few canned items such as pork and beans, all under the Green Valley brand name. Its notable sales success has been a soup product that has been marketed for many years, Green Valley Tomato Soup.

It is of passing interest to note that the company was founded by Daniel Webster Green in 1912 as the Farmers' Cooperative Soup Company, but in the thirties, having been impressed by a book he read called *How Green Was My Valley,* Mr. Green was inspired to change the company name to its present form. Mr. Green ruled the firm with an iron hand until he retired in 1963 at the age of 80. His attitude toward company advertising was strictly nononsense, and his concept of an excellent ad invariably consisted of a large plate of steaming soup dominated by a larger-than-life soup can alongside. The advertising slogan, "Green Valley Soups Are Best," was also an inspiration of Mr. Green's. It was perfect for the early growth stage of his company, when marketing was a relatively unsophisticated operation.

Current Marketing Decision

Things have changed at Green Valley since the founder's retirement, and new marketing and advertising thinking is in evidence. At a major meeting of key marketing executives late in March, it was decided to promote tomato soup with a special campaign of its own, rather than include it as part of the general soup line advertising. The theory behind this decision was that since tomato soup sales were better than those of other soups in the line, and since the market for tomato soup was larger than for other varieties except chicken, perhaps promoting tomato soup at a heavier rate would result in (1) taking tomato soup business from Campbell's and Heinz, the principal competi-

tors, and (2) creating new buyers who were not now buying tomato soup at all. This idea had been discussed, off and on, for a couple of years, and in the current fiscal year marketing and promotion budget, money had been set aside for the project. The dollar figure listed was definitely of the "ball park" variety; a formal project budget would be worked out later with the ad agency. At this point in the Green Valley special campaign, the first three steps of the advertising task had been completed (the nine advertising steps were listed in Chapter 4).

In another instance, the idea of promoting tomato soup might easily have originated with the advertising agency. Proposals such as this often do, but in this case the client was the originator.

Implementing the Decision at Green Valley and at the Agency

On April 2, the Green Valley advertising manager, Ted Griswold, passed on the marketing decision to the account supervisor at the advertising agency, Turnkey and Sesame, in Detroit. Agency personnel liked the decision because it offered additional promotional opportunities beyond the proposed advertising campaign itself, and these opportunities, it will be seen, were exploited at a later date. A tentative timetable for producing the advertising was agreed on, with a goal of starting the campaign by September 30. June 15 was set as the date for a formal presentation to the client of the campaign, proposed media, a budget, and any corollary promotional material involved in the project.

Company Activities With the marketing decision made to promote Green Valley Tomato Soup in a separate campaign, Griswold, the advertising manager, faced some new tasks. In addition to his regular work, he would now oversee the agency's work on the new project, initiating certain jobs in his collateral department and alerting company salesmen at the proper time to this new development. He set up the following projects in his department.

1. Creating display material for food stores, featuring Green Valley Tomato Soup. Suggested: end-of-aisle cardboard bins holding cans and carrying a sign tying in with the ad campaign theme; store banners for soup sections; photos of suggested store displays, such as pyramids of soup cans topped by signs. Work not to begin until receipt and approval of agency campaign theme so that display material can make use of it. Copy and art people in collateral section alerted and time scheduled for completion of creative work. Deliver copy and layout of all display material to display firm by August 7 for September 7 completion.

2. Presentation to sales force of all facets of new campaign September 15. Various visual aids needed, including slide presentation of marketing facts and selling opportunities presented by the new tomato soup campaign. Canned food products brand group to prepare.

3. Brochure in color summarizing important facts of new campaign addressed to sales force to be passed out at sales force presentation. This brochure to be used by sales force in selling food wholesalers and supermarket buyers. Assignment given to head copywriter in collateral section. Due date to printer: August 7.

4. Inclusion of facts on new campaign in Green Valley's regular direct mail campaign to the food trade. Responsibility of head copywriter, collateral department.

5. Griswold keeps his management informed of status of above projects, plus progress (or lack of it) on the new campaign at the agency.

The ad manager and his department people have their usual tasks to perform, so this new assignment will keep them quite busy over the next few months. The ad manager will rely heavily on the canned products brand group as a liaison between the company and the advertising agency on this product. Green Valley's advertising department has recently changed to the brand group system, with one person responsible for all advertising activities of a product or a related group of products.

Advertising Agency Activities Meanwhile, the account supervisor has alerted people in the following agency departments: creative, media, print production and traffic, television and radio traffic, merchandising, and research. Those assigned to the Green Valley account and agency management people are kept posted by *call reports,* or contact reports, memorandums that report on meetings and correspondence with the client and that outline decisions made and "next steps." The account supervisor, because this was an important project, also called several department heads to a meeting immediately after the get-together with the ad manager on April 2 to outline the new project.

The traffic person assigned to Green Valley in the print production department prepared a time schedule, based on a first-insertion date of September 30 for magazines and newspapers, with a series of due dates for creative work. The necessary job orders based on this schedule were issued to the creative people involved. The *job order* is a form that contains due dates for copy and layout and a job order number used by the accounting department for cost accounting purposes and by all agency personnel when ordering work from outside suppliers.

Creative Department Activities All the initial preparations are to no avail unless someone at

Turnkey & Sesame

Copywriter   *J. Pierce*

Traffic-Production Job Order-Print

Client/Product   *Green Valley Tomato Soup*   Job Order #   *GV 18-75 - Ad 11*

☐ New

Date   *April 9, 19- -*

☐ Other

Acc't Exec. Okay _____

Due Date	Copy Ordered/Due		Received	Layout Ordered/Due		Received	Client OK Received
Orig.	4/9	4/30	4/20	4/30	5/14	5/14	6/30
Revise 1.							
Revise 2.							
Revise 3.		6/1					
Special Instructions	☐ Copy		☐ Art	☑ Prod./Traffic		☐ Conf. request	

Publication	Issue	Closing	Extension	Space/Color	Size	Materials
STAR SUNDAY Sup. (Plus bal. of MID-WEST LIST)*	9/30	9/20	NONE	1p./b+w	1,200 l.	Offset

This ad will appear in the 8-paper Midwest Sunday supplement group. Eight b+w repro proofs needed.

An advertising agency job order form, filled out by the agency traffic department. It is used to initiate creative work.

the T & S agency can come up with a first-class creative idea that will appeal to the client and that can sell Green Valley Tomato Soup in the marketplace. Fortunately, T & S has a good copywriter assigned to Green Valley. Her name is Joan Pierce; she is 28 years old and very imaginative. She joined the agency seven years ago as an apprentice and succeeded from the start.

Joan Pierce received the job order on the new assignment from the traffic department on April 9. It set a date 3 weeks ahead for copy needed for the June 15 presentation. This was not Miss Pierce's only assignment during those

3 weeks. In that time she also wrote two ads and three radio spots for another account, attended a shooting, or filming, of a Green Valley frozen food commercial in New York, and worked on package copy (the words making up such things as recipes and instructions that appear on food product packages) for two new Green Valley frozen foods.

Meanwhile, she had already had her idea for tomato soup, and there were several parts to it. One might think that she would search for some great exclusive feature of the product itself or some special way the tomato soup was made. These areas are fine to explore and might help the body copy, or text, of future advertisements become more convincing or colorful. But Joan kept the marketing objective firmly in mind. She was after two goals: (1) increasing Green Valley Tomato Soup market share, or taking existing tomato soup customers from Campbell's and Heinz, and (2) adding new customers from among those not using tomato soup, or seldom using it. A product-oriented story would need to be unique indeed to deliver such sales results.

At a short conference with the head of the creative department, the following discussion took place:

Creative Director: "We need to get the homemaker to reach for the tomato soup can in her cupboard more often. And we need some new customers to reach for the brand on the supermarket shelf."

Joan: "We ought to use recipes."

Creative Director: "Right. But keep looking for a handle we can use all over the place."

Joan: "I will. And maybe we could have a contest for the best tomato soup recipes and use the winning recipes in our follow-on ads."

Creative Director: "Good thinking. Old Man Green would never have bought this one!"

Thus, it was decided that the campaign should be based on new uses of Green Valley Tomato Soup via appealing recipes. This approach will make consumers look at the brand in a new, fresh way and, if successful, will make them use Green Valley Tomato Soup more often. It can also attract new customers who rarely buy tomato soup. It is a "service" campaign—it serves the homemaker's interest in preparing attractive meals. By "handle" is meant a short theme or headline idea that sells the recipe concept and that can be a rallying point for all parts of the promotion.

It is often heard that recipe advertising has a flaw. The consumer can conceivably substitute a competing product in the recipe—in this case Campbell's or Heinz tomato soup. However, consumer research confirms that the consumer generally does not do so but stays with the advertised product when the recipe is used. The consumer has more confidence in the outcome when the recipe recommendations are followed, and this includes using the brand specified.

In the next few days, Joan wrote many themes, collected recipes featuring tomato soup, made up a few herself, and talked to a food editor of a women's magazine while in New York on the television production trip. This resource was a good one, for the editor assigned her test kitchen to the task of developing recipes for the project.

By April 20, a theme Joan liked was approved by the creative director. It was "Souperb Recipes—From Green Valley Tomato Soup." As this is a happy story, everybody liked it, including the Green Valley management at the June 15 presentation. It was practical, jibed with marketing objectives, had some freshness to it, and could be used in all components of the promotion.

Joan, working closely with the art director assigned to the Green Valley account, prepared copy for a half-dozen four-color recipe ads featuring two or three recipes each, several newspaper ads of varying sizes, plus scripts for one 1-minute and two 30-second television commercials.[2] These ads in rough layout and storyboard form were presented to the account handling group and then to the Green Valley advertising manager on an informal basis June 1. Ted Griswold wanted to see how the creative effort was progressing. (See Color Plates 6 and 7 for examples of the stages of an ad.)

During this time the following agency tasks were accomplished:

Merchandising Department Store display ideas passed on informally to Green Valley ad manager. Details of tomato soup recipe contest worked out and an estimate of contest cost prepared. Store display ideas for contest prepared.

Media Department Media recommendation developed for June 15 presentation. Media consists of regional editions of two national women's service magazines (*McCall's* and *Ladies' Home Journal*), newspapers and newspaper Sunday supplements, and spot television commercials in key markets in 1-minute and 30-second lengths.

Account Handling Department Worked with other departments, expedited, contacted client as needed, developed overall budget of $1,200,000 for a 1-year campaign including contest and point-of-sale material, and prepared marketing analysis for June 15 presentation.

Postpresentation Activities

Ted Griswold recommended acceptance of all agency projects attached to what was now called the Souperb campaign. This recommendation was bought with minor changes by cli-

---

ent management at the June 15 presentation in the oak-paneled Green Valley board room, with Mr. Green observing the proceedings from an oil painting on the wall. This picture always made the account supervisor, Pete Peruzzi, very nervous because he had heard many stories about Mr. Green and the good old days on the Green Valley account.

Activities at Green Valley The advertising manager and brand group approved revised copy and layout for the basic campaign on June 22. The ad manager then ordered the tasks outlined completed, as the company had in hand the campaign theme to be used in all collateral material. Ted approved a somewhat revised overall budget (it was cut by 10 percent) and the media schedule. He worked with the agency merchandising man on contest details. He approved *production estimates,* estimated costs of physically producing print ads and television commercials for use by media, and he approved the choice of a film production company to produce the commercials. He attended various agency meetings on such subjects as casting the commercials and obtaining media merchandising cooperation. The client sales force in the field started "selling in" an increased volume of tomato soup on September 15.

Activities at the Agency The art director ordered photography for three ads, based on approved copy and layout. On completion, the production department ordered materials prepared for the various media based on approved production estimates. The media buyer ordered space and time in media approved for the campaign. The print traffic department followed through on all creative schedules to see that insertion deadlines were met. The agency television producer received bids from three studios for producing one 1-minute and two 30-second commercials. Selection was then

---

[2] See the 30-second Green Valley TV script in Chapter 17.

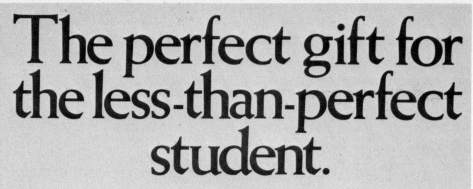

The perfect gift for the less-than-perfect student.

The patented snap-in Correction Cartridge.

One thing most students do a lot is type. Unfortunately, many of them are not what you'd call perfect typists.

That's where the Smith-Corona® Cartridge Ribbon portable with the Correction Cartridge can help. With it, you can correct most typing errors easily and neatly in only seconds.

It comes with a long-life nylon ribbon. There's also a film cartridge ribbon available in five colors, to give a sharper, crisper typing image. The film cartridge ribbon makes special papers look even more special.

We can't promise you the sun and the moon on a platter, or even an A in biology. But what we can promise you is great typing and easy correcting with America's favorite portable, the Smith-Corona Cartridge Ribbon typewriter.

And in an imperfect world, maybe that's enough.

SCM **SMITH-CORONA**
SCM CORPORATION

What people in the advertising agency were involved in the preparation of this national brand advertisement? What were their tasks? (Courtesy SCM Corporation)

made on the basis of which film studio could do the best job filming appetizing food shots (the price was in line) and the client approved the production estimate and choice of studio. The commercial was cast in New York 3 days before the TV shoot date. Several people involved in the project were on hand for the film session on August 20; Ted Griswold for the client, Pete Peruzzi, Joan Pierce, the agency producer, and a New York food stylist. The post-filming schedule, the time needed to process the commercials for station use, was tight, but all advertising started September 30 on schedule. Bills were paid, based on proof of insertion, within a month after submission by the media, and the agency was reimbursed subsequently by the client. Steps 4 to 8 of the advertising task had now been completed.

Campaign Results

Six months after the start of advertising, Green Valley total soup sales were up 6 percent, and tomato soup sales were up 19 percent, slightly under forecast objectives. The agency heard about this at length but offered the point of view that the original objectives were overambitious. The client's overall attitude was that the program would be a success when completed. The consumer contest results were particularly gratifying. On a personal note, at the agency, Joan Pierce received a spot raise for outstanding contributions to the Green Valley Tomato Soup campaign.

In this fictitious advertising campaign, every element came out right. It is important to note that many of the tasks could have failed. The original advertising might not have been acceptable to the client, with consequent postponement of the overall schedule until satisfactory ideas were developed. The television commercials might have been produced unimaginatively or with poor casting. The sales force in the field might have done a bad job in talking up and selling the campaign to the trade. But a good agency and a good client generally work as a team to avoid most of these mishaps.

Vocabulary

Define the following terms, and use each one in a sentence.

Advertising campaign	Package copy
Advertising request	Production estimate
Call report	Proof
Cut	Rough
Insertion date	Slick
Job order	Swipe
Marketing strategy	Tearsheets
Mat (matrix)	Wait order
Mat service	

Review Questions

1. List the basic steps of the advertising process that every advertiser must take.
2. What is the rule that helps a local merchant determine what particular goods or services should be advertised?
3. Name five local media generally available to local merchants.
4. List three resources that a local merchant could utilize to obtain illustrations for ads.
5. Describe ways in which a local appliance dealer could obtain copy help at no cost.
6. What are some of the pieces of information a department store buyer should include in the departmental advertising request?
7. What might a department store copywriter do to obtain information about merchandise beyond that listed on the advertising request?
8. Describe the differences between the advertising tasks performed by a department store advertising department and the tasks performed by an advertising agency.
9. Describe typical tasks that an advertising department's collateral section might be called upon to accomplish in order to support an ad campaign developed by the company's agency.
10. List five postpresentation activities undertaken at the agency after the tomato soup campaign was approved at the Green Valley Soup Company.

Activities

1. Study the following list of local advertisers. Write down possible subjects for profitable advertisements for each merchant. Depending on the type of business, subjects for ads could be goods on sale, timely items, services rendered, or image of the business. Bear in mind this rule: advertise best-selling goods and services.

   Example: florist. Possible ad subjects: springtime—forced bulbs (tulips, jonquils, lily of the valley, etc.); Easter—Easter lilies; Mother's Day—cut roses; fall—chrysanthemums, cut and potted; Christmas—plants. Cut-flower specials throughout the year. Image ads on freshness and quality of merchandise, quality of service.

   Car dealer   Dry cleaner
   Department store, medium-sized   Hardware store

Italian restaurant Savings bank
Real estate agent Travel agent

2. Suppose that you are a local merchant selling farm and garden supplies and equipment. From this chapter, you are familiar with the resources available for the preparation of advertising material. In making your ads, what resources do you decide to use for headlines, copy, and illustrations? List them, and give reasons for your choices.

Project

From observations of local newspaper, broadcast, and outdoor advertising, determine the objective or goal of the advertising for the types of businesses listed below. Write out the objective, and include the type of market at which the advertising is aimed (homemakers, upper-income men, all adults, teen-agers, etc.). In each case, attach an example of the concern's advertising that exemplifies the strategy.

Appliance store Jewelry store
Discount store Men's sportswear shop or sport-
Drive-in movie or movie theater ing goods store
Furniture store Women's high-fashion dress shop

Career Ladder

You have a job in an advertising agency as a member of the account group on a large packaged foods account. You have received a blind offer from a management consultant, or "head hunter," to compete for a job in a manufacturer's ad department. The job entails considerable responsibility for a person your age. Raises might be slower, but the job probably offers more security.

You decide to investigate. Although your advertising agency has been good to you, things are a little slow for you because the account you work on has not grown in size. By a startling coincidence, you discover that the job you're investigating is with another packaged food client serviced by your present advertising agency. This company is noncompetitive with the manufacturer you and your agency are presently servicing, but it's obvious that your general food background is why you got the nibble in the first place.

Do you now continue to pursue the job you're being considered for or drop out of competition? Give your reasons in class.

Jerome Atwood managed to combine his love for fishing with a business career. As a boy in his native Maine he fished in all the lakes and streams he could find. In 1949 he invented the famous Atwood lure, a patented basic design that proved irresistible to fresh- and saltwater fish. He manufactured it in Portland, Maine, and soon added more than 50 variations—colored differently and in various sizes.

Atwood was perfectly satisfied with his business achievement, but his son, Henry, who joined the business in 1968, had bigger ideas. Over a few years, he bought United States distribution rights to a first-quality reel of French manufacture and expanded manufacturing facilities to include tackle boxes, rods, and other fishing accessories.

Currently the Atwood Corporation has national distribution of its lures, fishing line, and reels. Distribution is spotty on rods and tackle boxes (volume on the latter item will never be large). The items are retailed through sporting goods stores, discount houses, and department stores.

Factory sales amount to approximately $1.4 million annually. There is a very small Atwood sales force in the field, and retail accounts are serviced directly from company headquarters in Portland, not through wholesalers. Consumers can also order goods directly from Portland at going retail prices through a small leaflet-catalog distributed in Atwood packaged items and through a direct mail operation.

Atwood believes in using only this catalog advertising. He thinks the best promotion is word of mouth and the excellent reputation of the basic Atwood lure among consumers. He is now in his seventies and is somewhat opinionated, but he will share decision making with his son, Henry.

The son has an aggressive expansionist attitude toward the business and has recently prevailed upon his father to hire a like-minded young sales manager, Joe Meyer.

Certain basic decisions are currently being faced. Retailers complain about the direct competition given by the Atwood catalog. Henry Atwood and Meyer are pushing for advertising because production facilities can handle more output. The father is dragging his feet, but he will go along.

1. Should the Atwood Corporation eliminate its catalog sales directed to the consumer and thus appease its dealers?
2. Should the company engage in other forms of advertising? If so, what kind of advertising? Toward what target groups should any advertising be directed? What types of media should be used and why?

U N I T

ADVERTISING MEDIA, RESEARCH

To perform its selling task, advertising requires a "vehicle" to carry it and the money to pay for it. In addition, the advertiser must obtain facts to guide judgment about what to say and where to say it. This unit covers

T W O

AND BUDGETS

these three vital areas: media (the "vehicles" that carry advertising); advertising research, or fact garnering; and advertising budgets.

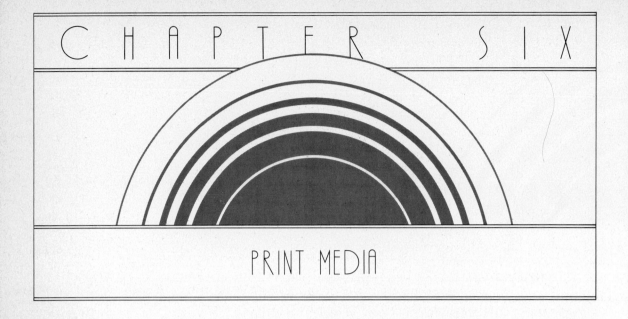

CHAPTER SIX

PRINT MEDIA

The three major classifications of print media are newspapers, magazines, and direct mail. Newspapers and magazines are discussed in detail in this chapter and direct mail in Chapter 7. In 1978, it was estimated that advertisers in the United States spent $12.7 billion in newspapers, $4.1 billion in consumer, business, and farm magazines, and $6 billion in direct mail.[1]

Other forms of advertising that use the printed word to communicate their message include outdoor advertising, nonstandardized signs, transportation or transit advertising, point-of-sale or point-of-purchase advertising, directory advertising, and advertising specialties. These supplemental forms of print advertising are discussed in Chapter 7.

Newspapers

According to *Editor and Publisher Year Book,* at the end of 1977, there were 352 morning papers, with a daily circulation of 26,742,000, and 1,435 evening papers, with a circulation of 34,753,000 for a combined daily circulation of 61,495,000. Twenty-one newspapers were published on an all-day basis, with both morning and evening editions. Their circulation is included in the combined circulation figures above. In addition, there were 668 Sunday papers, with a circulation of 52,429,000. It is estimated that there are also approximately 8,000 weekly newspapers in the United States, with an average circulation of about 3,000.

Characteristics of Newspapers

It is hard to imagine life without newspapers. Locally produced and locally oriented, the newspaper is an accepted and important part of community life. It presents a way through which the individual can identify with, or feel a part of, the immediate world. To the consumer, the newspaper is "now"—practical, important, and to a great extent, authoritative.

Editors gear the contents of newspapers to the needs and interests of the reading public. This is a diverse public. Although different

[1] McCann-Erickson, Inc., New York.

types of papers appeal to different types of readers, the readership of any newspaper is made up of every age group, many income classifications, and a multitude of occupations. A newspaper's circulation is mass circulation, a cross section of the city or town; yet, there is a unity of interest within all this diversity. People are most interested most of the time in what's going on in their immediate surroundings, and newspapers cater to this interest, espousing local causes, reporting local news in detail, and featuring service articles that have local application, as well as carrying national and international news.

Newspaper Advertising

Because newspapers are familiar and accepted, it is not surprising that more advertising dollars are placed in them than in any other medium. But it is important to note the kind of advertising that appears on the local newspaper's pages. It is estimated that 86 percent of this advertising is local advertising. Only 14 percent of it is placed by national and regional advertisers.

Local Advertising in Newspapers Newspapers serve the same area that local merchants serve. The newspaper's coverage may be wider than the area served by a particular merchant, but even if the merchant draws customers from only a small part of the city, the store's newspaper advertising reaches most of the store's potential customers in its sales area. The merchant considers, too, the reader's acceptance of the important role the paper plays in community life, relying on this acceptance to carry over to the ads when they appear in the newspaper. And the merchant knows that newspaper advertising is considered by the reader as a form of news, because it often contains information about prices and descriptions and illustrations of new merchandise, new styles, and fashions. We have seen (Table 1-5) that newspaper advertising is thought to be more informative and less annoying than other forms of advertising. Consumers generally like newspaper ads and turn to the newspaper's advertising pages as a matter of course.

In recent years, local advertisers have been increasing their use of radio and television, and this has apparently affected newspaper advertising revenue to a small degree. In 1970, newspapers accounted for 59 percent of total local advertising volume, local radio advertising, 9 percent, and local television advertising, 9 percent. By the end of 1978, these figures had changed to 55.3 percent for newspapers, 9.2 percent for local radio, and 12 percent for local television.

Whether or not this trend will continue depends on two factors: (1) Local merchants try to evaluate the relative pulling power of their advertising in one medium versus another. The most efficient mix of media will always be used. (2) Relative costs of different media must always be considered. If, for example, local television rates and production costs increase in comparison to the costs of preparing and running ads in newspapers, the slow trend of increased television use will cease. If newspaper rates show sharp rises, the trend to broadcast media will increase.

Evening newspapers in large cities suffered circulation losses in the late seventies, and some dailies were forced out of business. A combination of circumstances had caused circulation to drop. Television evening news programs have always competed with newspapers, but when stock markets changed their closing to a later time each day, large evening papers were unable to carry closing prices. According to *Media Decisions*,[2] this factor and the success of suburban newspapers, competing for some of the same readers as the big city

[2] *Media Decisions,* May 1978, pp. 68 and 69.

Poached ivory.

On May 19, 1977, the Kenya government announced a ban on big game hunting. The move was heralded as a victory for wildlife and its protectors. But, in fact, it may have been more of a smokescreen to cover the continued activities of certain wealthy illegal hunters — poachers — who had some very interesting connections and who sold ivory, hides, horns, and claws.

Among the hardest-hitting critics of the continuing slaughter was Field & Stream's editor Jack Samson. Perhaps you read his myriad article, "The Great Kenya Wildlife Ripoff." It was part of the international outpouring that led to the recent total ban on Kenya's ivory trade, once and for all — finally.

The article was part of conservation-minded Field & Stream's fight to keep wild places wild and wildlife alive. And it was just one of the surprising articles in Field & Stream that compel the interest even of indoorsmen.

When you want to reach men you have to consider us. 76% of our readers are men and we deliver them at a lot lower cost than Time, Newsweek, Sports Illustrated, and U.S. News. And your ad will be around four times longer in us than in them.

We have the largest circulation of any outdoor magazine in the entire world. Let us lead you through the woods to more than 8 million readers.

Field & Stream

Circulation: 2,033,135*
Readership: 8,472,000**
6,400,000 men

SURPRISING FIELD & STREAM: THE MONTHLY ALTERNATIVE

*ABC 12/31/77 **MRI Spring 1977-78

Prominent Ad Woman Relieved of Duties

Edith M. Tucker

It was a grim-faced Edith Tucker who confronted the press yesterday in an unprecedented question-and-answer session.

Miss Tucker, Ad Woman of the Year a short decade ago, and the creator of the beloved "Happy, Happy" campaign, could hardly conceal her chagrin:

"I made a big mistake not to insist on a sizeable chunk of our ad budget for The Boston Globe," Miss Tucker admitted. "After all, 50% of all adults in Boston's SMSA read The Globe – and 58% of all adults owning electric dishwashers, according to the new *Boston Today* study."

Miss Tucker's eyes misted slightly:

"Now I know better: Capture The Globe reader and you capture the Boston market."

Prominent Media Director Fired

Hank Bowman

Amos P. Bowman, Media Director at one of the city's more obscure advertising agencies, has been dismissed, according to an announcement today from his agency's Executive Committee:

The announcement explains why:

"We had a big new campaign breaking in Greater Boston for a heavy-spending bourbon client of ours. So what does Bowman do? Instead of concentrating most of the advertising dollars in The Boston Globe, he recommended sky-writing. He hadn't even heard about that new study called *Boston Today* which clearly proves that 55% of all men in Boston's SMSA read The Globe – and 65% of all bourbon drinkers..."

Mr. Bowman, who will announce his plans in the near future, now seems convinced of The Globe's superiority. "Capture the Globe reader and you capture the Boston market."

---

dailies, have caused circulation losses. In contrast, morning newspapers have not faced these problems, and their total circulation has shown annual increases.

Largest Retail Users of Newspaper Advertising Department stores are the largest local users of newspaper advertising. Their spending constitutes more than one-fourth of total retail advertising volume in newspapers, according to 1978 tabulations made by the Newspaper Advertising Bureau, a trade association of the newspaper world. The next largest advertisers are food stores and the major general merchandise stores. Table 6-1 lists retail and service classifications and their percentages of total retail advertising volume.[3]

National Advertising in Newspapers Since newspapers provide excellent coverage of local markets, national advertisers often use them to bolster local sales efforts. Usually this will not represent the total advertising effort of a national advertiser; instead as a part of its advertising program, a national advertiser may buy a newspaper ad schedule in its 50 or 100 largest markets.

Newspapers offer flexibility to the national advertiser. If coverage of a particular sales territory via national magazines or national television is thin, the addition of a newspaper ad schedule in that sales territory can increase it. Adding to newspapers' flexibility is their short *closing time,* or deadline for acceptance of an advertisement. In newspapers, the closing time is 2 days, or at the most 3 days, before

---

[3] The tabulations do not include one important local advertising category, automotive advertising. Car ads are run in newspapers by local dealers, regional dealer associations, and manufacturers. In addition, classified ads are heavily used by individual sellers and prospective purchasers of used cars and by local car dealers as well. As a result, the Newspaper Advertising Bureau has been unable to estimate the amount of automotive advertising with any degree of accuracy.

These ads, run in the advertising trade press, are all directed at advertisers and media buyers who buy space in magazines and newspapers. (Courtesy *Field & Stream; The Boston Globe; Southern Living; Lawrence Eagle-Tribune*)

BATON ROUGE

"Baton Rouge was clothed in flowers, like a bride—no, much more so; like a greenhouse...The magnolia trees in the Capitol grounds were lovely and fragrant...The scent of the flower is very sweet, but you want distance on it, because it is so powerful. They are not good bedroom blossoms—they might suffocate one in his sleep."

—*Mark Twain, Life on the Mississippi,*
Harper & Row, New York.

Southern literature abounds in verdant descriptions of its beautiful cities which, thanks to the region's benign climate and sufficient rainfall seem to bloom year-round. But, looking beyond the magnolias, it should be noted that today's Southern cities are active marketplaces for most goods and services; at least half the South's 69 million people live in their metro areas; and if they seem less awkward and cluttered than most cities it is because so many are no more than 50,000 to 250,000 population—a most agreeably manageable size.

Southern Living®

Put your money where The South is

You'll look great in our Sunday best!

On October 1, 1978, we proudly introduce the Sunday Eagle-Tribune: the newest and biggest edition of the award-winning Lawrence Eagle-Tribune.

As the only Sunday paper serving the central Merrimack Valley, the Sunday Eagle-Tribune is a natural for your advertising message. With our guaranteed circulation of 50,700 homes delivered, you'll reach over 80% of the market area!

Special introductory allowances and discounts make our new Sunday paper even more attractive. For more information, call one of our sales representatives today at 617-685-1000. Ask about the Sunday Eagle-Tribune – our Sunday best!

Introducing the Sunday Eagle-Tribune.

Our Sunday best.

Lawrence Eagle-Tribune, Box 100, Lawrence, MA 01842.
Represented Nationally by Story & Kelly-Smith.

TABLE 6-1 Retail Advertising Volume in Newspapers

Type of Store or Business	Percent of Total Newspaper Retail Advertising Volume, Based on a Sample of 40 Newspapers
Department stores	26.0
Food stores	8.9
Major general merchandise stores	7.5
Furniture stores	6.0
Theaters	5.6
Other general merchandise stores	5.0
Building materials, hardware, and farm equipment	4.0
Tires, auto supply stores, service stations	3.2
Real estate dealers	2.9
TV, radio, and record stores	2.8
Drugstores	2.5
Women's and girls' apparel, accessory stores	2.4
Home furnishing stores	2.3
Eating and drinking places	1.8
Boating, sporting goods, and hobby stores	1.6
General amusements	1.6
Not elsewhere classified	1.6
Family and infants' apparel, accessory stores	1.5
Banks, trust companies	1.4
Household appliance stores	1.3
Jewelry stores	1.1
Men's and boys' apparel, accessory stores	1.1
Savings and loan associations	0.8
Business, professional, home services	0.7
Shoe stores	0.7
Book and stationery stores, print shops	0.5
Florists, nurseries, garden supply stores	0.5
Variety stores	0.5
Camera, photo supply stores	0.4
Educational services	0.4
Health clubs, equipment	0.4
Help wanted (display)	0.4
Liquor stores	0.4
Hotels, motels, resorts	0.3
Musical instrument stores	0.3
Beauty salons, barber shops, hair goods	0.2
General financial	0.2
Gift, novelty, and souvenir shops	0.2
Religious organizations	0.2
Stock and bond brokers, investment houses	0.2
Stock issues and tender offers	0.2
Cleaners, laundries	0.1
Funeral directors, cemeteries	0.1
Loan and credit organizations	0.1
Mutual funds	0.1

Source: Newspaper Advertising Association, Inc., 1978.

publication. In contrast, magazine closing dates can be as long as 2 months before publication. The extremely short closing time allows the newspaper advertiser to place advertising at the last minute and thus take advantage of special selling opportunities as they arise.

Certain national advertisers, because of the nature of their businesses, consider newspaper advertising of vital importance. Among the top 25 national newspaper advertisers are the three largest car manufacturers, some distillers, several airlines and the largest cigarette makers. The car makers want to give their local dealers active support on the local level with advertising in the highly accepted local newspaper. The distillers, by self-regulation, are limited to advertising in newspapers and magazines. The cigarette makers no longer can use the television medium and have increased their newspaper advertising as a result. The airlines' ads contain "news" of air schedules; the airlines need to keep their destination and departure times constantly before the eyes of their potential patrons. So, for different valid reasons, these industries choose newspapers as an important medium.

Limitations of Newspaper Advertising

While newspapers are of paramount importance to local merchants and offer flexibility to national advertisers, they do have their limitations, as all media do. A newspaper's primary reason for being, to present the news, also means that the paper has a short life-span, measured in hours. The newspaper ad is seen briefly, for a reader usually goes through the paper only once before discarding it. Magazines, in contrast, are usually kept until the next issue is published, a week or a month later. Thus advertising in magazines has a longer life, and there is a chance that the reader will

return to a particular advertisement again. Then, too, magazines have "pass-on" readership; that is, they are usually read by more than one person. This may be true of a family newspaper, too, but the life-span of pass-on readership is shorter for newspapers.

Because of the nature of the printing process involved, daily newspapers do not offer the clarity and fidelity of ad reproduction found in magazines, except when Hi-Fi or SpectaColor advertising is used. These special methods of reproducing color ads in newspapers are discussed in Chapter 15; they must be considered in relation to the production and insertion costs involved.

Specialized Forms of Newspaper Advertising

The forms newspapers take have proliferated over the years, and today there is a wide variety available to the local and national advertiser. The word "newspaper" may call up an image of the familiar daily paper, but in reality the term covers many kinds of publications.

During-the-Week Sections   Large metropolitan dailies have during-the-week sections that appeal to their readers' special interests. These sections offer new, selective audiences to advertisers. The *Chicago Tribune* pioneered in this area by introducing "Feminique" in 1965. This special section offers full color to advertisers and concentrates on fashion. *The New York Times* introduced "Weekend," appearing in the Friday edition, in 1976. "Sports Monday," "Living," "Home," and "Science Times" sections appear on other days. Business news has been reorganized into a special section of its own. Seventeen newspapers in the ten largest metropolitan markets offered sections in 1979. Sections have increased circulation and advertising revenues.

Sunday Sections The Sunday newspaper contains sections that are difficult to classify. They have some of the characteristics of magazines, but they appear in newsprint form. There is the magazine supplement, the comic supplement, the television program supplement, and, in very large cities, sometimes a book section. In addition, department stores, manufacturers, and trade and tourist associations often prepare special sections for inclusion in the large metropolitan Sunday papers. All these supplements contain advertising, and all present specialized advertising opportunities.

Shopping Guides Another specialized newspaper advertising opportunity is found in the shopping-guide newspapers available in many urban markets. These free guides are not really newspapers, but they are printed in the general form of a newspaper and on newspaper stock. Any news included relates to the shopping scene, and the pages are filled with advertisements, almost wholly of the local variety. Before advertising in shopping guides, the local merchant should carefully analyze circulation figures and coverage areas and compare rates with those of local newspapers to determine the best value per advertising dollar.

Special-Interest Newspapers Some types of publications, *special-interest newspapers*, appear in newspaper form but cover a specialized editorial area and are directed at specific audiences. The *Wall Street Journal* deals with business news and is a national daily with four regional editions. *Women's Wear Daily* concentrates on the fashion field and is distributed nationally. Although its name suggests that the *Christian Science Monitor* is a special-interest newspaper, it is actually a national newspaper written for a general audience. The *National Enquirer* and the *Star,* both of which have en-

joyed exceptional circulation growth, are really magazines in newspaper form. Dealing with relatively sensational material, they are edited to appeal to a "youthful family audience" according to their publishers' editorial statements. Labor, religious, and trade groups all have newspapers oriented to their interests.

There are 214 newspapers throughout the country editorially directed to black audiences. Most of these newspapers are weeklies. Advertisers can buy space in them individually or through such representatives as Amalgamated Publishers, Inc., which can deliver a circulation of almost 4 million black newspaper readers nationwide.

The foreign-language press consists of 235 newspapers, mainly weeklies and monthlies. National groups, from Albanians to Yugoslavians, are represented. Among the larger groups, there are twenty-four Spanish newspapers. And there is one Korean newspaper, and two are printed in Urdu.

All these special kinds of newspapers offer a selected readership that many advertisers find of value in selling goods and services.

Buying Advertising Space in Newspapers

Newspaper advertising rates are lower for local advertisers than for national advertisers for two reasons: (1) The newspaper rate charged to national advertisers is paid by the advertiser to the advertising agency. The agency deducts its 15 percent commission and then pays the newspaper the remainder of the fee. Then the client is usually entitled to a 2 percent cash discount from the newspaper for payment of the bill by the tenth of the month following the advertisement's insertion date. (2) Newspapers often hire *newspaper representatives,* firms that sell newspaper space, or represent, the newspapers. These firms, located in major cities where the large ad agencies are, charge the newspaper a commission for all space sold to national advertisers. So newspaper revenues from national advertisers are reduced by commissions and discounts. But advertising revenues from local merchants are not reduced in these ways. Therefore, newspapers establish higher rates for national advertisers than for local ones.

Local Advertising Rates Local merchants find out their newspaper advertising costs through the use of a *rate card,* a pamphlet, published by the paper, that lists the categories of rates charged for advertising in its pages. On pages 134–135 is the rate card of the evening *Cincinnati Post.* It is typical of rate cards in general, and any local merchant who is involved in advertising should understand its contents.

Advertising space is, in most cases, measured in lines, or *agate lines.* This term comes from typography. It refers to a very small size of type that measures 14 lines to the inch. Fourteen agate lines of 6-point type, unleaded can be set in a one-inch depth per column, as the following example shows:

This copy has been set in 6-point Century, a typeface often used by newspapers. The type size is one of the smallest sizes generally available. Here the copy is "unleaded" or "set solid," which means there is no spacing between the lines. Advertising space in newspapers is generally measured in lines, but it can be measured in inches. So it should never be forgotten that 14 of these 5-point lines always are equal to 1 column inch depth. This copy has been set in 5-point Century, a typeface often used by newspapers. The type size is one of the smallest sizes generally available. Here the copy is "unleaded" or "set

For further discussion of the spacing of lines of type, see Chapter 16.

These lines have a definite width, which depends on the width of the newspaper column. In the case of the *Cincinnati Post,* the column width is 1 9/16 inches. (See "mechanical information" on the rate card.)

Some papers use the column inch, rather than the agate line, as the basic unit of measurement for retail advertising space, but this system presents no difficulty if it is remembered that 14 lines equal 1 column inch. For example, if the agate-line rate of a newspaper is 20 cents, the rate for an inch would be 14 lines times 20 cents, or $2.80.

Ads can appear in different forms and yet take the same amount of linage and cost the same amount. Suppose that an advertiser had decided to use 300 lines for an ad. The 300 lines could be used as an oblong ad, 150 lines deep by 2 columns wide, or 100 lines deep over 3 columns, resulting in an ad that is wider than it is deep.

In the *Cincinnati Post* rate card note that the basic retail rate is listed first. It is called the *open rate* (sometimes *transient rate* is used). The *Post's* open rate is 90 cents per agate line. If a local merchant advertises only once or twice, using a small ad, this is the rate paid. For example, if a candy store owner announced the opening of a new branch store with one 300-line ad and then stopped advertising, the bill would be $270 (less a 2 percent cash discount if paid by the tenth of the month following date of insertion). If a larger ad had been used, the rate would have decreased, and it would have kept decreasing the more the linage increased. Newspaper advertising managers prefer consistent advertising and offer reduced rates to the regular advertiser, who is a dependable source of revenue for the medium.

The advertiser who runs ads weekly for a year qualifies for rate reductions; the line rate can be cut still further through quarterly discounts, as an examination of the *Post* rate card shows.

Advertisers can request a particular position for their ad in the newspaper, but while the publisher will try to grant this request, it is not obligatory unless the advertiser pays a special position charge. Some advertisers prefer that their ad be placed near the beginning of the paper, while others request that it be above the fold (on the upper half of the page). The owner of a women's fashion shop might prefer to place an ad in the general news section or on the society page, whereas the owner of a sporting goods store often requests the sports section. Sometimes particular positions on the page are requested. The following terms are used to describe position on the page: *full position,* next to and following reading matter or at the top of a column and next to reading matter; *NR* (next to reading) *position,* with reading matter on one side but not at the top; *ROP* (run of paper) *position,* at the publisher's discretion. The ad in ROP position can be surrounded by other advertisements. See the illustration of typical page positions on page 136.

National Advertising Rates Advertising agencies placing national advertising in newspapers use the Standard Rate & Data Service (SRDS) to determine costs of advertising. This firm produces monthly publications listing national rate-card information for all types of advertising except outdoor, specialty, and point-of-purchase advertising. The SRDS listing for the *Cincinnati Post* is shown on page 137, and a national advertiser will refer to it if a schedule of newspaper advertising is to be run in this paper. The listing gives some mechanical information and certain raw data that can help the advertiser evaluate the *Post* as a medium.

Here are explanations for the most important items in the SRDS for the *Cincinnati Post.*

Line Rate (item 5)   The open agate-line rate for the national advertiser is $1.35, whereas it is only 90 cents for the local retailer. Contracts for over 500 lines obtain progressive discounts on the $1.35 open rate.

Color Rates and Data (item 7)   Color ads may be run in the *Post* at an additional charge. The

RETAIL DISPLAY RATES

PER AGATE LINE

OPEN RATE . . . . (No Contract) 90

TO BE USED WITHIN ONE YEAR: (With Contract)

500 lines	.77
1,000 lines	.76
2,500 lines	.75
5,000 lines	.74
7,500 lines	.73
10,000 lines	.72
15,000 lines	$.71\frac{1}{2}$
25,000 lines	$.71\frac{1}{4}$
50,000 lines	.71
75,000 lines	$.70\frac{1}{2}$
100,000 lines	.70
150,000 lines	$.69\frac{1}{2}$
200,000 lines	.69
250,000 lines	$.68\frac{1}{4}$
300,000 lines	.68
400,000 lines	$.67\frac{3}{4}$
500,000 lines	.67
600,000 lines	$.66\frac{1}{2}$
750,000 lines	.66
1,000,000 lines	$.65\frac{1}{2}$
1,250,000 lines	.65

$150.00 DISCOUNT ON FULL PAGE ADS

WEEKLY RATES (WITH CONTRACT)

28 lines weekly for one year	.75
90 lines weekly for one year	$.72\frac{1}{2}$
175 lines weekly for one year	$.71\frac{1}{2}$
350 lines weekly for one year	.70
700 lines weekly for one year	$.67\frac{1}{2}$

QUARTERLY DISCOUNT QUOTA PLAN

On contracts which have been in effect for a year, an increase in linage over the same calendar quarter of the previous year will earn a discount off the existing contract rate on all linage used in the quarter. The schedule of increases and discounts that may be earned are listed below:

5% increase earns a discount of .01 per line
10% increase earns a discount of .03 per line
15% increase earns a discount of .05 per line
20% increase earns a discount of .07 per line

Contracts covering multiple operations and billed separately will have individual quotas.

1 page (or less) 1 color and black. . . . . $325.00 extra
1 page (or less) 2 colors and black . . . . $425.00 extra
1 page (or less) 3 colors and black . . . . $600.00 extra

COLOR DEADLINE: All color ads ready for release 12 noon two days preceding publication.

COLOR FREQUENCY DISCOUNT
ON COLOR CHARGES ONLY
Second color ad within calendar month 5% discount
Third color ad within calendar month 10% discount
Fourth color ad within calendar month 20% discount

AMUSEMENT—MOTION PICTURES

Up to 2,500 lines (no contract). 91

With Contract:

2,501— 5,000 lines in 1 year	.86
5,001— 7,500 lines in 1 year	.85
7,501— 10,000 lines in 1 year	.84
10,001— 15,000 lines in 1 year	.83
15,001— 25,000 lines in 1 year	.82
25,001— 50,000 lines in 1 year	.81
50,001—100,000 lines in 1 year	.79
Over 100,000 lines in 1 year	.76

$150.00 Discount on all Full Page ads

Directory Theatre
Base Rate (no contract) 91
*14 lines—5 days per week 84
*14 lines—6 days per week 80
        *Plus 2 line charge for heading

MECHANICAL INFORMATION

9 columns to the page, depth of column 315 lines. 2,835 lines to the page.

COLUMN WIDTHS:

1 col.	9.9 picas or 1⁹/₁₆''
2 col.	19.9 picas or 3¼''
3 col.	29.9 picas or 4¹⁵/₁₆''
4 col.	39.9 picas or 6⁹/₁₆''
5 col.	49.9 picas or 8¼''
6 col.	59.9 picas or 9⁷/₈''
7 col.	69.9 picas or 11⁹/₁₆''
8 col.	79.9 picas or 13³/₁₆''
9 col.	89.9 picas or 14⁷/₈''

DOUBLE TRUCKS

Each page is 15¼'' wide
Minimum depth—200 lines
Double trucks will be sold in 19, 17 and 15 column widths only. Note: a 17-column ad must run either flush left or flush right

It is required that double trucks be complete in every detail and ready for release 24 hours in advance of regular deadline. An additional column of space is charged for the gutter on all double trucks.

TABLOID SIZE PAGES
Tabloid size printed page—11⁹/₁₆ x 14''
7 columns per page
196 lines per column
1,372 lines per page

Tabloid advertising is charged on the basis of one regular size page for every 2 pages of tabloid size.

NON-SUBSCRIBER INSERT
DISTRIBUTION AVAILABLE.
Consult your Post account executive
for complete details.

✳ ✳ ✳

Selected pages from the *Cincinnati Post* local rate card. The information is used by local advertisers to determine the cost of buying ad space in the paper. These rates are lower than national rates. (Courtesy *Cincinnati Post*)

abbreviation *b/w* stands for black-and-white, or ordinary noncolor, ads. The advertiser may run an ad of black and white plus one color (1c), two colors (2c), or three colors (3c) with certain size requirements involved.

Mechanical Measurements (item 15)　This item tells the *Post* advertiser that the *Post* uses the photocomposition direct letterpress method of printing. It should be noted that most newspapers are printed by the offset method. According to Adelaide Santonastasa of *Editor and Publisher,* 70 percent of United States daily newspapers, or about 1,260, are printed by offset. Item 15 also lists a few basics such as number of columns and width of columns in picas (a pica is $1/6$ inch; see also Chapter 16).

Circulation (item 18)　This is a very important piece of information. The *Post,* an evening and Saturday morning newspaper states that its total evening circulation is 190,303. In the city zone (CZ) 148,280 copies are sold. In the outlying trading zone (TrZ), suburban or satellite areas outside the city zone, 38,836 papers are sold. "Other" circulation covers copies mailed or distributed to areas beyond the trading zone. A more detailed circulation breakdown is available through another service of SRDS and is based on ABC, or Audit Bureau of Circulation, data. The ABC, founded in 1914, is a service that verifies circulation claims of the newspapers and magazines that are ABC members.

"Max" and "mil" stand for maximil-minimil rates. According to SRDS, the *maximil rate* represents the maximum cost of one line of advertising per million circulation at the open or flat line rate. The *minimil rate* represents the minimum cost of one line of advertising per million circulation at the lowest rate available from a particular newspaper.

For example, if the open line rate is 8 cents and the circulation is 10,000, the following calculation is done to determine the maximil rate:

$$\frac{0.08 \times 1,000,000}{10,000} = \$8 \text{ maximil rate}$$

If the paper's greatest discounted line rate is 6 cents, the following calculation applies:

$$\frac{0.06 \times 1,000,000}{10,000} = \$6 \text{ minimil rate}$$

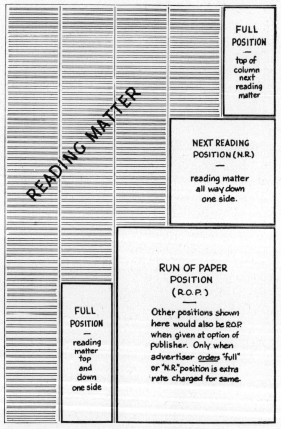

This diagram shows the typical newspaper positions: full position, NR position, and ROP position. (From Donald W. Davis, *Basic Text in Advertising,* Printers' Ink Books, Pleasantville, NY, 1955, p. 339.)

A more elaborate formula is required when a 2 percent cash discount is given by the newspaper. As a rule of thumb, the max and mil rates decrease as newspaper circulation increases. Certain expenses are fixed in the newspaper business, and additional circulation spreads these expenses over more copies of the newspaper.

The maximil and minimil figures are important to those who buy advertising space in newspapers when comparing newspapers of somewhat similar circulation. Cincinnati is also served by the *Enquirer,* which is published mornings and Sundays.

Judging by maximil and minimil rates, the morning *Enquirer* is slightly less expensive to advertise in than the *Post,* but the Sunday *Enquirer* minimil rate is the least expensive of all. See the SRDS listing for *Post* maximil and minimil rates. Other factors enter into choice of media, of course, such as advertisers' preference for running ads in the morning rather than in the evening and their judgment of the quality of the circulation.

POST

800 Broadway, Cincinnati, Ohio 45202.
Phone 513-352-2000.

(ABC) ads C

Media Code I 136 2000 9.00
EVENING (except Sunday) AND SATURDAY MORN.
Member: INAE; Newspaper Advertising Bureau, Inc.

1. PERSONNEL
Business Manager—John L. Feldmann.
Advertising Director- Robert W. Keim.
Mgr., Gen. Adv.—Robert A. Huninghake
Accounting Mgr.—Jack H. O'Bryan.

2. REPRESENTATIVES and/or BRANCH OFFICES
Story & Kelly-Smith, Inc.
Resort & Travel, Florida—Metropolitan Publishers Representatives, Inc.

3. COMMISSION AND CASH DISCOUNT
15% to agencies; no cash discount.

4. POLICY—ALL CLASSIFICATIONS
Alcoholic beverage advertising accepted.
8 column ads not accepted.

ADVERTISING RATES
Effective January 1, 1978. (Card No. 25.)
Received October 27, 1977.

5. BLACK/WHITE RATES
Open, per agate line........................ 1.35

BULK LINAGE CONTRACT RATES
500- 999 lines	1.19
1,000- 2,499 lines	1.18
2,500- 4,999 lines	1.17
5,000- 9,999 lines	1.16
10,000- 19,999 lines	1.13
20,000- 29,999 lines	1.12
30,000- 49,999 lines	1.11
50,000- 74,999 lines	1.09
75,000- 99,999 lines	1.08
100,000-149,999 lines	1.07

Discount rates apply within contract year. Discounts do not apply to color costs. Advertisers signing contracts billed at applicable contract rate and rebilled at higher rate if contract is not fulfilled, or refunded if lower rate is earned.

7. COLOR RATES AND DATA
Available daily, 600 line minimum on b/w 1 c, 1,000 line minimum on b/w 2 or 3 colors.
Use b/w line rate plus the following applicable costs:
	b/w 1 c	b/w 2 c	b/w 3 c
Extra	375.00	500.00	625.00

Closing dates—7 days in advance for reservations; 72 hours in advance for printing material; cancellations 9:00 a.m., 2 days in advance.

9. SPLIT-RUN
Two-way split-run, extra 50.00 (commissionable).

11. SPECIAL DAYS/PAGES/FEATURES
Best Food Day: Wednesday.
Automobile, Friday; Resort and Travel, Tuesday; Real Estate and Builders, Saturday; Garden News, Friday; Church, Saturday.

12. POP DEPTH REQUIREMENTS
One column over 287 lines deep charged full column. Minimum sizes on 9 col. ads: 2 inches deep; all others at least same number of inches deep as cols. wide.

13. CONTRACT AND COPY REGULATIONS
See Contents page for location of regulations—items 1, 2, 18, 19, 20, 23, 25, 26, 32, 35, 46.

14. CLOSING TIME
Closing 2 days before publication.
Cancellations not accepted after 12:00 noon, 2 days before publication date; 9:00 a.m. Friday for Wednesday food section.

15. MECHANICAL MEASUREMENTS
PRINTING PROCESS: Photo Composition Direct Letterpress (Letterflex).
For complete, detailed production information, see SRDS Print Media Production Data.
9/9-9/3—9 cols/ea 9 picas-9 pts/3 pts betw col.
Lines to: col. 315; page 2835; dbl truck 5985.

16. SPECIAL CLASSIFICATION/RATES
Amusement, Motion Picture, Financial, Help Wanted (Display), Recruitment (Display), Public Opinion—Bulk linage contract rates apply.
DAILY COMIC PAGE
Regular rates apply. Space available subject to prior sale and to current editorial requirements. Maximum depth 60 lines. Cartoon strip style permitted. Alcoholic beverages, tobacco products and proprietary remedies not accepted on comic page.

17. CLASSIFIED RATES
For complete data refer to classified rate section.

18. CIRCULATION
Established 1881, per copy .15.

Net Paid—A.B.C. 9-30-77 (Newspaper Form)
	Total	CZ	TrZ	Other
Eve	190,303	148,280	38,836	3,187

Rate: Eve Max 6.97, Min 5.53.
For county-by-county and/or metropolitan area breakdowns, see SRDS Newspaper Circulation Analysis.
Submitted by Robert Huninghake.

The Standard Rate and Data Service listing for the *Cincinnati Post* is used by national advertisers to determine the cost of ads. (Courtesy Standard Rate and Data Service)

TABLE 6-2 Circulation and Rate Figures for the *Enquirer*

Edition	Total	CZ	TrZ	Other	Max	Mil
Morning	190,407	139,049	45,050	6,308	6.83	5.36
Sunday	291,012	215,502	67,174	8,336	6.01	4.98

Source: SRDS.

Magazines

In spite of competition from television, consumer magazines continue to do well in terms of advertising revenue. *Consumer magazines* are magazines with an editorial approach appealing to specific classes of consumers. In a very few instances, consumer magazines are edited to appeal to the broad general interests of consumers. An example of a consumer special-interest magazine is *Skin Diver Magazine*. *Reader's Digest* is an example of a general-interest magazine.

Almost 1,500 consumer magazines are published in the United States. The 373 magazines or groups of magazines that are members of the Magazine Publishers Association alone had a total circulation per issue of 263,948,552 copies at the end of 1977. *Business publications,* magazines directing their editorial content to specific business and industry groups, numbered about 4,000 and had ad revenues of $1.4 billion in 1978. And the 300 *farm magazines,* which cover every type of agricultural operation, generated advertising revenue of an additional $105 million.

Because most magazines have national distribution, local advertisers seldom use them. The goods and services advertised are mainly nationally distributed.

Selectivity, the Chief Value of Magazine Advertising

Newspapers, with their mass circulation, offer a cross section of the local consumer market, from low-income households to high; but the circulations in magazines, in contrast, are selective. The news weeklies, *Time, Newsweek,* and *U.S. News & World Report,* offer, in their circulations, readers with high incomes and also high educational levels, a form of selectivity. Circulation characteristics such as these are known as *demographic* or socioeconomic characteristics.

The days of the high-circulation general magazines such as *Collier's, Life, Look,* and the *Saturday Evening Post* are past. Competition from television and steadily increasing postal rates contributed to their failure, and media people do not foresee their return in their old form. The titles of some of these magazines are still seen on newsstands, however. The *Saturday Evening Post,* formerly a very popular weekly, is now published nine times a year. It appeals editorially to an older than average audience. In mid-1978, its paid circulation was just under 600,000. As a weekly, *Life* once had a circulation of 8.5 million per issue. It expired in December 1972 and was revived as a monthly in September 1978. The new *Life* has different aspirations from the old one. A circulation of 1 million is all that is planned, and editorially, *Life* understresses news and features photographic essays. In keeping with the trend, these revived magazines are now selective, rather than general, in their editorial approach to readers.

Special-Interest Consumer Magazines The factor of selectivity is especially apparent in special-interest magazines. There are consumer magazines for every type of individual, every taste, and every life style, and the titles reveal the audiences they cater to. Here are the names of some of the most popular magazines or "books," each of which indicates its selective audience: *National Geographic*, *Playboy*, *Better Homes and Gardens*, *Sports Illustrated*, *Parents' Magazine*, *Ebony*, *Woman's Day*, and *TV Guide*. The list is endless. Some of the less familiar special-interest consumer magazines are *American Square Dance*, *Archery World*, *Cats Magazine*, *Fate*, *Firehouse*, *Popular Hot Rodding*, *Sky and Telescope*, *Stereo Review*, *Trailer Life*, *Van World*, *Weight Watchers*, and *Woodall's Retirement and Resort Communities*.

More than 200 new consumer magazines were introduced between January 1976 and January 1978. All were highly selective and reflect the changing special interest and special life styles of today. Among them were four magazines for singles, two devoted to soccer, and three magazines directed to the television soap opera audience and containing summaries of plots and daily story lines in case the episode was missed.[4] Obviously, there are available ready-made, highly selective magazine audiences for the ads of every type of manufacturer and service company.

Flexibility of Consumer Magazines While they have not yet attained the market flexibility of newspapers, magazines have made progress in this area, too. In the case of large-circulation magazines, it is no longer necessary for a manufacturer to advertise on a national basis. There is a wide choice of geographic or demographic editions to choose from. The regional distributor, or the manufacturer who wishes to bolster sales in certain important areas, can buy magazine circulation

[4] *Media Decisions*, December 1977, p. 64.

THE SATURDAY EVENING POST
welcomes back
LIFE and LOOK

Come on in—the water's fine!

The *Post* has had an exciting circulation growth in the past year.

In 1977, *Post* guaranteed 450,000 paid circulation. For the six months ending December 31, 1977, we averaged 467,000 paid—a 17,000 copy bonus per issue for our advertisers.

In 1978, *Post* guaranteed 475,000 paid circulation. For the six months ending June 30, 1978, we averaged 560,000 paid—an 85,000 copy bonus per issue.

At 6.1 adult readers per copy, (per T.G.I.) *Post* delivered a bonus to our advertisers in the year ending June 30, 1978 of 2,074,000 adult readers.

More exciting is the fact that the growth continues! The July/August 1978 issue will have a paid circulation in excess of 590,000.

For 1979, the *Post* will guarantee 600,000 paid circulation—a 26% increase over our 1978 guarantee . . . and we'll probably deliver a bonus to boot!

But paid circulation isn't the whole story. At 6.1 adult readers per copy, a minimum of 3,600,000 people will read every issue of the *Post* in 1979.

THE SATURDAY EVENING POST

. . . healthy growth,
enthusiastic, loyal readership,
discriminating advertisers. . . .

But, whether you are an advertiser or a competitor, get in the swim with us. Our success can be your success. Our growth proves the nation loves a family magazine!

1100 Waterway Blvd., Indianapolis, In. 46202 (317) 634-1100

The Saturday Evening Post, revived as a monthly, addressed this ad to media people to promote its circulation figures. Note the last paragraph of body copy. Here the *Post* is stressing its total "pass along" audience of readers, rather than its circulation figures of those who actually buy copies of the magazine. (Courtesy *The Saturday Evening Post*)

in selected areas. In its 1978 advertising rate data, *Reader's Digest* offered 17 separate regional and major markets. For example, the advertiser can restrict ads to circulation confined to the North Central or Pacific states, or to the Pittsburgh area.

Thus *Reader's Digest* can be used as a regional advertising medium and in some cases as a local advertising medium. Advertisers, however, pay a premium over national rate structures for using these regional or metropolitan parts of the magazines circulation. For example, in 1978, one black-and-white page in the national *Reader's Digest* edition, with a circulation of 18 million, cost $57,920. For the same space in the metropolitan New York edition with a circulation rate base of 1 million, the advertiser was charged $6,990.

Large-circulation magazines offer both geographic editions and demographic editions, with circulations among the different kinds of readers that make up their audiences. *Time* offers an elaborate and extensive variety of geographic editions (regional, large metropolitan, and spot-market editions for smaller cities such as Bryan, Texas, and Cumberland, Maryland). The magazine also has available "vertical," or demographic, slices of its readers. There is a college edition, with student circulation exclusively, a doctor's edition, and *Time B,* with circulation among subscribers who are primarily business executives.

Suburban areas, large cities, or even parts of large cities now have magazines which cater editorially to their local audiences. These are classified as *metropolitan magazines. Westchester Magazine* covers this suburban county adjoining the New York metropolitan area. *Chicago* and *Los Angeles Magazine* editorially appeal to local audiences. And within New York City, for example, *Avenue* is written to upper-income New Yorkers with its content devoted to business, investments, the arts, food and fashions. These metropolitan magazines are mainly used by local advertisers but include a few national advertisers as well.

Selectivity in Business Magazines Selectivity is a particular characteristic of the business-publication field. Business magazines, often referred to as trade journals, plan their editorial content to appeal to specialized parts of the business world and thus offer a selective market to advertisers who need to reach their prospects without wasting circulation. For example, perhaps a manufacturer of bedroom and living room furniture wishes to advertise to department store buyers and owners of home furnishing stores. To reach these people, several business publications are available, such as *Professional Furniture Merchant, HFD,* or *The Market Place.* Their editorial content attracts the buying audience the manufacturer needs. This same manufacturer needs equipment and supplies to produce furniture. There are trade papers that are written for the furniture manufacturer, too. Examples are *Furniture Design & Manufacturing* and *Furniture Production,* which keep the furniture maker posted on new manufacturing trends and methods and offer an ideal location for suppliers' ads.

There are classification groupings of business publications in SRDS listings, from advertising and marketing to woodworking. The medical and surgery grouping contains almost 300 publications. In contrast, those in the nut culture, nut, and popcorn trade have only one publication catering to their business needs, the *Peanut Journal and Nut World.* Newly listed publications appear in SRDS at an average rate of fifteen per month, and of course delistings occur as some publications fall by the wayside.

Included in the business publication category are the general business magazines, which are written for a nationwide audience of managerial and executive people. Magazines like *Fortune* and *Business Week* are in this group.

Selectivity in Farm Magazines Farm magazines are selective in a different way. While there are a few national farm magazines that speak to the farming community as a whole, such as *Farm Journal* and *Successful Farming,* the bulk of the farm publications are editorially oriented to particular geographic or vocational groups. The *Nebraska Farmer,* dedicated to Nebraskan agriculture, is an example of a geographic publication, while *Cotton Farming,* directed to commercial cotton growers across the United States cotton belt, is an example of a vocational one. Some magazines are both geographic and vocational in nature. *Western Livestock Journal* is an example.

Other Values of Magazine Advertising

Magazines offer generally excellent reproduction facilities for advertisements. The paper stock is of finer quality than newspaper stock and permits clear, crisp, black-and-white reproduction and excellent color reproduction, much prized by food and fashion advertisers.

Magazine advertisements have a longer life than newspaper advertisements because a magazine issue is often kept in a household until the next one arrives. The members of the family may look through it more than once during this period, so the advertisement has more than one chance of being seen.

Many magazines can also carry pop-up elements, separate coupons bound into the book adjoining an ad. They flag the reader's attention more than a coupon included as part of the ad would.

Buying Advertising Space in Magazines

The basic sources for magazine rates and data are two monthly publications of the Standard Rate and Data Service: *Business Publications* and *Consumer Magazines and Farm Publications.* The SRDS listing for *House Beautiful,* a women's service magazine; *Professional Furni-*

ture Merchant, a trade journal; and the *Oklahoma Cowman,* a regional, vocational farm magazine are shown in this chapter. It is important for the buyer of advertising space and the student of advertising to understand the contents of these listings.

Editorial Profile At the beginning of each listing is the publisher's *editorial profile,* a brief description of the editorial policy of the magazine that tells the prospective buyer of advertising space the kinds of readers reached and the types of articles that will attract these readers. When two or more magazines appealing to the same general type of audience are available, the advertiser should compare the profiles as well as the rate structures, circulations, and special services of the competing magazines to see which offers the best opportunity for the advertising campaign.

Rates Items 4 to 10 of the illustrations of SRDS listings give the buyer basic rate information for a magazine. Suppose that a furniture maker wishes to run six ads in *House Beautiful.* The ads are one-page size, four-color (meaning reproduced in the full color range), and bleed. (*Bleed* means that the ad will extend to the edge of the page rather than be surrounded by a margin of white space.) Item 6 tells the buyer that the basic cost of a one-page four-color ad will be $13,300. But ordinary bleed will cost the advertiser 15 percent more (item 9), or an additional $1,995 per ad. Six insertions will come to $91,770. When an advertiser runs six color pages, a volume discount of 5 percent is given. Volume discounts are found under item 5. Even though the heading of item 5 reads "black/white rates," the volume discounts listed there also apply to color rates. The cost of the six bleed color ads now becomes $87,181.50. If the bill is paid by the thirtieth of the month preceding the date of the

House Beautiful

A Hearst Publication

Media Code 8 403 1900 8.00
Published monthly by Hearst Corporation, 717 Fifth Ave., New York, N. Y. 10022. Phone 212-935-5900.

PUBLISHER'S EDITORIAL PROFILE

HOUSE BEAUTIFUL is a class-oriented home magazine designed for families interested in their homes and home furnishings. Architectural and decorating articles range from advance design concepts to practical home planning and maintenance information. Articles report trends of lasting significance that will serve professionals as well as consumers. The editorial content's primarily devoted to home furnishings, management and building; secondly, as a guide to good living, it regularly includes articles on travel, gardening, entertainment, food, liquor, and music.

I. PERSONNEL

Publisher—Thomas P. Losee, Jr.
Editor—Doris Shaw.
Advertising Director—David J. Moore.
Prod. Mgr.—Joseph A. Enterlin (212-935-8577).

2. REPRESENTATIVES and/or BRANCH OFFICES

Chicago 60606—Tom H. Welch, 1 N. Wacker Dr. Phone 312-372-0640.
Charlotte, N. C. 28204—Donald Rose, 1 Charlotte-town Center Bldg. Phone 704-376-2704.
Los Angeles, San Francisco — Perkins, Stephens, Von der Lieth & Hayward, Inc.
South Weymouth, Mass.—Thomas L. Masson Co.

3. COMMISSION AND CASH DISCOUNT

15% to agencies; 2% of net billed 20th of month preceding date of issue and discounted 30th of month preceding date of issue. New advertisers may either remit with order or furnish satisfactory references. Payment in U. S. currency required.

4. GENERAL RATE POLICY

Orders beyond 2 months at rates then prevailing. As part of the consideration and to induce House Beautiful to accept and publish the advertising for the advertiser, the advertiser's agency, if there be one, and the advertiser each agrees to indemnify The Hearst Corporation against all loss, liability, damage and expense of whatsoever nature arising out of copying, printing or publishing the advertising. Rates, conditions and space units subject to change without notice.

ADVERTISING RATES

Rates effective January, 1978 issue.
Rates approved August 25, 1977.

5. BLACK/WHITE RATES

1 page	9,080.	1/3 page..................3,085.
2/3 page	6,100.	1/6 page..................1,590.
1/2 page	4,900.	Agate line..................25.

FREQUENCY DISCOUNT

Apply to national advertising only, within a 12 month period.

6 issues	5%
9 issues	10%
12 issues	15%

Minimum 1/4 page.

VOLUME DISCOUNT

For advertisers not using frequency discounts:
Rates:

6 pages	5%	18 pages	17.5%
9 pages	10%	24 pages	20%
12 pages	15%	36 pages	25%

Issues must be used within 12 month period. Discounts apply to national advertising only.

6. COLOR RATES

	b/1 c	4 color
1 page	11,650.	13,300.
2/3 page	8,150.	9,565.
1/2 page	6,665.	8,955.
1/3 page	4,190.	6,570.

7. COVERS

2nd cover (4 color)	14,350.
3rd cover (4 color)	13,585.
4th cover (4 color)	16,210.

8. INSERTS

8 page 4-color Spectacular rate available—see Good Housekeeping listing in Classification No. 49.

9. BLEED

Extra..15%

10. SPECIAL POSITION

Special position other than covers not sold. Orders specifying positions other than covers not accepted.

II. CLASSIFIED AND READING NOTICES

DISPLAY CLASSIFICATIONS

WINDOW SHOPPING

	b/w	b/1 c	4 color
1 page	7,870.	10,860.	12,020.
1/2 page	3,955.	5,960.	8,700.
1/4 page	1,985.	3,570.	——
1/6 page	1,320.	——	——
1/12 page	665.	——	——

WINDOW SHOPPING DISCOUNTS

4 consecutive issues, earn	5%
8 consecutive issues, earn	10%
12 consecutive issues, earn	15%

Discounts apply only to consecutive advertisers, regardless of space size and units used, with the exception of card or booklet inserts. Ads of divisions of parent companies will earn maximum discounts provided the parent company shows satisfactory proof (incorporation papers, or financial statement) that the advertising subsidiary is a division of the parent company, or the divisions of parent company states in its ad that it is a division of the parent company

VOLUME DISCOUNTS

For advertisers not using consecutive insertions:

8 pages	20%	12 pages	25%

Volume discount advertisers may mix their schedules with any size or coloration space and need not appear in consecutive issues.
References to dealers or distributors, or soliciting agents or dealers, not permitted and requires use of general rate section in standard sizes and at general rates. All advertisers excepting those selling personalized merchandise agree to refund full price of merchandise should reader return it dissatisfied. All advertisers agree that, if shipment of merchandise ordered is not made within two weeks, the purchaser, be notified of the delay with the right to have money refunded if delivery date given is not satisfactory to purchaser. To avoid shopping trips by readers, it is requested, but not obligatory, that advertisers other than retail stores include in their copy "sold by mail order only."
No merchandising nor promotion of any type to trade distribution by Window Shopping advertisers is allowed. House Beautiful reserves right to reject at any time the copy of advertisers who merchandise Window Shopping advertising as this type of activity is confined to advertisers using general rate section. A legitimate retail store or mail order advertiser may list up to five different addresses. Manufacturers, wholesalers, growers are restricted to one address. Depilatory ads, objectionable patent medicines and personal ads not accepted.
If incorrect rate is specified on order it is understood that advertiser will be billed at correct card rate. On units larger than 1/4 page of acceptable advertising for the Window Shopping Section it is understood that due to mechanical difficulties position in this section cannot always be guaranteed. All Window Shopping advertisers and/or their advertising agencies must furnish finished copy, layout and cuts. Duplicate plate material is required for ads to be repeated in successive issues. Such statements and copy as "Sold direct from factory," "50% savings-buy direct from factory," or other words with the same meaning are not eligible for Window Shopping ads. Any retail store or mail order advertiser mentioning a trade-mark, brand or identifying name in heading or subcaption of ad will be charged the general rates where or when a manufacturer is contributing in any way whatsoever to part of the cost of such an ad. The Window Shopping Section is for retail mail order advertising only. The closing date for the Window Shopping advertising section is 1st of 2nd month preceding date of issue.

Dimensions for Window Shopping Ads:

1	7-3/8 x 10-3/16	1/6	1-3/4 x 6-3/4
1/2	7-3/8 x 10-3/16	1/6	3-5/8 x 3-5/16
1/2	7-3/8 x 5-1/16	1/12	1-3/4 x 3-5/16
1/4	1-3/4 x 10-3/16	1/12	3-5/8 x 1-5/8
1/4	3-5/8 x 5-1/16		

*RETAIL, HOTEL, TRAVEL AND NURSERY RATES

(Position outside of the Window Shopping Section)

	b/w	b/1 c	4 color
1 page	7,870.	10,860.	12,020.
2/3 page	5,295.	7,600.	9,135.
1/2 page	4,250.	6,210.	8,700.
1/3 page	2,650.	3,910.	5,726.
1/6 page	1,336.	——	——
Agate line	20.		

(*) Including seeds, bulbs or nursery stock sold direct or by mail order only.

Restricted to retail stores whose business is derived mainly from retail over-the-counter sales, not wholesale or mail order. Order must be placed by store or its advertising agency. Ads must be prominently signed by store or use accepted store logotypes. Use of brand names and trade marks permitted. A retailer may list up to five addresses of the same name in a single ad, but not stores of different names even though wholly owned and operated. Retail rates do not apply to national chain store operations.
All advertisers, excepting those selling personalized merchandise, agree to refund full price of merchandise should reader return it dissatisfied.

magazine's issue (see item 3), the advertiser will be entitled to an additional 2 percent cash discount.

If the prospective advertiser wishes to run a series of ads to the retail trade in *Professional Furniture Merchant,* rates will be found in SRDS's *Business Publications.* Six ads are wanted, each one to appear on the second cover (or the page that is on the reverse of the magazine cover) in four-color process and bleed. The six-time rate is used (item 7) and this second cover position rate, when purchased, includes four-color process and bleed. The charge for each insertion is $1,842, and for six ads, the cost to the manufacturer will be $11,052. There is also a 2 percent cash discount available if the bill is paid within 10 days of date of invoice (item 3).

There are no separate local advertising rate cards for magazines as there are for newspapers because local and retail advertising is not an important factor in the magazine field. The so-called *shelter books* such as *Woman's Day,* have advertising sections that are retail in scope. These sections are filled with mail-order ads for gifts, clothing, and housewares. The advertiser may be wholly in the mail-order business or may operate a retail store with a mail-order sideline. The Window Shopping feature of *House Beautiful* (item 11) is an example of this type of advertising section. It has a separate and lower rate structure and is restricted to businesses whose sales volume is based mainly on retail or mail-order sales.

Items 15 and 16 in the figures of SRDS listings tell the advertiser mechanical requirements that the ad must meet and dates when ad plates or offset mechanicals must arrive at the magazine. Circulation data (item 18) contain information very important to the advertiser. They indicate how much circulation is by subscription and how much by single-copy sales. Advertisers look for a high proportion of subscription circulation as an indication of reader loyalty and stability. When someone subscribes to a magazine, the advertiser running a series of ads has the opportunity of reaching that person more than once.

Note under item 18, *Professional Furniture Merchant* listing, the initials "B.P.A." They stand for Business Publications Audit of Circulation, a service similar to the Audit Bureau of Circulation. This service verifies circulation claims of member magazines in the trade journal field. If a trade journal is not a member, circulation figures are often listed as "sworn," or supported by a publisher's sworn statement that the circulation is as stated. The *Oklahoma Cowman* listing has such a sworn circulation statement.

Cost-per-Thousand Analysis Magazine circulations are not judged by the maximil-minimil method used by newspapers, described earlier in this chapter, but by the *cost-per-thousand* method, which is established by dividing the black-and-white one-page rate by the number of thousands of circulation. Thus, in the case of *House Beautiful,* with a black-and-white one-page rate of $9,080 and a paid circulation of 800,000, as noted in the publisher's statement at the end of the SRDS listing, one should divide $9,080 by 800 (the number of thousands of circulation) to get a cost per thousand of $11.35.

Total Audience Analysis Another method of judging circulation is by the magazine's total audience. The theory is that a single copy is not merely read by the subscriber or newsstand buyer. The copy is passed along to others in the household or to someone outside the household. The total audience figure is not

Professional Furniture Merchant

A Gralla Publication
See Advertisement on Fourth Cover

Media Code 7 315 5300 4.00
Published monthly by Gralla Publications, 1515 Broadway, New York, N. Y. 10036. Phone 212-869-1300.
For shipping info., see Print Media Production Data.

PUBLISHER'S EDITORIAL STATEMENT
PROFESSIONAL FURNITURE MERCHANT is editorially directed to the business management, operation and profit goals of retail furniture stores and departments. About 80% is devoted to in-depth study of business topics such as recruitment, compensation and management of salesmen; store location and layout; control and reduction of operating cost; effective merchandising, promotion and selling procedures; product and market trends; legal, tax and accounting methods, store hours; expansion; etc. About 15% of space is devoted to new products and product trends, with the remaining 5% containing condensed analyses of news and markets. Rec'd 10/17/77.

1. PERSONNEL
Editor/Assoc. Pub.—Marcie Lynn Avram.
Ad Sales Manager—John Blysick.
Production Manager—Susan Benvenuto.

2. REPRESENTATIVES and/or BRANCH OFFICES
New York 10036—John Blysick, Jim Bodino, Gralla Publications, 1515 Broadway. Phone 212-869-1300.
Chicago 60659—Gralla Publications, 3601 W. Devon Ave. Phone 312-588-7622.
High Point, N. C. 27260—John C. Jackson Jr., Gralla Publications, 3639 Malibu Dr. Phone 919-869-3938.
Encino, Calif. 91436—Neil Silverstein, Gralla Publications, 16200 Ventura Blvd. Phone 213-788-0271.
England—Jon Rose, All American Media, 54 Burton Ct., Franklin's Row, London SW3 SWY4.

3. COMMISSION AND CASH DISCOUNT
15% to agencies on space, color, bleed and special position if paid within 30 days of invoice date. Other charges not commissionable. 2% 10 days from invoice date; net 30 days.

4. GENERAL RATE POLICY
All billing subject to short-rate or rebate to earned rates, depending on frequency actually used during 12-month period. Advertisers will be protected for duration of contracts which are in effect at time rate changes are announced.

ADVERTISING RATES
Effective June 1, 1977. (Card No. 8.)
Rates received April 8, 1977.
Card received May 23, 1977.

5. BLACK/WHITE RATES

	1 ti	6 ti	12 ti
1 page	1150.	1050.	990.
2/3 page	950.	875.	830.
1/2 page (island)	770.	725.	680.
1/2 page	720.	675.	630.
1/3 page	520.	485.	450.
1/4 page	410.	385.	360.

6. COLOR RATES

Standard AAAA red, orange, yellow, green, blue, per page, extra	245.
2-page spread, extra	395.
Matched color, per page, extra	325.
2-page spread, extra	495.
4-color process, per page, extra	625.
2-page spread, extra	975.

7. COVERS

	6 ti	12 ti
2nd cover	1842.	1742.
3rd cover	1712.	1612.
4th cover	1942.	1842.

Rates include 4-color process and bleed at no additional charge.
Cover frequency rates apply only to cover contracts. An advertiser running 6 covers and 6 pages inside the magazine will be billed at the 6-time rate for covers and at the 12-time rate for inside pages.

8. INSERTS
Furnished inserts, earned black and white rates apply. Mechanical charges, non-commissionable, apply if printed one side.
Special insert discounts apply on inserts of 4 pages and larger.

1 page, reverse side blank, mechanical charge	245.
2 page spread, reverse side blank, mechanical charge	295.
2 pages, single sheet printed 2 sides, mechanical charge	125.

Special discounts for furnished inserts, 4 pages or more:

4 or 6 pages, per page, earned rate less	10%
8 or 12 pages, per page, earned rate less	15%
16 or more pages, per page, earned rate less	20%

Each page of an insert counts as 1 insertion toward earning the frequency rates of an advertiser's annual program. Hence, a 6 or 8 page insert automatically earns the 6-time rate. A 4-page insert, combined with 8 additional pages during the year, will earn the 12-time rate for all space in the program.

9. BLEED

Extra on space and color	10%
2-page spreads that bleed into gutter only, extra on space and color	5%

10. SPECIAL POSITION

Extra on space and color	10%

11. CLASSIFIED AND READING NOTICES
Per column inch, non-commissionable ... 24.
Add 5.00 if box number is used.

14. CONTRACT AND COPY REGULATIONS
See Contents page for location—items 1, 2, 4, 5, 12, 15, 17, 19, 24.

15. MECH. REQUIREMENTS (Web offset)
For complete, detailed production information, see SRDS Print Media Production Data.
Trim size: 8-1/2 x 11-1/4; No./Cols. 2&3.
Binding method: Side-stitched; Special issues Perfect.
Colors available: Publisher's Choice, AAAA/ABP; Matched.

DIMENSIONS—AD PAGE

1	7	x 10	1/2	4-9/16 x 7-3/8
2/3	4-9/16	x 10	1/3	2-3/16 x 10
1/2	3-3/8	x 10	1/4	3-3/8 x 4-7/8
1/2	7	x 4-7/8		

16. ISSUE AND CLOSING DATES
Published monthly; issued 1st of each month.
Orders due 1st of preceding month; offset film 5th of preceding month; furnished inserts 10th of preceding month.

SPECIAL FEATURE ISSUES
Mar/78—The Bedroom
Apr/78—Southern Market Preview
May/78—Lifestyle
June/78—Summer Market Previews
July/78—Summer Market Previews
Aug/78—Recliners
Sept/78—Casual Furniture Market Preview
Oct/78—Southern Market Preview
Nov/78—Wall Systems
Dec/78—Carpets & Rugs

17. SPECIAL SERVICES
1978 Ad Readership Studies—March.

18. CIRCULATION
Established 1969. Single copy 2.00; per year 20.00.
Summary data—for detail see Publisher's Statement.

B.P.A. 6-30-77 (6 mos. aver. qualified)

Total	Non-Pd	Paid
20,078	20,078	

Average Non-Qualified (not included above):
Total 4,239

TERRITORIAL DISTRIBUTION 5/77—20,168

N.Eng.	Mid.Atl.	E.N.Cen.	W.N.Cen.	S.Atl.	E.S.Cen.
1,160	3,494	3,603	1,910	3,569	1,444
W.S.Cen.	Mtn.St.	Pac.St.	Canada	Foreign	Other
1,993	852	2,128			15

BUSINESS ANALYSIS OF CIRCULATION
TL Total.
1 —Retail furniture stores.
2 —Dept. stores.
3 —Warehouse showrooms.
4 —Discount chain & chain stores; owners of leased furniture depts. & resident buyers.
5 —Furniture wholesalers & distributors.
6 —Independent & manufacturers's sales reps.

TL	1	2	3	4	5	6
20168	16359	1098	810	800	355	746

Submitted by Arlene Cohen.

listed in SRDS; it is supplied by the magazine. This figure is then substituted for paid circulation in the formula described above. Some advertisers prefer a cost per thousand figure of this nature. However, there is controversy on the subject of whether pass-along readership has the same value to the advertiser as readership by a magazine subscriber or newsstand purchaser.

These methods are important in judging magazines in the same category but are not the only criteria for choosing a magazine as an advertising vehicle. They may have no bearing on the quality, or lack of it, of a particular magazine's circulation.

Limitations of Magazine Advertising

Magazines lack the flexibility and immediacy of newspapers in spite of availability of geographic and demographic editions and in spite of the "fast close" national editions such as *U.S. News & World Report* offers, where black-and-white ads can be received 14 days before issue date. Also, the cost of advertising in magazines is generally higher than in newspapers, on a per-thousand circulation basis.

These limitations must be weighed against the advantages that magazines offer: selectivity, long life span, and excellent reproduction.

OKLAHOMA COWMAN, THE

Media Code 8 917 3380 0.00
Published monthly by the Oklahoma Cattleman's Assoc., 2500 Exchange Ave., Oklahoma City, Okla. 73108. Phone 405-235-4391.

PUBLISHER'S EDITORIAL PROFILE
OKLAHOMA COWMAN is directed to members of the OCA, who are actively identified with beef cattle production. It is also edited for cattlemen throughout seven (7) Southwestern states, schools of agriculture and other beef promotion bodies. Featured articles deal with beef production methods, cattle industry legislation, personalities of the beef industry in Oklahoma and surrounding states, cattle theft prevention, brand registration, etc. Regular monthly departments report on more specific interests with OCA, i.e.: scientific research, new medical techniques, live animal evaluation, recent equipment developments and activities of surrounding state associations. Approximately 65% editorial matter is devoted to features of general interest for beef raisers, the remainder to news of departments as above mentioned.

1. PERSONNEL
Executive Vice President—Ellis Freeny.
Advertising Manager—Nancy Bryan.

3. COMMISSION AND CASH DISCOUNT
15% to agencies; 2% cash discount 15 days.
ADVERTISING RATES
Rates effective January 1, 1974. (Card No. 4.)
Card received October 26, 1973.

5. BLACK/WHITE RATES

1 page	220.00
2/3 page	160.00
1/2 page	120.00
1/3 page	80.00
1/4 page	65.00
1/6 page	42.00
1/8 page	34.00
1 column inch	3.50

6. COLOR RATES
Standard colors red, orange, yellow, blue and green; per page, per color, extra......... 65.00
Metallic colors copper, gold, silver and bronze, per page, extra......... 9.00
4 color process......... 380.00

7. COVERS
Gloss enamel stock.
2nd or 3rd cover......... 250.00
4th cover......... 275.00

8. INSERTS
Available.

9. BLEED
Extra......... 5.00

15. MECH. REQUIREMENTS (Offset, sheet fed)
For complete, detailed production information see SRDS Print Media Production Data.
Trim size: 8-3/8 x 10-7/8; No./Cols. 2&3.
Binding method: Saddle-stitched.
Colors available: Publisher's Choice, Publisher's Standard, Matched, 4 color process (AAAA/MPA), Metallic.

DIMENSIONS—AD PAGE			
1	7-1/4 x 10	1/3	7-1/4 x 3-1/3
2/3	4-3/4 x 10	1/4	7-1/4 x 2-1/2
2/3	7-1/4 x 6-2/3	1/4	4-3/4 x 3-3/4
1/2	7-1/4 x 5	1/6	7-1/2 x 1-2/3
1/2	4-3/4 x 7-1/2	1/6	2-1/4 x 5
1/3	4-3/4 x 5	1/8	2-1/4 x 3-3/4
1/3	2-1/4 x 10	1/8	4-3/4 x 1-7/8

16. ISSUE AND CLOSING DATES
Published monthly; issued 1st of each month. Closing date for plated ads 15th of month preceding publication date. Closing date for copy 12th of month preceding publication date.

18. CIRCULATION
Established 1961. Per year 2.00.
SWORN 12-31-77 (6 mos. aver.)

	Total	Non-Pd	Paid	(Subs)	(Single)	[Assoc]
Total	5,296	533	4,763	4,763		4,545

Unpaid Distribution incl. Bulk (not included above):
Total 160

TERRITORIAL DISTRIBUTION 12/77—5,296

N.Eng.	Mid.Atl.	E.N.Cen.	W.N.Cen.	S.Atl.	E.S.Cen.
1	6	13	137	20	5

W.S.Cen.	Mtn.St.	Pac.St.	Canada	Foreign	Other
5,069	30	14	1	....	....

Submitted by Nancy Bryan.

This listing for a regional and vocational farm magazine is found in the farm magazine section of the SRDS *Consumer Magazine and Farm Publication Rates and Data,* published monthly. (Courtesy Standard Rate and Data Service)

Vocabulary

Define the following terms and use each one in a sentence.

Agate line
Bleed
Business publication
B/w
Closing time
Consumer magazine
Cost per thousand
Demographic
Editorial profile

Farm magazine
Full position
Maximil rate
Metropolitan
   magazines
Minimil rate
Newspaper
   representative
Open rate

NR position
Rate card
ROP position
Shelter book
Special-interest
   newspapers

Review Questions

1. What are the three major classifications of print media? What are the supplementary print media?
2. Discuss the advantages that newspapers offer to local advertisers.
3. Why would a national advertiser use the newspaper medium?
4. What are the limitations of newspaper advertising?
5. A local advertiser uses 75,000 lines on a contract basis in the *Cincinnati Post* in a year, taking a 2 percent cash discount. How much does the advertising cost for the year? (Use *Post* rate card shown in this chapter.)
6. Discuss the values to a manufacturer of a nationally distributed brand of canned ham of advertising in a women's service magazine. What advantages do magazines offer that are not offered by newspapers?
7. What two causes were responsible for the failure of several high-circulation general magazines?
8. A cattle feed marketer runs twelve ads in the *Oklahoma Cowman*, each being one-half page, black and white. The 2 percent cash discount will be taken. What do the twelve ads cost? (See SRDS listing shown in this chapter.)
9. Discuss the limitations of magazine advertising.
10. If the black-and-white page rate of a magazine is $10,000 and its circulation is 1.5 million, what is the cost-per-thousand circulation rate? (See page 143 for method.)

Activities

1. Select a magazine with which you are familiar. From an examination of its editorial and advertising pages, try to determine the types of consumers the magazine's contents are prepared for, and write out a short profile of the consumer group or groups the contents are selecting. List some of the advertisers of goods and services that are attempting to reach this selective audience through the pages of the magazine. Also list brand names or services not appearing on the advertising pages of this issue that might profitably be advertised to the readership.

2. Your local paper carries local advertising and national advertising. From a current issue, make a list of some of the national advertisers. Do you remember noticing their ads in other media such as magazines, outdoor advertising, radio, and television? If so, note in what media. Give an opinion on whether newspaper advertising should or should not be the main advertising medium of such national advertisers.

Project

One student should obtain a copy of a local newspaper's retail advertising rate card from the paper's advertising department. With this resource available, individual students should contact important local advertisers (one per student) and attempt to determine space size and frequency of annual advertising on an estimated basis. Using these figures and the rate card, it will be possible to determine with fair accuracy the annual newspaper advertising expenditures of these advertisers. The following local businesses should be covered:

Banks	Department stores	Movie theaters
Car dealers	Furniture stores	Real estate firms
Clothing stores	Home appliance dealers	Supermarkets

Career Ladder

You are the media department buyer in an advertising agency, and a friend of yours has asked you for some advice concerning employment. Your friend is a space representative on an urban evening newspaper and knows of a job opening on a new and successful metropolitan magazine in the same city. The salary for both jobs is about the same. Should you advise your friend to try for the magazine job? How would you assess for your friend the future growth prospects of an evening newspaper? What factors would you point out that can affect its circulation growth?

CHAPTER SEVEN

PRINT MEDIA (CONTINUED)

The printed word and the printed illustration are used to convey advertising messages through other media besides newspapers and magazines. Another major medium is direct mail advertising. Other print advertising media receiving smaller annual advertising expenditures are outdoor, transit, point-of-sale (or point-of-purchase), specialty, and directory advertising. These print advertising media are discussed in detail in this chapter.

Direct Mail

Advertising sent directly to prospective customers through the mail is called *direct mail advertising.* This medium is used by every type of advertiser. It is estimated that over 300,000 businesses in the United States use direct mail advertising. According to the Direct Mail Advertising Association, direct mail sells almost $80 billion in goods and services annually for local and national direct mail advertisers.

Local Users of Direct Mail

The local merchant makes frequent use of direct mail. When a bank sends out monthly statements to its customers, it may include a pamphlet promoting its travel bureau department or its safe-deposit facilities. The hardware store owner, when mailing bills, may include advertising material on merchandise that is carried. Department stores invariably include direct mail pieces with their bills; these ads feature merchandise and carry a coupon so that the items described can be ordered by mail. A local merchant may write letters to customers informing them of a special sale restricted to charge-account holders or describe a special department that has just been opened.

National Users of Direct Mail

Most manufacturers and service companies selling nationally often use direct mail. The copywriters and layout people in the advertising department prepare the material as part of their responsibilities, or a direct mail concern may be hired to handle such arrangements.

Here are several ways that a manufacturer of toys and games, for example, can use this medium. The manufacturer wants to tell wholesalers and retailers of new additions to the product line for Christmas selling. The maker's salespeople will be giving out this information on their calls, and trade advertising will be used to announce the new toys and games in a series of ads. But the manufacturer decides that these efforts are insufficient, and a short-term direct mail campaign is launched to introduce the products to the retail trade. This campaign supports the sales force and supplements the trade-paper advertising. The manufacturer also orders the company ad director to have a four-color illustrated pamphlet prepared; this pamphlet is directed at consumers and is prepared in an appropriate size for mailing out with the bills of retail stores. Through the manufacturer's sales force, the manufacturer supplies the pamphlets to stores for inclusion in November and December bill mailings. One of the new toys is an arithmetic game that teaches children the principles of addition and subtraction; it could be sold to educators for use in kindergarten and first grade. Since this game has sales potential outside the usual distribution area, the manufacturer orders another mailing that will be sent directly to educators. In all these activities, the manufacturer is applying direct mail advertising to many facets of business.

Sources of Mailing Lists

The most important prerequisite for direct mail advertising is a mailing list that delivers precisely the type of consumer who would be a logical prospect for the product or service offered and that eliminates those who would not. A homeowner would be a logical prospect for a roofing repair ad, and the holder of a season ticket to the opera would be a logical prospect for an announcement of a concert series, but a mailing promoting stamps is of no value to a person who does not collect stamps, and a life insurance offer receives no attention from people on social security.

A local merchant already has the addresses of charge customers, and can expand this mailing list by trading it for the lists of other merchants who are not competitors and whose trade appeals to the same class of customers. The local merchant's other sources include membership lists of local clubs and associations, phone and town directories, local magazine and newspaper circulation lists, and the like. Manufacturers and large service suppliers rely on mailing-list firms, which sell the use of their lists. These lists contain names and addresses of consumers in every conceivable grouping. SRDS semiannually publishes Direct Mail List Rates and Data. Here is a list of just a few of the larger groupings:

Accountants	Chemical engineers
Administrators, college	College students
Advertising agencies	Community-college students
Alumni, college	Contributors
Antique-car owners	Corporations
Associations	Credit-card holders
Attorneys	Divorced people
Bankers	Doctors
Black college students	Dog owners
Bowling-alley owners	Engineers
Car owners	Fire chiefs
Chamber of Commerce members	Gasoline stations
	Golfers
	Homeowners

Junior-college students

Manufacturers

Minority groups

Music lovers

Pop art buyers

Real estate brokers

Stock brokers

Tennis players

Vacationers

Women executives

People with very specialized interests, life styles, and employment can readily be reached by direct mail as well. Some of the more esoteric lists, for example, supply names and addresses of people interested in astrology or horoscopes, karate coaches, and members of the fan club for *Six Million Dollar Man*. There is even a list consisting of firms which sell mailing lists.

Lists must be constantly checked and revised to avoid duplication and because people move and change their occupations and marital status.

Factors to Consider Before Using Direct Mail

An important factor to consider before deciding to use direct mail is cost. Because this medium is so selective and carefully controlled, and because it contains the minimum amount of waste circulation, it is expensive in comparison with other forms of advertising. If a local merchant uses a list of charge customers already at hand and prepares a simple postcard announcing a special sale, it can be produced and mailed first class to 500 customers for a total cost of about $80. But a 100-line ad in the local newspaper, which has a retail line rate of 35 cents and a circulation of 10,000, would cost only $35.

Therefore, before a final decision is made, the advertiser should consider the advantages and disadvantages of direct mail listed here as they apply to the business requirements involved in the particular situation.

■ It can be directed, with a high degree of accuracy and control, toward specific target audiences.

■ Unlike the messages in other media, the advertising message can be personalized or addressed to a specific individual.

■ The message is not restricted by space limitations, as are ads in other print and broadcast media; any size or form of advertising message, from a simple postcard to a catalog, can be delivered to a prospect by mail.

■ Timing of advertising is completely under the control of the advertiser, and the time when the advertising is to be received can be pinpointed.

■ The sales results of direct mail advertising can be more precisely measured than is possible in other media.

■ Direct mail "asks for the order;" that is, it requests some type of consumer action and invites the reader to respond through return postcards or other devices not generally available when other media are used.

■ Cost is the major drawback of direct mail advertising, a drawback that for some advertisers may be outweighed by the special advantage of personally and directly addressing customers.

■ Direct mail advertising lacks the support of editorial surroundings that publications offer.

■ It does not have the prestige of a magazine or newspaper backing up the advertising message.

Outdoor Media

Outdoor signs are used widely by both local and national advertisers. (See Color Plate 9.) These signs can be nonstandardized (built in any size or shape that suits the merchant's fancy). Standardized signs are uniform types of signs that can be rented to display an advertising message. The term *outdoor advertising,* adopted for such standardized signs, should be used with caution because it can lead to confusion when all the outdoor media are under consideration. These two areas of outdoor media, nonstandardized and standardized signs, are discussed below.

Nonstandardized Signs

Nonstandardized signs are used by local merchants as identification advertising at their places of business or are placed along the roadside or throughout the neighborhood to attract customers. If the merchant runs an independent company, these signs can be made up at the local sign shop. If the business is a chain store, franchise establishment, or service station, the parent organization supplies the sign. When the sign appears elsewhere than on the merchant's own premises, the merchant must rent the space used from the owner of the property.

Outdoor Advertising (Standardized Signs)

A standardized sign available to advertisers nationally, regionally, or locally is the outdoor poster. According to the Institute of Outdoor Advertising, the trade organization of this advertising medium, there are about 270,000 structures, or frames, for outdoor posters available in 9,000 communities in the United States. The number of structures has declined from the 300,000 available in 1970, not because the medium is considered less attractive to advertisers but because the outdoor industry has eliminated many billboards on lightly traveled roads. More than 95 percent of all outdoor standardized signs are now situated in areas zoned for commerce and industry, where traffic is heavy and exposure greater. According to traffic counts by government and private agencies, 10 to 20 percent of highways carry up to 90 percent of the traffic. In 1978, advertisers spent $465 million on the standardized outdoor medium, 67 percent of which was national or regional advertising and 33 percent of which was local. The structures are owned and maintained by outdoor advertising companies, called plants, and are built on land either owned or leased by these companies. The plants sell the space on these structures to advertisers.

The standard poster panel frame can accommodate three sizes of advertisement: 24-sheet, 30-sheet, or bleed. As the figure on page 154 reveals, the 24-sheet size has a wider margin than the 30-sheet size; in the bleed size, the illustration extends to the edge of the panel frame. The names 24-sheet and 30-sheet are holdovers from an earlier day, when the posters were made up of 24 or 30 sections of paper pieced together. The panel frame always measures 12 feet 3 inches high by 24 feet 6 inches long.

Purchasing Outdoor   In most markets, poster panels are sold to advertisers by the month in packages of *gross rating points* (*GRP*). GRPs stand for the number of impression opportunities (without regard to audience duplication) expressed in terms of a percent of the total population of a specific market.[1] This means that if riders in a car pass an outdoor billboard, they have the opportunity to see the sign. Whether they note it or not is immaterial. And if the same riders pass the same sign in the same day, they are counted again in the GRP. In a market with a population of 1 million if a combination of panels purchased by an advertiser adds up to 750,000 impression opportunities every day, the package of panels would

[1] *Outdoor Advertising and Gross Rating Points,* Institute of Outdoor Advertising, New York, 1974, unpaged.

These standard outdoor posters are examples of reminder advertising. They concentrate on a single, quickly perceived idea. (Courtesy Institute of Outdoor Advertising)

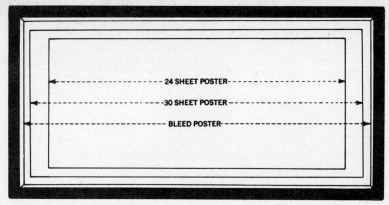

Outdoor posters are available in three sizes, each of which can fit within the standard frame.

deliver 75 GRPs each day. Since panels are sold on a 30-day-month basis, the advertiser would be buying 2,250 GRPs monthly.

Formerly, outdoor advertising space was bought in terms of outdoor showings, but with this method, one market purchase could not be compared with other market purchases. GRPs standardize purchases in different markets. The basis of gross rating points is circulation, in this case official federal, state, and local counts of cars traveling on roads between the hours of 6:00 a.m. and midnight. A private-sector organization, the Traffic Audit Bureau, also measures circulation and audits panels to develop information needed to establish GRPs.

Painted Bulletins and Other Types of Outdoor Advertising The local outdoor advertising plant supplies another form of outdoor sign known as the *painted bulletin,* which has an advertising message painted on the face of the sign area. Larger than outdoor posters, the painted bulletins are illuminated and placed at high-traffic locations. They are more costly for the advertiser to use. The purchase units are not packages of GRPs. Bulletins are usually

sold for longer periods than outdoor poster panels, 1 year being the typical sales period. Bulletins are sold individually, although an advertiser may buy a package of several in a market. Some painted bulletins remain at the same location for the life of the showing. Under the rotary plan however, an advertiser can display several different bulletin designs in one market and have them shifted between locations if that is desired.

Painted bulletins have tended to become more and more elaborate, featuring three-dimensional effects, elements that extend beyond the frame, and sometimes motion. A multivision or trivision effect can be obtained if part of the bulletin is made up of vertical triangles that turn mechanically at intervals to form three different messages or illustrations.

Other types of stationary outdoor signs available to national and local advertisers are 6- and 3-sheet posters and giant electric spectaculars. The 6-sheet poster is a small-scale version of the 24- or 30-sheet poster and is used in highly built-up areas where space for larger posters is not available. The 3-sheet poster is a small vertical oblong, and it is usually placed near retail outlets or on the exterior walls of stores. Soft-drink, packaged-food, and tobacco advertisers are typical users of the 3-sheet poster medium, and the messages serve as incentives to trigger consumer purchases at the point of sale. The enormous electric spectaculars are found in areas of concentrated traffic flow in the largest cities—in places such as Chicago's Loop or the Times Square area of New York City. These spectaculars often include moving elements and are costly prestige advertisements for consumer-goods manufacturers.

Usefulness of Standardized Outdoor Advertising Standardized outdoor advertising is a mass medium, similar to the newspaper medium. It is not in any sense selective as far as sorting out a specific audience is concerned; instead it attempts to reach every type of person that passes by the poster or bulletin. It attracts potential customers at a low basic cost to the advertiser and can be used on a national scale, regionally, or in one or more selected markets. It is therefore used by both national and local advertisers. National advertisers use 67 percent of the showings.

Basically, outdoor advertising is reminder advertising. It reminds the viewer of the values of the goods and services advertised, but because of its nature, it cannot sell in depth. Posters and bulletins are quickly passed by. They rely on a provocative illustration and a few brief words of copy to convey the message. There is no time to develop the sale or give reasons why a product or service is better than competing ones. A fresh turn of phrase or an evocative word or two are all that can be included. Advertisers of products whose images have been well established in other media and advertisers of products with entrenched mass appeal can profitably use this medium to remind the consumer of a simple selling point.

Public Attitude toward Outdoor Signs

Outdoor advertising suffers from much public criticism. Roadside signs, it is argued, often destroy the natural beauty of the countryside; the numerous signs in and around towns and cities give an impression of ugliness and clutter. There is a code of practices for the users of outdoor advertising that is placed and maintained by the outdoor advertising plants. The code attempts to eliminate public criticism. It is policy, for example, to avoid building sign structures in locations of natural scenic beauty, parks, and historical areas. But nonstandardized signs are governed by no such code of practice. The public, which does not realize the differences between types of signs, often condemns all forms of outdoor advertising.

Federal and state legislation and local ordinances have been developed to exercise control over the whole medium of signs. The Federal Highway Beautification Act of 1965 prohibits signs within 660 feet of interstate highways and primary roads. This has resulted in such phenomena as gas stations at intersections and cloverleafs beyond the 660-foot zone using station identifiers almost 100 feet high in an attempt to continue to obtain business from passing highway motorists. In counties, cities, and towns, the trend is to establish tighter zoning ordinances that dictate standards of size and taste for nonstandardized signs. With the growth of consumerism, a movement that includes definitions of public rights, it is anticipated that there will be more, rather than less, regulation of the outdoor advertising field by governments at the local, state and national levels.

Transit Advertising

Another form of sign advertising is the standardized medium known as *transit advertising*.

Examples of transit advertising. Note that the bus exterior card and the subway poster contain only reminder copy, while the bus interior card, viewed by riders for a longer time, can include several selling points. (Courtesy The Transit Advertising Association)

This medium uses public transportation facilities to bring advertising messages to the traveling public in urban centers and consists of *car cards,* ads used inside buses, commuter trains, and subways; *exterior cards,* messages on the sides and ends of buses; and *station posters,* signs of 3-sheet size or smaller, located near or in subway stations or railroad and bus terminals. According to the Transit Advertising Association, the trade organization for this medium, $50 million was spent on transit advertising in 1978. Joseph Palastak, executive director of TAA, estimates that about 50 percent of transit advertising was local advertising. Space is usually rented on a monthly basis.

Types of Transit Advertising

The usual size of a car card is 11 inches high by 28 inches long, but some cards can be as long as 84 inches. The cards are placed along the length of the vehicle interior, above the windows, and at the ends of subway cars and at the front of buses. Exterior cards are much larger than car cards, running 21 to 30 inches high and up to 12 feet long. Station posters are available only in large metropolitan areas.

A recent development in bus advertising is Moods in Motion, an advertising buy available in eight large metropolitan areas. One advertiser purchases exterior cards and also the entire showing within the bus. This offers complete dominance and an environment of no competitive ads. Current price per bus per month for Moods in Motion is $35 in these eight areas.

Usefulness of Transit Advertising

Transit advertising is a mass advertising medium very similar to outdoor posters in the brevity of its messages, although car cards can carry considerably more copy than exterior cards and station posters because the average bus or subway rider can be exposed to the advertiser's message for as long as 30 minutes and can reasonably be expected to read a longer message. The limitation on length of message is thus visibility rather than time of exposure.

Local advertisers find transit advertising advantageous when the bus or subway route passes near their stores. Because transit ads are run monthly, however, the medium lacks the immediacy and news value of newspaper and broadcast media. Transit advertising is relatively inexpensive. For car cards, circulation is based on "per thousand monthly rides," and the cost of advertising averages around 5 cents per thousand estimated circulation. See the illustration of a typical transit advertising rate structure on pages 158–159.

National advertisers use transit advertising as a supplementary medium. The Wm. Wrigley Jr. Company, the chewing gum maker, is a consistent user of transit advertising. The major distillers and cigarette makers have traditionally been large users of transit advertising. Locally, banks, savings and loan associations, and broadcast media often include transit in their budgets. B. V. Batchelder, chairman of the TAA, states that new categories, including movies, restaurants, and political ads, have recently increased use of the medium. He also points out that transit advertising is an effective way to reach women who work, a steadily increasing group in the labor market.

Transit advertising offers flexibility, as do the radio, television, direct mail, newspaper, and outdoor media. Transit advertising can be used nationally (in 380 United States markets), regionally, and locally.

Like outdoor advertising, transit advertising is fundamentally a reminder in nature, except for interior car cards. Because transit advertising reaches people when they are on the move in

THE BATCHELDER COMPANY

Rotary Transit Advertising

SPACE RATES
MARKET DATA
EFFECTIVE 1/1/76

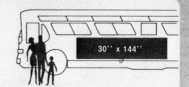

PEORIA

HOME OFFICE: 502 E. WAR MEMORIAL DRIVE, PEORIA, ILLINOIS 61614 309-688-8508

KING SIZE ROTARY POSTERS

"BIGGEST SIZE — BIGGEST IMPACT"

30'' x 144''

Showing	Displays	Monthly Rate	3 Month Rate	6 Month Rate	12 Month Rate
Intensive	30	$1575.00	$1497.00	$1371.00	$1218.00
# 100	20	1050.00	998.00	945.00	840.00
# 50	10	525.00	499.00	473.00	420.00
# 25	5	263.00	250.00	237.00	210.00
Unit Rate		53.00	50.00	48.00	42.00

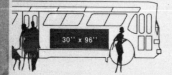

30'' x 96''

QUEEN SIZE POSTERS

"BIG FOR STRONG VISUAL"

Showing	Displays	Monthly Rate	3 Month Rate	6 Month Rate	12 Month Rate
Intensive	30	$1182.00	$1124.00	$1064.00	$945.00
# 100	20	788.00	749.00	709.00	630.00
# 50	10	394.00	375.00	355.00	315.00
# 25	5	197.00	187.00	178.00	158.00
Unit Rate		40.00	38.00	36.00	32.00

MALL

21'' x 36''

HEADLIGHT DISPLAYS

"UP FRONT FOR ALL TO SEE"

Showing	Displays	Less Than 12 Month Rate	12 Month Rate
Intensive	30	$473.00	$378.00
# 100	20	315.00	252.00
# 50	10	158.00	126.00
# 25	5	79.00	63.00
Unit Rate		16.00	13.00

LONDON ROOF DISPLAY: ADD ⅓ TO SPACE COST BELOW

TAILLIGHT SPECTACULARS

"ON MOTORISTS FRONT BUMPER"

21'' x 72''
21'' x 72''

Showing	Displays	Monthly Rate	3 Month Rate	6 Month Rate	12 Month Rate
Intensive	30	$1182.00	$1124.00	$1064.00	$ 945.00
# 100	20	788.00	749.00	709.00	630.00
# 50	10	394.00	375.00	355.00	315.00
# 25	5	197.00	187.00	178.00	158.00
Unit Rate		40.00	38.00	36.00	32.00

The dictionary says UBIQUITOUS comes from the Latin *ubique* which means *everywhere or present everywhere at the same time.* That's what Rotary Transit is all about. Many alert advertisers who want outstanding out-of-home market coverage know this. They know Rotary Transit is a people medium, operating to reach people wherever they are . . . on busy traffic streets, in shopping centers, residential areas, downtown and uptown. And they get all this UBIQUITOUS coverage and documented highest Reach & Frequency at the lowest CPM. Check out Rotary Transit. You'll see why it's smart to transfer some of the ad budget to the all-day DRIVE TIME medium.

THE BATCHELDER COMPANY — *rotary transit advertising*

INTERIOR ADVERTISING RATES

11'' x 28'' 22'' x 21'' 11'' x 56''

Size	# Displays	Less Than 12 Mo. rate	12 Mo. Rate
11'' x 28''	47	$150.00	$100.00
11'' x 56'' or 14'' x 20''	47	270.00	180.00

Klean Tear Service: 35c per card monthly charge—Non-Commissionable

MARKET AND TRANSIT FACTS

AREA SERVED: Peoria

TRANSIT SYSTEM
- 43 : Number of Buses
- 10 : Number of Transit Routes
- 127 : Total Miles of Streets Covered by Routes
- 132,500 : Fleet Miles Traveled Per Month
- 130 : Miles Per Bus Per Week Day
- 396 : Number of bus trips into Central Business District in an average Week Day

POPULATION
- 247,355 : SMSA Population served by Transit System
- 52% : Est. % of SMSA Population that Works, Shops, or Passes through Central Business District Average Week Day
- 15,624 : Numbers of Blacks in SMSA Served by Transit
- 12% : Blacks in SMSA as a Per Cent of Total SMSA

RIDERS
- 163,500 : Average Number of Passengers Per Month
- 60% : Est. % of Total Rides = WOMEN
- 28% : Est. % of Total Rides = STUDENTS
- 14% : Est. % of Total Rides = BLACKS

1/8'' tempered masonite or adhesive-backed vinyl is acceptable for KING, QUEEN and TAILLIGHT DISPLAYS. The only acceptable short term alternative is 80# waterproof paper with coat of varnish. .060 Polystyrene is preferred for HEADLIGHT and TRAVELING DISPLAYS. Vinyl is the short term alternative. INSIDE DISPLAYS require five ply stock with grain running horizontally. Advertising art and materials are provided by advertisers or their agencies. They should arrive one week before contract commencement.

This transit advertising rate card shows positions available on buses and also lists costs. (Courtesy The Batchelder Company)

shopping areas, it serves as a last-minute reminder to buy a certain product or service or to go to a certain store in the vicinity of the vehicle's traffic route. It reinforces basic advertising ideas that have been developed more fully in other media. In summary, transit advertising is inexpensive and flexible, and for these reasons it is often a part of an advertiser's total effort.

Point-of-Sale Advertising

Display advertising, point-of-purchase advertising, and POP are synonyms for *point-of-sale advertising,* advertising placed at or near the point where an item is to be selected by the consumer on a self-service basis or sold to the consumer by a salesperson. Its purposes are to remind consumers to buy the goods advertised and to stimulate impulse purchases. Point-of-sale material appears in store display windows and almost everywhere within the store's interior. It is estimated by Harold Stumpf, president of the Point-of-Purchase Advertising Institute, that $3.3 billion was spent by manufacturers on this medium in 1977.

Point-of-sale advertising can increase purchases far beyond customary sales levels; controlled tests indicate the increase can be as great as 500 percent. Placing this form of advertising in stores is good for the manufacturer, too, because it offers an important selling advantage over manufacturers of competing products not supported by this medium.

The disadvantage of point-of-sale advertising is that the merchant's space for such material is limited, and unless a special effort is made by the manufacturer, most of the display material will be discarded unused by the local merchant. Consequently, manufacturers do make a great effort to avoid this possibility. Manufacturers' and wholesalers' salespeople take the time to set up point-of-sale displays in retail outlets themselves, and they rent key counter positions for their products. Retailers are bombarded with mailing pieces urging them to take advantage of national advertising promotions by displaying tie-in signs and banners. Manufacturers devise expensive and at-

This point-of-sale display attracts the attention of the prospect and makes reaching for the product easy. (Courtesy Thermos Division of King-Seeley Thermos Company)

tractive dispensing racks that feature their merchandise—and sometimes even their competitors'—and they sell them to dealers at or below cost. Shipping cartons are constructed so that when opened they serve as self-dispensers, carrying a point-of-sale message on the side and folded-back top. Thus every attempt is made to obtain valuable in-store display space.

The manufacturer makes this effort to develop and place practical point-of-sale material because it is in the retail store that the payoff occurs. The manufacturer is stimulating consumer interest at the place where sales are made, attempting to get extra mileage from all the previous efforts made to sell the product and capitalizing on advertising in a final effort to make the sale.

Specialty Advertising

The Specialty Advertising Association International, the trade association of the medium, defines *specialty advertising* as a form of advertising that employs useful articles imprinted with the advertiser's name, address, or message. Specialty advertising is directed at a preselected audience to whom articles are given at no cost or obligation as a goodwill item.

Richard G. Ebel, director of public relations of the Specialty Advertising Association, estimates that the industry's sales volume amounted to 2.1 billion in 1977. He points out, however, that the total spent on the medium is considerably larger because some companies prepare calendars and other specialty items outside normal industry channels.

The most common form of specialty advertising is the calendar, and calendars account for about one-third of the total business of the industry.[2] In a consumer survey conducted for the Specialty Advertising Association International, it was found that out of 1,000 homes, 980 contained at least one calendar, and in 1,000 business establishments there were 8,441 calendars. Today there are between 10,000 and 15,000 specialty advertising items from which the advertiser can choose. Some of the more popular items are listed below.

Almanacs	Magnifying glasses
Ashtrays	Marking pens
Balloons	Matchbooks
Ball-point pens	Mechanical pencils
Belt buckles	Memo pads and holders
Bookmarks	
Bottle openers	Mending kits
Business card holders	Money clips
	Nail files
Calendars	Padlocks
Can openers	Paperweights
Carton cutters	Penknives
Charm bracelets	Playing cards
Cigarette lighters	Pocket secretaries
Coffee mugs	Purses
Cufflinks	Rulers
Glassware	Shoehorns
Golf tee packs	Swizzle sticks
Hand mirrors	T-shirts
Hats and caps	Thermometers
Key holders or rings	Tie bars
Letter openers	Windshield scrapers
Magnets	Wood pencils

[2] Walter A. Gaw, *Specialty Advertising*, 2d ed. Specialty Advertising Association, Chicago, 1966. p. 16.

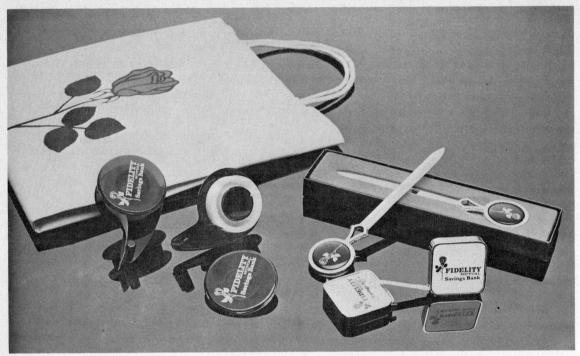

These specialty advertising items from Fidelity Mutual Savings Bank carry the advertiser's name and are given free to customers and prospects. (Courtesy Specialty Advertising Association International)

Use of Specialty Advertising

Every kind of business uses specialty advertising as part of its total advertising program. Local merchants use specialty advertising to gain the goodwill of present and prospective customers and to remind them that the merchants are in business to serve them. Manufacturers of goods and equipment and service companies give away specialty items to business customers for the same reason. Manufacturers also distribute specialties to wholesalers and jobbers to keep product names before them.

Need for Careful Selection of Items

The value of specialty advertising is in direct proportion to the desirability of the item to the receiver. As in direct mail, specialty advertising can be carefully directed to groups of consumers who are potential customers without wasting the novelties on those who have no need for the advertiser's goods or services. Having selected the target groups, the advertiser must take care to offer an item that is desirable to them. For example, business card holders would be of little use to a group of high school students but would be useful to a target group of salespeople. Business executives would find little value in a gift of marking pens or carton cutters, but shipping clerks would appreciate them.

Of course, the ideal novelty item or specialty is one that not only generates goodwill but also is tied in some way to the advertiser's business. Thus, car-key holders and windshield scrapers are excellent items for a service station manager to distribute, and shoehorns are appropriate items for the shoe store owner to give away.

Advantages and Limitations of Specialty Advertising

The calendars and novelties carrying advertising messages can be useful for some time if the items are carefully selected to match the interests and habits of the group receiving them. And as long as the item is useful to the recipients, the advertising message is reminding them of the donor. Specialty advertising thus has a longer life than advertising in any other medium. The initial cost of the item is the only cost, and the message is delivered over and over at no additional expense. In addition, as has been stated, specialty advertising is a controlled medium, and waste circulation can be minimized by careful development of target audiences. Another advantage is its ability to work well with its sister medium, direct mail. Often, specialty items such as calendars, nail files, or plastic rulers can be included in direct mail pieces to add interest and goodwill.

Specialty advertising is a supplemental, rather than a mass, medium. One of its limitations, as Walter Gaw states, is that the cost of purchasing and distributing novelties and calendars precludes building the large audiences available through other media.[3] A second limitation is that specialty advertising is basically reminder advertising, carrying little more than the name and address of the advertiser, or a brief message. This form of advertising cannot be expected to do a job of selling a product or service in depth, although, as Gaw points out, more copy points could be included on many novelties than are, in fact, usually listed.

Specialty advertising is often confused with premiums and business gifts. *Premiums* are

used as an inducement to buy a product or service; they are offers of merchandise, either at no cost or for a small charge, in conjunction with the purchase of a product. *Business gifts* are expensive specialty items. Both premiums and business gifts rarely carry an advertising message, and they are thus not considered advertising media, although their costs may be included in the advertising promotion budget.

Directory Advertising

Alphabetical listings of city and rural dwellers, businesses, supply sources, or trade and professional people are called *directories,* and because they offer specific audiences, advertising space is sold in them. The best-known listing is the telephone directory and its Yellow Pages or classified section. In the largest cities, the Yellow Pages are published separately. In the main telephone directory, business listings can be printed in boldface type for a fee, and ad space may be sold at the top or bottom of the page. All businesses and stores are listed free of charge in the Yellow Pages under classified categories such as handbags, insurance, lawn mowers, and real estate. An effort is made to sell boldface listings and separate display ads in the Yellow Pages on an annual basis.

Advertisers spend over $1 billion annually on Yellow Pages boldface listings and display ads. About $150 million of this is national advertising, and the balance is spent by local advertisers on their own or by local advertisers using cooperative advertising funds. Previously, the local telephone company's sales office handled the details of selling space in Yellow Page directories, a method which was cumbersome and time-consuming for national advertisers. Today, publishers of 4,500 telephone directories are members of the National

[3] Ibid., p. 19.

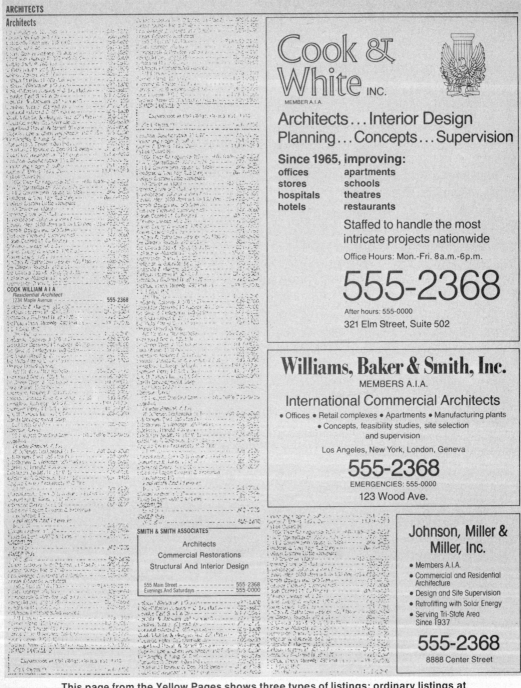

Yellow Pages Service Association (NYPSA). Through this organization, advertisers can buy space in directories up to a total of 120 million circulation, all with one order and one bill.[4]

Yellow Pages advertising offers several advantages. It is relatively permanent because the Yellow Pages are distributed once a year with the telephone book (or are part of the telephone book itself). The book is unlikely to be discarded and consequently has a long period of use. Market coverage of a town or city borders on "saturation"; the Yellow Pages are found in almost every household.

A characteristic of directory advertising such as the Yellow Pages is that it reaches people after they have decided to buy, and it then leads them to sources where their buying needs can be accommodated. In this regard, Yellow Pages advertising is similar to newspaper classified advertising.[5]

[4] Statistics and ordering and billing procedures from *Media Decisions,* June, 1976, pp. 72 and 90.
[5] *The Yellow Pages in Marketing and Advertising,* American Telephone & Telegraph Company, Chicago, 1970, p. 6.

Local merchants and service organizations find Yellow Pages advertising to be a valuable part of their advertising programs. It is particularly useful for businesses that supply services that people need infrequently and unexpectedly, such as the services of plumbers, electricians, or veterinarians. Manufacturers of nationally distributed goods use the classified pages to list their dealers. Often in national magazine advertising the line "See your local dealer's listing in the Yellow Pages" will appear. Such a listing is another attempt to carry the sales impulses generated by national advertising through to the local level, where the sale can actually be made. Yellow Pages advertising is not expensive and is a helpful supplement to other advertising efforts.

There are many specialized directories with pages available to advertisers. The most famous directory is the *Thomas Register of American Manufacturers,* which lists all the manufacturers in the United States, but almost every industry and trade group has its own published directory. These publications, like trade journals, are valuable when the advertiser wishes to reach a selective market.

Vocabulary

Define the following terms, and use each one in a sentence.

Business gift
Car card
Direct mail advertising
Directory
Exterior card
GRP
Outdoor advertising

Painted bulletin
Point-of-sale advertising
Premium
Specialty advertising
Station poster
Transit advertising

Review Questions

1. You are opening a menswear shop and want to run a direct mail campaign. How would you go about building a mailing list?
2. What are the chief advantages that a direct mail campaign offers an advertiser? What is its principal drawback?
3. Distinguish between standardized outdoor signs and nonstandardized signs.
4. Be prepared to discuss the advantages to national and local advertisers of the outdoor advertising medium.
5. What kind of manufacturer or service organization would be unlikely to use outdoor advertising?
6. What are your attitudes about outdoor advertising—standardized, nonstandardized, and in general? Discuss in class.
7. What are the three types of transit advertising?
8. What pieces of point-of-sale advertising might a manufacturer of a deodorant soap consider producing for use in supermarkets?
9. What are the purposes of point-of-sale advertising? What are its values to merchants and manufacturers?
10. List the advantages and disadvantages of specialty advertising.
11. How is Yellow Pages advertising similar to newspaper classified advertising?

Activities

1. Check your student living quarters or your home for advertising specialties. What are they, what do they advertise, and what do you think of their usefulness? What is the most effective advertising specialty that you have seen and why do you think it did a good job?
2. Make a list of direct mail advertising you have received recently. If you have responded favorably and "bought" a direct mail offer, be prepared to discuss why the offer appealed to you and why you acted favorably. Collect some samples of direct mail currently on hand, bring them to class, and be prepared with opinions on why the direct mail material was or was not effective for the advertiser.

Project

Make a survey of the outdoor advertising media in your neighborhood. List the principal national advertisers using outdoor advertising posters. List local advertisers, if any, using outdoor advertising posters. Look for painted bulletins erected by the local outdoor advertising plant. (The plant's name usually appears at the base of the poster or bulletin.) See if you can find any 3-sheet posters. Where are they located, and what do they advertise? Also, list a few local merchants who use nonstandardized signs. Are they located at or in the immediate vicinity of the place of business, on roads leading to it, or both? Describe any unique bulletin, with elements extending beyond the frame, that you may have seen.

Career Ladder

In your job as assistant ad manager in a manufacturing company, you have recently been given responsibility for choosing a printer for the company's annual report. Two printers have bid on the job. As far as you can tell, they are about equal in capabilities. They have entered bids that for all practical purposes are identical. Printer A did the annual report satisfactorily last year, but it's occurred to you that new thinking, as represented by Printer B, might be a good idea. A week before decision time, you receive at home two cases of very expensive liquor as a gift from Printer B.

What do you do about the gift? Does this present influence your decision in any way, and if so, how? To whom would you give the job, A or B?

CHAPTER EIGHT

BROADCAST MEDIA

The broadcast media, radio and television, are big business in the United States today. Television generated advertising revenues of over $8.8 billion in 1978 and is second only to newspapers in ad volume. Because television advertising requires large investments, the bulk of these TV dollars (77 percent) is spent by national advertisers who have the budgets to afford it. Radio, with about $3 billion of income from advertising in 1978, is a larger medium than consumer magazines. The bulk of its income comes from local advertisers, who sponsor about 73 percent of radio advertising.

Besides being big business, television and radio are also show business. People making advertising decisions for the large national advertisers become heavily involved in program content when they buy advertising time in the broadcast media. When advertisers buy space in magazines, they examine the quality and characteristics of the publication's circulation and try to determine whether the readers will be a good audience for their products. This same approach generally applies to the broadcast media, but television does not provide the magazines' continuity and stability of audience. Usually, the particular program—not the channel—determines the type of audience. On any one channel, a western may be followed by a news documentary or a sports event, and because all these shows appeal to different audiences, the national or local advertiser must constantly be aware of program content and must consider the program's appeal to the group of consumers most likely to be in the market for the product.

The advertiser's problem of choosing proper surroundings for the setting of the message is not as intricate in radio because radio stations today generally specialize in reaching a particular market—teen-agers, for example, or adult listeners—and all their programs are geared to a single audience.

Television

In the United States in 1979 there were 728 *commercial stations,* or stations that accept advertising messages and depend for support on the sale of commercial time. Of these, 516 were very-high-frequency (VHF) stations and 212 were ultra-high-frequency (UHF) stations.[1] The VHF stations use channels 2 to 13, the channels originally authorized for station use, and most of the television sets purchased in the early days of television's growth were built to receive VHF channels only. By the late 1950s, however, it was apparent that more channels could be used, and channels 14 through 83 were made available. Today, all sets manufactured are able to receive the signals of both VHF and UHF stations. Because VHF stations got there first, they will undoubtedly continue to dominate the medium.

There are 260 noncommercial television stations, of which 102 are VHF and 158 are UHF. Most of these carry educational programs; the balance are *public television stations,* carrying general programming which compete with the commercial stations for share of audience.[2] Educational television and public television are supported by government grants, private foundations, and individual contributions; they have no advertising revenues. The techniques of advertising nevertheless do serve public television stations. Such stations appeal on their channels for public contributions from time to time, and also run promos, just like commercial stations. *Promos* are messages that promote a future program in an effort to build audience.

Cable Television

The fastest-growing segment of the television industry is cable television, also called community antenna television (*CATV*). It operates by means of an antenna capable of receiving distant television station signals. Attached to

the antenna is a cable to bring the signal to subscribers' homes. Signals may also be received by microwave. Originally developed as a means of bringing television programming into remote or isolated areas incapable of receiving television signals directly because of terrain or distance, cable television is now available in many urban areas, supplying better reception than the ordinary direct systems of local stations when large buildings stand between the station and the receiving set.

In 1978, there were 3,700 cable systems serving 8,000 communities in the United States. The systems reach 11.9 million subscribers, representing more than 30 million individuals, or 16.8 percent of United States television homes. The subscriber pays a monthly fee for cable TV, somewhere between $7 and $10. The Federal Communications Commission has jurisdiction over cable systems, and has ruled that in major markets systems must have a potential capacity of a minimum of 20 channels available to serve the public interest. All educational stations within a 35-mile radius must be carried on the local cable system.

Cable systems originally offered only programming picked up by antenna or microwave from originating television stations some distance away. By 1978, 2,500 cable systems were originating their own programming for an average of 23 hours per week consisting mainly of automated time and weather signals and film and video tape programs. This program origination, called *cablecasting,* eventually should result in increased coverage of the local scene.

When cable systems originated cablecasting, a new medium for local advertisers was created. The programs the cable stations import from distant TV stations of course contain their own commercial messages which the cable subscriber receives. But the programming produced locally in the cable system stu-

---

[1] *1979 Broadcasting Yearbook,* Broadcasting Publications, Inc., Washington, D.C., p. A-2.
[2] Public television station viewers constitute 2 or 3 percent of the total local viewing audience.

dios has presented an advertising opportunity for local retailers. In 1977, more than 2,700 cable systems carried advertising on the programs these systems originated and the systems received $2.6 million in revenue from this source.[3]

In 1978, WTGC, Atlanta, (now WTBS) initiated programming to cable systems by satellite. Such stations are called "superstations." Local commercial TV station executives fear this competition. Superstations might siphon off advertising dollars that might be spent locally on commercial TV channels. While cable TV is growing, it is still limited in scope, and loss of revenue to local TV commercial stations from the new superstations lies far in the future.

Pay Television

Pay television, or subscription TV, is available over 364 systems in 45 states. In 1977, there were almost 1 million pay-television subscribers. Special programming is offered to those who pay a fee. The program is transmitted in scrambled form, which is translated by a device attached to the subscriber's television set. According to *Broadcasting Cable Sourcebook,* pay television is considered as a supplemental service to conventional broadcasting. The FCC has set up safeguards that prevent pay-television stations from siphoning audiences from already existing local conventional stations. Movies older than 2 years cannot be shown, for example, and there are restrictions on showing sports programs on pay television.

The special programming features of subscription TV can be combined with already existing cable TV systems. The subscriber pays the usual monthly fee for cable plus additional fees when special programming is made available and received.

[3] Information on cable systems from *Broadcasting Cable Sourcebook, 1978,* Broadcasting Publications, Inc., Washington, D.C., p. 7.

Qube Cable TV

Warner Communications, Inc., initiated a unique new TV system in Columbus, Ohio in the fall of 1977 through its division, Warner Cable Corporation. Called *Qube,* it is a two-way medium that for the first time allows people at home to participate actively in the programming brought to them by Warner Cable TV.

Customers receive programs on ten channels for their regular monthly fee. This is ordinary cable fare, with the Qube channels bringing Cleveland, Indianapolis, Cincinnati, and other TV stations to the subscriber. There are available nine channels of premium entertainment, sports, and education on Qube. Subscribers pay an additional fee to receive these shows on a per program basis. There are special Columbus-oriented channels, too, offering local religious programs, consumer shopping news and comparative prices, news, time and weather, children's programs without violence, and *Columbus Alive,* a channel of live programs developed for Columbus subscribers only.

Talking Back to the TV Screen Two-way response capability is part of the *Columbus Alive* channel programming and other local channels as well. Each subscriber's home is provided with a small, limited-capability computer terminal which has five response buttons (in addition to channel selectors) that permit the viewer to press a button and respond to what is appearing on the home TV screen. If, for example, a public official making a talk asks for an opinion requiring a yes or no answer, the viewer can "vote" by pushing the proper button on the terminal and the viewer's answer is registered instantaneously at the originating studio. The viewer can signal a TV teacher to slow down, for example, and even direct camera movements. In effect, the viewer "talks back" to the TV screen.

Advertising Potential Since local and national advertising time is available on many of the "free" channels, advertisers have a new tool to work with in two-way response. An advertiser can describe and show a product or service, and "ask for the order." The viewer can respond by pressing a button and order the merchandise or service on the spot. If merchandise with no appeal is being promoted, the advertiser gets the bad news instantaneously. If the advertiser has a "winner," more commercials can be run in short order. Qube also offers the fastest way conceivable for advertisers to test two different advertising approaches. Instead of waiting weeks for magazine coupons or direct mail orders to arrive or days for all the telephone orders from radio or TV offers to be received, orders are tallied by computer at the station within minutes.

Confirmation Procedures It may have occurred to you that children at home watching a Qube program with two-way response would find it great fun to order any or all of the merchandise or services being offered. This problem has been overcome to a great extent by confirmation procedures. The computer at the station "knows" which subscriber pushed the order button at home. Shortly, the home receives a call from a confirmer at the station, who checks the order, screens it, and answers delivery questions and the like.

Qube cable TV has generated controversy because the system by its nature can make available information concerning the viewer who uses two-way response. Recorded is such information as what programs the viewer watches, what goods are purchased, and how poll questions are answered. Possession of this information is, in reality, an invasion of privacy, and the subscriber should in fairness be made aware of this fact. Some of these criticisms can also be leveled at other forms of direct-order advertising such as mail order and direct mail.

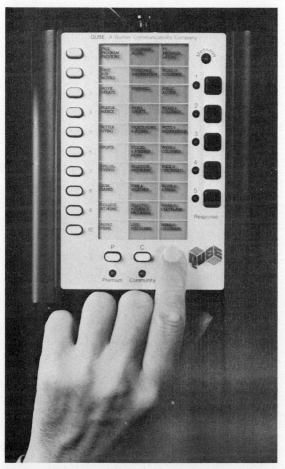

Subscribers to the Qube system in Columbus, Ohio, use this black box to respond to what appears on the screen. By pushing a button, a viewer can register opinions on the program being seen or order what is being advertised. (Courtesy Warner Cable/QUBE)

Commercial Television

By January 1979 almost every home in the United States boasted one television set or more. A total of 73 million, or 98 percent of all homes, were equipped with sets. About 47 percent had two TV sets or more. Color sets in use numbered 58 million.

Three television networks serve the United States, ABC, NBC, and CBS. Most commercial television stations are network-affiliated, or part of one of the three national networks, and some of them are affiliated with more than one network. Characteristically, these network affiliates accept the big evening network shows and some network-originated material during daytime hours, but the major portion of their broadcast time (on the average, about 60 percent) is devoted to programs and newscasts that are originated locally.

Network shows offer a mass advertising medium that blankets all principal markets. Television is an extremely effective medium, but network television advertising is very expensive and consequently beyond the reach of small- or even medium-size businesses.

To buy a network program during daytime hours, place three 1-minute commercials in it, and run this schedule for a year costs between $1.5 and $2 million. In *prime time,* the evening hours when television audiences are greatest, the advertising costs for time alone can be more than five times greater. The cost of buying a single 1½-hour special, including time and programming, can amount to $1.5 million.

National advertisers can reduce expenses by purchasing only part of a network program. A sponsor may buy the program either on an every-other-week basis or on a cosponsorship basis, where two or more advertisers (or several brands of a single major advertiser) each buy part of a program's available advertising time. But these measures don't make television sponsorship cheap; expenses still run into million-dollar figures.

Spot Television Because of the expense of purchasing or cosponsoring programs, adver-

tisers in general have turned to the purchase of *spot television,* whereby advertisers buy *commercial availabilities* for their messages. Time can be bought locally on network programs or through spot television. In spot television buying, national, regional, and local advertisers purchase availabilities on local TV stations. Availabilities, or local station time slots, can be bought during all broadcast hours on locally originated programs or on network participation programs, where local announcements or commercials are cut in. A national or regional advertiser can obtain complete national coverage for a product or service by purchasing spot television in key markets or can bolster sales areas in need of advertising support by buying special television spot coverage on a regional or local basis. Large local merchants can cover their sales territories by using spot television.

Syndicated Shows Advertisers seeking to reduce television costs have an alternative in the use of syndicated shows. In this case, the advertiser sponsors the production of a ½-hour film or taped sports program, for example. The advertiser's commercials are then integrated into the program, which is offered free to local TV stations. There is a constant need for new programming material, and if the content of the program being offered is of good quality, the advertiser has no problem making syndication deals in various markets that need coverage. In this barter transaction, the advertiser does not pay time charges for the ad messages included in the program when they are aired. The station gets a program free and can sell availabilities on this program to other local advertisers as well. On syndicated shows, some program time is usually left open for local sale of availabilities.

Local Advertisers Using TV Small merchants find local television rates prohibitively high

ONO says
O Yes to
WGAL-TV

WGAL-TV enjoys enthusiastic acceptance not only in the Lebanon County community of Ono, but also in hundreds of other Pennsylvania cities and towns in the prosperous 9-county DMA of some 1,200,000 persons. This rewarding reception is due to a combination of excellent programs and strong coverage consistently delivered to all segments of the market area. In your media buying, contrast WGAL-TV depth and reach with the partial coverage provided by other stations in the market. WGAL-TV is your obvious choice for outstanding superiority in area-wide coverage and sales.

Source: Nielsen 1977 County Coverage Report

WGAL·TV 8
STEINMAN TV STATION
LANCASTER-HARRISBURG-YORK-LEBANON, PA.

Represented by
THE
MEEKER
COMPANY, INC

Another Steinman TV Station WTEV *Providence R.I.-New Bedford-Fall River, Mass.*

This ad appearing in the trade press is typical of messages sponsored by local TV stations and addressed to media buyers. The copy lists market data and stresses viewer acceptance of WGAL-TV's programming. Note the area coverage map, lower left. (Courtesy WGAL-TV8, Steinman TV Station)

TABLE 8-1 Television Audience Composition

Time	Homes Using TV (HUT), %	Number of Viewers per Home (VPH)	Audience Composition, % (Horizontal Figures Add to 100%)			
			Women 18 and Over	Men 18 and Over	Teens	Children
Monday to Friday						
7–10 a.m., "early morning"	14.1	1.42	46	20	6	28
10–4:30 p.m., "day network"	24.1	1.36	59	19	8	14
4:30–7:30 p.m., "early evening"	45.6	1.72	41	29	10	20
Monday to Sunday						
7:30–8 p.m. "prime access"	58.8	1.96	40	32	10	18
8–11 p.m., "prime"	61.2	1.94	43	35	10	12
11:30 p.m.–1 a.m., "late night"	26.0	1.48	48	41	8	3

Source: *Nielsen Television Index,* November 1977; data for Monday through Sunday, 11 to 11:30 p.m. not available.

and unaffordable in relation to their sales volume. But according to the Television Advertising Bureau, the trade association of the television industry, many local merchants with high sales volume find the medium profitable. The ten leading local categories, in order of rank, are restaurants and fast-food establishments, department stores, banks and savings and loans institutions, food stores and supermarkets, auto dealers, movie theaters and drive-ins, furniture stores, discount department stores, amusements and entertainment other than movies, and clothing stores. Classifying restaurants and fast-food establishments as a local category, is something of a misnomer, as much of this advertising includes that of national fast-food chains such as McDonald's.

National Advertisers Using TV Television has proved to be the most effective advertising medium for many of the nation's leading advertisers. In the brand, or packaged goods, category, the industry giants continue to favor tele-

vision as a primary way to sell the consumer.

In 1977, Procter & Gamble placed 92.7 percent of its advertising on television; Gillette, 90.5 percent; General Foods, 85.2 percent, Bristol-Meyers, 85 percent; and General Mills, 83.4 percent.[4] For the national advertiser whose sales volume can support it, television advertising pays off.

Television Audiences

It is very important for the advertiser to know as much as possible about the potential audience that can be reached with commercials. While the number and composition of television audiences vary market by market, national research samples of the population give us general ideas of who the audience is and when they are looking or listening. Table 8-1 shows who is

[4] *Advertising Age,* August 28, 1978, p. 32.

watching television at different times of the day.

The month of November has been used because it is typical of fall, winter, and early spring viewing patterns. TV watching falls off in the summer months. In the time column terms media people use to describe times of the day are included. Prime access is the period when audiences build up as people turn on sets in anticipation of the most popular programs on prime time, which runs from 8 p.m. to 11 p.m. As we shall see, advertisers pay a premium to place their commercials in the more popular viewing periods. The next column shows the steady increase in homes where sets are being used that occurs as the day goes on, falling off abruptly at the end of prime time. In early morning 14.1 percent of all TV home sets are in use; in prime 61.2 percent of all TV home sets are in use. Note that the number of viewers per home rises irregularly and peaks in the evening hours.

The columns giving audience composition can be misleading at first glance. Remember that there are more sets in use as the day goes on. During day network, 59 percent of those who watch TV are women; in prime time 43 percent of the viewers are women. Actually, because over twice as many sets are being used in prime as in day network time, there are many more women watching television in the evening than in the morning. Prime time delivers an audience of more men, women, teen-agers and children than any other period.

Another way to study viewing habits is to determine the amount of time spent watching television. On a typical day, the average set was in use for well over 6 hours. It is not known whether people were actually watching for all this time; sets can be left on when viewers leave the room. Television viewing compared with radio listening at various times of the day is shown in the graph on page 185.

Buying Time on Television

Purchasing programs or spots for major television advertisers is an extremely specialized job. The media buyers at the advertising agency must thoroughly know their accounts, the brands or services that are their assignments. The buyers must be knowledgeable about sales distribution patterns and the types of consumers who are present or potential customers. They must understand a brand's "character," or the image it projects in the minds of those who buy it, and must cast this image against the programs where the spot TV buys are available. Does the program add to the prestige of the brand? If the program is long on sex or violence, is it really compatible with the brand's image, or will viewers blame the advertiser if they dislike the show? What is the quality of the audience, and do the demographic characteristics of the audience coincide with the profiles of users of the product?

Questions like these run through media buyers' minds, and not all of them can be easily answered. Buying availabilities remains an art and depends heavily on experience and judgment, in spite of all the research that is available today to agency media departments and their clients. And above these questions of program quality, demographics, and brand image, media buyers are fundamentally concerned with costs and budget structures. It is their ultimate responsibility to get the best buy for the money.

Buying on Network Programs

If the media buyer is considering buying availabilities on a network program and does so because the purchase fits the media strategy, this is not the end of the job. The buyer has purchased an existing audience for the client's

What kind of audiences would these programs attract? What products or services could be advertised effectively on each of these programs? (Jared D. Lee)

advertising messages that is ideally right in all respects. But programs wax and wane in popularity. The buyer must watch carefully to see that audience size is maintained and that the program continues to deliver a good advertising buy for the product. Continued analysis is required.

When it comes to the new programs aired for the first time every fall, the media buyer's task is to predict their appeal and gamble literally millions of dollars on their future success. The buyer sees pilot films or tapes of new shows before they are aired and judges their prospects on the basis of experience, but there is no guarantee that the buyer is right. The number of unsuccessful new programs is disastrously high. When a new program is developed, it is with the expectation that it will last more than one season, but there are out-and-out failures that are replaced by the networks at midseason or sooner and other programs with low ratings or small audiences that linger on and are replaced at the beginning of the following fall season.

In the fall of 1978 the networks offered advertisers a total of 63 programs, 24 of which were new. Sixteen of them, or 67 percent, were soon canceled because of lack of audience. There were high hopes for expensively produced programs like *Apple Pie, Dick Clark, Mary, Sword of Justice,* and *Undercover Cop,* all of which subsequently disappeared from home TV screens.

Successful specialists in the task of evaluating the future worth of new programs practice an intuitive art, aided, it is true, by all the facts and figures that can help in making judgments.

TV Rating Services

Because of the paramount importance that large national advertisers understandably attach to the size of the audience a given program develops, there are several companies that supply audience rating services. The A. C. Nielsen Company, the American Research Bureau, Simmons, and Trendex are such companies. In all cases a sample of the national viewing audience is studied, and ratings are projected in national terms under the assumption, valid in such research activities, that the percentage of the national audience tuned in to the program under consideration is the same as that indicated by the sample.

Several different methods are used to obtain program ratings. Nielsen attaches an Audimeter to television sets in selected homes. It is a device that records when the set is in use, and it is supplemented by a diary in which the householder lists the programs watched. Another method used in establishing ratings is the telephone survey, whereby telephone interviewers query television owners about the programs they are watching. Other methods are questionnaires, sent by mail, and personal interviews. All these methods serve the purpose of obtaining a sample that indicates program popularity.

Television Buying in Local Markets

In contrast to newspapers, which have different advertising rates for local and national advertisers, television stations generally maintain a single rate structure for both kinds of advertisers. The basic source of rate information is, once again, Standard Rate & Data Service, which issues a thick publication every month, *Spot Television Rates and Data.* Among other data, it lists television station representatives (companies in the business of acting as sales agents for local TV stations) and individual listings of all commercial TV stations.

Since we have used Cincinnati newspaper rates as an example in Chapter 6, we will use Cincinnati television rates here. Cincinnati offers a multitude of choices to the merchant interested in television advertising. There are four television stations available. The rate and data listing for WKRC-TV, ABC's television network station is shown on page 179.

At first glance, the listing for WKRC is a bewildering variety of rates, times, and qualifying statements, more complicated than listings for newspapers and magazines. Here is how to interpret it.

Under section 5, note the paragraph captioned Product Protection. This subject is of continuing concern to advertisers and advertising agencies. On the air, if a commercial for deodorant A were immediately preceded or followed by an ad for deodorant B, neither deodorant manufacturer would be happy about the situation because of viewer confusion and the theory that two commercials on similar products back to back would cancel out each other's effectiveness. Advertisers want some time to pass before a competitive product's message is aired. There is no real solution offered to the problem in this rate listing for WKRC or in any other rate listing. The station states it "will make every effort to schedule competitive products with a reasonable separation" but guarantees nothing.

On network programming, NBC, for example, will separate competitive products by 10 minutes of air time; but as a trade journal points out, difficulties occur at the local station level. It states, "where the situation gets thorny is when [the local TV stations] try to merge the positioning of their own commercials at the station break" with the commercials that are part of the network program being carried.[5] Product conflicts can't help occurring from time to time. What a media buyer of local commercial availabilities must do is negotiate firm product protection rules *before* purchasing the time slots.

[5] *Media Decisions,* January 1978, p. 116.

Section 7 lists programs, their times, and the cost of running 30-second announcements in these programs. Merely because the programs appear in the rate listing does not mean that any advertiser at any time can buy time slots on them. Program availabilities may be sold out, and substitutions must be made. The programs listed are either originated by ABC or produced locally by WKRC. The advertiser may want participation spot announcements on *Dinah,* a network-originated show at 4 p.m., or buy in on the local *News Combo* program. On *Dinah* the local station cuts in the advertiser's spot at a certain time designated by the network; on *News Combo* all spot integrations are made at the local studio.

Note the three prices listed for one 30-second commercial on *Dinah:* $180, $150, and $120, under columns F, P, and IP. F stands for fixed or nonpreemptible. The advertiser is paying a premium to ensure that the time that was purchased cannot be canceled and sold to another advertiser. P (preemptible) means that for $30 less, on *Dinah,* advertisers can take their chances that the spot time they bought will not be preempted and resold at a higher price. IP, or immediately preemptible, offers the advertiser even less security.

The last part of section 7 is devoted to prime-time television, the peak viewing hours between 8 p.m. and 11 p.m. Note that prices per 30-second spot are much higher than for the daytime hours. The advertiser must pay for exposure of the advertising message to the increased number of viewers watching television at these times.

Section 13 lists when material for commercials must be received by WKRC. Commercials already produced on film or tape and prepared slides must be received 72 hours before the time the commercials are to be aired. If a commercial is to be produced "live," or on

WKRC-TV
CINCINNATI, OHIO
(Airdate April, 1949)

ABC Television Network

 HARRINGTON, RIGHTER & PARSONS, INC.

TvB

A Taft Station
Subscriber to the NAB Television Code
Media Code 6 236 0150 7.00
Taft Broadcasting Co., 1906 Highland Ave., Cincinnati, Ohio. 45219. Phone 513-651-1200. TWX 810-461-2606.

1. PERSONNEL
Vice-Pres. & Gen'l Mgr.—Robert C. Wiegand.
General Sales Manager—James O'Shields.
National Sales Manager—Randall E. Smith.

2. REPRESENTATIVES
Harrington, Righter & Parsons, Inc.
Taft Sta. Sales Offices: See Rep & S/O pages.

3. FACILITIES
Video 316,000 w., audio 31,600 w.; ch 12.
Antenna ht.: 1,000 ft. above average terrain.
Operating schedule: 7:15-approx 1 am. EST.

4. AGENCY COMMISSION
15% to recognized agencies on net time charges.

5. GENERAL ADVERTISING See coded regulations
General: 1a, 2b, 4a, 5, 6a, 7b, 8.
Rate Protection: 14, 16a.
Contracts: 20a, 21, 22a, 23, 25, 26, 27a, 31b, 31c, 32a, 32d.
Basic Rates: 40a, 40b, 41d, 42, 43a, 43b, 44b, 45a, 46, 47a, 49, 51a.
Comb.; Cont. Discounts: 60a, 60f, 61a, 62b.
Cancellation: 70a, 70n, 71, 72, 73a.
Prod. Services: 83, 84, 86, 87b, 87c.
Affiliated with ABC Television Network.
When network or local programming delays the start of regularly scheduled programs, regular rates will apply; except in instances when the regularly scheduled programs start is delayed until after 12:00 midnight EST.

Product Protection
Scheduling of competitive products adjacent to or near each other is contrary to station policy; the station will make every effort to schedule competitive products with a reasonable separation. However, no rebate, credit, or makegood will be issued except when all three of the following conditions prevail:
1. Station has control over scheduling of both conflicting commercials.
2. Commercials are directly and totally competitive.
3. Such commercials are telecast directly adjacent to one another.
It is understood that product separation is not otherwise part of any contractual agreement.

Multiple Products Announcements
Station accepts 1 minute multiple product announcements in accordance with the NAB code. Station will not accept multiple product announcements in which 2 or more products are not manufactured by the same company even though they may be related in character, purpose or use. Piggyback announcements under one minute in length are not acceptable.

6. TIME RATES
No. 48 Eff 9/5/77—Rec'd 8/12/77.

7. SPOT ANNOUNCEMENTS
30 SECONDS

MON THRU FRI:	F	P	IP
7-9 am, Good Morning, America	90	70	50
9-10:30 am, Mike Douglas/Extra	70	50	30
10:30 am-noon, ABC AM Rotation	120	100	80
PM:			
1-2, All My Children	250	220	190
Noon-4, ABC PM Rotation	160	130	100
4-5:30, Dinah	180	150	120
5:30-6, Eyewitness News	280	240	200
6:30-7, The Rookies	220	190	160
7-7:30, Liar's Club	280	240	200
7:30-8, Newlywed Game	300	260	220
11-11:30 Tues thru Sun, Eyewitness News	300	250	200
11:30-concl Tues thru Thurs, Wide World of Entertainment	100	80	60
11:30 pm-1:30 am, Fri Night Flicks	120	100	80
11:30-concl, Saturday Night Late Movie	120	100	80
11:30 pm-12:40 am Sun, Baretta	160	130	100
SAT:			
7 am-noon, Kids Rotation	160	140	120
PM:			
Noon-1, TV Bowling	120	80	60
1-1:30, Hogan's Heroes	120	80	60
1:30-5, NCAA Football	1000	800	600
5-6:30, Wide World of Sports	500	400	300
6:30-7:30, Hee Haw	350	300	250
SUN:			
7 am-noon, Various/Religious, flat.	75	75	75
PM:			
Noon-2, When Movies Were Movies I	200	170	140
2-4, When Movies Were Movies II.	180	150	120
4-6, When Movies Were Movies III	180	150	120
6-7, Wild Wild World of Animals/ Wild Kingdom	300	250	200

News Combo:
5:30-6 pm Mon thru Fri, Early News; 11-11:30 pm Tues thru Fri, Late News.
2 per wk.. 370

PRIME TIME

MON:	1	2	3	4
8-9, San Pedro Beach Bums	1000	800	700	600
9-concl, NFL Football	1200	1000	900	800
TUES:				
8-9, Happy Days/Laverne & Shirley	2000	1700	1400	1200
9-10, Three's Company/Soap	1200	1000	900	800
10-11, Family	1000	800	700	600
WED:				
8-9, Eight Is Enough	1100	900	800	700
9-11, Charlie's Angels/ Baretta	1400	1200	1100	1000
THURS:				
8-9, Kotter/What's Happening	1100	900	800	700
9-10, Miller/Carter Country	1100	900	800	700
10-11, Redd Foxx	1000	800	700	600
FRI:				
8-9, Donny & Marie	1200	1000	900	800
9-11, ABC Movie	1100	900	800	700
SAT:				
8-9, Fish/Operation Petticoat	900	700	600	500
9-10, Starsky & Hutch	1000	800	700	600
10-11, Love Boat	900	700	600	500
SUN:				
7-8, Nancy Drew & Hardy Boys	950	750	650	550
8-9, Six Million Dollar Man	1000	900	800	
9-11, ABC Movie	1200	1000	900	800

Adjacencies to all programs may be rotated with spots within the program.
1—Fixed.
2—Preemptible.
3—Immediately preemptible.
4—Package.

11. SPECIAL FEATURES
COLOR
Schedules network color, film, slides, tape and live
Equipped with high and low band VTR.

13. CLOSING TIME
72 hours prior film, slides; 1 week artwork 3 days musical content and commercial copy
Submitted by Pierce H. Foster.

This is the SRDS station listing for WKRC-TV, an ABC affiliate in Cincinnati. The data are used by spot television buyers, both local and national, to determine costs of television time purchases. (Courtesy Standard Rate and Data Service)

camera using local studio facilities and artwork (display lines of copy, photos, and the like), the artwork must be received 1 week ahead of airing. Copy scripts of commercials to be read live on the air and accompanying tapes of musical effects must meet a deadline of 3 days before airing.

Negotiating Rates for TV Time Unsold slots for commercials naturally produce no advertising revenue for TV stations. When advertising sales are slow for magazines and newspapers, the publishers can cut back on the size of publications to cut operating costs. Television stations, which are licensed to present programs for a certain number of hours day and night, do not have this option. The pressure of competition for advertising dollars has often been so great that published rates have been ignored and bargaining, or negotiating, is done between the advertising agency or media buying service and television salespeople.

In 1979, for example, published rates remained firm in some markets but in others, local advertisers and spot television buyers were dickering for spot availabilities and were often successful in gaining price concessions. It is, of course, unknown whether this situation will continue. In any case, it is wise for local and national spot television buyers to investigate local time-buying conditions before committing advertising dollars at published rates.

Other TV Buying Criteria for Local Advertisers Beyond the raw cost data for local television stations listed in SRDS, local advertisers considering use of TV must search for other information to be assured of the value of this form of advertising. Advertisers should obtain all available information on the market coverage of each local station and match their sales territories against it. (See the illustration of a coverage map for a TV station.) Merchants should learn what they can about the listening and viewing habits of the audiences tuning in to the city's stations, and they should ask sales reps for facts on size of audience by time of day. If purchase of participation spots is being weighed, the kinds of audiences each program attracts should be considered, in order to see if these viewers are potential buyers for the merchandise the store offers. For example, feed and grain merchants look for farm programs as logical locations for their commercials. Local car dealers favor newscasts and sports events because of the male audience they attract. Advertising managers of local department stores might consider women's service programs logical for women's fashion items, furniture, and housewares.

Advantages and Limitations of Television

Because it employs sight, sound and motion, television is an ideal medium for showing products and services in use and for demonstrating their advantages. On color television especially, a product can be realistically presented in and out of its packaging. Television is a "personal" medium that tries to involve the viewer by means of direct person-to-person selling.

Much has been said negatively of the brevity of television commercials from the point of view of delivering a full sales message. But in a 30-second commercial, the main vehicle used by television advertisers today, the time available allows an advertiser to include one or more selling ideas in surprising depth and permits a reasoned, well-developed sales approach going far beyond reminder advertising.

A television campaign behind a product or service is highly promotable to dealers and

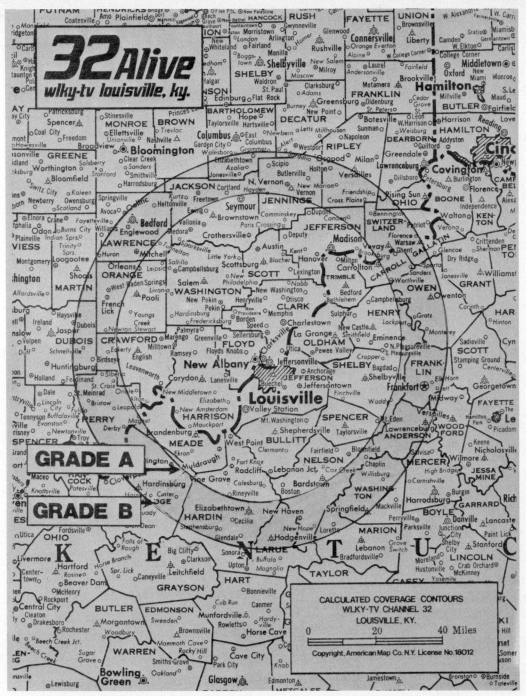

On this coverage map for station WLKY-TV 32, Louisville, KY, the inner circled area is Grade A, indicating the strongest signal. The outer circled area is Grade B, or next strongest signal area. (Courtesy WLKY-TV 32)

WKLV-TV				
Time	**Program Content**	**Advertiser and Good or Service**	**Commercial Length**	**Local (L), National (N), or Regional (R)**
6:30 p.m. station break	None	Muscular Dystrophy (public service)	30 sec.	N (spot)
		Stroh's Beer	30	R
		Timex (watches)	10	N (spot)
		Chevrolet dealer	30	L
6:30 6:45	Sports news	Shop'n Save Discount (house paint)	1:00 min.	L
		Larry's Sportshops (golf clubs)	30	L
		Getty Gasoline	1:00	N (spot)

Do you think that this schedule is an example of the clutter problem?

local merchants. Television has more prestige than competitive media, and people working in the distribution channels are more impressed by TV advertising plans than ad plans geared to print. Thus television advertising can aid distribution. A television ad plan is a stimulus to the manufacturer's sales force too.

Television, like radio and newspapers, is a highly flexible medium that can be used locally, regionally, or nationally. Manufacturers can advertise to selective audiences, as well, buying time slots on programs that appeal to the special segments of the population that would be most likely to use their products.

One limitation of television advertising is that the commercial message has a brief life. Once it is heard and viewed, it is gone; it does not remain in the household like an ad in a monthly magazine or an advertising message on a wall calendar.

Cost is a major consideration in mounting a television advertising campaign. In recent years TV rates have risen at a faster clip than newspaper, magazine, outdoor, and radio rates. Inflated costs for TV advertising have resulted in reduction of TV use by some advertisers, and studies are regularly made by such major marketers as Procter & Gamble and

General Foods on the use of advertising alternatives to television. As an added incentive to using alternatives, average costs of producing TV commercials have also risen at a rate of 10 percent or more each year.

Television advertising suffers from the clutter problem. *Clutter* simply means crowding several commercials into a short air-time period. It is not the consumer alone who complains about "too many commercials on TV"; the advertiser does too. There is a strong and often expressed opinion among major advertisers that the medium has oversold itself and crowded too many commercials within and around the program segments. Currently, 9 minutes 30 seconds of commercial time is allowed on prime-time hours, but according to many in the industry, the rule is violated.[6] Advertisers feel that clutter reduces the value and effectiveness of TV commercials. Industry studies and recommendations on clutter are

[6] In June, 1979, the Justice Department filed a civil antitrust suit against the National Association of Broadcasters claiming that limitation of TV commercials to 9 minutes 30 seconds during prime time deprived television advertisers of the benefits of free competition and drove up advertising costs. If the case were won by the Justice Department, the result would be even more clutter during prime viewing time.

being made by the AAAA, Station Representatives Association, and various network groups.

Factors Influencing Future TV Advertising

While television will undoubtedly be a powerful medium in the future and will continue to be favored by large national advertisers over other media for reasons already discussed, several developments will affect the size of viewing audiences to a certain extent.

Working women are a large segment of the total adult female market. As of 1978, working women constituted over 50 percent of the total number of women between the ages of 18 to 54. Ten years ago, it was around 40 percent. This trend obviously reduces the daytime viewing audience; when a woman has a job, she isn't at home watching a game show or a soap opera. A media mix of daytime and prime-time TV and magazines is a logical way to reach working as well as nonworking women, and this type of allocation of media dollars will diminish revenues received from daytime TV slot sales. Sale of evening television time should continue to hold up well.

The advent of TV games and video tape recorder systems still has an unknown effect on television viewing habits. When a family uses the TV screen to play Odyssey, for example, it is not watching *M.A.S.H.* It is estimated that over 3 million video games are sold annually. According to Arbitron Television Corp., a TV viewing measurement service, use of video games was heaviest during prime television time in a 1977 survey of New York and Los Angeles viewers in 1977. Unless video games turn out to be a novelty, used for a while in a home and then put aside, TV viewing will suffer a minor decline. The effects of video tape recorders are more difficult to determine. This system enables an owner to record a program for playback at a later time, and playback interferes with regular viewing habits.

Radio

At the end of 1978, there were 8,608 radio stations on the air in the United States. Of these, 4,547 were commercial AM stations, 3,079 were commercial FM stations, and 982 were noncommercial FMs.[7] AM stands for amplitude modulation, a form of radio transmission that curves with the earth's surface and therefore can carry over long distances. FM stands for frequency modulation, a type of transmission that does not have the reach of AM but produces better-quality sound, with less static and no fading. FM radio is consequently excellent for musical programs. A special kind of radio set is required for home reception of FM programs, and this, plus FM's lack of reach, inhibited the growth of this medium in the past. FM stations are mainly found in large urban areas, and many of them are owned by AM stations, which broadcast similar programs simultaneously. The advent of stereo FM has revitalized the growth of FM stations. Stereo AM broadcasting, a new development, is becoming increasingly available also.

Radio stations come in three sizes: 250-watt local stations with a limited transmission power capable of carrying an audible signal perhaps 25 miles; larger regional stations of up to 5,000 watts, capable of blanketing hundreds of miles with their signals; and a relatively few clear-channel stations of up to 50,000 watts, so powerful that other stations in their area are not permitted to broadcast in the evening hours on the same frequency.

[7] *Broadcasting Yearbook, 1978,* p. A-2.

Things your ad agency might have never told you about radio.

Do you sell spaghetti? Golf balls? X-Ray equipment? Maybe yogurt? Or perfume? Whatever you sell, we'd like to give you a few mind-bogglers about radio that might amaze you, and your advertising agency.

98.6% of homes have radio

Hard to believe, but it's true. There is virtually no escape from radio. There's one in practically every home in the United States. And there are more than *five* radios in the average American residence, more than *three* times the number of TV sets. Is this madness? No. Because people listen to radio everywhere. In their living rooms, bedrooms, kitchens, dens, workshops, patios, at the beach, at sporting events, in their cars, and on the job. There's even a "rubber ducky" radio, designed to float in the bathtub. Is it any wonder that radio reaches almost everyone (96% of the U.S. population, 12 and over) within one week?

People spend almost as much time with radio as they do with TV

Ready for some more surprises? Adults, 18 plus, spend almost as much time listening to radio (3 hours, 27 minutes per day) as they do watching the picture tube (3 hours, 49 minutes) and much, much more time than they spend with other media such as newspapers (37 minutes daily) and magazines (20 minutes daily). Some folks, in fact, such as working women, spend more time with radio than they do with TV. What's more, radio's listening patterns are more consistent, hardly varying from season to season.

The last of the great salesmen

And if you do sell spaghetti (or anything else, for that matter), consider this important fact. Among all the major media, radio has the last word when it comes to selling shoppers. Why? Because most Americans drive to the marketplace and you can't read a newspaper or watch TV while you're driving a car. But you can listen to the car radio. And most people do. Which is the reason why so much radio advertising comes from retailers, a shrewd breed known for their exceptionally hard noses. Want to know more about this low-cost, hardworking medium? Write to Kevin Cox, VP Sales, NBC Radio Network, 30 Rockefeller Plaza, NY, NY 10020

Hearing is believing

NBC Radio Network

Radio people often feel that their medium is overlooked because of TV's dominance and glamor. NBC Radio Network's trade ad attempts to go over the heads of agency media buyers and talk directly to clients, selling the benefits of radio advertising. (Courtesy NBC Radio Network)

RADIO LISTENING COMPARED TO TV VIEWING AT DIFFERENT TIMES OF THE DAY

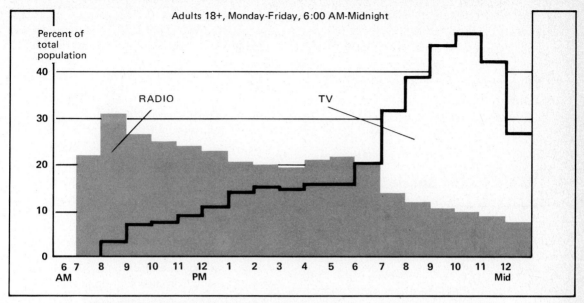

This chart compares radio listening with TV viewing at various times of the day. Note how radio listening peaks early in the day, while TV viewing is just the opposite, building to evening prime time. (Courtesy RAB)

Radio Networks

The largest radio network is the Mutual Broadcasting System. The three television networks maintain their own national radio networks. ABC has four networks, American Contemporary, American Entertainment, American FM, and American Information. There are also several regional radio networks. Today, network radio is not as important as it was before the amazing growth of the television industry. Before the 1950s, radio was the national habit, and millions tuned in regularly to the big musical and variety shows, such as the *Carnation Hour,* the *Jack Benny Show,* and the *Fred Allen Show.* When television put an end to this type of radio network programming, the radio industry survived by adapting itself to other consumer needs. Stations held their audiences by specializing in service programs, newscasts, and music and by tailoring their programming to selective audience segments.

Radio's Status Today

At present radio broadcasting is healthy and growing. Radio advertising revenues, network, spot, and local, are more than four times what they were in 1950 when television started its growth. In 1978, according to the Radio Advertising Bureau, 98.6 percent of all homes in the United States have at least one radio in working order, and there are 5.7 sets in the average home. The number of sets in use in 1978 totaled 444 million, of which 106 million were car radios. The percent of car radios is almost at the saturation point; 95 percent of cars have them.

Radio listening (compared with television viewing at various times of the day) is shown on page 185. Note the strength of radio listening in the early morning hours from 7 to 10 a.m. The audience steadily declines thereafter, as television viewing starts building throughout the day, peaking out in prime time evening hours. The public wants news and weather reports from radio in the early morning; this is also *drive time,* the period when people going to work use their car radios. Later in the day, the public turns to the television set for visual entertainment, and radio listening falls off.

Radio Station Specialization

A few programming description paragraphs that appear in Standard Rate & Data Service station listings will give you an idea of how radio stations specialize their programming and tailor it to their particular area or for specific target audiences. Here is the description for KHMO, in Hannibal, Missouri, a farming area.

FARM: 5–7 a.m. and noon–1 p.m. M–Sat. Four-man farm and news block with interviews, live markets, county agent reports. NEWS: on hour in 5-, 10-, & 15-minute segments except 7–8:15 a.m. and 11:55 a.m.–12:30 p.m. Four-man news, two auto, one aircraft mobile unit. Audience phone participation 10:05–11 a.m. M–Sat. SPORTS: local area high school football and basketball and college football. MUSIC: 100% Country & Western.

KUFF, in Albuquerque, New Mexico, offers this programming description:

Modern country format featuring middle of road country music with crossover into MOR soft rock; blend of currently popular music, better classics back to 1966 and super classics.

But KZZX, also in Albuquerque, bills itself as "The Young Adult Powerhouse" and offers a great contrast to KUFF's programming. Its description reads:

Programmed for young adults 18–44 and teens. MUSIC: mass appeal contemporary music by super-star artists.

In New York City, there are sixteen AM and thirteen FM radio stations. WCBS and WINS specialize in news. WBLS (FM) offers "contemporary, adult disco." WLIB is programmed for the black audience, with emphasis on the West Indian community. WQXR features classical music, news, and personalities. WADO and WBNX are programmed completely in Spanish. WBNX's profile follows:

MUSIC: Traditional and current Spanish vocals and instrumentals in morning. Spanish salsa featured afternoons and evening. NEWS: at :60 & :30. 2 5-minute summaries per hr. featuring local, regional, national and international coverage with sources including Latin-American and Puerto Rican AP wires. Emphasis on community involvement through public service campaigns.

Radio Time Buying in Local Markets

SRDS's *Spot Radio Rates and Data* is the source book for local radio spot buying. Continuing with Cincinnati as an example, this city and its satellites offers thirteen AM stations and five FM stations. The figure on page 187 reproduces the rate and data listing for WKRC-Radio.

Section 5 refers to standard coded regulations listed at the front of SRDS. This is a space-saving way of indicating that the station has the usual contract regulations; for example, all programs and commercials are subject to station approval and hard liquor advertising is not acceptable.

Section 6 lists costs of 1-minute and 30-sec-

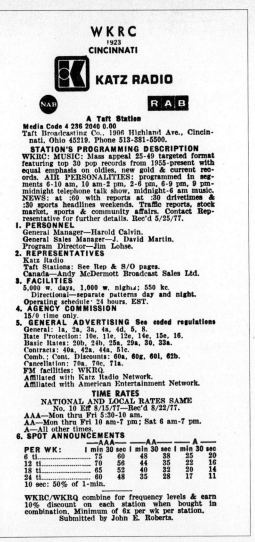

The SRDS listing for radio station WKRC, Cincinnati, tells radio time buyers what they need to know about the station's time rates. (Courtesy Standard Rate and Data Service)

ond commercials at different times of the day. Note that costs decrease when more commercials are added to the schedule. The 24-times-per-week rate for 1-minute commercials in class AAA time is $60 per message; the 6-times-per-week rate is $75 per message. AAA commercials are more expensive than AA and A because they run at the highly desirable times between 5:30 and 10 a.m., when listeners are greatest.

No local advertiser should automatically buy from the rate book before checking to see if rates are firm or negotiable. Just as in TV spot buying, there are times in local markets when rates are firm and times when bargaining can be done.

Advantages and Limitations of Radio Advertising

Radio is a specialized advertising medium that offers selective audiences to advertisers on network and local programs. It can cover national, regional and local markets with a high degree of flexibility. Radio is listened to almost everywhere—in cars and outdoors as well as in homes. Radio commercials can be produced in a hurry, compared with the time involved in making TV commercials or magazine ads for nationally advertised products and services. When speed in breaking new advertising is essential, radio can be even faster than newspapers. Radio advertising is also not expensive to use.

Employing only sound, radio can be an extremely creative medium for advertisers, as we shall see in Chapter 18. It is ideal for products where sound effects can help make the sale. Radio is not merely suitable for reminder advertising, like billboards. An in-depth sales pitch can be accomplished in 30-second and 1-minute commercials.

Because radio visualizes only through words, music, and sound effects (listeners create pictures in their minds when they hear a commercial), it lacks the advantages other media offer in showing product packages and visually demonstrating product advantages.

A radio commercial, like a TV commercial,

DAYTIME COVERAGE AREA

WLW RADIO 7

Legend:

- ■ 7 COUNTY METRO CINCINNATI AREA
- ▨ 45 COUNTY AREA OF DOMINANCE (ARB)
- ○ 216 COUNTY DAYTIME COVERAGE AREA
- 0.5 MV M DAYTIME CONTOUR

MARKET DATA

	7 COUNTY METRO AREA	45 COUNTY SURVEY AREA
Population	1,401,100	3,285,200
Households	471,530	1,100,460
Passenger Cars	698,540	1,679,490
Total Spendable Income	$6,583,078,000	$15,223,742,000
Total Retail Sales	$3,568,859,000	$ 8,201,940,000
Food	$ 840,027,000	$ 1,905,303,000
Drugs	$ 114,293,000	$ 243,623,000
Apparel	$ 138,979,000	$ 315,459,000
Home Furnishings	$ 194,295,000	$ 405,577,000
Automotive	$ 621,057,000	$ 1,475,701,000
Farm Population	24,800	178,800
Gross Farm Income	$ 89,977,000	$ 1,055,565,000

Copyright, American Map Company, New York   License No. 18214

SOURCE: Standard Rate and Data, 1976

On this coverage map for radio station WLW, Cincinnati, shaded counties indicate the dominant signal area, but the station can also be heard within the circled area. (Courtesy WLW Radio, Cincinnati and American Map Company, Inc.)

has a short life compared with other media. Advertisers make up for this lack by increasing frequency of message.

Regulation of the Broadcast Industry

Although broadcasting is a private industry in this country, it is licensed and regulated by the Federal Communications Commission (FCC). The FCC allocates space in the radio-frequency spectrum to all radio broadcasters, commercial and noncommercial, and to other services that must use the airwaves such as aviation, military, and weather. Within these radio-frequency bands, the FCC makes assignments of locations, power, and frequency to local radio stations. For the TV industry, the FCC makes the same kind of determinations with regard to channels. The FCC also has the responsibilities of regulating existing TV and radio stations, acting on station applications, assigning call letters, and seeing to it that stations adhere to a myriad of technical rules.

When applications to operate a radio or television station are made to the FCC, hearings are held and the agency decides whether or not the new broadcast facility is needed by the public. If a license is granted, it must be renewed every 3 years. One of the requirements for renewal is that a certain percentage of broadcast time be devoted to public-interest and educational programs. Thus potentially the FCC has great control over the broadcast media. In actuality, however, refusals to renew licenses are rare.

The Fairness Doctrine and Counter Commercials

For the past 30 years, the FCC has enforced its *fairness doctrine,* a standard requiring broadcasters airing one point of view on controversial public issues also to make available air time for the views of the opposition. For most of that period, the fairness doctrine had not been applied to commercials, but in 1967 the FCC took a stand that television and radio spots for cigarettes were controversial, in that they presented one side of the argument about cigarettes and health even though no health claims were being made.

The FCC ruling opened the way to a new broadcasting phenomenon, the *counter commercial.* Public-interest groups prepared anti-cigarette commercials presenting the other side of the cigarette-smoking controversy, and television and radio stations, under the fairness doctrine, broadcast them. Cigarette advertising is no longer broadcast, but counter advertising has also been prepared and run against leaded gasoline and high-powered cars.[8]

In 1974, the FCC revised the fairness doctrine, and under these revisions commercials for products are no longer considered controversial and subject to counter advertising. Commercials by advertisers which are in effect editorials, attempting to sway public opinion, can be considered controversial, however, and if public-interest groups demand time to rebut the points of view expressed, broadcasters must run counter advertising that presents these opposite views.

Radio spots in favor of nuclear power sponsored by a utility and a TV commercial of a petroleum advertiser on its methods of doing business have been considered editorials by the FCC. The stations running these commercials were required to broadcast counter advertising in rebuttal.

The result of the counter-advertising controversy is that the clearance divisions of the net-

[8] *Advertising Age,* June 5, 1978, p. 12.

works have become increasingly tough on advertisers submitting copy that is editorial in nature or seeks to sway public opinion. Most of such material is rejected by broadcasters.

Vocabulary

Define the following terms, and use each one in a sentence.

Cablecasting
CATV
Clutter
Commercial availabilities
Commercial station
Counter commercial
Drive time
Fairness doctrine

Pay television
Prime time
Promo
Public television
  stations
Qube
Spot television

Review Questions

1. Why must television or radio advertisers concern themselves with program content?
2. As a television viewer, would you prefer pay television to current sponsored television? Discuss your ideas.
3. How does Qube television differ from ordinary CATV?
4. What alternatives to purchasing entire network television programs are available to advertisers?
5. Describe some of the considerations faced by a media buyer in purchasing commercial availabilities on a television network show.
6. What is the function of rating services and why are they important?
7. You are a car dealer in Cincinnati and you have decided to buy sixty 30-second spots on participation programs on WKRC-TV during the next month. Using the WKRC rate and data listing, what programs in section 7 would you like to use? How many spots would you use on each program? Based on your choice, how much would your sixty spots cost in F or nonpreemptible time?
8. What criteria besides advertising costs would you, as a local advertiser using television, consider before purchasing time?
9. Discuss the advantages and limitations of television advertising.
10. Name three factors influencing future TV advertising.

11. At what time of the day is radio listening greater than television viewing? Give reasons why this is so.
12. In your opinion, what kinds of products could be profitably advertised on radio station KHMO, based on its programming description in this chapter?
13. Discuss the advantages and limitations of radio advertising.

Activities

1. Examine the programming of a local radio station and analyze it from the point of view of selectivity. If the program content is aimed at a selective audience, write out a brief profile of a typical consumer who might be attracted to the station. List the advertisers who buy spots, and state whether or not these advertisers fit the program content and the profile of the audience you have established. You may find that the station has programs for different types of audiences at different times of the day, for example, farm news at 7 a.m., home service and shopping programs at 1:30 p.m., and rock music at 8 p.m.
2. From your television viewing experience, list three network shows and the products that are advertised regularly within these programs (not at station breaks before and after the programs). In your opinion, are these programs appropriate settings for the products advertised? Write out your reasons for thinking as you do.
3. For one week, Monday through Sunday, make a daily record of the amount of time you have spent (a) watching television, and (b) listening to the radio. What is your daily average? How does your television viewing compare with the average daily set-in-use figures of over 6 hours? How does your television and radio daily average compare with your classmates' averages?

Project

Monitor a television station's broadcast pattern during the evening hours. List the programs and their times. Then list the commercial sponsors of each program and the goods and services that are advertised. Make notations of the station-break period between the programs, when between two and five commercials of various lengths appear. Who are the advertisers using these station breaks? With the data at hand, make up a log of the evening's broadcast pattern, indicating in the process whether the commercial sponsor is a local merchant or a national advertiser buying spot television or participating in a network program. The start of a typical log is constructed on page 182.

Career Ladder

You are the general manager of a radio station in a city with a population of 100,000 and you run far and away the best radio station in the area. A writer on your staff has just quit. The job that's now open consists of writing promos (radio messages that promote future programs), program continuity when required, and ads for local merchants when they want help.

You're looking at three applicants. One is the son of an advertiser who spends a fair amount of money with your station. This young man has no experience in writing other than a couple of short story efforts (unsold) and a strong feeling that he's highly "creative," which he expresses freely. Another is a girl who has been writing advertising copy for a small advertising agency that just folded. The material she has shown you looks good. The third applicant is a former public relations man with much experience in that area but with no advertising background.

What qualifications would you look for when interviewing the applicants? Which applicant would you hire and why?

CHAPTER NINE

USING ADVERTISING RESEARCH

Advertising is not a science. There are no advertising rules or formulas that will automatically produce sales results. Successful advertisers depend on experience, intuition, and judgment, although judgment is supported by as many pertinent facts as possible. It is in this last area—obtaining pertinent facts—that research activities are of great help. They can remove much of the guesswork from advertising decisions. It is important to realize, however, that research in itself does not make the decision; it is simply a tool that helps the advertiser to come to a decision.

Measuring Advertising Results

Why is advertising relatively unscientific? Why isn't it possible to establish procedures that can guarantee sales successes? The reason is the many variables at work in advertising. Taking an example from the measurement of

advertising results, one could reasonably assume that when X dollars are spent advertising product Y with a new campaign in market Z, a certain percentage of sales could be attributed to the advertising and that if the same plan were followed in other markets, this same relation of advertising to sales would prevail. If all markets operated under identical conditions at all times, this assumption would be valid; but, alas, such is not the case. Here are some non-controllable situations that might have occurred that would make interpreting and projecting the results of this X-Y-Z assumption difficult.

There were no competitive products on sale in market Z, but there will be in other markets.

Competitive products were available but not advertised.

Competitive advertising came in heavily halfway through the campaign and hurt Y's sales.

Competitive advertising is generally heavier (lighter) in other markets.

A major competitor broke in with a "price-off" deal midway through Y's campaign; sales of the competitive product increased at the expense of Y.

Distribution of the product in retail outlets was spotty. Potential customers asked for the product but were unable to buy it.

A tie-in merchandising effort at the point of sale was too late (too early).

All tie-in point-of-sale merchandising activities were accomplished, but it was not possible to determine whether consumers bought product Y because of the advertising or because of the merchandising.

It was not possible to determine whether consumers were buying the product because of its previous advertising or because of its new advertising.

The national economy turned down near the end of the test, putting national expansion in jeopardy.

Events like these, which are often beyond the control of the manufacturer, constantly occur in the ever-changing marketplace, making evaluation of results difficult and forecasting risky. Advertising is only one of many factors influencing the sale of a product or service; it is in trying to isolate and determine its pulling power that we run into trouble.

In Chapter 1 we noted that of ten major new products introduced into the marketplace, three have unsatisfactory sales and one is withdrawn completely. But these estimates only indicate the results of "major" marketers. These are the large companies, with ample resources for testing, where management could be expected to do very well indeed in the new-product field. When all companies are included, the new-product failure rate is awesome. More than 10,000 new items are introduced in retail outlets annually, and it is estimated that 80 percent do not reach planned sales levels and do not meet the manufacturers' profit targets.[1] In all these cases, the fickle public did not act as anticipated because the new items did not come up to consumer expectations. It is easy to understand why major marketers, faced with these statistics, spend heavily on research activities.

Leading advertisers and agencies annually spend millions of dollars to develop better evaluation yardsticks. Paul Gerhold, president of the Advertising Research Foundation, a non-profit organization to promote effectiveness in advertising through research, has listed five developments aiding the measurement of advertising results:[2]

■ There is a trend toward buying all types of media locally. This permits small-scale market tests that can approximate national media usage.

■ Local sales data are easier to secure than in the past.

■ Computers have greatly simplified analysis of marketing information.

■ New facilities have been developed for experiments within markets, splitting markets in half for testing purposes.

■ There is a new emphasis on research in major corporations.

So progress will be made in removing some of the inexactitudes in measuring and forecasting; and even the present tools are far better than none. As Mr. Gerhold said, "I had an adding machine once, with a broken gear, that subtracted a thousand dollars from every total it computed. But I learned to live with it, because it was the best machine I had."

[1] AdTel, Ltd.
[2] Paul E. J. Gerhold, "Measuring Results—The Almost Impossible Dream," speech made at the annual meeting of the AAAA, April 25, 1969.

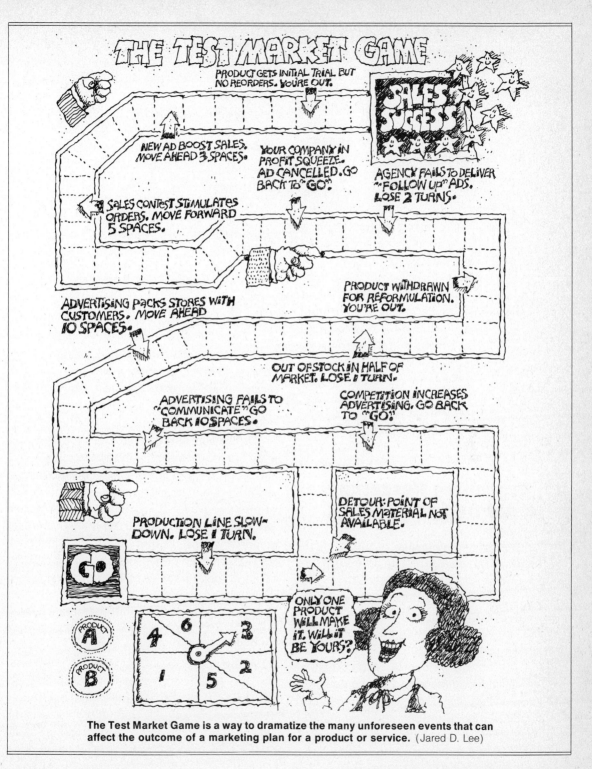

The Test Market Game is a way to dramatize the many unforeseen events that can affect the outcome of a marketing plan for a product or service. (Jared D. Lee)

Market Research and Advertising Research

Advertising people often distinguish between *market research* and *advertising research.* Advertising research is concerned only with the advertising process, while market research may or may not apply to the advertising process. Market research is concerned with facts about a market, its composition, and the demographic characteristics of the consumers within it. Advertising research restricts itself to determination of facts about the advertising, its impact, and its effectiveness. Both kinds of research are needed by advertisers. To sell their products and services properly, they must have market research to tell them what they need to know about customers and prospects. And they must have advertising research to help them find out whether or not the advertising is doing its job with these consumers. In practice, market research and advertising research overlap, and it is not necessary for our purposes to distinguish between them.

Organizing Research to Aid Decision Making

Since advertising people are trying to eliminate as much guesswork as possible from advertising, we should know what research activities are available for this purpose. We should be able to evaluate the practicality and usefulness of the research activities. For all the steps that advertisers customarily take (listed in Chapter 4) Table 9-1 outlines research aids that are useful along the way, for both national and local advertisers. The most important research aids will be described and their usefulness evaluated in the sections following the table. The subject of market and advertising re-

search is a separate study; here only highlights can be discussed, and the outline in Table 9-1 is by no means all-inclusive.

It is not necessary for an advertiser to use all the research aids listed in Table 9-1. Many of them are options, and if all the options were taken, duplication of findings would result. While it is foolish to attempt advertising with no research support, too much research can be a waste of time and money. The advertiser must ask whether a research project will truly be a help in making a better advertising decision. If it will help and it's affordable, it should be undertaken.

Secondary Sources

In developing information about marketing and and advertising, it is important for the national and local advertiser to check available material before initiating fresh research. The answer to the advertiser's question may already be known and may be located in what are called *secondary sources* —published or generally available data.

A television set manufacturer, for example, need not independently gather statistics on the incidence of color television set ownership, for this information is made known at regular intervals by the National Association of Television Set Manufacturers. A local department store ad manager who wants to know the occupations of wage earners in the sales area, the average income of these people, and something of their buying habits can usually find what is wanted in reports prepared by the chamber of commerce, the local newspaper, and various state authorities.

Principal sources of these types of information are the federal government (particularly the Department of Commerce, the Department of Agriculture, and the Bureau of the Census), state governments, trade and industrial associations, business books, media, and trade and industrial directories and publications.[3] Many of these sources are available at no cost.

Market Testing

The surest way for an advertiser to discover whether an ad program is producing sales is to prepare and run the advertising in the market —national, regional, or local, as the case may be—and make periodic sales audits of the advertised product or service. However, in the case of national advertisers, often as many as 6 months pass before enough data accumulate to judge a new campaign fairly. Local advertisers see sales results faster, sometimes in a matter of hours. But in either case advertising money has been irretrievably spent, and if results are bad, the money is wasted. Therefore, large advertisers with multi-million-dollar advertising budgets, who do all they can to protect their investments, rely heavily on market testing. This is a method whereby various elements of the advertising or marketing program can be tested on a small scale before funds are committed to a national advertising program.

Areas selected for test-market activites should reflect the composition of the national market as closely as possible. They should be small-scale versions of the country as a whole, containing a rural section as well as suburban and urban sections, and they should contain age groups, income classifications, and family compositions that are fairly comparable to their national counterparts. Within these areas, a wide choice of media should be available to the test marketer so that when a media plan is tested, it can include all the elements that will be used nationally. Certain cities and their outlying areas have been found to be projectable, or indicative of how the total consumer market might react to an advertising plan backing a given product or service. Medium-size cities often used as test markets are Albany, New York; Cincinnati, Ohio; Columbus, Ohio; Denver, Colorado; Des Moines, Iowa; Hartford, Connecticut; Omaha, Nebraska; Portland, Oregon; Rochester, New York; and Syracuse, New York. Smaller cities often used for test purposes include Flagstaff, Arizona; Herkimer, New York; and Stockton, California.

Here are some of the reasons for using test markets:

■ To introduce a new product or service to the marketplace.

■ To introduce an improved product and compare its sales with the sales of the product now being sold nationally.

■ To test a new media mix. For example, perhaps the product is backed nationally by network and spot television only. In the test market, television advertising expenditures are reduced and print media added.

■ To test a "heavy-up" media plan. If the national advertising budget were increased by 25 percent, would enough additional sales be generated to increase company profits? Before increasing the budget on a national scale, the advertiser establishes test markets for advertising at the increased rate and checks sales results.

■ To test the effectiveness of a new creative idea for an existing product or service.

■ To test sales promotion ideas on a limited scale before using them nationally. Such ideas include consumer contests, sales force contests, on-pack or write-in consumer premium offers, or price-off deals, the latter being temporary reductions in the product's price.

An alternative to going national after successful test-market results are obtained is to use *the roll-out method* of advertising and distribution of goods and services. This

---

[3] The U.S. Department of Commerce publishes *Market Research Sources,* which lists market data sources in business, government, and education.

TABLE 9-1 The Nine Advertising Steps with Research Correlations

Advertising Step	Research Activities	
	National	**Local**
1 Advertiser establishes an objective or goal for advertising	**a** Utilization of consumer qualitative and quantitative studies (see step 2) **b** Analysis of advantages and limitations of own products and competitors' **c** Analysis of competitors' goals and advertising **d** Collection and analysis of secondary source material on consumer wants, demographic characteristics of consumers, market statistics, etc. **e** Analysis of sales (current and past), market share, sales growth potentials, changing market	**a** Gathering and analysis of facts on type of store, customers appealed to, demographic characteristics of customers, untapped prospects in market **b** Analysis of competitors' goals and advertising **c** Sales analysis to determine goals and timing of advertising

2 Advertiser selects goods or services to be advertised	**a** Product development; R&D (research and development) activities
	b Qualitative consumer studies:
	  (1) Depth studies
	  (2) Focus group sessions
	  (3) Consumer panels
	c Quantitative consumer studies:
	  (1) Usage and attitude
	  (2) Demographic characteristics of customers and prospects
	  (3) Brand image
	d Product testing of own product and competitors':
	  (1) Laboratory
	  (2) With consumer groups
	e Market testing
		a Consideration of sales history and experience
		b Observation of competitors' experience
		c Study of industry, suppliers' sales trends; fashion trends
		d Analysis of composition of local market
		e Determination of store's selling area
		f Study of demographic characteristics of customers
		g Learning about local customer preferences, customs, life styles
		h Small-scale advertising tests in various media
		i Small in-store test promotions

3 Advertiser determines how much should be spent	**a** Analysis of own past advertising expenditures and effectiveness **b** Observation of competitors' activities; determination of size of competitors' budgets **c** Test-market activities **d** Affordability studies; cost-of-selling analysis of media needed for market coverage (see step 4)	Same as national

TABLE 9-1 (*Continued*)

Advertising Step	Research Activities	
	National	**Local**
4 Advertiser chooses advertising media	**a** Determination of coverage of market by type of media **b** Comparison coverage studies among individual components of media groups (paper A versus paper B, etc.) **c** Media demographic studies, quality-of-circulation research **d** Media cost comparisons based on cost-per-thousand circulation figures, maximil and minimil rates, GPRs, total audience, etc. **e** Market testing	**a** Same studies as national advertiser when practical and when information is available **b** Advertising tests in various local media
5 Advertiser prepares the advertising	**a** Advertising communications research: (1) Pretesting the ads (2) Posttesting the ads **b** Comprehension research **c** Measurement of selling strength of ad copy **d** Qualitative and quantitative consumer research	**a** Observation of competitors' strategies and advertising **b** Utilization of secondary source information on advertising readership **c** Informal investigations of consumer reactions to own and competitors' advertising
6 Advertiser produces the advertising in the form required by the media	No research aid required	No research aid required
7 Advertiser places advertising in the chosen media	No research aid required	No research aid required
8 Advertiser pays bills and does other paperwork	No research aid required	No research aid required
9 Advertiser evaluates results of the advertising	**a** National sales analysis **b** Market test sales analysis **c** Studies of brand image and usage, of consumer attitude and awareness **d** Quantitative study of consumer attitude and awareness and communications studies (of own advertising and competitors')	Sales analysis of advertised products; sales analysis of total business

method is slower but safer. In roll-out, a manufacturer does not immediately start selling and advertising everywhere at once. The manufacturer will first expand in 25 percent of the country, for example, and then add other areas at 4- or 6-month intervals until complete coverage is achieved. This way, advertisers can make changes and fine-tune the marketing and advertising plans as they go along, guided by experience in the field.

Store Audits An actual sales count at the point of sale of the items being tested is essential to any market-testing operation. This count is called a *store audit,* and the stores selected for the sample to be studied are called the panel. In a store audit, inventory, items on the shelf, and shipments received are examined at regular intervals, usually every 2 months, to reveal the actual sales of the product to the consumer. With this method, sales of competing products can also be watched to help evaluate the effectiveness of the promotional effort behind the test-market product.

A manufacturer always has sales figures showing how much product is shipped to distributors. These are called shipment figures. But they do not help explain actual movement of the product through the retail store, and they shed no light on the effect of a manufacturer's promotional activity on competitors' sales. Store audits are necessary to complete the manufacturer's picture of the total market.

Store audits are generally made by a research company hired by the manufacturer, not by the manufacturer's sales force, which has a full-time job of its own. A panel of 1,200 stores is used, and results can be projected to sales figures nationally. The A. C. Nielsen Company is the largest company in the store audit field. The manufacturer may subscribe to Nielsen's *Food and Drug Index,* which supplies store

Employees of the A.C. Nielsen Company conducting a store audit to determine the monthly sales of grocery store products. (Courtesy A.C. Nielsen Co.)

audits on a wide range of products, or have a special store audit set up—at considerable expense.

Warehouse Shipments Another method of analyzing food store sales is to monitor movement of all product shipments from warehouse to retail outlet. SAMI (Selling Areas Marketing, Inc.), a division of Time, Inc., offers this service to manufacturers. While SAMI does not offer information on movement of products through stores, as a store audit does, its data reveal warehouse shipments to retail outlets of an individual manufacturer's product and all competing brands. SAMI records shipments in thirty-nine major markets which account for about three-quarters of total United States retail food store sales. Its reports thus can be said to reveal national sales trends and the data are supplied faster than is possible through store audits.

Split-Market Testing We have already seen that many variables may exist in the marketplace during the period of a manufacturer's testing activities. If two test markets are used for comparison purposes and all factors do not remain equal in each market, the results of the research are ambiguous. And even if a single test market is used, it may have changed by the end of the test period so that it is no longer comparable to the national market. In recent years a new television research technique, *split-market testing,* has been developed that gives the marketer control over every variable in the test area except the one being tested. It is similar in some respects to split-run newspaper and magazine testing. A single market is used, and the television audience is split in half, each portion receiving a different advertising message about the product being tested.

One example of split-market testing is the AdTel system, based on CATV (Community Antenna Television). Instead of a single cable carrying television programs to viewing homes, a dual cable is installed in the test city. Half the homes involved in the test tie in with one cable, the other half with the second cable. Through a cut-in system, shown in the illustration, A homes can receive a test commercial, while B homes can receive regular advertising, and the advertising effectiveness can be checked by studying purchase diaries maintained by cooperating familes who own televisions linked to CATV cable. A and B homes number 1,000 families each.

AdTel has three test markets available to advertisers, AdTel City, AdTel West, and AdTel Midwest. It has avoided publishing the specific locations of these markets (although they are an open secret in the advertising community) to ensure that people in the test cities react to the advertising as ordinary customers

In the AdTel system of split market testing, technicians use this console to cut in test commercials shown to half the local CATV audience; the other half receives regular advertising, and the results are compared. (Courtesy AdTel)

would. If people were aware that their purchase decisions were the basis of future marketing decisions, this information might color or change their reactions.

The advantage of systems such as AdTel is that the market test is made on a one-city basis; if noncontrollable situations, such as increased competitive activity, occur during the test period, they affect both halves of the audience equally, making such changing market conditions less important to the research.

There are disadvantages, too, to such systems. For example, it is difficult to determine whether a consumer purchased the product because copy story A was seen on the set or because the consumer received a recommendation from someone else in town who had been exposed to copy story B. However, no system is perfect, and the disadvantages are not important enough to keep marketers from making these useful split-market tests.

Market Testing by Local Merchants The activities of progressive local merchants in their own sales areas often parallel those of national advertisers. Local merchants are constantly besieged by salespeople of local media who ask for advertising orders. Merchants can test the sales pulling power of these local media relatively inexpensively and compare results very quickly.

For example, a local department store buyer and the advertising manager know the sales history of an item that has been advertised successfully in the evening newspaper. Two weekly newspapers that cover suburban areas within the store's sales territory are available. They can now advertise the item exclusively in these supplemental media and compare ad costs and sales results with known figures to determine whether or not the two weekly newspapers should be added to the advertising schedule. The Meyersons, the hardware store

owner-operators discussed in Chapter 4, can try a small experiment in a medium they haven't used, in this case local radio. They pick an item of known sales appeal and advertise it exclusively in this medium. If they feel the results in increased sales, and if the results obtained are comparable to those from the local newspaper they have used in the past, they may well consider adding radio advertising to their ad program. If nothing happens, the Meyersons are out only a small amount of money. Direct mail and local television spots can be similarly tested.

Within the store, merchants can use test market activities. Before they commit themselves to taking on a new item or a new line of goods, they can devote a display window to the merchandise or set up a counter display and check sales results. If customers buy the new merchandise, the merchants know they have new promotable items on their hands.

Consumer Studies

At every stage in the life of a product, the manufacturer can make better marketing and advertising decisions if consumer attitudes, wants, and motivating forces are understood as they relate to what is to be sold. This understanding even helps shape new product concepts. Various types of consumer studies can help in the following ways:

- Help product development and product improvement
- Help determine advertising strategy
- Contribute to test-market activities
- Shed light on competitors' weaknesses and indicate sales opportunities
- Offer valuable assistance in developing advertising creative work
- Help media selection

It is important to distinguish between two types of consumer research. *Qualitative re-*

search is conducted with small groups of consumers, and the findings are not considered an accurate reflection of the consuming public as a whole. In research terminology, qualitative research is not projectable. It is valuable in gaining an insight into the consumer's mind, but it does not intend to be definitive. *Quantitative research,* on the other hand, attempts to reflect accurately the attitudes, preferences, reactions, habits, or wants of the entire target group, and it accomplishes its aims by means of a scientifically selected sample of the target group. Quantitative research is projectable and accurate within certain statistically defined percentage points. A sample of 3,000 homemakers might be found adequate for a survey on the use of, and preference for, household detergents, and the findings would be projectable to the "universe" of all United States homemakers. If a maker of a stomach settler for children wanted to discover the attitudes of pediatricians toward the product and similar competing products, a properly designed sample of 500 pediatricians would probably be adequate and projectable to the universe of all United States pediatricians. The sample size is checked by continuing interviewing or questionnaire completion to a point where additional results do not change those already obtained.

We will now examine some popular forms of qualitative and quantitative consumer studies.

Focus Group Sessions Up to nine people are brought together in relaxing surroundings in *focus group sessions* to discuss marketing or advertising, and subjects are introduced by a trained group leader or moderator. Such sessions are a valuable aid to research at many steps in the advertising process. The findings are qualitative rather than quantitative. The group leader knows that certain defined areas should be covered in the course of the 1- to

1 ½-hour session and keeps the conversation from wandering. The proceedings are usually taped for future reference.

It is important for an advertiser to know as much as possible about customers and potential customers, their thought processes, what makes them like or not like the product or service, how their attitudes are changing, and what their unsatisfied wants are. This knowledge will enable the advertiser to meet their needs and thus increase sales. Ideally, copywriters, brand people, advertising directors, and everyone involved in the creative process of advertising would frequently interview consumers; unfortunately, this is such a time-consuming procedure that it is not possible. Focus group sessions are a good substitute for face-to-face contact with consumers. Here are some ways these sessions can be used.

If a new product (such as a new brand of instant coffee) is to be developed in an already existing category, a group of the category's customers (here, coffee drinkers) can be brought together to discuss their likes and dislikes for brands already on the market.

Users of the manufacturer's brand or of competitive brands can be asked to discuss reasons for their preference, with the reasons cross-checked against current copy claims.

In copy development work, sessions are valuable in revealing how the consumer actually talks about products and services. The words and phrases used sometimes make good copy in themselves and often open up new ideas for the creative process.

Focus group sessions are used by most national advertisers today. They are an inexpensive form of research and can be completed quickly. Their drawbacks are that findings are not projectable, participants are sometimes too shy to open up and talk frankly about the

PARTICIPANT 1: I gave'em TV dinners last Friday and everybody --
I mean everybody -- groaned. It was those fish
sticks and I don't know what kind of fish they put
into them.
(LAUGHTER. SEVERAL SIMULTANEOUS COMMENTS)

GROUP LEADER: Did you feel guilty about serving them?

PARTICIPANT 1: Like I said, I do feel guilty. But some are better
then others. I don't mind, once in a while. The
costly ones taste good.

PARTICIPANT 2: A couple down the block where we lived last year,
she served TV dinners all the time and all I know
is, they got a divorce.
(LAUGHTER)

GROUP LEADER: Getting back to our gourmet TV dinners. If the
dinners were truly tasty, if the recipes were a
little different, would you ladies be willing to
try them?

PARTICIPANT 1: You said they'd be 30 percent higher and that's
okay as long as they're 30 percent better.

PARTICIPANT 2: I'd certainly try that beef bordelaise with the
noodles or that other one you said -- the one with
the corn pudding and I wouldn't mind a bit spending
more money for them.

GROUP LEADER: Now ladies, I want to get your thoughts on the names
for these new gourmet TV dinners. If you'll pass
the list down, Harriet. . . . Just look over the
names and I'll be asking you what thoughts they
bring up. . . just your off-hand thoughts.

PARTICIPANT 2: That first one's a lulu. Fancy Fixin's. I don't
go much for that one . . .

This is an excerpt from a focus group session. The group leader introduces subjects of interest to advertisers and obtains reactions from the panel, in this instance consisting of homemakers.

subject, and responses may be influenced by a domineering member of the group. But these drawbacks do not outweigh their usefulness.

Local merchants have not taken advantage of the opportunities presented by focus group sessions, largely because this form of research has not been brought to their attention. Bringing store customers and prospects together informally and at regular intervals can shed valuable light on the convenience of shopping hours, the adequacy and helpfulness of salespeople, the adequacy of stock, the image of one's own store and that of competitors, and local media reading and listening habits.

Individual Depth or Motivation Interviews

Sometimes it is desirable to learn not only what consumers think about products and services but also why they think the way they do. In the process of discovering consumers' motivations for their actions and attitudes, valuable help may be given in developing new products, improving existing products, and developing ways to talk to consumers through advertising. Focus group sessions help here, but this technique can inhibit individuals from revealing their true attitudes because of fear of social embarrassment and loss of face or because of lack of composure. The *depth interview* tries to overcome these obstacles. It is conducted by a trained researcher, who interviews a series of consumers individually. Most such sessions last for at least an hour, and notes are taken, or a tape recording is made by the interviewer.

Depth research can be extremely helpful to the manufacturer. For example, depth interviews among housewives revealed that some of them added ammonia to ordinary floor cleansers for more cleaning efficiency. Manufacturers in the cleaning field saw opportunities for new product development, and the result was a new category of cleaning products with ammonia already added.

Comet Cleanser is a product which benefited from depth interviewing. Before the product was formulated, homemakers were asked about how they cleaned their kitchen sinks. They were currently using cleansers containing a mild abrasive but no ingredient to get rid of the sink stains remaining on the porcelain after scrubbing. Some women had discovered that when a mixture of liquid bleach and water was allowed to stand in the sink for a while, the stains would disappear, and interviewers noted this fact. The manufacturer, through its product research and development people, was able to produce a dry, chlorine bleach in stable form which was then made part of the Comet formulation. This product improvement was featured in introductory advertising, was recognized and preferred by consumers, and was one of the main reasons why Comet became a leader in its category—from a standing start of no sales at all.

Depth research of this nature is qualitative, expensive, and time-consuming, but it is regarded as a valuable aid in understanding the consumer. It is often used to obtain consumer information on products of a personal nature.

Concept Testing and Consumer Juries

Many attempts have been made to develop research methods that forecast sales by pretesting the selling power of advertising with consumer groups. Unfortunately, in spite of claims to the contrary, no consumer testing method has yet been devised that guarantees sales success. The problem with such methods lies in the artificiality of the tests themselves. When shown samples of advertising and asked whether the sales messages make them want to buy the products or services, consumers become self-conscious, and the statements they make in these contrived situations are not necessarily borne out by subsequent sales.

In the past, the *consumer jury* was popular.

In this setup, typical consumers are asked which of two advertising layouts is preferred or which advertising theme or idea would make them want to buy the product. This approach places the consumer in the role of judge, an unreal position that does not correspond to the actual buying process. Research of this unrealistic type should be avoided.

Another method, *concept testing,* can be of value in certain areas. In this technique, advertising concepts, slogans, selling themes, and storyboards or layouts are presented to consumers in individual interviews for their comments. Ideally, only a single concept is presented; a choice between two or more is avoided. The other concepts are presented to other interviewees, and the results are compared. Because of the artificiality of the situation, the selling power of the concepts cannot legitimately be measured, but other factors can. For example, concept testing can help in determining whether the advertising idea is understandable and registers the selling idea as intended. In other words, it can test for comprehension—an important test, for the written message does not always convey the meaning desired. Concept testing can also indicate the relative interest to the consumer of a selling idea. In addition, it can determine whether the idea evokes positive or negative reactions. Concept testing can be accomplished not only by the individual interview method but also by the focus group method.

The concept testing and the consumer jury methods are both forms of qualitative research.

Experimental Consumer Research The elusive goal of finding a foolproof technique to measure the selling power of advertising before running advertising campaigns has preoccupied marketers for years, and some of the methods developed are esoteric, as a couple of examples will show.

In a method called VOPAN, the voice of a consumer being interviewed is recorded, then voice "bench marks" are established, and the whole track subjected to computer analysis. Various voice inflections, to a trained listener, may indicate that when the person interviewed says something like "Yes, I would buy the product," what is *really* meant is "Maybe I won't buy it after all." This method attempts to discover if the answers interviewees give really reflect their attitudes or are just given in an effort to please the person conducting the interview.

TELCOM, a viewing mechanism, actually audits the eye motion of the person being interviewed. When shown sample advertising layouts, for example, how many times does the eye move back and forth? Where on the ad does the eye linger? What doesn't it see at all? The procedure attempts to determine what is interesting and what is not in the advertising message. Ideally it guides the advertiser in development of advertising that sells the product efficiently.

New methods of this nature come along constantly. But the best method available to evaluate the selling efficiency of advertising continues to be costly and time-consuming. This method consists of putting products in test markets and evaluating results. Various split-run media techniques can be included in test-market activities and can produce helpful findings.

Questionnaires The questionnaire is frequently used in quantitative research. It is presented to the consumer in a personal interview or by mail or phone. The *questionnaire* is a structured technique in which a number of predetermined questions are asked in a certain order. Care must be taken to ensure that the form the questions take delivers the desired results. Vague propositions and questions that are open to misinterpretation produce poor research results. Often questionnaires are pre-tested with small groups to determine whether they will produce the desired information when the survey is actually made.

Let us assume that we must prepare a questionnaire on behalf of a nationally advertised soft drink to discover consumer habits and likes and dislikes in the soft-drink field. Here is a partial list of questions we should NOT include in a questionnaire:

1. Do you usually drink soft drinks? Yes No

2. In the past week, which of the following brands—Coca-Cola and Pepsi-Cola—have you tried?

3. What do you like about Coca-Cola?

4. What do you like about Pepsi-Cola?

5. Which brand do you like better, and why?

6. Disregarding taste, how do you feel about the shape of the bottle?

This questionnaire is an example of how not to prepare a survey, because the questions are not specific enough. The answer to question 1 wouldn't be particularly helpful. Question 2, although more specific, doesn't indicate whether the brand was bought by the interviewee or served to him or her. Questions 3 and 4 force a positive answer by assuming that the interviewee likes Pepsi and Coke. Question 5 wanders; it does not ask for specifics. Question 6 is too complicated, and individuals are unable to disregard taste.

The following series of questions is more direct and not subject to misinterpretation by the person being interviewed or the interviewer.

1. In the past week, how many bottles of soft drinks have you consumed?

2. In the past week, which of the following brands—Coca-Cola and Pepsi-Cola—have you bought? Have you been served?

3. What do you like about Coca-Cola? What do you dislike about Coca-Cola? (Interviewer probes for negative and positive answers.)

4. What do you like about Pepsi-Cola? What do you dislike about Pepsi-Cola? (Interviewer probes for negative and positive answers.)

5. Which do you like better (Pepsi) (Coke) in taste? In effervescence? In refreshing qualities?

6. Which bottle is easier to handle?

There are problems connected with using questionnaires. If the field worker doing the interviewing is tired at the end of a long day, answers may be written down incorrectly or not at all. An unethical interviewer may merely make up answers and fill out questionnaires without bothering to interview anybody. These problems are eliminated by validation. In validation, the interviewer always records the name and phone number of the person being interviewed on the questionnaire. Later a certain percentage of these people are phoned by personnel of the research company responsible for the job and a check is made on whether or not the answers given are what really was said to the interviewer. Validation should be done on all questionnaire surveys. At Spencer Bruno Research Associates, a firm that is a leading proponent of this system, staff members routinely call back and reinterview 10 percent of all people originally interviewed by field workers.

Brand Image or Reputation Studies Quantitative research, usually in the form of questionnaires, can be used to determine the image or reputation that a national or regional brand has in the minds of consumers. Usually a brand's reputation is compared with that of its competitors. Brand image studies are most useful when they are made on a regular basis, preferably annually. With regular image studies, the trend of a brand's popularity may be determined. If the popularity is diminishing, this can be an early warning that something is seriously amiss.

Usage and Attitude Studies Usage and attitude studies are quantitative studies made to determine consumer usage of a product and its competition over a period of time. Typical questions are "Do you have X product on hand?" "When did you last buy it?" "How often in the past months have you purchased it?" Usually included are rating questions that ask the consumer to indicate likes and dislikes about principal products in a particular category. Questions on likes and dislikes about package design and the use to which a product is put may be added. The usage information is a helpful cross-check on sales, and the other information received can be helpful in eliminating product weakness or in indicating what profitable selling approaches might be.

Copy-Testing Procedures

As market and advertising research have become more sophisticated, it has been natural for marketers to try to develop research tools to determine whether advertising messages are effective with consumers. The advertiser is vitally interested in how many people actually read the print advertising or pay attention to the broadcast message, so techniques have been developed to test advertising before and after it appears.

Pretesting Copy Several of the methods already discussed in this chapter can be used to test advertising messages for their ability to communicate and for the degree of interest they arouse in the consumer before the advertiser decides to use them on a national or regional basis. It is wise to determine, before in-

vesting one's national advertising dollars, whether the advertising arouses interest. If the message attracts relatively little consumer attention on a test basis, the campaign usually is killed.

AdTel is a useful pretesting facility, and concept testing with focus groups or individual interviews can supply a limited amount of knowledge on consumer interest in a given advertising campaign or selling idea.

Testing Recruited Audiences In recruited-audience tests, consumer groups are invited to a theater or auditorium, ostensibly to preview television shows. Included in the program is a series of television commercials. Later, the group is quizzed on what they remember about the commercials, which are rated according to the responses. In the *Schwerin method* of testing sales effectiveness of commercials, consumers are asked to choose their favorite products before viewing commercials and again after viewing to determine whether the commercials caused them to switch brand preferences. There are many variations of this method.

This kind of research is costly for advertisers because they must undergo the expense of producing a commercial for the test, and even the simplest television test commercials cost from $1,000 to $6,000 each. Some marketers insist on recruited-audience research in spite of a major drawback: the recruited-audience system is artificial in that it does not realistically parallel real-life television viewing habits. The unusual environment can produce misleading research results.

Recall Testing It is possible to test the ability of a television commercial to attract attention and communicate its sales points and to quantify the results of the test. From the reactions of a relatively small sample of the television viewing audience, it can be determined how the national viewing audience will react to a tested commercial. The method used is to telephone households at random 24 hours after a commercial has been aired to determine whether the person answering the phone was watching the television program containing the commercial being tested; if the person did see the program, questions are asked to establish whether or not the commercial is remembered, or recalled, and to find out what the viewer can repeat concerning the commercial's main points. The telephone interview is written up in a form called a *verbatim,* using the viewer's exact words. Here is an example of a verbatim:

There was a man in a restaurant, and the waitress asked him what he wanted for dessert. He didn't know. But he said he wanted something not too sweet but sort of sweet, and not too filling but just filling enough. He kept going on like this, and finally the waitress left without saying anything and brought him some Jell-O. The idea was Jell-O was just right. Then another guy at another table started the whole thing all over again. I thought it was a cute idea.

When about 200 verbatims are obtained in three or more test cities, a tabulated profile of the main points of the commercial can be drawn up and the score of the commercial compared with the scores of other tested commercials to determine the relative strengths of their communicating power.

Recall testing is nevertheless an expensive research method. A recall test of a commercial, with complete verbatims, costs an advertiser over $3,000 per test. To this must be added the costs of purchase of time in test cities and producing the commercial for the test. Burke International Research Corporation and Gallup & Robinson, Inc., are leading research firms in recall testing. It is considered worth the investment because it culls out the duds, or commercials that do not arouse viewers' interest and that would waste advertising dollars if they were run nationally.

Recall testing is done on commercials before they are aired to check viewers' interest and the ability of commercials to communicate. In television pretesting, advertisers have discovered that simple inexpensive messages without full production values of expensive casting and elaborate location shooting will score just as well as the more expensively produced commercials, and testing money can be saved in this area. A simple form of commercial known as an *animatic* can be produced for $1,000 or $1,500. An animatic consists of a series of colored drawings sometimes including

In TV recall testing, groups of television interviewers phone at random to determine how many individuals reached have seen and remembered TV commercials aired 24 hours earlier. (Courtesy Burke Marketing Research, Inc.)

limited animation. Research has shown that animatics, when tested, deliver a relatively similar recall score to those of full-production commercials.

Although it is unproved that high-scoring TV commercials or print advertisements necessarily result in higher than average sales, major advertisers want high-scoring commercials because of their ability to communicate. As a result, accounts have been lost by advertising agencies when campaigns get low scores consistently. High-score psychosis is a phenomenon present in copy departments of large agencies. When a good score comes in, it's a happy day for the copy group involved. When a bad score shows up, gloom prevails, and the account executive then has the difficult job of breaking the bad news about the recall score to the client.

Recall testing can also be used to pretest magazine advertising for communications efficiency through the use of a dummy magazine or newspaper supplement, which is placed in selected homes with the aim of duplicating home magazine readership habits. The dummy magazine or newspaper supplement is prepared by a research organization and contains several ads for which test results are desired. After 24 hours, interviewers call in person and determine the readership and attention-getting power of the ads in the same way that phone interviewers check on television commercials. The interviewers also obtain profiles and scores. Gallup & Robinson, Inc., conducts this kind of testing and can make available to its clients the records of literally tens of thousands of tested ads.

Posttesting Copy After a campaign breaks, major advertisers often check the ability of the television commercials or print ads to communicate a sales message. They might do this to check out a new campaign or to see if their TV messages, for example, are still retaining their original ability to score, as already determined by pretesting. This is called checking for wear-out factor. After a period of time, varying from commercial to commercial, the message becomes boring to viewers and is ignored. When this occurs, scores plummet, and the commercial is taken off the air. Recruited-audience methods are used for this purpose as well as the 24-hour recall system. The Daniel Starch service provides a widely used method of measuring readership of magazine ads. On the basis of interviews, ads in magazines are rated on the percentage of men and women who "noted" the ad, associated it with the product advertised, and read all or some of the copy. A typical Starched ad, showing the "noted," "seen-associated," and "read most" percentage ratings is shown on page 211. These figures can be used to compare the attention-getting power of one magazine ad with that of another in the same issue.

It is important to remember the assumption that underlies communications testing. It is not necessarily true that an ad will sell because it communicates well, but if it doesn't communicate, it won't sell. Other forms of research such as depth and focus interviews, questionnaires, and product tests help determine whether the advertiser's selling message is on the right track and help guide the advertiser to messages that can reasonably be expected to motivate the consumer to buy.

Research and the Local Advertiser

We have discussed local merchants' test-market activities and the value of focus group sessions earlier in the chapter. Research can aid the local advertiser in other important ways. It can help determine the extent of the area in which the merchant's goods or services can be

Bobby Woo, the 200 Millionth American ...10 years later.

Meet Bobby Woo, the 200 Millionth American. His diapers are done in a Maytag.

Two weeks before Bobby arrived, Mrs. Woo got a Maytag Washer and Dryer. She was following her mother's example.

MAYTAG
THE DEPENDABILITY PEOPLE

The Maytag Company, Newton, Iowa 50208

The Maytag that washed his diapers in 1967 is now washing his baseball uniforms, says Mrs. Woo.

David, 6; Angie, 11; Bobby, 10
Mrs. Sally Woo; Mr. Robert Woo; Cindy, 8

Whatever became of Bobby Woo, born a celebrity on November 20, 1967, when the Census people in Washington designated him the 200 Millionth American?

Well, since appearing in the Maytag ad reproduced here, "There are many changes in Bobby's life," writes his mother, Mrs. Sally Woo, Tucker, Georgia. "He has two sisters and one brother . . . he is a fifth-grader . . . he plays Little League baseball."

But one thing hasn't changed, states Mrs. Woo. The same Maytag that did Bobby's diapers in 1967 is washing for him today. The family laundry runs about 10 loads a week. But that washer has only [one] repair in 10 hard-working [years]. This doesn't surprise [her,] Mrs. Woo, because she [knows] Maytag Washers are built to last longer and need fewer repairs.

Of course, we don't say all Maytags will equal that record. But long life with few repairs is what we try to build into every Maytag Washer, Dryer, Dishwasher, and Disposer.

MAYTAG
THE DEPENDABILITY P[EOPLE]

This ad has been tested for its readership by Daniel Starch & Staff. The tabs pasted on the ad show what percentage of the readers who were checked "noted" various elements, saw and associated the ad with the product ("seen-associated"), and "read most" of the copy. (Courtesy Starch INRA Hooper, Inc. and Maytag)

sold, supply knowledge of the types of customers who buy from the merchant, and help determine the timing of promotions.

Trading Area A merchant should determine the firm's trading area, the geographic sections from which customers are drawn. This is important because the advertising must do an efficient job of covering the sales area. The merchant may find that the newspaper that carries the advertising has a smaller circulation than another paper in a section where good customers are located, and the advertising may be switched as a result. A city newspaper may not cover a suburban or rural area where the store's customers live, so a combination of radio and weekly suburban paper would be a better media buy.

The merchant can obtain information on where customers live (or work, if trade is drawn from a center-city area) from several sources, including a study of delivery records and charge accounts and brief interviews with customers to obtain a profile of part of the merchant's trade.

Demographic Characteristics of Customers
To serve customers best and to build sales volume, a merchant should know as much as possible about the kinds of people who come into the store. The merchant should know their occupations, age groupings, family size, income, and interests. The chamber of commerce and the local media can supply some of this information, and more specific facts can be obtained through the use of questionnaires mailed to customers or by telephone interviews.

A thorough knowledge of present customers will be an invaluable aid to the merchant in deciding what to stock and what to promote. And once a typical customer profile is established, the merchant can search for similar potential

customers through sales promotion and advertising efforts.

Determining Advertising Timing In order for advertising to be most effective, the right merchandise, realistically priced, must be promoted at the right time, and research aids the local advertiser in the matter of timing. Sales analyses should be made of seasonal patterns in the movement of merchandise and advertising plans subsequently tailored so that advertising schedules are increased during peak selling periods and cut down or eliminated during dull periods. In departmentalized stores, such as discount houses and department stores, various departments have differing periods of sales strength, and an analysis of departmental sales over the year will determine when each department's items should be featured.

A study of customer buying habits and daily sales volume figures aids in determining which day of the week is best for advertising. Each merchant must make an individual study, for often even stores carrying similar lines of merchandise have different daily sales patterns. As Edwards and Brown point out, paydays, local customs, and night openings can all affect daily sales volume[4] and these days can vary in different parts of the same community. Observing competitors' ad schedules is helpful as a check on a merchant's own timing of advertising, but too much consideration of what the other person is doing hampers initiative, develops a follow-the-leader or "me-too" psychology, and may be wrong for the merchant's own situation.

Market Data Supplied by Local Media The local advertiser should be familiar with the substantial amount of market data supplied by

[4] Edwards and Brown, p. 637.

local media. While some of it is obviously prepared to promote the particular medium and sell advertising space and time, the advertiser who keeps this fact in mind will still find useful information and help.

For example, the San Diego *Union and Evening Tribune,* in a promotion advertisement run in an advertising trade journal, lists the following market information that it has available for the asking: "San Diego Market Analysis," "Annual Review of San Diego Business Activity," "San Diego's Auto Market," "Automobile Dealer Map of San Diego County," "San Diego County Shopping Center Map," "Map of Major Food Outlets," "Grocer and Market Route Book," "Route List of Drug Outlets," "The San Diego Liquor Market," "Newspaper Readership and Family Characteristics," "Circulation Analysis by Regional Marketing Areas," and other pamphlets as well.

Vocabulary

Define the following terms, and use each one in a sentence:

Advertising research
Concept testing
Consumer jury
Depth interview
Focus group session
Market research
Qualitative research
Quantitative research

Questionnaire
Roll-out method
Schwerin method
Secondary source
Split-market testing
Store audit
Verbatim

Review Questions

1. Why is it difficult for a national marketer to forecast advertising sales results?
2. Do you think it is easier for a local merchant to forecast advertising sales results? If so, why?
3. Why is it important to check secondary sources before initiating new research studies?
4. Why might a national manufacturer of an established brand open a test market?
5. What are the advantages to the marketer of using the roll-out method of advertising and distribution rather than going national after successfully test marketing a product?

6. Describe the process of validation used by research companies to check on the accuracy of questionnaire surveys.
7. What kind of information do store audits deliver that a manufacturer's shipment figures cannot supply?
8. If you were a manufacturer of a women's complexion soap, what kind of information would you want to obtain from a series of focus groups?
9. Would a focus group session be helpful to a local department store ad manager? What could the ad manager find out that might be of value in preparing the advertising program?
10. Discuss how research activities can help the local advertiser.
11. Why should a local merchant establish a customer profile?

Activities

1. With another student, prepare a consumer questionnaire for the maker of a high-protein cold breakfast cereal that appeals to adults. Review the questionnaire text first. The maker is interested in obtaining information on purchase and usage habits of consumers of the maker's brand and of competitive high-protein cereal brands.
2. You have just been hired as the ad manager of a chain of discount houses selling a wide range of items including proprietary (brand name) drugs, housewares, clothing, sporting goods, garden equipment, electric appliances, and television and radio sets. No research has been done. What research activities would you suggest?

Project

You are a local, part-time interviewer for a national research firm and have been asked to obtain answers to questions listed on a couple of questionnaires. For this project, however, choose the questionnaire that you prefer; you need not do both.

Your instructions are to approach shoppers (perhaps outside a supermarket) and politely ask for their cooperation. Try to obtain at least five completed questionnaires. (As a student, your approach to obtain answers would be to state that you are an undergraduate, tell where you are enrolled, and tell the interviewee that you are studying market research. Then ask the shopper to answer a few brief questions.)

On completion of your five questionnaires, add the results of the questionnaires of other students, and obtain for your locality a "sample" of consumers' buying habits concerning household cleansers or light bulbs.

Household Cleanser Questionnaire

1. What product do you usually buy to clean your bathtub and kitchen sink?
2. How long have you used this product?
3. Why do you use it in preference to other products?
4. Why did you buy this particular product in the first place?
5. If you are aware of any advertising for this product, where have you seen it (in magazines or on television?)
6. Is there anything about this product that you think could be improved?

Light-Bulb Questionnaire

1. What make of light bulb do you usually buy for your home?
2. How long have you used this brand?
3. Why do you buy this particular brand? (Probe for reasons.)
4. What wattage bulb do you usually use for a reading lamp? Check one.
   50_____ 75_____ 100_____ 150_____
5. Have you ever bought a three-way light bulb?
6. If yes, what make was it?
7. Did you find the three-way bulb satisfactory?
8. If satisfactory, in what way?
9. If unsatisfactory, in what way?

Career Ladder

You are a project director in a medium-sized research firm and have done a good job for the past 3 years. Two openings offering more responsibilities and more pay have opened up in your firm, and you have been given your choice of either position. One job consists of guiding and programming the work of the three project supervisors the firm employs. This would be more of the same kind of work you have been doing but with additional responsibilities. The other job is in the selling area: presenting the firm's abilities to new business prospects and current clients. In this job, there could be even more money involved because in addition to your salary, you would get a commission on any new business you obtained. In addition, you would plan research projects for present clients and new ones. Which job do you want, and why?

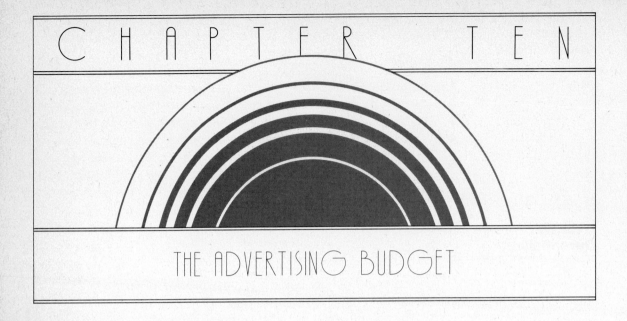

CHAPTER TEN

THE ADVERTISING BUDGET

The advertiser's most important guide to achieving goals and objectives is the advertising budget, or advertising appropriation. An *advertising budget* is a plan that sets a limitation on advertising expenditures, states how expenditures will be allocated, and controls the disbursement of advertising over a designated period of time, usually a year.

The advertising manager of a firm is the person responsible for the advertising budget. The ad manager prepares the budget, presents it to management for approval (trying hard to "sell it"), and then controls the approved advertising expenditures throughout the year.

How advertising dollars are spent is essentially a matter of choice. There are several tempting ways in which the advertiser can spend money, mainly in the purchase of media; if the ad manager succumbs, financial disaster is the result. But the very act of building a budget usually forces the advertiser to consider the various advertising possibilities carefully. And if the ad manager isn't able to re-

sist temptation, the comptroller or treasurer will be.

What Expenditures a Budget Covers

The costs of placing ads in various media are the advertiser's major costs, usually taking more than 65 percent of the advertising budget. But other expenses are incurred in operating an advertising program that must be taken into consideration. If all these costs are not included in the budget, there will be no way of determining how much the total program costs or of whether the expense is too great.

The following are the major expenditures that are involved in an advertising program:

1. Media costs; space charges for newspapers, magazines, directories, etc.; time charges for television and radio; costs of direct mail programs; outdoor and transit advertising; specialty advertising items

2. Point-of-sale advertising materials; sales force, dealer, and wholesaler advertising brochures; pamphlets; fliers; package inserts; window displays, in-store displays, and signs (retail advertisers) (all these items can be handled separately in a sales promotion budget)

3. Costs of producing advertising material

4. Advertising research

5. Payroll expenses of advertising department; costs of outside advertising technicians

6. Advertising department supplies and equipment

7. Travel expenses of advertising department personnel when such travel relates to the advertising program

In the course of a year, most of these expenditures will vary, although payroll expenses and the cost of supplies are relatively stable and, when forecast on an annual basis, can be allocated equally to each month.

Ways to Arrive at an Advertising Budget

There are several ways of determining the size of a budget, and they apply to national and local advertisers alike. Not all the methods used are of equal value; some are poor guides and should be avoided, while others can be very helpful to business growth. But no matter which method is used, it is important to remember that the factors determining the size of a budget are subject to change as time passes. As is done in all parts of the advertising process, the advertiser determining budget size must make a decision relying on judgment, which is based on all the facts that can be brought to bear on the project.

Percentage of Actual Sales

A simple way to arrive at an advertising appropriation is to multiply past sales figures by a

percentage; the resulting figure becomes the advertising budget for the coming fiscal or calendar year. The percentage could be any figure—perhaps as little as 2 percent or as much as 6.5 percent—based on the firm's custom in past years, estimates of what competition is spending, or advice received from trade associations and trade journals. This method is often used by retail advertisers.

Aside from its simplicity, the advantage of this method is that it doesn't get the advertiser into trouble through overspending. The advertiser knows that the amount allocated can be afforded because it's been afforded in the past.

On the other hand, this method forces the advertiser to look at the ad program in a narrow way. The purpose of advertising is to help sales. When the advertising appropriation is based on past sales, the advertiser tends to think of advertising as a result rather than a cause. Perhaps more important, in using this method the advertiser is assuming that past decisions were right and therefore feels bound to these decisions in the future.

Percentage of Anticipated Sales

Another way to arrive at an advertising budget is to make an estimate of sales for the coming year, based on current sales volume trends, forecasts of business conditions, and guesses about the competition's future sales and promotion activities. A percentage of the anticipated sales volume is figured—in the same way as when the budget is based on the percentage of actual sales.

When a budget is established by figuring a percentage of anticipated sales, it at least causes the advertiser to plan ahead and forces the advertiser to acknowledge the fact that advertising causes sales. For these reasons, this method is better than the one based on the percentage of actual sales; however, it is most useful only when the sales volume for a product doesn't change very much over a period of several years.

Percentage of Profits

The essence of the percentage-of-profits method is affordability. An arbitrary percentage figure is applied to the previous year's profits or to anticipated profits for the coming year, and the resulting figure becomes the advertising budget.

The problem with a budget system based wholly on profits is that profits may deteriorate rapidly in a given year because of a business recession or heavy competition. If low profits are due to a recession, and if business conditions improve the following year, the advertiser is stuck with a budget too small to cope with the heavy promotional effort that may be called for because of improved business conditions. If low profits are due to competition, a big promotional campaign is desirable, but this can't be provided for in a budget based on a percentage of profits. On the other hand, a budget established in this way might, in a good year, overlook forecasts of bad times to come and call for too much spending.

Another drawback of the percentage-of-profits method is that it does not allow for investment spending plans, whereby advertising expenditures are deliberately increased to introduce and establish a new brand or to relaunch an established brand that has been improved. In these instances, brands do not return a profit to the manufacturer until the introductory phase is successfully completed. The advertiser must make an investment and overspend to achieve future success.

Affordability Method

The affordability method covers those instances when planning an advertising budget is arbitrary and capricious. Unplanned budgeting goes hand in hand with a lack of understanding or appreciation of the advertising process. Retailers, in particular, sometimes have no formal budget at all and respond irregularly to the salesmanship of media representatives, advertising extensively when they have the money and curtailing advertising when money becomes tight. But unplanned budgeting is by no means confined to retailers. One national manufacturer of a line of branded products that have mass appeal has often cut the advertising appropriation in the fourth quarter of the year so that money would be available for a dividend payment to company stockholders.

Task Method

In the task method, the advertiser first studies market objectives. What are the long- and short-range sales goals, and what are the plans to realize them? Are there changes evolving in consumer target groups, and is the marketing territory expanding or stable? During the next 12 months, what parts of the marketing objective must be completed? When these matters are reviewed in the course of preparing an advertising budget, the budget itself becomes a method of achieving the advertiser's goals.

In the task method, the first step is to estimate the amount of advertising expenditures needed to accomplish sales objectives for the coming year, and the second step is to pare this amount—because it is usually so large that it is unaffordable. In this case, however, budget cutting is done on a priority basis. The elements considered most important for achieving marketing objectives are retained as much as possible, and less important elements are sacrificed.

Psychologically, the task method does the most for the advertiser. It causes the advertiser to review the entire selling effort, and it acknowledges the power of advertising to create sales. In addition, the task method does not impose a budget figure on an advertising department, like the other methods discussed, and it has many parts, each of which performs a necessary and agreed-upon task in line with overall marketing strategy.

The task method has its drawbacks, but they are not so serious that they can cause an advertiser to make big mistakes, such as underspending or not responding to competitive pressures. Its drawbacks are that more time is needed to prepare the budget and that research facts must be established in order to justify every step.

Recently there has been much discussion of zero-base budgeting. This is a method sometimes used in governmental budget planning and overall corporate budget planning that starts from scratch and places the burden on the budget planners to justify every forecast expenditure. Applying this method to advertising budgets would mean that all elements of the budget, such as payroll expenses, supplies and equipment, and costs of producing advertising material, would be reevaluated along with media expenses annually. Few advertisers go to this length in budget procedures. It is a refinement of the task method and, as far as advertising budgets are concerned, the time needed cannot be justified.

Recommended Budget-Planning Procedure

The task method, although it requires the most marketing sophistication and the most budget preparation time, is recommended to national and retail advertisers alike. Preferably, other methods will also be used as a cross-check on final budget figures, for such methods are relatively simple to accomplish. For example, a manufacturer of fishing tackle whose current annual sales volume is $6 million establishes by the task method that the budget for the coming year should be $312,000. Looking at the past sales volume figures and advertising expenditures on the basis of a percentage of actual sales, the manufacturer finds that advertising spending has amounted to 4 percent of sales. The new budget will be higher, amounting to 5.2 percent of sales. Trade sources indicated that the average sporting goods manufacturer spends about 4 percent of annual sales for advertising, and it's a pretty good guess on the manufacturer's part that the principal competitor spends 4.5 percent. Considering these various pieces of information, it looks as though the manufacturer will be overspending. However, the task method shows why the manufacturer should spend more in the coming year. Several new tackle items are being introduced, and if they're promoted aggressively, they could increase profits substantially. The task method budget supports the need for extra spending.

Those planning a budget must take into consideration forecasts of the state of the national economy and of the advertiser's own area. General business trends do not necessarily carry over to individual businesses. Sales of staples such as soaps, detergents, and packaged foods do not decline as much as the sales of luxury goods when the economy is soft. They also do not expand at the same rate as the sales of luxury goods when the economy is booming. When planning a budget, advertisers should try to anticipate conditions that will affect their products.

Variations in Ad Spending by Industry and Type of Business

In the planning of advertising budgets, it is always helpful to know as much as possible about what the other fellow is spending. Specific figures are often hard to come by, but

TABLE 10-1 Percentage of Sales Invested in Advertising for Major Businesses and Industry Groups

Classification	Percentage of Sales Invested in Advertising
Agriculture, crops	2.1
Airlines	1.2
Animal feed and pet foods	3.6
Automotive vehicles	0.3
Beer and brewed beverages	4.3
Book publishing	4.7
Bread, cake, and cookie bakers	1.6
Building contractors	0.1
Canned foods	2.9
CATV companies	1.1
Computer and data processing equipment	0.8
Cosmetics, health and beauty aids	9.3
Dairy products	1.9
Department stores	2.5
Distilled alcoholic beverages	5.3
Drugs, ethical	5.5
Over-the-counter	10.7
Wholesale	0.7
Educational services	4.6
Engines and turbines	0.9
Food chains	0.7
Forest products	0.5
Furniture, retail	4.8
Hardware products	1.5
Home furnishings, manufacturers	1.6
Hospitals and health care institutions	0.1
Industrial machinery	0.7
Machine tools	0.6
Mail order, retail	16.1
Motion picture producers	7.0
Newspaper publishing	0.8
Office and business equipment	1.3
Packaged confections	3.5
Packaged foods	2.8
Periodical publishing	4.0
Petroleum refining and retailing	0.2
Pottery and china	3.7
Radio-TV broadcasters	2.2
Radio, TV sets, home entertainment equipment	3.5
Real estate	3.1
Restaurant and fast-food chains	2.5
Shoes and footwear, manufacturers	1.8
Soft drinks	5.9
Tobacco, cigars	4.9
Cigarettes	1.6
Trucking	0.3

Note: Figures based on a study of advertising and promotion expenditures by more than 1,000 major United States corporations and industry sectors. Study compiled by Schonfeld Associates, as reported in *Advertising Age,* October 3, 1977, p. 95.

media sources, government publications, trade associations, trade journals, and observation can supply some information on competitors' advertising expenditures. Budgets vary from industry to industry, and within industries there are big differences. In Chapter 1 we explored how much advertising costs, and in Table 1-2 we listed advertising expenditures and advertising as a percentage of sales for leading marketers. Table 10-1 lists percentages of sales invested in advertising for major business and industry groups.

The reason for these great variations in advertising expenditures is that methods of distribution vary from industry to industry, as was pointed out in Chapter 1. The importance of advertising as a method of distributing goods and services is a relative matter, subject to great variation depending to a great extent on the type of industry involved.

The figures in Table 10-1 are of interest to manufacturers in the fields involved. But it should be kept in mind that there are companies that do no advertising, or very little; this fact is reflected in the figures. The aggressive, growth-minded company obviously spends considerably more than these average figures indicate.

Let's turn now to retail classifications. Table 10-2 lists average percentages of sales invested in advertising according to type of retail outlet.

Again, it is important to point out that these figures are only averages, based on the advertising expenditures of the sporadic advertiser and the dedicated, consistent advertiser. If a retailer spends less than the average figure, it's a good indication that the retailer is underspending. On the other hand, these figures should not be considered as maximums beyond which the retailer should not venture. They should only be used as a cross-check of a budget that has been prepared according to the task method.

Building the Media Plan

An advertising budget is not merely a series of figures that cover how much will be allocated to media, payroll, departmental expenses, and advertising research. It is a plan for action that specifies precisely how money will be allocated to media and that justifies these spending decisions with available facts and research. In spite of the availability of facts and figures, many media decisions must, in the final analysis, be a matter of judgment. In media selection there are countless alternatives, and choosing the right one is often more of an art than a science.

The *media plan* is that part of the advertising budget that lists which media will be used, gives reasons for choices based on available facts, and itemizes the costs involved. It can include a *media schedule,* which outlines when the advertising will run and the size of insertions or the length of commercials.

In the retail field, the advertising manager prepares the media plan. With relatively few local media to choose from and compare, the task is not particularly difficult or time-consuming. The media plan of a national advertiser is far more complicated and difficult to develop. Responsibility for developing this part of the national advertising budget is usually left with the client's advertising agency.

Marketing Strategy and Media Plan

The basis of the media plan is the marketing and advertising strategy of the company concerned. Fundamental factors that must be considered are size of market, composition of market, product characteristics, customers' profiles or demographic characteristics, distribution of the product or service, competitive outlook, necessity of obtaining dealer or

TABLE 10-2 Average Percentage of Sales Invested in Advertising by Retail Businesses

Class of Business	Average Percentage of Sales Invested in Advertising
Appliance, radio, TV dealers	2.3
Auto dealers	0.8
Auto parking and repair service	0.8
Bakeries	0.7
Banks, commercial	1.3
Beauty shops	2.0
Book stores	1.7
Camera stores:	
Under $500,000 sales volume	0.8
$500,000 sales volume and over	0.9
Cocktail lounges	0.9
Credit agencies, personal	2.4
Department stores:	2.8
$1,000,000–$2,000,000 sales volume	2.5
$2,000,000–$5,000,000 sales volume	2.9
$5,000,000–$20,000,000 sales volume	2.8
$20,000,000–$50,000,000 sales volume	2.7
$50,000,000 and over sales volume	2.4
Discount houses	2.4
Drugstores, chain	1.7
Independent	1.3
Dry cleaning	1.7
Florists and garden supply stores	2.1
Food chains	1.1
Furniture stores	5.0
Gasoline service stations	0.8
Hardware stores	1.6
Insurance agents, brokers	1.8
Jewelry stores	4.4
Liquor stores	0.9
Menswear stores:	
Under $300,000 sales volume	2.4
$300,000–$500,000 sales volume	2.6
$500,000–$1,000,000 sales volume	2.8
$1,000,000–$5,000,000 sales volume	3.2
$5,000,000 and over sales volume	3.4
Motion picture theaters	5.5
Real estate:	
Operators	0.6
Subdividers, developers	3.1
Brokers	4.0
Restaurants	0.8
Savings banks	1.5
Savings and loan associations	1.5
Sporting goods stores	3.5
Tire dealers	2.2
Travel agents	5.0
Variety stores	1.5

Source: The "I-Wonder-How-to-Set-Up-an-Advertising-Program-and-How-Much-to-Budget" Book, Newspaper Advertising Bureau, Inc., 1977, pp. 20–26. Percentages for certain retail categories not available.

wholesaler support, and short- and long-range sales goals. Obviously media people must be more than mere technicians or specialists. They must be advertising people versed in all phases of the marketing operation. Beyond this, as they develop their plans, they must be aware of the creative side of the advertising. A plan that conforms to the marketing strategy in all respects may be unusable because it does not consider the advertising campaign itself.

For example, a swimsuit manufacturer might find regional network radio satisfactory to cover the principal sales territories; however, because in this case it is very important to have customers see the new styles, radio would not be used. A food advertiser featuring long, involved recipes would not use broadcast media in spite of possible cost efficiencies; instead, magazines would be used, where there is the space to print the recipes and full-color illustrations to show how appetizing the end product will look.

Given the characteristics of a product or service and a complete knowledge of what kind of consumers buy the product, where these consumers are located, and where the product or service is distributed, media people must build a media plan that does the most effective job of handling these factors. This is really a balancing act because of the many options.

Reach and Frequency   A media planner may decide on maximum coverage of the target audience. Here the emphasis is on *reach,* a term

Universal Rent-A-Car Advertising Budget Summary Chart			
Category	Pages, b/w	Space Costs	Circulation (Millions)
Magazines:			
Time	13	$ 470,000	4.4
Newsweek	13	333,000	3.0
Sports Illustrated	13	299,000	3.0
U.S. News/World Report	13	228,000	2.1
Air Group One	12 monthlies 6 bimonthlies	164,000	1.0
		$1,494,000	
Print production costs		150,000	
Reserve fund print		75,000	
Print budget		$1,719,000	
		Time Costs	Coverage, % of U.S. Population
Drive Time Radio:			
10 airport cities	30-second commercial, 12 per week for 13 weeks	$340,000	33
Radio production costs		10,000	
Radio budget		$350,000	
Total media budget		$2,069,000	

This advertising media summary chart shows proposed expenditures and coverage for 1 year. Figures are rounded off and based on 1979 data. Air Group One consists of the in-flight magazines of five airlines, bought as a package. Reserve fund print is unallocated and is available for opportunity print medium purchases if they arise.

referring to the total number of people or households exposed to the advertising message. In this case, the goal is to communicate the message to as many prospects as possible within the limits of the ad dollars available. For example, a car maker introducing the new models wants the maximum number of people to read and hear about the new styling and performance features during the introductory period. On the retail level, the management of a department store chain opening a branch in a suburb wants all the local residents to know the store's location and the opening date. In both these situations, reach will be emphasized in the media plan, and the ad dollars will be used across the board in several media.

Frequency refers to the number of times an advertising message is delivered to a given audience within a certain period of time. For some product categories, particularly those with repeat purchases, frequency of message registration is more important than broad reach. Decisions about reach and frequency are not arbitrary; the type of product and its sales pattern help media people decide on the proper balance between these two factors.

An importer of fine watches knows that sales are best around Christmas, graduation, Father's Day, and Mother's Day. Maximum coverage of upper-income groups is wanted at those times, yet frequency is important too. The importer will strive for these twin goals within the budget. The rest of the year, the importer settles for sporadic reminder ads or none at all. Reach and frequency peak up and then fall off during slack selling periods to supply the dollars for heavy sales periods. A food manufacturer who sells a popular cake mix line or a maker of a kitchen and bathroom cleanser have different selling situations. Consumer demand is steady throughout the year. Frequency of advertising is most important, because people are in the market for these products constantly. A steady advertising program spread evenly over the months with as much coverage as can be afforded is the desirable goal in these cases.

Gross Rating Points   By using gross rating points, advertisers can achieve the desired weight or impact of their ad messages in a given market through applying a mathematical formula. Gross rating points (GRPs) stand for the number of ad messages aired or printed in a medium in terms of percentage of market population. Originally developed as a measurement tool for broadcast advertising, GRPs can be used in other media as well, as we discovered in our discussion of purchasing outdoor advertising (Chapter 7).

The concept is difficult to understand, but examples may make it clear. TV program rating services tell an advertiser in essence how popular a program is with audiences compared with other programs. A rating point of 1 means that 1 percent of the total TV home sets within the station's area tuned into the program, a rating point of 6 means that 6 percent of the total home sets are tuned in, and so on. This percentage figure is then applied to commercials run on the program. The commercial then is considered having a GRP of 1 or 6, as the case may be. If a commercial with a GRP of 6 is run five times weekly on the program, its weekly GRP would be $5 \times 6 = 30$. When other program availabilities for commercials are bought in the same market, their GRPs are added to the total. A media buyer might determine that a "weight" of 100 GRPs is right for a product and continue buying availabilities until that figure is reached.

GRPs are a way of enabling media buyers to apply a single yardstick to different markets and achieve the same weight of message in each of them. Important though GRPs are, they do not tell an advertiser anything about the quality of the audience. This information the buyer determines separately. A program may deliver high GRPs but the audience may not be a desirable one for the advertiser. For instance, buying high GRPs on a football program would be excellent for a life insurance company or a brewer because of its predominately male audience. A maker of cake mixes will look for gross rating points on programs holding more interest for women.

Wave or Pulse Technique "Wave," "pulse," and "flighting" are words identifying a method of scheduling advertising for a period of time, usually for 3 weeks or a month, ceasing advertising for the same length of time, and then continuing to alternate. There are variations of this method, as when advertising is run heavily and then lightly in sequence.

The method is controversial, but it has its advocates. As originally conceived, the purposes of the *wave technique* are to save money or to stretch a limited budget. Steadily mounting costs of TV advertising forced marketers to examine ways of keeping ad budgets in line, and wave advertising was first used to accomplish this goal. There is no reason why the wave advertising approach cannot be used in media other than television and radio, however.

Aside from saving money, there are other reasons given for using the technique. By running ad messages at a heavier weight for a short period of time, the advertiser increases "voice share" during that period. If advertising for a brand suddenly seems to be "everywhere" on TV channels or radio frequencies, the voice of competition is temporarily overwhelmed. The advertiser who is "pulsing" at a heavy rate also, it's claimed, can break through the clutter barrier (Chapter 8) and become dominant over all other advertisers using the medium during the heavy-schedule period. The wave technique can be used as a sales weapon against competition, blunting the efforts of another advertiser currently involved in introducing a new product.

Some advertisers consider pulsing a necessary evil, forced upon them by increasing media costs, others justify its use for the reasons stated above, and still others are dead set against it. The main reason for not using a wave or pulse technique is concern about whether sales will hold up during the hiatus when no advertising is running. Much market testing has been done to check the validity of the concept. Unfortunately, no generalities or rules have been developed. Every sales problem is different. Ideally, every marketer would like to run a consistent ad program. Sometimes, that just isn't possible because of budget limitations.

Campaign Requirements In addition to all the considerations already described in building the media plan, media people must keep in mind the kind of advertising campaign that is being proposed. The size of the ads when print media are being used or the length of the message in the case of broadcast media must be determined. What sizes of space (or length of broadcast message) are affordable at the desired reach and frequency levels? Can the product story be told in small space print ads, or are full-page color ads needed to do justice to it? In television or radio, should 30-second commercials, which are a very efficient buy, be used, or will 20- or even 10-second commercials be satisfactory?

As this stage, agency people should make sure they are communicating with the creative staff to gain complete understanding of copy space and time needs. An excellent buy, checked out for reach, frequency, GRPs and audience, may be completely wrong for the product because of special requirements of the creative department.

The media person at the advertising agency must consider a host of variables when putting together a media plan for a new product, such as golf clubs. (Jared D. Lee)

Financial Considerations

Any media plan is a compromise between reach, frequency, and size or length of message, on the one hand, and availability of funds on the other. Obviously, many media plans can be devised for a particular sum of money, and the media person must weigh one plan against another. If the product has mass appeal and universal distribution and is bought by homemakers, a combination of daytime network television supplemented by spot television in key markets that need bolstering plus a print campaign in four or five women's service magazines will deliver the largest number of messages to the target audience on a lower cost-per-thousand basis than a different plan. On the other hand, if the product appeals to upper-income men and is a luxury item, it may be found that advertising in *Time, Esquire, Playboy,* and a couple of sports magazines plus some spot radio in better markets constitute what in the buyer's opinion is an ideal plan. A national liquor advertiser, unable to use broadcast media because of trade restrictions for alcoholic beverages, will prepare a list that includes newspapers, magazines, and outdoor and transit media.

The task is further complicated by the necessity of choosing between two or more television stations or magazines that supply comparable audiences. The buyer must be intuitive and experienced in analyzing the quality of the audiences and is often guided in this case by cost-efficiency comparisons. This is an area of hard choices for the smaller advertiser, who cannot afford to place ads for the product in all the magazines but instead must choose one or two "best" publications for the ads.

Media people working on large advertising budgets use computers to help them in their preparation of alternate media plans. They can feed in data on product distribution and demographic characteristics of customers and cast against these knowns various facts about the circulations of different media, specific demographic data on audiences of individual components of these media, and costs of media schedules—accomplishing in days what would take thousands of hours with the pencil-and-paper method.

Experimentation over the years is necessary when planning national advertising budgets, and a willingness to try new media combinations should be cultivated. Markets and the media that cover them are constantly changing, and one year's media plan may not deliver adequate sales if repeated the following year.

Establishing a Retail Ad Budget

When the recommended task method of budget preparation is used, certain factors must be considered before actual budget planning begins. These factors include the type of business, the relative newness of a store, store location, the competitive situation, and the condition of the local economy. These factors apply to all retail establishments.

The merchant's type of business is extremely important in determining budget size. If the merchant is a supermarket operator selling staples on a high-volume basis, the advertising expenditures will be relatively low, averaging 1 to 3 percent of sales. Hardware stores, bakeries, drugstores, and service stations also sell goods that are relatively low-priced with small profit margins. Women's specialty apparel shops, with high-fashion lines, and stores concentrating on luxury merchandise have high profit margins to work with and are usually aggressive advertisers who spend relatively large sums. The owner of a high-fashion dress shop in a high-income suburban area stated that the average advertising appropriation ran 18 percent of sales. Another store owner, with a line of fur coats as well as dresses, spent 20

percent, and another, who advertises heavily and seeks orders by mail, spent 25 percent.

The relative newness of a store is a factor in determining budget size. The new store, or a store moving to a new location, must advertise more heavily to establish itself in the consumer's mind. If a store has expanded or has added new departments, it, too, must advertise more heavily.

The store location has a bearing on the size of the store's advertising budget. If a store is in a high traffic count area, in the downtown shopping area, or in an established shopping center on the outskirts of a market, the budget can be smaller than that needed for a store in a low traffic count area off the beaten track.

The competitive situation must be considered in budget planning. If a home appliance store, for example, has a sales territory all to itself, there is less need to advertise aggressively than if it has a nearby competitor seeking the same customers.

The condition of the local economy has a bearing on budget size. When the economy is booming, the local merchant will spend more money on advertising to take advantage of the tendency of consumers to spend. The merchant will follow a policy of spending more to increase sales volume. In periods of recession, the first expense item to get the ax is usully advertising. This is characteristic of national and local advertisers alike. But while advertising budgets should undoubtedly be reduced when sales volume forecasts are gloomy, elimination or drastic cutting of advertising is an unwise—even fatal—step. As one home appliance advertiser stated, "In bad times I can rely on my competition to cut ad budgets to the bone. I curtail plenty, but I keep the ads going. That way I get more than my share of the business that's around, and if I'm supplying wanted goods and my service holds up, I'll keep some of the new customers that have come to me."

Need for Budget Experimentation

All advertising budgets should be subjected to testing and trial. The advertiser should experiment. The budget size that is right for one merchant may be wrong for another in the same line of business because of different locations and types of customers. Even if a budget seems right and is developing adequate sales, it should not be assumed that it is right. As Budd Gore points out,

Expenses . . . rarely rise in proportion to sales increases. Rent, heat, light and power costs, for example, tend to remain the same. Once a store has learned from experience how much important additional volume and profit can be achieved through good budgeting and planning, experimentation with larger budgets should be started. The aim should be to find the level at which the greatest profit from advertising may be gained.[1]

A Sample Department Store Budget

To illustrate how a retail store's advertising budget is built, we will use as an example simplified budget-planning procedures for a medium-size department store with a forecast sales volume of $10 million for the following year. Having considered all its objectives on the basis of the task method, the advertising department has concluded that an advertising budget of $500,000 will accomplish the store's goal.

From this figure a reserve fund of 10 percent should immediately be subtracted. This cushion is necessary so that funds are available to promote special purchases, to take advantage

of unforeseen fashion trends, or to clear out unsold merchandise.

The "year" is looked at from the point of view of a spring and a fall selling season, spring covering the months from February through July, and fall from August through January.

Certain stable, recurrent expenses can now be charged to the advertising budget on a monthly basis. These include the advertising department payroll and the costs of supplies, outside services, and travel.[2] These stable expenses, figured according to past experience and forecasted sales are:

Payroll	$100,000
Supplies	35,000
Outside services	10,000
Travel	1,500
	$146,500

$146,500 ÷ 12 months = $12,208.33 per month

This sum can be allocated across the board and each month of the selling year charged with stable expenses of $12,208.33. We have already determined via the task method that we should spend approximately $300,000 in various media to accomplish our sales objectives for the coming year, so our budget breakdown now looks like Table 10-3.

Our store is typical of United States department stores in that 57 percent of the sales volume is accounted for in the fall selling season and 43 percent in the spring period. We should spend our media dollars in proportion to our sales volume. But our next challenge is to determine what store departments should receive

---

[1] Budd Gore, *How to Budget Advertising for Bigger Volume, More Profits,* Newspaper Advertising Bureau, Inc., 1967, p. 23.

[2] The major part of the "supplies" category consists of material to create in-store signs and displays. "Outside services" charges are incurred when free-lance copy, layout, or photography is needed, or window display services or publicity is purchased from an outside firm.

TABLE 10-3 Budget Breakdown

			Percent of Total Budget
Media:			
Newspapers, shopping publications	$228,000		
Broadcast	60,500		
Direct mail	10,500		
Transit advertising	4,500		
	$303,500	$303,500	
Media reserve fund		50,000	
Total media expenses		$353,500	70.7
Stable expenses:			
Payroll	$100,000		20.0
Supplies	35,000		7.0
Outside services	10,000		2.0
Travel	1,500		0.3
	$146,500		100.0
Total stable expenses		146,500	
Total advertising budget		$500,000	

advertising backing and when they should receive it. Some departments generate a large sales volume, and others generate a small sales volume. What's more, the sales volume for each department varies during the year.

Table 10-4 shows what percent of the year's total sales is made by each department each month. These figures are national averages. Note how sales in almost all departments peak during the Christmas selling season.

Table 10-5, also based on national averages, indicates the relative sales-generating importance of the various departments. Note the strength of the women's and misses' apparel department and of the home furnishings department, between them accounting for half of the store's sales volume.

These tables indicate that a store advertising manager must study the monthly percentages-of-sales figures of the store's departments so that the departments can be ranked according to the sales volume they generate. With these figures in hand, the ad manager allocates the monthly media expenditures to departments where a good sales volume exists. The general rule of supporting these high-sales-volume departments with advertising is followed. But the ad manager makes some exceptions to this rule. Store management may have decided that certain departments should be built up and others deemphasized. Its budget, based on the task method, will reflect these goals. Past departmental sales figures for these departments will therefore not determine monthly media advertising expenses. The new departmental sales goals will be the guides. Also, it's known, for example, that the pre-Christmas season is the store's period of biggest sales volume, and it's also known that the store will receive some of this business as a matter of course. The store's sales force, even with extra help, will hardly be able to serve the customers satisfactorily at this time. Additional advertising, attracting more patrons, would be too much of a good thing. Considering the sales volume breakdown of 57 percent business in the fall period and 43 percent in the spring, the advertising manager will probably allocate 53 percent of the expenditures for the fall period and 47 percent for the spring. This allocation attempts to even out these two major selling periods.

Budgets for Other Retail Businesses

The procedures described above can also be applied to other types of retail businesses, but as store volume decreases, the procedures become less complicated. The main problem becomes how to allocate advertising media ex-

TABLE 10-4 Percent of Year's Total Sales Made Each Month

	Jan.	Feb.	Mar.	Apr.	May	June	July	Aug.	Sept.	Oct.	Nov.	Dec.	Five-Year Average, %
Grand total, entire store	6.4	5.8	7.5	7.6	7.9	7.6	6.6	7.5	8.0	**8.8**	**10.1**	**16.2**	100
Main store, total	6.4	5.9	7.5	7.5	7.8	7.5	6.6	7.5	8.0	**8.7**	**10.1**	**16.5**	100
Women's and misses' apparel and accessories	5.9	5.7	**8.4**	**8.4**	8.2	7.0	6.1	7.6	**8.7**	**9.2**	**9.7**	**15.1**	100
Men's and boys' wear	5.3	4.9	6.2	6.7	7.2	**8.9**	5.9	6.5	7.1	8.2	**11.1**	**22.0**	100
Home furnishings	6.8	6.8	7.5	7.2	8.0	7.8	7.6	7.9	**8.4**	**9.2**	**10.3**	**12.5**	100
Piece goods and household textiles	**12.3**	6.1	6.7	6.6	7.9	6.7	**8.4**	**10.1**	7.6	8.1	**8.5**	**11.0**	100
Small wares	6.4	6.0	6.7	6.6	7.6	7.5	6.0	6.7	7.2	7.8	**10.1**	**21.4**	100
Miscellaneous merchandise departments	5.1	4.9	6.0	6.4	6.6	7.6	6.4	6.2	5.7	6.8	**11.9**	**26.4**	100
Basement store, total	5.9	5.4	7.8	8.2	8.1	7.9	6.3	8.0	**8.4**	**8.9**	**9.9**	**15.2**	100
Domestics and blankets	**10.8**	5.5	6.3	**9.2**	7.2	7.0	**8.3**	**9.5**	7.6	**8.3**	**8.8**	**11.5**	100
Women's and misses' ready-to-wear	5.3	5.3	**8.4**	**8.5**	**8.4**	7.6	6.2	8.1	**8.5**	**9.1**	**9.8**	**14.8**	100
Men's and boys' wear	4.9	4.9	7.1	7.5	7.5	**8.8**	5.6	7.7	7.7	8.0	**10.5**	**19.8**	100
Home furnishings	6.5	6.7	8.0	**8.4**	**8.5**	7.3	6.7	7.7	**8.4**	**10.4**	**11.2**	**10.2**	100
Shoes	5.9	5.8	**9.1**	**9.1**	**8.5**	7.9	6.0	8.2	**9.2**	**8.9**	**8.8**	**12.6**	100
Nonmerchandise, total	7.0	6.8	**8.3**	8.0	7.5	8.2	8.0	**8.3**	7.8	**8.6**	**9.7**	**11.8**	100
Barber and beauty shop	7.1	7.6	**9.3**	**10.3**	**9.8**	**9.5**	**9.8**	7.9	6.8	7.0	7.3	7.6	100

Note: Boldface indicates months when the merchandise division did 8.3 percent or better of its annual volume. (If sales were constant across the year, each month would account for approximately 8.3 percent.)
Source: *1978 Newspaper Advertising Planbook,* Newspaper Advertising Bureau, Inc., p. 51.

TABLE 10-5 Percent of Month's Total Sales Made by Merchandise Divisions

	Jan.	Feb.	Mar.	Apr.	May	June	July	Aug.	Sept.	Oct.	Nov.	Dec.	Five-Year Average, %
Grand total, entire store	100	100	100	100	100	100	100	100	100	100	100	100	100
Main store, total	**86.4**	**86.1**	85.1	84.7	85.5	85.1	85.6	84.7	85.4	85.6	**86.1**	**87.3**	85.8
Women's and misses' apparel and accessories	33.5	35.0	**40.0**	**39.8**	**37.4**	33.4	33.4	**36.1**	**38.7**	**37.9**	34.6	33.5	36.0
Men's and boys' wear	8.5	8.6	8.4	9.0	9.3	**12.0**	9.2	8.8	9.0	9.6	**11.2**	**13.8**	10.2
Home furnishings	**21.7**	**23.3**	19.9	19.1	**20.5**	**20.8**	**23.1**	**20.9**	**21.1**	**21.2**	**20.5**	15.5	20.1
Piece goods and household textiles	**8.8**	**4.8**	4.1	4.0	**4.6**	4.0	**5.9**	**6.1**	4.3	4.2	3.8	3.1	4.5
Small wares	**9.5**	**9.7**	8.3	8.2	9.1	9.3	8.7	8.3	8.4	8.4	**9.5**	**12.4**	9.5
Miscellaneous merchandise departments	4.4	4.7	4.4	4.6	4.6	**5.6**	5.3	4.5	3.9	4.3	**6.5**	**9.0**	5.5
Basement store, total	10.3	10.4	**11.6**	**12.1**	**11.6**	**11.6**	10.7	**12.0**	**11.7**	**11.4**	11.0	10.5	11.2
Domestics and blankets	**1.4**	0.7	0.7	**1.0**	0.7	0.7	**1.0**	**1.0**	**0.8**	**0.8**	0.7	0.6	0.8
Women's and misses' ready-to-wear	4.8	5.2	**6.3**	**6.4**	**6.1**	5.7	5.4	**6.1**	**6.0**	**5.9**	5.5	5.2	5.7
Men's and boys' wear	1.9	2.1	2.2	**2.4**	2.3	**2.8**	2.1	**2.5**	2.3	2.3	**2.6**	**3.0**	2.4
Home furnishings	**0.9**	**1.0**	**0.9**	**1.0**	**0.9**	**0.9**	**0.9**	**0.9**	**0.9**	**1.0**	**1.0**	0.6	0.9
Shoes	**0.8**	**0.8**	**1.0**	**1.0**	**0.9**	**0.8**	**0.8**	**0.9**	**1.0**	**0.9**	0.7	0.6	0.8
Nonmerchandise, total	**3.3**	**3.5**	**3.3**	**3.2**	2.9	**3.3**	**3.7**	**3.3**	2.9	**3.0**	2.9	2.2	3.0
Barber and beauty shop	**0.4**	**0.5**	**0.5**	**0.5**	**0.5**	**0.5**	**0.6**	**0.4**	0.3	0.3	0.3	0.2	0.4

Note: Boldface indicates months when the merchandise division contributed the same or a bigger percent of the whole store's volume than it did during the year as a whole (as shown in last right column).
Source: *1978 Newspaper Advertising Planbook,* Newspaper Advertising Bureau, Inc., p. 51.

penditures throughout the year. Merchants who specialize in one line of merchandise or one type of service do not have a group of departments with differing sales volume patterns throughout the year to consider.

The figure on page 232 shows sales volume patterns for total retail establishments and eight various kinds of retailers. Gasoline service stations, grocery stores, eating and drinking places, and auto dealers all have pretty much the same sales volume each month of the year. The sales of the other kinds of retail stores shown in the illustration all build to the Christmas selling period. Media allocation by month can closely follow sales volume for these specialized retailers.

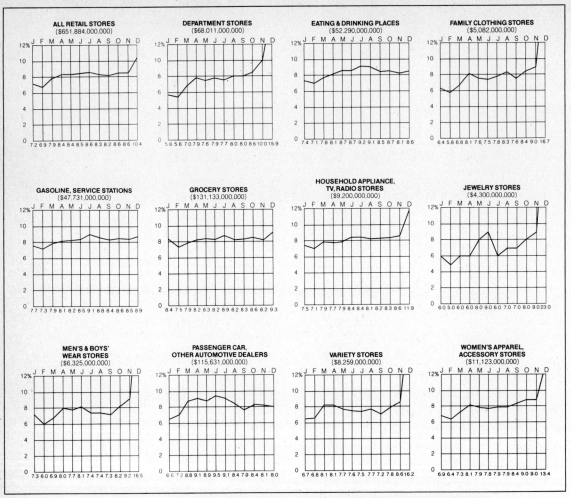

The graphs show the percentage of total annual retail sales made each month. The first graph is the average of all retail businesses tabulated. Note that some types of retail businesses have fairly even sales, while others have sales that peak at year's end. (Courtesy *Newspaper Advertising Plan Books*, Newspaper Advertising Bureau)

Vocabulary

Define the following terms, and use each one in a sentence.

Advertising budget
Frequency
Investment spending plan
Media plan

Media schedule
Reach
Wave technique

Review Questions

1. What is the purpose of an advertising budget?
2. What expenses in addition to the cost of media should be included in the advertising budget?
3. Discuss the various methods that can be used to arrive at a budget. Which one offers the most advantages and why? Does it have any drawbacks?
4. Tables 10-1 and 10-2 list percentages of sales invested in advertising for selected industry groups and retail stores. In preparing an advertising budget, how should you be guided by these figures and when should you not be guided by them?
5. In addition to the cost of running ads in an advertising medium, what other factors should be considered in making a decision to use the medium?
6. In your opinion, which of the products or businesses listed below should be advertised steadily throughout the year, and which would require heavier advertising at certain times of the year? Discuss your reasons.

Airline	Garden weed killer
Book club	Kitchen cleanser
Color television	Perfume
Dessert mix	Soft drink

7. If you were opening a large supermarket chain store unit in a city with a population of 75,000, would you emphasize reach or would you emphasize frequency in your introductory advertising? Give your reasons.
8. You, as a media buyer, have purchased one commercial a day, Monday through Friday, on program A, TV station WOOZ, and one commercial a day Tuesday through Friday on program B, TV station WWRY. Program A has a GRP of 4; program B has a GRP of 6. How many GRPs have you bought per week?
9. What is the main reason some advertisers do not use the wave (or pulse) technique of scheduling advertising in media?
10. What factors must be considered in determining the size of a retail store's advertising budget?
11. Describe the steps involved in preparing an advertising budget for a department store, using the task method.
12. For specialized retailers, how should monthly media allocations relate to monthly sales volume? Discuss your reasoning.

Activities

1. You have the responsibility of building a media plan for a manufacturer of quality power lawn mowers and leaf blowers. List what marketing and advertising questions you would want answered before you put the plan together.
2. From your own observation, list the names of magazines that would be worthwhile to consider in building media plans for any six of the following products and services:

A high-priced perfume, nationally distributed

A medium-priced line of cosmetics

Garden furniture

A nationally distributed beer

Power tools for home workshops

Kitchenware

A soft drink

Spaghetti sauce

Color television sets

A coast-to-coast airline

An automobile

A credit card

A correspondence school course

Camping equipment

Project

Select a local advertiser, stop by at a convenient time (preferably making an appointment in advance), and try to discover how the advertiser determines the amount of the annual advertising budget. Since merchants normally do not care to state the amount of their budget, steer clear of this subject. As a student of advertising, you are interested only in how the advertising budget figure is arrived at. Which of the methods described in this chapter does the advertiser seem to be using? Report your findings to the class.

Career Ladder

In your new job as an assistant advertising manager of a medium-sized maker of fine china and dinnerware, you have been assigned the task of putting together a preliminary advertising budget for the coming year. A couple of new china patterns will be introduced, along with a new line of inexpensive "patio style" dinnerware.

You know that your management is quite conservative and noninnovative in company policy although the company makes excellent products. Your boss, while an affable man, is 64, about to retire, and doesn't much care for controversy and boat rocking. To your consternation, you find that the affordability method—really not a budget-preparation method at all, in your opinion—has always been used in the past and the media schedule has been canceled in midstream for whimsical reasons. You know better than to use this method of budget preparation and believe that the task method should take over.

How would you handle this situation? What are your possible moves, and what do you plan to do now?

The home appliance firm of Brownell & Levy has been doing business in the city of Rockland for 35 years. Lawrence Brownell and Joseph Levy were successful retail salespeople in an appliance store and decided to strike out for themselves. They chose to start a store in Rockland because there was relatively little competition, and this proved a wise decision. Today, Brownell & Levy is the largest home appliance store in the city, and sales volume has grown over the years.

Rockland has a population of 75,000 (22,500 households) and is the largest city within 60 miles of an urban center with a population of 1 million. Rockland was formerly the center of a farming area, but today farming is less important to the city's economy.

The firm is now run by two partners, sons of the original owners. Larry Brownell, Jr., concentrates on service activities, and Charlie Levy handles the store, but both are involved in the business decisions. Retail sales are estimated at $930,000 for the coming year, which is $70,000 less than sales for the current year. The reason for this is the state of the local economy. There has been a national recession, and all business in Rockland has suffered.

Brownell & Levy carries Maytag washers and dryers; Frigidaire refrigerators, freezers, air conditioners, dishwashers, and ranges; Fedders air conditioners; and Zenith radios, televisions, and stereos—as well as small appliances made by several leading manufacturers. The store will sell a little over 3,700 major appliances in the current year.

Competition has become severe. The opening in Rockland of a discount house with a large home appliance department 2 years ago intensified competitive pressures, and there are four other local appliance dealers. Brownell & Levy has done well, however, because it has kept its prices competitive and has built an excellent service department. Larry Brownell coined an ad slogan for the store ("When we sell it, we service it") in an effort to compete against the discount house, which does not service the brands it sells, and Brownell & Levy's reputation in the service area is good.

Local advertising media consist of the following:

Newspaper *Rockland Times.* Published evenings except Saturday and Sunday. Circulation: City zone, 14,370. Trading zone, 16,572. Rate: 18 cents a line, flat (no volume discounts).

Radio WBZL, local station. Programming is generally directed to adults. Station estimates 60 percent of households tune in for at least one program daily. One-minute spot announcements cost $15 in the evening hours, $13 all other times.

Shopping guide Free local weekly newspaper, limited editorial content. Claims 10,000 circulation, unsubstantiated. Rate: 7 cents a line, flat.

Outdoor posters and painted bulletins Service available through metropolitan outdoor plant.

TV No local station. Three stations in metropolitan area cover Rockland.

Direct mail At initiative of local merchant.

During the preceding year, when the retail sales volume was $1,000,000, the advertising budget was $35,000, or 3.5 percent of sales. Larry Brownell and Charlie Levy have decided to cut the budget for the coming year to 2 percent of estimated sales, or $18,600 because of slower sales. The Frigidaire and Zenith sales reps calling on the store urged the partners not to reduce advertising to this extent, pointing out that on the average, 80 percent of Brownell & Levy's advertising budget was reimbursed through co-op programs. It is now December, and a budget for the coming year is being discussed. The manufacturers' sales reps have both stated that since sales are heading up again, the budget should be at least 3.5 percent of sales.

Advertising has been consistently run in the *Rockland Times* twice a week in one-page, or 1,000-line, size. No experiment of schedules in other media has ever been tried. The partners have no knowledge of the demographic characteristics of their customers, nor have they attempted studies of where their sales trends come from. The partners have also not concerned themselves with the industrial growth rate of their city, the income level of local wage earners, or any other basic research data.

1. If you were developing the advertising program for the coming year, what decisions would you make about the size of the budget and the selection of media?
2. What method of budget preparation would you use? If other media besides the newspaper are to be used, on what basis would you use them, and what percentage of the budget should be allocated to them?
3. Should research be undertaken, and if so, what kind?
4. What would you feature in your ads?

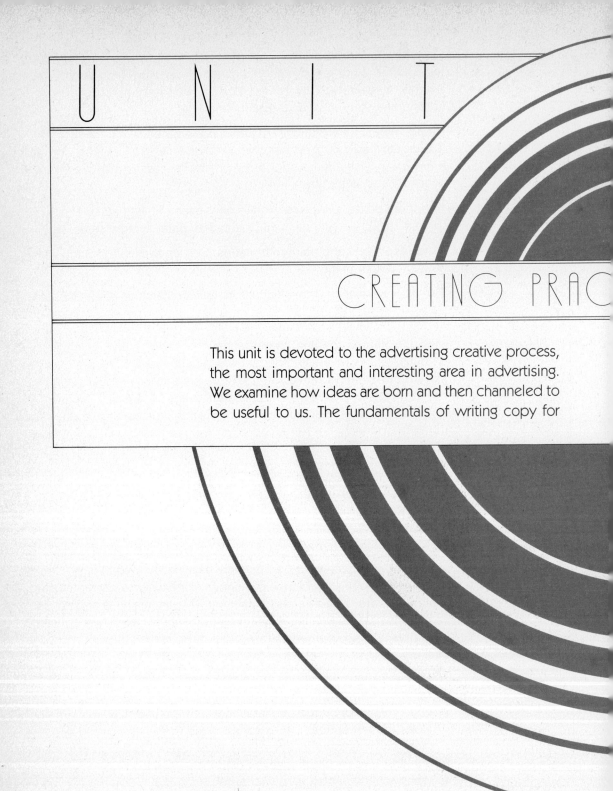

U N I T

CREATING PRAC

This unit is devoted to the advertising creative process, the most important and interesting area in advertising. We examine how ideas are born and then channeled to be useful to us. The fundamentals of writing copy for

T H R E E

CRITICAL ADVERTISING

print and broadcast media are discussed, together with basic art direction and layouts. Also described are production methods needed to prepare advertising material for use by media.

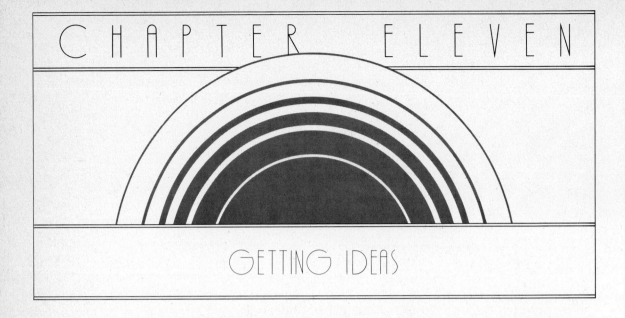

CHAPTER ELEVEN

GETTING IDEAS

In advertising, words and sounds and pictures are put together to convey a message to a person in the hope of getting some action favorable to the advertiser. This task of assembling is a creative process. When the message is put together, it may not appear "creative" in the sense of being original or fresh or provocative. It may, indeed, be dull, obvious, and ordinary; unfortunately, much advertising, particularly in the retail area, falls into this category. The best advertising people, however, try as hard as they can to rise above the ordinary.

These ad makers are convinced that the more creative and original their work becomes the more likely it is to interest and involve their audience in the message and the more chance there is for favorable audience response.

Importance of the Creative Process in Advertising

The most important part of advertising is the advertising message. Everything else is merely supportive. A prestige magazine may present a good environment for an advertisement appearing on its pages, and this may be good for the advertiser. But this effect is an intangible and not measurable in actual sales. The media in which the messages appear do not of themselves make a consumer buy a product or service, in spite of Marshall McLuhan's provocative statement that "the medium is the message"; media can only present an advertising message. Advertising budgets, research activities, production, traffic controls—all make the advertising message possible, and this is their only purpose. In themselves, they do not sell.

Since the creative side of advertising is the important side of advertising, we should know as much as possible about how it works, about how ideas are born, and something about the workings of the mind, which is responsible for the creation of ideas.

Creativity

When someone shows an ability to combine what is perceived by the senses in a way that is new and novel to him or her, we say that person is demonstrating *creativity*. There are many definitions of this term. Rollo May, the psychologist, defines creativity as "the process of bringing something new into being." Margaret Mead, the anthropologist, called it "a statement of process in the individual; to the extent that a person makes, invents, thinks of something that is new to him, he may be said to perform a creative act." John Haefele, the research chemist, defines it as "the ability to formulate new combinations from two or more concepts already in the mind."[1] *Creative* may mean possessing the ability to create, or it may be an adjective characterizing originality. Persons involved in the act of creating or inventing approach their task by not accepting objects or facts or things in general as they are. They consider their projects as being completely subject to change or modification. We recognize this attitude when we say, "I looked at it in a new way," or "So-and-so has an inquiring mind," or "I see the possibilities." These comments are indicative of an open-minded, objective attitude rather than one of satisfaction with the present state of things. "Creativity," says Don Fabun, "is a state of mind."[2]

By adopting this state of mind, we can create anything—from a rocking chair (a combination of a straight chair and rounded surface) to the theory of gravity. These examples may seem far removed from the world of advertising, but the creative process is similar in all fields, from physics to sculpture—to advertising.

Are Some People More Creative than Others?

Are there creative people and noncreative people—those who get ideas and those who use the ideas that others get? James W. Young says, "I think we all recognize that these two types of human beings do exist. Whether they were born that way, or whether their environment and training made them that way, is beside the point. They *are*."[3] But this is a rather fatalistic attitude, and we would not be very creative if we accepted it, for one criterion of creativity is to not accept things as they are.

Another theory is that everybody starts out as a creative individual, but early training and environment eradicate creativity. Some proponents of this theory believe that people can relearn creativity.

Children are indeed creative. They are seeing the world for the first time, and they describe and portray it with a sense of wonder and freshness. Children's drawings constantly surprise adults because of their originality, and the same is true of the stories they invent and the descriptions they write. They observe, they ask questions, and they project their experiences in a novel way. Fabun points out,

In time, through social pressures to conform and the repetition of experience, most of them lose this sense of wonder, and become less and less creative, trapped in a concrete mold not of their own making. It has been said that the creative person is essentially 'a perpetual child.' The tragedy is that most of us grow up.[4]

[1] The quotations from May and Mead and many other definitions are found in Harold H. Anderson (ed.), *Creativity and Its Cultivation*, Harper & Brothers, New York, 1959. The Haefele quotation is from his book *Creativity and Innovation*, Reinhold Publishing Corporation, New York, 1962.
[2] Don Fabun (ed.), "You and Creativity," *The Kaiser Aluminum News*, Vol. 25, No. 3, 1968, p. 5.
[3] James W. Young, *A Technique for Producing Ideas*, Advertising Publications, Chicago, 1943, pp. 19–20.
[4] Fabun, p. 5.

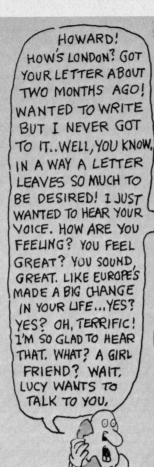

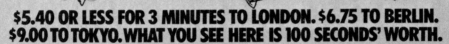

$5.40 OR LESS FOR 3 MINUTES TO LONDON. $6.75 TO BERLIN. $9.00 TO TOKYO. WHAT YOU SEE HERE IS 100 SECONDS' WORTH.

It's only $6.75 (plus tax) when you pick up the phone and call most countries in Western Europe. That's for the first 3 minutes of talk, station-to-station. But there are nighttime and Sunday discounts to many countries. Check it and save.

Best of all, there's the pleasure (and wonder) of talking to family and friends overseas. It's so easy to do. And it costs no more than treating one or two of them to the movies.

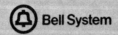 **Bell System**

In what ways could this ad for Bell System's overseas phone service be considered creative? What creative ideas are represented in this ad? (Courtesy The Bell System)

These drawings represent the fresh outlook of children, who express a creativity often lost when they grow older. (Erika Lang; Julia Ring)

Must you be "highly intelligent" in order to be creative and get good ideas? Silvano Arieti, the psychiatrist and professor of clinical psychiatry, states that the prevailing opinion is that highly intelligent persons are not necessarily creative. He says:

Although creative people are intelligent persons, an exceptionally high I.Q. is not a prerequisite for creativity. On the contrary, it may inhibit the inner resources of an individual because his self-criticism becomes too rigid or he learns too quickly what the cultural environment has to offer. We must add that a great ability to deduce according to the laws of logic and mathematics makes for disciplined thinkers but not necessarily for creative people.[5]

It's obvious that a person must have intelligence in order to think creatively. So there's hope here for all of us who have a high school education behind us and are now involved in higher education. These career steps are good evidence that we possess intelligence.

[5] Silvano Arieti, *Creativity, the Magic Synthesis*, Basic Books, Inc., New York, 1976, p. 342.

Exercises in Creativity

Acceptance of the world as it is leads to non-creativity; looking at it in a fresh and questioning way leads to creativity.

It is encouraging to think that even if we aren't creative now we once were. Here are a few exercises to encourage this latent creativity. And don't become discouraged; after all, it's difficult not to accept things as they are presented.

1. Here are three simple symbols: a cross, a triangle, and a circle. What does each of them remind you of? What could they possibly be?

As a start, the X could remind you of a wrong answer on an examination, the spot where the body was found, a multiplication sign, a road crossing, the sign of the cross, suspenders, one-half of a double-cross, and the mark of a person who can't write. How many more things can you think of? What do you "see" when you think about the triangle and the circle?

Limber up your thinking. Your answers can be matter-of-fact, romantic, humorous, prophetic, grandiose—or, with effort and practice, all these things.

2. Here is the start of a story. What do you think happens next?

I remember that morning so well. I awoke and had the strangest feeling that something was different. I turned over in bed and my husband was not there where he should be! But no, this was not the "different" thing; he had said he'd go to work very early. I put on my bathrobe and hurried downstairs, all the while feeling this oddness inside me. For some reason, I headed for the cellar door. I opened it and. . . .

Most people will describe something ominous, or at least mildly catastrophic. Now try for humor, a harder test of your creativity.

3. The following figure is a type of test that is often used to gauge creativity. At first glance, there appear to be meaningless black smudges on white space. But you're expected to look for something else. What do you see when you think for a minute about these shapes? Do you see different things at different times? Compare what you see with what another student sees. Do you each see different things?

4. Six common objects are shown in the following figure. How many uses can you find for each of them? What can you use them for beyond their obvious purpose? Give yourself only 3 minutes per object to list the uses that occur to you. Next compose a paragraph that makes use of all six objects.

5. Giving yourself 15 minutes or so, "invent" a new product, or several of them if you are particularly inspired. Think about what's needed that isn't available to your knowledge, starting with your immediate surroundings and broadening out to the world at large, if you like. The product can be as practical as developing grass seed that only grows 2 inches high and then stops. You would never cut a lawn again, and it would be bad news for the power mower manufacturers. Or think of something grander; a way to harness tides to create a new energy source, for example. Then discuss your new "product" in class.

The purpose of these exercises and other word and object games is to stimulate thinking about things in an unobvious way; that is, to encourage the use of creativity.

Where Do Ideas Come From?

Edmund W. Sinnott, dean of the Yale Graduate School, describes an experience of poet Robert Frost as follows:

One winter evening the poet had opened his front door and strode out into the snowy darkness for a breath of fresh air when there came into his mind the whole of that lovely poem "Stopping by Woods on a Snowy Evening." The strange pattern of rhymes continued in his mind through the verses as he wrote them down, and to bring the poem to a close he had to break the rhythm in the final quatrain.[6]

Rollo May tells the following anecdote about a famous chemistry professor:

He had been searching for a particular chemical formula without success. One night while he was sleeping, he had a dream in which the formula was worked out and displayed before him. He woke up and in the darkness he excitedly wrote it down on a piece of tissue, the only thing he could find. But the next morning, he could not read his own scribbling. Every night thereafter, he would concentrate his hopes on dreaming the dream again. Fortunately, after some nights he did, and he then wrote down the formula for good. It was the formula he had sought and for which he received the Nobel prize.[7]

Rollo May also writes that Albert Einstein once asked a friend, "Why is it I get my best ideas in the morning when I'm shaving?" The friend answered that often the mind needs the relaxation of inner controls, needs to "daydream" for those rare ideas to come forth.[8]

Does this mean that ideas, already formed and articulated, appear from some deep void in the mind—come out of nothingness? We do often say, when we think of something novel, that the idea "came out of the blue." If this were the case, it would entail incredible luck on the part of the creator. But obviously other factors are involved. We would not expect Henry Ford to create "Stars and Stripes Forever" or John Philip Sousa to originate the automobile assembly line. It seems clear that the person who creates an idea has been thinking about a problem and seeking a solution to it, perhaps unconsciously, for some time. Sinnott, discussing Frost's and other people's experiences, points out that these inspirations rarely happen unless an individual has been immersed in a problem.[9]

Poincaré was a great French mathematician, and his experience in solving a problem, as described in his autobiography, emphasizes the importance of thinking steadily about it.

Every day I seated myself at my work table, stayed an hour or two, tried a great number of combinations and reached no result. One evening, contrary to my custom, I drank black coffee and could not sleep. Ideas rose in crowds; I felt them collide until pairs interlocked, so to speak, making a stable combination. By the next morning I had established the existence of a class of Fuchsian functions, those which come from the hypergeometric series; I had only to write out the results, which took but a few hours.[10]

Apparently the mind receives input relevant to the problem. Facts, figures, observations, conversations with others, and the like are all fed into the consciousness. Then, amazingly, these related and unrelated thoughts sink deeper into the *subconscious,* that part of mental action beneath the conscious level. It seems as if all these thoughts have been forgotten; but subconsciously, the mind is working on them. Suddenly an idea comes forth at a most unexpected time. It may not be whole, or complete, but it is enough to work with and develop. It may offer a solution, or it may be discarded and the process repeated.

It is interesting that this moment of the birth

[6] Anderson, p. 24.
[7] Rollo May, *The Courage to Create,* W. W. Norton & Company, Inc., New York, 1975, pp. 45–46.
[8] Ibid., p. 63.
[9] Anderson, p. 24.
[10] May, p. 63.

An idea must be of use and "verified," or it's back to the drawing board, as this cartoon shows. (Courtesy *anny*, *Advertising News of New York*, and Paul Lippman)

of an idea is accompanied by great pleasure and enthusiasm. The creator feels good and usually wants to talk about the idea to anyone available who will listen. Before this happens, as Arieti points out, there is a time of worry, discontent, and anxiety. These unpleasant feelings can actually be incentives that keep a person working on the problem until it yields a solution.[11] Uncomfortable as they may make the creator feel, they are completely outweighed by the sensations of accomplishment, satisfaction, exhilaration, and pure pleasure that occur when an idea comes forth. A person who never discovers these feelings that accompany "getting an idea" has missed a great deal in life.

Steps in the Creative Process

It is apparent that when an individual gets an idea, certain steps have been taken in the conscious and subconscious levels of the mind. There is a logical, sequential development in the creative process, and several writers have listed what they believe the steps to be. Fabun describes the following seven steps.[12]

[11] Arieti, p. 369.
[12] Fabun, pp. 9–12.

Desire: The first step, naturally, is to want to develop an idea or create something. The person is motivated to seek a solution.

Preparation: All types of information are sought, both relevant and irrelevant.

Manipulation: The information is examined, studied, arranged in unusual combinations, and synthesized whenever possible.

Incubation: The problem may defy solution at this stage and may be put aside. The subconscious, however, doesn't take time off at this point.

Intimation: This is the feeling that something is brewing, that the individual is on the brink of a helpful discovery. Something deep in the mind is about to surface.

Illumination: Fabun calls this the "A-ha!" stage. The solution has come into view, and the conscious mind grasps it with feelings of pleasure and relief.

Verification: This is a cold and fearful period, a period of examination. Is this created thing of use? It is tested, looked at from all angles— and sometimes it's back to the drawing board for another go at the problem.

These steps do not all necessarily occur in

every case of problem solving, either in advertising or in any other situation. Incubation is often a luxury that cannot be afforded because of the pressure of deadlines, when it becomes necessary to force an idea by keeping steadily at the problem until a solution is found. The most important steps in the advertising creative process are the preparation stage and the manipulation stage.

There is one, simple additional step that one must take when an idea occurs, and that is the step of writing the thought down immediately. This sounds obvious, but it should be remembered that there is nothing more fleeting than a thought. Unless it is immediately recorded, it often disappears for good, and this can be very frustrating.

Creativity in Advertising

Creativity is necessary at many stages of the advertising process, not just in the construction of the advertising message. Making up a good media plan requires creative thinking, and a successful marketing plan for new-product introduction is fueled by imagination and creative ideas.

Sources of Advertising Ideas

There are two kinds of sources for advertising ideas. *Primary idea sources* are those that help to solve a specific advertising problem. *Secondary idea sources* consist of a body of general, nonspecific information that has been built up over a period of time and that may on occasion prove to be useful and stimulating in solving a specific advertisng problem.

Suppose a copywriter for a large department store must write an ad for expensive matched crystal glassware. The primary source is all the material that can be gathered about the product itself and about the company that produces it. (This information includes "lore," or interesting facts about the manufacturer that will help sell the prospect on quality. Example: "This French factory supplied glassware to the Empress Josephine.") Here are some of the questions the copywriter must answer:

- How much do the items cost?
- How much do they weigh, and what do they "feel" like?
- Are they etched by hand?
- Are they imported?
- When was such quality merchandise last available?
- What is the "lore" about the manufacturer of these items?

The answers to such questions will give the copywriter an idea for a headline and ideas to help construct the tone and flow of the copy. Naturally, the writer will ask an artist to prepare illustrations of the crystal; but the writer feels the quality of the merchandise requires special distinction. Thinking about secondary sources, the writer remembers a type of illustration called scratch board that can give the ad a quality look.

The above example may seem mundane; however, it may serve as a reminder that the creative process is needed to develop even the simplest advertising ideas. In the history of advertising there have been many ideas that required a high degree of creative imagination and that generated exceptional sales in the marketplace. Consider the following famous campaign themes:

CLAIROL Does she or doesn't she? Only her hairdresser knows for sure.

DE BEERS A diamond is forever.

DIAL Aren't you glad you use Dial? Don't you wish everybody did?

JELL-O There's always room for Jell-O.

LADIES' HOME JOURNAL Never underestimate the power of a woman.

These provocative combinations of words came about because creative people used information gathered from primary sources and had a deep understanding of consumer psychology and what motivates people to buy (secondary sources).

Creative people in advertising must be investigators. They constantly ask questions about products and services. They approach a product with an inquiring mind, poke at it, work with it, and find out how it's made and why it's made that way. They are exploring their primary sources so that later they can take the body of information they have developed and make radical statements based on it. Facts are played with and put into new relationships, and in the process ideas are born.

Creative people in advertising must also be collectors of general information. These secondary, background sources can often stimulate advertising ideas at unexpected times. Copywriters and art directors stay informed on what's new in all the art forms. Theater, motion pictures, new film techniques, museum exhibits, new television programming, and the editorial pages of service and shelter magazines are all sources of inspirations for advertising ideas. Most creative people keep scrapbooks and files of unusual turns of phrase, illustrations, magazine and newspaper articles, and other odd pieces of information seemingly unrelated to anything practical but interesting in their own right. Surprisingly, such collections often serve as sources of ideas for headlines, illustrations, themes, and body copy.

A person responsible for preparing an advertising message must have maximum information about the subject. The more input the more opportunities there are to get ideas. A copywriter in an agency developing advertising for a new dentifrice, for example, typically uses the following sources:

■ Library sources, agency, media, or public library; available research studies on consumer brushing habits, brand preferences and reasons for preferences, consumer wants and relative importance of these wants; published results of dental studies

■ Original research developed by the agency or its client; taste-test comparisons between the brand and competing brands; controlled experiments conducted by dental schools to determine the efficacy of the brand as a tooth decay inhibitor, if available; focus group interviews with consumers to determine toothpaste preferences and reasons for preferences; quantitative studies of brand image, usage, and consumer awareness

■ Writer's own sources; face-to-face questioning of consumers to learn about their habits, opinions, and attitudes concerning toothpaste; writer's own experiments with the product; current and past advertising (examination of what has already been done in dentifrice ads)

In other words, to prepare the mind to create ideas, the writer saturates it with all the information related to the problem that can be found. In the case of the writer preparing to write copy for a new toothpaste, we have noted all the kinds of material that can be made available. An assignment on a new product often does involve this much preparation. Most copy assignments don't require this depth of background. A copywriter working for a discount house chain, for example, needs only brief information and prices for the many items that are featured in such an ad.

Methods of Stimulating the Creative Process

The most difficult moment a writer faces when given an assignment to create an ad comes after the input stage, when staring at a blank piece of paper. It is a very lonely time. The writer feels frustrated and inadequate and may procrastinate by sharpening pencils, pacing the room, looking out the window, and hoping for interruptions. But the assignment cannot be avoided forever.

Here is how you can overcome this problem in your own writing. The important thing is to make some attempt. You may hesitate to do so because you know that what you put down won't be right. No matter; set it down anyway. To get started, write out the requirements of the assignment or what the ad must accomplish. State the problem. Every idea that occurs to you at this point should be put on paper, even if it doesn't seem to apply or make sense. As much as a page of thoughts may be written without getting anywhere; on the other hand, correct word combinations that accomplish your objectives may start to turn up right away.

Once something is on paper, sometimes it's a good idea to turn to another task for 15 minutes or so and then reread what you have written. Often you will see something in your stream-of-consciousness material that will suggest a headline or a copy idea. Then the job will be well on the way to completion.

The above method won't work for everybody. Some people find it necessary to talk out an ad with another person, both of them developing material as the discussion continues. Copywriters and art directors often work together in this mutual-stimulation method.

But the key, however the individual goes about it, is to start, even though the first draft may not be satisfactory.

It is absolutely necessary to set a deadline for the completion of an ad. This in itself is a method of stimulating the creative process. The deadline date should not lie too far in the future. It should be a reasonable date; but the granting of "plenty of time," while kind in intent, does not help the cause. Bad or just average advertising ideas often come from writers who have spent too much time creating their ads. The best ideas seem to come when a little deadline pressure is applied.

Brainstorming   Alex Osborn, the advertising agent, developed a widely followed method for stimulating the creative process. Osborn firmly believed that individuals can be taught how to be creative and how to get ideas. His method is called brainstorming.[13] It can be used in any field where ideas are needed. *Brainstorming* involves a group session of from five to twelve people, under one person's leadership, in which ideas are developed mutually or individually on a no-holds-barred basis. The session lasts no more than an hour, and all ideas are recorded, either in writing or by tape. The session must follow these rules in order to be successful:

1. Criticism of any idea presented is forbidden.

2. The modification of an idea, or its combination with another, is encouraged.

3. As many ideas as possible are developed. Quantity is a goal.

4. Unusual, off-beat, and far-out ideas are encouraged.

[13] Alex Osborn, *Applied Imagination,* Charles Scribner's Sons, New York, 1957.

The leader is the key to the operation. The leader must maintain some semblance of order, keep would-be humorists under control, suggest a fresh direction when the group seems to run out of gas, and cut off the session when fatigue occurs.

Criticisms of the brainstorming method are that individuals do not receive credit for ideas that they originate and that time for incubation in the creative process is eliminated. But the former drawback can be overcome by recording who thought of what; the latter, by allowing an incubation period as an aftermath of the session. If the participants are asked to continue thinking at their own pace about the problem after the formal session, they can let their ideas incubate at their own convenience.

Task Force Another method commonly used in advertising to develop ideas is the *task-force method*. A number of agency copy, art, and research people are selected and given an assignment to develop an advertising idea, campaign, or slogan in an attempt to solve a specific advertising problem. The problem is usually one that has defied solution for some time. The people in the task force need not have previous knowledge of or experience in the area to be explored. Fresh minds can often develop a fresh solution.

The procedure is to brief the people selected and to give them kits of material that outline the problem and the strategy for solution and that contain all the information that is considered helpful. A deadline is set, and the members of the group work individually or in teams on solutions. This method lacks the free-wheeling aspects of brainstorming, but it is useful in obtaining practical results.

Characteristics of Creative People

People can learn how to develop creative solutions to problems. Nevertheless, there are certain people whom we expect to be creative; the way they think and their past accomplishments indicate that they are likely to succeed in the task of getting ideas.

Creative people are usually inquisitive and curious about their surroundings and, specifically, about people, their motivations, and what makes them tick. The creative individual is probably a good reporter of facts and one who digs for information. He or she should have a sense of humor and an awareness of the ludicrous and the bizarre. The creative person should love words and appreciate good writing.

When hiring a copywriter, a copy chief will look at a person's previous experience record for evidence that the individual has been able to apply creative solutions to problems that have been encountered. One person might write in a job résumé that he or she was circulation manager of the campus weekly newspaper. Another might write, "I was circulation manager and was able to increase the number of subscribers by 30 percent. All new subscribers got a ticket in a lottery we held, and the circulation staff members received a cash bonus for every twenty-five students they signed up." Employers will rate the second applicant higher than the first.

The student interested in advertising should not concentrate exclusively on advertising and marketing courses. Literature, sociology, psychology, music, drama, and the arts add the broad perspective and the stimulus that an individual in the creative area of advertising needs as background.

Vocabulary

Define the following terms and use each one in a sentence.

Brainstorming
Creative
Creativity
Primary idea sources

Secondary idea sources
Subconscious
Task-force method

Review Questions

1. "Creativity is a state of mind." Discuss the meaning of this statement.
2. Do you agree or disagree with the idea that all intelligent people have the potential for creativity? Give reasons that support your point of view.
3. List steps in the process of creativity.
4. Which are the most important steps in the advertising creative process?
5. What current advertising themes impress you as being highly creative? What are your reasons for thinking so?
6. Describe various methods for stimulating advertising creativity.
7. What are the rules to follow in a brainstorming session?

Activities

1. Can you think of any examples in your own life of successful applications of the creative process? What problem have you faced where "getting an idea" on your part resulted in a solution? Write out a brief description of the situation, or be prepared to discuss it in class.
2. You are a copywriter in the advertising department of a large metropolitan department store, and you have received an assignment to prepare copy for a sale of particularly fine framed reproductions of the works of such artists as van Gogh, Renoir, Matisse, Monet, and Degas. List examples of primary source material that you would expect to be given for background by the store buyer to help you write the copy.

Project

By this time in the course, you may have been noticing the advertising efforts of local merchants more closely. Now consider these efforts from the point of view of creativity. Over the next two days look for examples of local advertising that you consider creative in the sense of being original, fresh, or provocative. The following local media can be checked: identification signs on merchants' stores, outdoor nonstandardized and standardized signs, newspapers, radio, television, and direct mail. Make a list of any outstanding creative advertising by local advertisers in these media. Be prepared to describe such advertising in class and to explain why you think your examples are creative.

Career Ladder

You have an entry-level job in a large ad agency and you're happy about this, up to a point. It's in the checking department, and it's pretty humdrum work for a person like yourself who's interested in the creative side of the business. You hear there's a beginning copy job open in the copy department. You're interested in writing and look on it as a great opportunity. What possible steps or actions would you take that would put you in a favorable light with those in the creative department who have the responsibility for filling the beginner's job? Discuss what you would do in class.

CHAPTER TWELVE

CHANNELING IDEAS

As we discussed in Chapter 11, ideas occur as a result of a complex mental process consisting of information input, information digestion, and information manipulation. People often get ideas without going through this process; but if they bring their "brilliant" insights to an expert in the area, unless they are unusually lucky, their ideas will be found to be impractical.

The expert has either thought of the amateur's idea before, or sees things wrong with it, or has seen it fail in the past. The expert has been doing things right, by absorbing information, thinking about it, and trying to solve possible problems by getting ideas. In other words, discipline is being applied to the problems, a discipline that the amateur, without knowledge of the problems and without a background of information, has been unable to apply.

Very often people not in the advertising business think of ideas, slogans, and illustrations for products and services. And very often these people send their ideas to the company con-

cerned in the hope of being paid for them. It may seem heartless and closed-minded, but unsolicited ideas are invariably returned to the sender. This is done for legal reasons. In the past, when such ideas were not returned, companies have been involved in legal actions when a previously submitted idea was thought by the originator to be similar in some way to an advertising idea used subsequently by the company.

The slogan, "Be happy, go Lucky" is an unusual case because the idea, suggested by people outside the business, was considered eventually to have merit and to be usable. It was submitted to the maker of Lucky Strike cigarettes literally dozens of times every month by people all over the United States, all thinking of the same slogan independently. In actuality, it was eventually used in a campaign for the brand, but not before it had been established to lawyers' satisfaction that it had also been created years ago by an individual working for the tobacco company.

Importance of Discipline

Discipline is essential to advertising creative work, just as it is to any creative process. Advertising often deals with large dollar expenditures; but even the smallest retailer, running a 2-inch ad in the local newspaper, can't afford to throw money away on an idea that won't help sell goods. Every advertiser must keep objectives in mind at all times, and no matter how pleased an advertiser may be with an advertising idea that has been developed, it should be discarded if it doesn't help achieve selling goals.

Walking away from one's own idea and looking at it in perspective is a very difficult thing to do. Having an idea is like having a baby; you love it and want it to have the best of futures. So it is natural to resist those who try to change or modify one's idea and to regard these people as enemies of progress. What is needed here is objectivity.

The Tyranny of Space and Time Limitations

Discipline starts with the form the advertising message takes. Form limits the content of the message. In print media, the copywriter or art director is confined by the size of the space that has been purchased—a page, a half-page, or perhaps 100 agate lines. In outdoor advertising, although there is ample space on a poster, the copywriter is limited by the fact that the message and illustration must be absorbed by motorists passing the sign at 50 miles or more per hour. A 12-word message will not do, no matter how provocative the copy; it must be cut to half that length to succeed in its purpose. In television and radio advertising, the time available for the message provides a form of discipline. While up to 200 words can be crammed into a 1-minute commercial, the resulting confusion to the viewer or listener defeats the purpose of the message. About 125 words per 1-minute commercial is comfortable, and a good rule to follow is two words per second. This timing does not allow for sound effects, dramatic pauses, and musical "punctuation," but we will be discussing these matters more fully in Chapters 17 and 18. It is enough to say that the length of the TV or radio commercial or the size of the ad in print media automatically cause advertisers to discipline themselves if they are not to undermine the effectiveness of their advertising messages.

Only one advertising medium is relatively unconfining. In direct mail, the prepared material can be highly flexible. Within the envelope (which can vary greatly in size), a message can conceivably be developed for a foldout measuring 4 by 6 feet. A letter, a pamphlet or two, and a specialty advertising item can all be included in a single mailing—and they often are. Cutouts, accordion folds, collapsible three-dimensional cardboard devices, and the like are all used, and the only limitations are the creative person's imagination and the budget for the job.

Most beginning copywriters tend to overwrite, with resulting problems in communication. In the print media, overwriting means that to fit the copy into the available space a small type size must be used and the leading between the lines cut down or eliminated. This makes reading the message difficult. In broadcast media, copy that is too long forces the announcer to hurry, and sales points slip by unheard. Retail advertisers occasionally overwrite and "crowd" ads with unnecessary elements. They sometimes try to get their "money's worth" by including every conceivable bit of information or by repetition. The advertiser should accept the discipline of space and time limitations.

The Basic Need for a Strategy

Space and time limitations impose discipline; advertising media budgets and cost-of-production budgets impose discipline; and there is a third very important discipline that is imposed by the need to develop an objective, or goal for the advertising and stick to this objective. Once this is done, a way to accomplish such goals is to put together an *advertising strategy*. This is a simple statement that briefly repeats the advertising objective and then lists primary, and possibly secondary, methods needed to reach it. Semantically speaking, a strategy statement should not contain objectives, but in the advertising business, it usually does. We need to refer to some kind of strategy statement when we start the process of creating advertising, and it's a good idea to remind ourselves of our ultimate advertising goals at the same time. These goals and strategies that advertisers impose on themselves are actually part of the advertising creative process itself.

The first step in communication is self-communication. The originator of an idea should think it through to make sure that it makes sense before attempting to explain it to others. In advertising, this is accomplished by thinking about the purpose of the ad; the advertiser must get into the habit of doing this before "getting ideas" and writing them down. An advertising strategy is basic to an advertisement because it channels thinking and helps develop problem-solving ideas that are practical and oriented toward selling goals.

The advertising strategy performs another important service, too. Once the advertiser has written the print media headline and copy or the television or radio message, the strategy is used as a yardstick to see whether what was intended has really been accomplished. It keeps the copy on the right track and prevents it from wandering.

Retail Strategies In retail advertising involved with uncomplicated or straightforward selling goals, a strategy statement need not be prepared or written out. The strategy is always present in the mind of copywriter, and the elements of the ad are developed almost automatically. If the job is to advertise a special purchase of men's poplin raincoats early in April, it's obvious that the copy will stress price, the water-repellent cloth, style features ("belted," "plaid-lined")—and the idea that the customer should be prepared for April showers. The strategy is to sell the store buyer's special-purchase raincoats on a price-value basis, and there's no need to "overthink" the advertising problem.

Suppose, however, that the management of the menswear store decides to initiate a new image-building institutional advertising campaign to supplement the regular advertising program. This involves subtleties that go beyond ordinary product advertising. The management must concern itself with the objectives and strategy of this proposed institutional ad campaign and must do some thinking about the long-term goals of the store. Perhaps the store's reputation is in the field of supplying moderately priced menswear; it is not thought of as a fashion leader, although some top men's fashion lines are carried. Now management decides to build business by featuring men's fashion trends in order to attract customers currently shopping at competing stores. The strategy statement might read as follows:

The goal of the institutional advertising campaign is to increase menswear business done in more

What is the main objective of this advertisement? What improvements could be made in copy, headline, and layout to further the main objective? Should any elements be omitted? (Courtesy Clavier Music)

expensive, style-oriented lines. The method to achieve this goal will be to feature top men's clothing designers whose goods are carried. In addition, it will be emphasized that the sales force is particularly knowledgeable in men's clothing trends.

A strategy is necessary for this advertising so that the individual institutional ads can be built along preconceived lines and each ad in the series can be checked to see if it meets the predetermined objectives.

National Brand Strategies All national advertising for goods and services should be written in accordance with a strategy statement. The statement should be clear, single-minded, and brief. It should be so constructed that a new copywriter hired by the ad agency, given product information and pertinent research on consumer profiles and desires, would immediately be able to write advertising that directs itself to solving the sales problems involved and doesn't wander into unproductive areas.

Copy strategy is based on marketing objectives and as much consumer and market research as can be brought to bear on the sales problem. It is usually developed by the manufacturer's marketing people working closely with the advertising agency team. Here are two strategies developed for a nationally advertised liquid dishwashing detergent:

Strategy A The advertising will convince housewives that X is the best possible product to use because it is exceptionally mild to hands. Proof of this is the fact that X contains some of the same ingredients that are found in hand lotions. A reassurance will be given that the product is an excellent dish cleaner.

Strategy B The advertising will convince consumers that X is the best possible product to use

"*Yes, offhand I'd say you _are_ hitting your serves harder with the Prince.*"

For people who, given the choice, would rather win than lose.

The strategy of this ad is to convince the reader that Prince Rackets are superior to other tennis rackets. How well do you think the ad accomplishes this strategy? (Courtesy Prince Tennis Racket)

because it is superior in dishwashing efficiency and is exceptionally mild to hands. Support will be found in its ability to remove grease and egg yolk and in the fact that it contains hand-lotion ingredients. Also mentioned will be product X's excellence in hand washing fine woolens and lingerie.

Strategy A is superior to Strategy B and will do a more efficient job of selling because it is single-minded in its thrust and features a major selling point. It doesn't attempt too much; the tendency to try to hook consumers by additional appeals is resisted. Strategy B is a "split," or fifty-fifty, strategy, selling dishwashing efficiency and mildness to hands equally. It is as if the advertiser couldn't decide which way to sell the product. The consumer seeing advertising based on this strategy is liable to be just as confused as the advertiser is.

Strategy statements are not the same thing as *execution,* which refers to how the strategy is actually carried out in the advertisement. Execution involves evoking a mood, attracting interest, and dramatizing facts; strategy statements are the selling "bones." Execution fleshes out the strategy with color, life, interest, and reader involvement. (See Color Plate 12.)

Understanding Human Nature

Working out copy objectives is a necessary task, but there is not much fun in it. It is a dry, semantic chore, lacking the life and involvement that actual copywriting holds. Copywriting involves the fascinating question of what motivates people to buy what the advertiser has to sell.

In a certain sense, advertising is an intrusion into our affairs. In most cases, the prospect has paid for the privilege of enjoying the media—and finds there a message that the advertiser has paid the media to carry. The prospect is interested in the editorial content of magazines and newspapers and in the entertainment content of radio and television; the advertising message must capture attention away from this competition and attempt to convince the prospect to buy something. And there are many advertisers competing for the attention of this same consumer through the same media.

So, on the face of it, to succeed in the advertising task seems to be an insurmountable job. And it would be if one did not understand human nature. But an understanding and application of the principles of human motivation help channel advertising ideas to gain the prospect's attention.

Motivating by Appealing to Self-Interest

If advertisers keep in mind the simple fact that people are interested in themselves, they will be able to climb over the barriers that the consumer builds against buying. By appealing to what really interests the consumer, advertisers will be heard, and their suggestions and appeals will have a greater likelihood of being acted upon.

Newspaper editors understand that people are interested in themselves, and they tailor their news and editorial content accordingly. Readers are most interested in events and editorial matter that relate closely to their own lives; they are least interested in things that are far removed from them. This is why today's weather always appears on the front page and why local events are often given as much

Crumple up this ad.

Then take it to your local Xerox office.

Tell a sales representative that if the new Xerox 5400 copier is so terrific, let's see if the ball of paper in your hand will go through its document feeder.

Chuckle to yourself as he smooths out the ad and carries it to the 5400. After all, you've never seen a document handler that could handle a problem like this.

Then he may pause to tell you how the 5400 can automatically copy on two sides of a sheet of paper. He may even point out its uncanny self-diagnostic systems and lightning-fast automatic bi-directional sorter.

But you both know why you're there.

At last, he slides the crumpled page towards the document handler and pushes the button. And...and...and...

Sorry. But what happens next is between you and your local Xerox representative. So pay him a visit, soon.

And find out if the original goes in.

And if it does, how the copy comes out.   **XEROX**

The purpose of this Xerox ad is to help sell the 5400 copier. What is the executional idea that captures reader interest? How does this idea help sell the Xerox 5400 copier? (Courtesy Xerox Corporation)

space as international developments, no matter how world-shaking. This is why local news stories are personalized with as many names as possible and why efforts are made to feature the opinions of local citizens in interviews.

In advertising, too, one must appeal to the self-interest of the individual and *motivate* that individual, or supply the incentives that make it more likely that the reader or viewer will take an action favorable to the advertiser. This is not as crass as it sounds. It means simply that the advertiser must talk in terms of what the product or service will do for the prospect. This is *the* important rule to remember in writing copy. The copywriter must give incentives, or motivate, by depicting, demonstrating, and telling how what is being sold will improve the lot of those who read or hear or see the message. Copy people must approach the selling problem from the consumer's viewpoint, not their own.

This is no different from the way salespeople sell their prospects face to face. A person selling life insurance knows that a certain number of policies must be sold in order to make a living. This is never brought up when talking to prospects. The seller of life insurance talks in terms of security for the family, meeting education needs, or building up an annuity for retirement years. The auto dealer has a back lot full of new models that must be moved. The sales approach never appeals to sympathy—the prospect couldn't care less—but stresses car leg room, driving ease, and good mileage. Then the dealer tries to sell air conditioning "to ensure summer comfort." The dealer is appealing to the self-interest of the prospect.

Appealing to Basic Desires

If the advertiser is to motivate a prospect to buy, something must be known about consumer psychology. It is for this reason that psy-

chology courses are so valuable to students of advertising, who must know what motivates people, what the needs and desires are that the individual strives to satisfy. The basic needs are for food and water, clothing, shelter, self-preservation, and sex. Today, most people are able to satisfy these needs in their simplest forms, but they desire more.

Some important needs and desires that the advertiser should be aware of are listed on the following pages.

Health People desire a feeling of well-being and physical health. They want "a good night's sleep." They want freedom from sicknesses or a cure for them as fast as possible. They don't want to be overweight or underweight, tired, lacking in energy, or depressed. Products that help people satisfy a desire for health or physical improvement should, in their advertising, make the most of their benefits. A few examples follow.

I LOST 30 POUNDS IN 30 DAYS.
(Weight-reducing plan)

WORKS FASTER THAN ASPIRIN TO RELIEVE HEADACHES. (Analgesic product)

TWICE AS MANY VITAMINS AS FRESH ORANGE JUICE. (Vitamin-fortified canned fruit drink)

TEN SIMPLE STEPS YOU CAN TAKE TO HELP YOU LIVE LONGER. (Life insurance)

Security Not many people thrive on insecurity. Most people want a well-ordered existence for themselves and their families. They want to be protected against financial disaster, fire, accidents, prowlers in the night, and the general vagaries of fate. Advertisers whose product or service can meet the desire for security make appeals such as these:

What basic desires do these ads appeal to? (Courtesy Whitehall Laboratories Division, American Home Products; American Insurance Association; Aetna Life & Casualty, Sterling Silversmiths Guild of America)

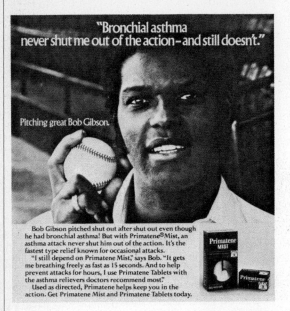

"Bronchial asthma never shut me out of the action – and still doesn't."

Pitching great Bob Gibson.

Bob Gibson pitched shut out after shut out even though he had bronchial asthma! But with Primatene® Mist, an asthma attack never shut him out of the action. It's the fastest type relief known for occasional attacks.

"I still depend on Primatene Mist," says Bob. "It gets me breathing freely as fast as 15 seconds. And to help prevent attacks for hours, I use Primatene Tablets with the asthma relievers doctors recommend most."

Used as directed, Primatene helps keep you in the action. Get Primatene Mist and Primatene Tablets today.

One of these homeowners is thrifty, safety conscious, and a sitting duck for financial disaster.

He doesn't even know it. He thinks he's done his best to protect his home and his possessions. He hasn't.

Many people, like the man on the left, believe they have adequate homeowners insurance. But inflation has been pushing up the value of their homes. They don't update their coverage every year. So when disaster strikes, they are unable to fully recover their losses.

Rising replacement costs are one reason. In the last 10 years the cost of re-siding a home jumped 132%, re-shingling a roof 155%, and repainting a living room 142%. In the last five years alone, the cost of building a new home has increased 63%.

As a group of property and casualty insurance companies, we don't want you to be a sitting duck by not having your insurance provide full protection for your home. Check with your agent to be sure your homeowners policy reflects the amount of additional coverage inflation has made necessary.

Here's what we're doing to help protect you:
■ Offering policies with a built-in inflation clause
■ Supporting strict building codes to reduce fire risk.

■ Designing new coverages to meet the special insurance needs of older homes.
■ Helping to develop safety standards which protect life and property.
■ Operating special claims assistance and damage repair programs in times of catastrophe.
■ Conducting fire prevention and arson control programs.

Here's what you can do to protect yourself:
■ Re-evaluate your home insurance needs annually with your agent.
■ Take a higher deductible if you can. It lowers your premiums.
■ Install a smoke detector or burglar alarm. Many companies offer premium discounts for such devices.
■ Get a receipt or appraisal for all major household items (furniture, antiques, jewelry, art). Duplicate it and keep it and all such records in a safety deposit box away from your home.
■ Inventory all your possessions and take photos of each room to document what you have.

This message is presented by The American Insurance Association, 85 John Street, New York, NY 10038.

Affordable insurance is our business...and yours.

HOW TO RETIRE AT 60 WITH $800 A MONTH. (Insurance annuity plan)

TURNS ON THE LIGHTS WHEN YOU'RE AWAY FROM HOME. (Burglar protection device)

THIS POLICY ENSURES THAT YOUR FAMILY BUSINESS STAYS IN THE FAMILY. (Insurance plan)

THE TIRE: SKIDPROOF ON WET, SLIPPERY PAVEMENTS. (Automobile tire)

Prosperity People want to feel secure financially. Whatever their net worth, it's never quite enough. They desire wealth beyond what they possess; consequently, they want to increase profits, save money when they make purchases, get exceptional values for their money, and increase their incomes. Advertising appeals that show how to improve one's financial lot consequently attract people's interest. Here are a few:

SPECIAL PURCHASE! FINE LUSTROUS COTTON BROADCLOTH SHIRTS. $14.50 VALUE FOR $9.99. (Menswear department store ad)

HOW TO MAKE MONEY IN THE MARKET—BY NOT FOLLOWING THE

Now, life insurance that gives you a hedge against inflation.

Rising inflation rates usually trigger rising rates of interest.

So a life insurance policy whose cost *dropped* when interest rates *rose* would lessen inflation's impact on your life.

That's how Æconomaster, from Ætna, is designed to work.

You start out paying one of the lowest premiums of any whole-life insurance policy in America.

Then, after the second year, Ætna adjusts your premium. The new premium reflects how we think our investments will fare, how long people are living, and other cost factors.

Higher annual interest rates mean higher income from Ætna's investments. That means we can afford to

lower your premium.

It's also possible (especially if interest rates should fall) that your premium could rise, but *never higher than the ceiling written into your Æconomaster policy.*

So you get a combination of the best features of several kinds of policies:

A very low premium to start with;

A very clear limit on how far that premium can rise;

And a very real possibility

of seeing that premium drop lower still.

Æconomaster policies begin at $25,000. Ætna Life & Casualty is the first major U.S. life insurance organization to offer them. And other Ætna inflation-fighting life insurance policies are on the way. To learn more about

them, contact your nearest Ætna Life General Agent soon. You'll find the number in the Yellow Pages.

Ætna
LIFE & CASUALTY

Ætna Life Insurance Company, Hartford, CT 06156. Æconomaster is already available in most states and Ætna is now working to make it available in states where it is not yet offered.

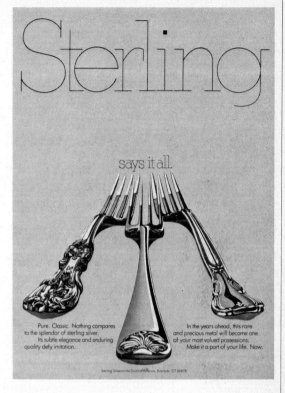

Sterling

says it all.

Pure. Classic. Nothing compares to the splendor of sterling silver. Its subtle elegance and enduring quality defy imitation.

In the years ahead, this rare and precious metal will become one of your most valued possessions. Make it a part of your life. Now.

Sterling Silversmiths Guild of America, Riverside, CT 06878

CROWD. (Book on timing of stock market trading)

HOW TO INCREASE SALES WITHOUT INCREASING YOUR SELLING STAFF. (Selling method course for salespeople)

20TH-CENTURY IRELAND PIONEERS THE GUARANTEED ANNUAL PROFIT. (Industrial development ad for Ireland)

Approval People want to be looked up to. Modesty prohibits most people from telling others about their own good taste, intelligence, and accomplishments, so they buy and use products that say it for them. Expensive

clothes, large homes, European vacation trips, even certain brands of liquor or cuts of meat all help establish the kind of image that people want to project. Individuals need to be accepted and liked.

Closely related to this area is the desire for self-fulfillment, taking advantage of one's abilities and developing them fully. Correspondence courses and the like cater to such wants. Self-fulfillment comes under the heading of approval because it is largely motivated by the hope that others will think well of you for your achievements.

Products and services that offer help in realizing the desire for approval are promoted in terms that make individuals feel they're "getting there" if they buy. Here are some appeals directed to this need for approval:

WE DO ALL THE WORK. YOU GET ALL THE GLORY. (Cake mix)

FOR PEOPLE WHO ARE NOT ASHAMED OF HAVING BRAINS. ("Masterpieces of literature" books)

THIS $1,000 WATCH TELLS YOU SOMETHING ABOUT YOURSELF. (Wristwatch)

WHILE YOU'VE BEEN WORKING YOUR WAY UP ALL THESE YEARS, WE'VE BEEN QUIETLY WAITING FOR YOU TO ARRIVE. (Liquor ad)

Attraction Sex is an important motivating drive, and a product that promises that a person will be more attractive, or charming, or somehow more appealing to the opposite sex is backed by a very strong sales approach. The promise of revived youth, or at least a younger appearance, is equally strong.

Here are some advertising approaches that directly or indirectly appeal to the desire for attraction. The first two are well written; the last two are so blatant that they run the risk of alienating the reader.

WHY BE PLAIN OLD BROWN WHEN YOU CAN BE A GORGEOUS BRUNETTE? (Hair-coloring product ad)

NEXT TIME YOUR HUSBAND TALKS TO A FASCINATING WOMAN, MAKE SURE IT'S YOU. (Magazine circulation-building ad)

WILL BALDNESS ADD FALSE YEARS TO YOUR AGE? (Men's hair-treatment ad)

. . . A REMARKABLE AFTER-SHAVE THAT HAS THE POWER TO MAKE MEN IRRESISTIBLE TO WOMEN. (After-shave lotion ad)

Comfort People like to be as comfortable as possible, and this need has created markets for products as diverse as air conditioners and foam rubber. Closely related to comfort are ease and convenience. If there's an easier, less complicated way to accomplish a task, people are all for it, if they can possibly afford it. Convenience products and services include TV dinners, take-home food services, power mowers, electric barbecues, golf carts, automated garage doors, electric typewriters, and other things that reduce time and effort.

Here are some examples of headlines and copy that take advantage of the desire for comfort, ease, and convenience:

BAKE YOUR OVEN CLEAN. (Self-cleaning oven ad)

THE HEAT PUMP THAT WARMS YOUR HOME IN WINTER, COOLS IT IN SUMMER—AND SAVES MONEY ALL YEAR 'ROUND. (Heat-pump installation ad)

KICK OFF YOUR SHOES AND SINK YOUR FEET INTO THIS DEEP, SCULPTURED CARPET. (Floor covering ad)

HOW DO YOU MAKE A DELICIOUS CAKE? JUST ADD WATER. (Cake mix)

Pleasure People want to get some pleasure out of life. If they can manage it, they'll pamper themselves with products and services that go far beyond satisfying their basic needs. Products that appeal to these powerful desires for pleasure are usually luxuries; they do well in good times, but sales dry up when the economy takes a turn for the worse. Real estate in Florida, Arizona, and southern California, boats and boat trailers, vacation trips, meals in luxury restaurants, expensive cars, home swimming pools, and gourmet foods are in the class of luxuries. Here are some typical ads:

OWN A PRIVATE BEACH, POOL, DOCK, AND A BEAUTIFUL APARTMENT ON LONG ISLAND SOUND. (Shore real estate development ad)

ADD A LOT OF LUXURY TO YOUR LEISURE. (Expensive automobile ad)

THE TROUBLE WITH HAVING YOUR OWN MULTIMILLION DOLLAR YACHT IS, YOU GET A LITTLE SPOILED. (Caribbean cruise ship ad)

Appealing to What Interests People

Besides appeals to the basic desires that motivate people, there are other ways to gain attention. Advertisers must understand human nature and discover what interests people. When copy is written in terms of these interests, it stands a better chance of being successful. People are curious about the lives and experiences of others. They are emotional in their reaction to people and events. They like to be entertained, and they love a good story. They appreciate humor and like to be amused. They want to be a part of things, not considered outsiders. Above all, they are interested in whatever is new.

These interests are particularly helpful to advertisers at a specific stage in the process of developing copy. When a strategy has been determined, the benefits of the product established, and the basic appeals worked out, the execution, or form of the advertising, must be considered. If advertisers understand people's interests, they can use various techniques to tie in with them. A humorous approach may be used if the humor is related to what is being sold and is not merely added for the sake of entertainment. The advertiser may tell a story, or appeal unabashedly to the emotions or write the copy from a first-person eyewitness point of view. A *testimonial* approach

may be chosen, in which the copy describes the actual experience of a real individual, famous or not, who recommends a product or service. Testimonial advertising personalizes the copy and tells the reader something of interest about someone else's life. In each of these cases the advertising executions are based on appeals to known basic interests.

Using Basic Desires and Interests Properly
An advertising approach appealing to a desire, such as health, security, or comfort, should develop easily and naturally from the strategy for an advertising message. It should not be forced or contrived. The advertiser must

This savings bank ad features more than one appeal in its headline: saving money and convenience. (Courtesy People's Savings Bank)

study the product and its benefits and then see how these benefits fit the needs, desires, and interests of the consumer. (See Color Plate 12.)

Just because the advertiser understands the importance of comfort to the consumer does not mean that a comfort appeal can be grafted onto a product that does not have benefits of this sort. An exercycle might have a comfortable seat and adjustable pedals (comfort features), but these features are not as important as its "health" appeal. An appeal to sexual attraction is a great motivator, but when it is dragged into copy where it doesn't apply, it deters rather than attracts the consumer.

Advertisers should make it a rule not to promise what the product or service can't deliver. They should not overpromise, or claim attributes for a product or service that are not really present. The consumer is intelligent, and while an item may be sold once on the basis of exaggerated claims, there will be no repeat sales.

This discussion of appeals refers to the main thrust of the copy. The headline is built around this idea, and the copy elaborates on it. This does not mean that the selling story must be limited to this single approach; the copy may include other appeals subordinate to the main idea. For example, an ad for a dishwasher features the fact that it scrubs pots clean. But it also states that it washes dishes and glasses "cleaner than ever," runs quietly because of a blanket of sound insulation, and saves water and energy when you press its special "energy saver" button. Thus this ad concentrates on a wanted feature, pot scrubbing, but includes money saving and other appeals as well.

Featuring More than One Appeal Sometimes the copywriter may decide to combine appeals to two basic desires in the headline. An example is: "Invest your money in a Villa on the Costa Smeralda. It's as worthwhile as blue

Strapped
For Time

Strap watches
of eighteen
karat gold by
Audemars Piguet.
Hers, $2,600. His, $2,950.

TIFFANY & CO.
NEW YORK FIFTH AVE. & 57TH ST. · ZIP: 10022 · TEL: (212) 755-8000
ATLANTA · CHICAGO · HOUSTON · SAN FRANCISCO · BEVERLY HILLS
Add sales tax where applicable · American Express · Diners Club · Master Charge · Visa

The appeal to self-indulgence in this Tiffany ad need not be explicitly stated in headline or copy; it is communicated by the prestige of the store, the prestige of the watchmaker, and the prices of the watches. (Courtesy Tiffany & Co.)

chips and a lot of fun." Here the real estate promoter is stressing two appeals, prosperity and pleasure, and the combination gives the prospect two good reasons to become interested.

Two headlines quoted earlier in this chapter feature more than one appeal. "We do all the work. You get all the glory," advertising a cake mix, combines appeals to convenience and approval. "The heat pump that warms your home in winter, cools it in summer—and saves money all year 'round" combines an economy appeal with a comfort appeal. Such combinations can be effective, but care must be taken to avoid confusing and overwhelming the reader.

Questioning the Need to Feature a Basic Appeal It's possible to write good advertising copy without any of the appeals we have listed.

The basic appeals are valuable and useful when they apply to the product and its benefits, but they are not absolutely essential. Use them when it is logical, but do not force the copy to include them.

Much retail advertising does not call for inclusion of appeals to basic desires. An ad may appeal indirectly to pleasure, comfort, or approval, particularly in the illustration—but the appeal is not explicitly stated.

Retail advertising often consists of a description of the merchandise, without elaboration. Much national advertising, too, is prepared under the assumption that the reader will buy the product because it appeals to basic

desires. The adverti... sary to spell out the ... luxury goods often un... not mention it at all. T... peal to self-gratificati... merely because a wel... product name is ment... mous New York jewelry... necessary when it advert... ...nd necklace to write a headline and copy that is addressed to the desires for self-gratification and approval. The illustration of the necklace, its price, and the name of the store are sufficient to awaken these basic desires in the reader's mind.

Vocabulary

Define the following terms, and use each one in a sentence.

Advertising strategy   Motivate
Execution   Testimonial

Review Questions

1. What kinds of disciplines are needed in preparing advertising?
2. What is the limiting factor that applies discipline to television and radio advertising? What is the limiting factor in preparing copy and illustrations for outdoor posters?
3. Discuss why it is important to develop an objective or strategy before advertising is written.
4. What basic approach must be taken in order to interest prospects and motivate them to buy a product or service?
5. List seven desires that individuals strive to satisfy.
6. What two basic desires might you appeal to if you were writing an advertisement for a savings bank?
7. Discuss why you think advertising in general goes too far in appealing to basic desires, or why you think it doesn't go overboard in this respect. Do you think specific advertising campaigns go too far in appealing to basic desires? Which ones come to mind?

8. What traits of human nature or individual interests can the advertiser cater to in order to interest the prospect in the selling story?
9. Why is it important not to overpromise in advertising copy?
10. Must an advertisement utilize a basic appeal? Why or why not?

Activities

1. Using current magazines, try to find examples of ads that, in headline, copy, or illustration, appeal to the following desires: health, approval, self-fulfillment, and pleasure. Bring either the ads or a brief description of them to class for discussion.
2. Some advertisers use a humorous approach, particularly on television or radio. Can you think of an example of humor being used in the broadcast media to sell goods or services? Describe the ad, and discuss its merits or faults.
3. Many advertisements feature a main selling idea in the headline, and then include other less important selling points in the body copy. In a current magazine or newspaper, find such an ad and list the main selling idea and the less important selling points. Do you agree or not that the most important selling point was listed in the headline? Discuss the ad and your point of view in class.

Project

Observe the advertising program of two local advertisers. Collect samples of their newspaper advertising, and if these merchants also use local broadcast media, write down the general content of their messages. Based on this material, write an advertising strategy for both these advertisers. Limit the strategies to 75 words. Are these, in your opinion, single-minded strategies featuring a main appeal and subordinate appeals, or are they dual strategies giving two appeals equal emphasis? Bring the strategies and ads to class for discussion.

Suggested local advertisers to choose from are the following: commercial bank, department store, discount house, home appliance store, home furnishings store, real estate dealer, savings bank, women's high-fashion specialty shop.

Career Ladder

You are head of a small ad agency and have been offered a land development account that would spend approximately $500,000 annually in advertising. The market consists of middle-income people who would be interested in retirement homes. You know the right copy appeals to make and feel sure you could prepare effective advertising.

Before accepting the business, you learn from reliable sources that the land developer has an unsavory reputation. Low-grade property has on occasion been sold to buyers, promised property improvements have not been made, and some previous buyers have lost their money. The developer, however, has a good reputation for paying the bills of suppliers such as yourself. Do you accept the account, or not? Discuss your reasons in class.

CHAPTER THIRTEEN

WRITING HEADLINES

The last chapter stressed two major points in preparing advertising: (1) objectives and a strategy must be established for every advertising creative task before it is undertaken, and (2) advertising must always talk in terms of what the product, service, or idea can do for the prospect or motivate the prospect in terms of self-interest. Both these points apply particularly to writing headlines. The writer's objectives will determine the kinds of headlines to build; effective headlines will tell what the product, service, or idea can do for the prospect.

Importance of Headlines

In a print advertisement the lead or featured idea is set in display, or large, type as a *headline* and is set apart from the *body copy,* or main copy story. In radio or television advertising, the first idea expressed in words or the first few seconds of the commercial perform a function similar to that of print headlines.

The headline is the most important element in an ad. The few words of the headline, working together with the illustration, make the difference between the success or failure of the ad. More creative time and effort should be spent on headlines than on any other part of an advertisement. They are not to be treated carelessly, nor be regarded as complete until the writer has tried hard to surpass initial efforts.

The Function of the Headline

The headline is so important because of its function: the headline must attract the attention of those readers who can be considered to be prospective customers for the advertised product or service. The headline may shout or whisper, be quiet or bold, understated or exaggerated, sophisticated or plain—or many other things. But whatever its tone, its function is to attract attention. If the headline fails in this function, it fails to communicate a message, and the advertiser might as well have saved the money the message cost.

It is very easy to write a bad headline, and many advertisers do this regularly. But it is very difficult to write great, selling headlines—this takes ingenuity, a high degree of creativity, and good business judgment. A good, efficient headline isn't hard to write if one keeps thinking about advertising objectives and clearly tells the prospective customers what the product or service will do for them.

The Selection Process

Individuals respond to very few of the advertising appeals that are offered to them. The "sorting" mechanism by which the consumer screens out advertising was discussed in Chapter 1. The headline allows the reader to sort out which advertising is of interest and which isn't.

To put it positively, the headline serves to select from all the people reading a magazine or newspaper those who are bona fide prospects for the product, service, or idea. Conceivably, the prospects can be almost all the readers. Sometimes what is being advertised has universal appeal. Examples are public-service campaigns, such as "Support Your Community Chest" or "Buy United States Savings Bonds." Nationally advertised packaged goods that are staples—such as soap, detergents, breakfast foods, and bread—also have wide audiences to which to appeal. But though there are a large number of prospective customers for these products, the selection process is at work. Generally, women purchase these products. The advertising and headline are thus directed at women, who are the prime prospects.

Selectivity is more obvious and more pronounced in the ads for other products—in ads that make up the great bulk of advertising. Misses' fashions, bikinis, maternity clothes, men's formal wear, and "portly" men's styles all must find buyers in specialized parts of the apparel market. Toupees, wheelchairs, and denture cleaners have their obvious and special audiences. Corn plasters are of no interest to people who do not have corns. Sales of thermometers and cold remedies soar during the months of February and March, when a large part of the total audience catches cold; ads for these products select those who are sick and try to sell them remedies. People in good health ignore the messages.

Guides in Writing Headlines

Since the headline occupies the most important position in an ad, it should be de-

In this ad, the headline relies completely on the illustration to promote what is being advertised. No other headline words are needed. (Courtesy Ford Motor Company)

The purpose of these headlines is to select from the total audience only those who are real prospects for what is being advertised. The rest of the audience will not be interested. (Courtesy Time Inc.; John Caples, member of the Advertising Hall of Fame and a vice president of BBDO, Inc., for Girl Scouts of the U.S.A.; The Woodsmith's Studio; National Institute of Fitness; Kindergard, GM; Moss Chemical Co., Inc.)

Wanted
Girl Scout Leaders
Assistants, Helpers

COLLEGE STUDENTS

Earn a sizable income with the TIME Inc. College Bureau

It doesn't matter whether you're a man or a woman...an undergrad or a grad student...at a big university or a small college...a resident on campus or a commuter—you could earn BIG MONEY as one of our Campus Reps. Maybe even enough to pay most of your tuition and expenses!

All you have to do is distribute our order cards, offering TIME, SPORTS ILLUSTRATED, FORTUNE, and MONEY at special campus rates.

You earn generous commissions and set your own hours. You invest no money. And we handle the billing and virtually all the paperwork. We even supply a kit that tells you how to make every working hour pay off!

Get full details now. Write: Campus Rep Program, Time Inc. College Bureau, Time & Life Building, Rockefeller Center, New York 10020. Please include your name, address, and telephone number.

K13

Here is your chance to do some good and have fun. No experience needed. You can begin as an observer. You can attend troop meetings or watch training sessions.

Or you can begin as a Helper. Will you take attendance at a meeting or help watch children while they cook? Will you help them with crafts or show them how to fix a snack? Whether you continue is up to you.

Anyone—from young singles to grandparents—can become a Girl Scout Leader. For free information, send this ad with your name and address and telephone number to Girl Scouts of the U.S.A., 830 Third Avenue, New York, N.Y. 10022.

Learn Woodworking
Learn Woodcarving
Learn Woodfinishing
Learn Framemaking
Learn Woodturning

The Woodsmith's STUDIO
142 East 32nd St.

Free lecture every Saturday 1 p.m.

For a brochure on day/evening classes call (212) 684-3642

voted to the selling idea that the writer considers of key importance. The headline is the essence of the ad; it should not concern itself with minor sales points. As has been stated, the function of the headline is to attract the attention of those who are conceivably interested in the product or service advertised; the headline attracts attention by talking in terms of what basic benefits the product or service can provide for the prospective consumer or what needs it can fulfill.

The headline writer must keep these guides in mind, and must also think about the ad's illustration. (Characteristics of good illustrations are discussed in detail in Chapter 15.) The illustration idea can heavily influence a headline. If the illustration is clear and furthers the objective of the ad, its forcefulness or what it pictures may eliminate the need for certain headline descriptive words or phrases (see the Ford ad and Color Plate 10). The headline does not stand alone and need not be self-sufficient; it can rely on the illustration for help in promoting what is advertised.

To summarize, in headline-writing, it is important to attract attention by appealing to the reader's self-interest, to include the main selling idea, and to think of an idea for an appropriate illustration.

These are the most important points, but there are several other suggestions for writing good headlines and a few don'ts for avoiding bad ones.

Include News Whenever Possible

New products and new services are interesting to people, and ads for them automatically attract more readers than ads for products and services that are already established in the marketplace. Obviously, the newness should be featured in a headline whenever possible because it will gain attention. Better still, if the new brand or service offers a tangible benefit that, for example, makes life easier or more convenient, this reward for buying should be strongly emphasized; it will involve the reader.

The following headlines all feature news about a product. See how the writer has tried to turn the news into a benefit that the reader might want.

THE NEW FIBER GLASS BOAT. IT TAKES THE ROCK AND ROLL OUT OF FISHING.
(Headline for a new, more stable two-man fishing boat)

SOLAR ENERGY NOW . . . AT A PRICE YOU CAN AFFORD. (Headline for solar home hot-water leased-equipment system)

FIBER GLASS REINVENTS THE WHEEL.
(Headline for automotive industry trade ad featuring a new, lighter wheel)

THIS ELECTRIC OVEN BROILS ON BOTH SIDES AT ONCE . . . THEN CLEANS UP AFTER ITSELF. (Headline for a self-cleaning oven that eliminates turning over broiled steak)

Notice that it is not necessary to include the word "new" when the benefit described is an obvious innovation.

Starting a headline with the words "How to" is a tried and true way to explain how the prospective buyer will benefit from buying a product, as these examples show.

HOW TO SAVE ABOUT 50% ON FAMILY PRODUCTS YOU USE EVERY DAY.

HOW TO CORRECT PHOTOCOPIES AS EASILY AS CORRECTING THE ORIGINALS.

HOW TO MAKE UP TO $100 A WEEK—IN YOUR SPARE TIME.

Include Specifics; Avoid Generalities

Headlines, and copy generally, should be as genuinely informative as possible. Facts and specific information are preferable to vague generalities. People are interested in specifics. They seek proof of performance or factual reasons for product superiority. Pertinent facts not only help convince; they are also "memory hooks" that serve to keep products and services in the prospect's mind. The writer cannot capture attention by using dangling comparisons such as "X brand gives you more" or empty claims such as "Y brand defies comparison" and "It's the best you can buy." The writer should make clear what is meant by "more," "comparison," or "best."

The first four of the following headlines make good use of specifics and involve the reader with the product or service. The last four are "soft" and unspecific and slide by almost unnoticed. They are a waste of the advertiser's money.

THERE ARE 23 DIAMONDS IN THIS DINNER RING. EACH ONE IS A FULLY CUT GEM. YET THE COST IS ONLY $1975.

PAPERBACK BOOKS AT ½ PRICE WHEN YOU BUY 5 OR MORE.

THIS RAINCOAT IS WATERPROOF, LIGHTWEIGHT, WASHABLE, AIR-CONDITIONED, STYLISH . . . AND ONLY $85.

TONIGHT! FIX REAL BARBECUED CHICKEN—WITHOUT A GRILL!

WHAT MAKES OUR GRAND PIANO SO GRAND?

WE'VE NEVER ANNOUNCED A CAR LIKE THIS BEFORE. BUT THEN NOBODY'S EVER ANNOUNCED A CAR LIKE THIS BEFORE.

OUR BANK DOES MORE FOR YOUR MONEY.

OUT-CLEANS 'EM ALL!

Use Simple, Uncomplicated Language

Since the function of a headline is to attract attention, the writer should not burden it with involved phrases, hard-to-understand words, or complicated figures of speech. These elements slow down the reader, distract from the benefit or reward that the writer is trying to communicate, and may make it difficult for the prospect to understand what the ad is all about.

Here are some headlines that are unnecessarily complicated. They give the reader the task of stopping to figure them out, and when this happens, the reader's attention wanders or is lost completely.

CAN TWO MEDIUM-SIZE SUCCESSFUL COMPANIES GET TOGETHER AND COMPETE MORE EFFECTIVELY IN AN INDUSTRY PEOPLED BY GIANTS AND POSSESSED OF A VORACIOUS APPETITE FOR CAPITAL? (Announcement of the merger of two companies)

THE WHEELS THAT POWER OUR CAR ARE ALSO THE WHEELS THAT STEER OUR CAR. THAT WAY THEY CAN'T DISAGREE.

AMAZING AUTOMATIC WEIGHT-LOSS PLAN! NOW! LIFETIME FREEDOM FROM UGLY FAT WITH A DOCTOR'S INCREDIBLE

The headlines of these ads work hard because they contain specifics, not generalities. (Courtesy The Kiwi Polish Co. (U.S.A.); Liquid Wrench)

"BEVERAGE-OFF" PROGRAM FOR CUP-TO-CUP LOSS OF EXTRA POUNDS!

Use Active, Colorful Words

The headline writer should use vigorous, active words and avoid the passive voice, or the headline will be passive instead of actively making its point. Interesting, colorful words add character and dimension to a headline, and the writer should use creativity and imagination in choosing pertinent words that make the headline come alive and that help attract attention.

Notice the use of colorful language in the following headlines:

FIRST GET INTO YOUR BRA THEN GET INTO YOUR CLINGY THING. (Ad for bra)

IF YOU WERE A LEAF, THIS WOULD REALLY GRAB YOU. (Ad for leaf raker)

THE STRAWBERRY. DIP IT. DUNK IT. SHAKE IT. BAKE IT. FREEZE IT. SQUEEZE IT. AND LOVE IT.

THIS TOWEL RUBS SOME PEOPLE THE WRONG WAY. OTHERS SWEAR BY IT.

Avoid Brag-and-Boast Headlines

It has been stressed that the copywriter must take the point of view of the reader at all times, talk in terms of the reader's interests, and show how the product rewards or benefits the potential buyer. This means no bragging about the manufacturer or boasting about the product's superiority. It's important to play down the interests of the seller. This approach applies particularly to headlines.

Beyond this common sense application of selling psychology, there is another good reason to avoid bragging claims. When reader-ship of headlines is analyzed, *brag-and-boast headlines* come through poorly in comparison with benefit-oriented approaches. Talking in boastful terms inhibits interest and readership. Advertisers who persist in using this approach probably do so because of pride, too much introspection, and an inability to see beyond their own needs and desires.

Here are some headlines that reflect self-interest rather than consumer interest.

OVER THE YEARS A FEW RARE CARS HAVE COMBINED CLASSIC ELEGANCE WITH GREAT PERFORMANCE.

WE'RE TWICE AS GOOD. (Headline for two salad dressings)

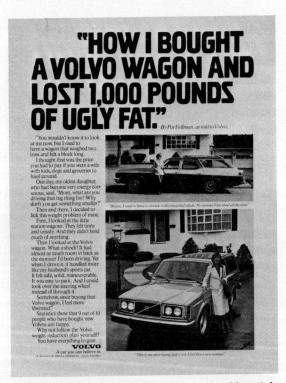

To communicate effectively, headlines should contain active, colorful words and be written in simple language, as this ad demonstrates. (Courtesy Volvo of America Corporation)

OUT FRONT BY A YARD. (Headline for a lawn tractor)

WE WERE FIRST FIFTY YEARS AGO. WE'RE FIRST TODAY. (Headline for a textile manufacturer)

MANY TRY, BUT NONE SUCCEED. YOU JUST CAN'T COPY AN ORIGINAL. (Liquor headline)

Don't Be Cute

Humor has a valuable and important place in advertising copy when it is properly used. The guide here is to use humor when it is related to the objectives of the ad and when it enhances the benefits or rewards that should be communicated to readers. Humor for the sake of humor may gain momentary attention, but it is pointless if it does not further the advertising objectives.

Here are some headlines that are "cute" but that really say nothing helpful to the prospect.

SAY AHHHHHHH (Headline for a concentrated mouthwash)

SALE! HELP YOURSHELF (Headline for a kitchen shelf covering material)

"MR. CAESAR, YOUR FRIEND BRUTUS THOUGHT I SHOULD TALK TO YOU ABOUT LIFE INSURANCE." "SEE ME AFTER THE IDES OF MARCH, SON." (Headline for a life insurance ad)

Don't Be Indirect

Sometimes you will see a headline that has nothing to do with the body copy that follows it. The headline is describing something else entirely. The thinking behind this type of headline is that the provocative, indirect words will serve as an attention getter and will so intrigue the reader that interest will be captured and the rest of the ad will be read.

Unfortunately, these assumptions are not valid. Good body-copy readership does *not* flow from indirect headlines. Just the opposite occurs. Readership tests show that reader confusion results, and the page is turned quickly to some other subject more interesting.

The following headlines fail in gaining attention and readership because they are indirect.

OUR EGGS ARE IN 3,000 BASKETS. (Headline for an independent phone company ad)

CRAZY OVER LINDY. MAD ABOUT AMELIA. (Headline for an aviation manufacturer's advertisement)

OH, THE PROBLEMS BEN'S WIFE CREATED WHEN SHE TOLD HIM TO GO FLY A KITE. (Headline for a chemical company's electrical insulating material)

Don't Write "Nothing" Headlines

It should be clear by now that headlines that do not advance the cause of selling and say nothing particular about the product or service being advertised are of no value in attracting attention to an ad. And yet the pages of magazines and newspapers are filled with lazy headlines that do not serve a purpose. After a headline is written, it should be checked against the following series of questions:

■ Is it clear and readily understandable?

■ Is its central idea a major sales point for the product or service?

■ Are the words fresh, vigorous, and hardworking?

■ Is it directed toward the reader's interest?

■ Does it accomplish its primary tasks of attracting attention and involving the reader?

■ Is it specific rather than general?

These "nothing" headlines do not pass the above tests:

FASHION RIDES HIGH IN (NAME OF STORE) COUNTRY! (Headline for a menswear store)

FASHION'S GONE SLEEK. (Headline for a department store)

SOARING TO NEW HEIGHTS. (Headline for a car)

BEYOND COMPARE. (Headline for a bourbon)

READ ALL ABOUT IT. (Headline for a car)

Headline Form

A headline may take any form that helps the writer accomplish the objectives. It can be an *imperative headline,* which "commands" the reader to take action: "Retire on $800 a month for life." It can be in the form of a question: "Will you be bald 6 years from now?" It can be a *declarative headline,* which puts forth a fact: "The best week of your life leaves for Bermuda every Saturday night" (ad for a cruise ship). It can be long: "And we went for a walk on the beach and there was a full moon over the Caribbean and that year and a half of saving really seemed worth it. Then Bob lost our money." (This headline for traveler's checks needs length to tell a pertinent and involving story.) It can be short, as Volkswagen's famous "Lemon" single-word headline attests.

The writer should feel completely free to use the form that fits the objectives best and that seems right for the ad.

Negative versus Positive Headlines

Some advertising people believe that headlines should always be positive; others think that headlines may, on occasion, be negative. John Caples, in his book *Tested Advertising Methods,* states, "Avoid, when possible, headlines which paint the gloomy or negative side of the picture. Take the cheerful, positive angle."[1] But Victor Schwab, in *How to Write a Good Advertisement,* says, "One of the principal objectives of a headline is to strike as directly as possible right at a situation confronting the reader. Sometimes you can do this with greater accuracy if you use a negative headline which pinpoints his ailment rather than the alleviation of it."[2]

Actually, negative headlines can be strong sales makers. "The oil without that oily taste" was an extremely effective headline that brought sales success to a salad and cooking oil. The ad for Neutrogena uses a negative headline to lead to a positive idea. Negative headlines can be extremely effective when they offer a benefit or reward.

Mention of the Name of the Product or Service

Perhaps half of all headlines contain the brand name or the name of the service being advertised. Mentioning the name is not a necessary headline requirement. If it helps to use the name, it should be included. The writer and the art director must keep in mind that somewhere in the ad the name of the product or service must be prominently featured, for reader identification purposes. This can be in the headline, at the base of the ad, or in an illustration of the

---

[1] John Caples, *Testing Advertising Methods,* Harper & Brothers, New York, 1932, p. 38.

[2] Victor Schwab, *How to Write a Good Advertisement,* Harper & Row, New York, 1962, p. 22.

Maybe you shouldn't have taken a bath last night.

If you have dry skin,

don't spend an hour soaking in a sudsy hot tub. Many dermatologists say those long sudsy soakings can take out too much of your skin's natural moisture. And actually leave it drier after bathing than before.

But that doesn't mean you have to give up on baths. Instead, make the water warm, not hot. Spend less time lingering in the tub. And avoid ordinary soaps or detergents, including bubble baths, that wash away even more of your natural oils.

There *is* a different way to bathe that gives you all the luxury you love about a bath plus some real help for dry skin. It's Neutrogena® Rainbath® Dry-Skin Bath Gel, a unique amber foaming gel made by Neutrogena, the people who specialize in sensitive-skin-care products.

Whether you use it in the bath or shower, this gel is specifically formulated to care for your dry skin.

It isn't a soap. But it cleans so mildly and effectively that it's been recommended for patients whose irritated skins can't tolerate soap.*

It isn't an oil. But it contains special nongreasy skin-smoothing ingredients that literally help the flaky, rough skin cells smooth down. Your whole body feels like satin—without an oily, sticky aftermath or a ring around your tub.

In fact, it isn't like any bath product you've used. Neutrogena Rainbath Dry-Skin Bath Gel. The luxury of a foamy bath or shower, fresh-scented as mountain rain. Plus help for dry, itchy skin that lasts all day long.

Who says your dry skin can't have everything it needs?

*In a clinical study involving patients with atopic dermatitis (very dry skin) 91% of the patients experienced good to excellent improvement of their skin conditions with the use of Rainbath as their only means of cleansing. "An Alternative Bathing Technique for use in Dermatitis." *Cutis*, January 1975.

Neutrogena® Rainbath® Dry-Skin Bath Gel

*Neutrogena Corp. 1977

Ask for it wherever Neutrogena Soap is sold.

Negative headlines can be effective salesmakers. This negative headline leads directly to a "dry skin" sale in an attention-getting way. (Neutrogena® Rainbath® Bath Gel is the current name of this product.) (Courtesy Neutrogena Corporation.)

product package itself, if the name is prominent there.

Headlines that start with the name of the product or service, however, are to be avoided. Headlines such as "The Mart presents fashion-right cruisewear" or "Old Froth Beer keeps its head when all about are losing theirs" are not good because by starting with the name of the product, the writer tends to develop a headline that stresses the interest of the maker rather than the interests of the prospect. Such headlines often wind up being in the brag-and-boast category.

Label versus Informative Retail Headlines

Headlines for both retail and national advertisements are guided by the principles outlined in this chapter. In defining types of retail ad headlines, however, Edwards and Brown[3] make some important distinctions that are helpful to retail advertising writers. Two types of retail ad headlines that they describe are label headlines and informative headlines. *Label headlines* are brief and merely identify the subject of the ad. Some examples of label headlines are as follows:

SPRING WOOL COATS, SALE—$119.

FAMOUS HARTWELL DRESS SHIRTS.

APCO MOCCASINS—$21.95 THE PAIR

Informative headlines tell the reader the main selling idea. Examples of informative headlines are as follows:

SALE! SAVE $20 ON OUR ITALIAN FOLDING BIKE. IT FOLDS UP AND SNAPS OPEN IN SECONDS . . . READY TO RIDE.

[3] Edwards and Brown, pp. 214–219.

THE HEAVIEST FURNITURE MOVES EASILY ON THESE ROLL-ABOUT CASTERS.

Label headlines do not require much thought, and although space in retail advertising layouts is often limited, the brevity of label headlines allows them to fit in easily. But, as Edwards and Brown point out, "the informative headline is by far the most productive of all types of retail headlines."[4] This is because informative headlines conform to the guides set down in this chapter. They include benefits and rewards for the reader and are specific and to the point. Label headlines should be avoided in retail advertising whenever possible.

═ Subheads and Lead-Ins ═

Some advertisements use words set in display type apart from the body copy but made less prominent than the headline. These *subheads* are really small-scale headlines, and they are used either to elaborate on the main idea or to introduce additional selling points or benefits. Subheads are developed by writers and art directors on an "as needed" basis to break up the solidity of the ad's appearance and to add importance to key selling words and phrases. Because little space is available for them, and because they are often surrounded by body copy, they are usually short and to the point.

Lead-ins (pronounced as in "leader") are phrases, words, or brief sentences that start copy paragraphs. To distinguish them from the copy that follows, they may be set in larger type, underlined, or italicized. They are really part of the body copy.

[4] Ibid., p. 217.

AVON.
IT'S A BEAUTIFUL WAY TO WORK.

Barbara Keve Gregory
Avon Representative
Mt. Vernon, N.Y.

Being an Avon
Representative is pride
and joy for me. The
business is my own, I've
gained good friends and
loyal customers. And, my
Avon earnings helped
to pay for my Master's
degree in Library Science.

Demonstrating all of the Avon colors
that are just right for my customers is
always a source
of news and fun.

My Avon experience has
increased my desire for
meeting people. I guess
that's what makes the
time I spend with the
Young Adult Advisory
Group so special.

If becoming an independent Avon Representative sounds interesting to you,
call 800-243-5000 toll free, in Connecticut 1-800-882-5577.
Or write: Avon Products, Inc., P.O. Box 4000, Pelham, N.Y. 10803.
©1979 Avon Products, Inc., N.Y., N.Y.

Think I'll fix up the pad.

*Now that the tads are grown
and gone. And Fred has decided
to make a new career for himself
as an appetizer at Bookbinders.
Well, he's not the only
croaker in the creek.*

*Anyway, it gives me a chance to stretch
my legs a little and think about
redecorating. Green's not a bad color,
but we never really planned all this
stuff around the lily pad. It just grew.*

Glunk.

*That's all it is: glunk. Plankton Provincial.
Think I'll go hopping at John Wanamaker
and get a few nice things.
Maybe a dropleaf table, some Queen Anne's
lace, and something in seaweed.*

*In fact, why not get a credenza?
All the girls are talking about them.
They sit up all night, and all you hear is Credenza, Credenza, Credenza. I could keep the stemware in it.*

*When Fred sees how I fix up the pad, I suppose he'll want to kiss and make up. He can go jump. What if I kissed him
and he turned into a prince? Glunk. Never saw a prince, and I never want to. I've heard them at night. They sound like rubber bands.*

Well, on to Wanamaker's. THEY know how to treat a girl. And they know how to fix up a pad.

John Wanamaker

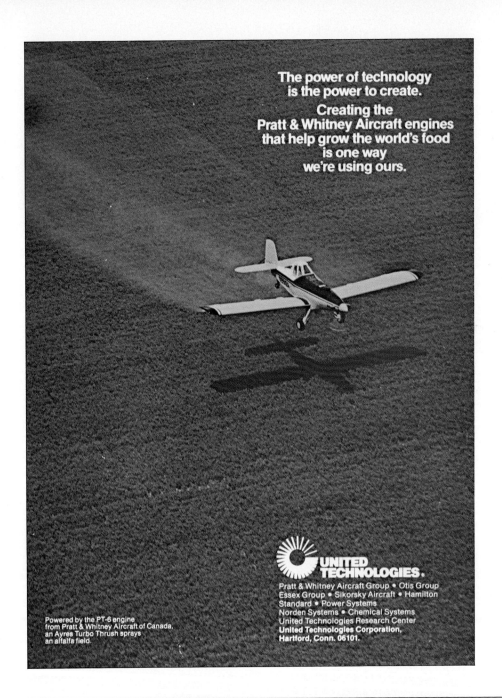

The power of technology
is the power to create.

Creating the
Pratt & Whitney Aircraft engines
that help grow the world's food
is one way
we're using ours.

UNITED
TECHNOLOGIES.

Pratt & Whitney Aircraft Group • Otis Group
Essex Group • Sikorsky Aircraft • Hamilton
Standard • Power Systems
Norden Systems • Chemical Systems
United Technologies Research Center
**United Technologies Corporation,
Hartford, Conn. 06101.**

Powered by the PT-6 engine
from Pratt & Whitney Aircraft of Canada,
an Ayres Turbo Thrush sprays
an alfalfa field.

COLOR PLATE 4 — This is a national institutional advertisement. It is addressed to the business community and appears in trade papers and business magazines. What is the impression this ad is trying to convey? (See Chapter Three.) Courtesy United Technologies Corporation. Agency: Marsteller, Inc.

Flowers.
To keep business blooming.

A natural part of that business is flowers. Especially for the holidays.

As a gift to the homes and offices of clients and customers, flowers and plants are an easy, spontaneous demonstration of your appreciation. But they also answer other business needs. As a tribute to employees on birthdays or anniversaries. As a way of brightening the office and the spirit.

To keep business blooming. just make an arrangement with your florist. One call is all that's needed. Your florist will do the rest.

Flowers and plants are for every business occasion. Naturally.

The customer pleaser. Hand-crafted holiday arrangements designed to brighten your best customer's desk.

The house call. Send a long-stemmed business gift to the home and receive double the appreciation.

The desk set. Give one or two dozen. Either way it's the flowery thought that pleases the office manager.

The senior partner. Plant an idea of good will and well wishes with this bold traditional gift.

AMERICAN FLORISTS MARKETING COUNCIL, Society of American Florists, 901 N. Washington St., Alexandria, Va. 22314

COLOR PLATE 5 — This ad, sponsored by a trade association, promotes the entire florists' trade rather than the products of one company. (See Chapter Three.) Courtesy American Florists Marketing Council. Agency: Henry J. Kaufman & Associates, Inc.

COLOR PLATE 6—At the left are "thumbnails" or minilayouts for a four-color consumer magazine ad. The art director is organizing ideas and coming to grips with the problems of how best to visualize an advertisement featuring recipes. The full-size color roughs to the right show the evolution of some of the ideas noted in the thumbnails. (See Chapters Five and Fifteen.)

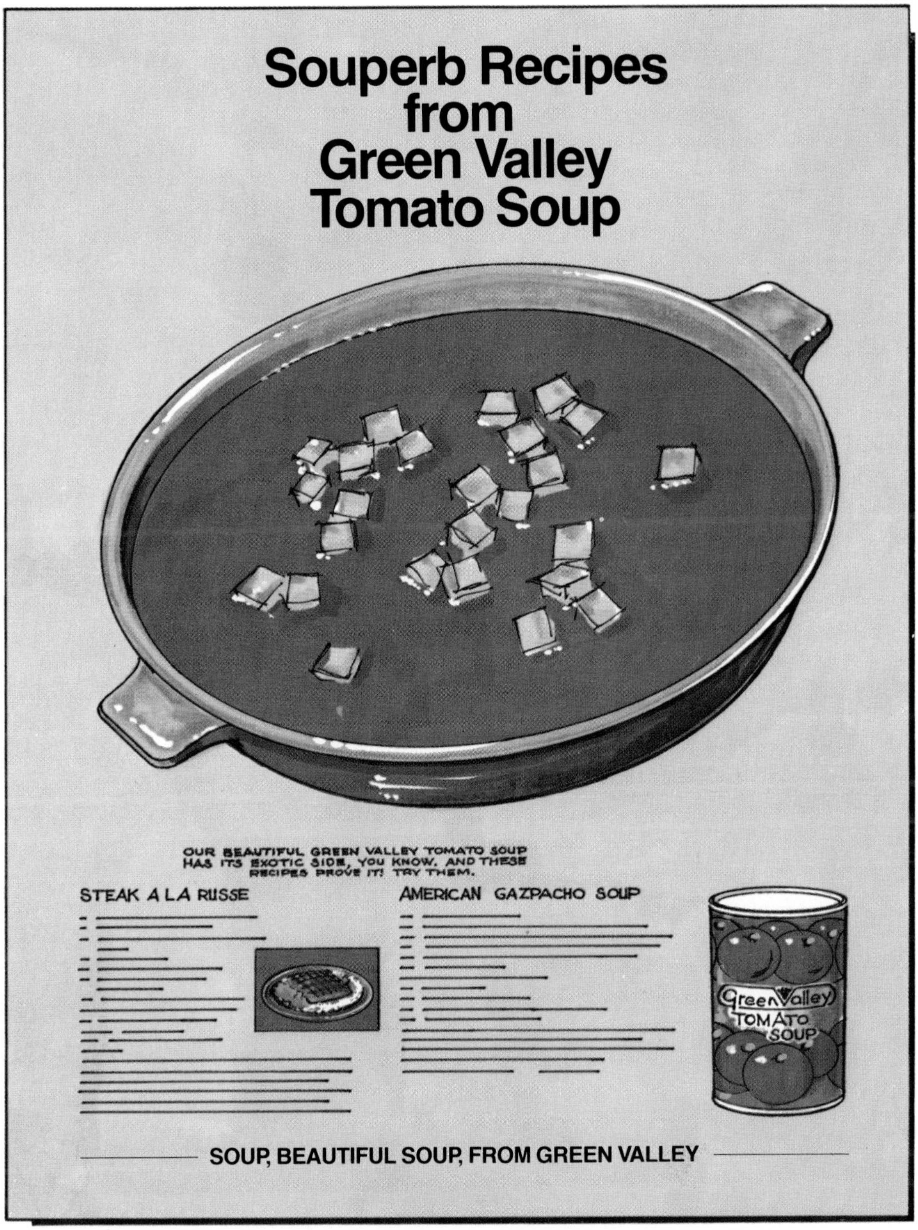
Souperb Recipes from Green Valley Tomato Soup
OUR BEAUTIFUL GREEN VALLEY TOMATO SOUP HAS ITS EXOTIC SIDE, YOU KNOW. AND THESE RECIPES PROVE IT! TRY THEM.
STEAK A LA RUSSE
AMERICAN GAZPACHO SOUP
Green Valley
TOMATO SOUP
SOUP, BEAUTIFUL SOUP, FROM GREEN VALLEY

COLOR PLATE 7 — The comprehensive is a refined layout based on the ideas developed in the thumbnails and roughs. A "tight comp," which closely resembles a finished ad, can be presented to the client for approval before the ad is actually run. (See Chapters Five and Fifteen.) Color Plates 6 and 7 prepared by David Carlson/Evelyne Johnson Associates.

Fairy Tales Long, long ago there lived a king and a queen, who owned wide forests, gr

Frogs A frog's life begins in a jelly-covered egg laid in water. When the baby frog hatches, it h

Flowers The flowers of a rose are different from those of a snapdragon. And both look very

Farms Each season of the year brings its own beauty to the farm. Fields are freshly green in s

Fossils Most fossils are the remains of plants and animals preserved in rock. Sometimes the

Feudalism Under feudalism, the king granted land to a man in return for the man's pro

Foreign Aid is a term used to describe the help provided by the government of one c

Fluoridation means adding a chemical, sodium fluoride, to the water supply in orde

Kids and The New Book of Knowledge grow up together.

To your four year old, The New Book of Knowledge is a "Read me a story" book that he can't wait to read as soon as he learns how to read. Then it grows into an answer-all-those questions book, an easy-to-do-your-homework book, a how-to book. As easy to look things up in as A to Z.

The New Book of Knowledge is all new. It's the children's encyclopedia that, subject by subject, follows the logical growth of the elementary school

curriculum. It grows in language and content to match a child's growing ability to read and learn. Simple words for first graders. More complicated words for fourth graders. And so it grows.

It takes a lot of growing up to understand what's happening in the world today. Home is where the growing begins. Just put The New Book of Knowledge into the hands of your kids and watch them grow up together.

The New Book of Knowledge
Putnam Valley, New York 10579

Please send me my free copy of your
booklet, "The Magic Carpet."
There are ____ children in my family.

Ages ____

Name ____

Address ____

City ____

State ____ Zip ____

Mail coupon now and we'll send you
a free 16-page bonus booklet, "To the
Moon and Beyond." (Supply limited).

Parents 3-70

A publication of Grolier Incorporated. Cash price $200 plus handling and shipping. Budget terms available.

WE SHAKE ALL NIGHT.

AMERICA'S FAVORITE. ASK FOR IT BY NAME."CHICAGO X." ON COLUMBIA RECORDS AND TAPES.

Coca-Cola adds life to...

COLOR PLATE 9—These ads were selected by the Institute of Outdoor Advertising as examples of excellence in the medium. (See Chapter Seven.) Courtesy Institute of Outdoor Advertising. Reproduced with permission of Jack-in-the-Box® Restaurants, Foodmaker Inc., a Subsidiary of Ralston Purina; Columbia Records; and The Coca-Cola Company.

LIGHT
A CRYSTAL
FIRE.

The light of
the stars.
The light of
the sun.
The light of
Waterford crystal.
A legend,
blown by mouth,
cut wholly by hand,
with heart.

WATERFORD

Photo Pean

COLOR PLATE 10 — Ownership of a luxury item such as Waterford Crystal satisfies a desire for prestige. The elegance of this product is featured in the illustration and headline, and the body copy elaborates on the theme. (See Chapters Twelve and Fourteen.) Courtesy Waterford Crystal. Agency: Pesin, Sydney & Bernard Advertising.

IS YOUR SALAMI GETTING OLD BEFORE ITS TIME?

Salami after 5 days in a Frost-Proof refrigerator.

Salami after 5 days in our Food-Life Preserver.

unwrapped food fresh for days by sealing air out and moisture in.

And it makes the storing of hard-to-wrap foods, like a piece of cake, a piece of cake.

So throw your food a life preserver and get a Frigidaire refrigerator.

After a few days in your refrigerator, does your juicy roast become nothing to boast about?

Can your custard still cut the mustard?

Does your chocolate mousse start getting mousey?

Maybe it's about time you took a look at Frigidaire's Elite Line of refrigerators.

Because aside from features like solid-state ice makers,* Electri-Saver

switches, and tempered-glass shelves, two models also have a Food-Life Preserver. It's a special section that not only has a vegetable Hydrator and a seven-day Meat Tender, but also an Unwrapped Food drawer. The drawer helps keep

Because with today's prices, losing an expensive cut of meat is the unkindest cut of all.

FRIGIDAIRE GM
WHY SETTLE FOR LESS?

*Available at extra charge

Look for our complete line of refrigerators and other Frigidaire appliances at your local Frigidaire dealer.

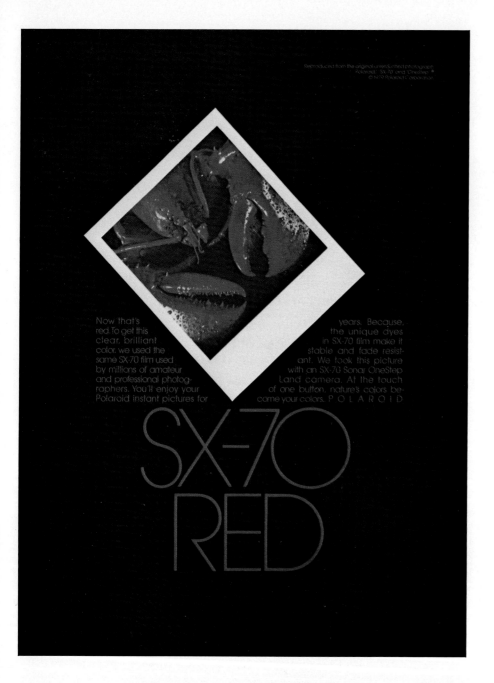

Bermuda. Get away to it all!

"Bermuda is a great place
to get the city out of your system. We've done
everything you can do on a vacation."

Kim and Sue Johnson talk about their first visit to Bermuda.

"The people here
are so courteous.
So friendly.
I really get a
kick out of the
Bermuda shorts."

"We've been to
a lot of the islands,
but I can't remember
any as beautiful
as this."

See your travel agent or write Bermuda, Dept. 507
630 Fifth Avenue, N.Y., N.Y. 10020 or Suite 1010, 44 School St., Boston, Mass. 02108
or 300 North State Street, Chicago, Ill. 60610

COLOR PLATE 13 — This travel ad is a good example of testimonial copy. Notice too how color is used to convey the resort atmosphere. The pink background duplicates the color of the sand on Bermuda's beaches. (See Chapters Fourteen and Fifteen.)
Courtesy The Bermuda Department of Tourism. Agency: Foote, Cone & Belding.

COLOR PLATE 14 — Black is combined with three colors, yellow, magenta, and cyan, to create a full-color picture. Each color is printed on a separate plate and the overlapping of the four plates gives a complete range of color in the finished ad, Color Plate 15. (See Chapter Sixteen.)

The Pittsburgh National Christmas Club makes some of our customers pretty smug this time of year.

Right now, when everyone else is just beginning to worry about Christmas, Pittsburgh National Christmas Clubbers earned the right to be a little smug. Their Christmas Club accounts are already full.

Pittsburgh National gives away free bayberry candles just for joining. And a few dollars every other week means the end to last minute scrimping and after-Christmas payments that stretch into the better part of next year.

Join the Pittsburgh National Christmas Club and brighten this year's Christmas with bayberry candles. Next year's Christmas will take care of itself.

PITTSBURGH NATIONAL

Member Federal Deposit Insurance Corporation
Each depositor insured to $20,000

COLOR PLATE 15 — This amusing ad promoting the Christmas Club for a local bank advertiser is an excellent example of the proper use of color in newspapers. The graphic design is simple and uncomplicated. Color adds immeasurably to the charm of the illustration. **(See Chapters Fifteen and Sixteen.)** Courtesy Pittsburgh National Bank. Agency: Ketchum, MacLeod & Grove, Inc.

THE PLEASURES OF TRAVELING IN MAY *continued from page 10*

the famous Fat Man Bar, once run by Ethel Waters, the noted black singer and actress (it's now called the New Fat Man Bar). Included too is Spanish Harlem, also known as *El Barrio*. The three-hour morning tour is $5. Write Penny Sightseeing Company, Dept. WD, 303 West 42nd Street, New York, N.Y. 10036 (telephone 212-247-2860).

The newest ethnic tour involves a boat trip to Ellis Island, the legendary reception center that welcomed a steady stream of immigrants for more than sixty years. Since the center closed in 1954, the island and its structures have gradually deteriorated, but the federal government has lately spent one million dollars as the first step in refurbishment. There will be walking lecture tours of the Main Hall and other buildings conducted by the National Park Service. For further information call 212-732-1236.

You've got to reach the Statue of Liberty National Monument by boat too. It's a delightful ferry ride from the Battery, at Manhattan's southern tip, "the shortest cruise in the world." Climb to the observation platform for thrilling views of ships and shoreline, but don't miss the American Museum of Immigration in the base.

ALASKA CRUISES

May is a key month for serious travel planning when you're considering a trip to someplace like Alaska, where the season is short and expenditures are likely to be substantial. This should, in fact, be a banner year for Alaska. More than a dozen cruise liners will soon be plying the scenic inland passage, a route becoming as popular in summer as the Caribbean in winter.

Cruises range from seven to fourteen days, and ships vary from yachtlike miniliners to some of the largest afloat, so you have a wide choice. The largest vessel entering the Alaska service this year, the 650-passenger *Monarch Star*, will sail on eight-day cruises from Vancouver from May 18 to September 15. If you're shopping for price, note that May sailings are the least expensive ($665 to $1,085 per person, double occupancy) compared with early June and September ($725 to $1,185) and June 19 to August 30 ($775 to $1,275).

122

Besides the big ships there are smaller ones such as the 380-passenger *Prinsendam*, which maneuvers into the spectacular glacial-flanked Tracy Arm inlet, and even more intimate crafts such as the 120-passenger *Xanadu*, with its charming public rooms called the Marco Polo Lounge and Library of Kubla Khan. Collect literature on the various cruises at the office of a competent travel agent.

You may want to go by ship and return by air to see more of Alaska. Write Robert Giersdorf, Alaska Tour and Marketing Service, Dept. WD, 312 Park Place Building, Seattle, Washington 98101, for a free copy of *Alaska 1977 Tour Destinations*. It covers tours ranging from one day to a week, to Mount McKinley National Park, Katmai and Glacier Bay National Monuments, Pribiloff Islands, Point Barrow and Prudhoe Bay. It's handsomely illustrated.

BIKE TOURING FOR ONE AND ALL

Bicycle touring is coming on strong, somewhat like backpacking ten years ago —not only for superenergized young people but for adults and families as well.

Now, as to where and how to go. In

1973 Tom and Susan Heavey, an enterprising young New Hampshire couple trained in outdoor education, started a summer bicycle-touring program strictly for teenagers and called it The Biking Expedition, or TBE. Last year they added a series of guided weekend and week-long trips in New England for adults and families, with overnight stops at country inns and campgrounds. It worked so well that this year they're expanding the program to include trips in New Hampshire and Vermont and in Holland and Denmark, two great cycling countries.

Beginner trips are exactly what they say, designed to cover only five to fifteen miles a day. Intermediates travel fifteen to twenty-five miles and the experienced more than twenty-five miles. An appealing and inexpensive three-day New Hampshire trip for novices to be given several times this season (starting May 27) travels through rural areas and small towns with minimal traffic, spending two nights at the Monadnock Inn in Jaffrey Center and one night at the Fitzwilliam Inn in Fitzwilliam. Total cost including meals and

lodging is $110 each for three. (Two in a room would be $110 each plus $3 extra per person per night.) An interesting seven-day intermediate trip through New Hampshire and Vermont with overnight camping stops at state parks and private campgrounds costs $165 per person.

Take your own bike, sleeping bag (for camping trips), saddlebags and/or handlebar bags; you can also buy or rent equipment, including bikes, from TBE. If you're arriving by train or bus, TBE will pick you up at the nearest terminal without charge. For teen-agers there are trips of twenty-four to forty-one days (covering twenty-five to forty miles per day) in the East, Canada and Europe. Write Terry Leedham, The Biking Expedition, Inc., Dept. WD, Box 547, Henniker, New Hampshire 03242; after June 1, the address will be RD 2, Hillsboro, New Hampshire 03244.

Bikecentennial, which last year had forty-one hundred cyclists touring one portion or another of the Trans-America Bike Trail, extending from Astoria, Oregon, to Yorktown, Virginia, is featuring trips of eight to fifteen days over three new loop trails in Oregon, Kentucky and Virginia. Rates ranging from $130 to $335 include meals, lodging (at hostels, churches, schools, campgrounds, motels and hotels) and services of the tour leader. Write Dan Burden, Bikecentennial, Dept. WD, Box 8308, Missoula, Montana 59807.

American Youth Hostels has been operating a bike-touring program since 1934 and is still going strong. Designed mostly for young people, AYH trips are now given in many parts of the world. They combine cycling with hiking, station wagon, train or bus travel and range from twenty-eight days in New England for $345 to a new 1977 summer French-language tour for $1,240 that combines four weeks of classes with two weeks of travel in France, Switzerland and Luxembourg. Trips are graded A, B and C, but even the C trips are not exactly easy, so you must be in shape. Write Robert A. Yarmy, American Youth Hostels, Dept. WD, Delaplane, Virginia 22025. AYH publishes worthwhile guides: *North American Bike Atlas* with one hundred mapped rides of one day to a month, from coast to coast ($3); and *Hosteling Guide and Handbook*, listing hostels and rates all over the country ($1.75, free to members).

Even if you don't pedal all the way, you'll find that national parks have developed routes strictly for cyclists. *The End*

Time for a new box. For a lot of little reasons.

Vocabulary

Define the following terms and use each one in a sentence:

Body copy
Brag-and-boast headline
Declarative headline
Headline
Imperative headline

Informative headline
Label headline
Lead-in
Subhead

Review Questions

1. Why is the headline the most important part of an ad?
2. What are the primary guides to follow when writing headlines? List three additional helpful guides.
3. Why is it important to include news in a headline?
4. Why are brag-and-boast headlines psychologically ineffective? Why do you think they are so often used?
5. Why should headlines be specific rather than general?
6. When should humor be used in headlines? What is your personal opinion of the use of humor in headlines? Discuss your reasons in class, and bring in, if possible, examples of good and poor uses of humor.
7. When can negative headlines be effective in selling goods or services?
8. Explain why label headlines often used in retail store advertisements are to be avoided and why informative headlines are more effective.
9. What are the purposes of subheads and lead-ins?

Activities

1. You are a department store copywriter and have as your assignment the task of writing an ad for a shipment of imported Finnegan Irish crystal that has just been received. The time of the year is late November. You know that Finnegan is a prestige name in crystal, expensive but worth the price. The price range is $15 to $85 for each item. You receive the following additional information: items include decorative bowls from 6 to 10 inches in diameter, vases, decanters, pitchers,

footed compotes, sugar and creamer sets, and stemware. Each piece is hand-blown and hand-cut and has Finnegan's "mark" on the bottom of the base. The shipment is a special purchase and an exceptional value. Your ad will appear as part of a one-page ad for your store in the local newspaper, and you have a generous area (approximately 60 square inches) to fill with your ad. Thus, if you like, you can write a headline of up to 15 words or a somewhat shorter headline with a subhead below it. Write three informative headlines for the Finnegan crystal, and check the one you like the best. Also write a label headline.

2. Copy for several imaginary products and services is given below. Assume that each product and service will be advertised in a magazine. Your task will be to write a headline for each ad. Use the appeals described in Chapter 12, if you care to apply them, and the guides described in this chapter. Be selective in your use of the information provided. Also describe briefly the illustration you plan for each ad.

   a. Slender Cola. Contains only a half a calorie in every ounce. Comes in bottles and cans. To be advertised in *McCall's.*

   b. Ajax pickup truck. For farm use. The cab is the biggest of any pickup and features the comfort of a car. I-beam design for both axles gives this pickup the ruggedness of a big truck. A quiet, level ride. Leaf-type rear springs for better load stability. To be advertised in *Farm Journal.*

   c. American Credit Card. Recognized by more restaurants, more merchants, and more motels than any other credit card. You never need cash, and you avoid the risk of loss or theft of money when you travel. To be advertised in *Fortune, Business Week,* and *Time.*

   d. Continental Insurance Company. Automobile insurance. If you have a safe driving record, you can qualify for a 10 percent rate reduction. Our agents are literally everywhere and lead the industry in fast settlement of claims. We write more automobile insurance than any other company.

Project

From your observations of the advertising of local merchants and from current national magazine advertising, try to find examples of headlines that fit into the categories discussed in this chapter and listed below. Choose ten categories. Under each category chosen, list the examples in your collection that seem to fit. Check the examples that you think are particularly effective headlines. Bring the list and examples to class, and be prepared to give reasons why the headlines you prefer are particularly effective.

Brag-and-boast headline

Complicated, hard-to-understand headline

Declarative headline

Headline appealing to a general audience

Headline using colorful words

Humorous headline

Imperative headline

Negative headline

News headline

"Nothing" headline

Question headline

Retail informative headline

Retail label headline

Specific headline

Career Ladder

As the copy chief in an agency billing about $30 million annually, you are going over headlines of ads that are part of a major forthcoming presentation to one of your clients. You are pleased with some of the headlines and ask one of the writers assigned to the account who it was who wrote them. The writer modestly admits authorship and accepts the praise. Subsequently this same writer asks you for a substantial raise. In the meanwhile, you have discovered beyond all doubt that a young copy apprentice actually wrote all those headlines you liked.

What do you think about this situation, and what action, if any, will you take?

CHAPTER FOURTEEN

WRITING THE COPY

Having gained the attention of the reader with the headline, the writer next faces the task of developing copy that builds on the headline promise, reward, or benefit. The copy's job is to do whatever is possible to cause the reader to take an action favorable to the advertiser. In institutional or corporate advertising, the goal is merely to implant an idea favorable to the company or service in the mind of the reader. But in the vast majority of ads, the purpose is to stimulate buying.

It won't be a difficult task to fill that blank sheet of paper with good, selling copy if two steps have been taken previously: (1) thinking through the objectives of the ad and (2) gathering all the necessary facts about the product or service to be sold. The copywriter's problem now is to stay on target, to organize the facts that seem important to the sale, and then to express them with as much vigor, freshness, and enthusiasm as can be mustered.

There are certain guides and aids in this process that will be described in detail. Many of

the guides that apply to writing headlines also apply to writing body copy. Copy for national advertising differs from copy for local and retail advertising and will be considered first.

How to Write Effective Copy

The purposes of copy are to elaborate on the headline idea, heighten the reader's interest and desire, offer proof in the form of facts and information, and then get the prospect to take action. This is selling in depth. The writer must make sure that the main benefit or promise is fully established; if the headline has not accomplished this completely, the copy must do so. If other, minor selling ideas can help, they should be put forth. The writer should aim to be as convincing as possible, presenting the information in terms that identify with the reader's interests, not those of the writer. This will hold the reader's attention. The writer may attempt to make the reader experience vicariously the benefits that will be enjoyed when the product or service is purchased. Like every good salesperson, the writer will do everything possible to keep the reader involved to the point where the writer "asks for the order."

Writing body copy is not a routine task. If the words the writer uses are dull and trite, if the writer just fills up the space with words and does not work hard to turn awakened interest into buying action, sales will be lost. The writer's enthusiasm must be apparent in all that is written.

Elaborate on the Headline Idea

It is often wise to dwell in depth on the headline in the first paragraph of copy. The writer fleshes out the headline idea, makes it more graphic and memorable, and emphasizes points to ensure full understanding. Here are some examples of copy that spell out a headline idea.

WHY WAIT TIL BREAKFAST TO ENJOY THOMAS' ENGLISH MUFFINS?

Thomas' English Muffins are the greatest thing that every happened to breakfast. But have you thought about how delicious they are as snacks? Some night when you're watching TV, whip up some savory cheese creams for the whole family . . .

Here, of course, the objective of the ad is to extend the use of the product beyond the usual breakfast period, and the first paragraph elaborates on this idea. By suggesting English muffin snacks at night, the maker hopes to get the reader to use up the package faster.

CAMPBELL'S VEGETABLE SOUP HAS SO MANY DIFFERENT KINDS OF VEGETABLES WE'LL BET YOU CAN'T NAME THEM ALL.

16 garden vegetables go into Campbell's Vegetable Soup along with a burly beef stock. So you get nutrition in every bite . . .

SEARS "FRENCH BOUQUET" SHEETS THAT NEVER NEED IRONING.

Because you're a woman who loves flowers and absolutely hates to iron, Sears brings you French Bouquet. Pink roses, yellow roses, even soft blue. Roses that never wilt. Perma-Prest sheets and pillow cases that machine wash and tumble dry without ironing . . . .

IS YOUR OFFICE A WAITING ROOM?

There you sit. Waiting while your secretary runs off copies of your report. Waiting while she sorts it. And (yawn!) waiting while she collates it.
(Ad for Xerox copiers)

All these ads use the headline idea in the first paragraph. They expand it, emphasize it, and make it more pertinent. They sustain the interest that has been aroused by the headline.

It is not always necessary to elaborate on the headline idea in the first paragraph of body copy. This decision is up to the writer. If the space in the layout permits it, if the headline calls for development, and if elaboration makes the benefit to the reader come alive, then the headline idea should be used. As the copywriter gains experience, it becomes easier to decide whether or not to expand on headline ideas.

Give the Reader Permission to Believe

In a typical advertisement, there are often two kinds of appeals at work. The first is basically an emotional appeal: the writer attempts to convince the prospect that the advertised item will deliver something of value, something that

Put your hand over this picture.

(And see how small the world's smallest standard cassette recorder is.)

Actual size

It's almost like carrying a little notepad with you.

Except it's infinitely faster, more efficient and more convenient. (It's more fun, too, for that matter.)

The Sony TCM-600 is the world's smallest tape recorder that takes a standard cassette. And although it couldn't be smaller in size, it couldn't be higher in quality.

It has a special Sony motor with a rotor that's so lightweight, it requires far less energy to operate

it. (Up to 8 hrs. of continuous recording with 2 "AA" batteries.) It also has a servo-generator built in for precise tape speed.

It has something called a "counter-inertial flywheel system" that insures tape stability when the unit is in motion. (Especially beneficial to all you highly emotional people who like to talk with your hands.)

And this ingenious little machine also has the utmost in con-

venience features, like total one-hand operation, one-touch review for switching from record to playback without going through stop, and a special "quick review button" that increases playback speed up to 50%.

All this plus our famous Sony sound fidelity, to boot.

Never before has so much been put into so little.

"IT'S A SONY."

© 1978 Sony Corp. of America. SONY is a registered trademark of Sony Corp.

Copy in this Sony cassette recorder ad is loaded with facts and specifics that give the reader permission to believe that the product is worth buying. (Courtesy Sony Corp. of America)

will make life more pleasant or easier and that will make the individual healthier, more attractive, wealthier, more secure, or more popular. The second appeal is a rational appeal: the writer offers proof, uses logic, adds facts, and often demonstrates that the benefit being offered will really deliver what is promised. The rational appeal that allows the reader to accept the emotional one is called *permission to believe*. (See Color Plates 11 and 12.)

The Need for Justification When people are asked to part with hard-earned money, there is a need to justify the expenditure to themselves and, in many cases, to others as well. A person may actually buy something to satisfy emotional needs but often won't admit it. Copy can provide such a person with rational justification.

In an ad for an expensive car, the main appeals in the headline and copy are usually to self-indulgence and status. But usually it is also pointed out that the car is a "sound investment because of exceptionally high trade-in value" or that upkeep and maintenance costs are remarkably low because of superior workmanship. The buyer, if it is found necessary to justify the purchase, will be highly unlikely to say, "I wanted to show the world how important I am." But the buyer may well say, "This car won't be a junk heap in 3 years. It will last for 10." Justification of this kind applies particularly to expensive purchases; it is not needed for less glamorous items.

Examples of Rational Copy The writer, at this stage of the ad, is out to prove to the prospect that the benefit or reward is really all that it is claimed to be. There are countless ways to accomplish this, as a half-hour spent reading the advertising copy in a magazine or newspaper can reveal. The following examples demonstrate the use of rational appeals—of facts that serve to make the ad more convincing.

ILLUSTRATION: PHOTO, PUZZLED WOMAN EXAMINING CARTON OF GE LONGLIFE LIGHT BULBS.

SUBORDINATE ILLUSTRATION: CARTOON OF WOMAN STRETCHING TO INSERT BULB IN HARD-TO-REACH CEILING FIXTURE.

HEADLINE: DON'T BE FOOLED BY LONGLIFE BULBS. EVEN OURS.

Longlifes seem long overdue. At first glance, longlife light bulbs seem like a great idea. After all, it says they last for years. And everybody wants a bulb that lasts longer. Right? Well, before you go out and spend money on longer-lasting bulbs to put around the house, GE wants to give you *all* the facts.

Longlifes cost you more long green. It's true longlife bulbs burn longer, but there's a catch! They cost more to buy and they use more electricity than regular bulbs to give you the same amount of light. So you *do* get long life. But you end up paying *more* for the same amount of light in the long run.

Longlife bulbs do have their place. If all this is true, why do all these manufacturers, including GE, make longlife bulbs? Good question. The answer is simple. Longlife bulbs *can* be a good investment. But only for certain places. For example, if you've got a fixture that's really difficult to get to, it's easier to put in a longlife bulb. . . .

ILLUSTRATION: BOB RYERSE USING HIS PITNEY BOWES TOUCHMATIC® POSTAGE METER.

HEADLINE: WHY BOB RYERSE USES A PITNEY BOWES POSTAGE METER TO MAIL AS FEW AS FIVE LETTERS A DAY.

For 25 years now, the people of Simcoe, Ontario have been buying their flowers from Bob Ryerse at Ryerse Brothers Flowers on Norfolk Street, North.

The place is a landmark with its breathtaking bloom of azaleas and geraniums planted around the grounds every spring. Bob runs the business with his wife Barb and their teenage daughter Shelley who helps out after school.

When Bob and Barb aren't taking care of their customers, they're taking care of outgoing mail. Correspondence, statements and invoices—it's all essential and it has to get out. As small as the flower shop is, Bob still found plenty of room to misplace or lose his stamps.

So just about five years ago, Bob and Barb got themselves a Pitney Bowes Touchmatic® postage meter mailing machine.

"Today getting the mail out every day is an easy job," says Bob. "My Touchmatic® not only meters stamps and moistens the envelopes fast, but it even keeps an automatic record of what I've spent on postage for the year."

Bob also likes the way the meter stamp can speed the mail through the post office faster, since it's already been postmarked, dated and canceled.

"Best of all," concludes Bob, "I always have the right denomination."

If you're beginning to think that your business could benefit from the conveniece of a Pitney Bowes Mailing System, fill out the coupon and mail it to us, or call toll free any time (phone number).

(Coupon and Pitney Bowes signature.)

The objective of the General Electric longlife bulb ad is to inform the reader on the proper use of this product; it is for hard-to-get-at light fixtures *only*. This is the only consumer benefit that these bulbs offer according to this manufacturer. Longlife bulbs have been "oversold" to consumers, who expect that the product will save them money in the long run. Such is not the case.

GE accomplishes its objective in a surprising way. It uses candor and a negative approach, seeking to identify with a consumerist point of view. The copy is completely rational, not emotional, and gives the reader permission to believe by stating prominently and often that savings do *not* occur when longlife bulbs are used.

The manufacturer does hope to sell longlife bulbs through this ad, of course, but only to people who understand how they are to be used. Customers who buy the bulbs to save money will be disappointed, and disappointed customers don't build a business.

The objective of the Pitney Bowes ad is to sell *small* merchants on the need for a postage meter. All the elements of the ad—headline, illustration, and text—work hard to accomplish this objective. The copy starts with a little "folksy" background on the Ryerse Brothers store, and then lists all the advantages of the Touchmatic postage meter. Stamps aren't misplaced or lost, because you don't need them anymore. The job is easier. The meter keeps a record of postage. Mail will move through the post office faster. Other reasons, too, are given. And it ends up "asking for the order" with a coupon. This rational copy contains plenty of facts that help small merchants convince themselves that buying a Pitney Bowes postage meter is a good investment.

Make the Writing Clear and Specific

The body copy examples quoted above are clear, specific, and to the point. In copywriting, as in headline writing, generalities, vague statements, and brag-and-boast claims are to be avoided. Watch out for big words that require some figuring out, and avoid the use of

5 MILES A DAY KEEPS THE DOCTOR AWAY.

Mavis Lindgren had been subject to colds all her life. At two she had whooping cough, at 13 tuberculosis, and until middle age she was afflicted by chest colds that turned into pneumonia three times.

Then, at age 62, with her doctor's blessing, Mavis started running because she thought it would help her.

Obviously, it has. Now 71, Mavis says, "After I started running I never had another cold. I've been sick once in nine years. I had a real bad flu. I had it for three hours."

Mavis Lindgren and an estimated 10 million other joggers in America feel running keeps them healthy. It's something Blue Cross and Blue Shield Plans believe in, too. We're convinced that people who exercise and stay fit help slow down the rise in health care costs.

Of course, there are other effective ways to fight rising costs besides asking you to stay fit. To do it, we've initiated many programs with doctors and hospitals.

Second surgical opinion, medical necessity programs, home care, health maintenance organizations, same-day surgery, pre-admission testing—these and other programs are being adopted by Blue Cross and Blue Shield Plans all over the country to help keep costs in line.

We're encouraged. The average length of hospital stays for Blue Cross Plan subscribers under age 65 dropped by almost a day between 1968 and 1977. That may not sound like much. But if the length of stay were the same today as it was in 1968, we would be paying an additional $1,249,869,813 a year. In addition, the rate of hospital admissions for these subscribers dropped by 4.9%, representing $554,938,847.

But controlling health care costs without sacrificing quality is a tough problem. One we all have to work on together.

That's why Blue Cross and Blue Shield Plans are actively promoting exercise, fitness and other health programs. Naturally, we'd like you to use common sense, see your doctor and don't overdo it at first.

But if you're concerned about high health care costs, do as Mavis Lindgren and millions of other Americans are doing.

Run away from them.

For a free booklet, "Food and Fitness," or for information on how your company can view a special film, "You Can't Buy Health," write Box 8008, Chicago, IL 60680.

Blue Cross®
Blue Shield®

ALL OF US HELPING EACH OF US.

® Registered Service Marks of the Blue Cross Association
®'Registered Service Marks of the Blue Shield Association

The body copy for this Blue Cross/Blue Shield advertisement is clear and specific and avoids generalities; it therefore helps the reader understand the subjects discussed. (Courtesy Blue Cross/Blue Shield)

the passive voice. Use colorful words that conjure up pictures in the reader's mind.

Don't Overdo It The use of colorful language is to be encouraged, but it can cause a problem, particularly for the beginning writer. The rule to follow is "Don't show off." The reader isn't at all interested in discovering how clever and original the writer is; the reader is interested in what consumer rewards and benefits the product will deliver.

Style of copy is most important and varies with the product or service advertised. Perfume or cosmetic ads obviously require a different style of writing from that used in copy for a menswear ad. Style for the sake of style is, however, to be avoided. The following retail copy goes too far.

LA! THEY'RE BUT COUNTRY LASSES

Putting on the prettiest milkmaid dresses that ever went to the fair. All wasped in at the midriff and scooped away up top. So cool and breezy with their little sleeves and barn-dancing skirts . . .

Avoid Generalities Generalities lead to bland writing. Vague, nonspecific words and clichés allow readers to glide over the copy (if they read it at all) and do not deliver hard facts and information. General statements are not convincing. Very often generalities lead to a series of brag-and-boast statements.

The following quotes from ads contain more generalities than specific, convincing facts.

Peace of Mind. This is peace of mind by the quart. Use it and you know you're giving your engine the best protection money can buy. (Name of brand) Motor Oil is deliberately de-

signed to exceed the motor oil requirements for every car maker in the world . . .

NOW. GET BEHIND A (NAME OF CIGAR BRAND)

They won . . . and he scored the winning touchdown. You couldn't be prouder. Now you can relax with an unforgettable cigar—the mild tasting (name of brand). You get real flavor from the (name of brand's) unique blend of fine imported and choice domestic tobaccos. And real flavor is the reason so many men are buying so many (name of brand).

The clichés in these examples include "the best protection money can buy," "deliberately designed," "fine imported and choice domestic tobaccos," and "real flavor." The copy is general in nature and does not prove the claims it makes—it gives no reason why the product is better than any other.

Here is copy from two ads for alcoholic beverages. This kind of product is expected to bring satisfaction and, in many cases, status to the buyer. The first example:

BEYOND DUPLICATION

. . . an exclusive American original. In no other country in the world could such a whiskey be made. There has never been a whiskey like it.

The maker of this brand is indulging in brag and boast and is not writing with the prospect's point of view in mind. It is a series of pompous statements. Advertising for Jack Daniel's Tennessee Whiskey, in contrast, has consistently used specific facts that add distinction and an atmosphere of quality to the product. The reader receives the impression that the brand is "the best," but these obvious cliché words are never used. Thus status is conveyed to the purchaser, and the purchaser's choice of the brand is confirmed by the high opinion that others have of it. It is a subtle, yet very convincing way to sell, and creative imagination is hard at work here.

A typical ad in the Jack Daniel's series shows a photo of a plainly dressed employee drinking from an outdoor fountain. There is no headline as such, but rather a bold lead-in to the copy. The copy reads as follows:

Folks who work at Jack Daniel's go out of their way to drink the cool limestone water coming from our Cave Spring. We only have two fountains. But folks could be working at the farthest warehouse and still find an excuse for getting by one of them. So, we know it's good for drinking. We also know it's good for Jack Daniel's. You see, it runs at 56° year-round, and it's completely iron-free. (Iron is murderous to whiskey; a nail dropped in a barrel would ruin every drop.) A sip of our whiskey, we feel, will tell you why we all appreciate our spring.

Include Price or Cost Data Whenever possible, it is a good idea to give the prospect information on price, or how much it costs to use the product or service. Copy for retail store ads frequently includes price information, but the national advertiser faces a problem when trade custom allows the retailer to set the actual selling price. Prices quoted in national advertising may at times bear no relationship to actual prices for the product in the marketplace unless the item is *fair-traded,* that is, sold in accordance with a practice whereby retailers agree with manufacturers not to sell products below established prices. In such cases, retail prices can be included in national advertising copy.

Price information does not have to be included in ads for certain classes of products, such as detergents, toothpastes, and certain food items, because consumers usually are familiar with the price ranges involved and because "price-off" deals or "limited time only" price reductions are so frequent at the retail level for these product categories.

Make the Reader Experience What Is Being Sold

An excellent way to sell the reader on an advertised product or service is to describe what happens when the prospect buys it. Through words and pictures, the copywriter allows the prospect to enjoy vicariously the pleasures

Price is featured in the national advertising of Mercury Bobcat. Subheads also feature comparative copy, naming higher-priced competitors. (Courtesy Lincoln-Mercury Division, Ford Motor Company)

and benefits that will result from the purchase. In car advertising, the copy often "puts the reader behind the wheel," enjoying the comfort, convenience, and performance that the car offers. Food advertising concentrates on taste sensations and the favorable reaction of guests and family members to the meal. Travel advertising traditionally "takes" the reader somewhere pleasant; for a few short moments, the reader is already there.

Here is some travel copy that helps a reader anticipate the trip and "experience" what is being sold.

WE'VE READ ABOUT SMOG, BUT WE'VE NEVER SEEN IT.

In New Zealand, the world hasn't passed us by, but the problems of the world have.

Unemployment is virtually unheard of. So is urban blight. Here, everything looks like it was just washed by a spring rain.

You don't believe such miracles? Wait, there are more.

You can ski down a glacier. See primeval forests and fjords. Stroll on subtropical beaches. Visit an authentic Scottish hamlet. And meet some of the world's friendliest people. All in a country no bigger than California . . .

INTRODUCING THE EUROPEAN VACATION WITHOUT JET LAG.

Why cross a whole ocean to enjoy a European holiday when easy-to-drive-to Quebec is a feast of sights, sounds and tastes with a refreshing European flavor?

Beautiful Montreal is truly an international city with everything from horse-drawn carriages to sidewalk cafes to a mountain in the centre, where you can picnic under the trees and enjoy lovely views of the city below. . . .

Close the Sale

The copy, like the good salesperson, should attempt to close the sale. The purpose of mail-order advertising is to sell merchandise right off the page, and the copy bears the entire selling burden. Most advertising, however, is one or two steps removed from the physical exchange of dollars for goods and services. In national advertising, the manufacturer's goals are to urge the prospect to visit a store specifically for the advertised item or to sell a prospect on the idea of buying, an idea that may be awakened and acted upon when the prospect sees the item on a shopping trip. Retail advertising, on the other hand, says, "Come to *my* store to buy such-and-such merchandise."

In any case, it is good policy to end copy with a suggestion, request, or command to take positive action. There are many ways to go about this. Following are some examples.

FOR COMPLETE INFORMATION, SEE YOUR DEALER.

THE NEW MODELS ARE NOW IN YOUR DEALER'S SHOWROOM. INSPECT THEM TODAY.

LOOK FOR IT THE NEXT TIME YOU GO SHOPPING.

SEE THE LIST IN THE RIGHT-HAND COLUMN FOR THE DEALER NEAREST YOU.

SEE THE DEALER NEAR YOU. LOOK HIM UP IN THE YELLOW PAGES.

ASK FOR (BRAND NAME) TOMORROW.

CALL THIS TOLL-FREE NUMBER FOR LOCATION OF THE DEALER NEAREST YOU.

Adding Incentives to the Closing Temporary buying incentives often made the demand for positive action more effective. For example, it is difficult to sell air conditioners in

March because the consumer isn't bothered by heat waves at that time of year. To even out yearly sales, manufacturers of home air conditioners frequently devote entire ads to special low-price offers in off-season selling periods. The offer gives the prospect a reason to buy immediately. This kind of planning can be used for many goods and services. It is particularly prevalent and useful in the retail field.

Here are examples of buying incentives added at the point in the ad where the copywriter is asking for positive action. Both national and local examples are given.

WE HAVEN'T MANY AT THIS LOW PRICE, SO COME IN EARLY.

STOP BY SOON WHILE WE HAVE A FULL SELECTION OF SIZES AND COLORS.

IT'S YOUR DEALER'S "UNBUSY" SEASON. ORDER NOW AND YOU'LL GET FAST SERVICE.

LIMITED TIME OFFER.

GO ON OUR OFF-SEASON RATES AND YOU'LL HAVE THE MONEY TO STAY FOUR DAYS LONGER.

Including Theme Lines The summary of the main selling idea of an advertising campaign or program is the copy *theme,* sometimes referred to as a slogan. The theme is not a necessary part of an ad. Styles in advertising constantly change, and one school of thought holds that themes are not necessary if headline and copy communicate the basic continuing selling idea of the campaign or program; if headline and copy do accomplish this, a theme just clutters up the appearance of the ad. But other advertisers insist on a theme because if it is provocative and strong enough, it serves in every ad as a constant selling reminder of what the product or service basically offers. As so often happens in advertising, individual judgment will prevail. Each opinion makes a good point.

Themes deal in big ideas and fundamental concepts. They tend to be general and not as specific, sharp, or pointed as headlines. When writing themes, the copywriter must keep the objectives of a campaign or program in mind and not be distracted by the specificity of any individual ad. "Maytag. The dependability people," "Beautiful Hair. Breck," "Meow Cat Food. Tastes so good, cats ask for it by name," are examples of themes that can continue over a series of ads and that carry out the strategy of the campaign.

Local advertising, particularly in the retail field, can make good use of themes to build store image and accomplish institutional advertising objectives. Themes need not be long or elaborate. Saks Fifth Avenue, a high-fashion New York department store, for some years ended its womenswear ads with the theme "Very Saks Fifth Avenue." The simple addition of the word "very" reminds women that fashion leadership is always to be found at this store. By implication the word says "style" and "prestige" and tells the reader that this store is confident of its top position in the fashion world. Sears often ends its ads with the theme "Only at Sears" to stress the fact that merchandise exclusive to its stores is being advertised.

Use the Basic Copywriting Guides

Keep the following checklist in mind; it will help you write effective selling copy. Soon the procedures will become automatic. Most professional copywriters don't go through these steps consciously; they follow them as a matter of course. But no matter how experienced the writer, it's a good idea to check written copy against the checklist from time to time, for sometimes essential copy requirements are forgotten.

1. Think through the objectives of the ad, and marshal all available pertinent facts.

2. Elaborate on the headline idea. (Optional)

3. Include permission to believe. Supply "reason why," the benefit or reward that the product or service can deliver. Give selling facts, and prove the main claim. Add rational appeals to support emotional appeals.

4. Be specific. Avoid generalities, brag-and-boast statements, and clichés. Include price whenever possible.

5. Close the sale, adding incentives when available.

Types of Copy

Categorized descriptions of different types of copy do not help an individual to write; they serve only to define what has already been written by others. This section therefore makes no attempt to list all possible kinds of copy. It will be confined to definitions of types of copy that are unique and call for special handling. Some words of advice will be given on how to treat these categories.

Testimonial Copy

In testimonial advertising, a satisfied user of the product or service acts as a "salesperson" for the advertiser. For an example of this kind of advertising, refer to Color Plate 13.

Testimonial copy is an extremely effective advertising tool. It permits a customer to bring out selling points about the item advertised, and the net effect is to say, "Don't just take our word for it. Here is the experience of a consumer that proves the validity of our claims." It has the added advantage of delivering in quo-tation form copy that is real and true to life. Often a consumer, using everyday language (which can be very colorful), can "write" more effective copy than a professional with a highly polished style. Since people are sometimes long-winded, the problem is to eliminate unnecessary, irrelevant thoughts without changing the intent of the quotations. Inventing sentences for a consumer to say should not be done under any circumstances. When testimonials are used, for legal reasons, the advertiser's agency must obtain a signed statement from the person whose words are being used that the copy is an accurate representation of what was actually said and that the ideas are a true expression of the person's opinions or experience.

Testimonial advertising, incorporating the words of actual users of a product or service, is effective in broadcast as well as in print media.

Endorsement Copy The term endorsement copy is often used to describe testimonial advertising, but here it is confined to the area that can be termed *celebrity endorsement advertising*. In such advertising, a well-known person is used to attract attention, and an endorsement of the product or service is given, either through a direct quotation or by using the third-person form. This is an effective technique only when the personality involved has some direct and obvious connection with the item being advertised. It makes sense for a famous professional golfer to endorse a set of clubs or a brand of golf ball; when the same person endorses a car or a brand of pizza, the effect is ludicrous. The personality presented must relate to the copy objectives of the product or service.

In all cases, the personality must be a user of the product or service advertised, or have some kind of direct knowledge of it.

The Federal Trade Commission pays particular attention to celebrity endorsement advertising. In a new enforcement dimension, singer Pat Boone agreed to an FTC settlement that held him personally liable for an acne product he endorsed. The settlement was not concerned with the fact that Boone had no knowledge of the product; he did because his four daughters used it. The FTC charged, however, that the maker of the product was making false advertising claims and argued that the endorser (Boone) must verify the claims about the product before the advertising is run.[1]

Case History Copy Closely related to testimonial advertising is *case history,* in which the successful results of using a product or service are explained in detail. Business and industrial advertisers are frequent users of case history ads. A typical case history advertisement describes how a manufacturer of women's apparel keeps department stores supplied by using the air cargo service of a leading airline. Another case history tells how an American firm exporting to Belgium was aided by the services of the overseas department of a United States commercial bank. Using a case history is an effective copy technique, based on the idea that "if our firm did this for so-and-so, it can do the same for you."

Reminder Copy

In leafing through magazines and newspapers or watching commercials on television, the student will soon be aware that there is a type of copy that does not conform to many of the copywriting guides described in this chapter. This copy, brief and to the point, is reminder copy. *Reminder advertising* aims to remind the prospect of a product or service without selling it in depth. It limits itself to one or two basic ap-

[1] *Advertising Age,* May 15, 1978, pp. 1 and 113.

peals and does not elaborate on them or offer the support of rational copy, "reason why," or proof of performance. Outdoor signs, because of their nature (Chapter 7) must use reminder advertising, but reminder copy also appears in other media that can use longer copy.

Advertisers who use reminder copy are either makers of mass-produced, volume-selling items of popular appeal or are offering a product about which little can be said, as in the case of cigarettes, candy, and beer. The burden of full explanation and a reasoned approach does not lie heavily upon the ads for such products, and the theory is that it is sufficient merely to remind consumers of the product's availability and to include a benefit or reward in order to sell the product.

Following are some examples of reminder copy.

Philip Morris, Inc.'s, Marlboro cigarette advertising in print media contains, in headline and copy, only the following words:

Come to where the flavor is. Come to Marlboro Country. Marlboro Red or Longhorn 100's— you get a lot to like. (Plus the obligatory Surgeon-General's warning about the dangers of cigarette smoking.)

Many other cigarette ads consist of equally brief copy.

Heineken has no copy in its advertising, merely a headline reading

---

HEINEKEN FROM HOLLAND. IT DIDN'T GET TO BE AMERICA'S NUMBER ONE IMPORTED BEER JUST BY LOOKING THIS GOOD.

For products other than those in mass-appeal, lower-priced category, reminder copy is not recommended. It is good sales technique, once attention has been gained, to elaborate on selling ideas in copy and, whenever possible, to add convincing reasons to buy.

Mood Copy

Another type of copy that does not conform to the copywriting guides is *mood copy,* copy that appeals wholly to the emotions. It never uses rational appeals, and it shuns proof, facts, information, and reasons why. Depending on the product category, mood copy can be a valid and sales-oriented approach to the prospect. Cosmetics, perfumes, and high-fashion items are products that appeal to emotions, and it is hard to make rational appeals for

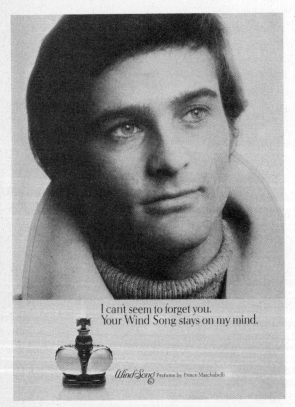

I can't seem to forget you. Your Wind Song stays on my mind.

Wind Song Perfume by Prince Matchabelli

This ad for Wind Song is an example of mood copy. It appeals only to the emotions because rational appeals have no place in advertisements for products in this category. (Courtesy Prince Matchabelli)

them. Selling them on a mood copy basis is a sound business practice. (See Color Plate 10.)

Teaser Copy

When introducing a new product or service, advertisers sometimes use a technique known as *teaser advertising.* This is actually "blind" advertising, usually consisting of a series of ads run in newspapers at close intervals and containing little or no identification of the advertiser. The purpose is to arouse the curiosity of the reader and stimulate interest in some forthcoming event or new arrival on the commercial scene. Sometimes teaser advertising contains no copy at all and relies on a visual symbol. New movies and store openings are often the subject of teaser campaigns.

There are many pitfalls in running teaser copy, and a high degree of creativity is needed to be successful. The short teaser campaign for New York's refurbished Chrysler building is shown on page 295. According to ESG, the managing agent, the campaign was extremely effective. In 1 hour alone, *The New York Times,* carrying the ads, received over 300 phone calls from curious people. More importantly, the building's rental goal was achieved.

Special-Incentive Copy

A marketing plan for a product or service may include a special drive period in which extra selling effort is concentrated. There are many merchandising aids and incentives available to marketers that serve to stimulate sales for relatively brief periods, and some of them require advertising support. A thorough discussion of drive-period merchandising belongs in marketing text books. But we should at least be knowledgeable of the most important incentives because consumers learn about them through advertising.

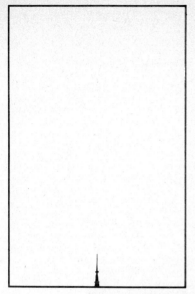

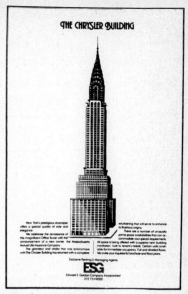

This successful teaser campaign for New York's Chrysler Building uses the visual symbol of the building's tower to stimulate interest in the building's modernization. These full-page newspaper ads were run on consecutive days. (Courtesy Edward S. Gordon Company, Incorporated)

Premiums, price-off coupons, and sweepstakes are common drive-period merchandising aids that are advertised.[2] Premiums and price-offs are primarily intended to stimulate trial purchases.

Premiums are items serving as sales incentives that are offered to consumers for purchasing goods or services. Premiums may be on-pack (attached to the merchandise) or obtained separately by the purchaser. They can be offered at no extra cost, or can be self-liquidating. In this latter case, the advertiser supplies the premium to the consumer at a price that approximates the premium's wholesale cost to the advertiser. Over time, the price liquidates the advertiser's premium's costs. The consumer benefits by obtaining the premium at wholesale prices.

Price-off coupons temporarily reduce the price of consumer items when the buyer turns in the coupon at point of purchase or returns the coupon (accompanied by proof of purchase) to the advertiser for a cash rebate. See the ad for Cott soda.

Sweepstakes are merchandising aids that distribute prizes to entrants on the basis of chance.

Ad copy and layout supporting these sales incentives have a tone and appearance unlike other forms of advertising. Often the primary purpose of such ads is to support the incentive; everything else is subordinate. The "news" is the offer itself, and the product or service tem-

[2] Although every major marketer of consumer products uses premiums and price-offs, some of the more sophisticated marketers strictly limit their use. When competitors use these techniques simultaneously, offers tend to cancel each other in effectiveness. Also, consumers have a tendency to switch temporarily to the brand featuring the offer (giving sales a short-term boost) and then to switch back to their regular brand. According to knowledgeable marketers, the best consumer reasons for buying a brand are the quality and satisfaction delivered by the brand itself when used. If these benefits are strong enough, special purchase incentives are rarely needed.

An example of special incentive copy featuring a priceoff coupon. How would Cott's usual brand advertising differ in layout from this ad? (Courtesy Cott Beverages)

porarily takes a back seat. See the example of special incentive copy in the Cott ad.

Comparative Copy

Rarely used in the past, comparative copy, or *comparative advertising,*[3] has today become an important strategic technique used by certain major advertisers. This type of advertising

---

[3] The term *comparative advertising* also can refer to advertising in which the competitor is referred to in unidentified terms such as "Brand X" or a "leading brand." In our discussion above, we are describing only comparative advertising that specifically identifies the competitor and compares the competitor's performance with the advertised brand or service.

compares by name or product illustration the competitors' brands or services with the sponsor's brand or service. Tests, statistics, and benefits that serve to prove the advertiser's product or service better than the named competition are marshaled in order to sell the consumer. Comparative advertising is brash and controversial.

Tracey Westen, deputy director of the FTC's Bureau of Consumer Protection, and some consumer groups hold that the use of comparative copy gives consumers more information than traditional advertising, and thus helps consumers become more knowledgeable.

Stanley Tannenbaum, chairman of the Kenyon & Eckhardt advertising agency, considers "comparative advertising as our industry's own brand of consumerism when properly executed."[4]

Andrew Kershaw, chairman of the Ogilvy & Mather agency, believed that "the widespread practice of comparative advertising will reduce the credibility and effectiveness of advertising, and intensify the distrust of business corporations."[5]

William Tankersley, president of the Council of Better Business Bureaus, believes that comparative ads have not produced hoped-for consumer benefits and stated, "the plethora of such ads has further damaged the credibility of advertising with equal negative effect on the mores of civilized business behavior."[6]

The subject is a hot potato that has meant more business for lawyers, kept research and development people busy proving claims, swamped the complaint log of the NAD-NARB self-regulation system (Chapter 1) and given the TV network copy-clearance divisions much extra work.

---

[4] AAAA, Comparative Advertising, paper from the 1976 Annual Meeting, p. 11.
[5] Ibid., p. 13.
[6] Advertising Age, October 17, 1977, p. 2.

Since advertising has the purpose of helping sell goods, services, and ideas, comparative advertising should be judged on its ability (or lack of it) to accomplish this end.

The makers of sales-leading products such as Tide detergent or Xerox copiers gain nothing from mentioning competitors by name in their advertising, and this is why they do not do so. Such a strategy would only result in the free promotion of lesser brands in the category. There is some evidence, however, that a *smaller* competitor can attract sales if it "names names" in its advertising. Savin Business Machines ran advertising naming Xerox and IBM (accompanied by a new marketing approach) and increased its sales.[7]

Television communications recall tests (Chapter 9) by several research companies indicate that there are no recall advantages to be gained by using comparative copy. In other words, comparative advertising commercials don't get higher scores than other types of advertising.

There is some research evidence that comparative television copy generates sponsor misidentification. People can be confused by copy that names competitors and as a result mistake the competitor for the sponsor. Research also indicates that comparative television copy creates increased consumer skepticism toward advertising as a whole.[8]

There is also a point of view that comparative advertising can violate a consumer's sense of fair play and may in fact be counterproductive. When a person using Brand A sees a commercial sponsored by competitive Brand B that says Brand B is "better" than Brand A (and names Brand A in the process), that person's brand purchase habit is being attacked and his or her judgment questioned. This is not a constructive or sensible way to sell. As Wright, Warner, Winter and Zeigler point out,

---

From an implementation viewpoint, there is a critical question whether a given (comparative) message constitutes disparagement of the competitor. . . . A case can be made that such comparisons hurt the advertiser.[9]

If a brand or service does indeed have provable advantages over competition, and if these advantages can be presented as benefits to the prospect, the brand can make its case in advertising very well indeed without the need for actually naming the competition. What is required in this case is good creative thinking. And considering that comparative advertising does not communicate better than other forms (at least in the TV medium), that comparative advertising can cause consumer confusion, and that it seems to add to consumer skepticism, its use must be seriously questioned.

Writing Local Retail Advertising Copy

The checklist found earlier in this chapter under the heading "Use the Basic Copywriting Guides" applies to local and retail advertising copy as well as to national advertising copy. Basically, local merchants and national manufacturers or national service suppliers have the same objective: selling goods or services to the public. But because of differences in methods of distribution, local merchants' advertising copy has a different look and feel from the copy of national advertisers. As dis-

---

[7] "It Pays to Knock Your Competitor," *Fortune,* February 13, 1978, pp. 110–111.

[8] Philip Levine, executive research director, Ogilvy & Mather, "Commercials That Name Competing Brands," *Journal of Advertising Research,* December 1976, p. 9.

[9] J. S. Wright, D. S. Warner, W. Winter, S. K. Zeigler, *Advertising,* 4th ed., McGraw-Hill Book Company, New York, 1977, p. 673.

cussed in Chapter 3, local advertising usually strives for immediate sales activity. It is also personal, direct, and price-oriented. National advertisers, however, are eager to sell their brands or services through a multitude of sales outlets; their advertising is indirect in the sense that they have no interest in specifically where the goods or services are sold. National advertisers also regard sales as occurring over a long period of time; they don't necessarily seek action "tomorrow," as the local merchant does.

The local advertiser[10] often faces the restriction of space limitations that the large national advertiser does not face. The total area of newspaper space may be 200 lines or less when frequency of insertion is desired. While individual department store ads may run to page size, several items may be featured; thus there is less space available for each item. For these reasons, local advertising copy tends to be short and to the point. It gets into its subject fast, and there is usually not sufficient space to elaborate on the headline idea in the first paragraph of body copy.

Promotional Copy

Promotional and institutional retail advertising were defined and discussed in Chapter 3. Promotional advertising copy can be broken down into regular-price copy and sale, price-off clearance, or special-purchase copy. Regular-price copy is used for all types of merchandise not currently being sold on a reduced-price basis. Price in such copy may be termed a "value" or "remarkably low," but it is not the major selling news. The quality features, style, or usefulness of the merchandise is featured in regular-price copy. In sale, price-off clearance, or special-purchase advertising, the

[10] See The Local Advertiser in Chapter 3 for an explanation of local advertising and its subdivision, retail advertising.

price of the item is featured in headline and copy. It is the main news, and quality, features, style, or usefulness become subordinate.

Regular-Price Copy Here is an example of regular-price copy that is tightly written and short and yet takes time to involve the reader by using graphic words and plenty of desirable facts about the merchandise.

OUR NEW FAMOLARE LINE . . . THE SHOES THAT PUT AMERICA BACK ON ITS FEET

The Famolare credo is walking for pleasure, for health and serenity. And with this in mind the Famolare shoe was designed with anatomically contoured inner sole honey-combed for lightness . . . rich Italian leathers and thick, bouncy, wavy soles to absorb shocks. Definitely the best of both worlds . . . fine craftsmanship of the old and 21st-century design of the new. Select your favorite style! "Just." Low wedge slip-on. Brown $38.00 "Soon." Oxford in Tan. $38.00 "Merlot." Sandal in rust. $39.00 "Albana." Sandal in rust. $39.00

Sale Copy In sale copy, the price is the news, and it is the focal point of the ad. The quality of the merchandise can be stressed in the copy, and features of the items are, of course, important to include. But quality and features are subordinate to price.

The retail appliance ad quoted below offers a substantial saving on a nationally distributed brand of dishwasher. The price reduction is a temporary one, so this news is the most important piece of information for the prospect. "Money" dominates the headline. The actual saving is listed, plus regular and sale prices.

The copy then describes performance features of the product.

SAVE $50
3-CYCLE (NAME) DISHWASHER,
CUTTING BOARD TOP
$235 REGULARLY $285

Dial normal wash or short wash for small loads. Crystal-clear rinse has even-drying action. This efficient toploading portable with handy lift-out rack, automatic detergent dispenser holds 14 place settings . . .

Generalities in Retail Advertising

Although the rule of avoiding generalities has been explored in the section on national advertising, it is of such importance that it deserves repeating in this section on local advertising. It is extremely important to be specific in local and retail advertising and to avoid generalities and clichés. The merchant is seeking immediate sales, and citing specific product features in copy is a sure way to obtain them.

This first example, from an ad for men's suits, is overdone, indirect, blatant in its appeal, and

KIDS LIKE 'EM

Good, sturdy Docksides. The brown leather moccasin with a white sole. School shoe and play shoe for children's sizes 12½ to 4, 26.00; youths' sizes 4½ to 6, 30.00. Children's Shoes, second floor, Fifth Avenue (212) MU9-7000, and branches.

B Altman Co

Although the layout appearance of these two B. Altman ads is similar, one ad features regular-price copy and the other sale copy. (Courtesy B. Altman & Company)

FLEECE SALE

Kick off your shoes, and slip on our soft, warm fleece robe of Arnel® triacetate/nylon. That's the way to relax. Gripper front, shirred shoulders in green, red or blue, P-S-M-L. **Now 21.90,** was 30.00. Robes and Loungewear, second floor, Fifth Avenue (212) MU9-7000 and branches.

B Altman Co

general in tone. It doesn't get down to business until the last sentences.

(NAME OF SUIT MAKER) BELONGS WHERE YOU'VE CLIMBED . . .

You're going up . . . up . . . And you're going to stay. Nice feeling. Nice knowing your suit reflects the way you feel. Confident! In form . . . in fashion. The new season suit . . . two button, single breasted. Sculptured front, widened lapels. Solids, mini-checks, plaid, bold stripes. From $165.

In the department store field, advertising managers and buyers should keep a close tab on the selling effectiveness of ads. It would be odd, therefore, to find copy that consists wholly of generalities—but, unfortunately, it is not hard to find examples. The copy below for men's shoes manages to offer no proof of fashion excellence, only empty boasts. It is unspecific until the last line, when it does list colors available.

(NAME OF MAKER) SHOES . . . FOR MEN WHO ARE PROUD TO BE IN THE FRONT LINE OF FASHION.

(Name of maker) has perfectly blended the best in creative styling with superior craftsmanship to produce these elegant classics. They coordinate excellently with just about anything in your wardrobe! Black and brown, subtle grained calfskin.

Here is another version of this copy, rewritten to deal with specifics.

There's a creative modern look about these square-toed moccasins that puts them in the front line of fashion. The 2-inch brass buckle and over-sized strap is part of their story; the elongated throat tells even more. Made on our extraordinarily comfortable Windsor last. In AA grade brown and black calfskin with interesting subtle graining.

Some retail stores have become deservedly famous for first-rate advertising copy written with style and feeling. This happens when top management is astute enough to plan for it— and when able advertising managers hire talented young people, help them gain experience, and encourage them with raises. Unfortunately, most retail advertising could be better and more effective than it is. But consider the bright side. Because there is so much to be accomplished, there are opportunities in the retail advertising field for talented young people.

In local advertising other than retail, some excellent campaigns and individual ads are turned out. But these successful efforts are relatively rare. In fact, good campaigns are talked about by the public and thus receive much valuable publicity just because they are unusual and don't face much advertising competition. Local businesses should be able to develop a favorable image—a good personality. But a great amount of the small-space local advertising for the small merchant is merely of the reminder variety.

The following quotes are typical of the entire message (except for the address) of many small merchants.

ROOF LEAK? CALL ACME ROOFING

J. L. STURDIVANT—REAL ESTATE AND INSURANCE

XEROX AND TYPING SERVICES—A. L. MULLER CO.

VISIT THE FIREPLACE RESTAURANT

TV REPAIR—ALL MAKES. CHARLIE SMITH.

Ads like these can be improved by as little as a line or two of copy that serves to distinguish the service offered from that of competing firms or that adds reasons why the merchandise is of superior quality. All that it takes to increase the effectiveness of much local advertising is ingenuity and a little effort on the part of the local advertiser. Here are brief copy blocks that add to the selling efficiency of the messages quoted above.

ROOF LEAK? CALL ACME ROOFING.

Our work is guaranteed. We find leaks and fix 'em. Get ready for a rainy spring with a sound roof. Call us today at 456-7890.

We sold six houses last week to happy buyers, because we know how. Come to the firm that sells more houses than any other agent in town. More listings available, more satisfaction for you.

J. L. STURDIVANT—REAL ESTATE AND INSURANCE

Fast, efficient service, competitively priced. Our typists really understand!
XEROX AND TYPING SERVICES—A. L. MULLER CO.

Enjoy a cozy dinner by the fireplace. Steak special—with vegetables, salad, rolls, coffee —$6.95.
VISIT THE FIREPLACE RESTAURANT

TV REPAIR—ALL MAKES

Factory-guaranteed parts, manufacturer-trained repairman.
Same-day service if you drop off your set.
CHARLIE SMITH

Vocabulary

Define the following terms and use each one in a sentence.

Case history advertising
Celebrity endorsement advertising
Comparative advertising
Fair-traded
Mood copy
Permission to believe

Premiums
Price-off coupons
Reminder advertising
Sweepstakes
Teaser advertising
Theme

Review Questions

1. What are the purposes of copy in an advertisement?
2. Can you find an example of copy that elaborates on the headline idea in the first paragraph. Copy it or bring it in for class discussion.
3. Describe the need in an advertisement for permission to believe and explain the importance of rational copy.

4. Why should a writer avoid generalities in the copy?
5. Give some examples of adding incentives to that part of the copy that asks for action.
6. In your opinion, are theme lines or slogans important in advertisements? Why, or why not?
7. Summarize the basic copywriting guide.
8. What are the values offered by testimonial and case history copy?
9. For what types of products is reminder copy sufficient as the total copy effort?
10. Name three common merchandising aids or incentives available to marketers.
11. What is your opinion of comparative advertising?
12. How does retail copy differ from national advertising copy?

Activities

1. The buyer of a department store has supplied you with the information below. Using one of the lists, write a headline and copy, and describe the illustration for an ad in the regular-price category. The number of words in your copy should be limited to 75. More points have been supplied than you will actually need. Make a duplicate of your headline and copy and keep it for an activity in Chapter 16.

   List 1 Ladies' and Misses' one-piece zippered ski suit. Denim look with ribbed acrylic neck and cuffs, very snug, plus ribbed acrylic vest effect. In quilted polyester and cotton, a smart fabric for this season. Lined with acrylic fiber plus aluminum. Excellent body-heat retainer. Warmth—no bulk.
   French styling. Cuffs are slightly bell-bottomed with a snow cuff inside to keep legs dry.
   In blue or rose. Sizes 6 to 18. $125.
   White crocheted wool cap with pom-pom, $10.
   The Ski Lodge, 2d Floor, Gingrich's, State Street.

   List 2 New Garamonde 16-band radio. Hand-assembled by European craftspeople.
   Reception from every part of the world.
   FM-AM; marine long wave (navigation and weather); very-high-frequency for police, fire department, and United States weather broadcasts; a total of 11 shortwave bands.
   Two built-in speakers.
   Extra tuner for ultra-high frequency.

Automatic drift control on FM.

Handsome vinyl-covered cabinet. Prize-winning design at Museum of Modern Art.

$169.95 The Sound Studio, Main Floor. Gingrich's, State Street.

2. You are a copywriter in an advertising agency and are assigned to the Geneva Watch account. Geneva is a Swiss-made, relatively inexpensive line of wristwatches with general distribution in discount houses, department stores, and drugstores. Your task is to suggest an illustration and write headline copy for a quarter-page ad for the Geneva Aquatic in a June issue of *Time*. Use your imagaination— and some of the following facts:

Black face, luminous dial

Day-of-the-month feature: calendar-date window on dial

Sweep second hand

Lapsed-time indicator

Stainless-steel case

Cloth "tropical" long-wearing strap

One jewel

Guaranteed waterproof, steamproof, moistureproof

Price: $29.95

Project

Check your understanding of this chapter by identifying the types of advertising copy listed below. Look for examples in magazines and local newspapers or, when pertinent, on outdoor posters. Bring to class tearsheets properly identified, or write out examples from advertising messages that fit the requirements. If you write out the examples, you need not copy the entire ad, only a sample that makes your point.

Comparative copy

Copy that utilizes an emotional appeal

Copy using a rational appeal

Copy consisting of generalities

Copy that closes the sale and adds incentives

Two or three themes used by local advertisers

Reminder copy (check outdoor posters in your area for examples)

Retail regular-price copy

Retail sale copy

Career Ladder

After graduation, you obtained your first job selling in a department store. You are doing well and have been told that you will be considered for an assistant buyer's job when one opens up in the near future. You think that you could have a good career in this type of business.

Your ambition, however, had been to go into advertising. One of your job interviews had been for a job in a large and successful mail-order house in town as a beginning catalog copy writer. Nothing was available at the time. You are now called by the person who interviewed you at the mail-order house, who says there is an opening as a beginning copy writer and asks if you would be interested. This is an excellent opportunity, but you would start at a salary that is less than you now earn as a salesperson. What is your decision? What factors have you considered in reaching this decision?

CHAPTER FIFTEEN

LAYOUT, ILLUSTRATION, COLOR, AND TYPE

Up to this point in Unit 3, the idea-getting process and the preparation of headlines and copy for print advertising have been discussed. Now the physical appearance of the ad must be considered. Aside from the obvious requirement that the elements of headline, copy, name of advertiser, and theme (if any) must fit the space contracted for, advertising craftspeople must concern themselves with the form of the ad, its illustrative elements, the use of color when necessary or desired, and the appearance of the type in which the copy is set. These considerations are discussed in this chapter.

Laying Out the Ad

Just as a writer plans what the copy should emphasize and what copy points should be included before actually putting words down on paper, an art director plans in advance the ultimate appearance of an ad. To accomplish this, the art director prepares a *layout,* a visualiza-

tion of the advertisement that serves as a guide during all phases of production.

Purposes of the Layout

In the layout all the elements of the ad are organized so that they are clear and easy to read. The layout helps ensure that the ad will attract attention and then hold the reader's interest as the eye is guided from one element to the next in logical order. (A layout alone cannot, of course, ensure readership of the finished ad if the headline and copy are dull or do not contain benefits or if the illustrations are not interesting and attention-getting.)

A layout also serves the following important purposes:

1. It organizes all the elements of the advertisement. The layout indicates positions of such elements as headline, subheadline, main and subordinate illustrations, copy blocks, copy subheads, boldface or heavy typesettings of key words and prices, picture captions, *logotype* (the company or brand name when it is featured as a separate element in the ad), and theme or slogan.

2. In its earliest stages, it serves as a basis of discussion between copywriter and art director to determine whether the ad's objectives are being accomplished.

3. It is used to "sell" the future ad to those who must approve it.

4. It is used as a guide for specialists such as typesetters and engravers, who must physically prepare the ad for use in print. When the ad is about to be produced, the layout is "marked up" to indicate *typefaces* (sets of type with the same design) and the size of type. The layout also carries any other instructions production people require.

Stages of the Layout

A layout is always made in the size that the advertisement will be in print. But in the conceptual stage of creating advertising, two forms of visualization are used that do not qualify as layouts because they are not made in the same size as the final ad. The first is a *copywriter's rough,* a necessarily crude indication of what the copywriter has in mind. Writers sometimes make copywriter's roughs as a matter of course. Depending on the temperament of the art director involved (and some art directors are very temperamental), these roughs are received with interest or ignored completely. For small retailers, a copywriter's rough is the only guide for the ad that will exist, and it at least serves as an indication to a newspaper's advertising department of what the retailer has in mind concerning the final appearance of his ad.

The second form of visualization that is not a layout is developed by the art director and is called the *thumbnail;* thumbnails are mini-layouts quickly sketched to present several alternative solutions to the arrangement of the ad's elements. The art director is thinking on

paper when sketching thumbnails and is working for the best possible choice.

Among forms of visualization that can be classified as layouts are *rough layouts,* which are sketchy but accurate guides to finished ads. They are usually all that is required to complete the ad-making process. Below we show a rough layout; notice that the copy area is indicated by rough lines. This extent of finish satisfies advertising department requirements in retail stores. Rough layouts also serve most purposes in advertising agencies.

A more complete picture of the advertisement is called a finished layout or *comprehensive.* A comprehensive looks very much like

This is a rough layout for a department store ad. It indicates in general how the illustration will look, and shows the positions of elements such as copy blocks, boldface prices, and store logotype.

the actual ad in that the illustration is carefully portrayed, and, in some cases, the copy block is actually set in type. Because comprehensives require the work of skilled artists as well as a layout person, and because they take more time to produce than rough layouts, they are costly. Comprehensives are mainly used as a selling tool to dress up presentations to agency clients. A sophisticated advertiser should be able to understand and visualize a completed ad from a rough layout, and the comprehensive stage should not be necessary. (See Color Plates 6 and 7.)

Mechanicals are a form of layout identical in appearance to the final ad, except that they do not include color (even if color will be used in the ad). The finished illustrations are photostated in proper size and pasted in correct position, and typeset copy blocks, headlines, logotypes, and theme lines are mounted on the mechanical as indicated by the rough layout. The mechanical is used as a guide in making plates from which the ad is printed or is prepared in camera-ready form when the offset process is used.

Considerations in Making Single-Item Layouts

It may be reassuring to the small local advertiser to realize that it is not necessary to be able to draw to make a simple, single-item layout (though it helps). Satisfactory layouts can be made by using "scrap" illustrations cut from finished ads or mat books, pasting them in place, and roughly indicating positions of headline, copy block, and store logotype, address, and slogan. In many instances, the advertising representative or other advertising personnel of the local newspaper can offer assistance, such as supplying a rough layout.

Determine the Advertisement's Area Since the layout is the same size as the final ad, the art director must know the ad size and print medium to be used before getting to work. In national advertising, the space size for a series of ads has usually been contracted for in advance. The art director may be dealing with space ranging from 14 lines to a double-page bleed. The page size varies in magazines, so it is important to check Standard Rate & Data listings for this information. In cases where the same ad is scheduled for several magazines of varying page sizes, one basic layout is made for a typical size, while mechanicals are scaled to conform to individual magazine requirements, and plates or film are made in the proper size.

Since newspapers have a larger page size, there are more shapes available to the art director. The ad can be long and thin, almost square, or a horizontal oblong; the shape chosen should be the one that best serves the purposes of the ad.

Make the Mood of the Layout Fit the Product or Service An ad for a luxury product has a look entirely different from that of an ad for a bargain-basement item. The illustration, copy, and typeface and the boldness or quietness of the headline can connote stability, conservativeness, fun, excitement, prosperity, or other qualities. The layout determines the feelings the ad will evoke, and it should handle all its elements in a way that contributes to the desired mood of the advertisement.

Determine What Elements Should Be Emphasized Before the layout is drawn, the objective or strategy of the ad should be considered. The layout should direct the reader's attention to the principal idea expressed in the ad and then lead to subordinate elements. For example, if a department store is advertising sale-priced merchandise, the merchandise and its low price will be emphasized; the price will be large and bold. In regular-price copy, the price is a subordinate element, and the merchandise and its special feature or benefit receive maximum attention. The two ads from B. Altman and Co. (in Chapter 14) are examples of these two types of layouts.

Put the Elements Together The qualities desired in good layouts are unity, simplicity, and cohesiveness. The layout must bring together the elements of the ad so that they are harmonious. Skilled art directors and layout people develop a "feel" that results in layouts that look right to the viewer. The factors that lead to this pleasing appearance are hard to analyze, but there are some basic guides to layout construction that help to create practical, hard-working layouts.

Balance the Ad If the top half of an advertisement has exactly the same weight and strength as the lower half, the ad appears top-heavy to the viewer. The *optical center,* or the point the human eye perceives as the middle, lies about one-third of the way down an ad rather than at the actual halfway mark. So the focus of interest in an ad should be slightly higher than the mid-ad point. Equal weights should not occupy equal halves but the top third and the lower two-thirds.

"Heavy" or large elements should be placed closer to the optical center than smaller elements. For example, in a simple retail ad containing an illustration, headline, copy block, and store logotype and address, the illustration, larger than any of the other elements, will lie nearer to the optical center than the logotype, a smaller element appearing near the base of the ad. This balancing of elements does not jar; it is pleasing to the eye.

Balance may be symmetrical or asymmetrical. If the ad is divided vertically, in symmetrical balance there is equal "weight" to both sides. In asymmetrical balance, various elements in each vertical section are laid out farther from or nearer to the optical center, depending on their mass or weight. Heavier elements are placed nearer the optical center than lighter, smaller elements. Asymmetrical balance is less formal than symmetrical balance and gives a sense of movement, as shown in the examples illustrated here.

Consider Borders Borders are occasionally used to set an ad apart from its competition and lend a distinctive look. A well-designed border can accomplish some of the same goals as a logotype; it can add the element of continuity to a store's advertising program. Borders can be obtained from advertising services or can be designed by an artist for the exclusive use of a store.

Consider Dark Backgrounds and Reverse Type Black, gray, or dark-toned backgrounds are often used in advertisements. These backgrounds may fill the entire area of the ad or only parts of the advertisement. Dark panels may be used in an otherwise white or lightly tinted background. On a dark background, the message must be set in *reverse type,* a technique whereby, to ensure legibility, the copy appears as white or etched-out lettering against a darker background.

Layouts with completely dark backgrounds or with a few dark panels should be avoided because they make ads harder to read and thus place an obstacle in the way of selling goods and services. Spencer Bruno, a specialist and innovator in readership analysis, stated to the author. "In nine cases out of ten the use of dark backgrounds and reverse type results in ads that are below average in consumer readership."

The use of *white space,* or unfilled areas in layouts, is much more likely to attract attention

(Shown actual size)

AZTEC PENDANT

The Sun god, Tonatiuh, in this miniature copy of the "Calendar Stone," the most important artifact of the Aztec civilization. The original stone, 11 feet in diameter, is in the Museum of Anthropology in Mexico City. A simpler sun disk, the Sacrificial Stone, is reproduced on the reverse side. Specify either 24K gold finish or sterling silver electroplate. Order by mail or phone: XH-100N $16.50, chain included ($1 shipping). Major credit cards. (N.Y., Conn. residents add sales tax.)

Free with your order—6000 years of art in our full-color catalog of fine sculpture and jewelry replicas from museums and private collections around the world, or send $1.

MUSEUM COLLECTIONS

Dept. TF-9, P.O. Box 7000, Greenwich, Conn. 06830

or call, 1-800-243-4492 toll-free

If not completely satisfied, return undamaged within four weeks for a full refund.

Finally. The European styles you've always admired in the Big and Tall sizes you could never find.

At London Majesty, we have an extensive collection of European styled suits, sports coats, trousers, sweaters and shirts: Made in Europe expressly for us. And expertly tailored in sizes expressly for you. Extra Tall 6' 3" to 6' 9". Kingsize 44 to 54.

Call or write for your free brochure.
London Majesty, 1211 Avenue of the Americas (at West 48th Street), New York, N.Y. 10036. (212) 221-1860

The Aztec pendant ad is symmetrical, with equal weight on each side. The London Majesty ad is asymmetrical, with elements extending from the optical center, giving a sense of movement. (Courtesy Museum Collections; London Majesty)

than the use of dark backgrounds. White space around illustrations and copy blocks lets the layout "breathe" and results in an uncluttered, clean appearance that adds interest and gains readership.

Considerations in Making Multi-Item Layouts

Up to this point layouts featuring a single item have been considered. But often retailers feature more than one item in their larger-size newspaper ads. The subjects discussed above—area, mood, emphasis, borders, etc. —must all be considered in building multi-item layouts. There are also some specific ways of handling the multi-item layout itself.

1. If items from several different departments are featured, the layout can give each item equal space. The space allotted to each item then becomes a separate ad within an ad, and the principles of cohesion, unity, and balance apply to each individual area. Borders may be used to separate these areas. Of course, it is not necessary to repeat the store logotype within each separate area—a logotype at the base of the whole ad will suffice.

2. When coordinated merchandise is displayed in a large ad, one item is featured, and the other items received secondary emphasis. For example, men's suits can be the featured item, with tie-in merchandise in the menswear area, such as neckties, shirts, and shoes, receiving second billing in illustration, copy, and price subheads.

3. In large ads including both coordinated merchandise and other unrelated merchandise, the coordinated items are treated as described above, and the unrelated merchandise is separated from the coordinated items by a border. Thus, the unrelated merchandise is treated as an ad within an ad, separate from the coordinated items.

Special Magazine Space Units

Unusual layout forms are available to advertisers in many of the large-circulation women's magazines.[1] These space units have the common goal of attempting to increase visibility of advertisements by placing them within (or adjoining to) magazine text. The units are usually used in bleed form with full color.

Checkerboard, junior page, and island are typical terms for such space units. A common form is *Reader's Digest size,* in which an exact duplicate of a full-page ad to be run in *Reader's Digest* is also run in a larger-sized woman's service magazine. The rest of the magazine page contains no additional advertising, only magazine text. Some of the more popular units are shown in the diagram.

In some of these units, the story the ad tells starts in the first unit and continues in the next. Because the space of each part of such continuing units is often small, the units are best used for reminder advertising. (See Color Plate 16.)

═Selecting the Illustration═

The purpose of an illustration in an advertisement is to further the ad's objective. The illustration does this by depicting the product or service and demonstrating its usefulness and benefits to the prospect or to enhance the basic selling ideas of the ad. If it does not accomplish these aims, the illustration is not needed and should not be included. Illustrations that serve merely decorative purposes and do not contribute to the selling objective are costly and useless. Most ads benefit from the inclusion of illustrative devices; some ads,

[1] Other types of large-circulation magazines offer special space units, but not to the extent of those available in *Woman's Day* or *Family Circle,* for example.

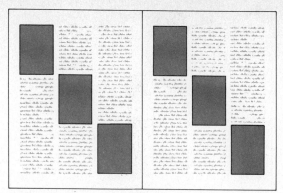

A. Checkerboard: total space, 2/3 page

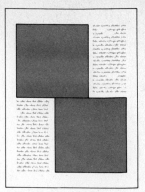

D. Modified checkerboard:
total space, 2/3 page

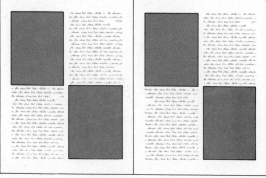

B. Checkerboard: total space, 1 page

E. *Reader's Digest* size

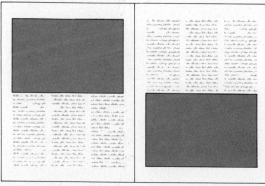

C. Two horizontal 1/2 pages

F. Island: 1/3 page

Diagrams of magazine special space units. (A) Checkerboard double page, total two-thirds page. (B) Checkerboard double page, total one page. (C) Two one-half pages horizontal on double-page spread. (D) Modified checkerboard, total two-thirds page. (E) *Reader's Digest* size. (F) Island, one-third page.

Does this illustration of Mom and Mom's apple pie serve a useful purpose in this ad, or is it a decorative addition? (Courtesy W. R. Weaver Company)

however, are "all headline and copy" and do very well without illustrations.

People in Illustrations

People are often pictured in illustrations. This adds human interest and serves to involve the reader. When people are shown using or demonstrating the product or service, the prospect can identify with the situation. The reader can see what it would be like to own the advertised item and can imagine the benefits that are outlined. Many national and local advertisement illustrations contain people. As Stephen Baker states in *Visual Persuasion,* "Department stores discovered long ago that the appeal of clothes is greatest when they are worn by people."[2] The presence of people lends a real-life atmosphere to inanimate objects.

But merely to add people to an illustration

[2] Stephen Baker, *Visual Persuasion: The Effect of Pictures on the Subconscious,* McGraw-Hill Book Company, Inc., New York, 1961, unpaged.

does not ensure reader involvement. People should perform as salesmen and saleswomen, not as decorative additions. They should act out product use or demonstrate a product advantage, not be mannequins or models who merely smile or point to the product. The ad for Allstate uses people effectively.

Type of Illustration

In national advertising, the art director can specify a photograph for the illustration or use a drawing, a painting, a watercolor, or one of many other forms of illustration. Every form other than photography is usually called *artwork.* The form used is determined by the mood and feeling required for the advertisement. A high-fashion item, for example, may be depicted by a high-fashion drawing if a certain look is required. In general, however, photography serves the national advertiser best.

The realism of photography provides for an excellent demonstration of products, and the high-quality paper stock available in magazines permits excellent photographic reproduction. Readership checks of thousands of ads reveal that photographs attract more attention than artwork does.

Illustrations Used by Local Advertisers

Functional illustrations are a vital part of every local advertiser's campaign. Just as in national advertising, illustrations should not be decorative but should fit in with the selling approach of the ad so that they support the sales message. Sources of illustrative material, such as ad services, manufacturers' ad folders of items on sale in the retail establishment, the local newspaper, ad clipping services, local advertising agencies, and free-lance illustrators, are described in detail in Chapter 5.

Large local retail stores in urban areas, including some department stores, furniture stores, specialized retailers of menswear and

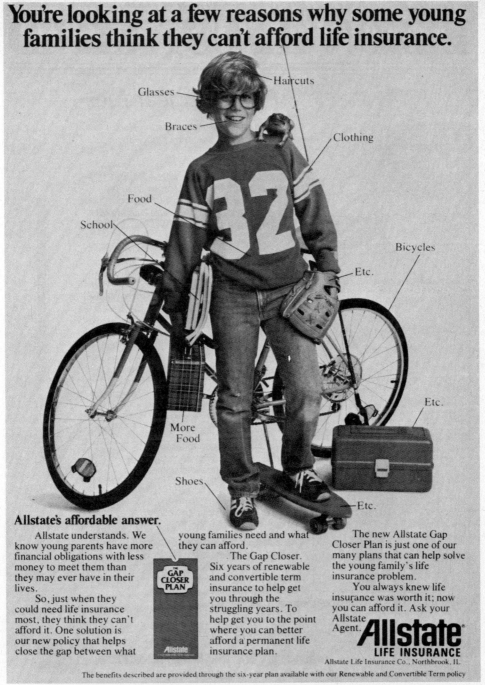

You're looking at a few reasons why some young families think they can't afford life insurance.

Glasses

Haircuts

Braces

Clothing

Food

School

Bicycles

Etc.

More Food

Etc.

Shoes

Etc.

Allstate's affordable answer.

Allstate understands. We know young parents have more financial obligations with less money to meet them than they may ever have in their lives.

So, just when they could need life insurance most, they think they can't afford it. One solution is our new policy that helps close the gap between what

young families need and what they can afford.

The Gap Closer. Six years of renewable and convertible term insurance to help get you through the struggling years. To help get you to the point where you can better afford a permanent life insurance plan.

The new Allstate Gap Closer Plan is just one of our many plans that can help solve the young family's life insurance problem.

You always knew life insurance was worth it; now you can afford it. Ask your Allstate Agent.

THE GAP CLOSER PLAN

Allstate

Allstate
LIFE INSURANCE

Allstate Life Insurance Co., Northbrook, IL.

The benefits described are provided through the six-year plan available with our Renewable and Convertible Term policy

The boy in the Allstate ad "demonstrates" all the cost items young families face that stand in the way of buying life insurance. It is an example of the effective use of people in an ad. (Courtesy Allstate Life Insurance)

womenswear, and discount houses, have their own artists and photographers on their staffs and also use free-lance talent. The typical advertisement of the small retail wearing-apparel shop includes an illustrated item or two supplied by a manufacturer's ad book or a local free-lance artist. No background or setting is used for the item because of space limitations. But the large department store often contracts for full pages of newspaper space, and illustrations are more elaborate. Settings are important. Garden furniture looks best when shown in an outdoor setting, and interior furniture appears at home in a scene where part of the room is shown along with the featured items. In a large ad, the ample space permits this embellishment so that the reader can imagine how the items will fit into real-life surroundings.

Photography or Artwork? The local advertiser uses the newspaper as the basic advertising medium, and newspaper stock is coarse compared with the coated stock available in magazines. The offset reproduction (or the engraving) of the photograph to be used in a newspaper ad must not be too fine or detailed, or the darker portions will appear muddy. Because of this lack of clarity and definition, many retailers use artwork in preference to photographs. A good rule to follow is to use artwork in small newspaper ads. When sizes of a quarter-page or larger can be afforded, and when ample space within the ad is available for the illustration, photography can be used with satisfactory results. (Types of artwork and techniques of reproducing them are described in Chapter 16.)

The Store Logo as Illustration The name of the store must appear in a prominent position in each of the store's advertisements. This element is called the logotype (or logo, or signa-

ture). While it is usually run at the base of the ad, there is no hard-and-fast rule about this, and some retail ads feature the store name at the top. Many sophisticated department store advertisers at times build their ads around their logos. The logo should be set apart from copy and illustration and be surrounded by white space.

Local advertisers realize the importance of the logo and treat it as an illustration. A distinctive typeface is used—or better still, the logotype is hand-lettered, the letters being designed by an artist. Once the style of the logotype is developed, it does not vary from ad to ad. Its familiarity helps the reader identify the ad and lends continuity to the advertising programs.

A well-designed and consistently used logotype is a valuable asset to an advertiser. The illustration on page 315 reproduces a variety of well-known store logos, all featuring excellence of design.

Using Color in Advertisements

When the layout stage is reached, it must be decided whether or not to use color in the ad. For the national advertiser, this is a simple decision. Will color help further the basic selling strategy of the advertisement? If it will, it should be used, in spite of the costs of preparation and the added charge set by the media. But not all ads call for color. Black-and-white photographs add realism, news value, and a documentary feeling to advertising, and the art director must determine whether these are qualities that fit in with the ad's objectives. Insurance company campaigns, financial ads, or advertisements for business machines such as office copying equipment and electric typewriters may all be well served by black-and-

F.R.TRIPLER & CO.
Established 1886
366 MADISON AVE., AT 46TH ST., N.Y. 10017 • (212) MU2-1760

—L.L.Bean—™
Outdoor Sporting Specialties

wallachs

Twenty-seven fine stores.

on the green at Boar's Head
Charlottesville, Va. 22901

Neiman-Marcus

FILENE'S

the•picket fence

San Francisco's British Goods Store Since 1939

I.magnin

These store logotypes, or signatures, are designed to stand out and be distinctive. Their repetition helps the reader identify the store and gives continuity to the advertising.

466 north rodeo drive, beverly hills, calif. 90210

white photographs. On the other hand, beauty aids need the full-color treatment to show skin tones and the color of the cosmetic. Foods look appetizing in color ads but lack appeal in black and white. Travel ads are more effective when color makes scenes come to life. (See Color Plate 13.)

Color adds fun, dimension, life, and excitement and should be used for products that benefit from these characteristics. Above all, the use of color allows the manufacturer to show precisely how the product's package looks on dealers' shelves and thus helps brand identification. The distinctive label on a can of Campbell's soup would look drab in black and white; so would the Heinz ketchup bottle and label.

But like illustrations, color should be used in a functional way to enhance the selling message. Color used merely as decoration is a waste of money.

The desire to use color to sell goods and services must also be controlled by the practical reality of the advertiser's budget. Sometimes color cannot be afforded. Check the SRDS listings for magazines reproduced in Chapter 6. Item 6 in the listing shows the premiums that must be paid when color is used.

Color in Local Advertisements

In outdoor and transit media, color is used in almost every instance. In newspapers while the use of one or more colors has become common, the bulk of local advertising is printed in black and white. But newspapers offer color in several ways, the most important being ROP (run of paper) color. ROP color is generally available in one color and black, two colors and black, and three colors and black (full color). Typical prices are listed in the *Cincinnati Post and Times-Star* local rate card illustrated in Chapter 6.

Because most newspaper advertising is black and white, the use of color in newspapers has more attention-getting value than it has in magazines, where many ads are printed in full color. But ROP color in newspaper ads will not guarantee selling success. Its cost can add 20 percent or more to the basic space charges so that more goods and services must be sold to pay for the ad. Retail stores using color should test the advertising for pulling power before committing themselves to its regular use. Many successful large retailers have in this way discovered that the use of ROP color, when it enhances the selling strategy, more than pays its way. (See Color Plate 3.)

A drawback in using color in newspaper advertising is that newspaper stock, coarser than that used in magazines, reduces definition, and ads appear muddy unless great care is taken in the application of color. Subtle effects must be avoided. Small details run the risk of being printed "out of register," or out of place. Small type printed on a color background will be unreadable. Bright, clean colors should be used, and the art director should try for marked contrasts, not delicate gradations. (See Color Plates 3 and 15.) Good reproduction can be achieved with *process color* (the ad is overprinted by a series of plates, each inked with a different color), but spot color is easier to use. *Spot color* refers to the use of color in portions of the ad only, to emphasize key elements such as headline, store logotype, or a large panel.

Preprinted Color Inserts

In recent years, the newspaper industry has made important advances in color reproduction. Preprinted inserts are comparable in quality to magazine color reproductions. *Preprinted inserts* are advertisements that are not printed on the newspaper press but are prepared in advance elsewhere and then by various methods incorporated into each copy of the newspaper. More than 1,100 newspapers now offer this service.

Types of Inserts   There are three kinds of preprinted inserts, Hi-Fi, SpectaColor, and Multi-Page. A Hi-Fi insert is a full-color ad printed on a roll of newsprint. The side containing the ad has a coated finish somewhat similar to the finish on magazine paper stock, and the reverse side is blank, with a finish of newspaper stock quality. After the ad has been prepared, the roll is fed into the newspaper presses and receives regular printing on the reverse side. In this roll-fed system, cutting off the paper to page size is at random and the page will be cut at different positions. It is, therefore, necessary for the art director to design a Hi-Fi ad so that it can be cut at any point and still deliver the basic message. Thus, various elements of the ad are repeated.

SpectaColor inserts are similar to Hi-Fi inserts except that the layout need not be designed to accommodate random cutting. A special electric-eye surveillance method is used to cut the page at the borders of the ad.

Multi-Page inserts are separate sections of eight pages devoted to advertising and promotion. They are preprinted at an offset plant and then incorporated into newspapers as separate sections. Often they are included in Sunday editions.

Use of Inserts   Local advertisers rarely use Hi-Fi and SpectaColor inserts. Their cost is considerable, and they require advance preparation time. Even after the insert has been produced, the newspaper sets a closing date several days in advance of the publication date. This cuts down on the traditional time flexibility offered by newspapers. However, if a local advertiser with a large budget can justify the cost and plan well ahead, these forms of inserts can be used successfully.

Choosing the Type

Typesetting is part of the advertising production process, but choosing type is an important creative act. Well-selected type can express moods and can add character to an advertisement. Hundreds of typefaces are available, and each one says something different. Type

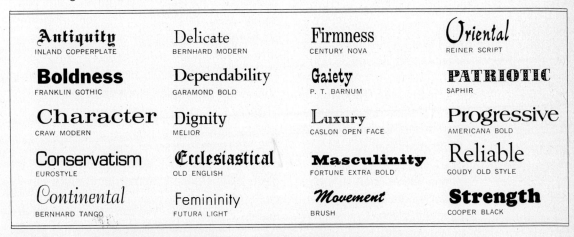

Typefaces can suggest moods, as these examples show. The name of each typeface is given directly below each word. (Courtesy Boise Cascade Envelopes)

can be loud and blatant, quiet and dignified, raucous or well-bred. The type chosen for a bank ad would be quite different from that used for a high-fashion women's retail shop. The illustration on page 317 shows how different typefaces can suggest different moods.

The main requirement for a typeface is that it be readable. The type should do its part in helping the reader get the message. If it is too ornate, distracting, crowded or too small for the average prospect to read, it has not served its main function of delivering a legible message.

Classes of Type

The largest division of typefaces is by class, and the most important class of type is roman. *Roman type* is characterized by letters that have contrasting thick and thin strokes and *serifs*, small lines that extend from the ends of the letters to give an ornamental effect. Within the roman class are many faces, such as Caslon and Bodoni, all with the same basic characteristics.

Other classes of type are block letter, cursive, and ornamental. *Block letter* uses uniform strokes of the same weight and is usually "sans" (without) serif—when serifs are used, the lines forming them are equal in weight to the lines of the balance of the letter. Helvetica is a typical face in the block letter class. The text of this book is printed in Helvetica light. *Cursive type* is found in either italicized form or scriptlike form. It resembles handwritten letters. Bank Script and Bernhard Cursive are examples of cursive faces. Because these typefaces are harder to read than roman and block, they should be used sparingly, and in headlines and captions rather than in body copy. They can suggest a note of formality or, in some cases, a feminine touch. *Ornamental type* is a catch-all group with many faces derived from the other three classes, and it is used for embellishment and decorative effect or to create a special mood—perhaps Old England or the Gay Nineties.

Typeface Subdivisions

As stated above, a class of type may have many different typefaces within it. For example, roman type can be further subdivided into Bodoni, Century, Caslon, Cheltenham, and other typefaces. Each typeface has a family: Trade Gothic may be further described as Trade Gothic Bold, a **boldface,** or more heavily imprinted type; Trade Gothic Condensed, a **condensed type** with less width to the letters than a regular Trade Gothic typeface; or Trade Gothic Italic, an *italic* type whose letters slant, or lean to the right. These different members of the family go well together because of their basic similarity of design.

The family contains many *series,* or sizes of typeface. The size of a letter is measured in *points,* an arithmetical system used to describe the height of letters. There are 72 points to an inch, which means that a letter of type one inch high is called 72-point type. Type is not generally made in sizes smaller than 6-point, and 8-, 9-, 10-, and 12-point sizes are commonly used for legibility. The following lines show words set in various points of type:

This is set in 6-point Helvetica Light.

This is set in 8-point Helvetica Light.

This is set in 10-point Helvetica Light.

This is set in 12-point Helvetica Light.

A *type font* is a set of type in one face and one series, such as 8-point Century Italic. It includes uppercase (capital) letters and lowercase (small) letters, numbers, and punctuation marks.

Understanding this terminology is necessary for the advertising person involved in any way in making layouts. The appearance of the type helps determine the character of the layout and the readability of the final ad. When the ad is ready for production, the layout must carry instructions to the typesetter about the faces and sizes to be used. Type specifying and composing procedures are described in Chapter 16.

Some Guides for Using Type

Selecting a typeface within a class of type can be a baffling task for the beginner trying to do it by using a printer's type book. The national advertiser employing an advertising agency has available art directors who have a feel for type or type specifiers, specialists whose only job is selecting type and "casting" it (measuring the copy as type-specified against the space allotted to it in the layout to determine whether it fits). The local advertiser's task is made simple because the newspaper carries only a limited number of popular typefaces, and it is therefore difficult to go wrong. And the newspaper's

advertising staff or local printers are usually pleased to offer advice in this area.

Unless one is an expert in the field, it is wise to stick to faces within the roman class for copy blocks or body text. Readers are most familiar with roman, so use of this type won't cause confusion. Certain sans serif faces, such as Helvetica—in which the text for this book is set —and Laurel, are very common and can also be used for copy. The use of ornamental and cursive faces should be restricted to headlines, subheads, short captions, and lead-ins; care should be taken not to overdo them. They are available to add character and feeling when it fits the strategy of the ad. Roman and block letters are, of course, satisfactory for heads and other words in display, when they are set apart from the rest of the copy.

It is a good plan to stay within a type class when using more than one face. If several different typefaces of varying classes are used, confusion and a busy appearance result.

Vocabulary

Define the following terms and use each one in a sentence.

Artwork	Preprinted inserts
Block letter	Process color
Boldface	*Reader's Digest* size
Comprehensive	Reverse type
Condensed type	Roman type
Copywriter's rough	Rough layout
Cursive type	Series
Italic	Serif
Logotype	Spot color
Mechanicals	Thumbnails
Optical center	Typeface
Ornamental type	Type font
Points	White space

Review Questions

1. What purposes does a layout serve? What is its primary purpose?
2. List three kinds of layouts and describe their uses.
3. What are three important considerations in making a layout?
4. Describe the difference between symmetrically balanced ads and asymmetrically balanced ads.
5. Name two types of special magazine space units.
6. Be able to discuss in class what the use of people in illustrations can accomplish.
7. What types of products benefit from the use of color in advertisements? Why?
8. What four methods of using colors are available today in newspaper advertising?
9. Name the four classes of type and select the one that is generally most satisfactory for use in setting copy blocks. Why is this so?
10. List the best uses of the three other classes of type in advertisements.

Activities

1. Prepare a copywriter's rough for the following assignment. Your task, as a copywriter, is to give some guidance to a department store art director in laying out the illustration, headline, and approximately 80 words of copy for an ad measuring approximately 8 inches wide by 12 inches deep. The subject is a sale of dining room furniture with a continental flavor. The main illustration is an oval dining room table and four chairs. Subsidiary items are a serving buffet and a breakfront. The headline is: "Continental dining group." A subhead is: "20% off regular prices." Prices of the units are to be separately listed in boldface. The name of the store is Gingrich.
2. Draw several thumbnail sketches for an ad featuring men's wristwatches. Several styles will be illustrated: luminous dials, dress watches, calendar watches, etc. Copy will be short (approximately fifty words), and the retail store name will be featured. Try to use symmetrical balance in at least one of the thumbnails.

Project

Try to find examples of ten of the types of ads described below in magazines and newspapers or on outdoor posters. Bring to class tearsheet examples of each, properly labeled. If examples from outdoor posters are used, make a rough sketch of the poster and label it.

1. Symmetrically balanced ad
2. Asymmetrically balanced ad
3. Ad in which layout and type say "quality merchandise"
4. Ad with a border
5. Multi-item retail ad
6. Retail ad featuring coordinated merchandise
7. Ad with dark-toned background and reverse type
8. Ad that uses people in its illustration as demonstrators or in another functional way
9. Ad that uses people merely as mannequins
10. Ad using a photograph
11. Ad using artwork
12. Store logo that is treated as an "illustration"
13. Ad that uses color in a functional way
14. Ad that uses roman type in headling or copy
15. Ad that uses more than one typeface
16. Example of a special magazine space unit

Career Ladder

As head art director in the collateral advertising department of a home appliance manufacturer, you need a young assistant. The job would mainly be preparing mechanicals, but there would be some simple layout work, too. You are considering two applicants. The first has the following background: college art major, with some courses in advertising layout, package design, and typography. Extracurricular activity: production manager of the yearbook. Summer jobs: camp counselor and working in a fast-food restaurant.

The second applicant has been working after graduation in a department store as a window display assistant. This applicant was head of student government and has painting as a hobby, turning out respectable watercolors. Summer employment: odd jobs on the local newspaper. Which applicant would you choose, and why?

CHAPTER SIXTEEN

ESSENTIALS OF PRINT PRODUCTION

Print production or *mechanical production* refers to all the steps of producing print advertising. Production for print media differs from the production phases called for in the broadcast media, and, of course, completely different mechanical techniques are used for each. Radio and television production will be discussed in Chapters 17 and 18; here we discuss print production.

It is necessary for anyone involved in advertising to have a basic familiarity with the various processes involved in the mechanical production of print advertising. Of course, to become proficient in these procedures, one needs a more specialized training and on-the-job apprenticeship. Advertising people must know how to call on the services of typesetters, engravers, and printers and be able to judge the quality of their work. But advertising people need not be skilled in these tasks themselves.

The last chapter described the creative aspects of one phase of print production, the area of type and its selection. Now we must study the mechanical aspects, how to prepare the

copy we write for typesetting. This is the first step in mechanically producing ads in a form that enables them to appear in newspapers, magazines, and other print media.

Making Copy Ready for Typesetting

When making copy ready for typesetting, the advertiser has in hand the layout, the finished illustration, and the copy. The advertiser marks up the page of written copy with instructions for the typesetter. A national advertiser will have the copy set by a typesetting company. A large department store may do the same in order to use distinctive typefaces not available in newspaper composing rooms. A small retailer will ordinarily use the services of the newspaper in which the ad will appear for assistance in preparing the ad as well as for typesetting.

The layout should also be marked up to indicate where the various blocks of copy, when set, will be placed. It will be helpful at this point to refer to three illustrations. In Chapter 15 is a rough layout for a retail store ad. The first figure in this chapter shows the same layout marked up, and the next figure shows the copy for this layout also marked up. Note on the marked layout that the circled copy blocks A through E correspond to the blocks of written copy similarly marked. The marked layout also contains handwritten instructions to the typesetter that specify face, size, and *leading* of type.

Leading (pronounced as in "led") refers to the white space that appears between the lines of type. Leads of various heights are measured in points, the same units of measurement used to determine the height of letters. (Remember, 72 points equal one inch.) When leads are not used, copy is said to be *set solid,* a form resulting in copy that is cramped and not easy or comfortable to read. Most of the copy for this book is set with 3-point leading, but an example of unleaded type appears in Chapter 6.

Photostating the Layout

The layout has served as a guide to the artist or the photographer. Now it performs the function of passing instructions along to the typesetter.

Often, as production proceeds, it is necessary to use duplicates of the original layout. Photostats, or stats, are made of the layout for this purpose. A *Photostat* is a relatively inexpensive camera-made duplicate of drawings, photos, or any flat-surface visuals, reproduced on sensitized paper. It is a rough reproduction with little clarity and definition, but it serves its ordinary purposes as a duplicate. A photostatic negative (black and white reversed) is made by the camera, and then as many positive copies (black and white reproduced as on the original) as are needed are made.

A reproduction of a layout made by an office copier such as a Xerox copier can often serve the same purpose as a stat, but in this case, the

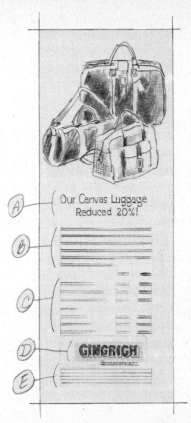

The layout has been marked up to indicate where the copy shown on page 324 is to be placed after it has been set in type.

layout can be reproduced only in a limited range of sizes. A photostatic negative of a layout or any of its elements can be increased or decreased in size as required and thus offers more flexibility.

Ensuring that the Copy Fits

Typesetting copy is an expensive procedure, and so when copy is too long or too short for the space allocated in the layout and copy additions or cuts must be made, costs spiral upward. Obviously, we should write copy that will fit the available space as closely as possible. Even when newspapers, for example, set type at no charge to the advertiser, it is good business to make sure the copy fits. Resetting wastes time.

One way of determining whether copy fits is measurement by the square inch; however, because this gives only a rough indication of copy-to-layout fit, it is not a recommended procedure. Briefly, in this method the total number of words of copy to be set in a designated copy area are counted and divided by the number of words that can be set in a square inch of a selected typeface. Then the layout space occupied by the copy block is measured in square inches, and the copy is expanded or cut as necessary before typesetting.

A more complicated but more accurate method of ensuring that copy to be set exactly fills the space allocated is to count the characters. This procedure is recommended when fit is essential. It is based on the typographical measuring term *pica* (pronounced "pyka"). A pica is a unit of measurement ¹/₆ of an inch long; 1 pica equals 12 points.

In this method, the number of letters, spaces, and punctuation marks, all called *characters*, in a block of copy are added up. Then the copy area of the layout is measured in picas. Having determined the typeface, type size, and leading (10-point Century Expanded with 2-point leading, for example), the specifier casts the copy. The specifier knows from the Century type book that 10-point Century Expanded contains 2.40 characters to the pica and also knows the width in picas of each copy line in the layout.

If the written copy totals 300 characters and the width of the copy lines in the layout is 3 inches, or 18 picas, each line in the layout set in 10-point Century Expanded would accommodate approximately 43 characters (18 picas times 2.40 characters per pica). Dividing 300 characters by 43 indicates that this much copy would run 7 lines deep, set solid. Since 2-point leading, or separation between lines, is indi-

cated, the depth of this copy block would be 70 points for the typeface (7 lines times 10 points per line) plus 2 points leading times 7 lines. This comes to 84 points, or 7 picas. Since there are 6 picas to the inch, the depth of the copy would be 1¹/₆ inches.

If a copy area 3 inches wide by 1¹/₆ inches deep closely fits the copy area indicated by the layout, the copy can be set with no additions or deletions.

The character count may seem overcomplicated, but it is routine practice where close fitting is essential. Some advertisers can be more relaxed; in most retail advertising, it doesn't matter if the copy runs a line shorter or a line longer than the layout area indicates. Here a shortcut can be used: type can be estimated from specimen blocks of copy of various lengths and widths that appear in type books. The specifier can count the number of words in

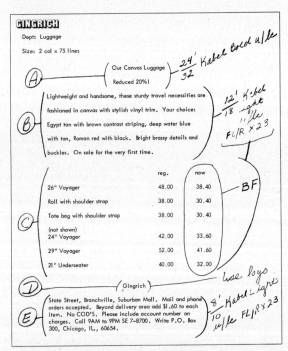

The typed copy is keyed to the layout on page 323. Typesetting instructions are indicated for each copy element.

12 point 2.1 Characters Per Pica

Simplicity and good taste are the keynotes of good typography. Type should be selected with an attempt to interpret appropriately the message to be printed. ABCDEFGHIJKLMNOPQRSTUVW ($1234567890)

12 point Italic 2.1 Characters Per Pica

Simplicity and good taste are the keynotes of good typography. Type should be selected with an attempt to interpret appropriately the message to be printed. ABCDEFGHIJKLMNOPQRSTUVW ($1234567890)

14 point 1.8 Characters Per Pica

Simplicity and good taste are the keynotes of good typography. Type should be selected with an attempt to interpret appropriately the mes- ABCDEFGHIJKLMNOPQRST ($1234567890)

These specimen blocks of typeset copy from a typesetter's book are used as a guide in estimating how the copy will fit in a layout.

a block of specimen 10-point Century Expanded or Caslon Old Style and then count the words in the copy to be set and get a fairly close idea of how the copy will fit.

Changing Copy Before Setting Type

Casting copy is one way to save the time and money involved in resetting type when it doesn't fit the planned-for space. It is also important to make copy changes of any kind before the copy is set, for these same reasons. Some advertising people develop an unfortunate habit of rethinking the copy after it has been set; this causes additional resetting. The time to improve the selling effectiveness of an ad is before copy goes to the typesetter. Written changes, inserts, and the like cost nothing before the type is set. The copy should be given a final look before it's sent to the typographer.

Composing Type

When copy and headlines have been specified, they are turned over to the typesetter for *composition,* or setting in lines, as required. Several methods of type composition are in use today. The earliest form originated in 9th-century China, when a process of printing using clay plates and wooden blocks was invented. Printing was not practiced in Europe until centuries later.

Handsetting

Handsetting type today is done in the same way that Johann Gutenberg used when he printed his famous Bible in Mainz in 1456. In *handsetting,* the compositor selects individual characters or type from a case or series of compartments in a tray or drawer and assembles them as the copy indicates on a composing stick, a hand-held small tray. The lines of type, composed and spaced, are then arranged and locked in a galley, a tray used for proofing purposes. Next the type is inked, and proofs, or copies, are "pulled." These *galley proofs* are then *proofread,* or compared for accuracy with the original typed copy.

This method is slow and expensive, but it gives the excellent results of craftsmanship. Because it is a process done by a person rather than a machine, words can be carefully spaced; thus handset type has a pleasing visual effect. It is sometimes used today for setting headlines and other display elements because they are so important in an ad.

Mechanical Typesetting

For the main body of the copy of an advertisement, *mechanical typesetting,* setting of type by machine, is used. In *Linotype* and Intertype machines, the typesetting mechanism is activated by an operator using a keyboard. When a key for a character or a space is struck, the matrix, or form of the character, is passed to a "line collector," a device that forms the predetermined length of a line of copy. The line is carried mechanically to a chamber where hot metal fills the matrices and molds the line into one long piece. The matrices are returned for reuse. The lines of type are cooled and ejected to a tray, where they are assembled in proper order.

The Linotype is a hot and noisy machine, but it can set newspaper columns of type, and some local advertising copy is set by this machine. If the copy format is irregular or complicated, requiring special characters or corrections, the Linotype method is slow and inefficient.

The *Monotype* machine avoids some of these difficulties. The operator uses a keyboard, but the keys punch a paper tape, which represents the matrices in Linotype. When inserted in the casting machine, the punched tape "instructs" and activates matrices. The

rest of the procedure is similar to Linotype operation. Monotype features some excellent typefaces.

Typewriter Composition A machine similar to a typewriter, but printing a much clearer, better-defined image than ordinary typewriter type, is used to "set" the copy in *typewriter composition.* The image is put on a printing plate by a photographic method. The quality of such reproduction is now excellent, and costs of using the method are relatively low. It is practical for intracompany use—for bulletins, pamphlets, and company magazines. It can also be used profitably for mailings, broadsides, and dealer booklets.

Photographic Typesetting Several machines use the process of photography to set type. This method, called *phototypesetting,* or photocomposition, operates by taped instruc-

In photocomposition, a keyboard on a computer terminal is used to type out the text. In place of manuscript, the text appears on a video screen. When completed, the text is stored in the computer's memory. (Photograph by Bruce Gilden)

tions issued from a keyboard or a computer. The "matrix" in this case is a photograph of all the characters in a specific size of a typeface, such as 8-point Caslon Old Style. These pictures of characters are scanned by a strobe lamp that, on instruction, selects the characters wanted and flashes them through a lens to a photosensitive surface that is subsequently developed. Various typefaces and type sizes are contained on photographs in the machine and can be retrieved by dialing as they are needed.

Large metropolitan newspapers are converting from Linotype to photocomposition, or "cold type." On July 3, 1978, *The New York Times* changed to this new method. Even the reporter's typewriter has been discarded at the *Times*. Instead, the reporter writes the story on a computer terminal with a keyboard like a typewriter, but with a black video screen on which the "typed" story appears in green letters. Special keys permit on-the-spot changes in the copy. The reporter's story then goes into computer memory and is retrieved by an editor on a video screen where changes are made as necessary, headlines added, and type faces and sizes specified.[1]

Electronic Typesetting Photocomposition is limited in production to the speed of the keyboard operator but has led to a revolutionary method known as electronic typesetting. The system is operated by a programmed computer. In this method, a cathode-ray tube "paints" characters on a screen, producing lines of text that are recorded on photographic film. The film can then be printed by the photo-offset process. RCA, Mergenthaler Linotype, Intertype, and IBM are currently producing machines using this method of typesetting.

[1] *The New York Times*, July 3, 1978, pp. 21L and 38C.

Justifying Lines

When copy is set in a block where the right-hand margin is a vertical straight line, as in this book, it is necessary to *justify* the line, spacing out the letters in words or adding spaces between words so that the lines are of equal length. Obviously, in handsetting this is done on a visual basis by the typesetter. In Linotype, the operator justifies by inserting expandable wedges in the line. Monotype "advises" the operator punching the tape when to insert spaces to justify, while typewriter composition machines contain a device that allows for spacing out lines for justifying. In electronic typesetting, the typed text is automatically formed into justified lines. Of course, when the layout indicates that the right-hand margin of the copy should be irregular or "run ragged," no justification is needed.

Proofreading Copy

Typographers make mechanical errors because they sometimes misinterpret and because they are human. The advertiser must check the galley proofs supplied by the typesetter against the original manuscript, make corrections as necessary, and send the marked-up proof to the typographer, who returns a new proof. Local advertisers must insist on seeing proofs of ads when newspapers set type and reproduce illustrations for them. This may seem like an obvious procedure, but some newspapers, particularly smaller ones, will not submit proofs unless specifically told to do so.

Principal Printing Processes

Three major printing processes are in use today, all requiring the use of plates: letterpress, gravure, and offset lithography. A fourth printing process is the screen process, formerly called *silk screen,* which uses stencils rather than plates. The screen process is mainly used on packaging and store displays. The plate systems of letterpress, gravure, and offset are discussed below.

Letterpress

The earliest printing process is still used extensively because it delivers high-quality, well-defined impressions. This is the *letterpress* method, or printing from raised inked surfaces. By various means, the inked plate is pressed onto the paper. The fastest method is the rotary press; curved printing plates are placed on a cylinder and under pressure, and they are rolled against another cylinder carrying paper fed from rolls.

Gravure

Printing can also be accomplished by a method that is the opposite of letterpress, called *gravure.* The area to be printed is etched below the surface of the plate and filled with ink. The rotary system is used, the printing cylinder rotating through a pool of ink that fills the recessed portion of the plate. The upper surface, or nonprinting area, is then wiped clean, and the cylinder is rotated against its paper-bearing companion, transferring the impression to the paper.

Offset Lithography

Lithography is a method in which a flat plate does the printing. The plate is chemically treated so that the printing areas accept ink while the nonprinting areas reject it. Direct lithography, in which the plate prints directly on paper, is not as important today as *offset lithography,* a method using a middle rotating "carrying" cylinder that takes the image from the plate cylinder and carries it to paper on the impression cylinder. These cylinders can rotate at tremendous speeds in modern offset presses. Quick production is the reason for the growth of offset lithography over direct lithography. In the United States 70 percent of all newspapers have converted from letterpress to offset.

The middle "carrying" cylinder is covered with rubber or a similar resilient composition. Sandage and Fryburger point out that "the use of rubber . . . makes it possible to print fine designs and photographs on fairly coarse paper, since the flexibility of rubber will adapt the printing surface to the rough paper area."[2]

Photoengraving

The plates used for printing purposes are produced by a photographic process called *photoengraving.* The plate can be in relief, in which case plate areas not to be printed are etched or cut away; or it may be just the opposite, as in gravure. A third alternative is printing from the completely flat surface of a lithographic plate.

Photoengraving reproduces illustrations as well as type. When the art work or photo of an advertisement is made, it is assembled with typeset proofs of the copy plus all the other elements, such as hand-lettered headlines and logotypes, and then is photographed. The image on the negative is then transferred to a metal plate that can print the now-completed ad.

Illustrations and Their Plate Requirements

Illustrations in advertising are restricted only by the imagination of the advertiser, as long as

[2] C. H. Sandage and Vernon Fryburger, *Advertising Theory and Practice,* Richard D. Irwin, Inc., Homewood, Ill., 1967, p. 419.

they can be executed on a flat surface. Many kinds of art forms have appeared in advertising layouts at one time or another, but we will discuss five principal types of illustrations—line drawings, line drawings with benday, wash drawings, halftones and dropouts—and the different photoengraving techniques required to reproduce them.

Line Drawings   Drawings that consist of black lines and black solids, with no intermediate tones, are called *line drawings.* Because of this contrast of black against a white printing surface, line drawings have a sharp, clear effect that is suitable for graphs, charts, simple sketches of people and merchandise items, and small-space illustrations, but it is difficult for a line drawing to illustrate texture or color differentiations.

For the sake of simplicity, the photoengraving process involved in reproducing line drawings and the other illustrations being considered will be described in terms of letterpress. However, other printing processes, such as gravure and offset lithography, can also be applied to all these types of illustrations.

Through the photoengraving process, the line drawing is reproduced as a line cut, an uncomplicated and inexpensive plate for printing purposes. The drawing is photographed, and the negative is transferred to sensitized metal. The metal is subjected to acid, but through chemical treatment, the "lines" are untouched. The acid etches away the nonprinting areas of the metal, and the lines are left in relief. When inked, the lines duplicate the original line drawing on a paper.

Line Drawings with Benday   To overcome to a certain extent the lack of tone and texture of simple line drawings, the *benday* method can be used. Benday is a pattern of tiny lines or dots of various degrees of density, which can

be placed as desired over any part of a line drawing. The benday method is often used in newspaper advertising, but care must be taken not to use too fine a benday screen or the printing ink will fill in the area between the dots, resulting in murkiness. Line cuts with benday are produced by the same photoengraving process as simple line cuts.

Wash Drawings   With application techniques such as paintbrush and ink or black watercolor, various tones and shades of gray can be achieved in a *wash drawing.* These tonal areas can be combined with the sharpness of a line drawing. Wash drawings are particularly suitable for portraying textures of materials. They can convey mood and feeling, while line drawings alone cannot, and by emphasizing the tone of certain important areas and deemphasizing tone in unimportant areas they can draw the reader's attention to features that are major

A title on the door...rates a **Bigelow** on the floor.

Whether it's a title on the door, or taking title on a house, be sure it's a Bigelow Carpet on your floor. For Residential Carpet information: send for our "Great Beginnings" Booklet. For Contract Carpet information: send for our "Proven Performers" Booklet. Bigelow-Sanford, Inc., P.O. Box 3089, Greenville, SC 29602.

A SPERRY AND HUTCHINSON COMPANY

Artwork in this Bigelow ad consists of a wash drawing combined with line drawings. Highlight dropouts have been used in the wash drawing to add texture. (Courtesy Bigelow-Sanford, Inc.)

selling points. Various painting techniques serve the same purposes.

Halftones All photographs and all artwork other than line drawings require a special photoengraving process because of their tonal variations. A *halftone* is a photoengraving plate with small dots of various sizes in relief that reproduce a variety of tones. The dots carry the printing ink and apply it to the surface to be printed in the letterpress method, and the smaller the dot, the lighter the impression. Halftone engravings cost more than line cuts.

In the preparation of halftones, the original illustration is photographed through a glass on which are imposed horizontal and vertical lines forming a screen. The crossing lines are reversed in printing so that they appear as white space, while the dots between the lines appear in final form as black-to-gray tones. The measurement of the screen is on the basis of lines per square inch; measurements vary from 55 lines for coarse screens to 150 lines and more. Newspaper stock is coarse, and for best reproduction it takes screens of 60- or 65-line size. Magazine paper can handle higher-count screens and thus give more defined reproductions of illustrations.

The halftone plate is created in the same way as the line cut, once the dot pattern is transferred to metal. Acid etches away the untreated areas between the dots, and the dots stand forth in relief, ready to take printing ink. Under a magnifying glass, the dot pattern in artwork and photos in magazines and newspapers becomes visible. Note the effects of the different screens in the photo below.

A line drawing can be combined with a half-

| 55 Line | 85 Line | 100 Line | 133 Line | 150 Line |

Here a photograph has been reproduced as a halftone engraving. Note that the reproduction becomes clearer as the number of lines per inch is increased. (Courtesy Allied Mills, Inc.)

tone picture on a *combination plate*. An item that looks better as a line drawing may be shown in the foreground of a photograph. Also, line borders and decorations can be added to photographs when a combination plate is used.

Dropouts Local advertisers can use a highlight dropout photoengraving method to allow the background white of the printing paper to appear within the illustration itself. If an ordinary halftone plate is made, it will be completely covered with dots, and thus all areas of the illustration will print as light gray to dark. But the advertiser may want certain areas of the reproduced illustration to be white, and in this case chemicals are applied to these areas of the plate to eliminate the dots.

Four-Color Process Engravings

The photoengraving method used in producing full-color letterpress advertisements is basically similar to that used in making black-to-gray halftones. This method is called *four-color process engraving* because only four colors are used: yellow, magenta (process red), cyan (process blue), and black. When combined, these colors will reproduce every other color.

In this four-color process, the color illustration is photographed through screened glass four times; in each case filters are used to block out all color but the primary color needed. This produces color separations. These color separations are transferred to sensitized metal, and the nonprinting surfaces are etched away by an acid bath, leaving dots that can carry ink.

The four resulting plates now represent the four colors that, when blended, will accurately reproduce the full color of the original artwork or photograph. A proof of each plate is pulled, along with a series of cumulative proofs that build up the colors one by one by surprinting until the final, correct result is achieved. These proofs are called *progressives* or *progs*. All these proofs are approved by the advertiser and given to the printer or magazine for guidance. When the illustration is printed, each plate is applied to the future color page in proper sequence, care being taken to achieve perfect *registration,* or alignment, to avoid a ragged or color halo effect. (See Color Plates 14 and 15.)

Vocabulary

Define the following terms and use each one in a sentence.

Benday	Justify	Phototypesetting
Character	Leading	Pica
Combination plate	Letterpress	Print production
Composition	Line drawing	Proofread
Four-color process engraving	Linotype	Registration
Galley proof	Mechanical typesetting	Set solid
Gravure	Monotype	Silk screen
Halftone	Offset lithography	Typewriter composition
Handsetting	Photoengraving	Wash drawing
	Photostat	

Review Questions

1. How is information on desired typeface and type size transmitted to the typographer by the advertiser?
2. What is the purpose of leading in setting lines of type?
3. Why is it important to make sure copy, when set, will fit the space allocated to it on the layout?
4. Briefly describe the recommended way of ensuring that copy will fit the space allocated for it. What is a shortcut that can be used?
5. In advertising, for what purposes is handset type used today?
6. List and describe five methods of composing type.
7. What are the principal printing processes, and how do they differ?
8. What is the purpose of using the benday method?

Activities

1. In Activity 1, Chapter 14, you were asked to write headlines and copy for department store merchandise and retain a duplicate of your work. Your task now is to mark up this written copy and make it ready for the typesetter. Specify the typeface (use one mentioned in this chapter, if you like) and point size for the headline and also specify the typeface, point size, and leading for the body copy. Typefaces for headline and body copy may be similar or different.
2. Below are listed several subjects for illustrations to be included in advertisements. What type of illustration would you recommend for each example, and what method of photoengraving would you use? Example: tools—hammer, power drills, plane, etc., to be featured in a local hardware dealer's newspaper ad. Type of illustration: Line drawings. Type of photoengraving: Line cuts.
   a. Women's wool dresses to be featured in a local department store's newspaper ad.
   b. New-model sports car to be announced in a national magazine printed by the letterpress method.
   c. Sirloin steak special, an item in a supermarket's newspaper ad.

Projects

1. Using your sources (newspapers and magazines), prepare a tearsheet file of examples of the following types of illustrations. Each should be properly identified.

a. Line drawing

b. Line drawing with benday

c. Halftone wash drawing

d. Halftone photograph, newspaper and magazine

e. Combination line and halftone picture

f. Halftone wash drawing or photograph with dropout technique

g. Four-color magazine advertisement

2. Visit your local newspaper, and observe its printing process. Be prepared to discuss the procedure in class. Also, examine the type books and make a list of the typefaces available for use by local advertisers.

Career Ladder

A production manager of a medium-sized advertising agency was checking bills submitted by a typographer for payment. Charges for setting type on one job (a pamphlet being prepared for a client of the agency) seemed high. The bill was for $500, but the typographer's written estimate of the cost had been only $300. On investigation, the production manager discovered from the typographer that the copy had been set, as instructed, but when galleys were returned to the agency for proofreading, the writer on the job had second thoughts on the copy and rewrote almost half of the text. Subsequent resetting entailed overtime to meet a deadline, and this explained the increase in charges.

The cost of setting the type would be eventually paid by the agency's client. The production manager knew that an explanation of the increase over estimate would be asked for by the client, whose nickname happened to be Old Eagle Eye. Several courses of action were open to the production manager. Which of the following would you advise him to do? (You can recommend more than one answer.) What are the reasons for your choice?

1. Ask the typographer, who does a lot of business with the agency, to reduce the bill to $300 as a favor.
2. Bill the client $300 and charge off the $200 as agency expense.
3. Take a long overdue vacation and forget about it.
4. Bill the client $500 and make the copywriter explain to the client why the amount was higher than estimate.
5. Bill the client $500, at the same time informing the agency contact person of all the details in case explanations are called for.
6. Inform the copy chief of the problem.

CHAPTER SEVENTEEN

WRITING AND PRODUCING TELEVISION COMMERCIALS

Writing television advertising requires many talents. Selling ideas based on copy strategy must be developed just as they are for ads for print media. But the copywriter must also constantly think in terms of visualization. Pictures must be kept in mind at all times as the commercial is written. Simultaneously, the writer must take advantage of sound—words, music, and sound effects—to enhance the values of the copy and the pictures that are created. This need not be an overwhelming task if the guides established in this chapter are followed.

As noted in Chapter 8, television advertising presents a superb opportunity to show what a product looks like and to demonstrate it in actual use. But message time is brief, and message content can't be referred to afterwards—the viewer can't reread or clip a television ad like a magazine or newspaper ad. This limitation requires that television advertising be simple, single-minded, and to the point.

Important Television Writing Terms

Following are definitions of some terms in television language that will be used in the discussion of the medium. The Green Valley script shows how these terms are used in a television script.

Script Television copy is first prepared in written form. The *script* contains copy and camera and sound instructions.

Audio Anything audible (words, music, and sound effects) that will be part of a television commercial is considered *audio*. In a script, the audio description is generally typed on the right-hand side of the page. If music is needed as a dramatic accent to copy—required to "run under" copy to create a background—or if a musical jingle is called for, such instructions appear on the audio side at the proper place.

Sound Effects *Sound effects* are noises that are not words and are part of the audio side of the script. They are indicated on a script in parentheses preceded by the initials SFX and appear in the copy at the called-for place. Typical sound effects are thunder, door slam, laughter, and the sound made by opening a soft-drink can.

Voice Over When an announcer, singer, or performer is heard but not seen, the copy is called *voice-over* copy and is prefaced on the script with the initials VO.

Direct Voice When an announcer, singer, or performer is seen as well as heard, the copy is called *direct-voice* copy. On the script it is prefaced with the initials DV.

Video Anything visual that will appear in a television commercial is classified as *video*. Video instructions appear on the left-hand side of a script opposite the accompanying audio.

Camera Instructions The writer must "instruct" the camera, when the video side of the script is being written, to film the scene from a distance or close up, to move in or out, to move across the scene, and so on. Here are some of the principal terms involved:

Extreme close-up (ECU) Camera concentrates on very tight head shot if a person is involved or concentrates very closely on an object.

Close-up (CU) Torso shot; could cover two or possibly three people.

Medium shot (MS) Middle distance. Can reveal considerable background (BG).

Long shot (LS) Distance shot.

Dolly in Camera moves into scene.

Dolly out Camera moves back.

Pan Camera moves across scene.

Cut The abrupt end of one scene and the immediate start of the next is a *cut*. The two scenes are "cut together."

Opticals *Opticals* are any visual devices added to the commercial after filming, such as *dissolve* (DIS), one scene fading out as the next fades on; *wipes,* an optical effect whereby one scene wipes another scene off the screen; *supers,* or printed copy superimposed on film or tape, *matting in,* superimposing an image on existing film or tape, and *freeze frame,* where the action is stopped and the picture becomes a still life momentarily. These opticals are prepared by an optical house when the commercial is produced on film, or are edited in immediately after shooting when tape production is used.

Length of Television Commercials

Television commercials are identified and measured by their timing, standard lengths being 1 minute, 30 seconds, 20 seconds, and 10 seconds. The 10-second length is often referred to as a 10-second *idee,* a shortened version of the word "identification." An important initial decision that an advertiser must make is how long the commercial should be. Time charges for running the various lengths must be considered, of course, but of even greater importance are copy requirements, the goals that the television message is expected to achieve in terms of sales, time for demonstration, and product or service identification. Some sales stories may require a full minute, but if the copy requirements can conceivably be handled in a shorter length, they should be; otherwise, advertising money is wasted, and the efficiency of the medium is weakened.

Turnkey & Sesame

CLIENT: Green Valley	TIMING (APPROX.):
PRODUCT: Tomato Soup - Recipe Series #3	LENGTH (APPROX.): :30
PRODUCT USE: Souperb Recipe Contest	WORD COUNT: 65 plus 4-sec. jingle

| TVO # 16-109 |
| TYPED: 7/6/-- |
| DRAFT # 2. |

TITLE: MOCK STROGANOFF DEMONSTRATION

VIDEO	SCENE NO.	AUDIO	LENGTH (APPROX.)
CU Helen Mears in Green Valley home kitchen. On table in foreground: Open can G. V. Tomato Soup, sliced pot roast on plate, attractive casserole--empty, sour cream, Worcestershire Sauce. Immed. super HELEN MEARS FROM GREEN VALLEY, and fade. On cue (*) she picks up can and holds it closer to camera.	1.	PRESENTER: (DV) Don't let a can of (*) Green Valley Tomato Soup just sit around! Here's a souperb recipe-- Mock Strognaoff.	:6
Cut. ECU. Down shot. Her hands arrange slices of pot roast in casserole.	2.	(VO) Put a pound of left-over sliced pot roast in a casserole. . .	:4
Pours in contents of can with one hand, showing label. Adds Worcestershire Sauce and mixes.	2a	(VO) Add a can of beautiful Green Valley Tomato Soup--and a tablespoon of Worcestershire Sauce.	:7
Dissolve to CU. Helen places casserole in oven.	3.	(DV) Heat 30 minutes at 350.	:3
Cut. Very tight shot. Bubbly casserole. Adds sour cream, folds in.	4.	(VO) Fold in half a cup of sour cream and heat again for 5 minutes.	:4
Dissolve to CU. She's starting to serve at kitchen table. Stack of four dinner plates.	5.	(DV) Serves four.	:2
Mat in ECU can of G. V. Tomato Soup over scene on cue (*).	5a	GREEN VALLEY QUARTET (SINGS): (VO) Soup--bee-youtiful soup... from (*) Green Valley!	:4

This is a script for a 30-second television commercial. Do you understand the camera instructions on the video side and the initials in parenthesis on the audio side? (See Chapter 5 for the Green Valley recipe contest.)

It is always easier to be long-winded than brief and to the point. Advertising writers rarely have too little to say—usually they have too much. Therefore it is easier to write a commercial in a 1-minute length than in a 30-second length. Top professional copywriters follow a simple dictum: "You don't know if it works until you try it." After a commercial is written in a 1-minute length, it should be attempted in a 30-second or 20-second length and then examined on the basis of what has been eliminated. If all that was left out was repetitive spoken words and mood or stage setting, the short version is better than the long one. Most commercials today are produced in the 30-second length, although 10-second commercials are becoming increasingly popular.

Determining Commercial Timing

Although determining commercial length is a production decision, it will be discussed here because of its importance to television copywriting. A major problem in making television commercials occurs when commercials are either too long or too short to be produced in their predetermined length. When commercials are too long, scenes and copy must be cut or eliminated altogether; and when they're too short, padding must be added—scenes lengthened and extra copy inserted. Producing material that is not used or padding short commercials is a frustrating waste of money, and usually proper planning can eliminate the need for these corrections.

Word-Count Method In broadcast media, a rule of thumb for timing is 125 words per minute of commercial broadcast time. This allows for comfortable, unhurried reading, with time available for pauses for emphasis. Copywriters often use a word count to give them a rough idea of timing. This works out to about 2 words per second of commercial time, as the following list shows:

1-minute commercial	125 words
30-second commercial	62 words
20-second commercial	41 words
10-second commercial	20 words

There is some "give" to these figures, but when the word count for a 1-minute commercial goes over 135, the prospective advertiser should be warned that there may be serious length problems.

Local advertisers are often guilty of crowding commercials with excess words, and 1-minute commercials containing 180 words are, unfortunately, not unusual. They can be read, but the result is a staccato, hurried, hard-sell rendition that cannot register selling points in an understandable way. Usually such commercials contain much repetition that could readily be eliminated.

The drawback of the word-count method is that writers relying on it tend to forget that visual action, which sometimes is not accompanied by words, also takes time; so if word count alone is considered, the commercial will run long.

Stopwatch Method In the stopwatch method, the writer reads the words aloud while timing the commercial, being careful to pause for necessary action that is unaccompanied by words, and also being careful not to rush the words but to read them at an unhurried, natural rate. This method is superior to word count, but overwriting may still occur if no time is allowed for action.

Acting-It-Out Method Sometimes, the commercial is actually acted out. Enough people to play all the parts indicated by the script perform the indicated action and read their parts.

This method is superior to other methods because it simulates the final produced version of the commercial as closely as possible and thus ensures more accurate timing.

Making Provision for Roll Time on Film Commercials

When a commercial is prerecorded on film for broadcast use, the actual length of the commercial will be 60, 30, 20, or 10 seconds, but not quite all this time can be filled with sound (voice, music, or sound effects). For 60 seconds, 90 feet of film or tape, or $1\frac{1}{2}$ feet per second, is needed, but the first $1\frac{1}{2}$ seconds of every filmed commercial are required to be silent. The picture starts $1\frac{1}{2}$ seconds before the sound; in other words, $58\frac{1}{2}$ seconds of sound are available for a 1-minute commercial, $28\frac{1}{2}$ seconds of sound for a 30-second commercial, and so on.

This requirement is necessary to give station personnel $1\frac{1}{2}$ seconds of leeway to ensure that the commercial is actually being projected on the air and that the first important words are not lost. These seconds are called *roll time* and should not be counted on by the advertiser to accomplish anything of importance. In many cases, these seconds of soundless picture will never be seen by the home viewer. When commercials are videotaped, a production method described below, the sound starts immediately, and no roll time is needed.

Choosing Live, Filmed, or Taped Commercials

Commercials can be broadcast live or filmed or videotaped in advance. *Live* means being broadcast at the moment when the video, audio, and performance of the actors are perceived by the viewer. *Filmed commercials* are pretranscribed on motion picture film containing an audio track. Previously, 35-millimeter film was preferred, but in recent years Kodak has sold a 16-millimeter film far superior to that previously available. This new film can produce excellent results and is cheaper to use than 35-millimeter. When the capabilities of the new 16-millimeter film are thoroughly understood, it can be a satisfactory substitute. A *taped commercial,* or videotaped commercial, is pretranscribed on a 2-inch plastic tape for broadcast purposes and contains an audio track.

Live broadcasting presents the possibility of human errors or "fluffs," and, of course, the live commercial cannot be repeated without additional live performances. If a one-shot is all that is needed, a live commercial is cheapest of all to produce. Filmed commercials can be repeated and, in production, shot in any scene sequence, the final film being edited and placed in proper order. This flexibility allows production to be efficiently organized.

When aired, a taped commercial is indistinguishable from a live broadcast. Also, once a scene or commercial is taped, it can be replayed on a monitor immediately without the time-consuming developing process required of film. A taped commercial, like a filmed one, can be shown repeatedly. And the tape itself can be erased, if need be, and used again.

Tape, because it can be immediately replayed, also offers another advantage. It can be approved on the spot if the advertiser is present on the set. In the early days of tape, editing was difficult. Today, computerized editing equipment is available, and editing can be done as soon as the commercial is taped. At the same time, supers can be added along with a number of opticals. One drawback of tape is that duplicate tapes are more expensive than duplicate film prints, and cost must be considered when many duplicates are needed for an extensive television spot campaign (Chapter 8). It is up to the individual advertiser to determine whether this higher cost is worthwhile.

If tape is faster and offers such superb clarity of image, why does film continue to be used in making commercials? The answer lies in the areas of quality and esthetics. To many directors, work done on film has a richer look than tape. Tape looks too "real" and gives a documentary flavor to some commercials where such an impression really doesn't belong. If time permits, many top directors prefer to use film because of its greater artistic potentials.

Types of Television Commercials

Commercial formats range from one simple scene to elaborate production numbers that involve a great deal of preparation and logistics. The important fact to remember is that complexity and large production expenses do not necessarily ensure the selling effectiveness of the commercial. Simple, inexpensive commercials can sell efficiently. One very large advertiser put it this way: "The more the commercial costs, the less it communicates to the prospect." This conclusion is overcynical; nevertheless, it is more realistic for this chapter to be devoted to simple commercials, and the more elaborate types will be treated briefly.

Presenter Commercials

The simplest commercial to execute is the one in which an on-stage announcer, actor, or actress presents the product or service to the viewer on a direct, person-to-person basis. The "presenter" can demonstrate a product, show it, talk about its good points, and compare it with competing products. The presenter generally approaches the selling problem as a salesperson would in selling face to face.

Much depends, of course, on the sincerity and conviction of the presenter.

This *presenter commercial*[1] is effective and often used. In its simplest form, it requires a single setting throughout; the setting can be a blank background (limbo setting) or a simple background such as a supermarket aisle, office, or living room. Close-ups can be included. Optical effects such as supers and dissolves can, of course, be added later as required, and if they can be afforded. Because of its simplicity, this type of commercial is often used by local advertisers. (See the storyboard of a presenter commercial for Green Valley.)

Slide Commercials

Another type of commercial that is simple to write and inexpensive to produce is a *slide commercial.* It consists of a series of still photographs or drawings that change via cuts or dissolves in synchronization with voice-over audio; that is, it consists of words illustrated by still pictures. It usually follows a classic advertising formula. The need for the product or service is established; the product or service is introduced; its advantages and benefits are extolled; and the conclusion is a call for action. Slide commercials are used by local advertisers rather than national advertisers.

Demonstration Commercials

Television advertising is most effective when the product or service is being demonstrated. Whenever possible, the writer should show the product being used or portray the product's benefits to the buyer. If a product or service contains a demonstrable advantage over its competition, often a *side-by-side demonstration* is used. Demonstrations of the ability of Bounty paper towels to soak up more moisture

[1] Sometimes called a *stand-up presenter commercial.*

than a competitive towel and of the ability of Comet Cleanser to remove stains more effectively than Brand X are typical television examples of side-by-side demonstrations.

Some of the most effective commercials consist of one continuous demonstration. The Mobil 1 motor oil commercial is simplicity itself. The selling point of the oil is that a motorist can drive for 25,000 miles without an oil change. Mobil chooses to demonstrate this mileage by showing in sequence the number of transcontinental trips a motorist could make with the product, the trips being indicated by glowing lines animated on a globe as a counter at the base of the TV picture clocks the miles. A demonstration need not occupy the

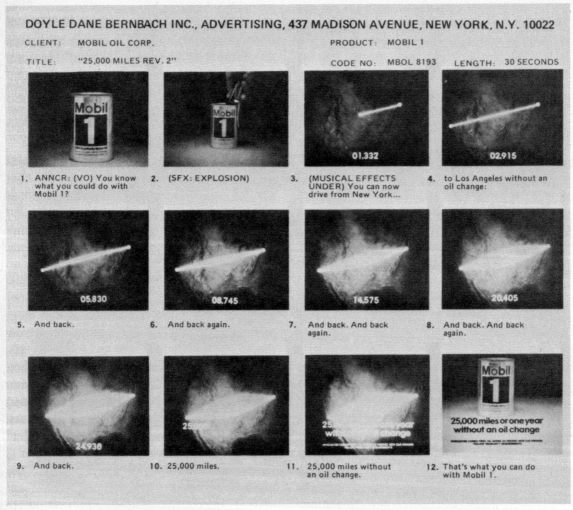

DOYLE DANE BERNBACH INC., ADVERTISING, 437 MADISON AVENUE, NEW YORK, N.Y. 10022

CLIENT: MOBIL OIL CORP.   PRODUCT: MOBIL 1

TITLE: "25,000 MILES REV. 2"   CODE NO: MBOL 8193   LENGTH: 30 SECONDS

1. ANNCR: (VO) You know what you could do with Mobil 1?

2. (SFX: EXPLOSION)

3. (MUSICAL EFFECTS UNDER) You can now drive from New York...

4. to Los Angeles without an oil change:

5. And back.

6. And back again.

7. And back. And back again.

8. And back. And back again.

9. And back.

10. 25,000 miles.

11. 25,000 miles without an oil change.

12. That's what you can do with Mobil 1.

This introductory television commercial for Mobil 1 motor oil is a single-minded visual demonstration of how far your car can go without an oil change when the product is used. (© 1978 Mobil Oil Corporation)

entire commercial; however, any commercial is improved when it contains a demonstration.

The Playlet

One of the most common forms of television advertising is the commercial that tells a story about a product or service in dramatized form. The *playlet* usually has a beginning in which actors and actresses establish a problem and an ending in which the problem is resolved by product use or demonstration.

This format is also called slice of life, problem solution, and dramatization. One of the first techniques developed in television advertising, it suffers from being overdone and is a major cause of irritation among television viewers because of its obviousness and "adiness" (a trade term used to describe blatant or corny copy). However, good casting and humorous dialogue can rescue a playlet from mediocrity. The playlet commercial is an effective format when professionally written and acted.

The Testimonial

An effective television commercial technique is the testimonial, in which a bona fide user of a product or service describes in his or her own words the satisfaction and benefits resulting from the purchase. This format, in interview form, is available to local and national advertisers alike and is a proved selling device. Naturally, this kind of commercial can't be written in advance; the copy is made up as the commercial is filmed or taped. The procedure is to find and interview interesting people (fans for a product or service), film or tape the interview, and edit the commercial to proper length, making sure that the editing does not in any way change the true meaning of the user's words. In testimonials using celebrities, the commercial script is written and rehearsed in advance.

The Mood Commercial

A mood commercial seeks through words (usually voice over) and pictures to create a feeling of acceptance for a product or service. Music, either as background or as an integral part of the commercial, often plays an important role. Some Clairol and Johnson & Johnson commercials are typical of this format.

Cosmetics, beauty aids, fashion products, and toiletries are often presented in mood commercials. But other products and services can be treated in this fashion. The controlling factor must be the advertising objective.

The Sing-and-Tell Commercial

In the sing-and-tell, or musical, commercial singers tell the product story, and sometimes dancing is thrown in to add visual interest.

A problem with commercials in which a group of singers carries the entire copy story is that the audience sometimes has trouble understanding words when they are sung and accompanied by a musical background. Important selling points may be lost. Also, musical commercials tend to be extremely expensive to produce.

These sing-and-tell commercials are not to be confused with *jingles*, short musical voice sequences mostly confined to the medium of radio and discussed in Chapter 18. A jingle is sometimes used in television as part of a commercial to express a theme or slogan and may be the entire content of a 10-second TV spot.

The Animated Commercial

The *animated commercial* achieves the illusion of movement through the filming of a series of sequential cartoon drawings. Commercials can be part animation and part live-action

Ogilvy & Mather	Client: **AMERICAN EXPRESS**
	Product: **CARD**
2 East 48th Street, New York 10017	Title: **PELE**
	Commercial No.: **XAPM 7173 (:30C)**

PELE: (IN PORTUGUESE) Do you know me?

I'm known for using my head on the soccer field, . . .

and I also use my head when I travel.

I carry the American Express Card. I've used it in more than 40 countries.

It's _known_ and _respected_ all over the world . . .

even in places where they speak strange languages . . . like English.

ANNCR (VO): To apply for an American Express Card . . .

look for this display wherever the card is welcome.

PELE: (IN ENGLISH) The American Express Card. Don't leave home without it.

This is a good example of a television commercial using a celebrity. In this campaign, attention is captured at the opening by quizzing the viewer on the celebrity's identity. (Courtesy Ogilvy & Mather/American Express)

film.[2] A commercial can start with animation and then switch to live-action film at points where reality in portraying selling features is needed.

Animation is more expensive to produce than straight live action. The production of a typical live-action film commercial might cost $25,000, whereas an animated commercial can cost $35,000 or more. The use of animation adds weeks to the film commercial's production schedule. Computer animation can now be used in taped commercials. An image is "painted" on a TV monitor screen by a technician operating a computerized system. It can be modified as desired and then edited into the commercial on the spot. The quality of the animated effect is now excellent. It is often used to add motion to corporate symbols or identifiers, for special effects and for "futuristic" imagery.

Stop motion is akin to animation. Movement is achieved by photographing a series of sequential scenes; in each scene the subject is posed in a slightly different position.

Writing Television Advertising

Unfortunately, the use of any particular commercial format won't guarantee advertising success. It is what a writer says and the strength of the selling ideas that make the difference between advertising success and failure, and if the writer remembers the guides established for writing headlines and copy explained in Chapters 13 and 14, there's a good chance of developing good television advertising. The selling principles are the same as in writing for print media, but because of the peculiarities of the television medium, execution of these principles is sometimes quite different.

Before beginning the actual script writing, the copywriter must have the product facts and selling points in mind and must work out the strategy or objective of the commercial. The writer must determine the length of the commercial. Above all, copy thinking must be simplified so that one principal selling thought will dominate the script.

Keep It Simple

Television copywriting must be more single-minded than print copywriting because of the short span of time involved. The viewer can be expected to retain only one main idea, although other ideas can be included if they support and enhance the main one. Look again at the Mobil commercial. All it sets out to achieve is to register the idea that the motor oil doesn't need to be changed for 25,000 miles, and everything visual and audible in the commercial serves to support this selling point.

In writing, stick to the important sales idea and resist the tendency to bring up an unrelated subject.

Emphasize the Visual

As the commercial is developed, the copywriter should constantly think visually. Sentences that don't suggest pictures should be avoided. Remember that television viewers are conscious first of what they are seeing; only later do they become aware of what they are hearing. Some writers make the mistake of first developing the audio side of the script completely and then filling in the video side, making up pictures to fit the words. The right way to go about developing the commercial is

---

[2] Live action should not be confused with "live" broadcasting. Live broadcasting is shown at the same time that the camera records the action in the studio. Live action refers to the photographing of actual action or objects, in contrast to animated drawings, for future commercial use.

to think visually as the words unfold, write down the video at regular intervals, and change the words when the pictures can't be made to conform.

Make Words and Pictures Work Together

Nothing confuses the viewer or kills interest more quickly than looking at a picture of one thing while the words are talking about something else. Words and picture should concentrate on the same thing at the same time. The feature should be shown and demonstrated, not just talked about. This is television's great selling opportunity, and the writer should take advantage of it.

Don't Overdo Changes of Scene

Thinking logically about scene sequence is a great asset to television copywriters. If the audience's viewpoint is firmly kept in mind, confusion can be avoided. An *establishing shot,* a scene that orients the viewer to what is about to unfold by showing a background such as a kitchen area or back-yard terrace, can then be logically followed by close-ups. When close-ups precede the establishing shot, the viewer can become disoriented.

Too many changes of scene can also be confusing. A good rule is no more than ten scenes to a 1-minute commercial and a maximum of three in a 10-second idee. Skilled writers can break this rule and get away with it, but beginning writers can't. Of course, ten scenes in a 1-minute commercial are not always necessary; a commercial can be very successful with just a single scene from beginning to end.

Copy paragraphs in scripts are sometimes written too long for the accompanying video. If the action is not interesting, or if the scene is static, the copy should be ruthlessly cut.

Use the Minimum Number of Players

Principals are actors and actresses with speaking roles or those who are seen full face on camera; *extras* are nonspeaking bit players who are nondistinguishable. Principals are expensive, for they are paid whenever the commercial is aired, whereas extras receive a single fee for their work. The copywriter should write in parts for the fewest number of principals possible, eliminating players who are not absolutely essential to the effectiveness of the commercial.

Don't Waste the Opening

The viewer is watching a favorite show, and it's time for the commercial. The fact that the set is in operation at that moment is no guarantee that the advertiser will have an audience, for the viewer does not need to leave the room to ignore the message. The viewer can "watch" without seeing, hearing, or comprehending the advertisement if it is dull, offensive, or irrelevant. Apathy is a bad climate for the advertiser. Because of this, the first few seconds of a commercial are of vital importance. Here it is necessary to capture attention and involve the viewer. This can be accomplished by video alone or by video plus audio. There are countless ways to capture attention, limited only by the creativity and imagination of the writer. Ways to capture attention include startling statements (voice over or direct voice), suspenseful scenes, humor including sight gags, conflict between two individuals, the statement of product news, statement of a problem subsequently solved by the product's attributes, and above all, scenes and words working together to establish the benefit or reward the viewer will receive if the product is purchased. If an efficient and newsworthy demonstration of a product's effectiveness has been developed, a commercial can concentrate completely on this asset.

What is important is that the opening scene, no matter how far-fetched or far out, should be related to the main selling idea or thrust of the commercial. Attention can be captured and then lost if the opening device does not relate to the rest of the commercial. This comment is, of course, true of print advertising headlines as well as TV commercials.

Follow Through after the Opening

Script development in its simplest form attempts to involve the viewer via the opening, to state a benefit or a problem, and then to indicate a solution. It identifies the product (often via a close-up), adds reasons to buy or permission to believe, includes a demonstration whenever possible, and winds up with a suggestion, request, or command to take action. The basic selling idea and the product name may be "supered" at the conclusion and included at other times in the body of the commercial. This kind of script development is only one of many commercial sequences, but it is a tried-and-true and fairly easy way to construct a commercial. This sequence is basically similar to the sequence of a print media ad and is an effective way to sell goods and services.

Although there are exceptions that have had great selling success, the product or service being advertised should be identified and pictured fairly early in a commercial. A good rule to follow is to accomplish this within the first 20 seconds of a 1-minute commercial.

While developing the commercial, the copywriter should keep a few simple guides in mind. Sentence construction should be uncomplicated and short, and cumbersome clauses should be removed and made into separate sentences. As time is short and

viewer interest fleeting, avoid big, difficult, or unusual words. State thoughts in a clear, unconfusing way. Important copy points can well be repeated, but the repetition should not follow immediately; when it does, the viewer is inclined to feel badgered.

Use the Copywriter's Checklist

Here is a handy checklist to use after the script has been written.

■ Do the words work with the pictures and support them?
■ Does the action of a scene take longer than the words indicate?
■ Are the words opposite any scene covered by no action at all?
■ Will the commercial run the proper length?
■ Are all the people necessary?
■ Is the commercial single-minded?
■ Does the opening attempt to involve the viewer?
■ Does the commercial talk in terms of benefits to the viewer?
■ Can the commercial conceivably be done in a shorter length?
■ Is the commercial padded with unnecessary scenes and words?
■ Does the commercial ask the viewer to take action?

The Storyboard

The purpose served by the layout in print advertising is served in television advertising by the *storyboard*. It is a visual plan for the advertising message. The storyboard consists of a sequence of illustrations that give a rough idea of the total commercial. Key scenes are sketched, and each is accompanied by its video instructions and the copy, or audio. The Green Valley storyboard reproduced here is typical.

A storyboard is merely an indication of the future look of a commercial. In an advertising agency, it is drawn by an art director, sketcher, or storyboard artist working with a copy of the script. Once the drawings are completed, the copy blocks are typed in or first typed on adhesive paper and then placed in proper position.

The storyboard is a handy device with which to explain the commercial to agency personnel and, later, the advertiser. It is also used as a basis for production bids by production houses

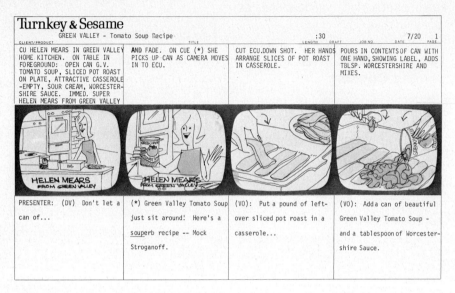

This is the storyboard of the script reproduced on page 336. It gives a rough idea of how the commercial will look when produced. Only key scenes are drawn. (Glenn Levy)

that will eventually make the commercial in film or tape.

Storyboards are a helpful but not completely necessary part of the television advertising scene. The local advertiser, developing simple one- or two-scene commercials, can dispense with them. Storyboards should be treated as an indication of a commercial's action, not as a hard-and-fast determinant of it. The producer or director of the commercial, dealing with actualities, may shoot the commercial so that it bears little resemblance to the original board.

Producing the Commercial

After the advertiser has approved a commercial, a complicated procedure involving many specialized services begins. In an agency, the producer,[3] who has often advised in the actual writing of the commercial, gives the storyboard to production houses for bids. Two or three houses submit their estimate of production costs, and one firm is selected. It may not be the lowest bidder; sometimes a higher bidder is judged best able to accomplish the objectives of the commercial.

Casting

An important part of planning the television commercial is casting the best available talent, or models, actors, and actresses, for the roles indicated by the script. Wooden, inanimate people without dramatic training can ruin a good commercial, so skill and some experience are needed to cast the right person for a role. In larger agencies, casting department members keep records and books of available talent, keep in touch with talent agencies, and stay informed on what's going on in the theater and in the movie and television industries.

Preproduction Meeting

During all these steps, key planning has been going on. The agency producer has been working out a production schedule with the chosen production house; scouting locations (if the commercial will be *on location,* or away from a studio stage); approving set designs proposed by the house; and arranging for the delivery of necessary items, such as the color-corrected product packages that will be used. This activity culminates in a preproduction meeting, where there is a final review of the commercial and decisions are made about how the commercial should be filmed or taped and what it should accomplish. Present are the agency producer, a client's representative, people from the production house (director, cameraperson, and stylist), and the agency account executive and creative people involved.

Production

The agency producer in charge of the set has the responsibility of achieving a successful filming; this responsibility can be a considerable burden, since the cost of 30-second commercials for national advertisers can run from $9,000 to $100,000 or more. (A 1-minute commercial for Levi's jeans, calling for many special effects, cost $250,000.[4]) The producer's challenge is to add "production values" to the commercial, or improve it if possible. Inventiveness in camera work and script readings can pay off in a better commercial. A good producer is part manager, part organizer, and part film maker.

---

[3] For an outline of the agency producer's job, see Chapter 4. In many advertising agencies, the writer or art director performs the producer's function, or a free-lance producer is hired for the job.

[4] *Advertising Age,* October 31, 1977, p. 56.

Postproduction Activities

At the conclusion of the shooting, if the commercial has been filmed rather than taped, the producer and the production house film editor view the rushes, or *dailies*. This material consists of all printed or developed film for the commercial. The commercial is then edited to proper length; the best shots are kept, and the others are eliminated. A rough cut, or *work print,* is made.

This stage of a film commercial is called an *interlock*. The audio (sound track) and video (pictures) are separate. On approval of the work print, opticals are added by an optical lab. At the same time, sound effects and a music track (when required) are added, and the sound levels of the commercial are balanced.

Next, the film commercial is assembled in *answer print* form. This is the complete stage of the commercial. Duplicate prints are then made and shipped to broadcast facilities for use on the air. A comfortable schedule for a film commercial is 6 weeks from production meeting to making duplicate prints.

In taping commercials, the same procedures are followed through the production day. But when tape is used, the commercial is complete as soon as it is taped and computer editing, including the addition of supers and opticals, is accomplished. Then duplicate tapes are made and shipped.

Producing Commercials
for the Small
Advertiser

It is not necessary for the small television advertiser to engage in the elaborate television production activity of the national advertiser. The national advertiser's budget and size of operation can support the production of top-quality filmed or taped commercials with full

Producing TV commercials. Left: Filming on a studio set. Right: Editing a tape commercial by computer. (Courtesy MPO Videotronics, Inc.; Orrox Corporation, photo by Kipp Baker)

production values. An adequate low-cost job can be done for local businesses and services such as banks, utilities, bakeries, department stores, and home appliance dealers. A simple slide commercial using still photos or a presenter single-set commercial can be produced at a cost measured in hundreds rather than thousands of dollars, particularly if it is produced outside the main film centers of New York and Los Angeles. Every city has its small production houses, and a local advertiser should talk to these firms, view their sample reel of commercials, and discuss prices. There is plenty of trained professional help available.

Sources of Produced Commercials

Manufacturers of products and national service companies routinely prepare commercials and make them available to retailers for local use on a cooperative advertising basis. The manufacturer produces a commercial that sells the product to consumers but leaves time at the end for the local merchant to add store identification in the form of a locally prepared card. A local station announcer can use the time when the sign is shown to read pertinent voice-over copy that also directs the viewer to the local sales outlet.

Independent syndicated film producers produce commercials for general sale to different kinds of local advertisers, too. These commercials also run short and leave room at the end for store identification. The independent firms perform the same function for local television advertisers that the syndicated mat services perform for local newspaper advertisers.

Production Facilities at Local Television Stations

The local television station sales management obviously has an interest in helping merchants prepare television commercials and can help the advertiser in many ways.

Stations maintain lists of local commercial film-producing outfits, free-lance writers and artists, and music men. Station personnel will make recommendations of these suppliers and will act as brokers for the job. They will also rent idle studios for commercial production and even construct simple sets, or backgrounds, at low cost. The local advertiser without an advertising agency or without an advertising department should talk over ideas for commercials with station representatives and let these experienced people do the production planning.

Some stations will create a commercial for a local advertiser at no cost provided the advertiser agrees to place all the broadcast advertising budget with the station. The drawback here is that the local advertiser is tied to a single station and has no opportunity to weigh the merits of one station against another.

When a local advertiser is planning to run co-op commercials supplied by a manufacturer whose line is carried, the advertiser normally personalizes the commercial by adding voice-over copy and visuals at the end. By using the local television station facilities the advertiser can go much farther than this toward owning and individualizing the commercial. The trick is to use the video part of the commercial as supplied by the manufacturer but discard the voice over or audio track completely. A new audio track is prepared that localizes the copy and gives important emphasis to the merchant's place of business. It is then recorded by a local announcer and synchronized with the existing video track. This results in a stronger commercial for the local advertiser. It combines professional video with localized audio.

Vocabulary

Define the following terms and use each one in a sentence.

Animated commercial
Answer print
Audio
Cut
Dailies
Direct voice
Dissolve
Establishing shot
Extra
Filmed commercial
Freeze frame
Idee
Interlock
Jingle
Live
Matting in
On location

Opticals
Playlet
Presenter commercial
Principal
Roll time
Script
Side-by-side demonstration
Slide commercial
Sound effects
Stop motion
Storyboard
Taped commercial
Video
Voice over
Wipe
Work print

Review Questions

1. List and identify five camera instructions used in television.
2. Describe three ways of timing television commercials and state which method is preferable and why.
3. Describe two television commercial formats that are simple to write and produce.
4. Why is simplicity important in television advertising?
5. In your opinion, can advertising copy for a newspaper or magazine ad be used without change for a television commercial? Be prepared to discuss in class the reasons for your viewpoint.
6. Why should an advertiser use the minimum number of principals in a television commercial?
7. What is the desired characteristic of the opening, or first few seconds, of a commercial, and why is the opening vital to a commercial's success?
8. Outline a checklist to be applied to a commercial after it is written.
9. What are the purposes of a storyboard?

10. List the steps in producing a commercial up to the day of shooting or taping.
11. What sources do small advertisers and local advertisers have available for producing a television commercial?

Activities

1. Be prepared to discuss in class television commercials you have seen that are examples of the following formats:
   a. Demonstration (it can be merely part of a commercial)
   b. Playlet
   c. Mood commercial
   d. Stand-up presenter
   Do you think these commercials did an effective selling job? Give reasons for your answer.
2. Write a 30-second commercial for one of the following imaginary products. Your script should include both audio and video. Include a slogan or theme.
   a. Gamble's Chow Down. A nationally sold leading dry dog food. Sold in 50-, 25-, and 10-pound bags and in 2-pound boxes. For all dogs 1 year old or older. Supplies a balanced diet, with a dog's complete nutritional needs. Can be served in dry form or moistened with warm water. More economical than canned dog food. Wins on taste tests over other leading dry dog foods.
   b. Kitchen Helper automatic dishwasher. 30-minute cycle. Handles a complete set of dishes and glassware plus silver for eight. Special speed-drive system cleans pots and pans beautifully. No need to rinse, just scrape the dishes.

Project

Arrange a visit to a local television station, and tour the facilities. From the point of view of a local advertiser, try to determine the amount of assistance available for the preparation of television commercials. Assume that a local advertiser buys time from the station.

1. If the local advertiser wishes to run a "live" commercial, how will the station help in the production?
2. If a taped commercial is desired, what facilities are available?
3. If a filmed commercial is desired, what facilites are available?
4. What sets, recorded music, sound effects, and talent can the station management line up to help in the production process?

Career Ladder

As general manager of a local TV station you need a general assistant to work in your studios, much of the time on TV commercials taped there for local advertisers. Some of the jobs that need doing are obtaining props around town as needed; constructing simple props; moving equipment; lettering cards, banners, signs, etc.; painting flats (nothing fancy); making up supers from press type (self-adhesive letters of various type sizes); and arranging sets for commercials. A little knowledge of studio lighting would be helpful, as would a little muscle. You've interviewed the following two applicants:

1. Head of drama society at college; acted in many plays. Stressed communications courses, achieving good marks. Summer jobs have been working for a tree surgeon and a landscape architect. Hobby: making old cars run.
2. Graduate of community college stressing advertising and marketing courses. Good marks. Also attended art school for a year, taking courses in print production, commercial layout, and design. Worked three summers as stage hand at the local community summer theater, helping in set construction. Hobbies: carpentry, stamps.

Which applicant would you hire? Why?

CHAPTER EIGHTEEN

WRITING AND PRODUCING RADIO COMMERCIALS

Radio today, as we learned in Chapter 8, is a highly specialized medium that offers selective audiences to the advertiser through station programming. The audiences can be broad, as when a station stresses news in its program content and thus appeals to the general public. On the other hand, many radio stations stake out a narrower part of the public and develop programming to appeal, for example, to teenagers, farmers, or upper-income groups.

Not only local radio stations specialize in program content to build certain specific audiences; radio networks have also done so. One of ABC's networks relies heavily on youth-oriented pop music, while another, trying to attract older groups, features middle-of-the-road music (MOR), semiclassical music, and the like.

The advertising message, to be most effective, should be tailored to the tastes of the audience it will reach—it should talk their language. The advertiser must keep in mind the distinctive characteristics of the radio medium

that make writing radio advertising a unique, specialized task.

Radio advertising, like television advertising, intrudes on the listener whether the listener wants it to or not. It is very different in this sense from print advertising, for readers can decide not to look at or read an ad if it doesn't interest them. Listeners can tune out a radio commercial or change the station, but this takes a conscious effort.

Because of radio's intrusiveness and because its advertising "invites itself in," the advertiser runs a risk, not faced in print advertising, of annoying or irritating the audience. For this reason, the advertiser should avoid bombastic commercials that seem to shout sales appeals; the advertiser should also avoid over-repetition of words, sound effects, and musical phrases. A high percentage of radio commercials today use entertainment, music, and humor, techniques that are likely to make a friend of the listener and that offset the intrusion factor.

Like television advertising, a radio commercial (or spot) is over in a few seconds. The consumer can't reread a key point for complete understanding as can be done in a print advertisement. This means that writing for radio must be simple, uncomplicated, and single-minded. The advertiser can't expect the listener to retain much more than one or two selling ideas.

Radio requires the listener to be creative. The imagination calls up the pictures that the words suggest, and settings and people are created as the commercial unfolds. This is not a drawback, as it allows the prospect to indulge in any amount of imagining that comes to mind. Radio can be a subtle medium. A tone of voice or a musical phrase can arouse any sort of emotion. Care must be taken to compensate for the lack of pictures by an adequate vocal description of products and benefits, a step that is not necessary in television, where products can be shown and demonstrated.

Length and Timing of Radio Commercials

Standard lengths of radio commercials are 1 minute or 30, 20, and 10 seconds. As in television commercials, length depends on the advertiser's budget and on copy requirements. If radio advertising is supplementing a major advertising effort in other media, and if the product is a soft drink or well-known packaged-goods item, reminder advertising may be satisfactory, and short commercials can be used. If the major effort is being made in radio, and if the product or service needs explanatory copy, 1-minute or 30-second lengths will be used.

A rule of thumb for measuring commercials consisting wholly of copy and not including music or sound effects is 150 words per minute. Some commercial scripts appearing in this chapter run much higher in word count.

When hearing a radio commercial, the listener supplies the pictures—which depend on an individual's point of view and vary from person to person. (Jared D. Lee)

These have been prepared by professionals, rehearsed many times, recorded with experienced talent, and edited tightly to eliminate pauses and "dead air." In the absence of these factors, it's better to keep the word count down.

On completion, scripts should be read aloud and timed by stopwatch or roughly timed with a wristwatch that has a sweep second hand. The Green Valley radio commercial script shown in this chapter is typical. This script has been prepared for recording purposes, and in such a case, capsule instructions on how lines are to be read by the "voices," or actors and actresses, are often included. Sounds other than voices are also indicated, prefaced by SFX for sound effects. The writer may also call for music as background under voices or for a jingle—or the entire commercial may be musical. In any case, music and how it is to be used are always indicated on the script.

Radio commercials are either read live on the air by an announcer or broadcast from pre-produced tapes. In the former case, the announcer reads the commercial as indicated by a script supplied by the advertiser, and the same procedure must be followed, of course, whenever the commercial is repeated. The *pre-produced commercial* offers the advertiser complete control of the broadcast message and eliminates the possibility of a live announcer fluffing.

Types of Radio Commercials

There are many different kinds of commercials broadcast today, and it is possible to categorize them by types, ranging from simple, straightforward single-voice announcements to commercials featuring electronic music and sound effects. There is much overlapping of

techniques, however. A humorous playlet commercial can contain a musical jingle, or a basically musical commercial may contain copy to be read by an announcer. Contents are limited only by imagination and by the production budget.

Commercial Based on a Fact Sheet

The simplest and easiest way for an advertiser to put a commercial on the air is to prepare a product or service *fact sheet.* This is not a commercial; it is merely a listing of selling points about the advertised item. The fact sheet is used by a radio station announcer or local radio personality as a basis for the commercial that is read over the air. In this case, the actual organization and flow of the commercial are developed by station personnel. Advertisers should regularly monitor commercials based on fact sheets to make sure that important copy points are being included.

This fact sheet is prepared for a local bank.

MERCHANTS NATIONAL BANK
RADIO COMMERCIAL FACT SHEET
BRANCH OPENING COPY

Grand Opening Week, November 1–6. We're located at 18th. and Broad.

Get a free address book or appointment book just for stopping in.

Full banking services.

Two convenient drive-up windows and 24-hour auto-teller service.

Lowest possible interest rates on personal loans. Investigate!

Come throw a coin in our beautiful indoor fountain and help the Town Thanksgiving Fund for those in need.

Member Federal Deposit Insurance Corporation.

There's a new Merchants National Bank branch in town—at 18th. and Broad. Come to our Grand Opening Week November 1 through 6 for your free gift.

Straight Announcement

The most common type of radio commercial and the simplest is the *straight announcement.* After it is written, no additional expense is incurred by the advertiser if it is broadcast live by local announcers. The straight announcement is read with no embellishments by an announcer in the course of a program. It is used by large and small advertisers alike. Here is a typical straight announcement for a local restaurant. It is 30 seconds long.

Anncr: They're all for the wife at Louisa's restaurant, Main and Sunrise. Every Thursday, pay the regular dinner price and your better half has her choice at half price. Try Louisa's great sirloin steak dinner. For you it's six ninety. For your bride, three forty-five. Complete dinners at five dollars. Come to Louisa's Thursday. Two dinners for the price of one and a half! Not married? Bring your date. Louisa's—Main and Sunrise. Famous for great food.

The straight announcement can either be broadcast live or preproduced on tape.

Commercial Using a Local Radio Personality

In local markets, disc jockeys and commentators often build up a loyal audience, and when the program of a local radio personality fits the product or service to be advertised, the advertiser can add effectiveness to the message by using the personality as the "voice" of the advertiser. A fact sheet is supplied, and the copy points are put into the personality's own words.

Local merchants should investigate the opportunities in this area.

Playlets or Dramatizations

Story-telling techniques are as common in radio advertising as they are on television. Playlets usually make use of two or more voices and spell out a problem that is solved by using a product or service. Unless the playlets involve some humor or slightly larger-than-life treatment, they tend to sound unreal and contrived with the result that the listener does not become involved in the message.

Interviews and Testimonials

Unrehearsed interviews and testimonials are tried-and-true techniques that are involving and believable. Portable taping equipment makes it possible for the interviewer to go almost anywhere for authentic copy, and the more natural the background noises picked up the more authentic the commercial sounds. Most products and services can benefit from this format, and it has proved particularly effective for local merchants. An interviewer for a bank talks to a person who uses the bank's travel service; a real estate firm features homeowners who bought their houses through the firm; and a retail store features its satisfied customers.

Note that in this kind of commercial, copy is usually disorganized, grammatically speaking. It is full of awkward expressions and unfinished sentences. The interviewer and the customer step on each other's copy lines and interrupt. It just happens that this is the way real people talk, and the lack of slickness and professionalism is all to the good. In such commercials we are not looking for rehearsed readings or carefully structured copy; we are looking for believable, realistic words and phrases, and

The interviewer is obtaining unrehearsed testimonial copy from a product user for use in a radio commercial.

we should not be concerned with a smooth reading.

Musicals and the Use of Music

Straight singing commercials, or musical commercials, rely on music as an entertainment factor to involve the listener and to make the copy points in verse form. Any number of singers can be used, and the musical background can range from none at all to full orchestration. Because professional musicians and songwriters should be used, musicals can run into high production costs. One serious problem encountered in such spots is that when more than one singer is used, clear projection of the words may not be possible, and the listener may fail to get the message.

Musical backgrounds under announcer copy are effective mood creators, and often musical "punctuation," or musical touches, can enhance the presentation of selling ideas. Instead of using original music especially scored for the commercial, *stock music* can be substituted at considerable savings. This is music that is either in public domain or already recorded. Stock music libraries are available where the radio commercial producer can search for background material and buy its use at a predetermined price.

The jingle, a short musical sequence supporting rhymed or unrhymed selling themes, became extremely prevalent in the 1930s and was overdone to the point of being repugnant. After these excesses, its use dropped off, but the jingle is still frequently heard. Jingles are effective for any number of products and services, either as reminder copy totally filling a 10-second spot or as thematic expressions in commercials that basically use another format such as the interview, playlet, or straight announcement. Jingles are used because they are memory hooks. Since they do not change from spot to spot, their repetition triggers recollection of the product image or selling theme. Jingles face the same cost problems as musicals, but a good, memorable jingle can be well worth the price.

Humorous Commercials

Entertainment in advertising is a controversial subject, but it is hard to understand why, if the use of humor and entertainment is properly handled. When entertainment is included only for its own sake, it accomplishes nothing; but when it enhances the selling idea and makes it meaningful and memorable, it is a valid and very useful technique. Particularly in radio, entertainment refreshes the viewer and gives the product or service a favorable, likable image. Radio's intrusiveness and radio's irritation factor are nicely counterbalanced by humor and entertainment in copy. Two award-winning commercials appear below, "Banana Boat" for *Time Magazine,* and "Mother's Day," a retail commercial for Norman's, including music and produced on a limited budget.

BANANA BOAT

Commissioner: All you had to do was pull the switch and raise the bridge.

Bridge Attendant: I know that, commissioner.

Commissioner: You were trained to raise bridges.

Attendant: I said I'm sorry.

Commissioner: Well, as commissioner of bridges and sidewalks, it is my duty to . . .

Attendant: There was a reason, you know.

Commissioner: What?

Attendant: I was reading a magazine.

Commissioner: . . . It is my duty to . . .

Attendant: Not just any magazine. A *Time Magazine.* You know you don't just look up when you're reading *Time.*

Commissioner: You do if it's a 40-ton banana boat from Guatamala.

Attendant: I didn't see it.

Commissioner: When it's sitting and tooting in front of a bridge for an hour and a half . . .

Attendant: Sir, you get caught up in a *Time Magazine.* What are your interests? Theater, art, books, cinema, it's all there in *Time Magazine.*

Commissioner: Taxidermy.

Attendant: Oh. Well, *Time* has a lot more color photography. Maybe there's a picture of something being stuffed. (SFX: *riffles pages*) Let's take a look here and . . .

Commissioner: It is my duty to . . .

Attendant: Sir, it was a *Time Magazine.* It's not like I was caught with my hands down and my pants in the till.

Commissioner: Good grief, man, the boat had to turn around. Go all the way back to Guatamala.

Attendant: You know I've had a perfect record for eleven years.

Commissioner: We haven't had a boat here in Herendon, Iowa for eleven years.

Attendant: Well that's being picky.

Commissioner: It is my duty to inform you . . .

Attendant: One lousy mistake and you make it a big . . .

Announcer: *Time* makes everything more interesting—including you.

MOTHER'S DAY

John: This is John over here.

Jack: And Jack over here.

John: With a little Mother's Day reminder song from Norman's, your Hallmark Store and so much more.

Jack: Downtown on the Trenton Commons, in the Oxford Valley Mall, the Lawrence Center, and the Quaker Bridge Mall.

John: Norman's has a fantastic variety of cards and gifts for Mother's Day.

Jack: So we've written this catchy little song.

John: Hit it, Jack!

(Duet: *corny piano background under*)

Both sing: N is for the nifty stuff they have there.
O is for the other stuff they have there.
R is for the real good stuff they have there.
M is for the many things they have there.
A is for all the stuff they have there.
N is for the real neat stuff they have there.
Stick an apostrophe S on the end there.
And Norman's is the word that you have there.

John: Well, I don't think it'll go very far on the charts.

Jack: No, but it's really popular at Norman's.

John: And you don't have to go very far to get to a Norman's.

Jack: Downtown at the Trenton Commons.

John: In the Oxford Valley Mall.

Jack: Lawrence Center.

John: And Quaker Bridge Mall.

Jack: So go to Norman's for Mother's Day gifts.

John: She'll love everything they have—there.

Demonstrations

In spite of the lack of pictures, effective demonstrations can be developed in radio commercials by fully describing product characteristics and capabilities. Sound effects can be helpful, as when a car engine valve lubricant is demonstrated. The stuck valve "pings" as the motor idles. The valve lubricant is added, and the valve quiets down. If the product can be demonstrated, it can often be demonstrated on radio, when imagination is used. Notice how a dictionary is demonstrated in this 10-second-spot aimed at middle- to upper-income audiences with higher education.

Announcer: And now, a word from the Random House College Dictionary.

Woman's Voice: Nitty gritty.

Announcer: If it isn't in your old dictionary, get our new one.

This copy is short, effective, interesting, and makes its sales point in a creative fashion.

Commercials Using Sound Effects

Some radio commercials successfully use sound effects as their basic and dominant technique; this can be done when the sound effect itself is an important part of the advertised product or service. However, sound effects are generally used as supplemental devices to lend color and life to other form of radio spots. A commercial for Gulf Pride Super G Motor Oil starts this way (only the opening seconds are reproduced):

(SFX: *sound of car starter; turns over and over unsuccessfully. Up strong, then under copy*)

Announcer: Want to know what makes your car so hard to start . . .

(SFX: *out*)

. . . on a cold morning? Come inside the engine and see for yourself. Down here, cold can make your motor oil . . .

(*Announcer's voice starts to wind down*) thicker . . . and . . . thicker . . . and thicker . . . (*Voice continues to slow down*) until . . . every . . . moving . . . part . . . can . . . . . . hardly . . . . move . . . . . (*voice grinds to a halt*).

RADIO SCRIPT
RECORDING XX) LIVE ( )
Turnkey & Sesame

PAGE # 1 TOTAL NO. PAGES:
CLIENT: GREEN VALLEY PROGRAM: RO # 73-131
PRODUCT: Tomato Soup OVERALL TIMING: 1 min. TYPED: 7/1/--
PRODUCT USE: Souperb Recipe Contest WORD COUNT: 115, plus 4 sec. jingle DRAFT # 2
TITLE OR NO. " NO JELLY BEANS" AIR DATE: 8/1/--

(CAST TWO GIRLS VOICES, AROUND 5 YEARS OLD. SIMULATE IF NECESSARY.
LET THEM READ THE LINES AS NATURALLY AS POSSIBLE.)

GIRL A: (AS IF CONTINUING A CONVERSATION) So will you go to Hawaii?

GIRL B: (MATTER-OF-FACTLY) Yes.

GIRL A: (POSITIVE TONE) We can when I win the Green Valley contest.

GIRL B: How are you gonna win it?

GIRL A: You send in a recipe for something good with Green Valley tomato soup

in it.

GIRL B: What's your recipe called?

GIRL A: "Good meat loaf." You take this hamburger meat and bread crumbs

and a can of Green Valley tomato soup. . .

(SFX: EXAGGERATED. CAN OF SOUP POURING)

and mix it up with a lot of jelly beans and marshmallows.

GIRL B: (CASUAL TONE) I don't like jelly beans. Just put in the marshmallows.

ANNOUNCER: (THEME MUSIC UP, THEN UNDER) Enter Green Valley's Souperb Recipe

Contest! Just be sure to include Green Valley tomato soup. Pick up

a contest blank at your food store . . . and some cans of beautiful

Green Valley tomato soup!

GREEN VALLEY QUARTET: (SINGS) Soup, bee-youtiful soup . . . from GREEN VALLEY.

This 1-minute radio commercial script promotes the Green Valley Tomato Soup recipe contest (see Chapter 5.) Note script instructions on how copy should be read, use of sound effects (SFX), and use of music.

Spalding uses musical effects dramatically to "describe" the way its new Australian tennis ball clings momentarily to the racket to establish better control, as the sound effect, a tennis ball being hit, punctuates the entire commercial. In this case, the effectiveness of the spot depends entirely on sound effects to make a selling point.

Writing Advertising for Radio

Before starting to write a radio commercial, the writer must do some homework. All available facts about the product or service should be reviewed and the copy strategy read. If no strategy has been determined, the writer must develop one. Then the writer must decide on the main selling idea that should be conveyed. Just as in writing advertisements for television, the writer is not going to attempt to cover too much territory in the commercials. Listening time is brief, so the writer must concentrate on one major point. The type of prospect most likely to buy what is advertised must be kept in mind and the copy directed to that individual. Finally, the writer must decide on the length of the commercial and be practical about what can be contained within the time limit.

Decide on a Format

What type of commercial can serve the copy strategy or objectives best? If the problem is to develop reminder advertising in short lengths, perhaps a musical jingle with an announcer *tag line,* a final line at the end of the spot that summarizes the message, will offer a solution. For a 1-minute commercial, a more elaborate format would be required. This length is useful in campaigns that advertise several items or introduce new products or services.

Whatever the copy problem, a straight announcement can always be satisfactorily used to deliver the selling message, and it is a good step to write this type of commercial first. It is simple to construct, and the process of writing it organizes the copy facts and gives the writer confidence. With a straight announcement in hand, the writer can then move on to other formats such as playlets, demonstrations, and humor, discovering in the process whether these treatments of the copy strategy are superior to the straight announcement version or do not work as well. A budget for production costs must be kept in mind. Using several different voices runs the cost up, and periodic payments to those who take part in a commercial must be made during the commercial's life. Original music or the preparation of a jingle can also be expensive, and the performance of the music also adds to the total cost.

Involve the Listener Immediately

The writer must always attempt to gain the listener's attention during the first few seconds of a radio spot. This can be done by the good advertising practice of appealing to a prospect's self-interest and talking in terms of a benefit or reward. It can also be accomplished by stating a problem that the use of the advertised product or service can solve. Attention-getting devices such as provocative dialogue, humor, and distinctive sound effects can also do the trick. These devices, sooner or later in the commercial, should be made to relate to the product or service being advertised or serve as a vehicle to carry along the flow of the advertiser's selling points.

Here are some examples of commercials that successfully involve the listener immediately. Only the opening seconds have been reproduced.

(Musical theme up for a couple of bars, then under copy)

Girl: Hello?

Man Phone Caller: Hello. I'll bet you just bought a new water bed.

Girl: Yeah!

Man: And I'll bet you bought it from that outfit on the highway.

Girl: Right.

Man: And I'll bet you didn't read in *The Trib* that they're being sued for defective merchandise.

Girl: You're kidding! Who is this anyway?

Man: This is David. The wet person. From downstairs.

(music up, voices sing jingle)

Voices: It was in *The Trib,* son. It was in *The Trib.*

(Opening of one of a series of circulation-building spots for the Oakland Tribune.)

Boss: And so, Shirley, welcome to the stenographic pool.

Man *(deep voice)***:** Thank you, sir.

Boss: Any questions?

Man: Yes. May I be excused to go to Dayton's fabulous warehouse sale?

Boss: Mr. Shirley, you've only been with the firm five minutes.

Man: Well I know, but Dayton's has this big sale. Appliances, . . .

Boss: No.

Man: Furniture.

Boss: No. Just get to work, Shirley . . .

(Opening of a spot for Dayton's Department Store, Minneapolis.)

(SFX: grunting, snorting animal noises)

First Man: Here you go, Bruno. Here's your last banana. Heh.

(SFX: one more grunt) Oh. Leave go my arm, Bruno. Bananas all bye-bye . . . No, No!

Second Man: What do you do here at the zoo, feed the gorilla?

First Man: Put me down, Bruno!

Second Man: Boy, that looks like fun.

First Man: Uh! Sir, do you know anything about gorillas?

Second Man: No. See, I work for A O Smith manufacturing data systems . . .

You may find it hard to believe, but the last commercial evolves into a logical sale for A O Smith systems in which a series of rather dull facts are registered with great conviction.

Develop Copy after the Opening

The opening seconds of a radio spot correspond in their function to the headline of a print advertisement in seeking to attract attention and to sort out specific prospects from the general audience. In the balance of the commercial the writer must make sure that the main selling idea is elaborated on, explained, demonstrated, repeated, or reinforced as necessary. If the copy strategy or objective of the spot is kept in mind, the writer will not stray into unrelated and unprofitable areas. Near the conclusion, the listener should be asked to take some kind of action if merchandise or a service is being sold. Obviously, where to obtain what is advertised is essential if a local advertiser is a sponsor, and this information should be included. If the advertiser had developed a recurrent theme or slogan, it's a good idea to use these words to wind up the message in a tag line. The conclusion can take the form of a summary statement if the advertiser has no slogan.

Be Conversational In writing, try for an easy, natural style, using words and sentences that sound like conversation rather than flowery, complicated word combinations. Maury Webster, CBS Radio Divisional Services vice president, says, "When a typewriter turns out radio copy that sounds more like talking than reading, listener involvement is the result." Remember that radio advertising is personal and addresses listeners one at a time. Write copy as if it were a conversation. After a commercial is written, always read it aloud a couple of times, and listen for awkward, nonconversational phrases. When they occur, revise them and smooth them out so that a natural, conversational flow results. As in writing television commercials, avoid too many words in a row beginning with an "s" sound.

Use Repetition It is often a good idea to repeat the main selling idea more than once if commercial time permits. The writer should assume that the brief seconds of a commercial are the only time when the listener will hear the message and should make the most of the opportunity. This means reiterating the main selling idea. The same words are not necessarily used each time the idea is repeated; the thought may be stated in different ways. The important thing is to register this essential selling thought.

Note again the commercial for Louisa's restaurant earlier in this chapter, under the head-

ing "Straight Announcement." The objective of this commercial is to establish the idea that the restaurant offers a half-price dinner on Thursdays for a wife or date. It states this fact twice in different words, and it also demonstrates the offer by quoting the half-price on the sirloin steak dinner. It would not be possible for the listener to miss the point of this commercial.

Don't Crowd the Commercial The writer should keep the spot single-minded and should reinforce the main selling idea. In department store or retail store copy, no more than two or three items should be advertised in a 30-second spot and no more than five or six in a 1-minute spot; the listener cannot be expected to retain or act upon more than this number. It is best if these items are related items, such as a dress and a handbag or belt accessory, a Father's Day special on pipes and tobacco, or a tent for camping and sleeping bags.

Use the Radio Commercial Checklist

Here's a checklist with which to compare the written commercial.

■ Does the opening attract attention?

■ Does the commercial talk in terms of a listener benefit or reward?

■ Does the main selling idea come through clearly?

■ Is the commercial single-minded?

■ Do the minor sales points relate to the main selling idea and reinforce it?

■ Are any of the sentences cumbersome and difficult to read aloud?

■ Does the commercial ask for listener action?

■ Does the commercial fit the time slot?

■ Can the commercial be produced within the budget?

Producing Radio Commercials

The quickest and easiest way for an advertiser to get a sales message to the public is through the medium of radio. A local advertiser can prepare a fact sheet, give it to the radio station representative, and have a commercial read live by a local personality or announcer. The entire process could conceivably be accomplished within a couple of hours if a time slot were available and if speed were that essential. The advertiser in this case would enjoy the pleasurable benefit of incurring no production costs.

Commercials for major local advertisers and national advertisers are not as simple to prepare because they are generally preproduced. Time is required to cast voices, compose original music when necessary, produce duplicate tapes, and ship the material to radio stations. In no case does this activity take the time required in producing television spots, and production costs are comparatively low. A rule of thumb for radio commercial production budgets is 5 percent of the radio time charges.

Producing Spots for National Advertisers

The production of radio commercials for national advertisers is the responsibility of the client's advertising agency. Actual production is contracted with outside suppliers, and the agency television producer usually handles the details. The producer makes up cost estimates; lines up a sound studio, where the commercial will be taped or recorded and then edited; arranges for original music and jingles or obtains stock music; and sees that the commercial is produced on time and according to directions.

Today there is an awareness of the many creative opportunities offered by radio advertising and a willingness on the part of national advertisers to spend the money it takes to obtain top acting, musical, and creative talent. Several talented and highly creative people have started firms that offer a combined creative and production service for radio spots. The advertising agency or national advertiser supplies the selling facts and strategy, and the firm develops and then produces the required number of spots. Dick & Bert, Chuck Blore & Don Richman, Inc., and Stiller and Meara are top names in this field, and although their work commands a high fee, it pays off in memorable, talked-about radio spots that in many cases have resulted in sales success.

Producing Spots for Local Advertisers

If the local advertiser has an advertising agency, it will supply the creative and production supervision facilities for the radio spots that are needed. Retail stores with advertising departments also have the staff to fulfill the creative and production needs. Small local advertisers who wish to use radio commercials but don't want to write them should deal with the local radio station.

Every station, no matter how small, has on its staff a *continuity writer* who prepares copy for radio programs as needed. Also available are a music library and a library of sound effects. As a service to the advertiser, the station will prepare simple commercials when radio time is purchased.

There are also syndicated services that have on hand and sell generalized radio commercials for a wide variety of retail businesses. For a fee, these commercials can be bought on an exclusive regional basis and tagged with the local advertiser's name, slogan, and address.

Vocabulary

Define the following terms and use each one in a sentence.

Continuity writer   Stock music
Fact sheet   Straight announcement
Preproduced commercial Tag line

Review Questions

1. What characteristics of radio advertising make it different from print advertising?
2. List the standard lengths of radio commercials.
3. Describe seven types of radio commercials.
4. Why is the opening of a commercial important?
5. After the writer decides on the opening words of a radio commercial, what should be covered in the balance of the commercial?
6. Why is it important to develop a conversational style in writing radio commercials?
7. Why is it important to read a commercial aloud after writing it?
8. Describe the elements of an advertiser's radio commercial checklist.

Activities

1. Using any format, write a radio commercial for one of the following:
   a. You are a successful real estate agent in a city of approximately 100,000 population. The city has a suburban area where your office is located. In the suburb (Glenville) yours is the largest firm. You employ ten salespeople, have the largest number of houses listed, and have established a reputation for fair dealing and turning over sellers' properties rapidly. Your listings are varied—small commercial properties, two-family houses, and single-family houses ranging in price from $65,000 to $150,000. Fresh, new listings are received every week. Houses (and their prices) currently listed could be included in your commercial if you desire. You've decided to write a 1-minute commercial (the start of a series of such commercials). You have no slogan or theme for your company, and you think you should have one. Your company's name is J. L. Sawyer Real Estate, and your office is located on Main and 4th, Glenville. You hope to incur no production expense.

b. You are a writer in an advertising agency and are assigned to the Shelby Motel Chain account. Shelby is a national advertiser, and there are 100 Shelby motels from coast to coast. These are luxury motels, and most are large enough to offer convention facilities and meeting rooms. Shelby motels boast heated swimming pools and the Rib Room, a restaurant featuring gourmet roast beef dinners. Special features are Saybrooke extra firm mattresses, a sauna, and a staff that is instructed by Shelby Motel "courtesy experts." Guests can obtain instant reservations (toll-free) by calling 800-757-5000. Your assignment is to write a 1-minute commercial (in any format) including a slogan. You have a generous production budget.

2. From your radio listening experience, are there any radio commercials that you believe are doing an especially effective job? Be prepared to describe such commercials in class and state reasons why you think they are effective. Are there commercials that you can't stand? Why?

Project

Arrange to visit a local radio station. While there, determine the station's programming approach to its audience. Is its policy to appeal to a single type of audience, or does the station attempt to appeal to different types of audiences throughout its daily broadcasting period? What facilities do the station and its sales department offer that can help local merchants to advertise? Be prepared to report your findings in class.

Career Ladder

For 4 years you have been working for a radio station in a midwestern city of 300,000 population. You like the city and you like your job as continuity writer. You have also done some selling of spot availabilities, as well as traffic work. In the course of your writing assignments, you've come up with a series of commercials for a large local bank. They're humorous, have warmed up the bank's chilly image, and have caused much complimentary talk.

A college friend of yours has formed a radio creative-production firm with a good reputation. The friend knows of your work and has offered you a job in New York. The Big Time beckons. When the radio station head hears of your offer, he tells you that you will eventually (in about 5 years) be general manager if you stay. It's a nice life, you have a good job, and now you are promised a fine future. What is your decision: join the New York production firm or stay? Give your reasons in class.

Bartlett and Geiss is an advertising agency located in Indianapolis, Indiana. It employs 22 people and has billings of approximately $1,300,000 plus several small accounts where agency reimbursement is made by fee. By a combination of a little luck and a great deal of hard work, Cy Bartlett, the president, and Bill Geiss, the general manager, have landed the Hillcrest Dairy account. Hillcrest markets milk and cream in Marion County, which is where Indianapolis is located, and in six neighboring counties. It's estimated that Hillcrest's annual budget will be approximately $475,-000 and this makes it B and G's largest account. There is high excitement about this fine acquisition. The agency principals are anxious to get off to a good start and are a little nervous about their ability to do so.

Hillcrest has done little advertising, and what it did, it placed directly. But a shakeup in management has caused a new emphasis to be placed on advertising and merchandising. Hillcrest has competition from other dairies, and one, Sunnyfield, is larger and particularly aggressive.

Hillcrest products have an excellent reputation for quality. The line of homogenized and "diet-light" milk, heavy cream, light cream, and "half and half" (cream and milk) is packaged in attractive green and white waxed cartons that include a pastoral scene. Package sizes are standard—quarts, half gallons, and gallons for milk and pints and half pints for the cream items.

The Hillcrest Farms near Indianapolis are a show place. Located in a beautiful rural setting, the white buildings are immaculate, and the dairy equipment is the most modern available. The Hillcrest owners welcome visitors, and tours by classes of schoolchildren are frequent. As a sideline, a small dairy bar is maintained at the roadside entrance to the Farms, but it is not a moneymaker. The Hillcrest herd of Guernseys is one of the finest in the country. Hillcrest is family-owned, and currently a son, Joe Stafford, is exerting new leadership, especially in the area of marketing decisions. He thinks the old slogan "Hillcrest Milk is good, good, good" is pretty corny and believes that advertising that conveys a quality image is called for.

The agency people agree with this objective, and they also feel that this need not lead to stuffy or pompous copy. Since Hillcrest's largest competitor is an aggressive advertiser, Hillcrest is less familiar to the average consumer. Although, as stated, the quality of the products enjoys a good reputation, there is not great awareness of the Hillcrest name in the marketplace. "Sunnyfield" comes to mind more often according to the small-scale consumer research that the agency has done. The account executive is encouraging the creative people to think in terms of humor as an executional device or, as he puts it, "sensational" ideas (not easy to come by!) to put the Hillcrest name in consumers' minds more often.

No media decisions have been made, but there are the usual options. Indianapolis has four television stations, any of which cover Hillcrest's marketing area well. There are eight local AM radio stations and five FM stations. Neighboring cities in Hillcrest's marketing area also have radio stations. Outdoor advertising is handled by the local outdoor poster plant. The Indianapolis *Star* is the city's morning paper, and the *News* is the evening paper. Both are under the same management. Circulation is concentrated in the city zone. Hillcrest's marketing area can be covered by adding additional regional newspapers.

1. If you were the agency account executive and had the task of roughing out a copy strategy for discussion purposes with the creative department people, what would your strategy for Hillcrest be? Write out a brief copy strategy.
2. If you were a copywriter and were assigned to this account you would be given the task of developing a theme or slogan for Hillcrest that could be used in all its advertising. What theme or themes can you think of? These creative assignments have been given to the creative department:
   a. Script (including audio and video) for a 30-second television commercial
   b. Three or four ideas for 24-sheet outdoor posters. Include the poster copy, suggested illustration, and copywriter's rough layout
   c. Headline and body copy for a 600-line newspaper ad; include suggested illustration or illustrations
   d. Script for a 30-second radio commercial
3. Choose two of these copy assignments and develop them. Include copywriter's roughs or copywriter's rough storyboard when the task requires you to give guidance to the art director. Use the theme for Hillcrest in these advertising executions, except in the outdoor posters. For that assignment, you need not use the theme if it crowds the space, but the theme may constitute the entire copy if you wish it to. Use any tone, including humor, that seems to you to be right.

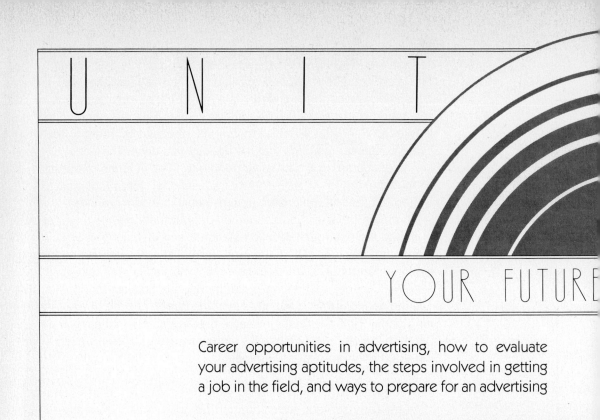

U N I T

YOUR FUTURE

Career opportunities in advertising, how to evaluate
your advertising aptitudes, the steps involved in getting
a job in the field, and ways to prepare for an advertising

F O U R

N ADVERTISING

career are described in Chapter 19. Future trends
in advertising and in the economy that may affect
your career are also discussed.

CHAPTER NINETEEN

CAREER OPPORTUNITIES AND FUTURE TRENDS IN ADVERTISING

The process of advertising uses the services of many different types of people with many different skills and aptitudes. Chapter 4 gives descriptions of the principal advertising jobs. This chapter is devoted to steps in career preparation and ways to analyze individual aptitudes. It also discusses future trends in the industry.

Advertising consists principally of several interrelated groups: advertising departments of manufacturers and service organizations, advertising departments of retail establishments, media advertising departments, marketing and advertising research suppliers, and advertising agencies. To this list should be added direct mail and catalog houses, manufacturers of advertising specialties, suppliers of advertising materials and services, and small local merchants in their function as part-time advertising people.

Many of these groups call for the services of similar types of employees: selling people, creative people, production people, and management people. These are the principal types, but other specialized employees are needed in the fields of accounting and budget and finance, for example. Clerical and secretarial personnel are also needed. Firms selling advertising services and supplies to ad agencies and to manufacturers use a sales staff. These sales representatives spend much of their time helping to solve advertising production problems.

Sales Careers in Advertising

Selling is needed in every part of the advertising field. An advertising manager working for a manufacturer must use selling techniques in presenting the annual budget to management. A copywriter finds selling ability very handy in explaining the copy to the copy chief or client. An agency research person must be able to sell research proposals. In these instances, an individual uses selling techniques to help accomplish a primary job function.

But there are many jobs in advertising where personal selling is the primary job function. Most of them are found in the media field. The media salesperson or representative must analyze the "product" (newspaper, radio station, or outdoor advertising plant), demonstrate how the use of the medium will benefit the advertiser-prospect, be skillful in organizing presentation of data, personally contact and often entertain the prospect, and generally do what can be done for the medium.

Other advertising jobs where personal selling is the primary job function include that of the person in charge of acquiring new business in an advertising agency, sales representative of advertising supplier firms such as tape or film production houses and photographic and art studios, and sales representatives for advertising specialties, typographers, printers, and engravers.

Aptitudes for Sales Careers in Advertising

Certain personal characteristics and aptitudes, developed or natural, can indicate future success in a sales career. If you can answer yes to at least eight out of the following ten questions, you probably would enjoy personal selling.

■ Are you outgoing and gregarious?

■ Are you relatively sure of yourself when you first meet people?

■ Are you known for possessing a good sense of humor?

■ Do you find satisfaction in convincing others to take some kind of action?

■ Do you maintain confidence when what you try to accomplish meets with no success?

■ Do you like people and enjoy being with them?

■ Can you organize and carry out a presentation of facts and figures?

■ Have you sought selling jobs in your life to date? (Sold tickets for amateur theatricals, sold magazine subscriptions, worked as a salesperson, etc.)

■ Have you enjoyed these tasks and been reasonably successful at them?

■ If you were told that a prospect was particularly difficult to sell, would you enjoy taking on the challenge?

Steps toward Sales Careers in Advertising

If you do some preparation while you are still a student, you will improve your ability to obtain an advertising sales job after graduation. Obviously, general advertising courses and courses in professional selling are helpful. Almost as important is summer or part-time work in selling or related fields. Employment in any job dealing with the public is good background. Selling door-to-door is difficult and often discouraging, but it is an excellent training job. Work as a retail sales clerk teaches patience and tact and offers opportunities to exercise selling ability. Working as a service station attendant permits a student to combine selling with the job routine.

Often local newspapers have bottom-of-the-ladder jobs for beginners, which are excellent training for a sales career in advertising or for any career in advertising. They usually consist of contacting local merchants, receiving instructions and material for ads, delivering proofs for approval, and similar tasks.

Copywriting Careers in Advertising

Every field of advertising requires writing and people to do it. Talented and experienced writers command salaries on a par with those of top advertising management people because ideas that sell goods and services are the keys to advertising success. There are plenty of jobs in this category, from copy cub all the way up to copy chief or creative director.

Although concrete figures are difficult to obtain, it is estimated that at least one-tenth of the 500,000 people involved in advertising devote their time to the creative aspects—writing and art. This figure doesn't include the hundreds of thousands of merchants who, in the course of their work, prepare their own advertising.

Copywriting Aptitudes

While everyone can develop the ability to create ideas, the art of copywriting, or expressing these ideas in selling prose, is not universal. Some people dislike writing and find it almost impossible to express themselves on paper.

However, if you have the necessary personal characteristics and aptitudes, you can develop copywriting ability. Here is a checklist to measure your potential in this field. A yes answer to nine of the following eleven questions indicates talent that can be cultivated.

- Do words and the imagery of words interest you?
- Do you enjoy reading?
- Are your high school and college grades in themes and compositions above average?
- Have you ever attempted creative writing?
- Have you made an effort to write for school and college publications?
- Would you enjoy selling to consumers via the written word?
- Does your writing keep to stated objectives without wandering?
- Can you take and apply constructive criticism of your written efforts?
- Do people and their habits and customs interest you?
- Can you dig for pertinent facts?

- Are your grades on copywriting and evaluating assignments in your advertising course above average?

Don't be discouraged if the task of writing is slow and arduous. Even for the most experienced writers, the assignment of writing a given piece of copy is often a painful process. The satisfaction of completing a good piece of selling copy is, however, an extremely gratifying experience.

Steps toward a Copywriting Career

Academically, survey courses in advertising and specialized courses in writing retail and national copy are an excellent background for copywriting. Studies in literature, history, sociology, and psychology are also desirable. Taking a course in creative writing is recommended. The more writing involved in a study program, the better prepared you will be for a future copywriting career. Writing experience develops word flexibility, writing ease, and confidence. If you have the time, extracurricular writing activities on college publications are excellent experience, and mention of them enhances job application forms.

Summer or part-time jobs that deal directly with the public are a good background for copywriting jobs, just as they are for any future advertising position, and also make a good impression on prospective employers.

When applying for work in a manufacturer's advertising department, a retail advertising department, an advertising medium, or an advertising agency, do not expect to be offered a job as an apprentice copywriter immediately. Such opportunities are rare. You should state your desire to write and offer service in any capacity just to break in. Once employed, pursue your goal of a copy job by doing writing tasks whenever you can. Many people take clerical jobs in

Part-time or summer jobs in sales or service fields are good steps in preparing for an advertising career. (Courtesy NCR Corporation; Stouffer's; Taylor Business Institute, Plainfield, Paramus, Manasquan, NJ)

order to join advertising departments or advertising agency creative departments.

It is important to impress a prospective employer with your desire to write and with proof of past ability to offer creative solutions to problems. It is also worthwhile to present a *portfolio,* or samples, of creative work. When looking for a job, experienced copywriters show some of their print advertising efforts and television commercials in order that their ability can be judged. Naturally, a beginner can't do this, but you can accomplish the same purpose by building a portfolio that reflects your creative ability. It should consist of a *résumé* (discussed later in this chapter), a typed itemization of your pertinent background and experience, plus examples of your writing, articles written for school publications, samples of copy written for advertising courses, etc.

An excellent idea is to do some ads. Select an advertised product or service and collect two or three ads that are representative of a campaign. Analyze their objectives, the kind of headlines that are used, and the style of artwork. Then assume that you are the copywriter for this account and write copy and heads for ads that continue the objectives. For the illustration, use scrap artwork cut from magazines or newspapers, or draw rough indications of what the artwork should be. The same result can be achieved by clipping ads for a local department store, studying them for style and content, and then writing and laying out more of the same in rough fashion.

This activity takes time and effort, but it indicates interest in the field and makes a first-rate impression on prospective employers.

The Sears Advertising Aptitude Review, which is taken by beginner applicants to Sears's large copy department, is reproduced in this chapter. It offers the kind of assignment actually undertaken daily by Sears's writers

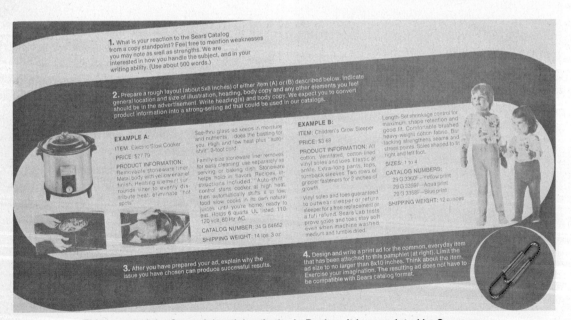

This is part of the Sears Advertising Aptitude Review. It is completed by Sears applicants for copywriting jobs. Applicants are judged in three areas: knowledge of advertising fundamentals, ability to apply this knowledge to actual problems, and skill in organizing and writing copy. (Courtesy Sears, Roebuck and Co.)

and permits the interviewer to judge the applicant's writing potential.

Careers in Advertising Art and Art Direction

The field of advertising art is a broad one, encompassing many career opportunities. Art directors, sketchers, and layout people are essential employees in advertising departments of manufacturers and department stores, ad agencies, catalog houses, direct mail firms, package design companies, and many other businesses. Photographers and producers of finished advertising artwork are needed on a free-lance basis, in art or photo supply firms, or in all the types of businesses listed above. Top art talent commands top pay, and creativity in this field is well rewarded.

Art Aptitudes

Possession of natural artistic talent is a basic requirement for the advertising artist or art director, and the development of this talent requires schooling. Unlike copywriting, art direction and the abilities to sketch and design are not taught on the job; professional training is essential. If you give a yes answer to eight of the following eleven questions, you have a good chance of succeeding in the art field.

■ Do you like to sketch or design?
■ Have you ever been encouraged to develop your talent in this area?
■ Have you entered original artwork in a local exhibition?
■ Are any of the following your hobbies: woodworking, carpentry or handicrafts, sketching, clay modeling, painting, photography?
■ Are you interested in the history of art and architecture?

■ Do you enjoy art museums?
■ Have you ever enrolled in art courses?
■ Can you work on your own as well as with others?
■ Has any of your artwork been used by school publications?
■ Have you a creative imagination? In other words, do you get ideas?
■ Can you meet work deadlines?

Steps toward Careers in Advertising Art

Survey courses in advertising are a good general background for advertising art careers, and specialized courses in drawing, layout and design, or photography are a necessity. Enrollment in a commercial art school is recommended at some stage.

Beginners who want to become art directors, layout people, or designers and who have a properly oriented educational background usually break into advertising jobs by doing the relatively simple tasks of pasting up mechanicals, assembling elements of ads, lettering charts and tables, and laying out display or point-of-purchase material. Much of this activity takes place in the bullpens of ad agencies, department store ad departments, and manufacturers' ad departments. Catalog firms, direct mail outfits, and chain store ad departments also offer opportunities to beginners.

You should prepare a portfolio before applying for a job. It should consist of samples of sketches, layouts, and designs you did for course assignments and any examples of original creative work you may have done on your own. It's a good idea to tailor the portfolio to the particular job you want. If you are checking on opportunities in a department store ad department, a couple of original layouts featuring typical merchandise should be worked out and included.

Production Careers in Advertising

The preparation of every type of advertising, from advertising specialties to national advertising, relies heavily on an efficient production department. If you are at home with figures and mathematics, like to see things through, and are efficient in organizing tasks, production work can be satisfying. Wage scales, except for top positions, are not as high as they are for copy and art jobs, but the work of technicians and artisans in such fields as photoengraving, type composition, and film production is extremely well paid.

Most beginners in the production field start in the traffic department, keeping track of the status of individual ads or projects and making sure deadlines are met. Ensuring the quality of engravings, plates, and typography is an acquired skill, achieved by apprenticing with an experienced production person.

General courses in advertising plus specialized courses in typographic arts and advertising production make a good background, and part-time or summer employment on a publication, with a local printer, or with a direct mail outfit shows effort and interest and offers some practical experience.

Research Careers in Advertising

Employment opportunities abound in the fast-growing marketing and advertising research field. It is particularly interesting work because research projects are so often concerned with the new and the experimental areas of the business scene. Yes answers to nine of the following eleven questions indicate that you would find job satisfaction in research work.

■ Do you have an aptitude for mathematics?
■ Do you like to work with others rather than work alone?
■ Do you like logic, and do you have a logical mind?
■ Can you talk freely and naturally to people you've just met?
■ Do you enjoy meeting new people?
■ Are your grades in the sciences generally good?
■ Do you like to dig for facts?
■ Can you organize facts and draw logical conclusions from them?
■ Are you a good reporter of events?
■ Do you have the ability to write clearly so that others can understand your conclusions?
■ Would you be able to give instructions to others and guide a project?

Survey courses in advertising and courses in mathematics, statistics, computer programming, and market research constitute a good academic background for future research work. Most cities have research firms that need part-time interviewers, tabulators, and coders. Because business can fluctuate depending on the number of research projects at hand, part-time employment is more prevalent in research firms than in other areas of advertising and marketing. Summer employment is a practical way to prepare for a career in research.

Management Careers in Advertising

Management jobs require years of nonexecutive departmental experience during which the employee shows skill in organizing tasks, communicating with others, managing and directing assistants to assume responsibility, and accomplishing assignments on time. The most valuable ability of all these is that of training employees well so that their acquired abilities aid in the growth of the business. Agency management trainees usually apprentice in assistant jobs in the media, research, and traffic departments and then spend some years in the account handling department. In the manufacturing and product marketing fields, management people usually start in the sales department or are hired as brand assistants in the advertising department. Management jobs in the advertising field are very well paid by general business standards.

Preparing for Job Interviews

At this point, as a prospective employee, you have analyzed your career to date and as a result have selected an employment opportunity in the field of advertising where you feel you can achieve success. Your next aim will be to land a job, and your next tasks are to prepare for job interviews and to make the interview itself as satisfactory as possible. There are several steps that can increase your chances of having a rewarding interview.

Writing the Résumé

The first step in preparing for job interviews is to type up a résumé and have duplicates made. The résumé should start with personal data: name; birth date; address and phone number; marital and health status. It should state employment objectives and desires, list educational institutions attended, specialized courses taken, and any pertinent information on honors, awards, or academic recognition. Extracurricular activities should be briefly detailed. Summer or part-time jobs should be listed. Hobbies and interests, including sports, should also be itemized. A few references should be included. They can be character ref-

erences, academic references, and references by former employers. Often employers, on request, write "to whom it may concern" letters that tell of satisfactory work performance. These can be duplicated and attached to the résumé. See the example of a well-planned résumé illustrated here.

Getting Interviews

Obtaining job interviews is not an easy task; plenty of perseverance is needed. An obvious place for an interview is a local employment agency, but for beginners, independent prospecting is more productive. People who make a job out of getting a job and who organize for

```
                        Jane L. Bertram
                     879 South Main Street
                     Winston, Illinois 07876
                        (313) 946-7254

EMPLOYMENT DESIRED

Copywriter in advertising department of manufacturer
Writing job for company publication

EDUCATION

Graduate of Winston High School, June 19--
AA degree from Acadia Junior College, June 19--
     Major courses:  Journalism, Advertising, Advertising
        Copywriting, Market Research

INTERESTS AND ACTIVITIES

Member of high school Drama Club
Ad Manager, Winston Senior Yearbook
Fiction Editor, The Beaver, undergraduate literary magazine
Member of ADS, national advertising fraternity
Winner of third-place prize in Writers' Magazine contest
Civil War history buff
Sports:  Bowling, swimming

BUSINESS EXPERIENCE

June to August 19--      Camp counselor

September 19--           A&P check-out clerk during weekends,
   to June 19--            holidays, winter and summer vacations.

June to September        Advertising staff assistant for Winston
   19--                    Herald.  Contacted local merchants, wrote
                           copy for S&J Sports Shop, Central Realty,
                           classified ads.


REFERENCES

Professor Susan McNalley, Journalism and Advertising
Acadia Junior College
Acadia, Illinois 07879

Mr. Max Sternberg, Advertising Manager
Winston Herald
Winston, Illinois 07876
```

This is a well-planned résumé. It should be presented at job interviews and mailed with letters requesting interviews. It contains pertinent data and qualifications, includes past experience, and states an employment goal.

the task will eventually wind up on a payroll; haphazard attempts usually don't succeed.

Make a list of potential employers, and conduct a campaign to obtain interviews. Phone calls are a possible method, but far better is a letter of application including a résumé. Try to couch the letter in terms of what you can do for your prospective employer. Use a phone call to discover who does the hiring, and write to that person. Always follow up a letter with a phone call. Employers are busy with their own affairs and need this reminder.

Business contacts are of immeasurable help in obtaining an interview. If you can locate a friend of a friend who can put in a word for you, obtaining an interview is sometimes easier. Remember, though, that such a contact can't get the job for you. The applicant who offers the potential of becoming a valuable employee obtains the job. But contacts do help in getting through the door.

Once a job interview has been arranged, it is extremely helpful to acquire advance information about the firm to be visited. If a retail store is the student's target, a trip through it is recommended, and any of the store's advertising that is available should be collected and studied. Mentioning this activity in the course of the interview shows interest and sincerity. If a writing or art career is sought, a portfolio should be brought along so that the interviewer can examine it.

Handling the Interviews

Remember that the employer is looking for intelligence and the ability to use it. It is in the employer's interest to fill jobs with capable people. Remember that you hope to solve some of the employer's problems; try to talk in these terms. When possible project what you can do for the company. This is the best way to sell—and to advertise, too, for that matter. Try to relax, but don't worry about awkwardness on your first interview. The process becomes easier with each new experience.

Unfortunately, applicants seldom write a "thank you" letter to a prospective employer after an interview. This presents a good opportunity to reiterate interest in the job, and often such a letter is a prime reason why one person is hired instead of another. Follow-up calls or notes expressing continued interest are also a good idea if not overdone.

The Creative Advertising Business

Employers look for certain qualities in job applicants. They seek evidence of intelligence, integrity, loyalty, and conscientiousness. Beyond these qualities, in the advertising business employers try to determine a person's ability to develop fresh solutions to problems, and this requires applied creativity.

The word "creativity" is in no sense restricted to the fields of advertising copywriting and art direction. Creativity, the ability to get ideas, is the keystone of the advertising business, and its cultivation is a sure way to a successful career. Original thinking and ideas can build a media list that puts advertising dollars to work more efficiently. Creativity and flair can make a presentation come to life and sell. An advertising budget can do a better job when a creative approach to it results in stretching dollars. Creative imagination can add insights to research proposals and research analysis. The habit of getting ideas should be cultivated. Unfortunately, most people don't take the time and trouble to do it. But it is a stimulating habit and one that is rewarding in job satisfaction and in financial return, particularly in the advertising business.

Future Trends in Advertising

If you are considering a career in advertising, you should of course give thought to the industry's future. Are there trends that will work to make it a less promising career field, or will the advertising industry continue to grow?

Growth Prospects

It is obvious that in the forseeable future the business community will continue to rely on advertising as an efficient contribution to the marketing of goods and services. Growth is another subject, however. A superficial consideration of population trends (approaching zero growth in the United States) and the prospective shortages of natural resources can lead to the conclusion that the *gross national product* (GNP), the total value of our goods and services, could stabilize and regress. And since advertising expenditures are tied to business activity, a "no growth" era for the advertising industry could lie ahead, according to this thinking.

However, it is not population size that determines the extent and success of commercial activities. The highly developed areas of the world have relatively small populations in contrast to the large populations of less developed areas. The factor determining the extent of commercial activities is the general availability of disposable income after the population's basic needs are met. Forecasting is a thankless task, but it appears that disposable income in this country will continue to rise, in spite of the toll of inflation and periodic recessions. Dwelling on the future shortages of natural resources as a limiting factor on the GNP is unnecessarily doleful. Estimates of available natural resources have a way of changing dramatically. Fairly recent prophecies of depletion of world petroleum reserves by the late eighties were negated in 1978 by the announcement of very large Mexican oil reserves, moving the depletion forecast into the twenty-first century.

An analysis of past annual advertising expenditures indicates future industry growth. On a year-to-year basis expenditures have generally risen. In 1967 and 1970 expenditures were approximately the same as the previous year, reflecting the effect of recessions in the economy. In 1975, expenditures rose by almost $1.5 billion in spite of a severe nationwide re-

New products, such as this RCA video cassette recorder, will continue to be introduced, and the need to promote them will contribute to the growth of the advertising industry. (Courtesy RCA)

cession. More recent years have shown annual increases well over the inflation rate.

New products and services continue to be introduced at a rapid rate, and advertising must be used to support them. Today, for example, according to the research department of *Progressive Grocer,* the average number of brands sold in supermarkets is 7,000. In 1972, the figure was 3,500. Over 55 percent of the products today on supermarket shelves were not available 10 years ago. It is a safe assumption that new product and service introduction will continue at high levels in the future, contributing to advertising's future growth.

The trend to increased consumer self-service in retail outlets will continue, with consequent reduction of emphasis on personal selling. In such an environment, manufacturers of goods must do their best to presell prospects before they shop, and this will mean more reliance on advertising and on point-of-purchase material.

In the media field, specialists agree that new consumer magazines emphasizing selectivity of audience will continue to be introduced (magazine selectivity is discussed in Chapter 6). As a result, there will be an increase in magazine sales and promotional jobs. Consumer purchasing from catalogs is expanding rapidly, a positive development for the direct mail medium. In 1978 it was estimated that Americans would buy $22 billion worth of catalog items.[1] This trend creates job opportunities in the catalog field for art directors, production people, and writers. If television costs continue to rise at a rapid rate, all competitive media will benefit modestly through the realignment of advertising media plans that increase the use of TV media alternatives. All these media trends should serve to give confidence to a belief in advertising's long-term growth.

[1] *Time Magazine,* November 27, 1978, p. 94.

Future Trends in the Climate of Advertising

Certain developments in public and governmental attitudes will necessarily affect advertising but not necessarily in a career-limiting sense. *Consumerism,* the defense by the public and government of consumer interests and rights as related to the products and services a consumer buys, has always been latent in the United States. The importance of consumerism increased in the early seventies, and it will continue to be an important factor influencing the business community. Advertisers, in reaction to this trend, will tend to be more specific and definitive in describing product contents in ads, in product pricing and sizing, and in providing fuller package information. Through advertising, the public will be able to learn more facts about what is for sale and thus will be better able to determine its value.

Advertising will continue to be extensively regulated by self-policing activities and government bodies. Because of the increased emphasis on consumerism and because of such types of advertising as comparative copy (Chapter 14) the advertising legal climate of the eighties will become increasingly tough. Legal approval of all national ad copy is today a reality, and most large local advertisers require a legal review of copy before it is run. In the seventies, the Federal Trade Commission's attitude toward advertising could be fairly categorized as that of an adversary; future attitudes cannot be forecast, as they will be determined by who is appointed to the staff and to the commission itself.

It is expected that two developments will occur in the area of television advertising. A resolution of the lengthy argument concerning television advertising to children will be made in favor of some sort of regulation of commercial content at times when the audience consists mainly of youngsters. And something will finally be done toward reducing clutter, the crowding of several commercials into a brief time.

The Future of Local Advertising

The field of local advertising will be a growing one. This growth in reality depends on the individual merchant's appreciation of the power of advertising as a selling tool and on understanding of how to use this selling power.

In certain areas of the local advertising scene, a high degree of advertising know-how and sound application of principles is in evidence. The large retail advertisers (department stores, supermarket chains, discount houses, clothing stores, furniture stores, auto dealers, appliance dealers, and some banks and ser-

vice businesses) are in general using the power of advertising fully and relying on it as an important part of the selling effort.

While there are outstanding exceptions, smaller local businesspeople do not have this appreciation of advertising, and much of their effort falls into the reminder advertising category. As we have pointed out, there is a great opportunity for applied creativity and imagination in the local advertising field. The local merchant who advertises with courage, conviction, and flair gains an immense selling advantage over competitors, and this fact should be firmly kept in mind by every student who enters the local business scene. There are opportunities to improve advertising output with resulting sales increases, in almost every merchant's business, when the nine steps of the advertising process are followed.

Vocabulary

Define the following terms and use each one in a sentence. Some of them, defined in previous chapters, are included as a review.

Consumerism
Gross national product

Portfolio
Résumé

Review Questions

1. What steps could an individual take during college years to prepare for an advertising sales career?
2. If you were hiring a copy apprentice, what aptitudes would you look for in the applicant?
3. What could an applicant who has no previous on-the-job copywriting experience include in a portfolio?
4. What kind of background would be helpful to an applicant for a bullpen job?
5. What background experience is helpful in obtaining a job in a marketing or advertising research firm?

6. List the contents of a résumé.
7. When a job interview is lined up, what preliminary steps should the applicant take?
8. Why is creativity so important in the advertising business?
9. Describe two developments in the media field that should help the growth of advertising.

Activities

1. Take stock of yourself, your abilities, and your scholastic and employment activities to date. What career in advertising do you feel you might be best suited for? Why do you feel this way? The job can be that of a local merchant who is a part-time advertiser, if you wish. In such a case, briefly describe the business and the advertising task involved.
2. Prepare a résumé of your qualifications and background for the career you selected in the above activity.

Project

Make a survey of businesses in your community that might offer part-time or summer employment of value in training for an eventual career in advertising. List the name of the company, define its business, describe the part-time or summer job it might offer, and explain why the employment would be valuable training.

Career Ladder

Assume you are interested in a career as art director, are a graduate of a community college, and have attended a commercial art school. You have been able to schedule an interview with the head art director in the advertising department of a large local department store with several branches. The job opening is for art assistant, and you believe it offers a good opportunity. What preparations would you make for the job interview? What kinds of material would you submit? What steps would you take after the interview that might help things along?

Larry Cole accomplished a lifetime ambition when he purchased a hardware store. All his business life (he is now 40 years old) he had been in the retail hardware business, first as a clerk and then as manager of a store.

His store, now called Larry's Hardware, is located on the outskirts of a 500,000-population coastal city in the Middle Atlantic states. The store draws trade from three suburbs with a total population of 40,000. There is competition. One hardware store is located in Cole's suburb, but it is a small, nonpromotional outfit. Cole's main competition for items such as garden supplies and equipment and tools comes from a large aggressive discount house located a mile away. Cole can't match the discount prices and make a profit. He'll compete by offering personalized services and repairs.

The store sells hardware items and tools; equipment such as snow blowers, power mowers, leaf sweepers, and the like; garden supplies, spreaders, and seeders; a line of household gifts; wallpaper; do-it-yourself tile; and wall, ceiling, and floor coverings.

The business's annual sales volume was $500,000. The former owner had rarely made promotional efforts. The efforts he did make consisted of having available at the store three catalogs a year, spring, fall, and Christmas time. These catalogs were also used as direct mail items sent to customers. The catalogs were prepared as a retailer service by a buyers' co-op, an association of hardware dealers who buy merchandise cooperatively and in volume. The buyers' co-op allows the store owner to buy items cheaper than by dealing directly with manufacturers' sales reps, and thus he can meet in part retail prices of businesses such as the neighboring discount house. Cole will maintain this buyers' co-op arrangement. The catalogs supplied by the buyers' co-op had created additional sales volume. If he uses them, Cole will have no say about their contents, and he must, of course, stock the items advertised in the catalogs. If the retailer desires, the buyers' co-op will supply ten catalogs a year. The cost averages about $600 per catalog issue.

Cole believes in advertising and feels that if he has a consistent ad program running, he can boost his annual sales volume to $600,000.

Larry Cole is a local character; outgoing and friendly, he likes to help people. The suburb is located on the shore, and Cole is an avid fisherman and sailing enthusiast. As a result, he has added an outboard motor line and is a sales agent for a small fiber glass sailboat.

Ever since Cole announced his intentions of promoting the store aggressively, he has had a series of visits from local media sales representatives. He has received the following information:

■ The local suburban newspaper covers the three suburbs that constitute Cole's marketing area with a circulation of 17,500. It publishes evenings, Monday through Friday. The local advertising rate is 24 cents a line. If 5,000 lines are run during the year, the rate is 22 cents.

■ The neighboring city newspaper's rep called on Cole; he claimed that Cole can attract some city business as well as local. The urban paper, published evenings Monday through Saturday, has a circulation of 8,382 in the three suburbs. Its total circulation (including the above figure) is 152,528, and the retail line rate is $1.20. Bulk discounts are as follows: 1,000 lines annually: 1 percent discount; 2,500 lines annually: 2 percent discount; 5,000 lines annually: 5 percent discount.

■ A local radio station rep also called with an interesting proposition. (The station does a good job of coverage in Cole's sales territory.) Knowing of Larry Cole's interest in fishing and boating and discovering that Cole is now distributing outboard motors and sailboats, the rep offered him a 15-minute program on Friday at 6:15 p.m. after a local news program. He proposed that in the summer and early fall Cole go on the air himself with weekend fishing forecasts and boating weather forecasts. The station would supply the material, and Cole would also add fishing and boating anecdotes. Other times of the year, Cole could discuss home workshop activities, hobbies, and garden topics. Two 1-minute commercials would be available per program and could be delivered by the staff announcer or by Cole himself. The cost to Cole would be $55 per program. If the summer and early fall segment were purchased alone, the cost would be $65 per program.

Larry Cole is faced with many advertising decisions. What would be your answers to the following questions?

1. Should Cole continue buying three catalogs a year, purchase more catalogs a year, or cancel catalogs?
2. Assuming Cole is right about his sales volume forecast for the coming

year, how much should he spend on advertising? (Include an estimated expenditure of 5 percent of the ad budget for production.) It may also be assumed that half the advertising expenses will be paid by manufacturers of the products he sells through a cooperative advertising program.

3. What media should he use?

4. Make up a media budget summary sheet for the media selected in answer to question 3. Consider the costs of annual newspaper linage, catalogs, and radio spots that your suggested media mix would require.

5. If the newspaper is used, what size ads should he run and how often?

6. What should his advertising theme or slogan be?

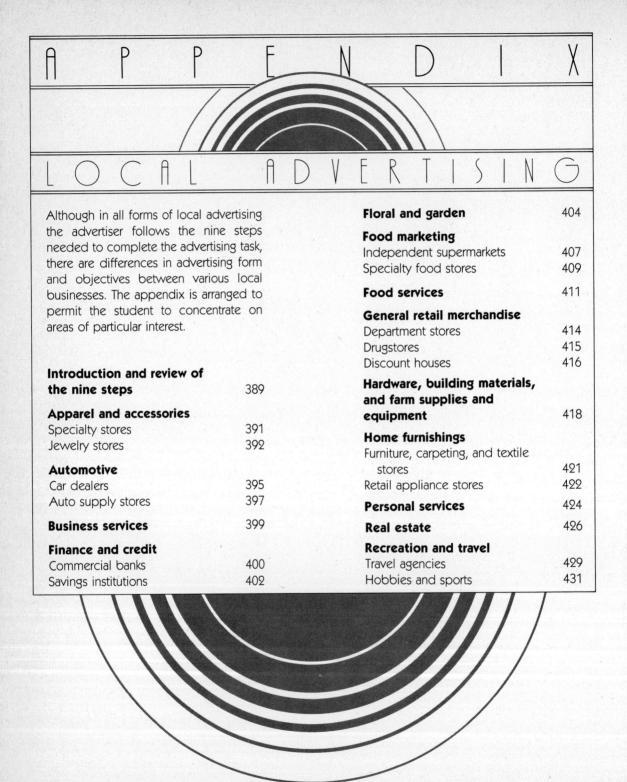

APPENDIX

LOCAL ADVERTISING

Although in all forms of local advertising the advertiser follows the nine steps needed to complete the advertising task, there are differences in advertising form and objectives between various local businesses. The appendix is arranged to permit the student to concentrate on areas of particular interest.

Introduction and Review of the Nine Steps

As a way to organize the many areas of local advertising, we will use in general the classification system for marketing and distributive education established by the U.S. Office of Education. Certain classifications, such as international marketing, have been omitted as they have no bearing on our subject.

Certain other classifications have not been included in this appendix because they apply to national or regional advertising or because they are small, measured on a basis of actual newspaper linage. These exceptions follow. Insurance is a small local advertising category, often included as part of real estate brokerage advertising when this service is offered by the firm. Hotel and motel advertising presents a special case. Large hotels and hotel and motel chains use national advertising and advertise lodging in markets that are a traditional source of patrons. Locally, hotels and motels generally restrict advertising to restaurant, banquet, and meeting facilities, with outdoor used near the unit's location. This advertising is not significant from a local point of view. The petroleum marketing and distribution classification includes, on the local scene, service stations, fuel oil dealers, and marine service companies. These are all very small local advertisers, relying on the parent petroleum marketer's national advertising for support for the brands they sell.

Advertising and display services are given a separate classification in the marketing and distributive education listing. It seems more logical to include this field under the business service classification in this appendix.

It will be helpful to review the nine steps that every advertiser must take to complete the advertising task. Table A-1 should be studied now and referred to when the local advertising sections that follow are read. Note that research is used in the table at several steps. Since the table is planned for the student or local advertiser, it includes more tasks than are usually required for the average local advertising program.

TABLE A-1 The Nine Steps Needed to Complete the Advertising Task, Applied to the Local Advertiser

Advertising Step	Local Application
1 Local advertiser establishes an objective or goal for the advertising	**a** Long-range objectives based on type of store, type of service, type of customers **b** Strategy for each individual advertisement or commercial **c** Research to support the objectives **d** Customer surveys—what current customers want; how to reach similar prospects not yet served
2 Local advertiser selects goods or services to be advertised	Research: analysis of sales records of merchandise carried or services sold, with aim of advertising best-selling items, not slow movers; observation of competitors' advertising; analysis of sales trends, fashion trends; analysis of local market—what customers want; determination of retailer's marketing area; in-store test promotions to determine advertising potential of merchandise
3 Local advertiser determines how much should be spent	Uses the task method of planning the advertising budget described in Chapter 10. Research; observation of competitors' activities; analysis of own past advertising expenditures and effectiveness; cost analysis of media required to cover marketing area
4 Local advertiser chooses the advertising media	Research: availability of media; data on type and number of prospects delivered by various media; testing media for advertising efficiency
5 Local advertiser prepares the advertising	Options: **a** Prepares it or has it prepared through own ad department **b** Uses media services **c** Uses service of local ad agency **d** Uses advertising material supplied by manufacturer Research: observation of competitors' strategy and advertising; investigations through surveys of customers' reaction to own and competitors' advertising
6 Local advertiser produces the advertising in the form required by the media	Options: **a** Produces it through production houses, or ad department production person buys services from suppliers **b** Uses media services **c** Uses services of local advertising agency which in turn deals with production houses
7 Local advertiser places the advertising in the chosen media	
8 Local advertiser pays advertising bills and takes care of paperwork	
9 Local advertiser evaluates the results of the advertising	Research: sales history of advertised goods and services; traffic counts on selling floor before and after advertising is run

Apparel and Accessories

Several types of stores carry and promote apparel and accessories. *Specialty stores* deal in narrow lines of clothing merchandise and related items appealing to specific consumer groups. Stores selling womenswear, menswear, childrenswear, men's furnishings, and shoes are typical. In larger cities, specialization can be profitably carried to extremes. There are tie shops, ladies' handbag shops, umbrella shops, and stores that specialize in larger garments or apparel for tall people. Specialty stores are discussed in detail here, as are jewelry stores, which are classified in the accessory category.

Of course, general retail merchandise stores have apparel and accessory departments. These stores include department stores, chain stores such as Sears and J. C. Penney, and *discount houses,* stores that eliminate service extras and count on volume and low prices for profit. For the department store, the promotion of apparel and accessories is only part of a larger strategy, but this category is often a crucial part. General retail merchandise stores are discussed later in the appendix. *Clothing outlets* are similar to discount houses in minimizing service and featuring low prices to obtain sales volume. Their advertising procedures are generally similar to discount houses (discussed later).

Specialty Stores

Step 1 For the specialty store, establishing a goal for the advertising is the most important of the nine steps. It must be based on the type of merchandise carried and the consumer group to which this merchandise appeals. For example, does the shop carry top fashion womenswear selling at high prices to a relatively small group of women? Or does it feature medium-priced apparel appealing to a wide audience of women? The advertising goal is very different in each case, as is the "look" or the image the advertising must communicate with its target audience.

Step 2 Selection of the goods to be advertised. For research activities see Table A-1, under step 2, Local Application.

Step 3 The task method of planning an advertising budget should be used to determine how much should be spent. Average percentage of sales invested in advertising for women's specialty stores is 2.8 percent. For menswear stores the average sales-to-advertising percentage ranges from 2.4 to 3.4 percent, depending on the store's sales volume. These averages are merely a guide. Aggressive merchandisers in this field spend 5 to 6 percent of sales on advertising. Co-op advertising funds are generally available from manufacturers, but owners of small shops often do not take the time to do the paperwork involved in order to make claims for such funds.

Step 4 Choosing media. The daily newspaper is the basic medium for specialty stores, receiving the bulk of the advertising dollars. Second in importance is local radio. Supplementary media which should be considered are direct mail, surburban weeklies, local magazines if available, and TV (for very large apparel stores and apparel chains). Demographic and circulation data on type and number of prospects should be studied.

Step 5 Preparing the advertising. In small shops, the owner usually prepares the advertising, writing the copy and using swipes (Chapter 5), manufacturer's artwork, or a local artist for illustrations. Stores with sales volume of 1 million or more have advertising departments. Local advertising agencies are seldom used except when advertising is run in broadcast media.

Step 6 Producing the advertising. Small apparel shops generally turn over artwork and manuscript of copy to local print media for production. Exceptions are stores where management insists on a distinctive "look" to the advertising. In such cases, type is set and mechanicals made for the print media. In large-volume stores, the ad department handles the production work through preparation of mechanicals. For radio, the small specialty shopowner or a delegate prepares announcer copy or has the commercials written by the local station's continuity writer. Larger apparel store advertisers often use professional talent to produce taped commercials or jingles.

Steps 7 and 8 Placing the advertising in the chosen media, paying bills, and taking care of paperwork are routine tasks.

Step 9 Evaluating advertising. Sales of each advertised item should be recorded and analyzed for effectiveness. Sales resulting from advertising placed in different media should also be consistently evaluated.

Jewelry Stores

Step 1 Establishing an objective. There are two principal groups of jewelry stores, the quality jeweler and the promotional jeweler. Advertising by the quality jeweler is not promotional; what are being sold are reliability, integrity, service, and high-quality merchandise. The advertising objective and strategy stem from store policy. The ads are restrained and dignified in appearance. Prices and extended payment plans are played down. The strategy of the promotional jeweler is quite different. This merchant seeks high volume and small profits per item. Advertising features layaway plans and reflects a slam-bang, hard-sell approach. Price is featured, and dignity and a high-fashion tone are avoided.

Step 2 Selection of the goods to be advertised. For research activities see Table A-1, under step 2, Local Application.

Step 3 Determining how much should be spent on advertising. The task method should be utilized. The average sales-to-advertising percentage for the category should be used as a check on the budget. It is high for jewelry stores, amounting to 4.4 percent. Some promotional stores spend 7 percent or more, however. Co-op advertising funds are available from manufacturers. The promotional opportunities of Mother's Day, Father's Day, graduations, and weddings result in increased advertising expenditures in May and June, and advertising peaks in mid-December for the Christmas sales period.

Step 4 Choosing media. Both promotional and quality jewelers rely on the local newspaper as the basic advertising medium. Radio receives some advertising dollars; jewelry stores rank fourteenth among local radio advertisers. Supplementary media are suburban papers and local magazines. Television is used mainly by the large credit jewelry chains at peak selling seasons.

Step 5 Preparing the advertising. There are many resources available to the jewelry store advertiser. Several services produce monthly brochures for the jewelry trade; the subscriber orders the ads wanted and on receipt of proofs, adds the store logotype. A jeweler may write the copy and pick out illustrations from the many illustration proof books at the newspaper office. Manufacturers supply brochures of illustrations and copy blocks for current items, and the jeweler can "build" ads from these elements, then including the store logotype. Or the jeweler can build ads from scratch, writing the copy and ordering artwork from local artists or photographers in order to give the campaign distinction and identity. For radio, the jewelry store owner can write simple commercials, have them prepared by a local radio station from a supplied fact sheet, or have commercials prepared professionally for a fee by a local ad agency. Large stores and chains can rely on a local agency for production of seasonal TV commercials.

Step 6 Producing the advertising. For print media, the small-store owner delivers copy and illustration to the newspaper or local magazine which then handle production. In larger stores, typesetters may be used and mechanicals made by a supplier. This permits complete control over the appearance of the advertising. Production for broadcast media has been discussed above, in step 5.

Steps 7 and 8 Placing the advertising in the chosen media, paying bills, and taking care of paperwork are routine tasks.

ALL BUSCHS STORES OPEN SUNDAY

LARGE STOCKS OF DIAMONDS, WATCHES & JEWELRY ON EASY CREDIT

SHIMMERING DIAMONDS
REGULAR $149.95, NOW...

DIAMOND EARRINGS

YOUR CHOICE **$99**

DIAMOND TRIO

DIAMOND BRIDAL SET

LADIES' DIAMOND

GENTS' DIAMOND

SUPER SAVINGS

DIAMOND PENDANT

FULL TRADE IN ON DIAMONDS
SELECTIONS MAY VARY FROM STORE TO STORE.

ENLARGED TO
SHOW DETAIL

CREDIT TERMS EASILY ARRANGED

BUSCHS
JEWELERS

35 WEST 14th ST. Bet. 5th & 6th • 573 FULTON ST. Near Flatbush Ave.
13 GRAHAM AVE. Near Broadway • 340 E. FORDHAM RD. at Kingsbridge Rd., Bnx.

The dignified appearance of the ad for a quality jeweler is in sharp contrast with the promotional jeweler's ad. The Lil'Duds and Orchard Leather ads are good small-space examples of apparel specialty shop advertising. (David Webb; Buschs; Lil'Duds; Orchard Leather)

Personalized Funwear

Boy's Shortall $25
Girl's Shoulder-tie
Sundress $25
not pictured

mini-stripe; blue-white
75% Poly 25% Cotton
name: 6 letter maximum
sizes: 9,12,18 mo.
2 thru 6 yrs.
$2.00 postage &
handling

LIL'DUDS

300 Fillmore
DENVER, COLORADO 80206
send 50 cents for brochure   303-322-9493

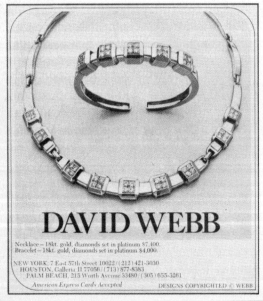

DAVID WEBB

Necklace — 18kt. gold, diamonds set in platinum $7,400.
Bracelet — 18kt. gold, diamonds set in platinum $4,000.

NEW YORK, 7 East 57th Street 10022 / (212) 421-3030
HOUSTON, Galleria II 77056 / (713) 877-8383
PALM BEACH, 215 Worth Avenue 33480 / (305) 655-3261

American Express Cards Accepted   DESIGNS COPYRIGHTED © WEBB

Orchard Leather

Custom leather
bags & garments

1570 2nd Ave. (81st & 82nd) N.Y.C. 628-4786

Step 9 Evaluating the advertising. A record of sales of each item advertised should be kept and regularly reviewed. Floor-traffic counts should be made occasionally, immediately after advertising is run. Best-selling merchandise should be featured, but even in such cases, advertised items that do not pull sales should be quickly eliminated from the advertising program.

Automotive

Two principal types of local businesses are discussed, car dealerships and auto supply stores. Automotive supplies are also sold by department stores, discount houses, and general merchandise chain stores, and such items are advertised in the normal course of promotional activities. Service stations also sell auto supplies, but managers of service stations are not aggressive advertisers.

Car Dealers

Step 1 Goals for the dealer's advertising. The goal of the dealer's new-model advertising is to increase showroom traffic. It is hoped that advertised values will attract many prospects and that their presence on the premises will create selling opportunities so that the salesperson can trade up to higher-priced models, which carry a higher profit margin. Ad goals for used cars and end-of-year models are obvious; the object is to move these cars at low profit and get them out of inventory as rapidly as possible.

Step 2 Selection of what is to be advertised. At new-model time in September and October, the best values in the line are advertised in major local media. In November, if there is a large inventory of last year's models, the dealer will cut prices on these cars and run clearance ads. Throughout the rest of the year, the aggressive dealer will run ads regularly featuring low-priced models, will run classified and display newspaper ads (plus broadcast ads) on used cars taken in on trades, and may schedule ads on rent-a-car service and leasing if this service is offered.

Step 3 Determining how much should be spent on advertising. As a retail advertiser, the local new-car dealer faces an unusual situation with regard to an advertising budget. The dealer is supported by the national advertising campaign of the car manufacturer. The dealer is also assessed a small amount of money, perhaps $35, for every car taken into inventory. This money is pooled and used to support a regional advertising campaign that appears locally, prepared by the manufacturer's ad agency. The dealer's name and address is included in this advertising. This regional advertising, as well as the national campaign, peaks at new-model time. The dealer has no say in the content or strategy of national or regional campaigns. Car dealers are also encouraged to run a local campaign at their expense. This should be prepared by the task method. But the car dealer's budget tends to be haphazard and unplanned, probably because major advertising campaigns are supporting the dealership anyway. The average car dealer is said to spend 0.8 percent of the annual sales volume on advertising; promotion-minded dealers spend twice this and more.

Step 4 Choosing media. The local newspaper still remains the car dealer's first choice and receives the bulk of budgeted advertising dollars. Other media utilized are, in order of importance, TV and radio, suburban weekly newspapers, direct mail, outdoor, Yellow Pages, and local magazines. Point-of-sale material, supplied by the manufacturer at cost, is heavily used at new-model time and generally throughout the year. Specialty advertising items may occasionally be used.

Step 5 Preparing the advertising. For the local newspaper campaign, the dealer or a delegate writes the headlines and copy although specific car-model copy blocks from the advertising proof brochures supplied by the manufacturer are often used. From these brochures, the dealer can order photos of the various models or complete ads, adding the dealership logotype. For radio advertising, the dealer's job is simpler. Copy can be written by the dealer, or scripts or taped commercials supplied by the manufacturer can be used, with the dealer adding name and address of the dealership.

Step 6 Producing the advertising. The local newspaper supplies page-size layout pads to the dealer who prefers to prepare advertising from scratch. A very rough layout is made, using the page linage previously contracted for, headlines and copy blocks are indicated, and illustrations pasted up. Nothing much need be known about specific typefaces; the dealer can rely on the paper's sales rep for help. The rough layout and attached copy are picked up 2 days or so before publication and the dealer is lucky if a proof of the ad is shown for approval before publication. Producing material for radio has been covered in step 5. For local TV commercials, the dealer will rely on the local station for production facilities and production help, or if the dealership is a very large one, hire a local production firm or an ad agency on a fee basis. For outdoor, the dealer can be supplied with material from the manufacturer, adding the logotype, or the local outdoor plant can supply art and layout assistance. Local direct mail campaign material is often available from the manufacturer.

Steps 7 and 8 Placing the advertising in the chosen media, paying bills, and taking care of paperwork are routine tasks.

Step 9 Evaluating the advertising. Showroom traffic counts should be made after advertising is run and sales records analyzed to evaluate advertising efficiency. Analysis of relative efficiency of local media is difficult because advertising in most media usually has the same content and showroom traffic attributed to specific media buys cannot be isolated. Over time, the dealer gets a "feeling" for the relative strengths of competitive media.

Auto Supply Stores

Step 1 Advertising objectives. Auto supply stores consist of independent merchants, chains, and franchised retail operations. Muffler and brake-relining shops, in this discussion, are also included in this category. This entire retail area is promotion-oriented, and the objective is to obtain business by featuring competitively priced items and service. Price is therefore the main feature of the advertising. In a line of tires, for example, the lowest-priced merchandise is usually advertised.

Step 2 Selection of what is to be advertised. The tire store, muffler shop, and brake-relining shop naturally emphasize their specialty merchandise or service; general auto supply stores offer a wide variety of goods. Here the rule of advertising best-selling items should be strictly followed. This means featuring tires, batteries, motor oil and filters, shock absorbers, and antifreeze in season. Many other items on sale receive small space in these "busy" ads.

Step 3 Determining the ad budget size. Auto supply stores consist of independent merchants, chains, and franchised retail operations. It is estimated that ad budgets run from 2 to 5 percent or more of annual sales. Because the business is competitive and promotion-oriented, underspending on advertising is a false economy. The dealer should spend a minimum of 5 percent of sales, and the task method of budget preparation should be used. Cooperative advertising dollars often make an important contribution to the ad budget.

Step 4 Choosing media. The daily newspaper is the mainstay of the ad budget, followed in importance by radio. TV is seldom used except by large-volume merchandisers in urban centers. Using the Yellow Pages is important to the auto supply store advertiser.

Step 5 Preparing the advertising. Large retail chains have an ad department. Personnel rely on manufacturer's proof books for the illustrations and copy blocks needed for print advertising, or copy can be written from the same sources. For radio advertising, manufacturers of tires and batteries supply scripts, or copy for these items and others can be written from scratch. Managers of franchised retail operations are supplied with advertising material by the advertising department of the parent organization.

Step 6 Producing the advertising. In the case of the small independent store, copy and illustration plus a very rough layout are usually given to the newspaper for production. The ad department of a chain supplies mechanicals to print media. The franchised dealer turns over proofs ordered from the parent organization's ad brochure, adding store logotype. When preproduced tapes of radio commercials are needed, the advertiser can rely on a local radio station for production or arrange for production through local suppliers or a local ad agency.

Steps 7 and 8 Placing the advertising in the chosen media, bill paying, and taking care of paperwork are routine tasks.

Step 9 Evaluating the advertising. The sales record of advertised items is kept and regularly reviewed.

The New Rochelle Dodge ad is a busy, hard-to-read example of an auto dealer's end-of-year clearance strategy. The ad for Carl's is typical of auto supply store multi-item advertising. (Courtesy New Rochelle Dodge; Carl's Auto Parts and Tire Center)

Business Services

In this category, the classification system of the U.S. Office of Education lists business such as carpet installers, employment agencies, interior decorators and planners, management consultants, marketing research firms, sales promotion firms, security systems, and telephone answering services. Advertising services are classified separately by the USOE but have been included here.

Step 1 Establishing objectives and an advertising strategy. As most of these services tailor their work to varying customer requirements, quality and reliability of service should be emphasized and price ignored, or generalized into adjectives such as "economical." Advertising should be placed at regular intervals as there are no seasonal peaks in these businesses. The advertising will be read (and hopefully acted upon) when the prospect has a need for the service.

Step 2 Selection of what is to be advertised presents no problem; these firms sell a particular kind of service, and advertising, when it is done, obviously concentrates on the service performed.

Step 3 Determining how much should be spent on advertising. Since most of the above businesses rely primarily on personal selling to obtain sales, advertising is merely supportive and not of key importance. It is estimated that services spend between 0.5 and 1 percent of sales volume on advertising annually. The exception is the employment agency. The advertising of jobs available and listed with the agency is a daily necessity. Here the advertising budget amounts to 5 percent (or more) of sales.

Step 4 Choosing the media. Direct mail and Yellow Pages advertising should be considered first in the media plan. A newspaper campaign should receive consideration from the large service firms. For employment agencies the daily (and Sunday) newspaper is a must.

Step 5 Preparing the advertising. Direct mail campaigns are handled on a do-it-yourself basis. Newspaper and Yellow Pages ad departments are available resources in preparing material. Large service firms should consider the use of a local advertising agency on a fee basis.

Step 6 Producing the advertising. Resources listed in step 5 handle production of advertising.

Steps 7 and 8 Placing the advertising in the chosen media, paying bills, and taking care of paperwork are routine tasks.

These advertisements offer business services and appear on the business pages of the daily newspaper. (Courtesy The Charles Brunelle Company; Hawthorne International Inc.; Telephone Answering Service Co.)

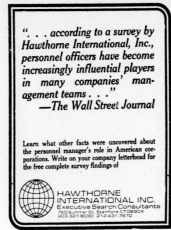

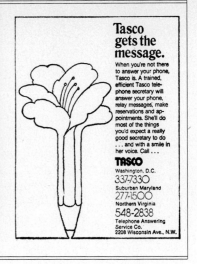

Step 9 Evaluating the advertising. When advertising is run, its job is to support the sales force. Evaluation of its effectiveness can be simplified by using keyed copy that offers prospects cost estimates or further information delivered in person by a sales representative. This method can yield information on the pulling power of individual ads or different media.

Finance and Credit

Two major advertising areas are discussed, commercial banks, and savings institutions. Stock brokerage firms and small loan companies are not included because they do little local advertising.

Commercial Banks

Step 1 Establishing objectives. The goals of the commercial bank's consumer advertising are to increase personal checking accounts and to sell its services to depositors and the general public alike. Commercial banks face a difficult problem because banking services are regulated by government bodies and one bank offers the same services as its competitor. However, bankers find it necessary to advertise to attract business. The general strategy for the advertising should be to convey a feeling of warmth and friendliness. imply stability, stress the personal service of its employees to customers, and try to convince prospects that service is "better," more understanding, and more convenient—if such is the case.

Step 2 Selection of services to be advertised. Typical advertised services are

- Personal checking accounts
- Personal loans (mortgage, home improvement, debt consolidation, and so on)
- Convenient hours, drive-up windows, 24-hour automatic teller
- Passbook savings accounts
- Credit cards
- Money management (purchase of stocks and bonds, trustee services, investment advisory and custodian services)
- Safe deposit boxes

The last three items receive little advertising support. Note that these are all consumer services. The important services that commercial banks give to businesspeople, such as extension of credit and commercial checking accounts, are sold on a basis of personal selling. Advertising is relatively unimportant, although direct mail is sometimes used.

Step 3 Determining the ad budget size. Bankers sell their services and thus create a sales volume, but attempting to determine what this figure is and using it as a basis for preparing an ad budget is difficult and results can be misleading. A gain in deposits might be the result of new business generated by promotion, or the result of one or two large corporate depositors temporarily adding to their accounts. Frequently the bank's total deposits are used as a budget basis and the small figure of 1 percent is applied to it. This is arbitrary and does not consider sales objectives. The task method, cross-checked by competitors' expenditures and by a percentage-of-total-deposits figure, is a better way to determine the budget. Average percentage of "sales" invested in advertising is 1.3 percent.

Step 4 Choosing the media. The daily newspaper remains the most important part of the media plan, although in the largest metropolitan markets, TV spending may top newspapers. Television advertising, when affordable and when the marketing area indicates its use, should be carefully considered. Commercial bank television advertising has experienced considerable growth in recent years. Radio usually is included in the media plan, and financial institutions rank first on the list of local radio advertisers. Outdoor, transit, local magazines, and suburban papers should also be considered in a media plan.

Step 5 Preparing the advertising. Depending on the size of the bank, preparing the advertising will be the responsibility of a bank officer, a small advertising department, or (for larger banks) an advertising agency. Advertising or mat services specializing in bank advertising are numerous and supply newspaper campaigns for principal banking services. Syndicated television and radio commercials with room for localization are also available.

Step 6 Producing the advertising. The small-town banker can operate on a do-it-yourself basis, writing the copy and choosing illustrations available in proof books at the newspaper office, with the newspaper handling production. When syndicated TV and radio material is used, production is completed with purchase of the material, and the localization of the spots handled at the TV or radio station. At larger banks, the production task is done by the ad department using local suppliers, or accomplished by the bank's advertising agency.

Steps 7 and 8 Placing the advertising, paying bills, and paperwork are routine tasks.

Step 9 Evaluating the advertising. The various media should ideally be tested for efficiency. When specific services such as 24-hour teller, new, more convenient banking hours, or personal loans are advertised, an effort should be made to compare business obtained with the cost of the advertising.

Savings Institutions

Step 1 Establishing a goal. The primary goals of savings institutions are to obtain new depositors and to keep present depositors' accounts growing. These goals are accomplished by stressing security in the advertising. Funds deposited are safe, guaranteed against loss (up to a certain figure) by a government agency, not subject to market fluctuation, and grow through the power of compound interest. Executions of the primary advertising goals consist of enumerating these security factors, pointing out the reasons to save (vacation, education, retirement, emergencies, etc.), featuring high interest rates and the growth power of compound interest, offering new checking accounts, and describing convenience services such as banking by mail.

Step 2 Selection of services to be advertised. Savings institutions differ from commercial banks in one principal way: savings institutions deal with the general public, while commercial banks deal with the general public and businesses. But, as noted, commercial banks do not generally use advertising to generate commercial business. Consumer services offered by savings institutions that are advertised parallel to a certain extent those advertised by commercial banks, particularly with the advent of checking accounts and NOW accounts permitted by certain state banking commissions. A list of savings institution services follows:

- Interest rates
- Savings incentives (gifts offered to depositors at the beginning of interest periods)
- Checking accounts, NOW accounts where permitted

The ad for Charter Oak Bank does a good job of conveying the idea that this commercial bank stresses personal service. The ad for the savings bank sells its Christmas Club with a special offer and features the interest rate. (Courtesy Charter Oak Bank and Trust Company; Home Savings and Loan Association)

- Loans (passbook, general-purpose, mortgage, home improvement, education, etc.)
- Banking by mail
- Savings Bank Life Insurance
- "The reasons to save"
- Automatic mail deposit of Social Security checks
- Christmas Clubs

All these services receive advertising support. Interest rates are first in importance from an advertising point of view, however.

Step 3 Determining the budget size. Savings banks and savings and loan associations should follow the same procedures as commercial banks as outlined in step 1, above. Average percent of "sales" (deposits) invested in advertising is 1.5 percent for savings institutions.

Step 4 Choosing the media. See step 4 for commercial banks.

Step 5 Preparing the advertising. See step 5, for commercial banks.

Step 6 Producing the advertising. See step 6 for commercial banks.

Steps 7 and 8 Placing the advertising, paying bills, and paperwork are routine tasks.

Step 9 Evaluating the advertising. Effectiveness of advertising can be estimated with a fair degree of accuracy by savings institutions. When higher interest rates are advertised, for example, the number of new accounts opened can be compared with the cost of advertising featuring the rates. When a series of ads is run on automatic Social Security check deposit, the number of customers who respond by filling out permission slips authorizing this procedure can easily be checked. If possible, advertisements featuring special services should be used to test the pulling power of various media.

Floral and Garden

In this section we will discuss garden supply stores, nurseries, and garden centers, concerns combining an enclosed sales area and an outdoor lot where plants, shrubs, and small trees are displayed and bulky merchandise stored. Advertising by florists is small in total volume and therefore will not be covered. Florists in general are do-it-yourself advertisers running small space ads on a limited basis. In season, garden supplies are often sold by discount houses and variety stores. This merchandise is advertised as part of store's regular promotional program.

Step 1 Establishing objectives. The objective of obtaining satisfactory sales volume is usually achieved by running promotional, competitive advertising that features price. Exceptions are nurseries specializing in rarer items for the garden; price is no object here, and quality of merchandise is featured. The promotional-type firm's manager will do well to include institutional copy in the advertising on occasion; the knowledge and expertise of the sales personnel should be stressed, as customers are full of questions about garden items. See discussion of one merchant's advertising program in Chapter 4.

Step 2 Selecting items to be advertised. The rule of advertising only best-selling items should be followed. This means featuring seeds, plants, garden equipment, fertilizer, peat moss, etc., in the spring; sprays, fertilizer, and garden utensils in the summer; and such items as shrubs and trees in the fall. See also Local Application, step 2, Table A-1.

Step 3 Determining how much should be spent. The task method of establishing a budget should be used, cross-checked by observation of competitors' expenditures, and by the average percentage of sales invested in advertising, which is 2.1 for the category. As sales are heavy in spring, summer, and early fall, advertising is concentrated in these periods. Pre-Christmas selling also receives advertising support. Co-op funds are generally available from seed companies and garden equipment manufacturers.

Step 4 Choosing advertising media. The local daily newspaper receives the bulk of the merchant's ad budget. The use of seasonal catalogs should be considered, as this can be a profitable promotion device. Other media are radio, direct mail to charge customers, and suburban newspapers when their circulation fits the concern's marketing area.

Step 5 Preparing the advertising. The merchant can operate on a do-it-yourself basis, writing headlines and copy and using stock artwork available in proof books at the local newspaper office. Seed companies, garden-equipment makers, and fertilizer manufacturers offer advertising brochures from which copy block and illustrations can be selected. Radio scripts, personalized with the dealer's name and address, are usually available from the same sources. Seasonal standard catalogs are available, which are imprinted with the local store's identification, but the dealer must then carry all the items included.

Step 6 Producing the advertising. When the dealer prepares the advertising from scratch, the local newspaper handles production. The local radio station's facilities can be used when tapes are made requiring special effects or stock music. Because of the small size of ad budgets in this field, advertising agencies are rarely used.

Lexington Gardens promotes seasonal merchandise in its well-designed adver-
tisement; type for the Christmas promotional ad for The Greenery was set by the
local newspaper, with less attention paid to layout. (Courtesy Lexington Gardens;
The Greenery)

Steps 7 and 8 Placing the advertising, bill paying, and paperwork are routine tasks.

Step 9 Evaluation advertising results. Sales history of advertised items should be checked to evaluate the efficiency of the advertising. Store traffic counts should be made immediately after advertising is run. Special offers advertised in a single advertising medium are a good way to judge the relative pulling power of elements on the media list.

Food Marketing

Included in the food marketing classification are retailers and wholesalers of consumer food items. Only the retailers are interesting to us from a local advertising point of view; wholesalers with relatively few trade customers are not local advertisers. National, regional, and local supermarket chains do not concern us either. The local unit manager has no say in the advertising for the unit; advertising is prepared in the ad department of chain store headquarters and placed in local media to support the store unit. For brief comments on chain store ad departments, refer to Chapter 4. Here we will concern ourselves with the advertising programs of independent supermarkets and specialty food stores such as bakeries, grocery stores, meat and fish markets, and gourmet food shops. Items carried in gourmet food shops and bakeries are of course also carried by food departments of large department stores, and advertising for this section receives its allocation in the store's monthly ad plan, its advertising volume depending on size of the food department.

Independent Supermarkets

Step 1 Establishing objectives. The purpose of the advertising is to stimulate store traffic. A promotional, price-oriented strategy for the advertising must be followed. The operator attempts to capture competitors' customers by advertising specials which are often loss leaders, selected items priced at no profit or even at a loss. The customer coming in for the special, it is hoped, will fill the shopping cart with other items while in the store. The advertising also features limited-time price-off coupons and sometimes promotions such as encyclopedias and dinnerware offered on a weekly basis, all in an effort to build traffic. Supermarket advertising shouts; it is characterized by large black faces for prices, little use of white space, and the maximum number of items the ad can hold.

Step 2 Selecting the items to be advertised. The rule of advertising only best-selling items should be followed. Meat and poultry specials are the mainstay traffic builders; they are featured in print layouts, and approximately 25 percent of total ad space is devoted to them. Next in importance are canned and package goods specials, followed by fresh produce and frozen food specials such as orange juice.

Step 3 Determining how much should be spent. The task method of budget preparation is the recommended procedure, cross-checked by observation of competitors' media expenditures and by the average percentage of sales invested in advertising, which is estimated at 1.5 to 2 percent. Since advertising is of highest importance to the supermarket operator, it is recommended that 2 percent of sales be the minimum ad budget figure. Co-op advertising dollars are available from marketers of branded products.

Step 4 Choosing advertising media. The local newspaper receives the bulk of the independent supermarket operator's ad budget. Supermarket advertising ranks second in importance in newspaper retail advertising volume. Large space units are used. One-page ads are characteristic, and sometimes double-page spreads, or "double trucks," are purchased. Radio advertising should be considered; supermarkets rank sixth among local radio advertisers. Television is generally unaffordable for the independent operator. Flyers featuring specials are valuable. Suburban weekly newspapers are used when circulation fits the store's sales area. Advertising during the week is usually run on Wednesday, although small-space newspaper ads are sometimes run on other days.

Step 5 Preparing the advertising. The independent operator (or delegate) is a do-it-yourself, part-time advertiser who sets prices, writes "label" headlines, hardly ever uses anything more than an adjective or two to describe items, and picks out stock illustrations from proof books supplied by the local newspaper. The operator can subscribe to one of several advertising (mat) services which mail out monthly seasonally oriented brochures. From these, headline, illustration, and border elements can be ordered, and ads put together by the operator. The continuity writer at the local radio station prepares commercials based on a supplied fact sheet if the operator doesn't want to write radio copy.

Step 6 Producing the advertising. When the operator prepares the advertising, the local newspaper handles production. A local print shop can prepare flyers. The local radio station personnel can make up tapes of commercials when required including special effects and stock music.

Steps 7 and 8 Placing the advertising, bill paying, and paperwork are routine tasks.

Step 9 Evaluating advertising results. In the course of time, the independent supermarket operator who carefully observes the sales results of featuring certain specials can learn to forecast precisely what will happen to store traffic and sales when certain advertising offers are made. These merchants contend for business with the supermarket chain but do not have their resources and buying power. One operator, for example, regularly features in advertising a sirloin steak special. The meat is top quality but is sold as a loss leader. The price per pound matches A&P. This particular offering has developed new customers for the quality meats sold in this independent store, even though the meat department prices are generally higher than those in the chain stores.

Specialty Food Stores

Step 1 Establishing advertising objectives. Specialty food shops are quality-oriented not price-oriented. The average patron is something of a gourmet, willing to pay more for quality foods. Therefore, the objective is to play down price and play up value and quality in the advertising. Occasionally, however, specials will be advertised to gain new customers and increase store traffic. A sound approach is to build the shop's image through a distinctive layout, logotype, and slogan in small-space newspaper ads. Institutional copy can be effective, particularly if a personality spokesman is developed such as "Sam the Cheese Man," or the "Saltwater Farmer."

Step 2 Selecting items to be advertised. The most popular merchandise with established sales appeal should be advertised. See also step 2, Local Application, in Table A-1.

Step 3 Determining how much should be spent. Specialty food stores and local specialty food chains have small sales volume and consequently small advertising budgets. The task method should be used for budget preparation, although it seldom is. General retail practice—among those merchants who do maintain a consistent advertising program—is to spend what amounts to 2 percent of sales volume on advertising.

Step 4 Choosing advertising media. Customers for specialty food stores are not numerous, have ample discretionary income, and are willing to make a special trip to obtain the best available product. Management must make an effort to find them and cover a wide area with advertising messages. The daily newspaper should head the media list, and a regular, small-space ad program should be initiated in the Wednesday edition food section. Radio is a profitable supplementary medium. Direct mail should be tested, if possible, exchanging customer lists with noncompetitive specialty food shops.

Step 5 Preparing the advertising. Most managers or their delegates do the creative job themselves. When illustrations are needed for print advertisements, they are obtained from newspaper proof books or principal suppliers of the store's merchandise. Continuity writers at local radio stations will write commercials from supplied fact sheets, or store managers can write their own copy if they wish.

Step 6 Producing the advertising. The production job is uncomplicated. Written copy, a very rough layout, and scrap illustrations are picked up by a newspaper sales rep and the newspaper handles production. Procedure for radio advertising is included in step 5, above.

Steps 7 and 8 Placing the advertising, bill paying, and paperwork are routine tasks.

Step 9 Evaluating advertising results. A record of sales results after advertising specific merchandise should be kept and analyzed. Store traffic counts should be made from time to time after ads are run.

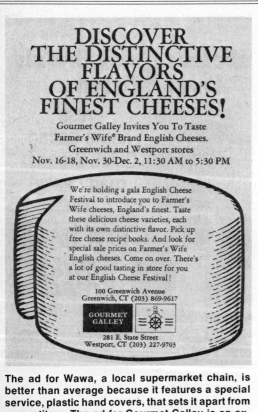

The ad for Wawa, a local supermarket chain, is better than average because it features a special service, plastic hand covers, that sets it apart from competitors. The ad for Gourmet Galley is an excellent example of specialty food store advertising. (Courtesy Wawa Food Markets, Wawa, PA and Gourmet Galley).

Food Services

The food service category includes restaurants, restaurant chains, hotel- and motel-operated restaurants, lunch counters, coffee shops, diners, catering concerns, and fast-food establishments. The latter are quick-service businesses offering a limited menu with items eaten on the premises and also sold from a take-out counter. Fast-food establishments are major advertisers, but since most are franchise operations or chain-operated outlets, the bulk of the advertising that supports them is national. The local franchiser is encouraged to support the unit with local advertising at the franchiser's cost, but material is supplied by chain headquarters. The job for the franchiser is therefore confined to selection of local media, and step 4, below, covers this activity. In this food service section it is sufficient to describe the advertising task for restaurants only; other merchants in this category operating diners, catering concerns and the like, when they advertise at all, can follow the steps below.

Step 1 Establishing an advertising objective. The variety of restaurant images is endless. Ads should project (in layout, illustration, copy, and theme or slogan) the restaurant's image. Is it North Italian, French, or Oriental? Is the restaurant a steak house or seafood house? The objective is to emphasize the type of restaurant. Much advertising in this field is of the reminder type, and while this is better than no advertising at all, it can't be expected to build much business. Successful restaurateurs today sell the restaurant's atmosphere almost as much as the food they serve. Decor and styling are increasingly important as a sales tool in attracting patrons. This merchandising approach calls for advertising that uses its appearance to help build the image the owners want for their business.

Step 2 Selecting what is to be advertised. The ads should be large enough to allow featuring specialties of the house *and their prices*. The most popular items should be emphasized, and if special nights (buffet, roast beef night, etc.) are the policy, ads should be based on these features. Other attractions such as valet parking, oversized drinks, and half-priced children's meals should be included in the copy when they apply.

Step 3 Determining how much should be spent. The task method of determining an annual budget should be followed, cross-checking with estimates of competitors' ad spending and the average percentage of sales invested in advertising for restaurants. The average for those under $50,000 in sales volume is only 0.6 percent; for restaurants with $50,000 to $100,000 sales volume, the average is 0.9 percent; for restaurants with $100,000 to $200,000 sales volume, the average is 1.7 percent, according to the Newspaper Advertising Bureau. It is essential that a restaurant advertise to be successful, and it is recommended that the *minimum* percentage of sales invested in advertising be 2 percent. A small-space ad campaign in print media (100 to 200 lines per ad) should be scheduled to run consistently throughout the year; people need to be reminded regularly of a restaurant's presence. The schedule should be expanded at such times as Mother's Day, Thanksgiving, and the Christmas holidays.

Step 4 Choosing advertising media. Newspapers and radio are the basic media. Outdoor, transit, and direct mail get a percentage of the budget, and outdoor and transit are reminder advertising. Local magazines and suburban weeklies are also used when circulation fits the market area. TV advertising is occasionally used, particularly in large metropolitan areas for local restaurant chains and large individual restaurants.

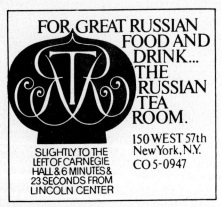

FOR GREAT RUSSIAN FOOD AND DRINK... THE RUSSIAN TEA ROOM.

150 WEST 57th
New York, N.Y.
CO 5-0947

SLIGHTLY TO THE LEFT OF CARNEGIE HALL & 6 MINUTES & 23 SECONDS FROM LINCOLN CENTER

The Proud Popover ad stresses price; the Russian Tea Room ad features restaurant atmosphere. (Courtesy The Russian Tea Room; The Proud Popover Restaurant and Tavern)

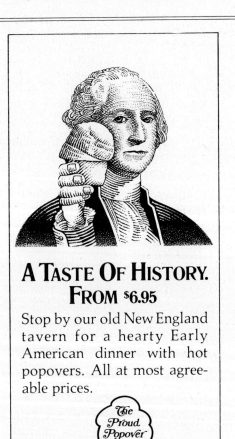

A TASTE OF HISTORY.
FROM $6.95

Stop by our old New England tavern for a hearty Early American dinner with hot popovers. All at most agreeable prices.

The Proud Popover

Restaurant & **Tavern**

Water Tower Place — 6th Level, Chicago

Step 5 Preparing the advertising. The owner of a small- to medium-sized restaurant usually operates on a do-it-yourself basis, writing heads and copy, using scrap illustrations for print ads, and writing radio copy or preparing a commercial fact sheet for local stations. The owner will do well to have a local artist design a logotype. Local advertising agencies are sometimes used by large restaurants and restaurant chains. A fee basis is the usual method of agency reimbursement.

Step 6 Producing the advertising. When the restaurateur prepares print advertising from scratch, the local newspaper (or local magazine) handles the production. Radio station facilities are available for production of tapes when required, and the continuity writer can prepare scripts (based on a supplied fact sheet) to be read live by an announcer. When an ad agency is hired, production of all material is done through this resource.

Steps 7 and 8 Placing the advertising, paperwork, and bill paying are routine tasks.

Step 9 Evaluating advertising results. The restaurateur can quickly check on the efficiency of individual ads by comparing business done when specialties (or special nights) are advertised compared with the same menu items when not promoted. A pretty good evaluation of the pulling power of a specific medium can also be made by restricting advertised specialties to one medium at a time and later comparing business done as a result of the ad.

General Retail Merchandise

Under this heading are grouped department stores, chain and independent variety stores, general merchandise chain stores (such as Sears), and chain and independent discount houses. All sell a wide variety of merchandise, but price ranges are not similar because of selling methods and (on occasion) the varying quality of goods sold. Drugstores are also included in this general retail merchandise category. The local manager of a general merchandise chain store, like the manager of a chain supermarket unit, has no local advertising task. Advertising is a headquarters activity and hence does not concern us in this local advertising appendix. Independent variety stores are a rarity, and the few there are follow advertising procedures basically similar to those of discount houses. Important to us are the advertising procedures of department stores, drugstores, and discount houses, discussed below.

Department Stores

Department store advertising ranks first in newspaper retail advertising volume by a very wide margin; 26 percent of all retail newspaper advertising is run by department stores, followed by 8.9 percent for food stores. In local radio advertising, department stores (together with clothing stores) rank second in volume. Because of the importance of department store advertising, it has been discussed in detail elsewhere. At this point the student should reread Advertising Departments in Larger Retail Stores, Chapter 4; Organizing for Advertising: The Department Store, Chapter 5; and A Sample Department Store Budget, Chapter 10. A summary of the nine steps follows.

Step 1 Establishing advertising goals. Is the store promotional, nonpromotional, or a combination of both? The sales objective of the promotional store is maximum sales volume of low- to medium-priced merchandising lines and the ad strategy is to feature sales events and low prices. Profits are minimal and depend on high volume. The nonpromotional store features regular-priced merchandise, and sales are not as frequent. It may carry better-grade, higher-priced items and appeal to customers wanting service and attention. The combination store obviously follows a sales policy which falls between these two extremes, featuring both sale-priced merchandise and regular-priced merchandise in its advertising. The look of the ads reflect these varying sales strategies.

Step 2 Selecting items to be advertised. The rule of promoting only best-selling items should be strictly followed. See also Local Application, step 2 in Table A-1.

Step 3 Determining how much should be spent. The task method of establishing the overall budget must be followed, supported by departmental advertising plans. Average percentage of sales invested in advertising is 2.8 percent. Average percentage by size of store sales volume is listed in Table 10-2. Competitors' advertising expenditures should be closely observed. A reserve fund (10 percent of the budget) should be available to promote unforeseen fashion trends and special purchases. Co-op dollars are generally available from large suppliers of merchandise; full use should be made of these opportunities.

Step 4 Choosing advertising media. Department stores rely first on newspapers in the allocation of budget dollars. Radio advertising is next in importance. In metropolitan areas, some stores include television in their media list. Direct mail, transit advertising, local magazines, suburban newspapers, and outdoor (for reminder copy) are also media used to a limited extent.

Step 5 Preparing the advertising. Copy is written and layouts made within the store's advertising department. Photographs and artwork are prepared by department staff; outside artists are occasionally used. In very large stores an advertising agency may be hired to prepare institutional advertising, but the usual method is to prepare institutional copy in the ad department.

Step 6 Producing the advertising. There are production people in the ad department for this task. Typesetting firms are usually used by large stores; smaller merchants rely on local newspaper facilities for this service. A broadcast section, when a part of the ad department, handles production of broadcast advertising material.

Steps 7 and 8 Placing the advertising, bill paying, and paperwork are routine tasks. The accounting department checks ads "as run" from tearsheets to determine whether their size is as ordered; this department handles claim procedure for available co-op monies.

Step 9 Evaluating advertising results. The buyer writes up sales results of departmental advertised merchandise, and this is a basis for measuring the success of the promotion. Department traffic counts should be made regularly, immediately following advertising.

Drugstores

Step 1 Establishing advertising objectives. Most drugstores are highly promotional. Managers seek volume through competitively priced merchandise. Consequently, strategy is to feature price on best-selling items. Advertising supports the seasonal aspects of the business; health aids are featured during the "cold season," back-to-school items in early September, and gift items during the pre-Christmas selling period. Advertising is run regularly throughout the year, however. In the few drugstores that are nonpromotional the sales emphasis is on over-the-counter drugs, prescriptions, drugs, and health and beauty aids. They are not miniature discount houses selling a wide variety of merchandise, as promotional stores are. Little advertising is done, and advertising strategy sometimes calls for institutional copy.

Step 2 Selecting the items to be advertised. As indicated in step 1, the druggist will feature only best-selling items in the advertising program; it does no good to promote poorly known brands.

Step 3 Determining how much should be spent. Ideally, the task method of budget preparation should be used. Average percentage of sales invested in advertising should be used as a cross-check; for chain drugstores it is 1.7 percent and 1.3 percent for independents. The drugstore advertiser is beseiged with offers of co-op advertising plans from suppliers. The druggist is selective in use of them and will accept co-op dollars only from makers of brands that are volume sellers.

Step 4 Choosing advertising media. Managers of promotional stores list the newspaper as first choice; drugstores rank eleventh in newspaper retail volume, and large-space ads are used. Radio is the second medium, thirteenth in rank among local radio advertisers. Transit and suburban weekly newspapers also appear often on media lists when circulation matches sales area.

Step 5 Preparing the advertising. In the case of independents, advertising preparation is the job of the manager or assistant manager, but the sales volume of the large chains makes a small advertising department affordable. A drugstore advertiser can use proofs supplied by the makers of the goods on sale or can deal with advertising (mat) services that offer brochures containing illustrations of best-selling items, borders, copy blocks, seasonal and standard heads, and complete ads.

Step 6 Producing the advertising. When the druggist prepares the newspaper ads from scratch, the local newspaper handles production. In chains, this function is accomplished in the ad department. For radio, the station's continuity writer can handle commercial production details when necessary.

Steps 7 and 8 Placing the advertising, bill paying, and paperwork are routine tasks.

Step 9 Evaluating the results. Very little is done. The drugstore advertiser should keep a sales record of advertised items to evaluate the advertising's efficiency.

Discount Houses

Step 1 Establishing advertising objectives. The discount house ad objective is to build maximum sales volume, selling leading brands at the lowest possible price. Prices are lower than those prevailing at department stores because frills are eliminated, service is minimal, decor plain and unvarnished, and delivery of merchandise is available (if at all) at a fee. In newspaper advertising the strategy dictates large multi-item ads featuring branded merchandise at low prices. Headlines tend to be label heads rather than informative ones and merely state the presence of merchandise on sale. Copy is factual and brief.

Step 2 Selecting items to be advertised. Promotional effort is in the main placed behind well-known brand names carried by the discount house. Home appliances, camera and film equipment, stereo, radio and TV sets, clothing items, small home furnishings, luggage—in fact, most of the merchandise carried by department stores—are featured. However, these items must do a good sales volume to be included.

Step 3 Determining how much should be spent. The task method of budget preparation should be stressed, and an over-all advertising plan, supported by departmental plans should be used. Department store planning practice is followed by discount stores (see Chapter 10). Budget figures should be checked against estimated competitors' advertising expendi-

Advertisements for drugstores and discount houses win no awards for appearance. Their promotional ads feature price and use multi-item layouts, label heads, and little or no copy. (Courtesy Jupiter Discount Store; Archer Kent)

tures, and against the average percentage of sales invested in advertising by discount houses, which amounts to 2.4 percent. Co-op advertising is an important source of budget funds.

Step 4 Choosing advertising media. Newspapers receive the bulk of the ad budget, and large stores sometimes run special color sections in the Sunday paper. Radio is second in importance. In large metropolitan markets some TV may be used. Suburban weeklies are used when circulation matches the sales area.

Step 5 Preparing the advertising. A very small advertising department is affordable. Print copy and layout are prepared there; resources are fact sheets, photos, and proofs of artwork supplied by manufacturers. Radio copy can be prepared in the department, or fact sheets can be supplied to continuity writers at the local radio station.

Step 6 Producing the advertising. For newspaper ads, this presents no problem, as the local newspaper handles the production. Copy and heads can be "pub set" (set by the newspaper), or a typesetter can be used if more control over the look of the advertising is desired. Radio production, if tapes or special effects are required, can be handled at the radio station's studios.

Steps 7 and 8 Placing advertising, bill paying, and paperwork, including co-op claims, are routine tasks.

Step 9 Evaluating advertising results. A sales history should be written up on all advertised merchandise and used as a basis for measuring the success of promotions. Department traffic counts should be made on occasion, immediately following advertising.

Hardware, Building Materials, and Farm Supplies and Equipment

Step 1 Establishing advertising objectives. Customers go to these retail outlets with specific needs in mind, although there is always the possibility of impulse buying at hardware and building materials outlets. These two types of stores therefore feature regular-price merchandise along with specials and if possible build the firm's reputation as a source of quality items and customer information. The farm supplies and equipment dealer carries much equipment with high price tags; price is not particularly emphasized, and the reliability and quality of the merchandise should be stressed.

Step 2 Selecting the goods to be advertised. The rule of only advertising best-selling merchandise should be followed.

Step 3 Determining the budget size. As in all cases, the task method is recommended for budget preparation. Very few dealers in these categories use it, however. Estimates of competitors' budgets are a budget cross-check. According to the Newspaper Advertising Bureau, average percentage of sales invested in advertising is 1.6 for hardware dealers and 0.5 for building material dealers. The figure for farm equipment dealers is unknown, but it is estimated that they spend the same amount as building material dealers. Co-op funds are available in this category from merchandise suppliers. Such allowances range from 20 to 50 percent of the cost of advertising the makers' items.

Step 4 Choosing the media. Retail merchants in the hardware and building materials business primarily use the local newspaper and catalogs. Radio also receives some of the budget dollars. Direct mail is also occasionally used, but television advertising is a rarity. The farm supplies and equipment merchant uses suburban and rural weeklies and places radio commercials on farm radio programs.

Step 5 Preparing the advertising. Hardware and retail building equipment dealers rely on two sources for their advertising material, manufacturers and suppliers of the items they carry and cooperative buying concerns if they use them. These sources supply offset proofs of illustrations, headlines, copy blocks, and complete ads which are devoted to seasonal or staple items. For broadcast media, they offer radio scripts and tapes and occasionally TV commercials for local use. The merchant may prefer to create the print advertising and radio commercials from scratch, basing them on materials received, often rewriting some of the copy. The merchant can rely on stock catalogs that can be ordered with modifications to local requirements. They are supplied by the cooperative buying service or by printing houses specializing in the field. The farm equipment dealer in general uses manufacturers' advertising materials as the primary source for whatever advertising is run.

Step 6 Producing the advertising. This step presents no problem to the merchant. Proofs or assembled ad elements are handled by the newspaper's production facilities, and radio commercials can be written from a supplied fact sheet by the station's continuity department. Tapes and special effects can be done by studio personnel.

Steps 7 and 8 Placing the advertising, paying bills, and paperwork, including co-op advertising claims, are routine tasks.

Step 9 Evaluating the advertising. An effort must be made to keep a record of the sales history of items advertised to measure the advertising's effectiveness. Some information on media efficiency can be obtained by restricting the advertising of specials to a single medium and analyzing results.

This ad is representative of the hardware and building supplies category. Note the offer of a free ceiling installation clinic, a good way to increase the store's reputation for customer service. (Courtesy W. G. Glenney Co.)

Home Furnishings

The classification system for distributive education includes in the home furnishings category furniture, household appliances, floor coverings, draperies, and specialized lines of home items. It is not necessary to describe individually the advertising tasks of the many specialized retailers in this field, as their tasks are generally similar. Furniture, carpeting, and textile stores will be discussed as a group, and appliance retailers will be covered separately as their advertising task is unique. Home furnishings are sold, of course, by department stores, chain general merchandise stores, discount houses, and other retail outlets. These items are included in the overall advertising plan of the store.

Furniture, Carpeting, and Textile Stores

Step 1 Establishing an advertising goal. The strategy for quality and regular-priced merchandise stores in this category is to feature name-brand merchandise at competitive prices to build sales volume. Customers visit these stores with a definite purchase in mind when the need occurs; there is little impulse buying. Therefore, a consistent advertising program should be run. Furniture outlets also require advertising consistency, but the advertising is different in other ways. These retailers resemble discount houses in their no-frills approach. Advertising is highly promotional, price is featured, and while name-brand merchandise is advertised, often the advertised specials promote merchandise of an anonymous manufacturer, referred to as a "leading maker" or "famous maker." Many small retail specialty stores, selling specific lines of merchandise such as lighting fixtures, modern furniture, Americana items and the like, obviously have a goal of creating an image in their specialized field. Their advertising tasks are generally similar to that of specialty apparel shops, described toward the beginning of this appendix.

Step 2 Selection of goods to be advertised. The rule of advertising only best-selling merchandise must be followed. Refer to Local Application, step 2 of Table A-1.

Step 3 Determining the ad budget size. The task method of budget preparation should be followed, cross-checked by observation of competitors' ad spending. The average percentage of sales invested in advertising for furniture stores is 5 percent; it is estimated that the average carpeting and textile store spends the same amount. Such average percentages should only be used as a general guide. Co-op advertising funds are available from large suppliers.

Step 4 Choosing media. Newspaper advertising (including suburban weeklies when circulation matches the store's sales area) is the mainstay of the ad budget. Radio is the second most important medium that should be considered. Television advertising is used by large stores in metropolitan areas. Transit, outdoor (for reminder copy), and direct mail can be valuable supporting media. Catalogs are sometimes used by furniture retailers.

Step 5 Preparing the advertising. For large-volume retailers, a small advertising department is affordable. The retailer, large or small, has ample advertising material available from represented manufacturers. This material ranges from proofs of complete ads (to which retailers add their logotype) to ad elements such as photos, proof pages of artwork, copy blocks, and headlines. Advertising services are in the business of supplying monthly or bimonthly brochures of similar material to subscribers. Radio scripts and tapes are also supplied by the same resources, or the retailer can prepare commercials from scratch.

Step 6 Producing the advertising. Pasted-up rough layouts of elements or complete ads from the above resources are turned over to the local newspaper for production, or the ad department handles production using outside suppliers as needed. The continuity department at the local radio station can write and produce commercials if desired. Other scheduled media have production facilities available.

Steps 7 and 8 Placing the advertising, paying bills, and handling paperwork are routine tasks.

Step 9 Evaluating the advertising. Records of sales of advertised merchandise are kept and analyzed to measure the advertising's effectiveness. Store traffic counts should occasionally be made after specials are promoted.

Retail Appliance Stores

Step 1 Establishing advertising goals. These goals differ, depending on four types of merchandise sold by the dealer. Typical advertising approaches, by type of merchandise, follow.

Major appliances: Up to 90 percent of this business is replacement. A consumer, for example, looks for a new refrigerator only when the old one can't be repaired. Therefore, these items are advertised consistently and low-end, price-value models are featured. An attempt is made at the store to trade up the prospect to higher-priced models.

TV sets: Replacement business is important, but advertising is increased at new-model introduction time and before Christmas.

Small appliances: These should not be advertised unless the dealer is willing to match or undercut discount house prices. These items are often sold as loss leaders, in an attempt to gain new customers.

Seasonal merchandise: humidifiers and air conditioners. The strategy, obviously, is to feature these items when they're most needed.

Advertising is highly aggressive and promotional. Price is emphasized and well-known brand names are featured.

Step 2 Selection of goods to be advertised. The rule of advertising only best-selling items must be followed.

Step 3 Determining the budget size. The task method of budget preparation should be followed but is seldom used. Appliance dealers are characteristically not painstaking in the budget area. This is because of the great availability of co-op advertising funds from manufacturers. In this field, co-op advertising can pay 80 percent or more of the dealer's ad expenses. This puts the retailer's ad budget in the hands of the manufacturer, because what the retailer spends is determined by the amount of merchandise purchased from manufacturers' distributors. Average percentage of sales invested in advertising is 2.3 percent, but most of it is not the dealer's money.

Step 4 Choosing the media. Newspapers, followed by radio, are the most important elements of the media plan for small outlets. TV comes second after newspapers in larger stores. Direct mail is often used for the customer mailing list at new-line introduction. Point-of-purchase material is important. Transit, outdoor (for reminder copy), flyers, suburban newspapers, and local magazines all have their supporting roles when the marketing area indicates use.

Step 5 Preparing the advertising. Unless the dealer (or local chain) does a business of over $1 million annually, full-time advertising specialists are not on the payroll. The manufacturers supply more ad material than the retailer needs or can use. There is no problem in obtaining coated proofs of ads, radio scripts and tapes, photos and proofs of artwork, and copy for every item in the line. Dealers tend to adapt this material for their own use. Manufacturers' collateral departments supply a series of ad and point-of-sale promotion brochures that outline complete packages for sales events. Point-of-sale material is usually supplied at cost.

Step 6 Producing the advertising. This is not a problem for retailers, as so much material is supplied by manufacturers. It is localized and turned over to the print media for production. The continuity department at radio and TV stations can handle simple production jobs for the dealer, as required. Ad agencies, occasionally used by large local chains, handle production details.

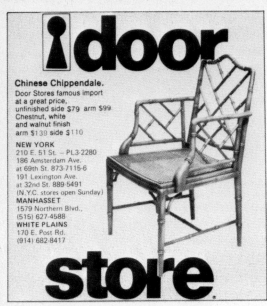

The ad for Algene's is a typical home appliance store ad. Elements have been picked up from a manufacturer's advertising brochure and the store name and address added. The Door Store advertisement is for a furniture chain noted for its good advertising design. (Courtesy Door Store; Algene's, Inc.)

Steps 7 and 8 Placing the advertising, paying the bills, and handling paperwork, including co-op claims, are routine tasks.

Step 9 Evaluating the advertising. The dealer tends to be haphazard about this, but sales records of advertised merchandise should be kept and analyzed in an attempt to measure ad efficiency.

Personal Services

Personal service retailers are defined in the classification system for distributive education as suppliers of services concerned with personal improvement and the care of a person and his or her personal apparel. Laundries, laundromats, dry cleaners, shoe repair shops, photo studios, beauty shops, health spas, reducing salons, dance studios, and the like fall into this category. They are relatively small advertisers and generally follow similar advertising procedures.

Step 1 Establishing advertising goals. As patrons visit these shops with a predetermined need in mind, advertising should be run consistently throughout the year. In print, small-space ads, up to 200 lines in size, are all that's required. Advertising should stress quality of service. While price should be included, it is not an important factor. Dry cleaners, dance studios, reducing salons, and health spas on occasion will find it profitable to offer specials.

Step 2 Selecting the service to be advertised. Since each retailer specializes in a single service, this presents no problem.

Step 3 Determining the budget size. In retailing of this nature, little attempt is made to follow any orderly procedure. Those who set advertising objectives and use the task method will profit in business growth if their service is competitive. The following average percentage of sales invested in advertising for some of these businesses are available from the Newspaper Advertising Bureau. They should be used as cross-checks on the task budget. Laundromats, 1.2 percent; dry cleaners, 1.7 percent; photo studios, 2.4 percent; beauty shops, 2 percent.

Step 4 Choosing the media. Newspapers are the primary medium. Weeklies and suburban papers are used when circulation fits the local marketing area. Radio is the second most important medium. Supplemental media are transit, outdoor, local magazines, and flyers.

Step 5 Preparing the advertising. The advertising preparation task is usually assumed by the owner-manager. The newspaper can supply individual ads, ad components, and complete campaigns from the advertising (mat) services to which it subscribes. The continuity writers of the radio station can prepare commercials from a supplied fact sheet. If retailers have the interest and the ability, they should do the creative and preparation job themselves, using local artwork sources, because this results in fresher, more individualistic copy.

Step 6 Producing the advertising. This task can be handled by the print media, and radio tapes, including special effects, can be produced by studio personnel.

Steps 7 and 8 Placing the advertising, paying bills, and taking care of paperwork are routine tasks.

Step 9 Evaluating the advertising. Because of the small budgets in the personal service field, very little evaluation is done. When special offers are advertised, some attempt should be made to record sales after ads are run and evaluate advertising efficiency.

Real Estate

Advertising by real estate brokers is an important local category and ranks ninth in newspaper ad volume. But real estate advertising takes other forms, too, although these forms are not as important as brokerage on a volume basis. Real estate developers and apartment managers advertise, as do builders of cooperatives and condominiums. All are discussed below.

Step 1 Establishing a goal. The advertising goal for brokerage firms is to develop a contact, or leads. Individual homes (or commercial properties) are featured. The particular offering may not necessarily be sold to the prospect contacting the broker as a result of the ad; once the contact is made, the full listing of homes or commercial properties in the prospect's price range is presented. Occasionally the broker will run institutional advertising that seeks to build the reputation of the firm on a long-term basis. This advertising is usually addressed to prospective property sellers. It will stress reputation, quick sales, and individual attention paid to selling the listed properties. The advertising objective of apartment managers is simple: list the selling features of the rental units and the rent in order to bring in prospects. Developers' advertising objective is to encourage visits to a model home, and amenities and price are featured in ads. The advertising objective of the builders of cooperatives and condominiums is to obtain prospects, and the strategy is to feature and describe the units and the surroundings and to list purchase prices and monthly maintenance charges.

Step 2 Selecting what is to be advertised. Brokers advertise listed properties for sale or rent and occasionally run institutional copy, discussed in step 3. The other real estate groups advertise their specialized offerings.

Step 3 Determining the budget size. The task method is recommended for budget preparation. The average percentage of sales invested in advertising can be used as a cross-check in budget preparation. Average for residential real estate brokers is 4 percent, but some brokers spend between 5 and 6 percent of sales on their advertising program. Developers spend an average of 3.1 percent of sales on their ad programs, and it is estimated that cooperative and condominium builders spend between 3 and 6 percent of sales on advertising.

Step 4 Choosing the media. For the broker, the local (or suburban) newspaper is the primary medium. Display ads and classified ads are used to advertise properties for sale or rent. Insertions tend to pile up on Fridays and on the weekend. Radio is second in importance, and commercials usually are institutional. Local magazines are used, when available. Classified newspaper advertising is the mainstay of apartment managers; depending on apartment building size, newspaper display ads are used. Developers are heavy users of the Sunday newspaper real estate section and also advertise in broadcast media. Local cooperative and condominium sales agents also use newspapers and radio. In print, large-space ads are generally run. For major projects, TV, outdoor, and transit are on the media list.

Step 5 Preparing the advertising. Real estate brokers, for newspaper display ads, hire a local photographer to shoot listings illustrations or even use the home owner's snapshot. Copy is written by a staff member. Real estate developers, apartment managers, and cooperative and condominium sales agents are also do-it-yourself advertisers who write simple copy

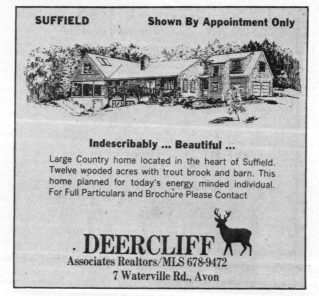
**Shown are ads sponsored by three types of real estate op-
erators. The Meadowlake ad is sponsored by a real estate
developer. The ad for The Caméron is a condominium advertisement sponsored by the builder and marketer. It sells
prestige and amenities. The purpose of the real estate
broker sponsoring the Dearcliff ad is to sell the property
and also to obtain contacts.** (Courtesy Timberwood Development; RAL Properties/Renophase; Deercliff Associates, Realtors)

consisting of features and amenities and use local suppliers for photos and artwork.

Step 6 Producing the advertising. Copy, rough layout, and illustration material is turned over to the newspaper for production. The continuity department of the local radio station can write commercials from a supplied fact sheet and handle production details as required.

Steps 7 and 8 Placing the advertising, paying bills, and taking care of paperwork are routine tasks.

Step 9 Evaluating the advertising. It is a simple matter for the real estate broker to measure the effectiveness of the advertising, and rank this effectiveness by medium used. Specific properties are advertised; a certain number of contacts are made in response to the ads. Cost per response is easy to establish. Similarly, developers, apartment managers, and sales agents for cooperatives and condominiums can effectively gauge advertising results. A specific offer is made in their advertising; results are felt within 48 hours after advertising is run.

Recreation and Travel

On the local scene, this category includes travel agents, movie theaters, drive-ins, bowling alleys, and the like. Movie theaters and drive-ins are important local advertisers, with an average percentage of sales invested in advertising of 5.5 percent. However, the advertising task for the movie theater operator presents no problems. Advertising material is supplied by the film distributor in the form of press books; the operator merely selects from this material and places the ads in local media. With the exception of travel agents, other retailers in this category advertise on a very small scale. Travel agencies are discussed below.

In the U.S. Office of Education classification system for marketing and distributive education, record stores and radio and stereo stores are listed under home furnishings. Camera stores and sporting goods stores are placed in general merchandise. Here we are not following this classification system and have arbitrarily included them in this appendix section under hobbies and sports. The advertising tasks for this group of stores are comparable.

Travel Agencies

Step 1 Establishing objectives. Promotional agents, booking charters with tie-in land accommodations and medium- to low-price cruises often advertise many such specials in a single ad. The objective of their advertising is to build a volume business. The nonpromotional agent with a relatively small clientele is interested in high markup. The objective is to obtain leads of well-to-do prospects through advertising by advertising quality trips and specialized knowledge. Once the customer is contacted, tailormade trips catering to the customer's interest can be developed. Such agents are interested in repeat business. Of course, the nonpromotional agent will sell low-priced package tours, too.

Step 2 Selecting what is to be advertised. Promotional travel agents with high volume and low markup feature budget package tours, and price is the main attraction. Nonpromotional agents with high-income clients advertise expensive package tours and do not emphasize price.

Step 3 Determining how much should be spent. The task method is recommended for budget preparation. The average ad budget runs approximately 5 percent of annual sales volume, according to the American Society of Travel Agents. This figure should be used as a check on budget size, and competitors' expenditures should be estimated and compared with the budget figure.

Step 4 Choosing media. The travel section of the Sunday newspaper (when the newspaper carries such a section) is first choice for travel agents. The daily newspaper is also used. Other media are radio, transit, direct mail, and local magazines. Advertising isn't usually scheduled on an all-year basis; ads are keyed to the important travel periods. Ads are placed in November and December for winter vacations and in the spring for summer trips.

Step 5 Preparing the advertising. The owner-manager or a delegate usually prepares the ads from scratch, writing the copy and using scrap art or relying on photos and artwork obtained from sources as foreign or local government tourist agencies, resorts, airline publicity departments and the like.

Step 6 Producing the advertising. The local newspaper production facilities are generally used. Very large metropolitan agents often use a part-time layout artist who can organize the production job. Continuity writers at the local radio station can write commercials from a supplied fact sheet, if desired, and handle production when tapes and special effects are required.

Steps 7 and 8 Placing the advertising, bill paying, and taking care of paperwork are routine tasks.

Step 9 Evaluating the advertising. An effort should be made to record the number of leads (and eventual business done) resulting from individual ad insertions to evaluate advertising efficiency. Business done as a result of direct mail is simple to determine, and a sales history of each mailing should be kept and analyzed.

Hobbies and Sports

Step 1 Establishing objectives. Most retailers in this category are highly promotional. Therefore a policy of featuring leading brands at a competitive price is followed. Record stores promote popular new items, usually fully priced, and also offer specials to generate store traffic. These retailers carefully follow the popularity ratings of recording stars, promoting whatever is current, and cutting prices on older records and albums.

Step 2 Selecting what is to be advertised. The rule of advertising best-selling items must rigorously be followed. Well-known and reliable brands, generating good sales volume, should be aggressively promoted.

Step 3 Determining how much should be spent. The task method is recommended for budget preparation. However, most store managers use a percentage of actual or anticipated sales to determine the budget or do not plan and spend what they think they can afford. The average ad budget for sporting goods stores is 3.5 percent of annual sales volume and between 0.8 and 0.9 percent for camera stores. The Newspaper Advertising Bureau includes radio stores with appliance and TV dealers for an average percentage of 2.3 of annual sales volume. Average advertising-to-sales percentages are not supplied for record shops. Manufacturers' co-op funds are available to managers of camera and radio and stereo equipment stores. Record retailers are offered co-op plans, but only from major record distributors. Co-op plans are a rarity in the sporting goods field. Manufacturers claim that plans have been abused by retailers and results are unsatisfactory. This attitude is unusual and impractical. Co-op plans can be adequately controlled by manufacturers, but such plans do take time and effort.

Step 4 Choosing media. Newspaper advertising is the first choice on media lists. Record retailers use the Sunday entertainment section when available. Camera stores, radio and stereo equipment stores, and sporting goods stores use both the weekday and Sunday editions. Radio advertising is second in popularity. Large urban camera and sporting goods stores use seasonal TV. Occasionally local magazines, transit, and outdoor find a place on media lists for institutional or reminder copy. Direct mail is sometimes used.

Step 5 Preparing the advertising. Proofs of illustrations, copy blocks, complete ads, and in some cases point-of-sale material are all made available by manufacturers. In preparing print ads, the manager, or delegate, uses this material as is or rewrites the copy as desired. The material is assembled in rough layout form. Larger retailers or local chains can af-

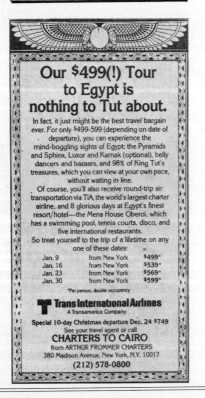

Representative of the travel agent field. The ad for the charter flight is promotional, and its purpose is to generate volume business at a low markup. The purpose of the Hanns Ebensten Travel ad is to seek out a few customers for an expensive tour, the price of which is not mentioned. The ad for a stereo store typically features reduced prices for brand items. (Courtesy Hanns Ebensten Travel, Inc.; Arthur Frommer Charters; Audio Breakthroughs)

ford a very small advertising department to do this work. A distinctive store logo and theme should always be used. Radio scripts are often supplied by manufacturers and the retailer adds store identification. The retailer may prefer to write commercials from scratch. A retailer doing large-volume business may choose to hire a local ad agency on a fee basis to do the entire preparation job.

Step 6 Producing the advertising. For print advertising, the retailer preparing copy and layout within the store can rely on local print media to handle typesetting and production. If complete control over the appearance of the advertising is wanted, the retailer should hire a typesetter and submit mechanicals for production. When required, local radio station personnel can supply special effects and stock music for commercials and produce tapes. All these activities can be accomplished, of course, by an ad agency when a retailer chooses this route.

Steps 7 and 8 Placing the advertising, bill paying, taking care of paperwork, and making co-op claims are routine tasks.

Step 9 Evaluating the advertising. A sales history of advertised items should be kept and analyzed. Efficiency of various media buys can be evaluated by running special offers exclusively in one medium, rotating the same offer in other media, and comparing sales results.

GLOSSARY

AAAA (American Association of Advertising Agencies) a trade organization representing member advertising agencies.

ABC (Audit Bureau of Circulation) an independent agency, founded in 1914, that verifies circulation claims of subscribing newspapers and magazines.

Account the company client or client's brand that an advertising agency serves. Example: the Texaco account.

Accrual in home appliance retail advertising, cooperative advertising dollars available.

AdTel a type of split-market testing system, using CATV, that divides the test area in half, each half receiving different advertising messages for the same product.

Advertiser the sponsor who pays the cost of preparing an advertisement and the cost of inserting it in the media of his or her choice.

Advertising a sales message, directed at a mass audience, that seeks through persuasion to sell goods, services, or ideas on behalf of the paying sponsor.

Advertising agency a business organization devoted to the development, preparation, and placement of advertising on behalf of sellers of goods and services.

Advertising budget a plan outlining and controlling advertising expenditures over a period of time, usually a year.

Advertising by professionals advertising sponsored by professionals such as members of the legal and dental professions.

Advertising campaign a series of advertising messages devoted to the same idea, concept, or theme.

Advertising department the department of a company charged with planning and executing the company's advertising program.

Advertising request a request to run an advertisement made by a department store buyer and directed to the advertising department for implementation.

Advertising research establishment of facts on matters pertaining to the creation of advertising or the effect of advertising.

Advertising strategy a statement of the selling problem to be solved by the advertising; it lists the primary and secondary methods needed to solve the selling problem.

Advocacy advertising advertising that presents one-sided ideas and opinions on controversial social issues.

Agate line a standard unit for measuring space in newspapers. Fourteen lines of 6-point unleaded type are equal to one column inch.

Agency commission system the method through which an advertising agency receives most of its income. The commission is 15 percent of the cost of placing an advertisement in the required medium.

AM amplitude modulation, a form of radio transmission that carries over long distances.

Animated commercial a television commercial that achieves the illusion of movement through the filming of a series of sequential cartoon drawings.

Animation the television advertising technique involving a series of drawings arranged sequentially and filmed to create the illusion of motion.

Answer print the completed stage of a television commercial.

Art work any form of illustration that is not a photograph.

Asymmetrical balance in a layout for an ad, an arrangement in which elements in each vertical half are laid out farther from or nearer to the optical center depending on their mass and weight.

Audio anything audible—words, music, sound effects—occurring in a television or radio commercial.

Benday a pattern of dots, which can be placed over any part of a line drawing to give a feeling of tone and texture when the line cut is made.

Bleed extension of a magazine advertisement to the edge of the page rather than its being surrounded by a margin of white space.

Block letter a class of type characterized by uniform strokes of the same weight for all parts of the letters. Usually without serifs.

Body copy the main paragraphs of copy in an advertisement.

Boldface a type that is darker, or more heavily imprinted than the regular or medium face.

Brag and boast headline a headline that brags about the manufacturer and boasts about the product's superiority.

Brainstorming an exchange of spontaneous thoughts by a group of people under leadership, in which ideas are developed mutually or individually.

Brand a distinctive name identifying the product of a manufacturer.

Brand image studies quantitative research to determine the image or reputation a brand and its competition have in the mind of the consumer.

Broadcast media radio and television media.

Bureau of Advertising an organization of the American Newspaper Publishers Association devoted to promoting newspaper advertising.

Business gifts expensive specialty items used to convey goodwill. They rarely carry an advertising message.

Business publications magazines directing their editorial content to specific business and industry groups.

B/w indication that an advertisement is "black and white" only, containing no color.

Cablecasting the transmission of original local programs by CATV systems rather than bringing in distant signals of programs originated by television stations and networks.

Call letters alphabetical series of three or four letters that designate a radio or television station. Call letters are assigned by the Federal Communications Commission.

Call reports, or contact reports in advertising agencies, memorandums that report on meetings and correspondence with the client and that outline decisions made and "next steps" to be taken.

Camera instructions instructions that indicate how the camera should film a scene.

Campaign see Advertising campaign.

Car cards interior advertising signs placed in buses, subway cars, and commuter trains.

Case in typography, a series of compartments in a tray containing individual characters or type of a single face and size.

Case history advertising advertising in which the successful results of using a product or service are described in depth.

CATV Community Antenna Television, first developed to bring distant television signals to isolated areas via a high pickup antenna and coaxial cable connected to a subscriber's home. Now spreading to urban areas as well. See also Cablecasting.

Circulation the number of copies per issue that a publication distributes.

Classified advertising in newspaper advertising, small-space ads containing a brief headline or lead-in to the copy and no illustration. Such ads are grouped together by category in a special "classified" section.

Closing time, or closing date the deadline for acceptance of an advertisement for a publication or broadcast medium.

Clutter the crowding of several television commercials into a short airtime period.

Collateral material advertising and advertising-related promotional devices, such as point-of-sale material, package designs, brochures, catalogs, and direct mail advertising.

Combination plate a printing plate that is prepared to contain both line drawings and halftone pictures.

Commercial availabilities in the broadcast media, local station time slots that can be used for advertising messages.

Comparative copy, or comparative advertising advertising that compares by name or product illustration the competitors' brands or services with the sponsor's brand or service.

Composing stick a hand-held small traylike device used to compose lines of type.

Composition in typography, setting or "composing" copy in type.

Comprehensive a finished advertising layout so complete in appearance that it closely resembles the actual advertisement.

Concept testing testing of advertising themes and layouts with consumers; valuable in checking on relative interest of ideas and on comprehension and understanding.

Condensed type type that has less width to the letters than regular type.

Consumer the individual who ultimately uses a product or service.

Consumer jury a research technique that asks consumers' opinions about advertising and its appeals.

Consumer magazine magazines of either general interest to consumers or of special appeal to specific classes of consumers.

Consumerism the defense by the public and government of consumer rights and interests as related to the products and services the consumer buys.

Continuity acceptance department, or commercial clearance department the television network department that approves or rejects advertising. All advertising must be submitted to this department.

Continuity writer a writer on the staff of a radio station, for example, who prepares copy for programs as needed.

Convenience products and services products and services that offer shortcuts of time and effort in preparation for use.

Cooperative advertising, or co-op advertising advertising prepared by a manufacturer or supplier and placed by local merchants in local media over the merchant's name. The manufacturer or supplier pays part of the cost of placing the ads.

Copy all written material that appears in an advertisement.

Copy-contact people advertising agency personnel who write copy and also handle client contact.

Copywriter a person responsible for writing the words that appear in advertisements.

Copywriter's rough a crude indication of a layout prepared by a copywriter.

Corporate advertising, or institutional advertising advertising that stresses the capabilities of the manufacturer or that has as its goal building a company's reputation or prestige.

Corrective advertising statements ordered by the FTC to be inserted in an advertiser's current advertising stating that previous claims for a product or service were not true.

Cost per thousand a method of cost analysis of a magazine's (or newspaper's) circulation; the black-and-white one-page rate is divided by the number of thousands of circulation.

Coverage the number of consumers who are exposed to an advertising medium.

Creative possessing the ability to originate or create. In an advertising department or agency, often used to describe the copywriting and art sections, although it is recognized that other sections also perform tasks that require creativity.

Creative boutique a company specializing in preparation of advertising copy and art. Television and radio production facilities may also be offered.

Creativity an individual's capability to combine what is perceived in ways that are new and novel.

Criers historically, people employed by merchants to "cry their wares" in the streets.

Cursive type a class of type resembling script or italic. *See* Italic.

Cut (n.) an engraving or plate of an illustrative element in an advertisement. (v.) To eliminate part of the copy in an advertisement or broadcast script. Also, in television, to change abruptly from one scene to the next.

Dailies, or rushes all the printed or developed film for a commercial.

Declarative headline a headline that states a fact or facts about the subject being advertised.

Demographic characteristics vital and social statistics of consumers and media audiences and circulations, such as average and median incomes, educational backgrounds, and occupational levels.

Depth interview *see* Motivation interview.

Direct mail advertising advertising letters, catalogs, or pamphlets mailed to potential buyers.

Direct placement placement of an ad without the help of an advertising agency.

Direct selling use of a sales force by a manufacturer to sell directly to the trade rather than through wholesalers. Use of a sales force to sell directly to the public.

Direct voice (DV) television copy spoken on screen by announcers, actors, and actresses.

Directory advertising use of advertising space in alphabetical listings or directories of city and rural dwellers, businesses, supply sources, or trade and professional groups.

Discount houses stores that eliminate service extras and count on volume and low prices for profit.

Display advertising in the newspaper field, ads that contain headlines, illustrative material, and other display elements.

Dissolve (DIS) in television, fading out one scene as the next fades in.

Drive time the period of the day when people going to work use their car radios.

Editorial profile a brief description of the editorial policy of a magazine that tells the prospective buyers of advertising space the kinds of readers they may reach and the types of articles that will be published.

Endorsement advertising *see* Personality endorsement advertising.

Execution the manner in which a strategy is carried out in the advertisement; it involves evoking a mood, attracting interest, and dramatizing facts.

Exterior cards a type of transit advertising placed on the sides and ends of buses.

Fact sheet a listing of selling points about an advertised item; it is for use by radio announcers or local radio personalities in building commercial messages.

Fair trade establish through an agreement between retailers and manufacturers the prices for merchandise that merchants cannot reduce.

Fairness Doctrine an FCC standard requiring broadcasters airing a controversial point of view to make available air time for opposing views.

Farm advertising advertising sponsored by a manufacturer of farm equipment or supplies, or by a seller of services to the agricultural community. Placed in farm-oriented media.

Farm magazines magazines that cover every type of agricultural operation.

Fast-food establishment a quick-service retail business selling a limited number of items that are eaten on the premises or taken out.

Federal Communications Commission (FCC) the Federal regulatory and licensing agency of the broadcast industry.

Federal Trade Commission (FTC) the government agency established in 1914 to prevent businesses from using unfair methods of competition.

Filmed commercial a commercial pretranscribed on motion picture film containing an audio track.

Focus group session a form of qualitative research using small groups of consumers, led by a moderator, to determine attitudes and opinions toward brands, consumer habits, etc.

Four-color process engraving a photoengraving technique used to produce full color.

FM frequency modulation or short-range radio transmission that is relatively static-free and delivers superior sound reproduction.

Free-lance work done on an assignment basis by specialists, who are not steadily employed by a company.

Freeze-frame action in a television commercial is stopped and the picture momentarily becomes a still life.

Frequency the number of times a consumer audience of an advertising medium is exposed to an advertisement.

Full position the position of a newspaper ad that is next to and also following reading matter or that is at the top of a column and next to reading matter.

Galley proofs first proof taken from type in galley trays before pages are made up, used for proofreading.

Gravure a printing method in which the area to be printed is etched below the plate surface and filled with ink.

Gross national product (GNP) the total value of a nation's goods and services.

GRP's—Gross Rating Points a method of measuring the number of impression opportunities offered to an advertiser when broadcast advertising time is purchased. GRP's are also used in purchasing outdoor advertising.

Halftone a photoengraving plate used to reproduce illustrations other than line drawings. Dots of varying sizes reproduce degrees of tone.

Handsetting in typography, composing lines of type by hand.

Headline the lead or featured idea of a print advertisement. It is the most important part of the ad's copy.

Hi-Fi a newspaper ad preprinted on a roll of newsprint and inserted in the newspaper.

High profit margin in retailing, a generous profit received when merchandise is sold.

House agency an advertising agency owned by a manufacturer or supplier of services.

Idee a ten-second commercial immediately preceding station identification between programs.

Industrial advertising advertising sponsored by suppliers of materials, equipment, machinery, and other goods and directed to manufacturers and service businesses.

Industrial agency an advertising agency specializing in serving industrial or trade clients.

Insertion date the specific calendar date when an advertisement is to appear in the medium selected by the advertiser.

Institutional advertising *see* Corporate advertising.

Interlock the stage in producing television commercials when the audio and visual are separate.

Intertype a typesetting machine activated by an operator using a keyboard. It casts a full line of type on a single metal slug, and therefore, any correction within a line requires the resetting of the entire line.

Investment spending heavy spending of advertising dollars during the introduction of new products or the promotion of improved products to achieve future profitable sales.

Italic a class of type in which the letters slant or lean to the right.

Jingle an advertising message, usually in verse form, sung to musical accompaniment.

Job order a form used in advertising agencies to initiate work on an advertisement or television commercial. It contains due dates and a job order number, which will identify the particular "job" through all stages of production.

Justify in typesetting, to space out letters in words

or add spaces between words so that typeset lines are of equal length.

Layout a rough visualization of what a finished print advertisement will look like. It serves as a guide in producing the ad.

Layout artist a member of an art department or a free-lance artist who prepares layouts.

Leading (pronounced as in "led") white space between lines of set type, created by inserting strips of blank metal between the lines of type.

Letterpress a printing method using raised inked surfaces for reproduction.

Line cut a photoengraving plate of a line drawing.

Line drawing a drawing consisting of black lines and solids with no intermediate tones.

Linotype a typesetting machine activated by an operator using a keyboard. It casts a full line of type on a single metal slug, and any correction within a line therefore requires the resetting of the entire line.

Lithography printing from a flat surface on which nonprinting areas are chemically treated to repel ink.

Live commercial a television or radio commercial received by the audience at the same time that the performance is being produced at the broadcast facility.

Local advertising advertising sponsored by local business people to reach the potential customers in their neighborhood, town, or city.

Logotype, or logo the name of a store or brand featured as a display element in an ad, usually at its base.

Loss leader an item sold at no profit or at a loss in order to build store traffic.

Mail-order advertising advertising that attempts to obtain orders from consumers by mail rather than through retail outlets. Print and broadcast media can both be used for mail-order advertising.

Market a group of individuals who are buyers or potential buyers of a product or service. Also, a geo- graphic area from which a seller draws his customers.

Market research establishment of facts concerning size, and demographic characteristics of a market for a product or service.

Market testing research conducted on a limited scale to determine product or service acceptability, sales efficiency of advertising copy or media programs, efficiency of sales promotion programs, and the like.

Marketing all the steps taken to speed up the movement of goods and services from production to consumption.

Marketing strategy the plan followed by merchants to speed up the movement of the goods or services that they see.

Matrix, or mat paper mold of type or newspaper printing plate. When filled with molten lead, it produces a duplicate printing plate used by the newspaper to reproduce an advertisement.

Maximil rate the maximum cost of one line of newspaper advertising per million circulation at the open agate-line rate.

Maximum coverage communication of an advertising message to as many prospects as possible.

Mechanical a layout form identical in appearance to the final ad, lacking color but including positioned photostats of the final illustrations and type set in position. It serves as a guide during production.

Mechanical typesetting setting of type by machine.

Media the various means that an advertiser uses to carry and communicate messages, including radio and television (the broadcast media); newspapers, magazines, direct mail, and outdoor and transit advertising (the print media); and point-of-sale and specialty advertising.

Media plan part of an advertising budget listing media to be used, costs involved, and reasons for choice.

Media schedule an outline of when ads will run and the size of insertions or the length of commercials.

Medical agency an advertising agency specializing in serving in industrial or trade clients.

Metropolitan magazines magazines with circulation limited to large cities, parts of large cities, or suburban areas.

Minimil rate the minimum cost of one line of newspaper advertising per million circulation at the lowest rate available.

Monotype a typesetting machine activated by an operator using a keyboard; the keys punch a paper tape, like the matrices in Linotype.

Mood copy copy that appeals mainly to the emotions.

Motivate in advertising, to supply the consumer with an incentive to take an action favorable to the advertiser.

Motivation interview research conducted with a series of individual consumers to determine why consumers hold opinions and attitudes toward a product or service and its competition. Also to determine consumer wants, both actual and unrealized. Qualitative research.

Multi-Page inserts preprinted inserts consisting of four or more pages of advertising and promotion material in full color; included in newspapers.

NAD National Advertising Division of the Council of Better Business Bureaus. Investigates complaints concerning truthfulness and accuracy of advertising claims.

NARB National Advertising Review Board. Reviews unresolved complaints referred by NAD.

National advertising advertising sponsored by a manufacturer of goods or a supplier of a service, on a nationwide basis, appearing in media with a national circulation.

Network a group of affiliated radio or television stations that can broadcast a program simultaneously. There are regional and national networks.

NR position the position of a newspaper ad that is next to reading matter.

Offset lithography a printing method using a rotating cylinder to carry the image from the plate cylinder to the paper on the impression cylinder.

On location in the production of television commercials, shooting scenes away from the studio stage.

Open rate the basic retail advertising rate found on a rate card.

Optical center the visual center of an advertisement, slightly above the mid-ad point, or one-third of the way down an ad.

Opticals visual devices such as dissolves and supers added to a commercial after filming.

Ornamental type a class of type derived from the three major classes—roman, cursive, and block letter—which is decorative in effect.

Outdoor advertising advertising utilizing the measurable standardized media of outdoor posters and painted bulletins.

Outdoor advertising plants outdoor advertising companies that lease and maintain poster structures of uniform size and that sell advertising space on these structures for specific periods of time.

Package copy copy appearing on product packaging, including instruction, product contents, and product descriptions.

Painted bulletins outdoor structures maintained by outdoor advertising plants. Usually larger in area than standardized posters. Painted bulletins are often embellished with dimensional effects and extensions of elements beyond the bulletin frame.

Permission to believe in advertising copy, an offer of rational appeals, facts, and information that support and make credible the ad's emotional appeal.

Personality endorsement advertising a method of advertising that makes use of a well-known person who says something favorable about a product or service. A direct quote or paraphrase is used in the copy.

Photocomposition *see* Phototypesetting.

Photoengraving a photographic process for making plates for printing purposes.

Photostat, or "stat" a crude camera-made reproduction of ad elements (type, illustration, or both) used in preparing advertising.

Phototypesetting a method of setting type using taped instructions (via a keyboard or a computer) that direct a strobe lamp to scan a photograph of typefaces, select needed characters, and flash them to a photosensitive surface that is subsequently developed. Teletypesetter, Linotron, Photon, and Fotosetter are examples of phototypesetting machines.

Pica a unit measurement in typesetting that is one-sixth of an inch long and divided into 12 points.

Playlet a commercial that tells a story about a product or service in dramatized form.

Point the unit of measurement for type. The height of letters is measured in points, with 72 points to the inch.

Point-of-sale advertising, or point-of-purchase (POP) advertising in-store signs, displays, pamphlets, and specification sheets at or near the point where an item is to be sold and featuring merchandise on sale.

Portfolio a collection of mounted samples of an individual's advertising work.

Premium an item of merchandise free of extra cost or for a small additional cost offered in conjunction with the sales of a product or service as an inducement to buy. On-pack premiums are physically attached to the product; write-in premiums must be requested by mail.

Preprinted inserts advertisements that are not printed on the newspaper press but are prepared in advance elsewhere and then by various methods incorporated into each copy of the paper.

Preproduced commercial a commercial that is prepared on tapes or records before it is broadcast.

Preproduction meeting the final review of a television commercial and the means of achieving its production.

Presenter commercial a commercial in which an on-stage announcer or actor presents the product or service to the viewer on a direct, person-to-person basis.

Price-off deal a manufacturer's reduction of product price to consumers for a short time.

Prime time the evening television viewing hours, usually between 8 p.m. and 11 p.m., that attract the largest audiences.

Process color reproduction of ads in full color by overprinting them with a series of plates, each inked with a different color.

Promotional advertising advertising of a specific item that is for sale.

Promotional mix activities, including display, sales promotion, publicity and public relations, personal selling, and advertising, designed to persuade a customer to buy a product or service.

Proof a copy printed by hand of an advertisement printing plate. Also, a hand-printed reproduction typeset copy.

Proofread to compare typeset proof to the original typed copy.

Public service advertising advertising that supports causes in the public interest.

Publicity a message about a product, company, industry, or service that is placed in editorial or news columns of media without cost to the organziation that is the subject of the message.

Qualitative research advertising or market research conducted with small groups of consumers and not projectable to the total market.

Quantitative research advertising or market research that reflects, within known statistical variations, the total market. Projectable research.

Questionnaire a series of questions used in research surveys and presented to consumers by interview, mail, or phone.

Rate card a listing in pamphlet form of rates charged by a newspaper for local advertising. Also, a listing of rates charged for national and local advertising by local television and radio stations and outdoor advertising firms.

Ratings in television, a measure of the popularity of a given program. The program rating indicates the percentage of all homes with sets in use that are tuned into a particular program.

Reach   the total number of individuals or households exposed to an advertising message.

Reason why   in advertising copy, the part that gives reasons for product or service superiority and that backs the claims made.

Regional advertising   advertising sponsored by a manufacturer of goods or supplier of services on a geographically limited or regional basis.

Registration   in photoengraving, proper alignment of colors.

Regular-price copy   in retail copy, all copy for merchandise that is sold at nonreduced prices.

Reminder advertising   advertising that merely reminds the prospect to buy and does not elaborate on reasons to buy.

Résumé   a typed itemization of an individual's background and experience.

Retail advertising   advertising for goods and services sponsored by a local merchant or retailer.

Reverse type   light or white type on dark panels or on a dark background that appears to be etched out.

Roll-out method   a procedure following successful test market results in which the advertiser distributes and advertises the product or service in stages across the country rather than distribution and advertising nationally all at once.

Roll time   the first 1½ seconds of a television commercial, containing video but no audio.

Roman type   the principal class of type, derived from Roman lettering, characterized by letters that have serifs and contrasting thick and thin strokes.

ROP position   the run-of-paper position. An ad can be placed at a newspaper's discretion and can be surrounded by other advertisements.

Rough layout   a roughly conceived diagram of the future ad, in exact size.

Sale copy   in retail advertising, copy for merchandise available at temporarily reduced prices.

Schedule   as used in advertising, a series of advertisements in print or commercials on broadcast media appearing at predetermined intervals.

Schwerin method   a procedure used to test sales effectiveness of commercials. Consumers are asked to choose their favorite products before viewing commercials and again after viewing to determine whether the commercials caused them to switch brand preferences.

Script   the written form of a television commercial containing copy and camera and sound instructions.

Secondary sources, or secondary idea sources   published or generally available data.

Series   a size of a particular typeface, such as 6-point Bodoni.

Serifs   in typography, small lines that extend from the ends of letters to give an ornamental effect.

Side-by-side demonstration   a technique used in television commercials whereby a product's advantages are emphasized by demonstrating the product along with competing products.

Siquis   an early English printed poster or sign.

Slide commercial   a commercial that consists of a series of still photographs or drawings that change via cuts or dissolves in synchronization with voice-over audio.

Sound effects (SFX)   sounds in radio and television commercials that are not words or music.

Specialty advertising   an advertising medium using useful articles, generally of small cost, imprinted with the advertiser's name, address, or message. Articles are distributed without cost or obligation to a preselected audience.

Specialty store   a store that sells small lines of clothing merchandise, for example, and related items—all appealing to a specific consumer group.

SpectaColor   a preprinted full-color advertisement insert available in many newspapers.

Split-market testing   a marketing research method that divides the consumers in a single test market into two groups, each of which is exposed to a different advertising message for the same product.

Split-run   a technique whereby an advertiser can

test his or her ads against each other in the same issue of a newspaper or magazine. The circulation is "split"—one-half of the circulation exposed to one ad, the remainder to another.

Spot color use of color in portions of an ad or illustration rather than overall, in order to emphasize key elements.

Standard Rate & Data Service (SRDS) the company that produces publications listing national rate card information for all types of advertising except outdoor, specialty, and point-of-purchase advertising.

Station poster a type of transit advertising placed in or near subway stations and railroad and bus terminals.

Stock music music already available for use in radio or television ads; not new music.

Stop motion a technique similar to animation. Movement is achieved by photographing a series of sequential scenes. In each scene, the subject is posed in a slightly different position.

Store audit a method to determine actual sales of a product and its competition by surveying at regular intervals stock on the shelf, stock in inventory, and shipments received. A "panel" or sample of drugstores or food stores is audited and the results projected to the total market.

Storyboard a rough visual plan of the action sequence of a television commercial prepared by an artist and accompanied by a copy script and video instructions.

Straight announcement a commercial delivered on radio by a single voice, and with no embellishments.

Subhead a collection of words standing apart from the body copy in display type that either elaborates on the main selling idea contained in the headline or introduces additional sales points. It is a small-scale headline.

Sweepstakes merchandise aids that distribute prizes to entrants on the basis of chance.

Symmetrical balance in a layout for an ad, a design which, when divided in half vertically, has equal weight of elements on either side.

Tag line the final line at the end of a commercial that summarizes the message.

Taped commercial a commercial pretranscribed on a plastic tape with an audio track.

Task force a selected group of people who work together to solve a particular problem.

Task method a way to prepare a budget based on tasks to be accomplished in the coming year.

Tear sheet an advertisement cut out from the publication containing it.

Teaser copy advertising containing little or no sponsor identification. Sometimes used to introduce new products and services.

Telecast programs that are originated by television stations and networks.

Television recall testing a research method used to test the ability of a television commercial to communicate its sales points.

Testimonial advertising advertising in which the spokesperson for the product or service is a satisfied user.

Theme a summary of the main selling idea of an advertising campaign or program that appears in every ad in the series. Also called a "slogan."

Thirty-sheet the size of an advertisement that measures 9 feet 7 inches by 27 feet 7 inches on a standardized outdoor poster structure.

Thumbnail a nonscale rough indication of a layout developed by an art director or layout artist in the experimental stage of layout preparation.

Trade advertising advertising sponsored by a manufacturer and directed to dealers, retail merchants, or wholesalers.

Trade association advertising advertising sponsored by an industry trade association that sells the generic product of an industry rather than specific brands.

Trade paper a magazine or newspaper directed to a specific trade or industry.

Trademark a name or design that is officially registered and used exclusively by a manufacturer or service supplier to distinguish this product or service from the competitors.

Transit advertising the mass advertising medium using public transportation and bus and subway terminals in urban centers.

Twenty-four sheet the size of an advertisement measuring 8 feet 8 inches by 19 feet 6 inches on a standardized outdoor poster structure.

Typeface a design of type letters within a class of type. Example: Bodoni is a typeface within the roman class.

Type family a group of different aspects of a typeface such as bold, condensed, or italic.

Type font a complete set of type in one face and series (or size), including upper- and lower-case letters, numbers, and punctuation marks.

Type series sizes of type within a typeface, usually running from 6-point to 72-point.

Typewriter composition a typesetting method in which a machine similar to a typewriter sets the copy. IBM Selectric is an example of the machines used. Plates are made by a photographic system.

Typo a typographical error.

Typographer a member of an advertising department, for example, who specifies type and who orders the copy "set," or composed.

UHF in television, the abbreviation for ultra-high frequency—using channels 14-83.

Usage and attitude studies quantitative research to determine consumer use of a brand and its competition over a period of time.

VHF in television, the abbreviation for very high frequency—using channels 2-13.

Video all the visual elements of a television commercial.

Video tape in television production, a magnetic tape that contains the recorded audio and video and that can be replayed immediately.

Voice over (VO) television copy read "over" a scene by an off-screen voice.

Wash drawings art work prepared by a technique such as brush and ink that portrays tone, shades, and texture.

Wave technique the scheduling of advertising to run for a period of time; for example, a month, then ceasing advertising for the same period of time. Also called pulse or flighting.

White space the blank area of a print ad.

Work print the edited commercial with audio and video on separate reels. No opticals are contained at this stage.

Yellow Pages the section of the telephone directory or, in larger cities, a separate publication listing by classification all the businesses and services in the area covered.